I0754954

N. P. Rogers

RECOLLECTIONS OF A BUSY LIFE:

INCLUDING

REMINISCENCES OF AMERICAN POLITICS AND POLITICIANS,

FROM THE OPENING OF THE MISSOURI CONTEST TO THE DOWNFALL OF SLAVERY;

TO WHICH ARE ADDED

MISCELLANIES:

"LITERATURE AS A VOCATION," "POETS AND POETRY," "REFORMS AND REFORMERS," A DEFENCE OF PROTECTION, ETC., ETC.

ALSO,

A DISCUSSION WITH ROBERT DALE OWEN OF THE LAW OF DIVORCE.

BY HORACE GREELEY.

NEW YORK:
J. B. FORD & CO., PRINTING-HOUSE SQUARE.
BOSTON: H. A. BROWN & CO. CHICAGO: J. A. STODDARD & CO.
SAN FRANCISCO: FRANCIS DEWING & CO.
CINCINNATI: C. F. VENT & CO.
1869.

University Press: Welch, Bigelow, & Co.,
Cambridge.

TO

OUR AMERICAN BOYS,

WHO,

BORN IN POVERTY, CRADLED IN OBSCURITY, AND EARLY CALLED FROM SCHOOL TO RUGGED LABOR,

ARE SEEKING

TO CONVERT OBSTACLE INTO OPPORTUNITY, AND WREST ACHIEVEMENT FROM DIFFICULTY,

These Recollections

ARE REGARDFULLY INSCRIBED BY

THEIR AUTHOR.

PUBLISHERS' CIRCULAR.

THE book herewith presented to the public is a collection of the series of articles originally published by MR. GREELEY in the *New York Ledger*, bearing, as now, the accurately descriptive title, "RECOLLECTIONS OF A BUSY LIFE." Revised, and in part rewritten, by the author, and enriched by the addition of much original matter, it is believed that these autobiographical reminiscences will be, not only entertaining and attractive to the casual reader, but of permanent value to all students of the times we live in. They form a record of the inner life and inspiration of one who has actively shared in the many strange intellectual and political phases through which America has gone during the past thirty years of intense vitality. MR. GREELEY himself gives the best indication of their nature: "I shall never write anything else into which I shall put so much of *myself*, my experiences, notions, convictions, and modes of thought, as these *Recollections*. I give, with small reserve, my mental history."

Whatever view may be taken of HORACE GREELEY's opinions and teachings, all will concede that he has been, and is, a man of untiring industry, of strong convictions, of continual and immense intellectual activity, and of wide-spread influence. Laboring in the metropolis of the country, he has there planted and nurtured with his own life a journal whose political and social ideas have been powerful in affecting the public mind beyond any other one agency; and he himself, intimately associated as he has been with all the great men and great events of the time, is a singularly interesting character. The mental history of such a man, and the varied reminiscences of his life and experience, cannot fail to attract the attention and excite the interest of all who take any pains to understand the history of the day; while the practical hints to young men, and the familiar chat about political, literary, agricultural, social, and personal topics contained in the book, must make it welcome to the general reader.

Of the illustrations, the views of MR. GREELEY'S various homes, &c., it is only necessary to say that they have been engraved from the most authentic sources, — generally photographs. The fine portrait of Mr. GREELEY is engraved on steel by MR. J. ROGERS, and that of the accomplished and lamented MARGARET FULLER is from the artistic hand of MR. W. J. LINTON, whose personal remembrance of that gifted lady has been aided by an excellent portrait. In every way, the publishers have endeavored to make the book one attainable and desirable by all, and feel sure that it will prove its own best commendation.

APOLOGY.

THESE Recollections owe their existence wholly to an impulse external to their author, who, of his own choice, writes on many topics, himself not included. When, years ago, he was introduced to Mr. James Parton, and apprised that he had been chosen, by that gentleman, as the subject of a biographic volume, he said that every person whose career was in some sense public was a fair subject for public comment and criticism, but that he could not furnish materials for, nor in any wise make himself a party to, the undertaking. As it had never occurred to him that he should have time and inclination to write concerning himself, he had never saved even a scrap with reference to such contingency; and he has chosen not to avail himself of Mr. Parton's labors, in order that the following chapters should, so far as possible, justify their title of Recollections.

Mr. Robert Bonner is justly entitled to the credit (or otherwise) of having called these Recollections into tangible (even though fleeting) existence. He had previously invited me to write for his Ledger, and had paid me liberally for so doing; but our engagement and intimacy had long ceased, when, on the occasion of the hubbub incited by my bailing of Jefferson Davis, he reopened a long-suspended correspondence, and once more urged me to write for his columns; suggesting a series of autobiographic reminiscences, which

I at first flatly declined to furnish. On mature reflection, however, I perceived that he had proffered me opportunity to commend to many thousands, of mainly young persons, convictions which are a part of my being, and conceptions of public events and interests which might never so fairly invoke their attention if I repelled this opportunity; and that, therefore, I ought not to reject it. Hence, I soon recalled my hasty negative, apprised him that I would accept his offer, and immediately commenced writing, as I could snatch time from other pressing duties, the Recollections herewith printed. That they are less personal and more political than Mr. Bonner would have wished them, I was early aware; yet he allowed all but two of them to appear, and to have the post of honor in successive issues of his excellent and widely circulated periodical. I have added somewhat, however, to nearly half of them, in revising them for publication in this shape; but the reader who may note the discrepancy will be so just as to attribute it to the proper source. In a single instance only, was I requested by Mr. Bonner to change an expression in one of the numbers he published; and therein he was clearly right, as I instantly conceded.

The papers which I have chosen to add to my Recollections, in giving them this permanent form, embody my views on certain topics which I was not able to present so fully in my contributions to The Ledger, yet which I hoped would reward the attention of most readers. That in which Protection is explained and commended was printed as it was hurriedly written more than twenty-five years ago; I present it now, without the change of a sentence, as a statement of views contemptuously rejected by most writers on Political Economy in our day, who never really gave them consideration or thought. That they deserve a different and more respectful treatment, I profoundly believe: the public must judge between me and their contemners.

I hope to be spared to write hereafter a fuller and more systematic exposition of Political Economy from the Protectionist stand-point; and I do not expect henceforth to write or print any other work whatever. If, then, my friends will accept the essays which conclude this volume as a part of my mental biography, I respectfully proffer this book as my account of all of myself that is worth their consideration; and I will cherish the hope that some portion, at least, of its contents embody lessons of persistency and patience which will not have been set forth in vain.

The controversy with Mr. Robert Dale Owen respecting Marriage and Divorce, which is printed at the end of the volume, was wholly unpremeditated on my part, yet I had so clearly, though unintentionally, provoked Mr. Owen's first letter, that I could not refuse to print it; and I could not suffer it to appear without a reply. My strictures incited a response; and so the discussion ran on, till each had said what seemed to him pertinent on a subject of wide and enduring interest. Before my last letter was printed, Mr. Owen, presuming that I had closed, had prepared those already in print for issue in a pamphlet, which accordingly appeared. The whole first appear together in this volume; and I trust it will be found that their interest has not exhaled during the eight years that have elapsed since they were written.

H. G.

NEW YORK, September 1, 1868.

CONTENTS.

MISCELLANIES.

LIST OF ILLUSTRATIONS.

LETTER FROM MR. GREELEY.

New York Tribune,
New York, June 1, 1868.

Gentlemen :—

I wrote my Recollections because Mr. Bonner urged and paid me to do so, and because I hoped thus to make clear to many of our younger generation several points in our country's internal history which have been widely misunderstood. Trusting that these unpretending papers may be found to embody some lessons of industry, integrity, self-reliance, truth, and hope, I commit them to you as the substance of a volume which I dedicate and commend to the portionless youth of this Republic.

Yours,

HORACE GREELEY.

Messrs. J. B. Ford & Co.,
104 Nassau Street, City.

New-York Tribune.

New York, June 1st, 1868.

Gentlemen: I wrote my Recollections, because Mr. Bonner urged and paid me to do so, and because I hoped thus to make clear to many of our younger generation some points in our country's internal history which have been widely misunderstood. That these Recollections may be found to embody some lessons of industry, integrity, self-reliance, truth and hope, I commit them to you as the substance of a volume which I dedicate and commend to the fortuneless youth of this Republic.

Yours, Horace Greeley.

Messrs. J. B. Ford & Co.
164 Nassau St. N.Y.

RECOLLECTIONS OF A BUSY LIFE.

I.

A SAMPLE OF THE SCOTCH-IRISH.

ULSTER, — the most northern of the four provinces into which Ireland is pretty equally divided, — being separated but by a strait from the western coast of Scotland, was doubtless the recipient of emigration thence from time immemorial; but, after the suppression, by Queen Elizabeth, of a bloody insurrection of the Celts under Hugh O'Neil against English domination, a large area of the soil previously held by the insurgents was confiscated; and "The Plantation of Ulster," with some English, but more Scotch emigrants, was effected under James I. More Celtic insurrections naturally followed; that of 1641 being marked as especially murderous; 40,000 of the Protestant settlers in Ulster having been speedily massacred, with small regard to age or sex. Eight years later, Cromwell, heading his terrible "Ironsides," swept resistlessly over Ulster not only, but all Ireland, crushing out her resistance, and leaving in his track but blood, ashes, and ruins; actually subjugating the entire island, for the first time, to British power, and confiscating four fifths of its soil.

Forty years of such peace as subjugation can make was suddenly broken by the expulsion of James II. from the throne of England, mainly because of his Romanism, while Papal Ireland still clung to his falling throne, and resisted the accession of Dutch William and his wife Mary, daughter of James. Ulster, in so far as she was Scotch-English and Protestant, hailed with rapture the new rule; while Catholic Ireland clung to James; who, having fled to France, landed thence at Kinsale, and was received with open arms. The Protestants of Ulster, unaccountably left to themselves, had already been nearly overrun by the French and Irish soldiers of James, who was eager to pass over to Scotland and recruit his forces from the Highlanders of that kingdom, who were already enrolled, under the banners of Grahame of Claverhouse, and eagerly awaiting their monarch's appearance. Londonderry (originally Derry, but re-named on being re-peopled, as above recited, under the patronage of a London company) for months stood up almost alone against the overwhelming forces of James, ably led by Richard Hamilton, and finally by Conrad de Rosen. A poorly walled town of perhaps a thousand houses, garrisoned by a few drilled soldiers, and three or four thousand armed citizens, partly fugitives driven in from the surrounding country, who, wretchedly armed, and most scantily provided with ammunition, commanded for weeks by a traitor (Colonel Lundy), who did all he dared to betray them to their enemies, nevertheless defied the most desperate efforts of their besiegers, with the still more terrible assaults of famine; and even their cowardly desertion by General Kirke, who was sent from England to relieve them with 5,000 men and a supply of provisions, but who recoiled with all his fleet without even seriously attempting to succor the famishing, heroic city. Yet the sorely disappointed and distressed Protestants, so far from despairing, resolved, five days afterward, that no man, on penalty of death, should propose a surrender, and fought on, eating horses, dogs, cats, rats, salted hides and tallow, while scores died of absolute starvation, until not two days' subsistence remained, or only nine lean horses in all, and one pint of meal per man, when, on the 28th of July, 1690, a frigate and two transports ran up the Foyle past the enemy's batteries, and, sadly peppered and cut up, anchored at the quay, — the transports laden with provisions.

Of 7,500 men enrolled for the defence at the outset, but 4,300 survived; and one fourth of these were disabled. That night James's army raised the siege, in which they had lost more than 8,000 men; and the signal defeat of their monarch by his son-in-law in the battle of the Boyne, a few days before, was speedily followed by the utter overthrow and expulsion of the former. Londonderry had saved the kingdom, and enabled William to fight the decisive battle under auspices far more favorable than if James had been allowed to cross into Scotland, and add the Highland clans and their great leader to the army wherewith he struggled for his crown.

A quarter of a century had elapsed. William and Mary were dead; so was their sister and successor, Anne; George I. had been called from Hanover to the throne; when a new migration was meditated and resolved on by a goodly company of the "Scotch-Irish" of Londonderry and its neighborhood. They were rigid Presbyterians, of the school of Knox; the faith and observances of their Celtic neighbors were exceedingly repugnant to them, and those of the Protestant Episcopal Church by law established, little less so. Acts of Uniformity and other prelatical devices bore hardly upon them; they resolved to seek homes where they would enjoy absolute religious freedom. Sending out to New England a young Mr. Holmes to examine and inquire, they were incited by his report to take the decisive step; and a considerable portion of four Presbyterian societies (one of them that of Holmes's father), resolved to cross the Atlantic. Early in 1718 they despatched Rev. William Boyd with an address to Governor Shute, of Massachusetts, signed by 217 of their number, of whom 210 attached their names in fair, legible chirography; nine of them being clergymen. The Governor's response was such that the colony, on receiving it, took passage on five small vessels, landing at Boston, August 4, 1718. Months were now wasted in seeking, in different lands, a location,—the ensuing Winter being passed with great privation and suffering by twenty families of these explorers, near Falmouth, now Portland, Maine, where they were saved from starving by a donation of one hundred bushels of Indian meal from the Massachusetts General Court.

But Spring at length opened. The colonists, returning from Casco Bay, dissatisfied with their experience in that quarter, entered the mouth of the Merrimac, and ascended it to Haverhill; where they heard of an inviting tract of wilderness, known as *Nutfield,* from the abundance of its indigenous chestnut, butternut, and hickory trees. Leaving their families at Haverhill, the men visited this tract, some fifteen miles northward; and, having found it worth their taking, they located thereon their grant from Governor Shute of any twelve miles square of unoccupied land which they should select within the boundaries of his colony, — to find, ultimately, that their Canaan was not in Massachusetts, but New Hampshire, and their grant, consequently, of no use. As many, if not most of them, including nearly all their leaders, had borne part in the defence of the Protestant stronghold of their native land, they, in memory thereof, discarded the name of Nutfield, and were, in 1722, incorporated under that of LONDONDERRY.

Having hastily erected a few huts of logs, the pioneers returned to Haverhill for their families; the day of whose arrival — April 11 (old style), 1719 — is regarded as that on which their settlement was founded. Rev. James McGregor, their chosen pastor, preached (from Isa. xxxii. 2) next day, under a great oak, the first sermon ever listened to in that locality. When he had left to seek his family in Dracut, but sixteen sturdy pioneers and their families remained; and these, for mutual defence against Indians, were located but thirty rods apart, facing a brook; each lot being a mile in depth, or sixty acres in area. But two stone houses of refuge, in case of attack, were soon built, affording some security against savage incursions; and the town was finally laid off into lots, each sixty rods wide on the road it fronted, and a mile deep, making each allotment one hundred and twenty acres. Such were the dimensions of the tract on "the High Range," allotted, in 1721, to my mother's grandfather, John Woodburn, and which was by his industry transformed into the farm whereon she was born, and which is to day the property of her youngest and only surviving brother, John,*

* Since this was first printed he has deceased, aged 72; but the farm descends to his numerous children.

now about 70 years old. The first framed house, wherein she was born, was superseded, about 1800, by that wherein she was married, and whence I first went to school, which is now the family homestead. No price was ever paid for the Woodburn farm, nor has a deed of it ever been given.

Though the infant settlement of Londonderry was rapidly augmented, not only by the flocking thither of the original colonists (whose sixteen families in April had thus been swelled to seventy by September), but by continuous accessions of relatives and friends from the old country, yet brave men long ploughed and sowed with a loaded gun standing as handy as might be, and with a sharp eye on the adjacent woods; and they never went to "meeting" on Sunday without carrying their trusty weapon, first seeing that it was in good order. Nay, their spiritual teacher and guide for months regularly entered his pulpit musket in hand, and, having cocked it and carefully scrutinized the priming, sat it down in one corner, and devoutly addressed himself to the ever-living God. His influence with the Marquis de Vaudreuil, then French Governor of Canada, who had been his classmate at college, and with whom he still maintained a friendly correspondence, was supposed to have averted from his charge the savage attacks by which so many frontier towns were desolated.

Mr. McGregor died in 1729, and was succeeded by Rev. Matthew Clark, a patriarch who now came out from Ireland on purpose, and whose memory deserves a paragraph. He never ate flesh, but said nothing on the subject; and his abstinence was regarded as an idle whim, until one day when my great-grandmother (his niece, as I remember), then a young girl and an inmate of his house, saw the pot wherein the family dinner was cooking boil over into the smaller vessel wherein was boiling his frugal mess of greens. Supposing this of no consequence, she said nothing until — the family being seated at the table, and its head having said grace and taken his first mouthful — he was observed to fall back insensible and apparently dying. Recovering his consciousness after a few moments, he calmed the general excitement by saying, "It is nothing — a trifle — I shall be well directly — only a little of the water from your meat has boiled over into my greens." He had been a lieutenant in the famous Siege, wherein he was wounded in the temple by a ball, which injured a bone so that it never healed; and, though a devoted evangelist, could never forget that he had been a soldier. Once, while acting as Moderator of an assembled Presbytery, the music of a marching company was heard, when his attention was wholly absorbed by it. Being repeatedly called to give heed to the grave business in hand, his steady reply was, "Nae business while I hear the roll of the drum." When death came to him at seventy-six years of age, and after forty years of blameless ministry, he said to sympathizing friends, "I have a last request which must not be denied." "What is it, Father Clark?" "Let me be borne to my rest by my brother soldiers in the Siege, and let them fire a parting volley over my grave!" The military parade was conceded; but, according to my mother's tradition, the volley, though promised, was withheld; it being deemed indecorous and unsuitable that so holy a man should be indulged in a dying freak so unbecoming his cloth.

II.

OUR FOLKS AT LONDONDERRY.

THE current notion that the Puritans were a sour, morose, ascetic people — objecting, as Macaulay says, to bear-baiting, not that it gave pain to the bear, but that it gave pleasure to the spectator — is not justified by my recollections, nor by the traditions handed down through my mother. The pioneers of Londonderry were so thoroughly Puritan that, while their original framed and well-built meeting-house was finished and occupied in the third year of the settlement, when there were none other but log huts in the township, nearly a century elapsed before any other than a Presbyterian or Orthodox Congregational sermon was preached therein, and nobody that *was* anybody adhered to any rival church, down to a period within the memory of persons still living. "The Westminster *Shorter* Catechism"— a rather tough digest of Calvinistic theology, which aroused my infantile wonder as to what a dreadful bore its *longer* counterpart must be — was, within my experience, regularly administered to us youngsters once a week, as a portion of our common-school regimen; and we were required to affirm that "God having, out of his mere good pleasure, from all eternity, elected some to everlasting life," &c., &c., as though it were next of kin to the proposition that two and two make four. If there was anywhere a community strictly, thoroughly Puritan, such was Londonderry down to at least 1800, as she mainly is to-day. And yet there was more humor, more play, more fun, more merriment, in that Puritan community, than can be found anywhere in this anxious, plodding age. All were measurably poor, yet seldom were any hungry; all wore coarse clothes, made in utter contempt of the fashions which, in the course of three or four years, had made their way from Paris to Boston; yet lads and lasses were as comely in each other's eyes, though clad in coarse homespun, as if they had been arrayed in purple and fine linen, and redolent of lavender and patchouli: and they danced with each other through long winter nights with a vigor and zest rarely evinced at Almack's or in Fifth Avenue mansions. Their weddings were far more numerously attended and more expensive than are the average in our day; for not to be invited was an affront, as it implied discredit or insignificance; and all who were invited expected to eat and drink bountifully of the best that could be had. A general discharge of musketry throughout the neighborhood ushered in a wedding-day; and the bridegroom's party, starting from his house, was met by the bride's at a point halfway to hers, when one of each party was chosen to "run for the bottle" to the bride's house; and whichever won the race returned with the prize to the waiting assembly; which, having drunk all around, proceeded, under a dropping fire of musketry, to their destination; where — the ceremony having been duly performed — drinking was resumed, and continued, with alternate feasting and dancing, often till broad daylight.

Nor was this the worst. Our ancestors had somehow caught from their Celtic neighbors, in the old country, despite their general antipathy, the infection of "wakes"; and the house in which lay a corpse awaiting burial was often filled through the night with sympathizing friends, who, after due religious observances, proceeded to drown their sorrow in the strong drink supplied in abundance, whereby strange transformations were sometimes wrought from plaintive grief to exuberant, and even boisterous, hilarity. Funerals were attended by nearly every one who seasonably heard of them, and all would have felt insulted if not asked to drink at least twice; while those who walked to the grave were entitled by usage to a third glass, and at least a lunch, on their return. As none were yet rich, while many were quite poor on their arrival, many families were absolutely impoverished by the expense imposed on them by the funeral of a deceased member; while, if a wedding and a funeral occurred within a few months in a household, it could hardly escape ruin. Happily, living in frugal plenty, almost wholly on their own products, spending much of their time in vigorous exercise in the open air, and having but one doctor within call, they had great tenacity of life; so that funerals were few and far between.

The pioneers of Londonderry brought with them the Potato, which, despite its American origin, was hardly known in New England till they introduced it from Ireland, where it had already taken root and flourished. Some of them, having spent their first winter in America in a neighboring settlement of Massachusetts, planted there a few of the valued tubers, which were duly tended by those to whom they were left; but, the plants being matured, they gathered the seed-balls from the stalks and tried to cook them into edibility; but by no boiling, baking, or roasting could they render them palatable; and they gave it up that those Scotch-Irish had unaccountable tastes.

Next Spring, however, when the garden was duly ploughed, the large, fair "murphies" were rolled out in generous abundance, and, being dubiously tasted, were pronounced quite endurable. Like too many ignorant people, these novices in potato-eating had begun at the wrong end. They could never have made *this* mistake in Londonderry; yet it is related that the first pound of tea ever seen there was received as a present from a Boston friend, and, being duly boiled as a vegetable, and served up as "greens," was unanimously pronounced detestable, and pitched out of doors.

Flaxseed was brought from Ireland by the pioneers; and the growth of flax and production of linen early became important elements of the industry and trade of Londonderry, though every operation, from the sowing of the seed to the bleaching of the cloth, was effected by the simplest manual labor; and I can personally testify that "breaking flax," in the bad, old way, is the most execrably hard work to which a young boy can be set. A skilful, resolute man could hardly make laborer's wages at it now, if the raw material were given him. When the matrons of the town had a neighborhood gathering, — tea, like coffee, being then happily unknown, — each took her "little wheel" under her arm to the house whereto she had been invited, and the flow of conversation and gossip ran on for hours to a constant "whir, whir" of swiftly flying wheels. Whitney's Cotton Gin and Arkwright's Spinning Jenny have long since dismissed those wheels to the moles and the bats; but, so late as 1819, my mother spun and wove a goodly roll of linen from the flax grown on our farm, bleaching it to adequate whiteness by spreading it on the aftermath of a meadow, and watering it thrice per day from a sprinkling-pot.

Poor folks have their vanities as well as the rich. Most of the pioneers had been small farmers or artificers "at home"; and the rude log huts, which were at first inevitable, seemed to many good wives to involve a sacrifice, not only of comfort, but of social standing. Hence it is related of the Morrisons, who were among the first settlers, that the good dame remonstrated against the contemplated homestead until assured that there was no help for it, when she acquiescingly entreated: "A-weel, a-weel, dear John, if it maun (must) be a log-house, *make it a log heegher nor the lave*" (a log higher that the rest).

The settlers knew that their homespun garments (often of tow) contrasted strongly with the trim, dapper apparel of the polished denizens of more refined communities; but they were not thereby disconcerted. Though Burns had not yet strung his immortal lyre, his spirit so flooded their log-cabins that he would have been welcomed and understood in any of them, but would have excited surprise in none. Thus it is related of the Rev. Matthew Clark, already mentioned, that, among the audience in attendance on his ministrations was once a young British military officer, whose scarlet uniform far outshone any rival habiliments, and so fixed the gaze of the young damsels present, that the wearer, enjoying the impression he was making, not only stood through the prayer with the rest, but remained standing after all others had sat down, until the pastor had proceeded for some time with his sermon. At length, noticing a divided attention and its cause, the minister stopped, laid aside his sermon, and, addressing his new hearer, said: "Ye 're a braw (brave) lad; ye ha'e a braw suit of claithes, and we ha'e a' seen them; ye may sit doun." The lieutenant dropped as if shot, and the sermon was resumed and concluded as though it had not been interrupted.

Rev. E. L. Parker's "History of Londonderry," to which I am indebted for many facts, gives the following specimen of Mr. Clark's pulpit efforts. His theme was Peter's assurance that, though all others should forsake his Divine Master, *he* never would; and this was a part of his commentary:—

"Just like Peter — aye mair forrit (forward) than wise; ganging swaggering aboot wi' a sword at his side; an' a puir han' he mad' o' it when he cam' to the trial; for he only cut off a chiel's lug (ear); *an' he ought to ha' split doun his head.*"

This was a gleam of the spirit evoked in the Siege of Derry.

I fear I have nowise portrayed the perfect mingling of humor and piety in the prevalent type of our Scotch-Irish pioneers, — all of them baptized in infancy, and growing up devoted members of the church, — all hearing the Bible read, a hymn sung and a prayer offered, each morning at the family fireside, and these exercises repeated at night, so uniformly, that one of the early pastors, having learned that a parishioner had retired without invoking the throne of grace, forthwith repaired to his dwelling, called up the delinquent and his family, made them kneel and renew their devotions, and did not leave till they were finished; and yet there was never a people who loved play better, or gave it more attention, than these. House-raisings, corn-huskings, and all manner of excuses for festive merry-making, were frequent, and generally improved; games requiring strength, rather than skill, especially wrestling (with, I grieve to say, some boxing), were favorite pastimes; and it is recorded of the pioneers of Peterborough, N. H.,— one of the several swarms sent out by the parent hive in Londonderry, — that, having cut each his hole in the great woods, and reared his log-cabin, a meeting was called to form a church, and generally attended. The object having been duly set forth, some one started the cavil: "I fear we are such a rough set — so given to frolic and drink — that we are not good enough to constitute a church"; but he was instantly silenced by another, who, like a true Calvinist, observed: "Mr. Moderator, if it be the Lord's will that He should have a church in Peterborough, I am sure He will be willing to have it made up of such materials as there are." So it was.

The present township of Londonderry embraces but a fraction of the original town, whose 144 square miles have been sliced away to form the several townships of Derry, Windham, and parts of others, until it now probably contains less than forty square miles. Though a railroad now crosses it, and accords it a station, it has no considerable village, no lawyer (I believe); its people nearly all live by farming, and own the land they cultivate; three fourths of them were born where they live, and there expect to die. Some families of English lineage have gradually taken root among them; but they are still mainly of the original Scotch-Irish stock, and even Celtic or German "help" is scarcely known to them. Simple, moral, diligent, God-fearing, the vices of modern civilization have scarcely penetrated their quiet homes; and, while those who with pride trace their origin to the old settlement are numbered by thousands, and scattered all over our broad land, I doubt whether the present population of Londonderry exceeds in number that which tilled her fields, and hunted through her woods, fifty to sixty years ago.

III.

"THE TIMES THAT TRIED MEN'S SOULS."

THE Scotch-Irish founders of *our* Londonderry indignantly eschewed the characterization of "Irish," which was sometimes maliciously, but oftener ignorantly, applied to them; stoutly insisting that, as stanch Protestants and zealous upholders of the Hanoverian succession, they should not be confounded with the savage and intractable Celtic Papists who were indigenous to Ireland. Devoted loyalty was their pride and boast, and was usefully evinced in the "Old French War," which lasted from 1756 to 1763, and effected a transfer of the Canadas from France to Great Britain; yet the British assumption, directly thereafter, of a right to impose taxes on the Colonies, without their consent, was here early, promptly, zealously, persistently resisted; and the tidings that Colonial blood had been shed by British soldiers at Lexington, Mass., on the 19th of April, 1775, operated like an electric shock on this rural, peace-loving community. Ten minutes after receiving it, JOHN STARK — who had served with distinction in the recent French war — stopped the saw-mill in which he was at work, mounted his horse, and rode off to Cambridge, leaving directions for his neighbors to muster and follow. The two companies of Londonderry militia were immediately assembled, and, though many had already hastened to the scene of action, a full company — the best blood of the township — volunteered, choosing GEORGE REED their captain. Six days after the Lexington fray, the two thousand New Hampshire men now confronting General Gage were organized by the convention sitting at Exeter into two regiments, with Stark and Reed as their respective colonels. Another regiment from this thinly peopled colony was soon formed, under Colonel Poor; but the left wing of our army, stationed near Medford, was composed of the two regiments commanded by Londonderry colonels; and these, under Stark and Reed, were soon deputed to join the Connecticut men under Putnam, and a Massachusetts regiment under Prescott, in throwing up and holding the breastwork on Bunker's or Breed's Hill, in Charlestown, which the British assailed next day with such memorable consequences. Londonderry had 130 men behind those slight defences. In the struggle for this position, the New Hampshire men lost 19 killed and 74 wounded.

The three New Hampshire regiments were detached from Washington's army to swell that which, in 1776, was organized in this State, under General Sullivan, for the conquest of Canada; but which, having invaded that Province, by way of the Hudson and Lake Champlain, found itself outnumbered and compelled to retreat to Ticonderoga, losing a third of its number by sickness, privation, and exposure. Rejoining General Washington, Stark's regiment was conspicuous in the brilliant affair at Trenton, where it had the advance, and participated in the succeeding actions at Princeton and at Springfield, N. J.

In the list of promotions made by Congress next Spring, Stark's name did not appear; whereupon, he promptly and indignantly resigned. But, on the alarm of Burgoyne's invasion from Canada, soon afterward, a fresh appeal to the patriotism of the people was made by the General Assembly of New Hampshire; when Londonderry raised another company of seventy men, besides contributing liberally to existing organizations. In fact, there was nearly a levy *en masse* of the able-bodied men of this State and the debatable lands now known as Vermont. Stark was asked to take command of the new militia, and did so; stipulating only that he should not be subordinate to any other commander. Hence, he refused to obey General Schuyler's order to advance to and cross the Hudson, giving excellent reasons therefor; but, remaining within the territory his men were called out to protect, he fought and won — Aug. 26, 1777 — the brilliant battle of Bennington, routing and killing Colonel Baum, the Hessian commander, and taking five hundred prisoners. His speech to his troops, on the brink of engaging, ran substantially thus: "Boys, you see them Hessians. King George gave £4 7*s.* 6*d.* apiece for 'em. I reckon we are worth more, and will prove it directly. If not, Molly Stark sleeps a widow to-night!" There have been more elegant and far longer speeches; but this went as straight to its mark as a bullet.

The danger to his State having thus been averted, Stark hastened to join General Gates on the Hudson, was in the council which fixed the terms of Burgoyne's surrender, and was soon thereafter restored to position in the Continental line, — Congress making reparation for its oversight by publicly thanking him for his victory at Bennington, and appointing him a Brigadier-General in the regular service. He remained in the army till the close of the war, and lived forty years thereafter, — dying May 8, 1822, in his ninety-fourth year.

Colonel Reed, though not awarded his rank in the Continental line, also served through the war, — taking part in the battles of Long Island, White Plains, Trenton, Saratoga, Stillwater, Brandywine, Germantown, and in Sullivan's Indian expedition. Having at length risen to a Continental colonelcy, he was in command at Albany in 1782, when he was favored with several letters from Washington, of whose military and political character he was evermore a passionate admirer. Having left his family in haste, on the tidings of the first shot, he paid it but two or three hurried visits in midwinter till honorably mustered out of service after the close of the war, in the Summer of 1783. Meantime his wife, Mary, sister of my grandfather Woodburn, was the ruler of his household, the manager of his farm and business, and the sharer in full measure of his fervid, unwearying patriotism. He lived to fill several public stations, including those of Brigadier-General and Sheriff of his county; dying in 1815, aged eighty-two years. His wife survived him; dying in 1823, at the ripe age of eighty-eight.

Never was a war more essentially popular than that waged in support of American Independence, and never were the issues involved more thoroughly debated or more clearly understood by a people. Congress having, early in 1776, requested the authorities of each township to ascertain and to disarm all persons "who are notoriously disaffected to the cause of America," the selectmen of Londonderry reported the names of 374 adult males in that town who had severally signed the following pledge:—

"We, the subscribers, do hereby solemnly engage and promise that we will, to the utmost of our power, at the risk of our lives and fortunes, with arms, oppose the hostile proceedings of the British fleets and armies against the United American Colonies."

Of course, those who had already enlisted, and were then absent in the Continental service, should be added to the above list, raising it nearly to five hundred; while barely fifteen men in that entire community refused to sign. Several "Tories," however, had already left, finding the place too hot for them: among them, Major Robert Rogers, of the "Rangers," raised in 1756, who had served with distinction throughout the French war; but who now, taking the wrong side, was proscribed, and fled to England, where he died. Colonel Stephen Holland, who had been one of the most eminent and popular citizens, and had held several important public trusts, after concealing and denying his Toryism so long as he could, finally proclaimed it by fleeing to General Gage at Boston; whereupon his property was confiscated. Nowhere was Toryism more execrated; and the suggestion in the Treaty of Paris that the Loyalists should be permitted to return to the communities they had, to serve the king, deserted, was unanimously scouted and defied in full town meeting.

Dr. Matthew Thornton, whose name heads the list of signers to the pledge aforesaid, soon afterward affixed his signature to the immortal Declaration of American Independence. He was born in Ireland in 1714, but brought over when but three years old; early commenced the practice of medicine in Londonderry, and steadily rose to esteem and competence. He was a surgeon of the New Hampshire forces in the expedition against Cape Breton, in 1745, and was a colonel of militia at the breaking out of the Revolution. He was President of the first Provincial Convention assembled in New Hampshire after the retirement of the royal Governor Wentworth, and was chosen by it a delegate to Congress, in which he did not take his seat till November, 1776, when — though it was the darkest hour of the struggle — he at once signed the Declaration. After peace was restored, though no lawyer, he was chosen a judge of the Superior Court, and afterward Chief-Justice of the Common Pleas. He died in 1803, aged eighty-nine.

From first to last, Londonderry furnished 347 soldiers to the Revolutionary armies, while her whole number of adult males cannot, as we have seen, have much exceeded 500. Some of these served but for short terms; yet, after making every deduction, this record, from a purely rural township, whose youth had for forty years been constantly drawn away to pioneer new settlements, not only in different parts of New Hampshire, but in Londonderry and Windham, Vermont, Truro, Nova Scotia, Cherry Valley, N. Y., &c., &c., is one which her children have a right to regard with affectionate pride. And not only were town bounties — liberal, considering the value of money in those days — paid to her volunteers, but their families were shielded from want by the provident care of her authorities and people. Food was scarce and dear; clothing was scarcer and dearer; but those who fought their country's battles were consoled by the thought that, whatever might befall them, their wives and little ones should not famish or freeze while bread or cloth remained. And, when independence and peace were at length achieved, it was a proud reflection that they had been won by the constancy and devotion, not of a class or a portion, but of the entire people.

IV.

RURAL NEW ENGLAND FIFTY YEARS AGO.

THREE brothers named Greeley (spelled five different ways) migrated to America in 1640. One settled in Maine, where he has many living descendants; another in Rhode Island, where he soon died; a third in Salisbury, Mass., near the south line of New Hampshire, into which his descendants soon migrated, if he did not. One large family of them hail from Gilmanton; another, to whom I am less remotely related, from Wilton; my own great-grandfather (named Zaccheus, as was his son my grandfather, and *his* son my father) lived in or on the verge of Londonderry, in what was in my youth Nottingham-West, and is now Hudson, across the Merrimac from Nashua (which was then Dunstable or nothing). I never heard of a Woodburn of our stock who was not a farmer; but the Greeleys of our clan, while mainly farmers, are in part blacksmiths. Some of them have in this century engaged in trade, and are presumed to have acquired considerable property; but these are not of the tribe of Zaccheus.

My grandfather Greeley was a most excellent, though never a thrifty citizen. Kind, mild, easy-going, honest, and unambitious, he married young, and reared a family of thirteen,— nine sons and four daughters,— of whom he who died youngest was thirty years old; while a majority lived to be seventy, and three are yet living, — at least two of them having seen more than eighty summers.

So many children in the house of a poor and by no means driving farmer, in an age when food and cloth cost twice the labor they now do, made economy rather a necessity than a virtue; but I presume none of those children ever suffered protractedly from hunger, while all of them obtained such education as was afforded by the common schools of sixty to eighty years ago; or, if not, the fault was their own. Still, the school-houses were ruder and rarer, the teachers less competent, and the terms much shorter, than now; while attendance was quite irregular, being suspended on slight pretexts; so that I have heard my father say that his winter's schooling after he came of age — when for three months he hired his board, attended constantly, and studied diligently — was worth more to him than all that preceded it.

My grandfather owned and worked small farms successively in Hudson, Pelham, Nottingham, and Londonderry, and was living in the latter town for a second or third time when, on the death of his wife, when he was about seventy-five years old, he sold out, and went to spend his remaining days with his son Gilbert, living in Manchester; but, that son dying before him, he found a home thenceforth in Londonderry, with his older son John, whose farm all but joins that of the Woodburns in "the High Range,"— the respective houses being but a hundred rods apart,— and here, in his fulness of days, he died, aged ninety-four. (My grandfather Woodburn had died at eighty-five, nearly thirty years before.) A devoted, consistent, life-long Christian,— originally of the Baptist, but ultimately of the Methodist persuasion,— exemplary in deportment and blameless in life, I do not believe that my grandfather Greeley ever made an enemy; and, while he never held an office, and his property was probably at no time worth $2,000, and generally ranged from $1,000 to zero, I think few men were ever more sincerely and generally esteemed than he by those who knew him.

My father — married at twenty-five to Mary Woodburn, aged nineteen — went first to live with his father, whose farm he was to work, and inherit, supporting the old folks and their still numerous minor children; but he soon tired of this, and seceded; migrating to and purchasing the farm whereon six of his seven children were born.

The old road to Amherst from the Merrimac, at what in my childhood was Amoskeag Falls, crossed by a rickety old bridge, with but two or three houses in sight, and is now the manufacturing city of Manchester, with twenty-five thousand inhabitants, passes through the little village of Piscataquoag, near the mouth of the creek of like name; thence through the township and village of Bedford, and, zigzagging over the gentler hills, descends, when about five miles from "Amherst Plain," or village, and just on the verge of the township, into the deep valley of a brook, not yet quite large enough for a mill-stream. (The road now travelled is far smoother and better, and passes a mile or two southward of the old one.) The "Stewart farm," of some forty acres (enlarged by my father to fifty), covers the hillside and meadow north of the road, with a few acres south of it, and lies partly in Bedford, but mainly in Amherst. The soil is a gravelly loam, generally strong, but hard and rocky; grass, heavy at first, "binds out" the third or fourth year, when the land must be broken up, manured, tilled, and seeded down again; and a breaking-up team, in my early boyhood, was made up of four yoke of oxen and a horse, whereby an acre per day was seldom ploughed. Across the brook were two or three little knolls, of an acre or so each, in good part composed of water-worn pebbles,—the *débris* of I know not what antediluvian commotion and collision of glaciers and marine currents, — which, when duly fertilized and tilled, produced freely of corn or potatoes; but which, being laid down to grass, utterly refused to respond, deeming itself better adapted to the growth of sorrel, milk-weed, or mullein. The potato yielded more bounteously then than it does now, and was freely grown to be fed into pork; but I reckon that Indian corn cost treble, if not quadruple, the labor per bushel that our Western friends now give for it; while wheat yielded meagrely and was a very uncertain crop. Rye and oats did much better, and were favorite crops to "seed down" upon; "rye and Indian" were the bases of the farmer's staff of life; and, when well made, no bread is more palatable or wholesome. The hop culture was then common in our section; and, though fearfully hazardous, — there being no yield one year and no price the next, — was reckoned inviting and productive. My father estimated hops at ten cents per pound as profitable a crop as corn at one dollar per bushel.

My father bought and removed to this farm early in 1808;

"The cot where I was born."

here his first two children died; here I was born (February 3, 1811), and my only surviving brother on the 12th of June, 1812. The house — a modest, framed, unpainted structure of one story — was then quite new; it was only modified in our time by filling up and making narrower the old-fashioned kitchen fireplace, which, having already devoured all the wood on the farm, yawned ravenously for more. This dwelling faces the road from the north on a bench, or narrow plateau, about two thirds down the hill; the orchard of natural fruit covers two or three acres of the hillside northeast of the house, with the patch of garden and a small frog-pond between.

It seemed to me that sweeter and more spicy apples grew in that neglected orchard than can now be bought in market; and it is not a mere notion that most fruits attain their highest and best flavor at or near the coldest latitude in which they can be grown at all. That orchard was not young fifty years ago; and, having been kept constantly in pasture, never tilled nor enriched, and rarely pruned, must be nearly run out by this time.

Being the older son of a poor and hard-working farmer, struggling to pay off the debt he had incurred in buying his high-priced farm, and to support his increasing family, I was early made acquainted with labor. I well remember the cold summer (1816) when we rose on the eighth of June to find the earth covered with a good inch of newly fallen snow,—when there was frost every month, and corn did not fill till October. Plants grew very slowly that season, while burrowing insects fed and fattened on them. My task for a time was to precede my father as he hoed his corn, dig open the hills, and kill the wire-worms and grubs that were anticipating our dubious harvest. To "ride horse to plough" soon became my more usual vocation; the horse preceding and guiding the oxen, save when furrowing for or tilling the planted crops. Occasionally, the plough would strike a fast stone, and bring up the team all standing, pitching me over the horse's head, and landing me three to five feet in front. In the frosty autumn mornings, the working teams had to be "baited" on the rowen or aftermath of thick, sweet grass beside the luxuriant corn (maize); and I was called out at sunrise to watch and keep them out of the corn while the men ate their breakfast before yoking up and going afield. My bare feet imbibed a prejudice against that line of duty; but such premature rising induced sleepiness; so, if my feet had not ached, the oxen would have had a better chance for corn.

Burning charcoal in the woods south and southwest of us was a favorite, though very slow, method of earning money in those days. The growing wood, having then no commercial value, could usually be had for nothing; but the labor of cutting it down and reducing it to the proper length, piling it skilfully, covering the heap with sods, or with straw and earth, and then expelling every element but the carbon by smothered combustion, is rugged and tedious. I have known a pit of green wood to be nine days in burning; and every pit must be watched night and day till the process is complete. Night-watching by a pit has a fascination for green boys, who have hitherto slept soundly and regularly through the dark hours; but a little of it usually suffices. To sit or lie in a rude forest-hut of boards or logs, located three or four rods from the pit, with a good fire burning between, and an open, flaring front looking across the fire at the pit, is a pleasant novelty of a mild, quiet evening; and many a jovial story has been told, many a pleasant game of cards, fox-and-geese, or checkers played, and (I fear) some watermelons lawlessly purveyed from neighboring fields and gardens by night-watching charcoal-burners. But the taste for turning out, looking for and stopping the holes that are frequently burnt through the covering of the pit, is easily sated; while a strong wind that drives the smoke of fire and pit into the open mouth of your shanty, and threatens to set fire to the straw flooring on which you recline, is soon regarded as a positive nuisance, especially if accompanied by a pelting storm. In a wild night, your pit breaks out far oftener than in calm weather; requiring constant attention and effort to keep it from burning up altogether; thus consuming the fruits of weeks of arduous toil. And, after a week of coal-burning, you find it hard to return to regular sleep, but hastily wake every hour or so, and instinctively jump up to see how the pit is going on.

Picking stones is a never-ending labor on one of those rocky New England farms. Pick as closely as you may, the next ploughing turns up a fresh eruption of boulders and pebbles, from the size of a hickory-nut to that of a tea-kettle; and, as this work is mainly to be done in March or April, when the earth is saturated with ice-cold water, if not also whitened with falling snow, youngsters soon learn to regard it with detestation. I filially love the "Granite State," but could well excuse the absence of sundry subdivisions of her granite.

"Hop-picking" was the rural carnival — the festive harvest-home — of those old times; answering to the vintage of southern France or Italy. The hop matures about the first of September, when the vines are cut near the ground, the poles pulled up and laid successively across forked sticks lengthwise of a large bin, into which busy fingers from either side rapidly strip the hops — each pole, when stripped, being laid aside and replaced by another. The bin having been filled, the hops are drawn to the kiln, wherein they are cured by exposure for hours to a constant, drying heat from a charcoal fire below; after which, they are pressed, like cotton, into bales so compact and dense as to defy easy disintegration. The pickers are mainly young women — the daughters of neighboring farmers — and the older children of both sexes; while the handling of the poles demands masculine strength and energy; the work is pushed with ardor, often by rival groups employed at different bins, racing to see which will first have its bin full. The evenings are devoted to social companionship and rustic merry-making; friends drop in to enjoy and increase the festivity; and, if hop-picking is not now an agreeable labor, despite the sore eyes sometimes caught from it, then rural life in hop-growing districts has lost what was one of its pleasantest features half a century ago.

V.

MY EARLY SCHOOL-DAYS.

MY mother, having lost *her* mother when but five years old, was, for the next few years, the especial protégée and favorite of her aged grandmother, already mentioned, who had migrated from Ireland when but fourteen years old, and whose store of Scottish and Scotch-Irish traditions, songs, anecdotes, shreds of history, &c., can have rarely been equalled. These she imparted freely to her eager, receptive granddaughter, who was a glad, easy learner, whose schooling was better than that of most farmers' daughters in her day, and who naturally became a most omnivorous and retentive reader. There were many, doubtless, whose literary acquisitions were more accurate and more profound than hers; but few can have been better qualified to interest or to stimulate the unfolding mind in its earliest stages of development.

I was for years a feeble, sickly child, often under medical treatment, and unable to watch, through a closed window, the falling of rain, without incurring an instant and violent attack of illness. Having suddenly lost her two former children, just before my birth, my mother was led to regard me even more fondly and tenderly than she otherwise might have done; hence, I was her companion and confidant about as early as I could talk; and her abundant store of ballads, stories, anecdotes, and traditions was daily poured into my willing ears. I learned to read at her knee, — of course, longer ago than I can remember; but I can faintly recollect her sitting spinning at her "little wheel," with the book in her lap whence I was taking my daily lesson; and thus I soon acquired the facility of reading from a book sidewise or upside down as readily as in the usual fashion, — a knack which I did not at first suppose peculiar; but which, being at length observed, became a subject of neighborhood wonder and fabulous exaggeration.

Two months before I had attained the age of three years, I was taken home by my grandfather Woodburn to spend a few weeks with him, and sent to school from his house, — the

My First School-House.

school-house of his district being but fifty rods from his door; whereas, our proper school-house in Amherst was two miles, and the nearest school-house (in Bedford) over a mile, from my father's. Hence, I lived at my grandfather's, and went thence to school, most of each Winter and some months in Summer during the next three years.

My first schoolmaster was David Woodburn Dickey, a nephew of my grandfather, a college graduate, and an able, worthy man, though rather a severe than a successful governor of youth. The district was large; there were ninety names on its roll of pupils,—many of them of full-grown men and women, not well broken to obedience and docility,—with an average attendance of perhaps sixty; all to be instructed in various studies, as well as ruled, by a single teacher, who did his very best, which included a liberal application of birch and ferule. He was a cripple; and it was all he could do, with his high spirit and unquestioned moral superiority, to retain the mastery of the school.

Our next teacher in Winter was Cyrus Winn, from Massachusetts,—a tall, muscular, thoroughly capable young man, who rarely or never struck a blow, but governed by moral force, and by appeals to the nobler impulses of his pupils. They were no better, when he took charge of them, than his predecessor's had been,—in fact, they were mainly the same,—yet his sway was far more complete, and the revolts against it much rarer; and when he left us, at the close of his second term, a general attendance of parents on his last afternoon, with a rural feast of boiled cider and doughnuts, attested the emphatic appreciation of his worth. For my own part, I could enjoy nothing, partake of nothing, so intense was my grief at parting with him. It was the first keen sorrow of my life. I never saw him again, but learned that he was drowned the next Winter.

There was an unruly, frolicsome custom of "barring out" in our New Hampshire common schools, which I trust never obtained a wider acceptance. On the first of January, and perhaps on some other day that the big boys chose to consider or make a holiday, the forenoon passed off as quietly as that of any other day; but, the moment the master left the house in quest of his dinner, the little ones were started homeward, the door and windows suddenly and securely barricaded, and the older pupils, thus fortified against intrusion, proceeded to spend the afternoon in play and hilarity. I have known a master to make a desperate struggle for admission; but I do not recollect that one ever succeeded,—the odds being too great. If he appealed to the neighboring fathers, they were apt to recollect that they had been boys themselves, and advise him to desist, and let matters take their course. I recollect one instance, however, where a youth was shut out who thought he ought to have been numbered with the elect, and resolved to resent his exclusion. Procuring a piece of board, he mounted from a fence to the roof of the school-house, and covered the top of the chimney nicely with his board. Ten minutes thereafter, the house was filled with smoke, and its inmates, opening the door and windows, were glad to make terms with the outsider.

The capital start given me by my mother enabled me to make rapid progress in school, — a progress monstrously exaggerated by gossip and tradition. I was specially clever in spelling, — an art in which there were then few even tolerably proficient, — so that I soon rose to the head of the "first class," and usually retained that position. It was a custom of the school to "choose sides" for a "spelling-match" one afternoon of each week, — the head of the first class in spelling, and the pupil standing next, being the choosers. In my case, however, it was found necessary to change the rule, and confide the choice to those who stood second and third respectively; as I — a mere infant of four years — could spell, but not choose, — often preferring my playmates, who could not spell at all.

These spelling-matches usually took place in the evening, when I could not keep my eyes open, and should have been in bed. It was often necessary to rap me sharply when "the word" came around to me; but I never failed to respond; and it came to be said that I spelled as well asleep as awake. I apprehend that this was more likely to be true of some others of the class; who, if ever so sound asleep, could scarcely have spelled worse than they did.

We very generally complain of frequent changes in our school-books, and with reason. Yet we ought to consider that these frequent changes have resulted in signal improvement; that our school-books of to-day are not only far better than those of fifty years ago, but that their improvement has not been fully paralleled elsewhere. When I first went to school, Webster's Spelling-Book was just supplanting Dilworth's; "The American Preceptor" was pushing aside "The Art of Reading"; and the only grammar in use was "The Ladies' Accidence," by Caleb Bingham, — as poor an affair as its name would indicate. Geography was scarcely studied at all; while chemistry, geology, and other departments of natural science, had never been heard of in rural school-houses. "Morse's Geography," which soon came into vogue, was a valuable compend of political and statistical information; but, having barely one map, would scarcely pass for a school geography now. Very soon, Lindley Murray's Grammar and English Reader came into fashion, — solid works, but not well adapted to the instruction of children of eight to fourteen years. In fact, I spent considerable time on grammar to little purpose, and made no decided progress therein, till I had learned to scan my authorities critically, and repudiate their errors. When I had pondered myself into a decided conviction that Murray did not fully understand his subject, and that his giving "Let me be" as an example of the first, and "Let him be" as its correlative in the third person singular of the imperative mood, were simply blunders, which a deeper knowledge of grammar would have taught him to avoid, I had broken loose from the shackles of routine and iteration, and was prepared to accept all the light from any quarter that might irradiate the science. Daniel Adams (a New Hampshire man, now lately deceased) had not then published his lucid and favorite Arithmetic, or, if he had, it had not reached us; Pike's far more difficult work was in general use. I cannot say what progress has very recently been made; but Greenleaf, some thirty or forty years since, shortened the time and effort required to gain a decent knowledge of English grammar by at least one half. I believe like progress has been made in elementary treatises in other departments of knowledge.

The first book I ever owned was "The Columbian Orator,"

given to me by my uncle Perry (husband of my father's oldest sister), as I lay very sick of the measles at my maternal grandfather's, when about four years of age. Those who happen to have been familiar, in its day, with that volume, will recollect it as a medley of dialogues, extracts from orations, from sermons, from speeches in Parliament, in Congress, and at the Bar, with two or three versified themes for declamation, such as "Columbia, Columbia, to glory arise!" and the lines (since attributed to Edward Everett,[1] but who must have written them very young, if he wrote them at all) beginning, "You 'd scarce expect one of my age to speak in public on the stage," — lines which I was dragged forward to recite incessantly, till I fairly loathed them. This "Orator" was my prized text-book for years, and I became thoroughly familiar with its contents; though I cannot say that I ever learned much of value from it, — certainly not oratory. The first large work that I ever read consecutively was the Bible, under the guidance of my mother, when I was about five years old.

I attended school, rather irregularly, during the brief term of my fifth and sixth summers, in the western district of Bedford, about a mile from my father's. For the next two years, we lived in that township, — my father having rented his own farm to a brother, and himself removed to the much larger "Beard Farm," in the eastern part of that town, which he had undertaken to work on shares. Here we were again nearly equidistant from two school-houses; living in the northeastern district, but often attending the school at the centre of the town, which was much larger, and generally better taught.

Here I first learned that this is a world of hard work. Often called out of bed at dawn to "ride horse to plough" among the growing corn, potatoes, and hops, we would get as much ploughed by 9 to 10 A. M. as could be hoed that day; when I would be allowed to start for school, where I some-

[1] Their author, I have learned since the above was first printed, was *Moses* Everett, a Massachusetts teacher of sixty to eighty years ago.

times arrived as the forenoon session was half through. In Winter, our work was lighter; but the snow was often deep and drifted, the cold intense, the north wind piercing, and our clothing thin; beside which, the term rarely exceeded, and sometimes fell short of, two months. I am grateful for much — schooling included — to my native State; yet I trust her boys of to-day generally enjoy better facilities for education at her common schools than they afforded me half a century ago.

The French have a proverb importing that in age we return to the loves of our youth. I have asked myself, "How would you like to return to that cot on the hillside, and spend the rest of your days there?" My answer, is that I would *not* like it, — that, though adversity drove me inexorably thence, I have been so thoroughly weaned that I have no wish to go back "for good." The cot still looks friendly and kindly when I (too seldom) pass it; the farm and the orchard are still familiar objects, and I would gladly muse a sunny, genial Autumn day there; but my heart no longer recognizes that spot as its home.

The last Summer that we lived in New Hampshire, an offer was made by the leading men of our neighborhood to send me to Phillips Academy at Exeter, and thence to college, — the expense being so defrayed that no part of it should fall on my parents. They listened thoughtfully to the proposal, briefly deliberated, then firmly, though gratefully, declined it; saying that they would give their children the best education they could afford, and there stop. I do not remember that I had then any decided opinion or wish in the premises; but I now have; and, from the bottom of my heart, I thank my parents for their wise and manly decision. Much as I have needed a fuller, better education, I rejoice that I am indebted for schooling to none but those of whom I had a right to ask and expect it.

VI.

ADIEU TO NEW HAMPSHIRE.

OUR tenancy of the "Beard Farm," in Bedford, answered very nearly to my seventh and eighth years. That was a large and naturally good farm, but in a state of dilapidation: overgrown with bushes and briers, its fences in ruins, and the buildings barely able to stand alone,—the large two-story house more especially far gone. My father had let his own farm, on shares, to a younger brother, whom he wished and hoped thus to serve, while he was led to expect payment for whatever improvements he should make on that which he had taken instead. He was disappointed every way; his health failed, and he was for nearly a year unable to work; his brother did not prosper on our place; while the promises which had lured us to the larger sphere of effort were not made good. To us children — by this time, four in number — the larger house and broader activities of the hired farm were a welcome exchange; but our fortunes, manifestly, waned there; and I think we were all soberly glad to return to our own snugger house and smaller farm, in the Spring of 1820. As we were trying to work off a lee-shore, I believe neither of us boys went to school at all that Summer, though I was but nine years old, and my brother not eight till June.

All in vain. The times were what is termed "hard,"— that is, almost every one owed, and scarcely any one could pay. The rapid strides of British manufactures, impelled by the steam-engine, spinning-jenny, and power-loom, had utterly undermined the homely household fabrications whereof Londonderry was a prominent American focus; my mother still carded her wool and flax, spun her yarn, and wove her woollen, linen, and tow cloth; but they found no market at living prices; our hops sold for little more than the cost of bagging; and, in short, we were bankrupt. I presume my father had never been quite out of debt since he bought his place; but sickness, rash indorsements (a family failing), and bad luck generally, had swelled his indebtedness to something like $1,000,—which all we had in the world would not, at current prices, pay. In fact, I do not know how much property *would* have paid $1,000 in New Hampshire in 1820, when almost every one was hopelessly involved, every third farm was in the sheriff's hands, and every poor man leaving for "the West" who could raise the money requisite for getting away. Everything was cheap,—dog-cheap,—British goods especially so; yet the comparatively rich were embarrassed, and the poor were often compulsorily idle, and on the brink of famine. I have not been much of a Free-Trader ever since.

We had finished our Summer tillage and our haying, when a very heavy rain set in, near the end of August. I think its second day was a Saturday; and still the rain poured till far into the night. Father was absent on business; but our mother gathered her little ones around her, and delighted us with stories and prospects of good things she purposed to do for us in the better days she hoped to see. Father did not return till after we children were fast asleep; and, when he did, it was with tidings that our ill-fortune was about to culminate. I guess that he was scarcely surprised, though we young ones ruefully were, when, about sunrise on Monday morning, the sheriff and sundry other officials, with two or three of our principal creditors, appeared, and—first formally demanding payment of their claims—proceeded to levy on farm, stock, implements, household stuff, and nearly all our worldly possessions but the clothes we stood in. There had been no writ issued till then,—of course, no trial, no judgment,—but it was a word and a blow in those days, and the blow first, in the matter of debt-collecting by legal process. Father left the premises directly, apprehending arrest and imprisonment, and was invisible all day; the rest of us repaired to a friendly neighbor's, and the work of levying went on in our absence. It were needless to add that all we had was swallowed up, and our debts not much lessened. Our farm, which had cost us $1,350, and which had been considerably improved in our hands, was appraised and set off to creditors at $500, out of which the legal costs were first deducted. A barn-full of rye, grown by us on another's land, whereof we owned an undivided half, was attached by a doctor, threshed out by his poorer customers by days' work on account, and sold; the net result being an enlargement of our debt,— the grain failing to meet all the costs. Thus, when night fell, we were as bankrupt a family as well could be.

We returned to our devastated house; and the rest of us stayed there while father took a journey on foot westward, in quest of a new home. He stopped in the township of Hampton, Washington County, N. Y., and worked there two or three months with a Colonel Parker French, who tilled a noble farm, and kept tavern on the main road from Troy into western Vermont. He returned to us in due time, and, on the 1st of January, 1821, we all started in a hired two-horse sleigh, with the little worldly gear that was left us, for the township of Westhaven, Vermont, where father had hired, for $16 per annum, a small house, in which, after an intensely cold journey, we were installed three days later.

Let me revert for a little to our New Hampshire life, ere I bid it a final adieu.

I have already said that Amherst and Bedford are in the main poor towns, whose hard, rocky soil yields grudgingly, save of wood. Except in the villages, if even there, there were very few who could be called forehanded in my early boyhood. Poor as we were, no richer family lived within sight of our humble homestead, though our western prospect was only bounded by the "Chestnut Hills," two or three miles away. On the east, our range of vision was barred by the hill on the side of which we lived. The leading man of our neighborhood was Captain Nathan Barnes, a Calvinist deacon, after whom my brother was named, and who was a farmer of decided probity and sound judgment,— worth, perhaps, $ 3,000. Though an ardent Federalist, as were a majority of his townsmen, he commanded a company of "exempts," raised to defend the country in case of British invasion, during the war of 1812.

The Revolutionary War was not yet thirty years bygone when I was born, and its passions, its prejudices, and its ballads were still current throughout that intensely Whig region. When neighbors and neighbors' wives drew together at the house of one of their number for an evening visit, there were often interspersed with "Cruel Barbara Allen," and other love-lorn ditties then in vogue, such reminiscences of the preceding age as "American Taxation," a screed of some fifty prosaic verses, opening thus: —

> "While I relate my story,
> Americans, give ear;
> Of Britain's fading glory
> You presently shall hear.
> I 'll give a true relation,
> (Attend to what I say,)
> Concerning the taxation
> Of North America."

The last throes of expiring loyalty are visible in this long-drawn ballad,— Bute and North, and even Fox, being soundly berated for acts of tyranny whereof their royal master, George III., was sole author, and they but reluctant, hesitating, apprehensive instruments.

The ballads of the late war with Great Britain were not so popular in our immediate neighborhood, though my mother had good store of these also, and sang them with spirit and effect, along with "Boyne Water," "The Taking of Quebec," by Wolfe, and even "Wearing of the Green," which, though dating from Ireland's '98, has been revived and adopted in our day, with so vast and deserved an Irish popularity.

We were, in the truest sense, democrats, we Scotch-Irish Federalists from Londonderry, where Jefferson received but two votes in the memorable struggle of 1800. When, for a single year at the "Beard Farm," our house echoed to the tread of a female "help," whose natural abilities were humble, and whose literary acquirements were inferior even to ours, that servant always ate with the family, even when we had the neighbors as "company"; and, though her wages were but fifty cents a week, she had her party, and invited the girls of the neighborhood to be her guests at tea, precisely as if she had been a daughter of the house. Nowhere were manners ever simpler, or society freer from pretension or exclusiveness, than in those farmers' homes.

Hospitality was less bounteous, and kinship less prized, than in the days of the Scotch-Irish pioneers; but there was still much visiting of relatives and social enjoyment, especially in Winter, when hundreds returned to the old Londonderry hive from the younger swarms scattered all over the East: some of them beginning to stretch away even to the far "Holland Purchase," in Western New York; then practically as distant as Oregon or Alaska now is. I remember when the Doles left the "Chestnut Hills" to pitch their tent in Illinois, — then a far bolder venture than migration to Sitka would now be. I have often seen my grandfather Woodburn's house crammed for days with cousins and nephews from Vermont and other 'Derry settlements, who could not be so many as to miss a hearty welcome. *Our* house was far smaller, and less frequented; but its latch-string was always out; and a free liver, with twelve brothers and sisters, to say nothing of their partners by marriage and their children, is not apt to be persistently shunned. In fact, we lived better than we could afford to (as poor folks are too apt to do), and this was one cause of our downfall. My father, as proud as he was poor, spared nothing when friends and relatives, especially those of higher social standing, favored him with their company, and was rarely found unable to fulfil their most sanguine expectations. When too many dropped in upon us at once, or we were found deficient in the luxuries they might fairly expect, he had a habit of telling them this anecdote: —

"When I was a boy of fifteen," said he, "I worked two summers in the great brick-yards of Medford, Mass. My employer, Mr. Marshall, was at first a new man in the community, whose wife deemed it incumbent on her to give her neighbors a tea-party, as a prelude to better acquaintance. In those ante-canal days, wheaten flour was a luxury, though nearly all had it for 'company' occasions; ordinarily, our bread was made of 'rye and Indian' exclusively. Mrs. Marshall, on the great occasion, had the inevitable 'short-cake' for tea,— of rye flour, as all could perceive: still, it was not imperative on common folks to proffer cake of wheaten flour; and all would have passed off without remark, and been soon forgotten, but for a maladroit explanation by the hostess. 'Ladies,' said she to her guests, 'I beg you not to infer that we have no wheat flour, from the fact that I give you rye short-cake. We *have* wheat flour in the house; but I thought I would save that for Mr. Marshall, when he comes to work hard in haying-time.'" The astonished guests tittered; the glee broadened into a loud laugh as the explanation galloped through the neighborhood; and it readily passed into a proverb, that anything deficient on a kindred occasion was saved for Mr. Marshall in haying-time. "Friends," added my father, in conclusion, "if you note anything deficient in our fare, consider that it is saved for Mr. Marshall in haying-time."

VII.

WESTHAVEN.

THE township of Westhaven, Vermont, comprises that irregular corner of the State which is bounded by Lake Champlain on the west, and by Hampton and Whitehall, N. Y., on the south and southeast, and may be roughly compared to a very blunt wedge driven into the State of New York; its point being formed by the rather sharp angle which the little Poultney river, which here divides the two States, makes with the Lake, in which it is finally lost. The general plain or level, widening from south to north, which separates the Green Mountains from that lake, is here repeatedly broken by gentle upheavals of limestone, and, less frequently, by higher and more precipitous ridges of gneiss or of trap, which increase in number and height as you approach the chain of verdant hills which have given the State her name.

This whole region was thickly covered by heavy timber, — in good part, white pine, — when its devastation by our race commenced; and its proximity to navigable water, with the abundance of mill-streams everywhere pervading it, incited its rapid monopoly for "lumbering" purposes. A Dr. Smith, from Connecticut, — brother of one and uncle of another Governor of that State, — pitched his tent in Westhaven (then a part of Fairhaven) some seventy to eighty years ago, and did great execution upon the pines; rapidly amassing wealth, and becoming an extensive landholder. Death stopped him in mid-career, paralyzing his activity, and dividing his property, whereof part was inherited by his brother, and the residue by his widow; who soon married Christopher Minot, a Boston banker, who thenceforth made his home in Westhaven; inhabiting the spacious mansion which his predecessor had barely lived to complete. Our first home in Vermont was on his estate, and within a few rods of his mansion; and we mainly worked for him, or on his land, while we lived in that town.

Westhaven might have been, and should be to-day, a rich grazing township; but for its original wealth of pines, it probably would have been. But its pioneers, high and low, were lumbermen; and it has never yet liberated itself from their baleful sway. As Moore says,—

"The trail of the serpent is over it all."

As the pines had begun to fail, I presume its population was declining when we settled there, or a house that might be lived in with frugal comfort could not have been hired for $16 per annum; but it had then a considerably larger population than it has to-day,—our school-district at least twice as much. "Going West" has ever since been the general proclivity; though I believe any one who understands and likes dairy farming can buy land and buildings there cheaper than anywhere beyond the Ohio. By and by some one will settle there who knows how to apply the superabundant lime to the strong but stubborn clay; making farms richly worth $100 per acre which now go begging at $30. Until then, let Westhaven sleep; for *I* lack power or time to wake her. I can heartily commend her remaining people—all farmers, after a sort—as too honest to need a lawyer, and too wise to support a grog-shop, even though the law had not forbidden any one to open it.

When we first set our stakes there, father was thirty-eight and mother was thirty-three years old. I was not quite ten; my brother and two sisters, eight, six, and four, respectively. A third sister—the youngling of the flock—was born two years later; and all five of us children have been spared through the intervening forty-seven years.

We now made the acquaintance of genuine poverty,—not

beggary, nor dependence, but the manly American sort. Our sum total of worldly goods, including furniture, bedding, and the clothes we stood in, may have been worth $200; but, as we had afterward to pay that amount on old New Hampshire debts, our material possessions may be fairly represented by 0, with a credit for $200 worth of clothing and household stuff. Yet, we never needed nor ran into debt for anything; never were without meal, meat, and wood, and very rarely without money. Father went to chopping at fifty cents per day, without repining or apprehension; and we children all went to school till Spring, though there were no school-funds in those days, and rate-bills for four children made quite a hole in a gross income of $3 per week. Hitherto, we had never lived within a mile of a school-house; now, we were within fifty rods of one, — in fact, of *two;* for a quarrel had split the district, and two schools were in full blast on our arrival, — one on either side of us. The Vermont schools were rather better than the New Hampshire, — better, at least, in this: their terms were longer. I never tried them in Summer, — except during one *very* rainy day; but I had a full opportunity in Winter; and I deeply regret that such homely sciences as Chemistry, Geology, and Botany were never taught, — were not even named therein. Had our range of studies included these, I had ample time to learn something of them; and this would have proved of inestimable value to me evermore. Yet, I am thankful that Algebra had not yet been thrust into our rural common schools, to knot the brains and squander the time of those who should be learning something of positive and practical utility.

Before the Spring of 1821 opened, father had taken a job of clearing fifty acres of wild land, a mile north of our cot; and here he and his sons were employed, save in Winter, for the next two years.

The work was rugged and grimy, but healthful. The land had been timbered with Yellow Pine, a thousand years before, — as a hundred giant trunks, long since prostrated, but not yet wholly mouldered back to dust, attested. This was followed by a forest of White Pines, of which hundreds were still standing, mostly lifeless; while a large number lay prone and dead, though the trunks were mainly sound. Black Ash in abundance formed a later and generally living growth; though a fierce conflagration, which swept over this whole region, during a great drouth, four years before we saw it, had devoured much, and killed more of the forest, but increased the undergrowth of Beech, Alder, Poplar, etc., which we were required to dispose of. When we first attacked it, the snow was just going, and the water and slush were knee-deep. We were all indifferent choppers, when compared with those who usually grapple with great forests; and the job looked so formidable that travellers along the turnpike which skirted our task were accustomed to halt and comfort us with predictions that we boys would be grown men before we saw the end of it. But, cutting trees and bushes; chopping up great trunks into manageable lengths, drawing them together, rolling up and burning great heaps of logs; saving out here and there a log that would do to saw; digging out rotten pines from the soil wherein they had embedded themselves, so that they might dry sufficiently to burn; piling and burning brush and rotten or worthless sticks, and carting home such wood as served for fuel, we persevered until the job was done; when I could have begun another just like it and managed so as not to require more than two thirds of the labor we expended on this. And now, if any one has a great tract of land to clear of trees, decaying logs, and bushes, I fancy that I might give him hints worth considering. N. B. — I work for pay.

We had been farmers of the poorer class in New Hampshire; we took rank with day-laborers in Vermont. We had lived freely, though not lavishly, much less sumptuously, in our earlier home; here, we were compelled to observe a sterner frugality. The bread of our class in this section was almost exclusively made of rye, — Indian corn being little grown on the clay soil of Western Vermont, — and, though there are always about six women alive who know how to make of rye the best bread ever tasted, our mother was not one of these, and never learned their admirable art. Then the clay itself, alternating with the weather from mire to rock, is not well adapted to bare feet; while the detestable Canada thistles, which infest every road and almost every field in Westhaven, are not conducive to placidity of temper or propriety of speech. Having the sharp lances of these thistles dug out of my festered feet with needles was long my daily terror and my nightly torture; the tough, horny integument with which their rough experiences had covered our naked feet rendering the dislodgement of the thistle-beards more laborious and painful than any soft-footed person can realize. I have never since been able to appraise stiff clay soils at their full value.

A precipitous ledge, eighty rods east of the turnpike from which we worked westward, afforded us good spring water, and supplied us also with rattlesnakes, whereof we killed some, which might have proved annoying to us barefoot boys, as we worked among the brush and weeds, had they caught the idea. Still, clearing land is pleasant work, especially when you have a hundred heaps of logs and brush burning at once of a dark, windy night; while ten or twenty acres of fallen, leafy timber, on fire at once, affords a magnificent spectacle. We were to have had $7 per acre, with the use of a team, and half the wood suitable for timber and fuel; and, though $350, even in those days, was not large pay for two years' work of a man and two boys, we were well satisfied. In the event, however, Mr. Minot died before we had effected a settlement; when his estate was declared insolvent, and we were juggled out of a part of our pay.

Our third year in Vermont was spent two miles farther west, where we inhabited and worked a little place known as Flea Knoll, while father ran a neighboring saw-mill on shares. As he sawed twelve hours on and twelve off, with a partner, I insisted on being his helper; but I think once working from noon till midnight satiated my ambition, and I never fully learned the art and mystery of sawing boards by water-power. My brother, though younger, was more persistent, and made greater progress. I gave that Summer pretty diligently to farming, with very meagre results. First, the season was wet till the 1st of June; and our corn, planted in mortar, encountered a brick-like crust when it undertook to come up; and, unable to pierce or break it, pushed laterally under it for two inches or so, until we dug off the crust, and introduced the pale, imprisoned shoots to sunshine. Next came a long Summer of intense drouth, baking and cracking our fields, so that the hoe made no serious impression on their rock-like masses, causing the corn to stand still and turn yellow, while the thistles came up thick, rank, and vigorous, covering the fields with a verdure most deceitful to the eye at a distance. We had failed in an attempt to make maple sugar that Spring: the season being bad, the trees distant, and our knowledge of the art very meagre; our crops amounted to little; while the water we drank here was so bad that the fever and ague struck down our parents in the Fall, and all of us children next Spring, when we beat a precipitate retreat from "Flea Knoll," — where it was said that no family ever remained more than a year, — and returned to the Minot estate; living in a larger house just west of our former tenement, cultivating the adjacent land on shares, and clearing off some twenty acres more of young White Pine, for which we were to be paid by two years' crops; which proved, in the main, a failure: our wheat being destroyed by the midge.

Thus ended my boyish experiences of farming, which may be said to have commenced in my sixth, and closed with my fifteenth year. During the whole period, though an eager and omnivorous reader, I never saw a book that treated of Agriculture and the natural sciences auxiliary thereto. I think I never saw even one copy of a periodical devoted mainly to farming; and I doubt that we ever harvested one bounteous crop. A good field of rye, or corn, or grass, or potatoes, we sometimes had; but we had more half crops than whole ones; and a good yield of any one product was generally balanced by two or three poor ones. I know I had the stuff in me for an efficient and successful farmer; but such training as I received at home would never have brought it out. And the moral I would deduce from my experience is simply this: *Our farmers' sons escape from their fathers' calling whenever they can, because it is made a mindless, monotonous drudgery, instead of an ennobling, liberalizing, intellectual pursuit.* Could I have known in my youth what a business farming sometimes is, always may be, and yet generally shall be, I would never have sought nor chosen any other. In the farmer's calling, as I saw it followed, there was neither scope for expanding faculties, incitement to constant growth in knowledge, nor a spur to generous ambition. To preserve existence was its ordinary impulse; to get rich, its exceptional and most exalted aim. So I turned from it in dissatisfaction, if not in disgust, and sought a different sphere and vocation.

Fairhaven, lying southeast of Westhaven, was the poorer of the two towns thirty years ago, producing no surplus but of rye, which was readily transmuted into whiskey, and drank at home to no profit; but the more recent development of her natural wealth in slate, with the erection of mills for sawing the marble abundantly found a few miles farther east, has given her a pretty rapid and quite substantial growth. Though limited in area, and nowise inviting in soil, Fairhaven now takes rank with the more prosperous townships of Vermont; a considerable accession of inhabitants, — mainly Welsh miners and Irish laborers, — with the erection of new dwellings and other structures, evincing the thrift which everywhere attends or follows the opening of a new field for productive industry. Fairhaven might to-day be mistaken, at a hasty glance, for a growing township of Pennsylvania or Ohio; while Westhaven — having no pursuit but Agriculture — lies petrified and lifeless as though located in Nova Scotia or Lower Canada. Clearly, Man was not intended to live by bread alone, — whether the eating or the growing of it.

VIII.

MY APPRENTICESHIP.

HAVING loved and devoured newspapers — indeed, every form of periodical — from childhood, I early resolved to be a printer if I could. When but eleven years old, hearing that an apprentice was wanted in the newspaper office at Whitehall, I accompanied my father to that office, and tried hard to find favor in the printer's eyes; but he promptly and properly rejected me as too young, and would not relent; so I went home downcast and sorrowful. No new opportunity was presented till the Spring of 1826, when an apprentice was advertised for by the publishers of The Northern Spectator, at East Poultney, Vt. That paper had just been purchased by an association of the leading citizens of the place from its founders, Messrs. Smith and Shute, who had started it as The Poultney Gazette three or four years before. The village, though larger and more active then than now, was not adequate to the support of a newspaper; but the citizens thought otherwise, and resolved to maintain one, under the management of a committee. So they hired from New York an editor, — Mr. E. G. Stone, brother of the more distinguished editor of The Commercial Advertiser, — paid handsomely for the printing-office and good-will, and went ahead. Much of the old force having left with the retiring publishers, there was room for a new apprentice, and I wanted the place. My father was about starting for the wide West in quest of a future home; so, not needing at the moment my services, he readily acceded to my wishes. I walked over to Poultney, saw the publishers, came to an understanding with them, and returned; and a few days afterward — April 18, 1826 — my father took me down, and verbally agreed with them for my services. I was to remain till twenty years of age, be allowed my board only for six months, and thereafter $40 per annum in addition for my clothing. So I stopped, and went to work; while he returned to Westhaven, and soon left in quest of a more inviting region. He made his way to the town of Wayne, Erie County, Pennsylvania, on the State line opposite Clymer, Chautauqua County, N. Y., — a spot where his brothers Benjamin and Leonard had, three or four years earlier, made holes in the tall, dense forest, which then covered nearly all that region for twenty to fifty miles in every direction. He bought out first one, then another pioneer, until he had at length two or three hundred acres of good land, but covered with a heavy growth of Beech, Maple, Elm, Hemlock, &c. Having made his first purchase, — which included a log hut, and four acres of clearing, — he returned for his family; and I walked over from Poultney to spend a Sabbath with and bid them farewell.

It was a sad parting. We had seen hard times together, and were very fondly attached to each other. I was urged by some of my kindred to give up Poultney, — where there were some things in the office not exactly to my mind, — and accompany them to their new home; whence, they urged, I could easily find, in its vicinity, another and better chance to learn my chosen trade. I was strongly tempted to comply; but it would have been bad faith to do so; and I turned my face once more toward Poultney with dry eyes but a heavy heart. A word from my mother, at the critical moment, might have overcome my resolution; but she did not speak it, and I went my way; leaving the family soon to travel much farther, and in an opposite direction. After the parting was over, and I well on my way, I was strongly tempted to return; and my walk back to Poultney (twelve miles) was one of the slowest and saddest of my life.

I have ever since been thankful that I did not yield to the temptation of the hour. Poultney was a capital place to serve an apprenticeship. Essentially a rural community, her people are at once intelligent and moral; and there are few villages wherein the incitements to dissipation and vice are fewer or less obtrusive. The organization and management of our establishment were vicious; for an apprentice should have one master; while I had a series of them, and often two or three at once. First, our editor left us; next, the company broke up or broke down, as any one might have known it would; and a mercantile firm in the village became owners and managers of the concern; and so we had a succession of editors and of printers. These changes enabled me to demand and receive a more liberal allowance for the later years of my apprenticeship; but the office was too laxly ruled for the most part, and, as to instruction, every one had perfect liberty to learn whatever he could. In fact, as but two, or at most three, persons were employed in the printing department, it would have puzzled an apprentice to avoid a practical knowledge of whatever was done there. I had not been there a year before my hands were blistered and my back lamed by working off the very considerable edition of the paper on an old-fashioned, two-pull Ramage (wooden) press, — a task beyond my boyish strength, — and I can scarcely recall a day wherein we were not hurried by our work. I would not imply that I worked too hard; yet I think few apprentices work more steadily and faithfully than I did throughout the four years and over of my stay in Poultney. While I lived at home, I had always been allowed a day's fishing, at least once a month in Spring and Summer, and I once went hunting; but I never fished, nor hunted, nor attended a dance, nor any sort of party or fandango, in Poultney. I doubt that I even played a game of ball.

Yet I was ever considerately and even kindly treated by those in authority over me; and I believe I generally merited and enjoyed their confidence and good-will. Very seldom was a word of reproach or dissatisfaction addressed to me by one of them. Though I worked diligently, I found much time for reading, and might have had more, had every leisure hour been carefully improved. I had been generously loaned books from the Minot house while in Westhaven; I found good ones abundant and accessible in Poultney, where I first made the acquaintance of a public library. I have never since found at once books, and opportunity to enjoy them, so ample as while there; I do not think I ever before or since read to so much profit. They say that apprenticeship is distasteful to, and out of fashion with, the boys of our day: if so, I regret it for their sakes. To the youth who asks, "How shall I obtain an education?" I would answer, "Learn a trade of a good master." I hold firmly that most boys may thus better acquire the knowledge they need than by spending four years in college.

I was kindly allowed to visit my father's family in their new Western home twice during my apprenticeship; having a furlough of a month in either instance. I made either journey by way of the Erie Canal, on those line-boats whose "cent and a half a mile, mile and a half an hour," so many yet remember. Railroads, as yet, were not; the days passed slowly yet smoothly on those gliding arks, being enlivened by various sedentary games; but the nights were tedious beyond any sleeping-car experience. At daybreak, you were routed out of your shabby, shelf-like berth, and driven on deck to swallow fog while the cabin was cleared of its beds and made ready for breakfast. I say nothing as to "the good old times"; but, if any one would recall the good old line-boats, I object. And the wretched little tubs that then did duty for steamboats on Lake Erie were scarcely less conducive to the increase and diffusion of human misery. I have suffered in them to the extent of mortal endurance; I have left one at Dunkirk, and walked twenty miles to Westfield, instead of keeping on by boat at a trifling charge, simply because flesh and blood could bear the torture no longer. I trust I have due respect for "the good old ways" we often hear of; yet I feel that this earthly life has been practically lengthened and sweetened by the invention and construction of railroads.

Among the incidents of my sojourn in Poultney that made

most impression on my mind is a fugitive slave-chase. New York had professed to abolish slavery years before, but had ordained that certain born slaves should remain such till twenty-eight years old; and the year of jubilee for certain of these had not yet come. A young negro, who must have been uninstructed in the sacredness of constitutional guaranties, the rights of property, &c., &c., &c., feloniously abstracted himself from his master in a neighboring New York town, and conveyed the chattel-personal to our village; where he was at work when said master, with due process and following, came over to reclaim and recover the goods. I never saw so large a muster of men and boys so suddenly on our village-green as his advent incited; and the result was a speedy disappearance of the chattel, and the return of his master, disconsolate and niggerless, to the place whence he came. Everything on our side was *impromptu* and instinctive; and nobody suggested that envy or hate of "the South," or of New York, or of the master, had impelled the rescue. Our people hated injustice and oppression, and acted as if they could n't help it.

Another fresh recollection of those far-off days concerns our Poultney celebration of the fiftieth anniversary of American Independence. I know we still celebrate the Fourth of July; but it does seem to me that the glory has departed. In those times, we had always from twenty to fifty Revolutionary soldiers on the platform,—veterans of seventy to ninety years, in whose eyes the recurrence of the nation's anniversary seemed to rekindle "the light of other days." The semi-centennial celebration brought out these in full force,—the gatherings were unusually large, and the services impressive; since few of those present, and none of the veterans, could rationally hope to see its repetition. The Declaration of Independence sounded far less antediluvian than it now does; the quarrel of the colonists with King George, if not recent, was yet real; and the old soldiers forgot for a day their rheumatism, their decrepitude, and their poverty, and were proud of their bygone perils and hardships, and their abiding scars. I doubt that Poultney has since been so thrilled with patriotic emotion as on that 4th of July, 1826; and when we learned, a few days later, that Thomas Jefferson and John Adams, the author and the great champion, respectively, of the Declaration, had both died on that day, and that the messengers bearing South and North, respectively, the tidings of their decease, had met in Philadelphia, under the shadow of that Hall in which our Independence was declared, it seemed that a Divine attestation had solemnly hallowed and sanctified the great anniversary by the impressive ministration of Death.

Time works changes, even where a hasty glance discerns but immobility and virtual stagnation. A railroad from Troy to Rutland (*via* Eagle Bridge and Salem, N. Y.) now runs through West Poultney; increasing the decided advantage which that village had already achieved over its rival by the establishment within its limits of a great Methodist seminary and of certain manufactures. East Poultney has fewer stores, fewer mechanics' shops, less business, and fewer inhabitants, than when I first saw it, forty-odd years ago; while scarcely a house has meantime been built within its limits. It is still a pleasant place to visit, however; and I live in hopes of spending a quiet week there ere I die.

Our paper was intensely Adams and Clay before, and in the Presidential struggle of 1828, and our whole community sympathized with its preference. The defection of our State's foremost politician, Governor Cornelius P. Van Ness, after he had vainly tried, while professing to be an Adams man, to vault from the Governor's chair into the United States Senate, created a passing ripple on the face of the current, but did not begin to stem it. A few active yet unpopular politicians went over with him; but the masses stood firm, especially in our section, where the influence of Hon. Rollin C. Mallary, our representative in Congress, was unrivalled. The Jackson party nominated him for Congress; but that did not affect his position, nor much affect his vote, which in any case would have been nearly unanimous. We Vermonters were all Protectionists;

and Mr. Mallary was the foremost champion of our cause in the House. He made a speech in Poultney the evening before the election, when, though the omens were sinister, we still hoped that Adams might be reëlected. The Jackson paper nearest us headed its Electoral Ticket, "For General Jackson and a Protective Tariff"; and Jackson men all over the North and West protested that their party was as decidedly for Protection as ours; pointing to the attitude of Pennsylvania, at once the leading Protectionist and the strongest Jackson State; but we could not help seeing that all the Free Traders were for Jackson; that Calhoun was running with him for Vice-President; and that South Carolina was threatening nullification and forcible resistance if the Protective policy were not abandoned; and we concluded that either Pennsylvania or Carolina must be cheated, and that the latter would take good care not to be. So Mr. Mallary urged us to stand fast by those whom we *knew* to be devoted to our cherished policy, rather than try those whose professions were discredited by notorious facts; and the response in our section was enthusiastic. Poultney gave next day 334 votes for Adams to 4 for Jackson. I doubt that her vote has ever since been so unanimous or so strong. And, though the general result was heavily adverse to our desperate hopes, — only New England, not quite half of New York, New Jersey, Delaware, and part of Maryland, giving Mr. Adams their votes; while Pennsylvania, the rest of New York, and all the South and West, went against him, — we had the poor consolation, that, for whatever disaster the political revolution might involve, no shadow of responsibility could rest on our own Vermont.

IX.

MY FAITH.

I MUST have been about ten years old, when, in some school-book, whereof I have forgotten the name, I first read an account of the treatment of the Athenians by Demetrius, called Poliorcetes (Destroyer of Cities), one of the successors of "Macedonia's madman." I cannot rediscover that account; so I must be content with the far tamer and less vivid narration of the French historian Rollin:—

"Demetrius had withdrawn himself to Ephesus after the Battle of Ipsus, [wherein he was routed,] and thence embarked for Greece; his whole resources being trusted to the affection of the Athenians, with whom he had left his fleet, money, and wife, Deidamia. But he was strangely surprised and offended when he was met on his way by ambassadors from the Athenians, who came to apprise him that he could not be admitted into their city, because the people had, by a decree, prohibited the reception of any of the kings; they also informed him that his consort, Deidamia, had been conducted to Megara with all the honors and attendance due to her dignity. Demetrius was then sensible of the value of honors and homages extorted by fear, and which did not proceed from the will. The posture of his affairs not permitting him to revenge the perfidy of that people, he contented himself with intimating his complaints to them in a moderate manner, and demanded his galleys; with which, as soon as he had received them, he sailed toward the Chersonesus."

Not many months elapsed before, through one of those strange and sudden mutations which were frequent throughout his career, the fortunes of Demetrius were completely restored, and he was enabled to settle his running account with those who had proved so treacherous in his adversity. I return here to the narration of Rollin: —

"Athens, as we have already observed, had revolted from Demetrius, and shut her gates against him. But, when that prince thought he had sufficiently provided for the security of his territories in Asia, he moved against that rebellious and ungrateful city, with a resolution to punish her as she deserved. The first year was devoted to the conquest of the Messenians, and of some other cities which had quitted his party; but he returned the next season to Athens, which he closed, blocked up, and reduced to the last extremity, by cutting off all influx of provisions. A fleet of a hundred and fifty sail, sent by King Ptolemy to succor the Athenians, and which appeared off the coast of Ægina, afforded them but a transient joy; for, when this naval force saw a strong fleet arrive from Peloponnesus to the assistance of Demetrius, besides a great number of other vessels from Cyprus, and that the whole amounted to three hundred, they weighed anchor and fled.

"Although the Athenians had issued a decree by which they made it a capital offence for any person even to mention a peace with Demetrius, the extremity to which they were reduced obliged them to open their gates to him. When he entered the city, he commanded the inhabitants to assemble in the theatre, which he surrounded with armed troops, and posted his guards on either side of the stage where the dramatic pieces were wont to be performed; and then, descending from the upper part of the theatre, in the manner usual with actors, he showed himself to the multitude, who seemed more dead than alive, and awaited the event in inexpressible terror, expecting it would prove their sentence to destruction; but he dissipated their apprehensions by the first words he uttered: for he did not raise his voice like a man enraged, nor deliver himself in any passionate or insulting terms; but softened the tones of his voice, and only addressed to them gentle complaints and amicable expostulations. He pardoned their offence and restored them to his favor, — presenting them, at the same time, with 100,000 measures of corn [wheat], and reinstating such magistrates as were most agreeable to them. The joy of this people may be easily conceived from the terrors with which they were previously affected; and how glorious must that prince be who could *always* support so admirable a character!"

Reflecting with admiration on this exhibition of a magnanimity too rare in human annals, I was moved to inquire if a spirit so nobly, so wisely, transcending the mean and savage impulse which man too often disguises as justice, when it is in essence revenge, might not be reverently termed Divine; and the firm conclusion to which I was finally led, imported that the old Greek's treatment of vanquished rebels or prostrate enemies must forcibly image and body forth that of the "King immortal, invisible, and only wise God."

When I reached this conclusion, I had never seen one who was called, or who called himself, a Universalist; and I neither saw one, nor read a page of any one's writings, for years thereafter. I had only heard that there were a few graceless reprobates and scurvy outcasts, who pretended to believe that all men would be saved, and to wrench the Scriptures into some sort of conformity to their mockery of a creed. I had read the Bible through, much of it repeatedly, but when quite too infantile to form any coherent, definite synopsis of the doctrines I presumed to be taught therein. But, soon after entering a printing-office, I procured exchanges with several Universalist periodicals, and was thenceforth familiar with their methods of interpretation and of argument; though I first heard a sermon preached by one of this school while passing through Buffalo, about 1830; and I was acquainted with no society, and no preacher, of this faith, prior to my arrival in New York in August, 1831; when I made my way, on the first Sunday morning of my sojourn, to the little chapel in Grand Street, near Pitt,—about the size of an average country school-house,—where Rev. Thomas J. Sawyer, then quite young, ministered to a congregation of, perhaps, a hundred souls; to which congregation I soon afterward attached myself: remaining a member of it until he left the city.

I am not, therefore, to be classed with those who claim to have been converted from one creed to another by studying the Bible alone. Certainly, upon re-reading that book in the light of my new convictions, I found therein abundant proof of their correctness in the averments of patriarchs,* prophets,† apostles,‡ and of the Messiah § himself. But not so much in particular passages, however pertinent and decisive, as in the spirit and general scope of the Gospel, — so happily blending inexorable punishment for every offence with unfailing pity and ultimate forgiveness for the chastened transgressor, — thus saving sinners from sin by leading them, through suffering, to loathe and forsake it; and in laying down its Golden Rule, which, if of universal application, (and why not?) must be utterly inconsistent with the infliction of infinite and unending torture as the penalty of transient, and often ignorant, offending, did I find ample warrant for my hope and trust that all suffering is disciplinary and transitional, and shall ultimately result in universal holiness and consequent happiness.

In the light of this faith, the dark problem of Evil is irradiated, and virtually solved. "Perfect through suffering" was the way traced out for the great Captain of our salvation: then why not for all the children of Adam? To say that temporary affliction is as difficult to reconcile with Divine goodness as eternal agony is to defy reason and insult common sense. The history of Joseph's perfidious sale into slavery by his brethren, and the Divine overruling ‖ of that crime into a means of vast and permanent blessing to the entire family of Jacob, is directly in point. Once conceive that an Omniscient Beneficence presides over and directs the entire course of human affairs, leading ever onward and upward to universal purity and bliss, and all evil becomes phenomenal and preparative, — a mere curtain or passing cloud, which hides for a moment the light of the celestial and eternal day.

I am not wise enough, even in my own conceit, to assume to say where and when the deliverance of our race from evil and suffering shall be consummated. Perceiving that many

* Gen. iii. 15; xii. 3.

† Isa. xxv. 8; xlv. 23–25.

‡ Rom. v. 12–21; viii. 19–21; 1 Cor. xv. 42–54; Eph. i. 8–10; Col. i. 19–21; 1 Tim. ii. 3–6.

§ Matt. xv. 13; John xii. 32.

‖ Gen. xlv. 5–8.

leave this stage of being depraved and impenitent, I cannot believe that they will be transformed into angels of purity by the intervention of a circumstance so purely physical and involuntary as death. Holding that the government of God is everywhere and always perfect (however inadequate may be our comprehension of it), I infer that, alike in all worlds, men will be chastised whenever they shall need to be, and that neither by suicide, nor any other device, can a single individual escape the penalty of his evil-doing. If man is punished because he *needs* to be, — because that is best for him, — why should such discipline be restricted to this span of life? While I know that the words translated hell, eternal, &c., in our version of the Bible, bear various meanings which the translators have befogged, — giving hell, the grave, the pit, &c., as equivalents of the one Hebrew term that signifies the unseen home of departed souls, — and while I am sure that the luxuriant metaphors whereby a state of anguish and suffering are depicted were not meant to be taken literally, — I yet realize that human iniquity is often so flagrant and enormous that its punishment, to be just and efficient, must be severe and protracted. How or where it will be inflicted are matters of incident and circumstance, not of principle nor of primary consequence. Enough that it will be administered by One who "doth not willingly * [that is, wantonly] afflict nor grieve the children of men," but because their own highest good demands it, and would be prejudiced by his withholding it. But I do not dogmatize nor speculate. I rest in a more assured conviction of what Tennyson timidly, yet impressively, warbles, in mourning the death of his beloved friend: —

"O, yet we trust that, somehow, good
Will be the final goal of ill,
To pangs of nature, sins of will,
Defects of doubt, and taints of blood;

"That nothing walks with aimless feet;
That not one life shall be destroyed,
Or cast as rubbish to the void,
When God hath made the pile complete;

* Lam. iii. 33.

"That not a worm is cloven in vain;
That not a moth, with vain desire,
Is shrivelled in a fruitless fire,
Or but subserves another's gain.

"Behold! we know not anything:
I can but trust that good shall fall
At last, — far off, — at last, to all,
And every Winter change to Spring."

Twenty years earlier, Mrs. Hemans, when on the brink of the angelic life, was blest with a gleam from within the celestial gates, and, in almost her last sonnet, faintly refracted it as follows: —

"ON RECORDS OF IMMATURE GENIUS.

"O, judge in thoughtful tenderness of those
Who, richly dowered for life, are called to die
Ere the soul's flame, through storms, hath won repose
In truth's divinest ether, still and high!
Let their minds' riches claim a trustful sigh;
Deem them but sad, sweet fragments of a strain,
First notes of some yet struggling harmony
By the strong rush, the crowding joy and pain,
Of many inspirations, met and held
From its true sphere. O, soon it might have swelled
Majestically forth! Nor doubt that He
Whose touch mysterious may on earth dissolve
Those links of music, elsewhere will evolve
Their grand, consummate hymn, from passion-gusts made free!"

If I pronounce timid and tentative these and many kindred utterances of modern poets, I mean only that the great truth, so obscurely hinted by one, and so doubtingly asserted by the other, had long before been more firmly grasped, and more boldly proclaimed, by seers like Milton and Pope, and has in our age been affirmed and systematically elucidated by the calm, cogent reasoning of Ballou, the critical research of Balfour, the fervid eloquence of Chapin, and hundreds beside them, until it is no longer a feeble hope, a trembling aspiration, a pleasing hypothesis, but an assured and joyful conviction. In its clear daylight, the hideous Inquisition, and all kindred devices for torturing heretics, under a libellous pretence of zeal for God, shrink and cower in shame and terror; the revolting gallows hides itself from public view, preliminary to its utter and final disappearance; and man, growing ashamed of all cruelty and revenge, deals humanely with the outcast, the pauper, the criminal, and the vanquished foe. The overthrow of a rebellion is no longer the signal for sweeping spoliation and massacre; the downfall of an ancient tyranny like that of Naples is followed by no butchery of its pertinacious upholders; and our earth begins to body forth and mirror — but so slowly, so faintly! — the merciful doctrines of the meek and loving Prince of Peace.

Perhaps I ought to add, that, with the great body of the Universalists of our day (who herein differ from the earlier pioneers in America of our faith), I believe that "our God is *one* Lord," — that "though there be that are called gods, as there be gods many and lords many, to us there is but one God, the Father, *of* whom are all things, one Lord Jesus Christ, *by* whom are all things"; * and I find the relation between the Father and the Saviour of mankind most fully and clearly set forth in that majestic first chapter of Hebrews, which I cannot see how any Trinitarian can ever have intently read, without perceiving that its whole tenor and burden are directly at war with his conception of "three persons in one God." Nor can I see how Paul's express assertion, that "when all things shall be subdued unto him, then shall the Son himself also be subject to Him that put all things under him, that God may be all in all," † is to be reconciled with the more popular creed. However, I war not upon others' convictions, but rest satisfied with a simple statement of my own.

* 1 Cor. viii. 5, 6. † 1 Cor. xv. 28.

X.

A YEAR BY LAKE ERIE.

WHEN I entered Poultney, an aspirant to apprenticeship in her printing-office, I knew no one of her citizens or residents; when I left that place, after a quiet sojourn of a little more than four years, I parted with many valued friends, of whom all who survive still, I trust, remain such. I have never since known a community so generally moral, intelligent, industrious, and friendly, — never one where so much good was known, and so little evil said, of neighbor by neighbor. There is no single individual among the many whose acquaintance I formed there, of whom I have other than a kindly remembrance; while of nearly all those with whom I was brought into immediate contact I cherish fervid and grateful recollections.

The two-story wooden house, whence our Spectator was issued, still stands on the east side of the street leading from north to south, a few rods southeast of the Baptist meeting-house, near the centre of the village green; but the printing materials were packed up directly after I left, and have been sold away, — I know not whither. No single number of a journal has been issued from that town since I left it in June, 1830.

A friend of like years accompanied me thence by wagon to Comstock's Landing, on the Champlain Canal, where we waited, scarcely twelve miles from Poultney, through a dreary day of pelting rain, for a line-boat from Whitehall, whereon we crept snail-like to Troy, and thence, by another such conveyance, to Buffalo; though my friend stopped to look about him not far westward of Rochester. I kept on by steamboat on Lake Erie to Dunkirk, and thence diagonally across Chautauqua County to my father's in Pennsylvania.

I think it was on this visit that I made my best day's walk, — from Fredonia, through Mayville and Mina, to my father's, which can hardly be less than forty miles now, and by the zigzags we then made must have been considerably farther. I have known my father to walk fifty-two miles in a day, — that is, betwixt morning and midnight, — and I had made thirty-six miles per day (from Salem, Washington County, N. Y., to Westhaven) before I was fifteen years old; but I caught a horseback ride for several miles of the distance. I estimated the route I travelled from Fredonia to Wayne at forty-five miles of bad road, equal to fifty of good. He who will measure his walk by mile-stones, as I have done, will discover that lively and persistent stepping, with no stopping to chase butterflies, is required to make four miles per hour. I have done this on the tow-path of the Delaware and Raritan Canal; but the sweat started freely pretty early in the second mile. Beginning at twenty-five miles per day, walking slowly, but keeping pretty constantly in motion, you may add two to three miles per day, till you have reached forty; all above that, I judge, must, for most persons, involve exhaustive fatigue. I once walked across a corner of Chautauqua Lake when it was freshly frozen, and learned that walking on smooth ice, no matter how firm and assured your tread, will start the sweat on the coldest day, though you have been quite cool enough while walking on hard, frozen ground.

The railroads have nearly killed pedestrianism, and I regret it. Days of steady, solitary walking I have found most favorable to patient meditation. To study Nature profitably, you must be left alone with her, — she does not unveil herself to babbling, shouting crowds. A walk of two or three hundred miles in a calm, clear October, is one of the cheap and wholesome luxuries of life, as free to the poor as the rich. I do not regard the modern student plan of tramping and camping, ten to twenty in a mess, as its fair equivalent. A solitary walk of day after day is inevitably sober, quiet, thoughtful; and the weary pedestrian washes his feverish feet and drops asleep very soon after he has halted at night. An encampment of several pedestrians, whether in tent or tavern, is prone to stories, songs, games, feasting, drinking, and often to boisterous hilarity, whereby rest is postponed or sacrificed, and health imperilled. Of course, these evils are often shunned or repelled; yet I would advise the young pedestrian, who seeks mainly enjoyment, to travel with a single, well-chosen friend; if his aim be meditation and self-improvement, let him swing his pack and step off entirely alone.

I was once travelling in the company of a chance companion, whom I had never seen before, and have not seen since, — a man of perhaps forty years, — when our route led us through the village of Mayville, Chautauqua County, N. Y. We were in doubt as to our road beyond that village, and civilly inquired our way of a thrifty citizen whom we met. He looked us well over, and, seeing that we were evidently of no account, vouchsafed us never a word of reply, but passed us in utter silence. We, too, walked on without remark, until, at length, my companion broke the stillness with the abrupt observation:

"I am glad I have got to die some time."

I did not see the point, and looked inquiry.

"Because," he resumed, "that man has got to die just the same as I have."

I saw.

On my first visit to my father's forest home, I had entered the little hamlet termed Clymer, — then of four or five very new houses, — just at dusk of a Saturday night, when I learned that the log-cabin I sought was three miles away in a southwesterly course. "But you can't make your way to it to-night," I was very properly advised. I tried to hire some one to guide me, but without success; there was no tavern to stay at; so I took the track pointed out, and plunged into the darkening woods. Half a mile on, the cart-tracks diverged; and I took the more easterly and wrong one. I went on till I found a log-cabin tenanted by a mother and her children, who responded to my inquiries that they knew the way to Zack Greeley's quite well, but that it was two miles off, through dense woods, away from any road, and could not be reached that night, especially as the two intervening cabins stood tenantless,—their usual occupants having gone off to work on the Pennsylvania State Canal, then being dug in the vicinity of Meadville. I was pressed to stay here till morning, and — there being no practicable alternative — consented. The house was quite new, consisting of a single room, some twenty by sixteen feet, and the logs of which it was built were still so green that the fire was made close to one side, on the bare earth, with no fireplace and no chimney save a hole through the bark-covered roof. The man of the house soon came home, and we all slept sweetly till morning, when I made my way to my destination.

The cabin which my father had bought with his land was a little better than that I have just described, but nothing to brag of. My mother — born half a century after the log-cabin stage of Londonderry — could never be reconciled to this, nor to either of the two rather better ones that the family tenanted before it emerged into a poor sort of framed house. In fact, she had plunged into the primitive forest too late in life, and never became reconciled to the pioneer's inevitable discomforts. The chimney of the best log-house, she insisted, *would* smoke; and its roof, in a driving, drenching rain, *would* leak, do what you might. I think the shadow of the great woods oppressed her from the hour she first entered them; and, though removed but two generations from pioneer ancestors, she was never reconciled to what the less roughly bred must always deem privations and hardships. I never caught the old smile on her face, the familiar gladness in her mood, the hearty joyfulness in her manner, from the day she entered those woods until that of her death, nearly thirty years later, in August, 1855. Though not yet sixty-eight, she had for years been worn out by hard work, and broken down in mind and body. Those who knew her only in her later years, when toil and trouble had gained the victory over her, never truly knew her at all.

My father had for many years — perhaps from boyhood — fixed his affections on Western Pennsylvania as his ultimate home; and the region to which his footsteps were at length directed is essentially a good one. Situated on high, moderately rolling land, just across the line from Clymer, Chautauqua County, N. Y., in Erie County, Pa., two miles from the line of Warren County, the region is healthy and the soil strong, though better adapted to grass than to grain. He never wished to move again. Still, it was a mistake, at his time of life, to plunge so deep into the primitive forest. The giant timber — Beech, Maple, Hemlock, Elm, Ash, Basswood, &c. — yielded very slowly to his axe; he and my brother were often a full Winter month in chopping off an acre; and logging up and burning made another serious job; still leaving the soil cold with green roots, and deformed by an eruption of stumps, which must be allowed years wherein to rot out. A wealthy pioneer, who can pay for slashing or winrowing forty to eighty acres at once of timber when in full leaf, and can afford to let it lie untouched for a full year (better still, two years), and then put fire into it when favored by a dry spell and a good breeze, then log off and put it into grain forthwith, may clear at a third of the cost to, and have his land in far better condition than the poor settler, who must burn up his timber green, because he needs the land to till, and cannot afford to lay out of the fruits of his labor for years. Thus, a poor man hews a farm out of the great woods at more than twice the proper cost, and injures the soil by the process. I presume my folks gave two thousand days' work to gathering ashes from their burned log-heaps, and leaching them into "Black Salts" (the base of Pot and Pearl Ashes), because they must have wherewith to pay store-bills, though the product did not give fifty cents' return for each fair day's work, and the removal of the ashes impoverished the soil by more than they brought. But the crops grown among green roots, in a small excavation from a vast, tall forest, are precarious and scanty at best, being preyed upon by pigeons in myriads, and by all manner of four-footed beasts; and the pioneer's family must somehow live while he slowly transforms the stubborn wilderness into fruitful fields and orchards.

After spending some weeks at home, I sought work at my trade in various directions: finding a little first at Jamestown, N. Y., and, after an interval, more at Lodi (now Gowanda), Cattaraugus County, where I received $11 per month for six weeks; but my employer could afford to hire a journeyman no longer; and I thence walked home across Chautauqua County, about January 1, 1831, and remained a full month — a bitter cold one — chopping with my father and brother, but not very efficiently nor satisfactorily. Fully convinced that the life of a pioneer was one to which I was poorly adapted, I made one more effort to resume my chosen calling. Having already exhausted the possibilities in the printing line of Chautauqua County, I now visited Erie, Pa., where I found work in the office of The Erie Gazette, and was retained at $15 per month well into the ensuing summer.

This was the first newspaper whereon I was employed that made any money for its owner, and thus had a pecuniary value. It had been started twenty years or so before, when borough and county were both thinly peopled, almost wholly by poor young men, and it had grown with the vicinage until it had a substantial, profitable patronage. Its proprietor, Mr. Joseph M. Sterrett, now in the prime of life, had begun on The Gazette as a boy, and grown up with it into general consideration and esteem; his journeymen and apprentices boarded at his house, as was fit; and I spent here five months industriously and agreeably. Though still a raw youth of twenty years, and knowing no one in the borough when I thus entered it, I made acquaintances there who are still valued friends; and, before I left, I was offered a partnership in the concern; which, though I had reasons for declining, was none the less flattering as a mark of appreciation and confidence. Mr. Sterrett has since represented his district acceptably in the Senate of Pennsylvania, has received other proofs of the trustful regard of his fellow-citizens; and, though he has retired from The Gazette, still lives in the enjoyment of competence and general esteem.

Erie dwells in my memory as a place which started with too sanguine expectations, and was thus exposed to a sudden check, from which it has never fully recovered. From time to time, its early dreams of greatness have been revived by a State canal, by railroads, by coal-mines, and at length by the oil developments of the Titusville region not far south of it; but they have never been fully realized. It was rather a busy borough for its size in 1831; it is much larger and more important now; yet it has seen Buffalo, Cleveland, Toledo, on either side, rise above it like meteors, and not merely achieve a preëminence, but retain it. I fancy it must have ceased even to dream of coming grandeur by this time.

The quality for which its people were most remarkable in 1831 was an intense addiction to partisan strife. An ardent politician from childhood, I was fairly appalled by the assiduity and vehemence wherewith political controversy was prosecuted by nearly every man and boy I met in Erie. I have seen individual politicians elsewhere who could never set eyes on a stranger without mentally measuring up the feet and inches of party capital that might be made out of him; but politics in Erie seemed the universal and engrossing topic, to an extent and in a degree I have never known paralleled. Possibly, however, there was a temporary frenzy on the subject while I stayed there, from which her people have long since recovered. At all events, I will *hope* so.

At length, work failed at The Gazette office, and I was constrained to take a fresh departure. No printing-office in all that region wanted a journeyman. The West seemed to be laboring under a surfeit of printers. One was advertised for to take charge of a journal at Wilkesbarre, Pa., and I applied for the place, but failed to secure it. I would gladly have given faithful labor at case and press through some years yet for $15 per month and board, or even less; but it was not to be had. So, upon full consideration, I decided to turn my steps toward the Commercial Emporium, while still considerably younger than I would have preferred to be on making such a venture. Paying a parting visit to my father's, under the reasonable expectation that my next absence would be a long one, I divided with him my Erie earnings, and, with $25 in my pocket, and very little extra clothing in my bundle, I set my face toward New York.

It was now midsummer, — dry and hot. I had but one friend on my rather long route, and I resolved to pay him a visit. He lived at Gaines, nearly forty miles westward of Rochester; and I traversed on foot the dusty "ridge road" eastward from Lockport the day before I reached him. That day was quite hot, and the water I was incessantly compelled to drink seemed very hard; by nightfall, I fancied that it had covered my mouth and throat with a scale like that often found incrusting a long-used tea-kettle. The region was gently rolling and very fertile; but I should have more enjoyed a saunter over New England hills and rocks, sweetened by draughts from New England wells and springs.

It was Saturday night when I reached my friend, and I remained with him till Sunday afternoon, when we walked down to the canal, and waited long for a boat. None came till after nightfall, when I dismissed my friend, confident that a boat must soon appear. After waiting in vain till near midnight, I started down the tow-path, and walked through the pitchy darkness to Brockport, some fifteen miles. Repeatedly, the head-light of a boat moving westward came in sight, when I was obliged to plunge down the often rugged, briery, off-bank of the tow-path, to avoid being caught by the tow-line and hauled into the not quite transparent and nowise inviting "drink." Though the almanac made that night short, it seemed to me quite long; and I very gladly hailed and boarded at Brockport a line-boat heading eastward. My sleepy tendencies amused my fellow-passengers thence to Rochester, to whom "sparking Sunday night" afforded a ready and natural explanation.

XI.

MY FIRST EXPERIENCES IN NEW YORK.

REACHING Schenectady from Buffalo by line-boat,—my sixth and last journey on "the raging canal,"—I debarked about 6 P. M., and took the turnpike for Albany. I think a railroad between the two cities first and last named was completed soon afterward; but I believe not a mile of iron track was then operated in the State, if (in fact) anywhere in America, save the little affair constructed to freight granite from the quarry at Quincy, Mass., to Boston. Night fell when I was about half-way over; so I sought rest in one of the many indifferent taverns that then lined the turnpike in question, and was directed to sleep in an ante-room through which people were momently passing; I declined, and, gathering up my handful of portables, walked on. Half a mile farther, I found another tavern, not quite so inhospitable, and managed to stay in it till morning; when I rose and walked on to Albany. Having never been in that city before, I missed the nearest way to the day-boat, and when I reached the landing it was two or three lengths on its way to New York, having left at 7 A. M. I had no choice but to wait for another, which started at 10 A. M., towing a barge on either side, and reached, in twenty hours, the emporium, where I, after a good view of the city as we passed it down the river, was landed near Whitehall at 6 A. M.

New York was then about one third of her present size; but her business was not one fourth so great as now; and her real size—counting her suburbs, and considering the tens of thousands who find employment in and earn subsistence here, though sleeping outside of her chartered limits — was not one fifth that of 1867. No single railroad pointed toward her wharves. No line of ocean steamers brought passengers to her hotels, nor goods to her warehouses, from any foreign port. In the mercantile world, her relative rank was higher, but her absolute importance was scarcely greater, than that of Rio Janeiro or San Francisco is to-day. Still, to my eyes, which had never till yesterday gazed on a city of even 20,000 inhabitants, nor seen a sea-going vessel, her miles square of mainly brick or stone houses, and her furlongs of masts and yards, afforded ample incitement to a wonder and admiration akin to awe.

It was, if I recollect aright, the 17th of August, 1831. I was twenty years old the preceding February; tall, slender, pale, and plain, with ten dollars in my pocket, Summer clothing worth perhaps as much more, nearly all on my back, and a decent knowledge of so much of the art of printing as a boy will usually learn in the office of a country newspaper. But I knew no human being within two hundred miles, and my unmistakably rustic manner and address did not favor that immediate command of remunerating employment which was my most urgent need. However, the world was all before me; my personal estate, tied up in a pocket-handkerchief, did not at all encumber me; and I stepped lightly off the boat, and away from the detested hiss of escaping steam, walking into and up Broad Street in quest of a boarding-house. I found and entered one at or near the corner of Wall; but the price of board given me was $6 per week; so I did not need the giver's candidly kind suggestion that I would probably prefer one where the charge was more moderate. Wandering thence, I cannot say how, to the North River side, I halted next at 168 West Street, where the sign of "Boarding" on a humbler edifice fixed my attention. I entered, and was offered shelter and subsistence at $2.50 per week, which seemed more rational, and I closed the bargain.

My host was Mr. Edward McGolrick; his place quite as much grog-shop as boarding-house; but it was quietly, decently kept while I stayed in it, and he and his family were kind and friendly. I regret to add that liquor proved his ruin not many years afterward. My first day in New York was a Friday, and, the family being Roman Catholic, no meat was eaten or provided, which I understood; but when Sunday evening was celebrated by unlimited card-playing in that same house, my traditions were decidedly jarred. I do not imply that my observances were better or worse than my host's, but that they were different.

Having breakfasted, I began to ransack the city for work, and, in my total ignorance, traversed many streets where none could possibly be found. In the course of that day and the next, however, I must have visited fully two thirds of the printing-offices on Manhattan Island, without a gleam of success. It was midsummer, when business in New York is habitually dull; and my youth, and unquestionable air of country greenness, must have told against me. When I called at The Journal of Commerce, its editor, Mr. David Hale, bluntly told me I was a runaway apprentice from some country office; which was a very natural, though mistaken, presumption. I returned to my lodging on Saturday evening, thoroughly weary, disheartened, disgusted with New York, and resolved to shake its dust from my feet next Monday morning, while I could still leave with money in my pocket, and before its almshouse could foreclose upon me.

But that was not to be. On Sunday afternoon and evening several young Irishmen called at McGolrick's, in their holiday saunterings about town; and, being told that I was a young printer in quest of work, interested themselves in my effort, with the spontaneous kindness of their race. One among them happened to know a place where printers were wanted, and gave me the requisite direction; so that, on visiting the designated spot next morning, I readily found employment; and thus, when barely three days a resident, I had found anchorage in New York.

The printing establishment was John T. West's, over McElrath and Bangs's publishing-house, 85 Chatham Street, and the work was at my call simply because no printer who knew the city would accept it. It was the composition of a very small (32mo) New Testament, in double columns, of Agate type, each column barely 12 ems wide, with a centre column of notes in Pearl, only 4 ems wide; the text thickly studded with references by Greek and superior letters to the notes, which of course were preceded and discriminated by corresponding indices, with prefatory and supplementary remarks on each Book, set in Pearl, and only paid for as Agate. The type was considerably smaller than any to which I had been accustomed; the narrow measure and thickly sown Italics of the text, with the strange characters employed as indices, rendered it the slowest, and by far the most difficult, work I had ever undertaken; while the making up, proving, and correcting twice, and even thrice over, preparatory to stereotyping, nearly doubled the time required for ordinary composition. I was never a swift type-setter; I aimed to be an assiduous and correct one; but my proofs on this work at first looked as though they had caught the chicken-pox, and were in the worst stage of a profuse eruption. For the first two or three weeks, being sometimes kept waiting for letter, I scarcely made my board; while, by diligent type-sticking through twelve to fourteen hours per day, I was able, at my best, to earn but five to six dollars per week. As scarcely another compositor could be induced to work on it more than two days, I had this job in good part to myself; and I persevered to the end of it. I had removed, very soon after obtaining it, to Mrs. Mason's shoemaker boarding-house at the corner of Chatham and Duane Streets, nearly opposite my work; so that I was enabled to keep doing nearly all the time I did not need for meals and sleep. When it was done, I was out of work for a fortnight, in spite of my best efforts to find more; so I attended, as an unknown spectator, the sittings of the Tariff Convention, which was held at the American Institute, north end of the City Hall Park, and presided over by Hon. William Wilkins, of Pittsburg, Pa. I next found work in Ann Street, on a short-lived monthly, where my pay was not forthcoming; and the next month saw me back at West's, where a new work — a commentary on the Book of Genesis, by Rev. George Bush — had come in; and I worked on it throughout. The chirography was blind; the author made many vexatious alterations in proof; the page was small and the type close; but, though the reverse of *fat,* in printers' jargon, it was not nearly so abominably lean as the Testament; and I regretted to reach the end of it. When I did, I was again out of work, and seriously meditated seeking employment at something else than printing; but the Winter was a hard one, and business in New York stagnant to an extent not now conceivable. I think it was early in December, when a "cold snap" of remarkable severity closed the Hudson, and sent up the price of coal at a bound to $16 per ton, while the cost of other necessaries of life took a kindred but less considerable elevation. Our city stood as if besieged till Spring relieved her; and it was much the same every Winter. Mechanics and laborers lived awhile on the scanty savings of the preceding Summer and Autumn; then on such credit as they could wring from grocers and landlords, till milder weather brought them work again. The earnings of good mechanics did not average $8 per week in 1831–32, while they are now double that sum; and living is *not* twice as dear as it then was. Meat may possibly be; but Bread is not; Fuel is not; Clothing is not; while travel is cheaper; and our little cars have enabled working-men to live two or three miles from their work without serious cost or inconvenience; thus bringing Yorkville or Green Point practically as near to Maiden Lane or Broad Street as Greenwich or the Eleventh Ward was. Winter is relatively dull now, but not nearly so stagnant as it formerly was. In spite of an inflated currency and high taxes, it is easier now for a working-man to earn his living in New York than it was thirty to forty years ago.

About the 1st of January, 1832, I found employment on The Spirit of the Times, a weekly paper devoted to sporting intelligence, then started by Messrs. William T. Porter and James Howe, two young printers, of whom the former, if not both, had worked with me at West's the previous Fall. I think it was a little after midnight, on the 1st of January, 1832, that we compositors delivered the forms of the first number into the hands of the pressmen in an upper story in Fulton Street. The concern migrated to Wall Street the next March, finding a location very near the present site of the Merchants' Exchange; and I clung to it through the ensuing Spring and Summer; its foreman, Francis V. Story, being nearly of my own age, and thenceforth my devoted friend. But the founders and editors were also quite young; they were inexperienced in their calling, without capital or influential friends, having recently drifted from the country to the city much as I did; and their paper did not pay, — I know it was difficult to make it pay *me*, — especially through the dreary cholera Summer of 1832. The disease was then new to the civilized world, while the accounts of its recent ravages in the far East were calculated to appall the stoutest heart; the season was sultry, the city filthy, and the water we drank such as should breed a pestilence at any time. New York had long enjoyed and deserved the reputation of having worse water than any other city of its size on earth; and the loose, porous sands whereon it was built rendered this fluid more and more detestable as the city grew larger and older. I am glad that it was my privilege to vote soon afterward for the introduction of the Croton, which I did right heartily, though a good many opposed it (some of them voting "Brandy"); two of the Wards, tenanted mainly by poor men, giving majorities against it. Twelve years intervened betwixt that vote and our celebration to welcome the actual introduction of the water, — the fluid we drew from the wells growing steadily more and more repulsive and unwholesome; but the glad day came at last; and New York has ever since been a more eligible, healthful residence for rich or poor than it previously was.

We have had cholera and other epidemics since; but our city has never since been paralyzed as it was in the Summer of 1832. Those who could mainly left us; scarcely any one entered the city; trade was dead, and industry languished during that fatal Summer. I think I sometimes met two, if not three, palanquins, bearing cholera patients to some hospital, in my short walk from dinner in Chatham Street to my work in Wall Street. One died at my boarding-house., I believe nearly all experienced symptoms of the plague, though it was most common and most fatal with those debilitated by intemperance or some form of sensual excess. But it passed off as cool evenings came on; our fugitives and our business came back to us; and all, save the dead and the bereaved, was as before.

In October I paid a visit, via Providence and Boston, to my relatives in New Hampshire; walking over the lower part of that State from Londonderry into eastern Vermont, and as far north as Newport, which I entered after dark of a stormy evening, having walked from Claremont (nine miles) in a rain, at first gentle, but steadily increasing to the last. I never enter, as a stranger, a private house if I can avoid it; and I kept hoping to see a tavern-sign until I was so wet that it was of no consequence. When at last I reached the village, where I expected (but failed) to find an uncle living, it proved to be court-week, with the two taverns crowded to overflowing. Making my way through a thick cloud of tobacco-smoke to the office of one, I procured a remnant of supper, and part of a bed in a private house at some distance, where I threw off my wet clothes and slept. In the morning, my clothes all responded to the call to duty till it came to my short boots; these utterly refused, until I had taken off my wet socks and thrust them into my pockets, when the boots were barely persuaded to resume their only serviceable position. I took breakfast, paid my bill, and walked off, in the frosty morning air, considerably less supple-jointed than one should be at one-and-twenty. I never saw this New Hampshire Newport before, and have not seen it since.

My relatives being pretty widely scattered, I had occasion to traverse southwestern New Hampshire in various directions; and I saw more of that State than ever before or since. I started, one clear, frosty morning, from Francestown, taking a mountainous by-way to Stoddard; and, as I recollect, I did not see a hundred acres of really arable soil in travelling twelve to fifteen miles. There was some rugged pasturage; but Hemlock and White Birch, alternating with naked rocks and mountain tarns or petty lakes, generally monopolized the prospect. I met one poor soul who had a horse and wagon, and heartily pitied him. He could rarely ride, while my walk was far easier and less anxious than his.

Reaching Stoddard (a small village half-way up a high hill), I stepped into a convenient tavern, and called for dinner. My breakfast had been quite early; the keen air and rough walk had freshened my appetite; I was shown into a dining-room with a well-spread table in the centre, and left to help myself. There were steaks, chickens, tea, coffee, pies, &c., and I did ample justice to all. "What is to pay?" I asked the landlord, on reëntering the bar-room. "Dinner 18$\frac{3}{4}$ cents," he replied. I laid down the required sum, and stepped off, mentally resolving that I would, in mercy to that tavern, never patronize it again.

I returned by the way I went; walking from Providence across to Norwich, Conn., where I took steamboat, and arrived in New York on the second of our three days of State election. I gave my vote right heartily for the anti-Jackson ticket, but without avail, — Jackson being overwhelmingly reëlected, with Marcy over Granger for Governor. I soon found work which paid fairly at the stereotyping establishment of J. S. Redfield, and was there employed till the close of that year, when an opportunity presented for commencing business on my own account, which I improved, as will be set forth in my next chapter.

XII.

GETTING INTO BUSINESS.

HAVING been fairly driven to New York two or three years earlier than I deemed desirable, I was in like manner impelled to undertake the responsibilities of business while still in my twenty-second year. My friend Story, barely older than myself, but far better acquainted with city ways, having been for many years the only son of a poor widow, and accustomed to struggling with difficulties, had already conceived the idea of starting a printery, and offering me a partnership in the enterprise. His position in Wall Street, on The Spirit of the Times, made him acquainted with Mr. S. J. Sylvester, then a leading broker and seller of lottery-tickets, who issued a weekly "Bank-Note Reporter," largely devoted to the advertising of his own business, and who offered my friend the job of printing that paper. Story was also intimate with Dr. W. Beach, who, in addition to his medical practice, dabbled considerably in ink, and at whose office my friend made the acquaintance of a young graduate, Dr. H. D. Shepard, who was understood to have money, and who was intent on bringing out a cheap daily paper, to be sold about the streets, — then a novel idea, — daily papers being presumed desirable only for mercantile men, and addressed exclusively to their wants and tastes. Dr. Shepard had won over my friend to a belief in the practicability of his project; and the latter visited me at my work and my lodging, urging me to unite with him in starting a printery on the strength of Mr. Sylvester's and Dr. Shepard's proffered work. I hesitated, having very little means, — for I had sent a good part of my past year's scanty savings to aid my father in his struggle with the stubborn wilderness; but Story's enthusiastic confidence at length triumphed over my distrust; we formed a partnership, hired part of two rooms already devoted to printing, on the southwest corner of Nassau and Liberty Streets (opposite our city's present post-office), spending our little all (less than $200), and stretching our credit to the utmost, for the requisite materials. I tried Mr. James Conner, the extensive type-founder in Ann Street, — having a very slight acquaintance with him, formed in the course of frequent visits to his foundry in quest of "sorts" (type found deficient in the several offices for which I had worked at one time or another), — but he, after hearing me patiently, decided not to credit me six months for the $40 worth of type I wanted of him; and he did right, — my exhibit did not justify my request. I went directly thence to Mr. George Bruce, the older and wealthier founder, in Chambers Street, — made the same exhibit, and was allowed by him the credit I asked; and that purchase has since secured to his concern the sale of not less than $50,000 worth of type. I think he must have noted something in my awkward, bashful ways, that impelled him to take the risk.

The Morning Post — Dr. Shepard's two-cent daily, which he wished to sell for one cent — was issued on the 1st of January, 1833. Nobody in New York reads much (except visitor's cards) on New Year's Day; and that one happened to be very cold, with the streets much obstructed by a fall of snow throughout the preceding night. Projectors of newspapers in those days, though expecting other people to advertise in their columns, did not comprehend that *they* also must advertise, or the public will never know that their bantling has been ushered into existence; and Dr. Shepard was too poor to give his sheet the requisite publicity, had he understood the matter. He was neither a writer nor a man of affairs; had no editors, no reporters worth naming, no correspondents, and no exchanges even; he fancied that a paper would sell, if remarkable for cheapness, though remarkable also for the absence of every other desirable quality. He was said to have migrated, while a youth, from New Jersey to New York, with $ 1,500 in cash; if he did, his capital must have nearly all melted away before he had issued his first number. Though his enterprise involved no outlay of capital by him, and his weekly outgoes were less than $ 200, he was able to meet them for a single week only, while his journal obtained a circulation of but two or three hundred copies. Finally, he reduced its price to one cent; but the public would not buy it even at that, and we printers, already considerably in debt for materials, were utterly unable to go on beyond the second or third week after the publisher had stopped paying. Thus the first cheap-for-cash daily in New York — perhaps in the world — died when scarcely yet a month old; and we printers were hard aground on a lee shore, with little prospect of getting off.

We were saved from sudden bankruptcy by the address of my partner, who had formed the acquaintance of a wealthy, eccentric Briton, named Schols, who had a taste for editorial life, and who was somehow induced to buy the wreck of The Morning Post, remove it to an office of his own, and employ Story as foreman. He soon tired of his thriftless, profitless speculation, and threw it up; but we had meantime surmounted our embarrassments by the help of the little money he paid for a portion of our materials and for my partner's services. Meantime, the managers of the New York lotteries, then regularly drawn under State auspices, had allowed a portion of their letter-press printing to follow Mr. Sylvester's into our concern, and were paying us very fairly for it; I doing most of the composition. For two or three months after Dr. Shepard's collapse, I was frequently sent for to work as a substitute in the composing-room of The Commercial Advertiser, not far from our shop; and I was at length offered a regular situation there; but our business had by this time so improved that I was constrained to decline. Working early and late, and looking sharply on every side for jobs, we were beginning to make decided headway, when my partner was drowned (July 9, 1833) while bathing in the East River near his mother's residence in Brooklyn, and I bitterly mourned the loss of my nearest and dearest friend. His place in the concern was promptly taken by another young printer, a friend of the bereaved family, Mr. Jonas Winchester, who soon married Story's oldest sister; and we thus went on, with moderate but steady prosperity, until the ensuing Spring, when we issued (March 22, 1834), without premonitory sound of trumpet, THE NEW-YORKER, a large, fair, and cheap weekly folio (afterward changed to a double quarto), devoted mainly to current literature, but giving regularly a digest of all important news, including a careful exhibit and summary of election returns and other political intelligence. I edited and made up this paper, while my partner took charge of our more profitable jobbing business.

The New-Yorker was issued under my supervision, its editorials written, its selections made, for the most part, by me, for seven years and a half from the date just given. Though not calculated to enlist partisanship or excite enthusiasm, it was at length extensively liked and read. It began with scarcely a dozen subscribers; these steadily increased to nine thousand; and it might, under better business management, (perhaps I should add, at a more favorable time,) have proved profitable and permanent. That it did not was mainly owing to these circumstances: 1. It was not extensively advertised at the start, and at least annually thereafter, as it should have been. 2. It was never really published, though it had half a dozen nominal publishers in succession. 3. It was sent to subscribers on credit, and a large share of them never paid for it, and never will, while the cost of collecting from others ate up the proceeds. 4. The machinery of railroads, expresses, news companies, news offices, &c., whereby literary periodicals are now mainly disseminated, did not then exist. I believe that just such a paper, issued to-day, properly published and advertised, would obtain a circulation of one hundred thousand in less time than was required to give The New-Yorker scarcely a tithe of that aggregate, and would make money for its owners, instead of nearly starving them, as mine did. I was worth at least $1,500 when it was started; I worked hard and lived frugally throughout its existence; it subsisted for the first two years on the profits of our job-work; when I, deeming it established, dissolved with my partner, he taking the jobbing business and I The New-Yorker, which held its own pretty fairly thenceforth till the Commercial Revulsion of 1837 swept over the land, whelming it and me in the general ruin. I had married in 1836 (July 5th), deeming myself worth $5,000, and the master of a business which would thenceforth yield me for my labor at least $1,000 per annum; but, instead of that, or of any income at all, I found myself obliged, throughout 1837, to confront a net loss of about $100 per week, — my income averaging $100, and my inevitable expenses $200. It was in vain that I appealed to delinquents to pay up; many of them migrated; some died; others were so considerate as to order the paper stopped, but very few of these paid; and I struggled on against a steadily rising tide of adversity that might have appalled a stouter heart. Often did I call on this or that friend with intent to solicit a small loan to meet some demand that could no longer be postponed nor evaded, and, after wasting a precious hour, leave him, utterly unable to broach the loathsome topic. I have borrowed $500 of a broker late on Saturday, and paid him $5 for the use of it till Monday morning, when I somehow contrived to return it. Most gladly would I have terminated the struggle by a surrender; but, if I had failed to pay my notes continually falling due, I must have paid money for my weekly supply of paper, — so that would have availed nothing. To have stopped my journal (for I could not give it away) would have left me in debt, beside my notes for paper, from fifty cents to two dollars each, to at least three thousand subscribers who had paid in advance; and that is the worst kind of bankruptcy. If any one would have taken my business and debts off my hands, upon my giving him my note for $2,000, I would have jumped at the chance, and tried to work out the debt by setting type, if nothing better offered. If it be suggested that my whole indebtedness was at no time more than $ 5,000 to $ 7,000, I have only to say that even $ 1,000 of debt is ruin to him who keenly feels his obligation to fulfil every engagement, yet is utterly without the means of so doing, and who finds himself dragged each week a little deeper into hopeless insolvency. To be hungry, ragged, and penniless is not pleasant; but this is nothing to the horrors of bankruptcy. All the wealth of the Rothschilds would be a poor recompense for a five years' struggle with the consciousness that you had taken the money or property of trusting friends, — promising to return or pay for it when required, — and had betrayed their confidence through insolvency.

I dwell on this point, for I would deter others from entering that place of torment. Half the young men in the country, with many old enough to know better, would "go into business" — that is, into debt — to-morrow, if they could. Most poor men are so ignorant as to envy the merchant or manufacturer whose life is an incessant struggle with pecuniary difficulties, who is driven to constant "shinning," and who, from month to month, barely evades that insolvency which sooner or later overtakes most men in business; so that it has been computed that but one in twenty of them achieve a pecuniary success. For my own part, — and I speak from sad experience, — I would rather be a convict in a State prison, a slave in a rice-swamp, than to pass through life under the harrow of debt. Let no young man misjudge himself unfortunate, or truly poor, so long as he has the full use of his limbs and faculties, and is substantially free from debt. Hunger, cold, rags, hard work, contempt, suspicion, unjust reproach, are disagreeable; but debt is infinitely worse than them all. And, if it had pleased God to spare either or all of my sons to be the support and solace of my declining years, the lesson which I should have most earnestly sought to impress upon them is, — "Never run into debt! Avoid pecuniary obligation as you would pestilence or famine. If you have but fifty cents, and can get no more for a week, buy a peck of corn, parch it, and live on it, rather than owe any man a dollar!" Of course, I know that some men must do business that involves risks, and must often give notes and other obligations, and I do not consider him really in debt who can lay his hands directly on the means of paying, at some little sacrifice, all he owes; I speak of *real* debt, — that which involves risk or sacrifice on the one side, obligation and dependence on the other, — and I say, From all such, let every youth humbly pray God to preserve him evermore!

When I at length stopped The New-Yorker (September 20, 1841), though poor enough, I provided for making good all I owed to its subscribers who had paid in advance, and shut up its books whereon were inscribed some $10,000 owed me in sums of $1 to $10 each, by men to whose service I had faithfully devoted the best years of my life, — years that, though full of labor and frugal care, might have been happy had they not been made wretched by those men's dishonesty. They took my journal, and probably read it; they promised to pay for it, and defaulted; leaving me to pay my paper-maker, type-founder, journeymen, &c., as I could. My only requital was a sorely achieved but wholesome lesson. I had been thoroughly burned out, only saving my books, in the great Ann Street fire (August 12, 1835); I was burned out again in February, 1845; and, while the destruction was complete, and the insurance but partial, I had the poor consolation, that the account-books of The New-Yorker — which I had never opened since I first laid them away, but which had been an eye-sore and a reminder of evil days whenever I stumbled upon them — were at length dissolved in smoke and flame, and lost to sight for ever.

XIII.

TEMPERANCE IN ALL THINGS.

ON the first day of January, 1824, while living in Westhaven, Vermont, I deliberately resolved to drink no more distilled liquors. At this time I had heard of persons who had made a kindred resolve, but I had not known one. I had probably heard that Temperance societies had somewhere been formed, though I do not now distinctly recollect the circumstance. I believe the first American society that adopted the principle of Total Abstinence — at least from distilled liquors — had been organized in a rural township of Saratoga County, N. Y., in 1817; but the American Temperance Society was yet unknown, and did not adopt the principle of Total Abstinence from Alcoholic Beverages until 1833.

Whiskey and Tobacco were the universal luxuries — I might say the poor man's *only* luxuries — in Vermont, as Rum had been in New Hampshire. The apple-tree flourished luxuriantly, and bore abundantly on the virgin soils wherein it was generally planted, and while each settler's "clearing" was shut in by the grand old woods which softened the harsher winds and obstructed the dissemination of fruit-destroying insects. Good peaches were grown in southern New Hampshire fifty years ago; whereas they can no longer be produced, save rarely and scantily, in southern New York. Cider was, next to water, the most abundant and the cheapest fluid to be had in New Hampshire, while I lived there, — often selling for a dollar per barrel. In many a family of six or eight persons, a barrel tapped on Saturday barely lasted a full week. Whoever dropped in of an evening expected to be treated to cider; a mug, once emptied, was quickly refilled; and so on, till every one was about as full as he could hold. The transition from cider to warmer and more potent stimulants was easy and natural; so that whole families died drunkards and vagabond paupers from the impetus first given by cider-swilling in their rural homes.

I believe I was five years old when my grandfather Woodburn's house in Londonderry was, one Winter day, filled with relatives, gathered, in good part, from Deering, Windham, and from Vermont towns originally settled from the old hive; who, after dinner, departed in their sleighs to visit some other relative, taking our old folks with them, and leaving but three or four little boys of us to keep house till their return. A number of half-smoked cigars had been left on the mantel, and some evil genius suggested to us tow-headed urchins that it would be smart and clever to indulge in a general smoke. Like older fools, we went in; and I was soon the sickest mortal on the face of this planet. I cannot say as to my comrades in this folly; but that half-inch of cigar-stump will last me all my life, though its years should outnumber Methuselah's. For a decade thereafter, it was often my filial duty to fill and light my mother's pipe, when she had lain down for her after-dinner nap; and she, having taken it, would hold it and talk till the fire had gone out, so that it must again be lighted and drawn till the tobacco was well ignited; hence I know that, if I had not been proof against narcotic seduction, I should have learned to like the soothing weed; but I never used, nor wished to use, it as a sedative or a luxury after my one juvenile and thoroughly conclusive experiment. From that hour to this, the chewing, smoking, or snuffing of tobacco has seemed to me, if not the most pernicious, certainly the vilest, most detestable abuse of his corrupted sensual appetites whereof depraved Man is capable.

In my childhood, there was no merry-making, there was no entertainment of relatives or friends, there was scarcely

a casual gathering of two or three neighbors for an evening's social chat, without strong drink. Cider, always, while it remained drinkable without severe contortions of visage; Rum at all seasons and on all occasions, were required and provided. No house or barn was raised without a bountiful supply of the latter, and generally of both. A wedding without "toddy," "flip," "sling," or "punch," with rum undisguised in abundance, would have been deemed a poor, mean affair, even among the penniless; while the more fortunate and thrifty of course dispensed wine, brandy, and gin in profusion. Dancing — almost the only pastime wherein the sexes jointly participated — was always enlivened and stimulated by liquor. Militia trainings — then rigidly enforced at least twice a year — usually wound up with a drinking frolic at the village tavern. Election days were drinking days, as they still too commonly are; and even funerals were regarded as inadequately celebrated without the dispensing of spirituous consolation: so that I distinctly recollect the neighborhood talk, in 1820, after the funeral of a poor man's child, that, if he had not been mean as well as poor, he would have cheered the hearts of his sympathizing friends by treating them to at least *one* gallon of rum. I have heard my father say that he had mowed through the haying season of thirty successive years, and never a day without liquor; and the account of an Irishman who mowed and pitched throughout one haying, drinking only buttermilk, while his associates drank rum, yet accomplished more, and with less fatigue, than any of them, was received with as much wondering incredulity as though it had been certified that he lived wholly on air. Nay: we had an ordination in Amherst nearly fifty years ago, settling an able and popular young clergyman named Lord (I believe he is now the venerable ex-President of Dartmouth College) to the signal satisfaction of the great body of our people; and, according to my recollection, strong drink was more generally and bountifully dispensed than on any previous occasion: bottles and glasses being set on tables in front of many farmers' houses as an invitation to those who passed on their way to or from the installation to stop and drink freely. We have worse liquor now than we had then; and delirium tremens, apoplexy, palsy, &c., come sooner and oftener to those who use it; but our consumers of strong drink are a class; whereas they were then the whole people. The pious probably drank more discreetly than the ungodly; but they all drank to their own satisfaction, and, I judge, more than was consistent with their personal good.

My resolve not to drink was only mentioned by me at our own fireside; but it somehow became known in the neighborhood, where it excited some curiosity, and even a stronger feeling. At the annual sheep-washing, in June following, it was brought forward and condemned; when I was required to take a glass of liquor, and, on my declining, was held by two or three youngsters older and stronger than I, while the liquor was turned into my mouth, and some of it forced down my throat. That was understood to be the end of my foolish attempt at singularity.

It was not, however. I kept quiet, but my resolution was unchanged; and, soon after my removal to Poultney, I "assisted" in organizing the first Temperance Society ever formed in that town, — perhaps the first in the county. It inhibited the use of distilled liquors only; so that I believe our first president died of intemperance some years afterward; but a number still live to rejoice that they took part in that movement, and have since remained faithful to its pledge and its purpose. I recollect a story told at that time by our adversaries of a man who had joined the Temperance Society just organized in a neighboring township, and, dying soon afterward, had been subjected to an autopsy, which developed a cake of ice weighing several pounds, which had gradually formed and increased in his stomach, as a result of his fanatical devotion to cold water. Alas that most of our facetious critics have since died, and no autopsy was needed to develop the cause of *their* departure! A glance at each fiery proboscis, that irradiated even the cerements of the grave, was sufficient.

Total Abstinence has never yet been popular in this nor in any other great city; and, as liquor grows unfashionable in the country, it tends to become less and less so. A great city derives its subsistence and its profits from ministrations therein, not only to the real needs of the surrounding country, but to its baser appetites, its vices, as well; and, as the country becomes less and less tolerant of immoral indulgences and vicious aberrations, the gains of cities therefrom, and their consequent interest therein, must steadily increase. Time was when the young man of means and social position, who shunned the haunts of the gamester, the wiles of the libertine, and never indulged in a drunken "spree," was widely sneered at as a "milksop," or detested as a calculating hypocrite. Sheridan's Joseph Surface admirably reflects the once popular appreciation of such absurd, fanatical Puritanism; but, as the world grows wiser and (in an important sense) better, a great though silent change is wrought in public sentiment, which compels the vicious to conceal indulgences that they formerly paraded, and maintain an exterior decency which would once have exposed them to ridicule. Thousands, who formerly gratified their baser appetites without disguise or shame, now feel constrained, not to "leave undone," but to "keep unknown," by hieing to some great city, — where no one's deeds or ways are observed or much regarded so long as he keeps out of the hands of the police, — and there balance a year's compelled decorum by a week's unrestrained debauchery. Fifty years back, a jug would readily be filled with any designated liquor at almost any country store; now, the devotee of alcoholic potations must usually send or take his demijohn to the most convenient city, where it will at once be filled and despatched to its impatient, thirsty owner; and so, as the Liquor Interest grows weaker and weaker in the country, it becomes stronger and yet stronger in the cities, whose politics it fashions, whose government it governs, by virtue of its inherent strength and apprehensive activity. And thus the Liquor Traffic has greater strength and vitality in our city to-day than it had twenty to forty years ago.

Sylvester Graham first appeared in New York as a lecturer, I think, in the Winter of 1831–32. He had been a Presbyterian clergyman, settled in New Jersey, and was styled "Dr.," though I do not know that he ever studied or practised medicine. He had an active, inquiring mind, and a considerable knowledge of physics, metaphysics, and theology; he was a fluent and forcible, though diffuse and egotistical, speaker; and he was possessed and impelled by definite convictions. He was at home in single combat alike with Alcohol and Atheism; but there was nothing narrow in his Temperance nor in his Orthodoxy. He believed, therefore taught, that Health is the necessary result of obedience, Disease of disobedience, to physical laws; that all stimulants, whether alcoholic or narcotic, are pernicious, and should be rejected, save, possibly, in those rare cases where one poison may be wisely employed to neutralize or expel another: he condemned Tea and Coffee, as well as Tobacco, Opium, and Alcoholic potables, — Cider and Beer equally with Brandy and Gin, save that the poison is more concentrated in the latter. He disapproved of all spices and condiments save (grudgingly) a very little salt; and he held that more suitable and wholesome food for human beings than the flesh of animals can almost always be procured, and should be preferred. The bolting of meal, to separate its coarser from its finer particles, he also reprobated; teaching that the ripe, sound berry of Wheat or Rye, being ground to the requisite fineness, should in no manner be sifted, but should be made into loaves and eaten precisely as the mill-stones deliver it. Such is, in brief, "the Graham system," as I heard it expounded in successive lectures by its author, and fortified by evidence and reasoning which commanded my general assent. A boarding-house was soon established, based on its principles, and I became an inmate thereof, as well as of others afterward founded on the same general ideas, though I never wholly rejected the use of meat. Tea I never cared for, and I used none at all for a quarter of a century; now, I sometimes take it in moderation, when black and very good. Coffee had for years been my chief luxury, — coffee without breakfast being far preferable, to my taste, to breakfast without coffee; but, having drank a strong cup of it one evening at a festive board, I woke next morning to find my hand trembling; and I at once said, "No more coffee!" and have not drank it since. My taste gradually changed thereafter, so that I soon ceased to crave, and now thoroughly dislike, the beverage. And, while I eat meat, and deem it, when unspoiled by decay or bad cookery, far less objectionable than hot bread, rancid butter, decayed fruits, wilted vegetables, and too many other contributions to our ordinary diet, I profoundly believe that there is better food obtainable by the great body of mankind than the butcher and the fisherman do or can supply; and that a diet made up of sound grain (ground, but unbolted), ripe, undecayed fruits, and a variety of fresh, wholesome vegetables, with milk, butter, and cheese, and very little of spices or condiments, will enable our grandchildren to live in the average far longer, and fall far less frequently into the hands of the doctors, than we do.

My wife, whose acquaintance I made at the Graham House, and who was long a more faithful, consistent disciple of Graham than I was, in our years of extreme poverty kept her house in strict accordance with her convictions; never even deigning an explanation to her friends and relatives who from time to time visited and temporarily sojourned with us; and, as politeness usually repressed complaint or inquiry on their part, their first experiences of a regimen which dispensed with all they deemed most appetizing could hardly be observed without a smile. Usually, a day, or at most two, of beans and potatoes, boiled rice, puddings, bread and butter, with no condiment but salt, and never a pickle, was all they could abide; so, bidding her a kind adieu, each in turn departed to seek elsewhere a more congenial hospitality.

"But what peculiar effects of a vegetable diet did you experience?" some will naturally ask. I answer generally, "Much the same as a rum-drinker notes after a brief return to water-drinking exclusively. I first felt a quite perceptible sinking of animal spirits, a partial relaxation or depression of natural energies. It seemed as though I could not lift so much, jump so high, nor run so fast, as when I ate meat. After a time, this lowering of the tone of the physical system passed away or became imperceptible. On the other hand, I had no feeling of repletion or over-fulness; I had no headache, and scarcely an ache of any sort; my health was stubbornly good; and any cut or other flesh-wound healed more easily and rapidly than formerly. Other things being equal, I judge that a strict vegetarian will live ten years longer than a habitual flesh-eater, while suffering, in the average, less than half so much from sickness as the carnivorous must. The simple fact, that animals are often diseased when killed for food, and that the flesh of those borne in crowded cars, from far inland, to be slaughtered for the sustenance of seaboard cities, is almost always and inevitably feverish and unwholesome, ought to be conclusive.

On the whole, I am convinced, by the observation and experience of a third of a century, that all public danger lies in the direction opposite to that of vegetarianism, — that a thousand fresh Grahams let loose each year upon the public will not prevent the consumption, in the average, of far too much and too highly seasoned animal food; while all the Goughs and Neal Dows that ever were or can be scared up will not deter the body politic from pouring down its throat a great deal more "fire-water" than is good for it. And, while I look with interest on all attempts to substitute American wines and malt liquors for the more concentrated and maddening decoctions of the still, I have noted no such permanent triumphs in the thousand past attempts to cast out big devils by the incantations of little ones as would give me reason to put faith in the principle, or augur success for this latest experiment.

XIV.

POLITICS.

AN eager, omnivorous reader, especially of newspapers, from early childhood, I was an ardent politician when not yet half old enough to vote. I heartily sympathized with the Northern uprising against the admission of Missouri as a Slave State, and shared in the disappointment and chagrin so widely felt when that uprising was circumvented and defeated by what was called a Compromise. I think few of us blamed the Southern politicians for their agency in our defeat; but the score of Northern Senators and Representatives who (as we thought) betrayed us were thenceforth marked men, and few indeed of them were ever again successful aspirants to popular favor.

When, in 1824, the country was freshly agitated and divided, after several years of general calm, by the nomination of William H. Crawford, of Georgia, for President, in a caucus attended by less than a third of the Members of Congress,—considerably less than half of those who were chosen by the dominant party,—all New England became zealously anti-Caucus, and her electoral vote was cast solid for John Quincy Adams; there being no serious opposition among the masses, though several of her leading politicians, and hitherto most influential journals, were vehemently for Crawford. The choice in the House of Adams for President, by the help of Mr. Clay and his friends, suited us exactly, and all the more that Mr. Clay was eminently National in his views and feelings, a leading champion of Internal Improvements, Protection to Home Industry, and every good work. But the hostile combination soon thereafter formed of the lately warring supporters of Jackson, Crawford, and Calhoun respectively, did not please us at all; Calhoun especially — having been a National man, a supporter of Protection, River and Harbor Improvement, &c., while in Congress, and having been generally sustained by our section for Vice-President — was regarded, up our way, as a renegade from principle for office and power. The fierce personal warfare waged upon Adams and Clay for their alleged coalition, by and in full view of this hostile combination, excited our wrath and scorn; but this did not overbear the fact that their three factions united were an overmatch for our two; and, as Crawford died soon after Adams's accession, they were enabled to achieve what would now-a-days be called a close connection, by running Jackson for President, with Calhoun for Vice-President. We ought to have countered this by nominating Clay with Adams, or (better still) by having Adams decline a reëlection, and running Clay for President, with Walter Forward, of Pennsylvania, or Smith Thompson, of New York, for Vice-President; but everything went wrong with us: the sudden death of De Witt Clinton consolidated many of his personal followers with their life-long adversaries in the support of Jackson for President, with Van Buren for Governor of New York; our nomination of Richard Rush, of Pennsylvania, for Vice-President was injudicious, and gave us no strength; and our reasonable hopes that the Tariff question would secure us Ohio with Kentucky, and give us a fair chance for Pennsylvania, were blighted by the tactics of our antagonists: Van Buren, Silas Wright, Buchanan, the Jackson delegations from Pennsylvania, Ohio, and Kentucky, in solid column, with all but two or three members from New York, uniting (in 1828) to frame and pass the highest and most Protective Tariff that had ever been proposed, over the votes of a majority of the Adams men from New England. Outmanœuvred on every side, we were clearly foredoomed to defeat; the loss of Mr. Clay's own Kentucky was a blow for which her preceding election of Members to Congress had partly prepared us, though we carried, by a close vote, her Governor (Metcalf) in the spirited August election of this year; but Indiana, and even Ohio, went with her, though we had carried the latter in her State election scarcely a month before the popular vote for President. Louisiana, too, voted for Jackson, though with us in her preceding State contest; New York (then choosing electors by districts) gave Adams but 16 votes to 20 for his opponent; and so we were badly beaten, carrying but 84 electors, while Jackson — having every vote below the Potomac, and all west of the Alleghanies — had more than double that number.

In the succeeding Presidential contest (1832) we had scarcely a chance. Anti-Masonry had divided us, and driven thousands of Adams men over to Jackson, whose personal popularity was very great, especially with the non-reading class, and who had strengthened himself at the North by his Tariff Messages and his open rupture with Calhoun. New Hampshire and Maine had already gone over to him; Vermont voted for Wirt, the Anti-Masonic candidate; Ohio, distracted by Anti-Masonry, went again for Jackson; New York (now choosing electors by general ticket) went solid for him, with Pennsylvania, and even New Jersey: so that Mr. Clay, though carrying his own Kentucky, made but a sorry figure in the electoral aggregate. Massachusetts, Rhode Island, Connecticut, Delaware, and part of Maryland (by districts), were all the States that voted for him, save his own.

South Carolina now threw away her vote for President on John Floyd, of Virginia, and proceeded to nullify the Tariff, which had just been somewhat reduced, — in part, to placate her. But Van Buren had been substituted for Calhoun as Vice-President, and she would not *be* placated. Her nullification was abandoned, rather than suppressed, and this only after the main point had been virtually yielded to her by a graduated reduction of the Tariff throughout the next ten years to a purely Revenue standard. Though overborne, she was practically triumphant. Mr. Clay proposed the Compromise Tariff, that gave her ample excuse for receding from her untenable position; but only after it had been rendered certain that a more immediate and sweeping reduction of the Tariff, already reported by Mr. Verplanck, from the Committee of Ways and Means, would be carried if this were forborne. So the land had peace again for a brief season.

The United States Bank war, which soon followed, had already been inaugurated by General Jackson's imperious will. Early in his first term, he had been prompted to require the removal of Jeremiah Mason, President of the branch at Portsmouth, N. H., who was obnoxious to his leading friends in that State. He was not gratified. Though the first charter of the bank would not expire till 1836, he demonstrated against its renewal so early as 1830; telling Congress that the question should be promptly acted on, so that arrangements might seasonably be made, in case it should not be rechartered, for supplying its place as a financial agent of the Government, and a commercial convenience to the people. A Jackson Congress, in due time, took the matter in hand, and, in 1832, voted a renewal of the charter, by large majorities in either House. The bill was vetoed, and the Veto Message complained that the act of rechartering was premature! That Congress, prior to its final adjournment, heard vaguely that the President intended to remove the deposits of public money from the detested Bank; whereupon the House voted, by three to one, that they ought *not* to be removed.

William J. Duane, of Pennsylvania, was then Secretary of the Treasury. The President required him to remove the deposits. He declined. Jackson thereupon removed *him;* appointing in his stead Roger B. Taney, of Maryland, who proceeded at once to do his master's bidding. When a new Congress assembled (December, 1833), the Federal deposits, as they accrued, were being dispersed among a multiplicity of State banks, — the least able being of course the most needy and clamorous for a share of the pap, on the strength of their directors' professed devotion to the Administration and its "revered chief."

I have always — at least, since I read Dr. Franklin's autobiography, more than forty years ago — been an advocate of paper money. But I want it to be *money*, — convertible at pleasure into coin, — not printed lies, even though they fail to deceive. From 1818 up to 1830, this country suffered from a dearth of money. Tens of thousands were unwillingly idle from month to month, who would have been usefully and profitably employed had the country been blest with an adequate circulating medium. Comparatively few houses were built in those years, because of the scarcity of money, which palsied enterprise and petrified labor. As a journeyman, I could rarely find work in the country, because there was so little money; and, on coming to the city, I found that payments by master mechanics to their men were mainly made in "uncurrent" notes of State banks, which must often, if not generally, be taken to a broker and "shaved" before they would pay board or buy groceries. The consequent loss was something; the inevitable bother and vexation were a far greater nuisance. A paper currency everywhere current, everywhere convertible into coin, was my ideal; hence I was not partial to local emissions of paper, but a zealous, determined advocate of a National Bank.

The United States Bank, being required to pay over the millions it held on deposit for the Government, receiving no more, began, of course, to contract its loans. It could do no otherwise; especially as an attempt, evidently inspired, had been made by Jackson brokers to break its branch at Savannah by quietly collecting a large quantity of its notes and presenting them at once for payment, hoping that they could not all be met, and that it might thereupon be claimed that the Bank had failed. It was charged by its adversaries that the contraction consequent upon the removal of the Deposits was too rapid and too great; in fact, that its purpose was the creation of commercial distress and panic. This may have been; but a very decided contraction by that Bank was inevitable; and it could have pursued no course that did not expose it to accusation and reproach. I presume it struggled for its life, as most of us would do, if assailed with deadly intent. With the removal of the Deposits, its power to regulate the currency lapsed, and its duty as well. Those Banks to which the Government had transferred its funds and its favors should unitedly have assumed and exercised the functions of a regulator, or confessed their inability.

As the pressure for money increased, the political elements were lashed to fury, and our city, the focus of American commerce, became the arena of a fierce electioneering struggle. Hitherto, the Jackson ascendency had, since the death of De Witt Clinton, been so decided, that our charter elections had usually been scarcely contested; but the stirring debates daily received from Washington, the strivings of merchants and banks to avert bankruptcy, the daily tightening of the money market, and the novel hopes of success inspired in the breasts of those who now took the name of "Whigs" (to indicate their repugnance to unauthorized assumptions of Executive power), rendered New York for some weeks a boiling caldron of political passions. Our three days' election (April, 1834) was the most vehement and keenly contested struggle which I ever witnessed. Our city was then divided into fifteen Wards, with but one poll to each Ward; and I should estimate the average attendance on each poll at little less than one thousand. I am certain that I saw the masses surrounding the Fourth and Sixth Ward polls respectively (then but two or three blocks apart), so mingled that you could not say where the one ended and the other began. There were some fights, of course, and one general collision in the Sixth Ward that might have resulted in deplorable bloodshed; but peace was soon restored. In the event, the Jacksonites elected their Mayor (Cornelius W. Lawrence) over the Whig candidate (Gulian C. Verplanck) by 384 majority, which was less than their overplus of voters naturalized on the last day of the poll. The total vote was nearly 35,000; which was probably a closer approach to the whole number of legal voters than was ever drawn out before or since. The Whigs carried both branches of the Common Council, giving them the control of most of the city patronage; so that the result was generally and justly regarded as a drawn battle.

My concern printed a daily campaign penny paper, entitled The Constitution, through most of that year, and I was a free contributor to its columns, though its editor and publisher was Mr. Achilles R. Crain, who died some thirty years ago. It did not pay, and the firm of Greeley and Winchester were losers by it, counting my editorial assistance worth nothing. William H. Seward, then thirty-four years old, and just closing with distinction a four years' term in the State Senate, was our candidate for Governor, with Silas M. Stillwell for Lieutenant; and we fondly hoped to carry the State in the November election. But meantime the State Banks, wherein the Federal revenue was deposited ("Pet Banks," we Whigs termed them), had been enabled to effect an enormous expansion of their loans and issues; and the country — not yet feeling the Tariff reductions which the Compromise of 1833 had barely inaugurated — was launched on the flood of a factitious but seductive semblance of prosperity. Money was abundant; every one had employment who wanted, and pay if he earned it; property was rapidly appreciating in value; factories and furnaces had full work, and were doing well; so, when the Fall election came, we made a gallant fight, but were badly defeated, — Marcy being reëlected Governor over Seward by some 13,000 majority,— more than he had over Granger in 1832,— and the Whigs, beaten pretty generally and decisively, relapsed into a torpor whence they were scarcely aroused by the ensuing Presidential Election, wherein General Harrison was made their candidate for President, with Francis Granger for Vice-President, while Hugh L. White, of Tennessee, ran for President, with John Tyler, of Virginia, for Vice-President, on an independent ticket which contested the South with the Jackson regulars, who alone held a National Convention, in which they nominated Martin Van Buren for President, with Colonel Richard M. Johnson, of Kentucky, for Vice. I was among the very few in the Eastern States who had taken any interest in bringing forward General Harrison as a candidate, believing that there was the raw material for a good run in his history and character; but this was not generally credited, at least in our State, which, in a languid contest on a light vote, went for Van Buren, Johnson, and Marcy, by some 28,000 majority. When, however, the returns from other States came pouring in, and it was found that General Harrison had carried, with Vermont only of the New England States, New Jersey, Delaware, Maryland, Ohio, Indiana, and Kentucky, and had barely failed to carry Pennsylvania, while White had carried Tennessee and Georgia, barely failing in North Carolina, and in two or three Southwestern States, and that Virginia had refused her vote to Johnson, so that he had failed of an election by the people, and had to be chosen over Granger by the Senate, there was a general waking up to the conviction, that either Harrison was more popular, or Van Buren more obnoxious, than had been supposed in our State, and that the latter might have been beaten by seasonable concert and effort. In that slouching Whig defeat of 1836 lay the germ of the overwhelming Whig triumph of 1840.

Mr. Van Buren's election to the Presidency always seemed to me anomalous, and I am not yet fully reconciled to it. He had none of that personal magnetism which made General Jackson and Mr. Clay respectively the idols of their contending parties. He was not even an orator, was far inferior to Silas Wright as a debater, and to William L. Marcy in executive ability. I believe his strength lay in his suavity. He was the reconciler of the estranged, the harmonizer of those who were at feud, among his fellow-partisans. An adroit and subtle, rather than a great man, I judge that he owed his election, first to the Vice-Presidency, then to the Presidency, to the personal favor and imperious will of Andrew Jackson, with whom "Love me, love my dog," was an iron rule. Had there been no Jackson, Van Buren would never have attained the highest office in the gift of his countrymen.

XV.

PLAY-DAYS.

WHOEVER has spent a few weeks in Paris has doubtless paused to witness, on the greensward enclosed by the Palais Royal, or elsewhere, groups of young children at play, and been charmed by their unconscious spirit, freedom, and grace of manner. The French chronicler's observation, centuries ago, — "The English take their pleasures sadly," — will be brought to his mind on almost every occasion when he witnesses an attempt at festivity on the part of the neighboring islanders or of their descendants on this side of the Atlantic. Our Scotch-Irish settlers in southern New Hampshire brought with them from the other side a broad humor, a love of fun, a spirit of hospitality, a regard for kinship and clanship, which had not wholly faded out in my boyhood, or been drowned in the sea of British nationality which in time rolled over the continent, submerging the islets of Scotch, Hollandic, Swedish, French, or other diverse origin, which had for a season gleamed above the waves. The low-born, rudely bred Englishman has but one natural fashion of enjoying himself, — by getting drunk. We have modified this somewhat; but, as a rule, our thrifty, self-respecting people have hitherto allowed themselves too few holidays, and failed to make the best use of those they actually took.

Fifty years have passed since I first stole down, one foggy morning, to the brook that ran through the west side of my father's farm in New Hampshire, and, dropping my line off the bridge, felt a bite almost instantly, and, hauling up, drew in a nice speckled trout. I had tried to fish before, but without success; henceforth, through boyhood, I was an enthusiastic, persevering fisherman, though never a master of the art. The modern sophistications of fly and reel were unknown in rural New England in those days; hook, line, and sinker gave adequate warning to every considerate, wary fish of what he had to expect if he bit; but fishermen were fewer and brooks more shady, less capricious in volume, than the clearing away of woods has since made them, while intellectual delights were rarer and less inviting: so fishing was largely the pleasure of the gay and the business of the grave. Our rivers, unvexed by mill-dams, swarmed in their season with shad, lamprey-eels, &c., and afforded some salmon, as well as fish of less consideration. Even the sea was not too far to be visited by adventurous parties, intent on a week's profitable sport. Winter brought its sleigh-loads of fresh cod, frozen as soon as fairly out of water, and so retaining the sweetness which soon vanishes forever; and I reckon that, down to 1800, the people of New England had eaten many more pounds of fish than of beef and mutton together, — perhaps of all meats save those obtained by the chase.

In Vermont, the clay soil of the Champlain Valley discolors the brooks when full and repels the trout; but the abundant lakes and lakelets used to abound in perch, bass, and sunfish, while the larger streams afforded, in addition, eels and pike. East Bay — the common estuary of the Poultney and Castleton creeks, and dividing Westhaven from Hampton, N. Y. — is, in Spring, the resort of a small, peculiar shad, which, with a few pike, bass, mullet, &c., come up from the Lake to spawn, and are caught with seines drawn by two fishermen, who wade through the swollen stream, — one of them sometimes obliged to swim, — while great blocks of ice, left aground by the receding floods, often lie slowly wasting along the bank. The melted snow from the mountains eastward stings like a hornet as you enter it; so that, if this were not sport, it would be disagreeable; but I have often, when ten to twelve years old, carried the in-shore staff while my father took the deeper track, which immersed him up to his neck; we dipping together at his word of command, and then gathering up our net and carrying out therein, from no fish at all up to six or eight. I have known a dozen taken at one haul; but this was most extraordinary.

In Summer, we sometimes caught a fine pike or eel with hook and line in the basin beneath the fifty-foot cataract by which the blended creeks tumble into the Bay; but fishing here was too slow for any sportsman less persistent than I then was. I have sat here alone in the dense darkness of a wooded abyss, where the fall drowned all sounds but its own, from 8 to 11 P. M., without being blest with a bite, and then felt my way up through the Egyptian darkness of the forest hillside to the road, and so home, pondering on the fickleness of fortune; yet eager to try again whenever opportunity should favor. I always had my week's work allotted me when I could, and generally succeeded in redeeming at least the Saturday afternoon for my favorite pastime. And I wish here to bear my testimony against a current theory which imports that boys are naturally lazy. My experience contradicts it. My schoolmates and neighbors, who had a great deal more leisure than I, were frequent visitors to the field wherein I was working out my "stint," and very rarely hesitated to turn in, with hearty good-will, and help me out, so that I might devote the rest of the day to fishing, ball, or other sport with them. A lazy man, in my view, is always the pitiable victim of miseducation. Each human being, properly trained, works as freely and naturally as he eats; only the victims of parental neglect or misguidance hate work, and prefer hunger and rags with idleness, to thrift won by industry and patient effort.

There came a day, early in June, 1824, when I had ransomed from toil the afternoon for perch-fishing in "Inman Pond," a lovely tarn, lying lonely among wooded hills in Fairhaven, some two miles east of our home. I was undeniably ill, in the forenoon, so that I was twice compelled to desist from labor and lie down; hence, my mother judiciously urged me to let the fish alone for that day, and care for my health. I had not fished for months, however; the day was glorious; I set off for the pond a little after noon, and was dropping the perch a line within the hour. But my head soon grew heavy; there was a strange ache in my every bone; the breeze that sped gently across the pond, though really warm and bland, seemed to chill me as never before. I was soon compelled to put aside my pole, and lie down, shivering, on the bare rock which here formed the shore; thus passing two hours in a semi-conscious state of mingled delirium and suffering. When the fit of ague passed off, I rose and started homeward, but was constrained to stop at the first house, half a mile from home, where I passed the night. I had seen fever and ague before, but never felt it; and I made haste to terminate the unpleasant acquaintance.

Judging solely from my own experience, I believe he who will begin with an emetic directly after his first fit, and follow this with heavy and frequent doses of Peruvian Bark (I distrust Quinine, as less natural and more perilous), taking care to eat very little, and that of the simplest vegetable food, and do absolutely no work at all, may break the fits directly, and return to work quite well after a fortnight. He who neglects or trifles with this scourge may lose a Summer by it, and never again be restored to his pristine health and vigor.

Ball was a common diversion in Vermont while I lived there; yet I never became a proficient at it, probably for want of time and practice. To catch a flying ball, propelled by a muscular arm straight at my nose, and coming on so swiftly that I could scarcely see it, was a feat requiring a celerity of action, an electric sympathy of eye and brain and hand, which my few and far-between hours snatched from labor for recreation did not suffice to acquire. Call it a knack, if you will; it was quite beyond my powers of acquisition. "Practice makes perfect." I certainly needed the practice, though I am not sure that any amount of it would have made me a perfect ball-player.

I like popular amusements, especially those which develop

and strengthen the muscles; but I *do not* like the modern matches made up between clubs located hundreds of miles apart. According to my notion, the prize should be awarded in these matches to the side which makes the shorter score. In awarding the palm for such a contest, count *my* vote always for the beaten party. They doubtless mind their proper business better, and perform their duties as fathers, husbands, sons, clerks, journeymen, apprentices, &c., more thoroughly than do the victors. It is an honor not to beat, but to be beaten, in a match of this sort.

I wish it were practicable to win our countrymen to a wiser and more equable frame of mind respecting recreations. Many sourly contemn and reject them altogether; and I think this was a prevalent mistake of our better class, up to a late period. Now, the excess seems to be of an opposite character. Too many make play a business, when it should be only a diversion from business. The youth, who has given his minority to study and play alternately, with no experience of work, is deplorably ill fitted to grapple with the stern realities of responsible life. His muscles need hardening; his sinews have not been disciplined to the work that solicits them. As between a youth all work and one all play, though neither is commendable, the former is preferable.

I never saw a game of Billiards played, and know nothing of Bowling; yet I judge this latter a capital in-door exercise for persons of sedentary pursuits and habits. These I would advise to shun such games as Chess, Cards, Checkers, Backgammon, &c., because of their inevitable tendency to impair digestion and incite headache. If played at all, they should be played by men who give their days to muscular, out-door exertion, and at night feel too tired to study.

I tried fishing again, after being weaned of it throughout my apprenticeship, while stopping with my father at the West, and had some little success in the creeks adjacent to his new home; but I was no longer fascinated by the sport, while the proceeds were of slender bulk and value. The

streams were full of trees and roots, while overgrown by a tangle of limbs and bushes; the sawdust gradually repelled or killed the trout; the business involved more plague than profit of any kind; and I soon deserted it. I had become, in my poor way, a fisher of men.

I protest against making a business of play. The Yankees are prone to "run the thing into the ground," be it what it may. We work immoderately, and play ditto. I have seen very few holidays during my thirty-six years' sojourn in New York; and such is the experience of a large class; while others have too many play-days, — far too many. We must somehow strike a general average, for mutual benefit and the promotion of public health.

I have often cooled my imagination, amid the fervid and sweltering heats of a summer of constant work in the city, with a dream of spending a week amid the lakes and mountains, under the dense forest-shades of "John Brown's Tract," as we term the great northern wilderness wherein the Hudson, Mohawk, Au-Sable, Racket, Black, and other rivers of the eastern half of our State, have their sources; and, though I never found time to set foot therein, I have hardly yet relinquished the hope that I may do so. I was ever the zealous advocate of all works of internal improvement, so called, save those which aim at the heart of that wilderness, threatening to hunt the deer from their last refuge on our soil, and denude of their forest-covering the springs which feed our most useful and valued streams. Strip "John Brown's Tract" of its timber, and the Hudson will, from June to October, cease to be navigable by floating palaces to Albany; while desolating floods, especially in Spring, will do immense damage from Utica down to Castleton.

I presume, if I were ever to have the week I covet, I should find it insufferably tedious, — the mosquitoes biting superbly; the trout shyly, or not at all, — and should long for a return to civilization, with its hourly toils and struggles, its thronged pavements, and its damp newspapers with breakfast. Still, I should like to try the experiment; and I hope our children will see, though I shall not, the greater portion of Pike and Monroe Counties, with other sterile mountain districts of eastern Pennsylvania, converted into spacious deer-parks of fifty to five hundred square miles each, enclosed by massive stone walls, intersected by belts of grass traversing each tiny valley (so as speedily to stop the running of any fires that might chance to be started), planted with the best timber, and held by large companies of shareholders for sporting, under proper regulations. These lands are not now worth five dollars per acre in the average; but the timber on them would soon be cheap at one hundred dollars per acre, if this plan were adopted. They are full of petty lakes, and of spring-fed, swiftly running streams, which would soon abound with the finest trout if they were simply let alone; with proper arrangements for breeding and feeding, they would produce more of this delicate fish than New York and Philadelphia ever yet saw. A century hence, were those bleak mountains thus dealt with, they would be covered, as of old, with a magnificent forest, containing more serviceable pine than is now standing in all our States east of the Potomac and Lake Erie, and then worth at least five hundred dollars per acre.

Yet the fact remains, that we do not enjoy our holidays, — do not know how to play judiciously and in moderation. Though often invited, I never yet went on a railroad excursion that was to outlast the day of starting; knowing by instinct that it would prove a failure so far as enjoyment was concerned. And my recollection of steamboat excursions, however brief, is, that they were generally bores. I recollect that, one Fourth of July, long ago, an excursion to Sandy Hook was advertised that seemed specially inviting; so I overruled my distrust, and went. At 11 A. M., we passengers, some hundreds in number, were debarked, by small boats, on the back side of the island, which we found a sand-heap, thinly bristled with bushes, — its solitary dwelling inhabited by the keeper of the light-house, whose limited stock of bread and bacon scarcely afforded us a fair mouthful each. Our steamboat had gone back to the city for a second load; so we bathed, and killed time as well as we could, until she returned, — running aground as she attempted to near the shore. We got aboard, and waited dreary hours — hungry, crowded, and sullen — for the tide to rise and float us off; being tantalized throughout the evening by the shooting up of abundant rockets over the city, barely within our range of vision. At length, we partly floated, partly pulled off; and, at midnight, we were landed at the Battery, — as thoroughly wearied and disgusted a lot of disappointed pleasure-seekers as ever crept silently to their homes. I have never since hankered after a seaward excursion.

We have teachers of every art, science, and ology; why not a teacher of the art of enjoying leisure, — of making play a little less wearisome than work? Take excursions to illustrate my idea. Why should not any person above ten years old know better than to embark on a crowded vessel or train with some hundreds of others, mainly total strangers, expecting to enjoy in their company a trip of several days? But if, instead of this, a small party of intimate, devoted friends, of reasonably accordant tastes, education, and habits, were to charter a little steamboat, or a train, or a dozen wagons, and so betake themselves to some quiet nook where they would be safe from intrusion or prying curiosity, — say an islet off the coast or in the St. Lawrence, a lake-side in our Northern wilderness, a cluster of deserted shingle-makers' huts on the mountains of Eastern Pennsylvania, where fish or game was procurable, and cool breezes in Midsummer might be confidently expected, — they surely might expect to redeem a full week from care and trouble, and return to their homes more vigorous, more healthful, more at peace with themselves and with others, — cured of these interminable headaches, and sound in body and soul. Who will teach us incessant workers how to achieve leisure and enjoy it?

XVI.

TRIUMPH.

MR. VAN BUREN was inaugurated President on the 4th of March, 1837; when General Jackson retired to his Hermitage, congratulating himself that he left the American people prosperous and happy. Never was man more mistaken. He had just before pointed to the immense sales of public lands, in 1835–36, as proof of increased and general addiction to agriculture, when, in fact, it proved only a plethora of currency, and a consequent high-tide of speculation. At length, convinced that something was wrong, the General attempted to dam the flood by a "specie circular," prescribing that only coin should thenceforth be received in payment for public lands. This device precipitated the catastrophe it was intended to avert. The harvest of 1836 had been generally bad, while our importations had been quite large; we were compelled to import grain, while heavily in debt to Europe for goods; thus our banks were drained of specie both ways, — to pay for lands in the West and South, and for grain and goods daily pouring in from the Old World. They held out so long as they could, and then gave way, — those of our city suspending specie payment on the 10th of May, and all others directly afterward, save that some of those located in the southwest had done so some days before. Samuel Swartwout, Collector of Customs at this port, at first proclaimed that he would continue to receive bank-notes for duties, notwithstanding the suspension (which was promptly legalized by our Jackson legislature); but he was soon overruled from Washington; and the duties on imports — indeed, the entire

Federal revenue — were thenceforth collected and kept in coin alone. The revenues of all the States, however, were still collected, kept, and paid out in bank-notes, which continued to be the currency of the people.

Mr. Van Buren promptly called the new Congress to meet in extraordinary session on the first Monday in September, when he addressed to it a Message which laid the blame of suspension on the banks, which were accused of over-issuing and over-lending; and he thereupon insisted that the Government should divorce itself from all connection with banks, and should thenceforth collect, keep, and pay out its revenues in coin only, through the agency of special depositories, forming what he termed the Independent Treasury. An able, earnest, searching debate in the House was elicited by this proposition, which was terminated by a motion of Hon. John C. Clark, of this State, that the bill providing for the Independent Treasury (so called) do lie on the table; which was carried in a full House by a small majority. Mr. Clark had been a Jackson-Van Buren Democrat, but was henceforth accounted a "Conservative," and acted openly with the Whigs, as did Hon. Nathaniel P. Tallmadge, one of our United States Senators, and many other leading men hitherto Democrats. The Independent Treasury, thus condemned by the House, remained in force, by the President's direction, until it was finally enacted in the Summer of 1840.

The commercial revulsion, which was rather apprehended than fully experienced in 1834, was abundantly realized in 1837. Manufactories were stopped, and their "hands" thrown out of work. Trade was almost stagnant. Bankruptcies among men of business were rather the rule than the exception. Property was sacrificed at auction — often at sheriff's or assignee's sale — for a fraction of its value; and thousands, who had fondly dreamed themselves millionnaires, or on the point of becoming such, awoke to the fact that they were bankrupt. The banks were, of course, in trouble, — those which had been Government depositories, or "pets," rather deeper than the rest. Looking at the matter from *their* point of view, they had been first seduced into a questionable path, and were now reviled and assailed for yielding to their seducers.

Soon were heard the rumblings of a political earthquake. Scarcely a State elected Members of Congress or a Governor in 1837, after the Suspension of Specie Payments; but the Legislative and local elections of Autumn sufficiently indicated the popular revulsion. When New York came to vote, in November, the gale had stiffened into a tornado. The Whigs carried New York City, — which they had never done before, — with Westchester, Orange, Dutchess, Greene, Oneida, Onondaga, and other counties hitherto overwhelmingly Democratic, giving them six of the eight Senate districts, including the First and Second. Herkimer, Jefferson, St. Lawrence, Suffolk, and a few smaller counties, were all that clung to the waning fortunes of Van Buren, — the Whigs choosing 100 out of the 128 Members of Assembly. The Senate, being chosen but one fourth annually, remained strongly Democratic.

I had been active, as usual, in the canvass, but not conspicuously so, — my personal embarrassments constraining me not to be. I had been privately tendered a place on the City Assembly ticket, but felt obliged to decline it. Outside of the city, I had no political, and little personal, acquaintance in the State; having never yet attended a State Convention. I was somewhat surprised, therefore, at a visit, in my rude editorial attic, a few days after the extent of our victory was ascertained, from a stranger, who introduced himself as Mr. Thurlow Weed, editor of The Albany Evening Journal, who, with Mr. Lewis Benedict, also of Albany, was stopping at the City Hotel, and wished to confer with me at their lodgings.

I accompanied Mr. Weed to his hotel, where the business which had brought the friends to New York was unfolded. Decided as had been our triumph in the State, it had been won on a moderate vote, and quite as much by the failure of

Democrats to exercise their right of suffrage as by their voting the Whig ticket. The next election would naturally bring many of these stay-at-homes to the polls, and — there being a Governor and Representatives in Congress to be then chosen, with a United States Senator in prospect — would inevitably draw out a heavy vote. To maintain and confirm the Whig ascendency, it had been resolved to publish, throughout 1838, a cheap weekly journal, to be called The Jeffersonian, which I had been pitched upon as the proper person to edit. I believe Mr. Weed first designated me for the post, though he knew nothing of me except by reading my paper, The New-Yorker; for though I had written for several Whig dailies, mainly of the ephemeral type, I had done so anonymously. The Jeffersonian was to be a small octavo, issued weekly for a year, and virtually given away for the nominal price of fifty cents per annum, — the expense of its issue being made up by voluntary contributions from wealthy or spirited Whigs. I was offered $1,000 to serve as editor, and concluded to accept it, though this would oblige me to spend a good part of my time — in Summer, half of each week; in Winter, nearly the whole — in Albany.

About two months thereafter, having put my affairs into as good a shape as possible, I took stage in Cortlandt Street, one cold Winter morning, and had a sleigh-ride thence up the west side of the Hudson to Albany, where I arrived in the afternoon of the third day. My No. 1 appeared in due time thereafter; but, as my small paper did not require all my time, I made condensed reports of the Assembly debates for The Evening Journal, and wrote some articles for its editorial columns.

The new era in politics had called many of our foremost men to Albany. The courtly and gracious Luther Bradish was Speaker of the Assembly. Our city was represented therein by several notables, — among them David B. Ogden, Willis Hall, Samuel B. Ruggles, and Adoniram Chandler. We had chosen as Senator Gulian C. Verplanck, whom we vainly tried to make Mayor in 1834. From Albany, Daniel

D. Barnard; from Troy, Day O. Kellogg; from Oneida, Fortune C. White; from Onondaga, James R. Lawrence, Victory Birdseye, and Azariah Smith; from Rochester, Derick Sibley; from Livingston, George W. Patterson, — were Whig Members of Assembly. On the other side stood Abijah Mann, of Herkimer, Preston King, of St. Lawrence, and Richard Hulbert, of Jefferson, with several others of decided ability and cleverness in parliamentary warfare. The Free Banking System — for which our State is specially indebted to Willis Hall — was developed and established that Winter, — a great and admirable improvement on the corrupting political monopoly it superseded. Our banks were again allowed to issue small bills, which the last preceding Legislature had forbidden. The partisan device whereby County Judges (there were then several in each county) were interpolated into the County Boards of Supervisors for the purpose of making certain county appointments, was knocked on the head. In short, I believe our State has, since 1824, had no other Legislature so able, nor one that did so much good and so little harm, as that of 1838.

The Jeffersonian was a campaign paper, but after a fashion of its own. It carefully eschewed abuse, scurrility, and railing accusations. Its editorials were few, brief, and related to the topics of the day, — rarely evincing partisanship, never bitterness. Its pages were mainly devoted to the ablest and calmest speeches made in Congress, — generally to those which opposed the Independent (or Sub-) Treasury scheme and its adjuncts, though other able essays also found place in it. In short, it aimed to convince and win by candor and moderation, rather than overbear by passion and vehemence. Its circulation was, throughout, about 15,000 copies; and, being mainly read by those who took no other paper, I think it did good. Had it been conducted on the high-pressure principle, it would probably have had a larger circulation, and perhaps done no good at all. I think its efficiency was somewhat evidenced by the fact that, while the Whigs were beaten that Fall in Maine, in Pennsylvania, in Ohio (which they had carried two years before), and in nearly or quite every State westward of Ohio, they were successful in the later election in New York, as the result of a desperate struggle, and on an average vote largely beyond precedent, — William H. Seward ousting William L. Marcy from the Governor's chair, and Luther Bradish succeeding John Tracy as Lieutenant-Governor, — each by more than 10,000 majority. We carried also the Assembly (though by no such majority as the year before), and gained somewhat in the Senate; but that branch was still adverse to us, owing to the dead weight accumulated in former years: so Governor Seward's nominations were all laid on the table, and our attempt to reëlect Hon. N. P. Tallmadge United States Senator was likewise defeated, — the law requiring each House to nominate a Senator, meet to compare nominations, and, in case of their disagreement, proceed to elect in joint ballot; but the Democratic Senators evaded its requirement by each voting for a separate candidate: so that the Senate made no nomination, and could not be compelled to go into joint ballot.

Considerable excitement was caused by this evasion of a strictly prescribed duty; and the Whigs, by desperate exertions, carried the State again in the ensuing election (November, 1839), though this city, which for two years had gone with them, now went against them. There were three Senators to be chosen this year in the Third (Albany and Delaware) District; and the Whigs just carried them all, — one of them (General Erastus Root) by barely *one* majority. They had never triumphed in this district before; and I think they never carried it again unless their adversaries were divided. And now, when the new Legislature met (January, 1840), we had, along with the Governor and Assembly, a clear majority (20 to 12) in the Senate, and a new chapter was to be opened.

I was writing at a reporter's desk in the Senate, when, very soon after its first sitting had begun, some Whig rose and moved that so and so (the Democratic incumbents) be removed from the posts of secretary, sergeant-at-arms, &c., and that so and so [nominees of a Whig caucus, held the night before] be appointed in their stead. At once, up rose the venerable but vigorous Colonel Samuel Young, of Saratoga, and for nearly an hour poured hot shot into the proposition, descanting on bleeding constitutions, outraged liberties, violated rights, &c., &c. When he had blown out, Uncle Harry Livingston, of Dutchess, — a humorous old Whig, who, in the general overturn of 1837, had blundered into the Senate from the Second District, to the amazement of himself and of everybody else, — sprang to his feet. As we all knew that he could not make a speech, — in fact, had scarcely, till now, attempted it, — curiosity was on tiptoe to catch his first sentence; but his consciousness that he had something good to say for a moment choked his powers of utterance. "Mr. President" (che-hee-hee), — "Mr. President," he at length managed to say, "I take it that *this* is one of those questions that are settled by the rule of *eighteen to fourteen*." [Throughout the preceding session, every attempt to confirm one of Governor Seward's nominees resulted in this entry in the journal: "Laid on the table, — 18 to 14."] The hit was decided; the spectators roared; the Senator from the Fourth was shut up; and the Senate proceeded to appoint the Whig nominees without further opposition or demur. Mr. Tallmadge was soon re-elected to the Senate, and everything put in order for the decisive struggle of this eventful 1840.

XVII.

LOG-CABIN DAYS.

NEW YORK, which gave Mr. Van Buren the largest majority of any State in 1836, had been held against him throughout his administration, though she was his own State, and he had therein a powerful body of devoted, personal adherents, led by such men of eminent ability as Silas Wright, William L. Marcy, and Edwin Croswell. She had been so held by the talent, exertion, and vigilance of men equally able and determined, among whom Thurlow Weed, William H. Seward (now Governor), John C. Spencer, and Willis Hall were conspicuous. But our majority of 15,000 in '37 had fallen to 10,000 in '38, and to 5,000 in '39, despite our best efforts; Governor Seward's school recommendations and dispensation of State patronage had made him many enemies; and the friends of Mr. Van Buren counted, with reason, on carrying the State for his reëlection, and against that of Governor Seward, in the impending struggle of 1840. Pennsylvania, Ohio, Tennessee, and all the Northwest, had been carried against the Whigs in the most recent contests; Mr. Van Buren's star was clearly in the ascendant at the South; while New England and New Jersey were nicely balanced, — Massachusetts, as well as Maine and New Hampshire, having chosen a Democratic governor (Marcus Morton) in 1839. Mr. Van Buren's Administration, though at first condemned, was now sustained by a popular majority: New York alone — his own State — stood forth the flagship of the Opposition. Both parties were silently preparing to put forth their very best efforts in the Presidential contest in prospect; but fully two thirds of the States, choosing about that proportion of the electors, were now ranged on the Democratic side, — many of them by impregnable majorities, — while scarcely *one* State was unquestionably Whig. Mr. Van Buren, when first overwhelmed by the popular surge that followed close upon the collapse of the Pet Bank system, had calmly and with dignity appealed to the people's "sober second thought"; and it now seemed morally certain that he would be triumphantly re-elected.

Such were the auspices under which the first Whig National Convention (the second National Convention ever held by any party, — that held in 1840 by the Democrats at Baltimore, which nominated Van Buren and Johnson, having been the first) assembled at Harrisburg, Pa., early in December, 1839. Of its doings I was a deeply interested observer. The States were nearly all represented, though in South Carolina there were no Whigs but a handful; even the name was unknown in Tennessee, and the party was feeble in several other States. But the delegations convened included many names widely and favorably known, — including two ex-Governors of Virginia (James Barbour and John Tyler), one of Kentucky (Thomas Metcalf), one of Ohio (Joseph Vance), and at least one from several other States. I recollect at least two ex-Governors of Pennsylvania (John Andrew Shultze and Joseph Ritner) as actively counselling and sympathizing with the delegates.

The sittings of the Convention were protracted through three or four days, during which several ballots for President were taken. There was a plurality, though not a majority, in favor of nominating Mr. Clay; but it was in good part composed of delegates from States which could not rationally be expected to vote for any Whig candidate. On the other hand, the delegates from Pennsylvania, Ohio, and Indiana said, "We can carry our States for General Harrison, but not for Mr. Clay." New York and New Jersey cast their earlier votes for General Scott, but stood ready to unite on General Harrison whenever it should be clear that he could be nominated and elected; and they ultimately did so. The delegates from Maine and Massachusetts contributed powerfully to secure General Harrison's ultimate nomination. Each delegation cast its vote through a committee, and the votes were added up by a general committee, which reported no names and no figures, but simply that no choice had been effected; until at length the Scott votes were all cast for Harrison, and his nomination thus effected; when the result was proclaimed.

Governor Seward, who was in Albany (there were no telegraphs in those days), and Mr. Weed, who was present, and very influential in producing the result, were strongly blamed by the ardent, uncalculating supporters of Mr. Clay, as having cheated him out of the nomination, — I could never see with what reason. They judged that he could not be chosen, if nominated, while another could be, and acted accordingly. If politics do not meditate the achievement of beneficent ends through the choice and use of the safest and most effective means, I wholly misapprehend them.

Mr. John Tyler, with nearly or quite all his fellow-delegates from Virginia, was for Clay first, last, and all the time; for him whether he could be elected or not. When it was announced that Mr. Clay was defeated, he *cried* (so it was reported); and that report (I think) gave him the nomination for Vice-President without a contest. It was an attempt of the triumphant Harrisonites to heal the wounds of Mr. Clay's devoted friends. Yet the nomination was, for several reasons, a strong one. Mr. Tyler, though a Jackson man, had received, in 1828, the votes for United States Senator of the Adams men in the Virginia Legislature, and been thereby elected over John Randolph. When Jackson removed the deposits from the United States Bank, he united with the Whigs in publicly condemning the act; and, having been superseded therefor, he was thereafter regarded as a Whig. He had voted alone in the Senate of 1832–33 against the Force bill, which provided for the collection of the Federal revenue in South Carolina in defiance of the nullifying ordinance of her Convention. He had run for Vice-President on the White ticket in 1836, and so had acquired a hold on the Southern opponents of Van Buren, which soon brought them all heartily into the support of the Harrisburg ticket. In short, the Convention made the strongest possible ticket, so far as success was regarded; and the Democrats in attendance all felt, though they did not confess it. Every one who had eyes could see that they desired and worked for the nomination of Mr. Clay. One of them, after the ticket was made, offered to bet that it would not be elected; but, his offer being promptly accepted, and he requested to name the amount, he hauled off. In short, we left Harrisburg with that confidence of success which goes far to secure its own justification; and we were greeted on our way home as though the battle were already won.

But it was well understood that the struggle would be desperate, especially in our State, and preparations were soon in progress to render it effective. Our adversaries now helped us to our most effective weapons. They at once commenced assailing General Harrison as an imbecile, dotard, granny, &c., who had seen no real fighting, but had achieved a good deal of tall running from the enemy; and one militia general, Crary, who represented Michigan in the House, having made a speech in this vein, provoked a response from Hon. Tom Corwin of Ohio, which for wit, humor, and withering yet good-natured sarcasm has rarely, if ever, been excelled. The triumph was overwhelming; and, when the venerable and grave John Quincy Adams, in a few casual remarks next morning, spoke carelessly of "the late General Crary," a spontaneous roar attested the felicity of the allusion.

General Harrison had lived many years after his removal to Ohio in a log-house, and had been a poor man most of his life, as he still was. A Democratic journalist, scoffing at the idea of electing such a man to the Presidency, smartly observed, in substance, "Give him a log-cabin and a barrel of hard cider, and he will stay content in Ohio, not aspiring to the Presidency." The taunt was immediately caught up by the Whigs: "log-cabins" and "hard cider" became watchwords of the canvass; and every hour the excitement and enthusiasm swelled higher and higher.

But the Democratic party claimed an unbroken series of triumphs in every Presidential election which it did not throw away by its own dissensions; and, being now united, regarded its success as inevitable. "You Whigs," said Dr. Duncan, of Ohio, one of its most effective canvassers, "achieve great victories every day in the year but one,—that is the day of election." It was certain that a party which had enjoyed the ever-increasing patronage of the Federal Government for the preceding twelve years, which wielded that of most of the States also, and which was still backed by the popularity and active sympathy of General Jackson, was not to be expelled from power without the most resolute, persistent, systematic exertions. Hence, it was determined in the councils of our friends at Albany that a new campaign paper should be issued, to be entitled The Log-Cabin; and I was chosen to conduct it. No contributions were made or sought in its behalf. I was to publish as well as edit it; it was to be a folio of good size; and it was decided that fifteen copies should be sent for the full term of six months (from May 1 to November 1) for $5.

I had just secured a new partner (my fifth or sixth) of considerable business capacity, when this campaign sheet was undertaken; and the immediate influx of subscriptions frightened and repelled him. He insisted that the price was ruinous,—that the paper could not be afforded for so little,—that we should inevitably be bankrupted by its enormous circulation,—and all my expostulations and entreaties were unavailing against his fixed resolve to get out of the concern at once. I therefore dissolved and settled with him, and was left alone to edit and publish both The New-Yorker and The Log-Cabin, as I had in 1838 edited, but not published, The New-Yorker and The Jeffersonian. Having neither steam presses nor facilities for mailing, I was obliged to hire everything done but the head-work, which involved heavier outlays than I ought to have had to meet. I tried to make The Log-Cabin as effective as I could, with wood engravings of General Harrison's battle-scenes, music, &c., and to render it a model of its kind; but the times were so changed that it was more lively and less sedately argumentative than The Jeffersonian.

Its circulation was entirely beyond precedent. I fixed the edition of No. 1 at 30,000; but before the close of the week I was obliged to print 10,000 more; and even this was too few. The weekly issues ran rapidly up to 80,000, and might have been increased, had I possessed ample facilities for printing and mailing, to 100,000. With the machinery of distribution by news companies, expresses, &c., now existing, I guess that it might have been swelled to a quarter of a million. And, though I made very little money by it, I gave every subscriber an extra number containing the results of the election. After that, I continued the paper for a full year longer; having a circulation for it of 10,000 copies, which about paid the cost, counting my work as editor nothing.

The Log-Cabin was but an incident, a feature of the canvass. Briefly, we Whigs took the lead, and kept it throughout. Our opponents struggled manfully, desperately; but wind and tide were against them. They had campaign and other papers, good speakers, and large meetings; but we were far ahead of them in singing, and in electioneering emblems and mottoes which appealed to popular sympathies. The elections held next after the Harrisburg nominations were local, but they all went our way; and the State contests, which soon followed, amply confirmed their indications. In September, Maine held her State election, and chose the Whig candidate for Governor (Edward Kent) by a small majority, but on a very full vote. The Democrats did not concede his election till after the vote for President, in November. Pennsylvania, in October, gave a small Democratic majority; but we insisted that it could be overcome when we came to vote for Harrison, and it was. In October, Ohio, Indiana, and Georgia all gave decisive Harrison majorities, rendering the great result morally certain. Yet, when the Presidential electors chosen were fully ascertained, even the most sanguine among us were astounded by the completeness of our triumph. We had given General Harrison the electoral votes of all but the seven States of New Hampshire, Virginia, South Carolina, Alabama, Illinois, Missouri, and Arkansas, — 60 in all, — while our candidate had 234; making his the heaviest majority by which any President had ever been chosen. New York, where each party had done its best, had been carried for him by 13,290 majority; but Governor Seward had been reëlected by only 5,315. With any other candidate for President, he could scarcely have escaped defeat.

I judge that there were not many who had done more effective work in the canvass than I had; but I doubt that General Harrison ever heard my name. I never visited nor wrote him; I was not of the throng that surrounded him on reaching Washington, — in fact, I did not visit that city, in 1841, until after his most untimely death. I received the news of that calamity on landing one morning from an Albany steamboat; and I mournfully realized, on the instant, that it was no common disaster, but far-reaching in its malign influence. General Harrison was never a great man, but he had good sense, was moderate in his views, and tolerant of adverse convictions; he truly loved and aspired to serve his country, and was at the summit of a broadly based and substantial popularity which, had he lived out his term, would have averted many impending evils. Our country, in my view, had lost many abler men, but none that she could so ill spare since Washington. He was President for one short month; and then the hopes born of his election were suddenly buried in his grave.

XVIII.

THE TRIBUNE.

ON the tenth day of April, 1841, — a day of most unseasonable chill and sleet and snow, — our city held her great funeral parade and pageant in honor of our lost President, who had died six days before. General Robert Bogardus, the venerable Grand Marshal of the parade, died not long afterward of exposure to its inclemencies. On that leaden, funereal morning, the most inhospitable of the year, I issued the first number of THE NEW YORK TRIBUNE. It was a small sheet, for it was to be retailed for a cent, and not much of a newspaper could be afforded for that price, even in those specie-paying times. I had been incited to this enterprise by several Whig friends, who deemed a cheap daily, addressed more especially to the laboring class, eminently needed in our city, where the only two cheap journals then and still existing — The Sun and The Herald — were in decided, though unavowed, and therefore more effective, sympathy and affiliation with the Democratic party. Two or three had promised pecuniary aid if it should be needed; only one (Mr. James Coggeshall, long since deceased) ever made good that promise, by loaning me one thousand dollars, which was duly and gratefully repaid, principal and interest. I presume others would have helped me had I asked it; but I never did. Mr. Dudley S. Gregory, who had voluntarily loaned me one thousand dollars to sustain The New-Yorker in the very darkest hour of my fortunes, in 1837, and whom I had but recently repaid, was among my most trusted friends in the outset of my new enterprise also; but I was able to prosecute it without taxing (I no longer needed to test) his generosity.

My leading idea was the establishment of a journal removed alike from servile partisanship on the one hand and from gagged, mincing neutrality on the other. Party spirit is so fierce and intolerant in this country that the editor of a non-partisan sheet is restrained from saying what he thinks and feels on the most vital, imminent topics; while, on the other hand, a Democratic, Whig, or Republican journal is generally expected to praise or blame, like or dislike, eulogize or condemn, in precise accordance with the views and interest of its party. I believed there was a happy medium between these extremes, — a position from which a journalist might openly and heartily advocate the principles and commend the measures of that party to which his convictions allied him, yet frankly dissent from its course on a particular question, and even denounce its candidates if they were shown to be deficient in capacity or (far worse) in integrity. I felt that a journal thus loyal to its guiding convictions, yet ready to expose and condemn unworthy conduct or incidental error on the part of men attached to its party, must be far more effective, even party-wise, than though it might always be counted on to applaud or reprobate, bless or curse, as the party's prejudices or immediate interest might seem to prescribe. Especially by the Whigs — who were rather the loosely aggregated, mainly undisciplined opponents of a great party, than, in the stricter sense, a party themselves — did I feel that such a journal was consciously needed, and would be fairly sustained. I had been a pretty constant and copious contributor (generally unpaid) to nearly or quite every cheap Whig journal that had, from time to time, been started in our city; most of them to fail after a very brief, and not particularly bright career; but one — The New York Whig, which was, throughout most of its existence, under the dignified and conscientious direction of Jacob B. Moore, formerly of The New Hampshire Journal — had been continued through two or three years. My familiarity with its history and management gave me confidence that the right sort of a cheap Whig journal would be enabled to live. I had been ten years in

New York, was thirty years old, in full health and vigor, and worth, I presume, about two thousand dollars, half of it in printing materials. The Jeffersonian, and still more The Log-Cabin, had made me favorably known to many thousands of those who were most likely to take such a paper as I proposed to make The Tribune, while The New-Yorker had given me some literary standing and the reputation of a useful and well-informed compiler of election returns. In short, I was in a better position to undertake the establishment of a daily newspaper than the great mass of those who try it and fail, as most who make the venture do and must. I presume the new journals (in English) since started in this city number not less than one hundred, whereof barely two — The Times and The World — can be fairly said to be still living; and The World is a mausoleum wherein the remains of The Evening Star, The American, and The Courier and Enquirer lie inurned; these having long ago swallowed sundry of their predecessors. Yet several of those which have meantime lived their little hour and passed away were conducted by men of decided ability and ripe experience, and were backed by a pecuniary capital at least twenty times greater than the fearfully inadequate sum whereon I started The Tribune.

On the intellectual side, my venture was not so rash as it seemed. My own fifteen years' devotion to newspaper-making, in all its phases, was worth far more than will be generally supposed; and I had already secured a first assistant in Mr. Henry J. Raymond, who — having for two years, while in college at Burlington, Vt., been a valued contributor to the literary side of The New-Yorker — had hied to the city directly upon graduating, late in 1840, and gladly accepted my offer to hire him at eight dollars per week until he could do better. I had not much for him to do till The Tribune was started: then I had enough: and I never found another person, barely of age and just from his studies, who evinced so signal and such versatile ability in journalism as he did. Abler and stronger men I may have met; a cleverer, readier, more generally efficient journalist, I never saw. He remained with me nearly eight years, if my memory serves, and is the only assistant with whom I ever felt required to remonstrate for doing more work than any human brain and frame could be expected long to endure. His salary was of course gradually increased from time to time; but his services were more valuable in proportion to their cost than those of any one else who ever aided me on The Tribune.

Mr. George M. Snow, a friend of my own age, who had had considerable mercantile experience, took charge of the Financial or Wall-Street department (then far less important than it now is), and retained it for more than twenty-two years; becoming ultimately a heavy stockholder in, and a trustee of, the concern; resigning his trust only when (in 1863) he departed for Europe in ill health; returning but to die two years later. A large majority of those who aided in preparing or in issuing the first number had preceded or have followed Mr. Snow to the Silent Land; but two remain, and are now Foreman and Engineer respectively in the Printing Department, — both stockholders and trustees. Others, doubtless, survive, who were with us then, but have long since drifted away to the West, to the Pacific slope, or into some other employment, and the places that once knew them know them no more. Twenty-six years witness many changes, especially in a city like ours, a position like mine; and I believe that the only men who were Editors of New York dailies before me, and who still remain such, are Mr. William Cullen Bryant of The Evening Post, and Mr. James Gordon Bennett of The Herald.

About five hundred names of subscribers had already been obtained for The Tribune — mainly by my warm personal and political friends, Noah Cook and James Coggeshall — before its first issue, whereof I printed five thousand, and nearly succeeded in giving away all of them that would not sell. I had type, but no presses; and so had to hire my press-work done by the "token"; my folding and mailing must have staggered me but for the circumstance that I had few papers to mail, and not very many to fold. The lack of the present machinery of railroads and expresses was a grave obstacle to the circulation of my paper outside of the city's suburbs; but I think its paid-for issues were two thousand at the close of the first week, and that they thenceforth increased pretty steadily, at the rate of five hundred per week, till they reached ten thousand. My current expenses for the first week were about five hundred and twenty-five dollars; my receipts ninety-two dollars; and, though the outgoes steadily, inevitably increased, the income increased in a still larger ratio, till it nearly balanced the former. But I was not made for a publisher; indeed, no man was ever qualified at once to edit and to publish a daily paper such as it must be to live in these times; and it was not until Mr. Thomas McElrath — whom I had barely known as a member of the publishing firm over whose store I first set type in this city, but who was now a lawyer in good standing and practice — made me a voluntary and wholly unexpected proffer of partnership in my still struggling but hopeful enterprise, that it might be considered fairly on its feet. He offered to invest two thousand dollars as an equivalent to whatever I had in the business, and to devote his time and energies to its management, on the basis of perfect equality in ownership and in sharing the proceeds. This I very gladly accepted; and from that hour my load was palpably lightened. During the ten years or over that The Tribune was issued by Greeley & McElrath, my partner never once even indicated that my anti-Slavery, anti-Hanging, Socialist, and other frequent aberrations from the straight and narrow path of Whig partisanship, were injurious to our common interest, though he must often have sorely felt that they were so; and never, except when I (rarely) drew from the common treasury more money than could well be spared, in order to help some needy friend whom he judged beyond help, did he even *look* grieved at anything I did. On the other hand, his business management of the concern, though never brilliant, nor specially energetic, was so safe and judicious that it gave me no trouble, and scarcely required of me a thought, during that long era of all but unclouded prosperity.

The transition from my four preceding years of incessant pecuniary anxiety, if not absolute embarrassment, was like escaping from the dungeon and the rack to freedom and sympathy. Henceforth, such rare pecuniary troubles as I encountered were the just penalties of my own folly in indorsing notes for persons who, in the nature of things, could not rationally be expected to pay them. But these penalties are not to be evaded by those who, soon after entering responsible life, "go into business," as the phrase is, when it is inevitable that they must be thereby involved in debt. He who starts on the basis of dependence on his own proper resources, resolved to extend his business no further and no faster than his means will justify, may fairly refuse to lend what he needs in his own operations, or to indorse for others when he asks no one to indorse for him. But you cannot ask favors, and then churlishly refuse to grant any, — borrow, and then frown upon whoever asks you to lend, — seek indorsements, but decline to give any: and so the idle, the prodigal, the dissolute, with the thousands foredoomed by their own defects of capacity, of industry, or of management, to chronic bankruptcy, live upon the earnings of the capable, thrifty, and provident. Better wait five years to go into business upon adequate means which are properly your own, than to rush in prematurely, trusting to loans, indorsements, and the forbearance of creditors, to help you through. I have squandered much hard-earned money in trying to help others who were already past help, when I not only might, but should, have saved most of it if I had never, needing help, sought and received it. As it is, I trust that my general obligation has been fully discharged.

The Tribune, as it first appeared, was but the germ of what I sought to make it. No journal sold for a cent could ever be much more than a dry summary of the most important or the most interesting occurrences of the day; and such is not a newspaper, in the higher sense of the term. We need to know, not only what is done, but what is purposed and said, by those who sway the destinies of states and realms; and, to this end, the prompt perusal of the manifestoes of monarchs, presidents, ministers, legislators, etc., is indispensable. No man is even tolerably informed in our day who does not regularly "keep the run" of events and opinions, through the daily perusal of at least *one* good journal; and the ready cavil that "no one can read" all that a great modern journal contains, only proves the ignorance or thoughtlessness of the caviller. No *one* person is expected to take such an interest in the rise and fall of stocks, the markets for cotton, cattle, grain, and goods, the proceedings of Congress, Legislatures, and Courts, the politics of Europe, and the ever-shifting phases of Spanish-American anarchy, etc., etc., as would incite him to a daily perusal of the entire contents of a metropolitan city journal of the first rank. The idea is rather to embody in a single sheet the information daily required by all those who aim to keep "posted" on every important occurrence; so that the lawyer, the merchant, the banker, the forwarder, the economist, the author, the politician, etc., may find here whatever he needs to see, and be spared the trouble of looking elsewhere. A copy of a great morning journal now contains more matter than an average twelvemo volume, and its production costs far more, while it is sold for a fortieth or fiftieth part of the volume's price. There is no other miracle of cheapness which at all approaches it. The Electric Telegraph has precluded the multiplication of journals in the great cities, by enormously increasing the cost of publishing each of them. The Tribune, for example, now pays more than one hundred thousand dollars per annum for intellectual labor (reporting included) in and about its office, and one hundred thousand dollars more for correspondence and telegraphing,—in other words, for collecting and transmitting news. And, while its income has been largely increased from year to year, its expenses have inevitably been swelled even more rapidly; so that, at the close of 1866, in which its receipts had been over nine hundred thousand dollars, its expenses had been very nearly equal in amount, leaving no profit beyond a fair rent for the premises it owned and occupied. And yet its stockholders were satisfied that they had done a good business, — that the increase in the patronage and value of the establishment amounted to a fair interest on their investment, and might well be accepted in lieu of a dividend. In the good time coming, with cheaper paper and less exorbitant charges for "cable despatches" from the Old World, they will doubtless reap where they have now faithfully sown. Yet they realize and accept the fact, that a journal radically hostile to the gainful arts whereby the cunning and powerful few live sumptuously without useful labor, and often amass wealth, by pandering to lawless sensuality and popular vice, can never hope to enrich its publishers so rapidly nor so vastly as though it had a soft side for the Liquor Traffic, and for all kindred allurements to carnal appetite and sensual indulgence.

Fame is a vapor; popularity an accident; riches take wings; the only earthly certainty is oblivion; no man can foresee what a day may bring forth; while those who cheer to-day will often curse to-morrow: and yet I cherish the hope that the journal I projected and established will live and flourish long after I shall have mouldered into forgotten dust, being guided by a larger wisdom, a more unerring sagacity to discern the right, though not by a more unfaltering readiness to embrace and defend it at whatever personal cost; and that the stone which covers my ashes may bear to future eyes the still intelligible inscription, "Founder of The New York Tribune."

XIX.

SOCIALISM.

THE Winter of 1837–38, though happily mild and open till far into January, was one of pervading destitution and suffering in our city, from paralysis of business and consequent dearth of employment. The liberality of those who could and would give was heavily taxed to save from famishing the tens of thousands who, being needy and unable to find employment, first ran into debt so far as they could, and thenceforth must be helped or starve. For, in addition to all who may be said to belong here, legions of laborers, servants, etc., are annually dismissed in Autumn from the farms, country-seats, and watering-places of the suburban districts, and drift down to the city, whence they were mainly hired; vaguely hoping to find work here, which a small part of them do: the rest live on the good-nature of relatives, if such they have here, or on credit from boarding-houses, landlords, or grocers, so long as they can; and then make their choice between roguery and beggary, or change from this to that, or take them mixed, as chance may dictate. Since the general diffusion of railroads and the considerable extension of our manufacturing industry, business is far more equable than it was, even in prosperous times, thirty years ago; but Winter is still a season of privation and suffering to many thousands who live in tolerable comfort through the warmer seasons. To say that ten thousand young persons here annually take their first lessons in debauchery and crime would be to keep quite within the truth; and, while passion, ignorance, and miseducation ruin their thousands, I judge that destitution flowing from involuntary idleness sends more men and women to perdition, in this city, than any other cause, — intemperance possibly excepted.

I lived that Winter in the Sixth Ward, — then, as now, eminent for filth, squalor, rags, dissipation, want, and misery. A public meeting of its citizens was duly held early in December, and an organization formed thereat, by which committees were appointed to canvass the Ward from house to house, collect funds from those who could and would spare anything, ascertain the nature and extent of the existing destitution, and devise ways and means for its systematic relief. Very poor myself, I could give no money, or but a mite; so I gave time instead, and served, through several days, on one of the visiting committees. I thus saw extreme destitution more closely than I had ever before observed it, and was enabled to scan its repulsive features intelligently. I saw two families, including six or eight children, burrowing in one cellar under a stable, — a prey to famine on the one hand, and to vermin and cutaneous maladies on the other, with sickness adding its horrors to those of a polluted atmosphere and a wintry temperature. I saw men who each, somehow, supported his family on an income of $5 per week or less, yet who cheerfully gave something to mitigate the sufferings of those who were *really* poor. I saw three widows, with as many children, living in an attic on the profits of an apple-stand which yielded less than $3 per week, and the landlord came in for a full third of that. But worst to bear of all was the pitiful plea of stout, resolute, single young men and young women: "We do not want alms; we are not beggars; we hate to sit here day by day idle and useless; help us to work, — we want no other help: why is it that we can have nothing to do?"

I pondered these scenes at intervals throughout the next two or three years, and was impelled thereby to write for The New-Yorker — I think, in the Winter of 1839-40 — a series of articles entitled, "What shall be done for the Laborer?" I believe these attracted the attention of Mr. Albert Brisbane, a young man of liberal education and varied culture, a native of Batavia, N. Y., which he still regarded as his home, but who had travelled widely and observed thoughtfully; making the acquaintance in Paris of the school of Socialists called (after their founder) St. Simonians, and that also of Charles Fourier, the founder of a different school, which had been distinguished by his name. Robert Owen, by his experiments at New Lanark and his "New Views of Society," was the first in this century to win public attention to Socialism, though (I believe) Fourier had not only speculated, but written, before either of his co-laborers. But Owen was an extensive and successful manufacturer; St. Simon was a soldier, and the heir of a noble family; while Fourier was a poor clerk, reserved and taciturn, whose hard, dogmatic, algebraic style seemed expressly calculated to discourage readers and repel adherents; so that his disciples were few indeed, down to the date of his death in 1837. Mr. Brisbane, returning not long afterward from Europe, prepared and published his first work — which was an exposition and commendation of Fourier's industrial system — in 1840. My acquaintance with the author and his work commenced soon afterward.

I sum up these three competing projects of Social Reform as follows: —

Owen. — Place human beings in proper relations, under favoring circumstances (among which I include Education and Intelligence), and they will do right rather than wrong. Hitherto, the heritage of the great majority has been filth, squalor, famine, ignorance, superstition; and these have impelled many to indolence and vice, if not to crime. Make their external conditions what they should be, and these will give place to industry, sobriety, and virtue.

St. Simon. — "Love is the fulfilling of the law." Secure to every one opportunity; let each do whatever he can do best; and the highest good of the whole will be achieved and perpetuated.

Fourier. — Society, as we find it, is organized rapacity. Half of its force is spent in repressing or resisting the jealousies and rogueries of its members. We need to organize Universal

Justice based on Science. The true Eden lies before, not behind us. We may so provide that Labor, now repulsive, shall be attractive; while its efficiency in production shall be increased by the improvement of machinery and the extended use of natural forces, so as to secure abundance, education, and elegant luxury, to all. What is needed is to provide all with homes, employment, instruction, good living, the most effective implements, machinery, &c., securing to each the fair and full recompense of his achievement; and this can best be attained through the association of some four to five hundred families in a common household, and in the ownership and cultivation of a common domain, say of 2,000 acres, or about one acre to each person living thereon.

I accept, unreservedly, the views of no man, dead or living. "The master has said it," was never conclusive with me. Even though I have found him right nine times, I do not take his tenth proposition on trust; unless that also be proved sound and rational, I reject it. But I am convinced, after much study and reflection, that the Social Reformers are right on many points, even when clearly wrong on others; and I deem Fourier — though in many respects erratic, mistaken, visionary — the most suggestive and practical among them. I accept nothing on his authority; for I find many of his speculations fantastic, erroneous, and (in my view) pernicious; but on many points he commands my unreserved concurrence. Yet I prefer to set forth my own Social creed rather than his, even wherein mine was borrowed from his teachings; and mine is, briefly, as follows: —

I. I believe that there need be, and should be, no paupers who are not infantile, idiotic, or disabled; and that civilized society pays more for the support of able-bodied pauperism than the necessary cost of its extirpation.

II. I believe that they babble idly and libel Providence who talk of surplus Labor, or the inadequacy of Capital to supply employment to all who need it. Labor is often most required and best paid where Capital is scarcest (as was shown in California in 1849-50); and there is always — even in China — far more work than hands, provided the ability to devise and direct be not wanting. Where Labor stands idle, save in the presence of some great public calamity, there is a demonstrated deficiency, not of Capital, but of brains.

III. I believe that the efficiency of human effort is enormously, ruinously diminished by what I term Social Anarchy. That is to say: "We spend half our energies in building fences and providing safeguards against each other's roguery, while our labor is rendered inefficient and inadequately productive by bad management, imperfect implements, a deficiency of power (animal or steam), and the inability of our producers to command and wield the most effective machinery. It is quite within the truth to estimate the annual product of our National Industry at less than one half what it might be if better applied and directed.

IV. Inefficiency in production is paralleled by waste in consumption. Insects and vermin devour at least one fourth of the farmer's harvests, which inadequate fertilizing and unskilful cultivation have already reduced far below the proper aggregate. A thousand cooks are required, and a thousand fires maintained, to prepare badly the food of a township; when a dozen fires and a hundred cooks might do it far better, and with a vast saving in quantity as well as improvement in quality. [I judge that the cooks of Paris would subsist One Million persons on the food consumed or wasted by Six Hundred Thousand in this city; feeding them better than they are now fed, and prolonging their lives by an average of five years.]

V. Youth should be a season of instruction in Industry and the Useful Arts, as well as in Letters and the Sciences mastered by their aid. Each child should be trained to skill and efficiency in productive Labor. The hours of children should be alternately devoted to Labor, Study, and Recreation, — say, two hours to each before, and a like allotment after, dinner each secular day. Thus each child would grow up an adept, not merely in letters, but in arts, — a skilful worker as well as a proficient in the lessons of the school-room, — able to do well, not one thing only, but many things, — familiar with mechanical as well as agricultural processes, and acquainted with the use of steam and the direction of machinery. Not till one has achieved the fullest command, the most varied use, of *all* his faculties and powers, can he be properly said to be educated.

VI. Isolation is at war with efficiency and with progress. As "iron sharpeneth iron," so are man's intellectual and inventive faculties stimulated by contact with his fellow-men. A nation of herdsmen, dwelling in movable tents, invents little or nothing, and makes no progress, or next to none. Serfdom was the general condition of the laboring class in Europe, until aggregation in cities and manufactories, diffusing intelligence, and nourishing aspiration, wrought its downfall.

VII. The poor work at perpetual disadvantage in isolation, because of the inadequacy of their means. Let us suppose that four or five hundred heads of families propose to embark in Agriculture. Each buys his little farm, his furniture, his implements, animals, seeds, fertilizers, &c., &c., and — though he has purchased nothing that he does not urgently need — he finds his means utterly exhausted, and his farm and future exertions heavily burdened by debt. He hopes and labors to clear off the mortgage; but flood and drouth, frost and fire, work against him; his poverty compels him to do without many implements, and to plough or team with inadequate force; he runs up an account at the store, and pays twenty per cent. extra for his goods, because others, who buy on credit, fail to pay at all; and so he struggles on, till his strength fails, and he dies oppressed with debt. Such is the common lot.

VIII. Association would have these unite to purchase, inhabit, and cultivate a common domain, — say, of two thousand acres, — whereby these advantages over the isolated system would be realized: —

1. One fourth (at most) of the land required under the old system would be found abundant.

2. It could be far better allotted and appropriated to Grain, Grass, Fruits, Forest, Garden, &c.

3. The draught animals that were far too few, when dispersed among five hundred owners, on so many different farms, would be amply sufficient for a common domain.

4. Steam or water power could now be economically employed for a hundred purposes — cutting and sawing timber, threshing and grinding grain, ploughing the soil, and for many household uses — where the small farmer could not think of employing it.

5. Industry would find new and powerful incentives in the observation and praise or censure of the entire community; uniforms, banners, and music, with the rivalry of bands of competing workers, would provoke emulation and lighten labor; while such recreations as dramas, concerts, readings, &c., — now utterly beyond the reach of rural workers, — would give a new zest to life. At present, our youth escape from rural industry when they can, — not that they really hate work, but that they find their leisure hours even duller and less endurable than those they give to rugged toil.

I must devote another chapter to a narration of my experiences as an advocate of the views above set forth, and a brief account of the efforts made within my knowledge to give them practical exemplification. That these efforts resulted in failures the world already knows: I will endeavor to set forth the facts dispassionately, so as to afford fair grounds for judgment as to how far these failures are due to circumstances, and how far they may be fairly charged to the system itself. I shall endeavor to lay little of the blame on well-abused Human Nature; since, if any system be ill adapted to Man as we find him, it may be excellently calculated for use on some other planet, but not on this one.

XX.

SOCIALISTIC EFFORTS.

THE propagation in this country of Fourier's ideas of Industrial Association was wholly pioneered by Mr. A. Brisbane, who presented them in a series of articles in The Tribune, beginning in 1841, and running through two or three years. The Future — a weekly entirely devoted to the subject — was issued for a few weeks, but received no considerable support, and was therefore discontinued. The Harbinger, a smaller weekly, was afterward issued from the Brook Farm Association, and sustained — not without loss — for two or three years. Meantime, several treatises, explaining and commending the system, were published, — the best of them being "Democracy, Pacific and Constructive," by Mr. Parke Godwin, now of The Evening Post. The problem was further discussed in a series of controversial letters between Mr. Henry J. Raymond and myself. Thus, by persevering effort, the subject was thrust, as it were, on public attention; a few zealous converts made to the new ideas, and probably more vehement adversaries aroused; while the far greater number could not be induced to read or consider, but regarded all Socialist theories with stubborn indifference. Those who were in good circumstances, or hoped yet to be, wished no such change as was contemplated by the new theories; the ignorant, stolid many, who endure lives of destitution and squalid misery, were utterly devoid of faith or hope, receiving with profound incredulity and distrust any proposal to improve their condition. My observation justifies the belief, that the most *conservative* of mankind, when not under the influence of some great, convulsive uprising like the French Revolution, are those who have nothing to lose.

Of the practical attempts to realize our social Utopia, I believe that known as "Brook Farm," in Roxbury, Mass., ten miles from Boston, was first in the order of time, and notable in many other respects. Its projectors were cultivated, scholarly persons, who were profoundly dissatisfied with the aims, as well as the routine, of ordinary life, and who welcomed in theoretic Socialism a fairer and nobler ideal. So they bought a cold, grassy farm of two hundred acres, added two or three new buildings to those which had served the last preceding owner, and bravely took possession. New members joined from time to time, as others left; the land was improved, and, I believe, some was added; boarders were taken occasionally; a school was started and maintained; and so the concern fared on through some five or six years. But, deficient in capital, in agricultural skill, and in many needful things besides, it was never a pecuniary success, and was finally given up about 1847 or '48,—paying its debts, I understood, to the last dime, but returning nothing to its stockholders. I believe this was the only attempt made in New England.

From this city, two bands of Socialist pioneers went forth,—one to a rugged, lofty region in Pike County, Pa., five miles from the Erie Railroad at the mouth of the Lackawaxen, which they called "Sylvania," after the State. The domain here purchased was ample,—some 2,300 acres; the location was healthy, and there was abundance of wood and water. But the soil was stony and poor; the altitude was such that there was a heavy frost on the 4th of July, 1844; the members were generally very poor, and in good part inefficient also; and the crops harvested were slender enough. I think "Sylvania" was founded early in 1843, and gave up the ghost—having little else to give up—some time in 1845. Its domain returned to the seller or his assigns, in satisfaction of his mortgage, and its movables nearly or quite paid its debts, leaving its stock a total loss.

The "North American Phalanx" had more vitality and a better location. The nucleus of its membership was formed in Albany, though it drew associates from every quarter. Several of them were capable mechanics, traders, and farmers. It was located in Shrewsbury, Monmouth County, N. J., five miles from the dock at Red Bank, on a farm of 673 acres, originally good land, but worn out by most improvident, thriftless cultivation, so that it was bought for less than $23 per acre, which was its full value. But there was an ample bed of marl on its eastern border, considerable timber along its creeks, two or three very dilapidated farm buildings, and a few large, old apple-trees, which were just better than none. Here we few, but zealous, Associationists of New York and its vicinity for a time concentrated our means and our efforts; each subscribing freely to the capital, and then aiding the enterprise by loans to nearly an equal amount. I think the capital ultimately invested here (loans included) was fully $100,000, or about one fourth the amount there should have been. By means thereof, a capacious wooden dwelling, one or two barns, and a fruit-house were erected, thousands of loads of marl dug and applied to the land, large orchards were planted and reared to maturity, and a mile square of sterile, exhausted land converted into a thrifty and productive domain. The experiment was finally abandoned, on the heel of a heavy loss sustained in the burning of our fruit-house, which, with some other set-backs, discouraged some of the best associates, and caused them to favor a dissolution. There was no pecuniary failure, in the ordinary acceptation of the term. The property was sold out at auction, — the domain in tracts of ten to eighty acres, — and, though it brought not more than two thirds of its cash value, every debt was paid, and each stockholder received back about 65 per cent. of his investment with interest. I reckon that not many stockholders in gold-mines or oil-wells can show a better result. (I can speak of gold-mines from personal experience; oil-wells — being older when they came into vogue — I have carefully kept out of.) As I recollect, the "North American

Phalanx" was founded in 1843, and wound up about 1850, when I think no sister Association was left to deplore its fate. Its means had been larger, its men and women, in the average, more capable and devoted, than those of any rival; if it could not live, there was no hope for any of them.

A serious obstacle to the success of any Socialist experiment must always be confronted. I allude to the kind of persons who are naturally attracted to it. Along with many noble and lofty souls, whose impulses are purely philanthropic, and who are willing to labor and suffer reproach for any cause that promises to benefit mankind, there throng scores of whom the world is quite worthy,—the conceited, the crotchety, the selfish, the headstrong, the pugnacious, the unappreciated, the played-out, the idle, and the good-for-nothing generally; who, finding themselves utterly out of place and at a discount in the world as it is, rashly conclude that they are exactly fitted for the world as it ought to be. These may have failed again and again, and been protested at every bank to which they have been presented; yet they are sure to jump into any new movement, as if they had been born expressly to superintend and direct it, though they are morally certain to ruin whatever they lay their hands on. Destitute of means, of practical ability, of prudence, tact, and common sense, they have such a wealth of assurance and of self-confidence that they clutch the responsible positions, which the capable and worthy modestly shrink from: so responsibilities that would tax the ablest are mistakenly devolved on the blindest and least fit. Many an experiment is thus wrecked, when, engineered by its best members, it might have succeeded. I judge not what may be done and borne by a mature, thoroughly organized Association; but a pioneer, half-fledged experiment — lacking means, experience, edifices, everything — can bear no extra weight, but needs to be composed of, and directed by, most efficient, devoted, self-sacrificing men and women.

That there have been — nay, are — decided successes in practical Socialism, is undeniable; but they all have that Communistic basis which seems to me irrational, and calculated to prove fatal. I cannot conceive it just, that an associate who invests $ 100,000 should stand on an equal footing, so far as property is concerned, with one who brings nothing to the common fund; nor can I see why an ingenious, efficient mechanic, whose services are worth $ 5 per day, should receive no more of the annual product than an ignorant ditcher, who can at best earn but $ 2 per day. To my mind, every one is fairly entitled to what he has earned, and to what he *shall* earn, unless he chooses to bestow it on some one else; and I hold, with Fourier, that Communism must destroy individual liberty. Credit me on the books with what I invested, and what I have since earned or otherwise added to the common wealth; and, if I choose to spend my day with a visiting friend, or go off for a week's fishing, it is no one's business but my own. But, say that all we have and all we make are common property, wherein each has rightfully an equal interest, and I shall feel morally bound to do my share of the work, and shall be dissatisfied when others palpably do less than I do. Hence, I can easily account for the failure of Communism,—at New Harmony, and in several other experiments; I cannot so easily account for its successes. Yet the fact stares us in the face, that, while hundreds of banks and factories, and thousands of mercantile concerns managed by shrewd, strong men, have gone into bankruptcy and perished, Shaker Communities, established more than sixty years ago, upon a basis of little property and less worldly wisdom, are living and prosperous to-day. And their experience has been imitated by the German Communities at Economy, Pa., Zoar, Ohio, the Society of Ebenezer, &c., &c. Theory, however plausible, must respect the facts.

I once visited the Society of Ebenezer, when it was located on lands seven miles from Buffalo, not long before surrendered by the Tonawanda Indians. The members were nearly all Prussians, led by a rich nobleman, who had invested his all in the common fund, and led his followers to this country, where they first located near Buffalo as aforesaid, but have since sold, and migrated to cheaper land, away from any great city, in Iowa. I did not see the "head centre," but the second man was from the Zoar Community, and I had a free talk with him, part of which (in substance) is worth recalling:—

"What do you do with lazy people?" I inquired.

"We have none," he promptly replied. "We have often disciplined members for working too hard and too long; for, whatever the world may think of us, we profess to be associated for spiritual edification, not temporal gain; and we do not desire our people to become absorbed in drudgery and money-getting."

"Yes, I understand," I persisted; "but suppose you *had* a lazy member: how would you treat him? How does your discipline provide for the possible contingency of his attaining to the membership of your body?"

"In this way only: we are a brotherhood and sisterhood for spiritual, not temporal, ends. Our temporal relations are a consequence of our spiritual union. For spiritual growth and improvement, we are divided into four classes, according to our presumed religious advancement respectively. If, then, a member of the fourth (highest) class were to evince a lazy, shirking disposition, he would, after some private admonition, be reported by that class to the next general meeting, as not sufficiently developed, or endued with Divine grace, for that class; and, on that report, he would be reduced to the third class. If, after due probation, he should evince a slothful spirit there, he would be reported by *that* class, as he had been by the higher; and, on this report, be reduced to the second class; and, on the report of this, in like manner, to the first or lowest class,—that which includes young children and all wholly undeveloped natures. Theoretically, this would be our course; we know no further or other discipline than this: practically, no occasion for such discipline has arisen. We often discipline members for working too much or too persistently; never for working too little."

I do not believe men naturally lazy; but I judge that they prefer to receive the fair recompense of their labor,—to work for themselves and those dear to them, rather than for hundreds, if not thousands, whom they scarcely know by sight. I believe in Association, or Coöperation, or whatever name may be given to the combination of many heads and hands to achieve a beneficent result, which is beyond the means of one or a few of them; for I perceive that vast economies, and vastly increased efficiency, may thus be secured; I reject Communism as at war with one of the strongest and most universal instincts,—that which impels each worker to produce and save for himself and his own. Yet Religion often makes practicable that which were else impossible, and Divine Love triumphs where Human Science is baffled. Thus I interpret the past successes and failures of Socialism.

Coöperation—the combination of some hundreds of producers to dispose of their labor or its fruits, or of consumers in like manner to supply their common wants of food, &c. more economically and satisfactorily than by individual purchases from markets, stalls, or stores—is one-sided, fragmentary Association. Its advantages are signal, obvious, immediate; its chief peril is the rascality of the agent, treasurer, or manager, whom it is obliged to trust. As it involves no decided, radical change of habits and usages, it is destined to achieve an early success, and thus to pioneer further and more beneficent reforms. It has already won signal triumphs in sober, practical England; it is winning the intellectual assent of earnest, meditative Germany. I shall be sorely disappointed if this Nineteenth Century does not witness its very general adoption as a means of reducing the cost and increasing the comfort of the poor man's living. It ought to add twenty-five per cent. to the average income of the thriftier half of the laboring class; while its advantages are free to all with whom economy is an object. And even above its direct advantages I prize the habits of calculation, of foresight, of saving which it is calculated to foster and promote among those who accept its principle and enjoy its more material blessings.

With a firm and deep religious basis, any Socialistic scheme may succeed, though vicious in organization, and at war with

Human Nature, as I deem Shaker Communism, and the antagonist or "Free Love" Community of Perfectionists at Oneida, N. Y. Without a basis of religious sympathy and religious aspiration, it will always be difficult, though, I judge, not impossible. Even the followers of Comte, the swallowers of his Pantheistic fog, will yet be banded or melted into communities, and will endeavor to realize the exaltation of Work into Worship, with a degree of success to be measured by the individual characters of the associates. And every effort to achieve through Association a less sordid, fettered, grovelling life, will have a positive value for the future of mankind, however speedy and utter its failure. I deem it impossible that beings born in the huts and hovels of isolated society, feebly, ineffectively delving and grubbing through life on the few acres immediately surrounding each of them, shall there attain the full stature of perfect manhood. They are dwarfed, stunted, shrivelled, by their petty avocations and shabby surroundings, — by the seeming necessity which constrains them to bend their thoughts and energies to the achievement of narrow, petty, paltry ends. Our dwellings, our fields, our farms, our industries, all tend to belittle us; the edifice which shall yet lodge commodiously and agreeably two thousand persons, giving each the requisite privacy and independence, though as yet unconstructed, is not a chimera; no more is the prosecution of agricultural and other labor by large bands, rendered picturesque by uniforms, and inspired by music. That "many hands make light work" is an old discovery; it shall yet be proved that the combined efforts of many workers make Labor efficient and ennobling, as well as attractive. In modern society, all things tend unconsciously toward grand, comprehensive, pervading reforms. The steamboat, the rail-car, the omnibus, are but blind gropings toward an end which, unpremeditated, shall yet be attained; in the order of Nature, nothing ultimately resists an economy; and the sceptical, sneering world shall yet perceive and acknowledge that, in many important relations, and not merely in one, "It is not good for Man to be alone."

XXI.

HARRY CLAY.

JOHN TYLER succeeded General Harrison in the Presidency. He was called a Whig when elected Vice-President; I think he never called himself, nor wished others to call him so, from the day on which he stepped into our dead President's shoes. At all events, he contrived soon to quarrel with the great body of those whose efforts and votes had borne him into power. If he cried at Harrisburg over Mr. Clay's defeat, Mr. Clay's friends had abundant reason to cry ever afterward over Tyler's success there. He vetoed the bill chartering a new United States Bank; and, having himself sketched the plan of a substitute, and given it a name, he, when Congress passed it, vetoed that. He having inherited General Harrison's cabinet, this veto compelled its members to resign; Mr. Webster, as Secretary of State, lingering for months after all the rest had left; but he, too, had to go at last; and Mr. Tyler stood forth an imbittered, implacable enemy of the party which had raised him from obscurity and neglect to the pinnacle of power. Men always hate those they have wronged; and Mr. Tyler fairly detested those he had betrayed. Before he had been a year in power, he was in full, though covert, alliance with the Democrats, and figuring for their next Presidential nomination. But such as he are often used, never trusted.

Of course, the blighting of the fond hopes of the Whigs, and the transfer to their adversaries of the power and patronage they had so arduously won, were disastrous. Their plunder-seekers went over to the adversary; their favorite measures were defeated, and their energies paralyzed: so State after State deserted their standard. New York, which had proved herself Whig at every State election held under Van Buren's administration, went strongly Democratic at the very first held under Tyler's, and remained so at the two following. Two thirds, if not three fourths, of the States were carried against us in the State elections of 1841, '42, '43.

On the 1st of May, 1844, a Whig National Convention assembled in Baltimore. The venerable Ambrose Spencer, of New York, then nearly eighty years old, presided. Henry Clay was nominated for President without a dissenting voice, and with rapturous enthusiasm. Theodore Frelinghuysen, of New Jersey, was, after a spirited contest, presented for Vice-President. The delegates separated in undoubting confidence that their choice would be ratified by the people.

The Democratic Convention met in the same city soon afterward. A large majority of the delegates had been expressly instructed to nominate Martin Van Buren for President, and such was the undoubted preference of the Democratic masses. But many of the managing politicians had other views. Some of them had rival personal aspirations; and these thought two chances for the Presidency enough for one person, even though he had but once succeeded. A good many were tired of the New York ascendency, and eager for a change. The question of annexing Texas — of which more hereafter — had been so manipulated as to render many Southern politicians bitterly, actively hostile to Mr. Van Buren, who had taken ground adverse to annexation under the existing circumstances. Hence, when the Convention met, a resolve was introduced and passed requiring the vote of two thirds of the delegates to nominate a candidate. Van Buren's pledged majority was thus rendered of no avail; and soon, as the ballotings progressed, delegate after delegate dropped away from him, until at length his remaining and earnest supporters, in order to defeat Cass, Buchanan, and Woodbury, went over in a body to James K. Polk, of Tennessee, and nominated him on the forty-fourth ballot. Silas

Wright, of New York, was quite unanimously named for Vice-President; but he declined, and George M. Dallas, of Pennsylvania, was set up in his stead.

Mr. Polk was a man of moderate abilities, faultless private character, and undeviating Jacksonism. He had briefly but positively avowed himself an advocate of the immediate Annexation of Texas. He had once been chosen Speaker of the House of Representatives, and once Governor of Tennessee; being beaten, when he stood for reëlection, by Colonel James C. Jones, the Whig candidate. The suggestion that such a man, whose very name was unknown, up to the hour of his nomination, by a majority of those whose votes he must obtain if he were to be elected, should be pitted against the world-known and admired Harry Clay, was deemed the height of absurdity. And not only did multitudes of Whigs deem the nomination of Polk a virtual surrender at discretion, but many Democrats privately cherished a similar conviction. The canvass, which opened at once with unusual spirit and determination, soon undeceived them. Yet I think I do not err in stating that thousands supported Mr. Polk who intended only to maintain their standing in the Democratic party, while they neither expected nor wished to defeat Mr. Clay's election.

The early nomination of Silas Wright for Governor of our State added immensely to Mr. Polk's strength. He was widely known as a life-long friend and devoted follower of Mr. Van Buren, and his refusal to be placed second on the Polk ticket had increased his popularity with those who felt as he did. It soon became evident that the party would be substantially united on its National nominees, — united rather by their common hostility to Mr. Clay than by their devotion to his competitor. A few eminent New York Democrats issued what was called a secret circular, advising their friends to vote for Polk and Dallas, but to be careful to send members to Congress who would oppose to the last the Annexation of Texas. This recommendation was not followed. Those Democrats who disliked Annexation generally held their peace;

Silas Wright, in two or more campaign speeches, proclaimed that Annexation should only take place under conditions that gave Free Labor equal advantages with Slave from the acquisition. In the event, though the repugnance to Annexation at the North had been strong and general, Mr. Polk lost very few Democratic votes on account of it, though his support of the measure was open and unequivocal. Mr. Clay, on the other hand, though always clearly hostile to the Tyler or any kindred project,—to *any* scheme of immediate, unconditional Annexation without the prior consent of Mexico,—yet wrote several letters on the subject that served to embarrass his friends and encourage his foes. He explained that he did not object to Annexation because of Slavery, which he regarded as temporary, while the acquisition of Texas would be permanent, and, under fit circumstances, desirable. These letters were written to two different friends in Alabama, and were probably not intended for publication,—at all events, they should not have been published. They gave Mr. Clay's opponents plausible grounds for saying that he was dissatisfied with his position before the public, and anxious to change it; they embarrassed his many friends who *did* object to Annexation on anti-Slavery grounds; and they did not help him anywhere. Alabama and all the planting States went against him,—all but Georgia and Louisiana heavily so. He would have been stronger with the people if he had stood on his letter written from Raleigh, N. C., before his nomination, which was sufficiently full and explicit. A candidate for a high elective office can hardly be too sparing of personal manifestoes and explanations.

On the other great issue of the canvass—the Tariff—Mr. Clay's position was unquestionable. He was for Protection as a cardinal feature of a beneficent National policy, and he was especially in favor of the Protective Tariff of 1842, then just fairly in operation, and giving profitable employment to much hitherto dormant labor, not only in existing mines, furnaces, factories, &c., but in opening new mines, and in erecting and fitting up many more furnaces and factories.

The country had unquestionably been poor, its industry paralyzed, its revenue deficient, when that Tariff was enacted; the subsequent change had been signal and rapid, and the Whigs believed and insisted that the Protection and the Prosperity stood to each other in the relation of cause and effect. Our opponents, of course, denied the relation: they could not plausibly deny the facts. And their metropolitan organ, — The Globe, — which issued a prospectus for campaign subscribers, in which Protection and the Tariff were fiercely assailed, circulated in Pennsylvania a revised and expurgated edition, from which the anti-Tariff fulmination was carefully expunged.

Nor was this the worst. Mr. Polk had been for years in Congress, and had always voted there against Protection, as all Southern Democrats had voted since 1828. He was as much a Free-Trader in his votes as Mr. Calhoun had been ever since 1824. And yet he was induced by the exigencies of the canvass in Pennsylvania to write (or sign) the following letter: —

COLUMBIA, TENN., June 19, 1844.

DEAR SIR: I have received recently several letters in reference to my opinions on the subject of the Tariff, and, among others, yours of the 10th ultimo.* My opinions on this subject have been often given to the public. They are to be found in my public acts, and in the public discussions in which I have participated. I am in favor of a tariff for revenue, — such a one as will yield a sufficient amount to the Treasury to defray the expenses of Government, economically administered. In adjusting the details of a revenue tariff, I have heretofore sanctioned such moderate discriminating duties as would produce the amount of revenue needed, and at the same time afford incidental protection to our home industry. I am opposed to a tariff for protection merely, and not for revenue. Acting upon these general principles, it is well known that I gave my support to the policy of General Jackson's administration on this subject. I voted against the tariff act of 1828. I voted for the act of 1832, which contained modifications of some of the objectionable provisions of the act of 1828. As a member

* Never given to the public. — H. G.

of the Committee of Ways and Means of the House of Representatives, I gave my assent to the bill reported by that committee in December, 1832, making further modifications of the act of 1828, and making also discriminations in the imposition of the duties which it proposed. That bill did not pass, but was superseded by the bill commonly called the Compromise Bill, for which I voted.

In my judgment, it is the duty of the government to extend, as far as it may be practicable to do so, by its revenue laws and all other means within its power, fair and just protection to all the great interests of the whole Union, embracing Agriculture, Manufactures, and the Mechanic Arts, Commerce, and Navigation. I heartily approve the resolutions upon this subject passed by the Democratic National Convention, lately assembled at Baltimore.

I am, with great respect, dear sir,

Your ob't serv't,

JAMES K. POLK.

JOHN K. KANE, Esq., Philadelphia.

It was impossible not to see that this was an elaborate attempt to darken counsel so as to break the force of the Tariff issue, which was telling strongly against him wherever Protection was the favorite policy, and especially in intensely, and all but unanimously, Protective Pennsylvania. The Whigs had felt confident of carrying Pennsylvania on the Tariff issue in her State (October) election, and thereupon carrying, not her only, but New York and other doubtful States, at the Presidential election in November; but this letter enabled those who saw fit to insist that Polk was as much a Tariff man as Clay, and thereupon to override us by appeals to Pennsylvania's Democratic and Jackson prepossessions. A remarkably clever and subtle speech by Silas Wright, at Watertown, N. Y., aided this effort. Mr. Wright had voted in Congress for both the Tariffs of 1828 and 1842,—the two most Protective of any ever yet passed. Yet he assailed the latter, not in principle, but in detail; arguing that it favored the woollen manufacturer at the expense of the wool-grower, by admitting cheap, coarse foreign wool at a low rate of duty. All our efforts to make a distinct issue, and obtain a popular decision as between Protection and Free Trade respectively, were thus baffled; and, while every Free-Trader went against us, — Gulian C. Verplanck leaving us expressly on that ground, — we lost the votes of thousands of Protectionists, who were unfairly induced to believe Polk as much a Protectionist as Clay! A "Native American" movement, which had originated in the Fall of 1843 among the native Democrats of this city, who revolted against what they considered a monopoly of office by our foreign-born population, had extended to, and almost absorbed, the Whig voters of this and other cities, — New York and Philadelphia being both swept by it in the Spring of '44. The first impression that Mr. Clay would gain more than he would lose by this side-wind was not justified by the result; as the Presidential contest grew hotter and hotter, the Democratic Natives returned to their old standard, while immigrants by tens of thousands were naturalized expressly to vote against Nativism, and all their votes told against us, as did those of thousands more who managed to vote without awaiting naturalization. Hence we failed to elect our Governor in Pennsylvania by 4,397 majority, — the vote standing: Shunk, 160,759; Markle, 156,352; and of course failed to carry the State at the following Presidential election, when Polk had 167,535 to 161,203 for Clay; and, as Pennsylvania then voted on the Friday before our election, which commenced on the following Monday and continued till Wednesday night, — the weight of that State's vote against us fell heavily on New York, and, by the help of a heavy illegal vote in this city, barely carried her against us; the votes cast being: Polk, 237,588; Clay, 232,482; and Birney (Abolition), 15,812. I think we should have had at least half of that Birney vote for Clay, and made him President (for he only needed the vote of New York), in spite of all other drawbacks, but for those fatal Alabama letters. And the result in Michigan was likewise decided by the Birney vote; while Louisiana was lost by the scandalous "Plaquemine" frauds, — a parish which had given 179 Democratic to 93 Whig votes in '42 giving 1,007 Democratic to but 37 Whig in '44: the voters coming down from New Orleans on a steamboat, and pouring in their illegal ballots with scarcely a fig-leaf of decency. Polk carried that State by 699 majority; and he had 970 in Plaquemines, where he was entitled to 200 at most. As it was, we carried for Mr. Clay the States of Vermont, Massachusetts, Rhode Island, Connecticut, New Jersey, Delaware, Maryland, Ohio, North Carolina, Kentucky, and Tennessee, — 11 in all, casting 105 electoral votes; while Mr. Polk's electors were chosen in fifteen States, casting 170 votes. And, so close was the contest throughout, that Mr. Clay had in the whole Union 1,288,533 popular votes to 1,327,325 for Mr. Polk: Polk's majority, 38,792. Mr. Birney had in all 62,263 votes: so that Mr. Polk was preferred by a plurality, not a majority, of the entire people. But that did not affect the fact nor the validity of his election.

I have admired and trusted many statesmen: I profoundly loved Henry Clay. Though a slaveholder, he was a champion of Gradual Emancipation when Kentucky formed her first State Constitution in his early manhood; and he was openly the same when she came to revise it, half a century later. He was a conservative in the true sense of that much-abused term: satisfied to hold by the present until he could see clearly how to exchange it for the better; but his was no obstinate, bigoted conservatism, but such as became an intelligent and patriotic American. From his first entrance into Congress, he had been a zealous and effective champion of Internal Improvements, the Protection of Home Industry, a sound and uniform National Currency, — those leading features of a comprehensive, beneficent National policy which commanded the fullest assent of my judgment and the best exertions of my voice and pen. I loved him for his generous nature, his gallant bearing, his thrilling eloquence, and his life-long devotion to what I deemed our country's unity, prosperity, and just renown. Hence, from the day of his nomination in May to that of his defeat in November, I gave every hour, every effort, every thought, to his election. My wife and then surviving child (our third) spent the Summer at a farm-house in a rural township of Massachusetts, while I gave heart and soul to the canvass. I travelled and spoke much; I wrote, I think, an average of three columns of The Tribune each secular day; and I gave the residue of the hours I could save from sleep to watching the canvass, and doing whatever I could to render our side of it more effective. Very often, I crept to my lodging near the office at 2 to 3 A.M., with my head so heated by fourteen to sixteen hours of incessant reading and writing, that I could only win sleep by means of copious affusions from a shower-bath; and these, while they probably saved me from a dangerous fever, brought out such myriads of boils, that — though I did not heed them till after the battle was fought out and lost — I was covered by them for the six months ensuing, often fifty or sixty at once, so that I could contrive no position in which to rest, but passed night after night in an easy-chair. And these unwelcome visitors returned to plague me, though less severely, throughout the following Winter. I have suffered from their kindred since, but never as I did from their young luxuriance in that Winter of '44–45.

Looking back through almost a quarter of a century on that Clay canvass of 1844, I say deliberately that it should not have been lost, — that it *need* not have been. True, there was much good work done in it, but not half so much as there should have been. I, for example, was in the very prime of life, — thirty-three years old, — and knew how to write for a newspaper; and I printed in that canvass one of the most effective daily political journals ever yet issued. It was sold for two cents; and it had 15,000 daily subscribers when the canvass closed. It should have had 100,000 from the first day onward; and my Clay Tribune — a campaign weekly, issued six months for fifty cents — should have had not less than a quarter of a million. And those two issues, wisely and carefully distributed, could not have failed to turn the long-doubtful scale in favor of Mr. Clay's election. Of course, I mean that other effective, devoted journals should also have been systematically disseminated, until every voter who could and would read a Whig journal had been supplied with one, even though he had paid nothing for it. A quarter of a million

Campaign Tribunes would have cost at most $125,000; and there were single houses largely engaged in mining or manufacturing who were damaged more than that amount by Mr. Clay's defeat, and the consequent repeal of the Tariff of '42. There should have been $1,000,000 raised by open subscription during the week in which Mr. Clay was nominated, and every dime of it judiciously, providently expended in furnishing information touching the canvass to the voters of New York, New Jersey, and Pennsylvania. To put a good, efficient journal into the hands of every voter who will read it is the true mode of prosecuting a political canvass; meetings and speeches are well enough, but this is indispensable. Mr. Clay might have been elected, if his prominent, earnest supporters had made the requisite exertions and sacrifices; and I cannot but bitterly feel that great and lasting public calamities would thereby have been averted.

Mr. Clay, born in poverty and obscurity, had not even a common-school education, and had only a few months' clerkship in a store, with a somewhat longer training in a lawyer's office, as preparation for his great career. Tall in person, though plain in features, graceful in manner, and at once dignified and affable in bearing, I think his fervid patriotism and thrilling eloquence combined with decided natural abilities and a wide and varied experience to render him the American more fitted to win and enjoy popularity than any other who has lived. That popularity he steadily achieved and extended through the earlier half of his long public life; but he was now confronted by a political combination well-nigh invincible, based on the potent personal strength of General Jackson; and this overcame him. Five times presented as a candidate for President, he was always beaten,— twice in conventions of his political associates, thrice in the choice of electors by the people. The careless reader of our history in future centuries will scarcely realize the force of his personal magnetism, nor conceive how millions of hearts glowed with sanguine hopes of his election to the Presidency, and bitterly lamented his and their discomfiture.

XXII.

MARGARET FULLER.

THE year 1840 — rendered notable by the Harrison canvass — was signalized by several less noisy reactions and uprisings against prescription and routine. One of these made itself manifest in the appearance at Boston of The Dial, — the quarterly utterance of a small fraternity of scholars and thinkers, who had so far outgrown the recognized standards of orthodox opinion in theology and philosophy as to be grouped, in the vague, awkward terminology of this stammering century, as *Transcendentalists*. Inexcusably bad as the term is, it so clearly indicates an aspiration, a tendency, as contradistinguished from a realization, an achievement, that it may be allowed to stand. Those to whom it was applied had alike transcended the preëxisting limitations of decorous and allowable thinking; but they were alike in little else. The chosen editor of this magazine was SARAH MARGARET FULLER, while Ralph Waldo Emerson and George Ripley were announced as her associates. After a time, Mr. Emerson became the editor, with his predecessor as his chief assistant, but there was in reality little change; and, while others contributed to its pages, The Dial, throughout the four or five years of its precarious existence, was chiefly regarded and valued as an expression and exponent of the ideas and convictions of these two rarest, if not ripest, fruits of New England's culture and reflection in the middle of the Nineteenth Century. The original editor was to have been paid a salary of two hundred dollars per annum, had the sale of the work justified so liberal a stipend; but I believe it never did. What was purposed by its projectors is thus stated in one of her private letters:—

"A perfectly free organ is to be offered for the expression of individual thought and character. There are no party measures to be carried, no particular standard to be set up. A fair, calm tone, a recognition of universal principles, will, I hope, pervade the essays in every form. I trust there will be a spirit neither of dogmatism nor of compromise; and that this journal will aim, not at leading public opinion, but at stimulating each man to judge for himself, and to think more deeply and more nobly, by letting him see how some minds are kept alive by a wise self-trust. . . . . We cannot show high culture, and I doubt about vigorous thought. But we shall manifest free action as far as it goes, and a high aim. It were much if a periodical could be kept open, not to accomplish any outward object, but merely to afford an avenue for what of liberal and calm thought might be originated among us, by the wants of individual minds."

I presume the circulation of The Dial never reached two thousand copies, and that it hardly averaged one thousand. But its influence and results are nowise measured by the number of its patrons, nor even of its readers. To the "fit audience, though few," who had long awaited and needed its advent, without clearly comprehending their need, it was like manna in the wilderness; and scores of them found in its pages incitement and guidance to a noble and beneficent, even though undistinguished, career.

S. MARGARET FULLER, the eldest child of Timothy and Margaret Crane Fuller, was born at Cambridgeport, Mass., on the 23d of May, 1810. Her father was a lawyer of humble origin, who had risen, by force of resolution and industry, to a respectable position at the Boston bar, though he was a Republican, and all the wealth and business of that city were intensely Federal; and he ultimately represented in Congress, for several terms, the Middlesex district adjacent. This did not increase his popularity nor his professional gains in Boston; so that, when he died of cholera (Oct. 2, 1835), after a life of labor and frugality, he left but a narrow competence to his widow and large family of mainly young, dependent children.

But that widow was a woman of signal excellence of soul and life. He was well established in practice, and must have been ten or fifteen years at the bar when he met her,—a young girl of humble family and little education, but of rare beauty, physical and mental; and, falling in love with her at sight, sought her acquaintance, wooed, won, and married her. And, though she never found time for extensive study, her natural refinement was such that the deficiencies of her education were seldom or never perceptible.

Her eldest daughter was too early stimulated to protracted, excessive mental labor by her fond, exacting, ambitious father, justly proud of her great natural powers, and ignorant of the peril of overtaxing them. I have heard that, when but eight years old, she had her "stint" of so many Latin verses to compose per day, ready to recite to him on his return to their suburban home from his day's work in the city. This may be idle gossip; I only know that, when I first made her acquaintance, she was, mentally, the best instructed woman in America; while she was, physically, one of the least enviable,—a prey to spinal affliction, nervous disorder, and protracted, fearfully torturing headaches. Those who knew her in early youth have assured me that she was then the picture of rude health,—red-cheeked, robust, vigorous, and comely, if not absolutely beautiful. Too much of this was sacrificed to excessive study. Her near friend and literary associate, Ralph Waldo Emerson, gives this account of his first impressions of her in her early prime of womanhood, ten years before I met her:—

"I still remember the first half-hour of Margaret's conversation. She was then twenty-six years old. She had a face and frame that would indicate fulness and tenacity of life. She was rather under the middle height; her complexion was fair, with strong, fair hair. She was then, as always, carefully and becomingly dressed, and of lady-like self-possession. For the rest, her appearance had nothing prepossessing. Her extreme plainness, a trick of incessantly opening and shutting her eyelids, the nasal tones of her voice, all repelled; and I said to myself, 'We shall never get far.' It is to be said that Margaret made a disagreeable first impression on most persons, including those who became afterward her best friends, to such an extreme that they did not wish to be in the same room with her. This was partly the effect of her manners, which expressed an overweening sense of power, and slight esteem of others; and partly the prejudice of her fame. She had a dangerous reputation for satire, in addition to her great scholarship. The men thought she carried too many guns, and the women did not like one who despised them. I believe I fancied her too much interested in personal history; and her talk was a comedy, in which dramatic justice was done to everybody's foibles. I remember that she made me laugh more than I liked; for I was, at that time, an eager scholar of ethics, and had tasted the sweets of solitude and stoicism, and I found something profane in the hours of amusing gossip into which she drew me; and, when I returned to my library, had much to think of the crackling of thorns under a pot."

Her beloved and loving cousin, Rev. William H. Channing, in his account of a visit he paid her, somewhat later, when she lived at Jamaica Plain, near Boston, in 1840, says: —

"As, leaning on one arm, she poured out her stream of thought, turning now and then her full eyes upon me to see whether I caught her meaning, there was leisure to study her thoroughly. Her temperament was predominantly what the physiologist would call nervous-sanguine; and the gray eye, rich brown hair, and light complexion, with the muscular and well-developed frame, bespoke delicacy balanced by vigor. Here was a sensitive yet powerful being, fit at once for rapture or sustained effort, intensely active, prompt for adventure, firm for trial. She certainly had no beauty; yet the high-arched dome of her head, the changeful expressiveness of every feature, and her whole air of mingled dignity and impulse, gave her a commanding charm. Especially characteristic were two physical traits. The first was a contraction of the eyelids almost to a point, — a trick caught from near-sightedness, — and then a sudden dilation, till the iris seemed to emit flashes, — an effect, no doubt, dependent on her highly magnetized condition. The second was a singular pliancy of the vertebræ and muscles of the neck, enabling her, by a mere movement, to denote each varying emotion; in moments of tenderness, or pensive feeling, its curves were swan-like in grace; but, when she was scornful or indignant, it contracted, and made swift turns, like that of a bird of prey. Finally, in the animation, yet *abandon*, of Margaret's attitude and look, were rarely blended the fiery course of northern, and the soft languor of southern races."

Margaret Fuller.

Such a woman could not live idly, especially in diligent, practical New England, even had she been shielded by fortune from the most obvious necessity for habitual industry. After the completion of her school-day education, and before undertaking the editorship of The Dial, she had taught classes of girls in her home, given two years to the conduct of a seminary in Providence, R. I. (for which she was never paid), had translated (in 1839) Eckermann's "Conversations with Goethe," and in the autumn of this year she planned and announced her most unique enterprise, — a series of conversations (in Boston), for women only, wherein she was to take a leading part; but every one who attended was required to contribute according to her ability, by written essay or spoken word, as should be suggested or found possible. The general object of these conferences, as declared in her programme, was to supply answers to these questions: "What were we born to do?" and "How shall we do it?" or (as I think she elsewhere said), "to vindicate the right of Woman to think," by showing that she *can* think nobly and to good purpose; but Life, Literature, Mythology, Art, Culture, Religion, were liberally drawn upon for material and stimulus in the progress of this most arduous undertaking.

But Margaret had higher qualifications for such a task than any other person that America had yet produced, being "the best talker since De Staël," as I once heard her characterized. And, as the ablest and most cultivated women in and around Boston were naturally attracted to her conversations, and incited to take part in them, I doubt not that they were more interesting and profitable than any intellectual exercises which had preceded them; and, while the attendance was necessarily limited, — averaging less than fifty persons, — there are still many living who gratefully recall them as the starting-point and incitement of a new and nobler existence. Yet an attempt by Margaret to extend their advantages to men proved a failure; and, even when repeated under the guidance of so eminent a conversationist as Mr. A. Bronson Alcott, I judge that no decided success was achieved.

In 1839, she had visited, with a party of friends, what was then "the Great West"; spending weeks in traversing the prairies of Illinois, as yet undeformed by fences and unvexed by the plough. Her observations and impressions, embodied in a volume entitled "Summer on the Lakes," evinced an un-American ripeness of culture, and a sympathetic enjoyment of Nature in her untamed luxuriance. But the alternating meadow and forest of that bounteous region in its primitive state evinced little of the rugged wildness of mountain or desert; and she remarked that it seemed a reproduction, though on a gigantic scale, and without enclosures, of the great baronial domains and parks of Europe; so that the traveller was constantly looking for the castles and other evidences of human occupation and enjoyment which, it seemed, must be just at hand. Half a century hence, Illinoians will read her book, and wonder if the region it vividly depicts and describes can indeed be identical with that which surrounds them.

But the work by which she will be longest and widest known first appeared in The Dial (1843) as "The Great Lawsuit," and, when afterward expanded into a separate volume, was entitled, "Woman in the Nineteenth Century." If not the clearest and most logical, it was the loftiest and most commanding assertion yet made of the right of Woman to be regarded and treated as an independent, intelligent, rational being, entitled to an equal voice in framing and modifying the laws she is required to obey, and in controlling and disposing of the property she has inherited or aided to acquire. Yet questions of property, personal rights, guardianship of children, &c., are but incidental, not essential. She says:—

> "It is the fault of MARRIAGE, and of the present relations between the sexes, that the woman *belongs* to the man, instead of forming a whole with him. . . . . Woman, self-centred, would never be absorbed by any relation; it would only be an experience to her, as to Man. It is a vulgar error, that love—*a* love—is to Woman her whole existence: she also is born for Truth and Love in their universal energy. Would she but assume her inheritance, Mary would not be the only virgin mother."

If you say this is vague, mystical, unmeaning, I shall not contradict you; I am not arguing that Woman's undoubted wrongs are to be redressed by the concession of what Margaret, or any of her disciples, has claimed as Woman's inherent rights; I only feel that hers is the ablest, bravest, broadest, assertion yet made of what are termed Woman's Rights; and I suspect that the statement might lose in force by gaining in clearness. And, at all events, I am confident that there lives no man or woman who would not profit (if he or she has not already profited) by a thoughtful perusal of "Woman in the Nineteenth Century."

My wife, having spent much time in and near Boston, had there made Margaret's acquaintance, attended her conversations, accepted her leading ideas; and, desiring to enjoy her society more intimately and continuously, Mrs. G. planned and partly negotiated an arrangement whereby her monitor and friend became an inmate of our family and a writer for The Tribune.

Up to the close of the Presidential canvass in 1844, I had lived thirteen years in New York, and never half a mile from the City Hall, — usually within sixty rods of it. The newspaper business requiring close attention, and being wholly prosecuted "down town," it seemed, when I once ventured to live so far up as Broome Street, that I had strayed to an inconvenient distance from my work; but, when the great struggle was over, and I the worst beaten man on the continent, — worn out by incessant anxiety and effort, covered with boils, and thoroughly used up, — I took a long stride landward, removing to a spacious old wooden house, built as a country or summer residence by Isaac Lawrence, formerly President of the United States Branch Bank, but which, since his death, had been neglected, and suffered to decay. It was located on eight acres of ground, including a wooded ravine, or dell, on the East River, at Turtle Bay, nearly opposite the southernmost point of Blackwell's Island, amid shade and fruit trees, abundant shrubbery, ample garden, &c.; and, though now for years perforated by streets, and in good part covered by buildings, was then so secluded as to be only reached by a narrow, devious, private lane, exceedingly dark at night for one accustomed to the glare of gas-lamps; the nearest highway being the old "Boston Road" at Forty-ninth Street; while an hourly stage on the Third Avenue, just beyond, afforded our readiest means of transit to and from the city proper. Accustomed to the rumble and roar of carriages, the stillness here at night seemed at first so sepulchral, unearthly, that I found difficulty in sleeping. Of the place itself, Margaret — who became one of our household soon after we took possession — wrote thus to a friend: —

"This place is, to me, entirely charming; it is so completely in the country, and all around is so bold and free. It is two miles or more from the thickly settled parts of New York, but omnibuses and cars give me constant access to the city; and, while I can readily see what and whom I will, I can command time and retirement. Stopping on the Harlem Road, you enter a lane nearly a quarter of a mile long, and, going by a small brook and pond that locks in the place, and ascending a slightly rising ground, get sight of the house, which, old-fashioned and of mellow tint, fronts on a flower-garden filled with shrubs, large vines, and trim box borders. On both sides of the house are beautiful trees, standing fair, full-grown, and clear. Passing through a wide hall, you come out upon a piazza stretching the whole length of the house, where one can walk in all weathers; and thence, by a step or two, on a lawn, with picturesque masses of rocks, shrubs, and trees, overlooking the East River. Gravel-paths lead, by several turns, down the steep bank to the water's edge, where, round the rocky point, a small bay curves, in which boats are lying; and, owing to the currents and the set of the tide, the sails glide sidelong, seeming to greet the house as they sweep by. The beauty here, seen by moonlight, is truly transporting. I enjoy it greatly, and the *genus loci* receives me as to a home."

We have seen that the first impressions made by Margaret, even on those who soon learned to admire her most, were not favorable; and it was decidedly so in my case. A sufferer myself, and at times scarcely able to ride to and from the office, I yet did a day's work each day, regardless of nerves or moods; but she had no such capacity for incessant labor. If quantity only were considered, I could easily write ten columns to her one: indeed, she would only write at all when in the vein; and her headaches and other infirmities often precluded all labor for days. Meantime, perhaps, the interest of the theme had evaporated, or the book to be reviewed had the bloom brushed from its cheek by some rival journal. Attendance and care were very needful to her; she would evidently have been happier amid other and more abundant furniture than graced our dwelling; and, while nothing was said, I felt that a richer and more generous diet than ours would have been more accordant with her tastes and wishes. Then I had a notion that strong-minded women should be above the weakness of fearing to go anywhere, at any time, alone, — that the sex would have to emancipate itself from thraldom to etiquette and the need of a masculine arm in crossing a street or a room, before it could expect to fight its way to the bar, the bench, the jury-box, and the polls. Nor was I wholly exempt from the vulgar prejudice against female claimants of functions hitherto devolved only on men, as mistaking the source of their dissatisfaction. Her cousin, Channing, narrating a day's conversation with her in 1840, delicately says: —

> "But the tragedy of Margaret's history was deeper yet. Behind the poet was the woman, — the fond and relying, the heroic and disinterested woman. The very glow of her poetic enthusiasm was but an outflush of trustful affection; the very restlessness of her intellect was the confession that her heart had found no home. A 'book-worm,' 'a dilettante,' a 'pedant,' I had heard her sneeringly called; but now it was evident that her seeming insensibility was virgin pride, and her absorption in study the natural vent of emotions which had met no object worthy of life-long attachment. At once, many of her peculiarities became intelligible. Fitfulness, unlooked-for changes of mood, misconceptions of words and actions, substitution of fancy for fact, — which had annoyed me during the previous season, as inconsistent in a person of such capacious judgment and sustained self-government, — were now referred to the morbid influence of affections pent up to prey upon themselves."

If *I* had attempted to say this, I should have somehow blundered out that, noble and great as she was, a good husband and two or three bouncing babies would have emancipated her from a deal of cant and nonsense.

Yet I very soon noted, even before I was prepared to ratify their judgment, that the women who visited us to make or improve her acquaintance seemed instinctively to recognize and defer to her as their superior in thought and culture. Some who were her seniors, and whose writings had achieved a far wider and more profitable popularity than hers, were eager to sit at her feet, and to listen to her casual utterances as to those of an oracle. Yet there was no assumption of precedence, no exaction of deference, on her part; for, though somewhat stately and reserved in the presence of strangers, no one "thawed out" more completely, or was more unstarched and cordial in manner, when surrounded by her friends. Her magnetic sway over these was marvellous, unaccountable: women who had known her but a day revealed to her the most jealously guarded secrets of their lives, seeking her sympathy and counsel thereon, and were themselves annoyed at having done so when the magnetism of her presence was withdrawn. I judge that she was the repository of more confidences than any contemporary; and I am sure no one had ever reason to regret the imprudent precipitancy of their trust. Nor were these revelations made by those only of her own plane of life, but chambermaids and seamstresses unburdened their souls to her, seeking and receiving her counsel; while children found her a delightful playmate and a capital friend. My son Arthur (otherwise "Pickie"), who was but eight months old when she came to us, learned to walk and to talk in her society, and to love and admire her as few but nearest relatives are ever loved and admired by a child. For, as the elephant's trunk serves either to rend a limb from the oak or pick up a pin, so her wonderful range of capacities, of experiences, of sympathies, seemed adapted to every condition and phase of humanity. She had marvelous powers of personation and mimicry, and, had she condescended to appear before the foot-lights, would soon have been recognized as the first actress of the Nineteenth Century. For every effort to limit vice, ignorance, and misery she had a ready, eager ear, and a willing hand; so that her charities — large in proportion to her slender means — were signally enhanced by the fitness and fulness of her wise and generous counsel, the readiness and emphasis with which she, publicly and privately, commended to those richer than herself any object deserving their alms. She had once attended, with other noble women, a gathering of outcasts of their sex; and, being asked how they appeared to her, replied, "As women like myself, save that they are victims of wrong and misfortune." No project of moral or social reform ever failed to command her generous, cheering benediction, even when she could not share the sanguine hopes of its authors: she trusted that these might somehow benefit the objects of their self-sacrifice, and felt confident that they must, at all events, be blest in their own moral natures. I doubt that our various benevolent and reformatory associations had ever before, or have ever since, received such wise, discriminating commendation to the favor of the rich, as they did from her pen during her connection with The Tribune.

In closing her "Woman in the Nineteenth Century," not long before she came to New York, she had said:—

"I stand in the sunny noon of life. Objects no longer glitter in the dews of morning, neither are they yet softened by the shadows of evening. Every spot is seen, every chasm revealed. Climbing the dusty hill, some few effigies, that once stood for symbols of human destiny, have been broken; those I still have with me show defects in this broad light. Yet enough is left, even by experience, to point distinctly to the glories of that destiny,—faint, but not to be mistaken, streaks of the future day. I can say with the bard,—

'Though *many* have suffered shipwreck, still beat noble hearts.'"

Though ten years had not passed since her first visit to Emerson, at Concord, so graphically narrated by him in a reminiscence wherefrom I have already quoted, care and suffering had meantime detracted much from the lightness of her step, the buoyancy of her spirits. If, in any of her varying moods, she was so gay-hearted and mirth-provoking as he there describes her, I never happened to be a witness; but then I was never so intimate and admired a friend as he became at an early day, and remained to the last. Satirical she could still be, on great provocation; but she rarely, and, I judge, reluctantly, gave evidence of her eminent power to rebuke assumption or meanness by caricaturing or intensifying their unconscious exhibition. She *could* be joyous, and even merry; but her usual manner, while with us, was one of grave thoughtfulness, absorption in noble deeds, and in paramount aspirations and efforts to leave some narrow corner of the world somewhat better than she had found it.

I may have already spoken of her quick, earnest sympathy with humanity under all diversities of temporal condition, her easy penetration of the disguise which sometimes seeks to conceal the true king in the beggar's rags, and her profound appreciation of nobleness of soul, wherever and however manifested. Here is an instance, from her newspaper article on "Woman in Poverty":—

"The old woman was recommended as a laundress by my friend, who had long prized her. I was immediately struck with the dignity and propriety of her manner. In the depth of Winter, she brought herself the heavy baskets through the slippery streets; and, when I asked her why she did not employ some younger person to do what was so entirely disproportioned to her strength, simply said, she 'lived alone, and could not afford to hire an errand-boy.' 'It was hard for her?' 'No; she was fortunate in being able to get work, at her age, when others could do it better. Her friends were very good to procure it for her.' 'Had she a comfortable home?' 'Tolerably so; she should not need one long.' 'Was that a thought of joy to her?' 'Yes; for she hoped to see again the husband and children from whom she had long been separated.'

"Thus much in answer to the questions; but, at other times, the little she said was on general topics. It was not from her that I learned how the great idea of Duty had held her upright through a life of incessant toil, sorrow, bereavement; and that not only had she remained upright, but that her character had been constantly progressive. Her latest act had been to take home a poor sick girl who had no home of her own, and could not bear the idea of dying in an hospital, and maintain and nurse her through the last weeks of her life. 'Her eyesight was failing, and she should not be able to work much longer; but, then, God would provide. *Somebody* ought to see to the poor motherless girl.'

"It was not merely the greatness of the act, for one in such circumstances, but the quiet, matter-of-course way in which it was done, that showed the habitual tone of the mind, and made us feel that life could hardly do more for a human being than to make him or her the *somebody* that is daily so deeply needed, to represent the right, to do the plain right thing.

"'God will provide.'—Yes, it is the poor who feel themselves near to the God of Love. Though He slay them, still do they trust Him.

"'I hope,' said I, to a poor apple-woman, who had been drawn on to disclose a tale of distress that, almost in the mere hearing, made me weary of life,—'I hope I may yet see you in a happier condition.'

"'With God's help!' she replied, with a smile that a Raphael would have delighted to transfer to his canvas; a Mozart, to strains of angelic sweetness. All her life she had seemed an outcast child; still, she leaned upon a Father's love."

In the summer of 1846,—modifying, but not terminating, her connection with The Tribune,—Margaret left New York for Boston, and, after a parting visit to her relatives and early friends, took passage thence (August 1) for Europe. As I last saw her on the steamboat that bore her hence, I might, perhaps, here bid her adieu. But my recollections of her do not cease with her departure; and I feel that my many young readers, whose previous acquaintance with her was but a vague tradition, cannot choose that she be thus abruptly dismissed from these reminiscences, but will prefer to hear more of the most remarkable, and in some respects the greatest, woman whom America has yet known. I therefore devote some pages to her subsequent career; only regretting that time and space do not serve to render that career ampler justice.

Leaving in the company of admiring, devoted friends, who welcomed her to the intimacy of their family circle, and writing to The Tribune whenever she (too seldom) found topics of interest that did not trench upon her deference to the sanctities of social intercourse, she first traversed Great Britain; meeting and conversing with Wordsworth, Joanna Baillie, De Quincey, Carlyle, Mazzini, Dr. Chalmers, the Howitts, and many other celebrities, — most of whom have since passed away, — thence crossing to France, where she met George Sand, Béranger, La Mennais, saw Rachel act, and listened to a lecture by Arago. The next Spring (1847), she, with her party, sped to Italy; coasting to Naples, and thence returning leisurely to Rome, where Pius IX. had just been made Pope, and had signalized his accession by words of sympathy and cheer for the aspirations to freedom of down-trodden millions, which he has long since recanted, but they refuse to forget.

Passing thence by Florence, Bologna, Ravenna, to Venice, she there parted with the friends who had thus far been her companions in travel, — they crossing the Alps on their homeward way; while she — fully identified with the new-born hopes of Italy — had decided to remain. After hastily visiting Vicenza, Verona, Mantua, Brescia, Milan, the lakes Garda, Maggiore, and Como, and spending a few days in southern Switzerland, she returned, *via* Milan and Florence, to Rome, august "city of the soul," which she had chosen for her future home, and whence she wrote (December 20) to her friend Emerson: —

"I find how true was the hope that always drew me toward Europe. It was no false instinct that said I might here find an atmosphere to develop me in ways that I need. Had I only come ten years earlier! Now, my life must be a failure, so much strength has been wasted on abstractions, which only came because I grew not on the right soil."

She was privately married, not long after her return to Rome, to Giovanni Angelo Ossoli, of a noble but impoverished Roman family. He had caught the infection of liberal principles from the air, or from her, — his three brothers being, as he had been, in the Papal service, and so remaining after the Pope had disappointed the hopes excited by his first words and acts under the tiara. In the troublous times then imminent, it was deemed expedient to keep their marriage a close secret, as their only hope of securing their share of the patrimony of Ossoli's recently deceased father; and she spent the ensuing Summer at the little mountain village of Rieti, where her son Angelo was born. Returning before Winter to Rome, she became at once a trusted counsellor of Mazzini during the brief but glorious era of the Republic; and, when the city was invested and besieged by a French army, she was appointed director of a hospital, and therein found a sphere of sad, but earnest and beneficent activity. While thus absorbed in the noblest efforts in behalf of Italy, of Freedom, and Humanity, she snatched time (May 6) to send me a letter descriptive of the situation, opening, trumpet-toned, as follows:—

"I write you from barricaded Rome. The mother of nations is now at bay against them all.

"Rome was suffering before.

"The misfortunes of other regions of Italy, the defeat at Novarra, —preconcerted, in hope to strike the last blow at Italian independence,—the surrender and painful condition of Genoa; the money difficulties,—insuperable, unless the government could secure confidence abroad as well as at home,—prevented her people from finding that foothold for which they were ready. The vacillations of France agitated them; still, they could not seriously believe she would ever act the part she has. We must say France, because, though many honorable men have washed their hands of all share in the perfidy, the Assembly voted funds to sustain the expedition to Civita Vecchia, and the nation, the army, have remained quiescent."

This letter closed as follows:—

"The Americans here are not in a pleasant situation. Mr. Cass, the Chargé of the United States, stays here without recognizing the government. Of course, he holds no position at the present moment that can enable him to act for us. Besides, it gives us pain that our country, whose policy it justly is to avoid physical interference with the affairs of Europe, should not use a moral influence. Rome has — as we did — thrown off a government no longer tolerable; she had made use of the suffrage to form another; she stands on the same basis as ourselves. Mr. Rush did us great honor by his ready recognition of a principle, as represented by the French Provisional Government; had Mr. Cass been empowered to do the same, our country would have acted nobly, and all that is most truly American in America would have spoken to sustain the sickened hopes of European Democracy. But of this more when I write next. Who knows what I may have to tell another week?"

She soon afterward wrote (June 6) to another friend as follows: —

"On Sunday, from our loggia, I witnessed a terrible, a real battle. It began at four in the morning: it lasted to the last gleam of light. The musket-fire was almost unintermitted; the roll of the cannon, especially from St. Angelo, most majestic. As all passed at Porta San Pancrazio and Villa Pamfili, I saw the smoke of every discharge, the flash of the bayonets; with a glass, could see the men. The French could not use their heavy cannon, being always driven away by the legions of Garibaldi and ——, when trying to find positions for them. The loss on our side is about three hundred killed and wounded; theirs must be much greater. In one casino have been found seventy dead bodies of theirs. . . . . The cannonade on our side has continued day and night (being full moon) till this morning; they seeking to advance or take other positions, the Romans firing on them. The French throw rockets into the town; one burst in the court-yard of the hospital just as I arrived there yesterday, agitating the poor sufferers very much; they said they did not want to die like mice in a trap."

She writes, five days later, to her friend Emerson as follows: —

"I received your letter amid the sound of cannonade and musketry. It was a terrible battle, fought here from the first till the last light of day. I could see all its progress from my balcony. The Italians fought like lions. It is a truly heroic spirit that animates them. They make a stand here for honor and their rights, with little ground for hope that they can resist, now they are betrayed by France.

"Since the 30th April, I go almost daily to the hospitals; and though I have suffered, — for I had no idea before how terrible gunshot wounds and wound-fever are, — yet I have taken pleasure, and great pleasure, in being with the men; there is scarcely one who is not moved by a noble spirit. Many, especially among the Lombards, are the flower of the Italian youth. When they begin to get better, I carry them books and flowers; they read, and we talk.

"The palace of the Pope, on the Quirinal, is now used for convalescents. In those beautiful gardens, I walk with them, — one with his sling, another with his crutch. The gardener plays off all his water-works for the defenders of the country, and gathers flowers for me, their friend.

"I feel profoundly for Mazzini; at moments, I am tempted to say, 'Cursed with every granted prayer,' — so cunning is the demon. He is becoming the inspiring soul of his people. He saw Rome, to which all his hopes through life tended, for the first time as a Roman citizen, and to become in a few days its ruler. He has animated, he sustains her to a glorious effort, which, if it fails this time, will not in the age. His country will be free. Yet to me it would be so dreadful to cause all the bloodshed, to dig the graves of such martyrs.

"Then Rome is being destroyed; her glorious oaks; her villas, haunts of sacred beauty, that seemed the possession of the world forever, — the villa of Raphael, the villa of Albani, home of Winkelmann, and the best expression of the ideal of modern Rome, and so many other sanctuaries of beauty, — all must perish, lest a foe should level his musket from their shelter. *I* could not, could not!

"I know not, dear friend, whether I shall ever get home across that great ocean; but here in Rome I shall no longer wish to live. O Rome, *my* country! could I imagine that the triumph of what I held dear was to heap such desolation on thy head!

"Speaking of the Republic you say, 'Do not I wish Italy had a great man?' Mazzini *is* a great man. In mind, a great poetic statesman; in heart, a lover; in action, decisive, and full of resources as Cæsar. Dearly I love Mazzini. He came in just as I had finished the first letter to you. His soft, radiant look makes melancholy music in my soul; it consecrates my present life, that, like the Magdalen, I may, at the important hour, shed all the consecrated ointment on his head. There is one, Mazzini, who understands thee well; who knew thee no less when an object of popular fear, than now of idolatry; and who, if the pen be not held too feebly, will help posterity to know thee too."

Her friend, Mrs. William W. Story, an eyewitness, writes of her in those heroic days as follows: —

"Night and day, Margaret was occupied, and, with the Princess [Belgiojoso], so ordered and disposed the hospitals, that their conduct was truly admirable. All the work was skilfully divided, so that there was no confusion or hurry; and, from the chaotic condition in which these places had been left by the priests, — who previously had charge of them, — they brought them to a state of perfect regularity and discipline. Of money they had very little; and they were obliged to give their time and thoughts in its place. From the Americans in Rome they raised a subscription for the aid of the wounded of either party; but beside this they had scarcely any means to use. I have walked through the wards with Margaret, and saw how comforting was her presence to the poor suffering men. 'How long will Signora stay?' 'When will the Signora come again?' they eagerly asked. For each one's peculiar tastes she had a care: to one, she carried books; to another, she told the news of the day; and listened to another's oft-repeated tale of wrongs, as the best sympathy she could give. They raised themselves up on their elbows, to get the last glimpse of her as she was going away. There were some of the sturdy fellows of Garibaldi's Legion there; and to them she listened, as they spoke with delight of their chief, of his courage and skill; for he seemed to have won the hearts of his men in a remarkable manner."

Of course, this most unequal struggle could have but one result. Rome, gallantly defended by the badly armed, ill-supplied, motley host of volunteers, who had gathered from all Italy to uphold the flag of the Republic, at last fell: the superiority of the French in numbers, in discipline, and in every resource, being too decided to leave room for hope. Margaret had accompanied her husband to the battery in front of the enemy, where his company was stationed on the last evening of the siege; but the cannonade was not renewed, and next morning the city surrendered. Husband and wife hastened directly to Rieti, where their child had been left at nurse through the storm; and whence she wrote her mother, saying: —

"Dearest Mother: I received your letter a few hours before reaching Rome. Like all of yours, it refreshed me, and gave me as much satisfaction as anything could at that sad time. Its spirit is of eternity, and befits an epoch when wickedness and perfidy so impudently triumph, and the best blood of the generous and honorable is poured out like water, seemingly in vain.

"I cannot tell you what I suffered to abandon the wounded to the care of their mean foes; to see the young men that were faithful to their vows hunted from their homes, — hunted like wild beasts, — denied a refuge in every civilized land. Many of those I loved sunk to the bottom of the sea by Austrian cannon, or will be shot; others are in penury, grief, and exile. May God give due recompense for all that has been endured!

"My mind still agitated, and my spirits worn out, I have not felt like writing to any one. Yet the magnificent Summer does not smile quite in vain for me. Much exercise in the open air, living much on milk and fruit, have recruited my health; and I am regaining the habit of sleep, which a month of nightly cannonade in Rome had destroyed.

"Receiving, a few days since, a packet of letters from America, I opened them with more feeling of hope and good cheer than for a long time past. The first words that met my eye were these, in the hand of Mr. Greeley: 'Ah, Margaret! the world grows dark with us! *You* grieve, for Rome is fallen; *I* mourn, for Pickie is dead.'

"I have shed rivers of tears over the inexpressibly affecting letter thus begun. One would think I might have become familiar enough with images of death and destruction; yet, somehow, the image of Pickie's little dancing figure lying stiff and stark, between his parents, has made me weep more than all else. There was little hope he could do justice to himself, or lead a happy life, in so perplexed a world; but never was a character of richer capacity, — never a more charming child. To me, he was most dear, and would always have been so. Had he become stained with earthly faults, I could never have forgotten what he was when fresh from the soul's home, and what he was to me when my soul pined for sympathy, pure and unalloyed. The three children I have seen who were fairest in my eyes, and gave most promise of the future, were Waldo [Emerson], Pickie, Hermann Clarke; — all nipped in the bud. Endless thought has this given me, and a resolve to seek the realization of all hopes and plans elsewhere; which resolve will weigh with me as much as it can weigh before the silver cord is finally loosed. Till then, Earth, our mother, always finds strange, unexpected ways to draw us back to her bosom, — to make us seek anew a nutriment which has never failed to cause us frequent sickness."

Having somewhat regained her health and calmness at Rieti, she journeyed thence, with her husband and child, by Perugia to Florence, where they were welcomed and cheered by the love and admiration of the little American colony, and by the few British liberals residing there, — the Brownings prominent among them. Here they spent the ensuing Winter, and Margaret wrote her survey of the grand movement for Italian liberty and unity, which had miscarried for the moment, but which was still cherished in millions of noble hearts. With the ensuing Spring came urgent messages from her native land, awaking, or rather strengthening, her natural longing to greet once more the dear ones from whom she had now been four years parted; and on the 17th of May, 1850, they embarked in the bark Elizabeth, Captain Hasty, at Leghorn, for New York, which they hoped to reach within sixty days at farthest.

Margaret's correspondence for the preceding month is darkened with apprehensions and sinister forebodings, which were destined to be fearfully justified. First: Captain Hasty was prostrated, when a few days on his voyage, by what proved to be confluent small-pox, whereof he died, despite his wife's tenderest care, and his body was consigned to the deep. Then Angelo, Margaret's child, was attacked by the terrible disease, and his life barely saved, after he had for days been utterly blind, and his recovery seemed hopeless. So, after a week's detention by head winds at Gibralter, they fared on, under the mate's guidance, until, at noon of July 15, in a thick fog, with a southeast breeze, they reckoned themselves off the Jersey coast, and headed northeast for the bay of New York, which they expected to enter next morning. But the evening brought a gale, which steadily increased to a tempest, before which, though under close-reefed sails, they were driven with a rapidity of which they were unconscious, until, about four o'clock the next morning, the Elizabeth struck heavily on Fire Island Beach, off the south coast of Long Island, and her prow was driven harder and farther into the sand, while her freight of marble broke through her keel, and her stern was gradually hove around by the terrible waves, until she lay broadside to their thundering sweep, her deck being careened toward the land, the sea making a clear sweep over her at every swell. The masts had been promptly cut away; but the ship was already lost, and her inmates could only hope to save their own lives. Making their way with great difficulty to the forecastle, they remained there, amid the war of elements, until 9 A. M., when, as the wreck was evidently about to break up, they resolved to attempt the perilous passage to the desolate sand-hills which were plainly visible at a distance of a few hundred feet; and, venturing upon a plank, Mrs. Hasty, aided by a seaman named Davis, reached the shore. But Margaret and her husband refused to be saved separately, or without their child; and the crew were directed to save themselves, which most of them did. Still, some remained on the wreck, and were persuading the passengers to trust themselves to planks, when, at 3 P. M., a great sea struck the forecastle, carrying away the foremast, together with the deck and all upon it. Two of the crew saved themselves by swimming; the steward, with little Angelo in his arms, both dead, was washed ashore twenty minutes later; but of Margaret and her husband nothing was evermore seen.

Just before setting out on this fateful voyage, she had written apprehensively to a friend at home:—

"I shall embark more composedly in our merchant-ship; praying fervently, indeed, that it may not be my lot to lose my boy at sea, either by unsolaced illness, or amid howling waves; or, if so, that Ossoli, Angelo, and I may go together, and that the anguish may be brief."

So passed away the loftiest, bravest soul that has yet irradiated the form of an American woman.

IN MEMORY
OF THE
MARTYRS TO HUMAN LIBERTY,
WHO FELL
DURING THE SIEGE OF MAY AND JUNE, 1849,
AS
DEFENDERS OF ROME;
STERNLY STRUGGLING
AGAINST OVERWHELMING NUMBERS, AGAINST AMPLE MUNITIONS,
AGAINST FATE:
THEIR HIGHEST HOPE THAT IN THEM, LIVING OR DEAD, THE
SACRED CAUSE SHOULD NOT BE DISHONORED:
THEIR PROUDEST WISH
THAT FREEDOM'S CHAMPIONS THROUGHOUT THE WORLD
MIGHT RECOGNIZE THEM AS BRETHREN,
NOBLY DYING
THAT SURVIVING MILLIONS MAY DULY ABHOR TYRANNY AND LOVE LIBERTY:
CLOSING THEIR EYES SERENELY,
IN THE GENEROUS FAITH THAT RIGHTS FOR ALL, DOMINION FOR NONE,
WILL SOON REVIVIFY THE EARTH BAPTIZED IN THEIR BLOOD.
STAY, HEEDLESS WANDERER!
DEFILE NOT WITH LISTLESS STEP THE ASHES OF HEROES!
BUT,
ON THE RELICS OF THESE MARTYRS, SWEAR A DEEPER AND STERNER
HATE TO EVERY FORM OF OPPRESSION:
HERE LEARN TO FEEL
A DEARER LOVE FOR ALL WHO STRIVE FOR LIBERTY:
HERE BREATHE A PRAYER
FOR THE SPEEDY TRIUMPH OF RIGHT OVER MIGHT, LIGHT OVER NIGHT;
AND FOR ROME'S FALLEN DEFENDERS,
THAT THE GOD OF THE OPPRESSED AND AFFLICTED MAY HAVE
THEM IN HIS HOLY KEEPING.

"They never fail who die
In a great cause; the block may soak their gore;
Their heads may sodden in the sun; their limbs
Be strung to city gates and castle walls, —
But still their spirit walks abroad."

BYRON, *Marino Faliero*, Act II. Scene 2.

XXIII.

BEGGARS AND BORROWERS.

NEW YORK is the metropolis of beggary. The wrecks of incapacity, miseducation, prodigality, and profligacy drift hither from either continent, and are finally stranded on our shore. Has a pretentious family in Europe a member who is felt as a burden or loathed as a disgrace? money is somehow scraped together to ship him off to New York; taking good care that there be not enough to enable him to ship himself back again. Does a family collapse anywhere in the interior or along the coast of our country, leaving a helpless widow and fatherless children to struggle with difficulties utterly unexpected and unprepared for? though too proud to work, or even beg, where they are known, they are ready enough to try their fortune and hide their fall in this great emporium, where they would gladly do — if they could get it — the very work which they reject as degrading in the home of their by-gone prosperity and consequence. Though living is here most expensive, and only eminent skill or efficiency can justify migration hither on the part of any but single young men, yet mechanics and laborers of very moderate ability, and even widows with small children, hie hither, in reckless defiance of the fact that myriads have done so before them, — at least nineteen-twentieths of them only to plunge thereby into deeper, more squalid, hopeless misery than they had previously known. Want is a hard master anywhere; but nowhere else are the sufferings, the woes, the desperation, of utter need so trying as in a great city; and they are preëminently so in *this* city; because the multiplicity of the destitute benumbs the heart of charity and precludes attention to any one's wants, while each is absorbed in his own cares and efforts to such extent that he knows nothing of the neighbors who may be starving to death, with barely a brick wall between him and them.

The beggars of New York comprise but a small proportion of its sufferers from want; yet they are at once very numerous and remarkably impudent. One who would accept a franc in Paris, or a shilling in London, with grateful acknowledgments, considers himself ill-used and insulted if you offer him less than a dollar in New York. With thousands, beggary is a profession, whereof the rudiments were acquired in the Old World; but experience and observation have qualified them to pursue it with veteran proficiency and success in the New. Even our native beggars have a boldness of aspiration, an audacity of conception, such as the magnificent proportions of our lakes and valleys, our mountains and prairies, are calculated to inspire. I doubt that an Asiatic or European beggar ever frankly avowed his intent to beg the purchase-money of a good farm, though some may have invested their gains thus laudably; but I have been solicited by more than one American, who had visited this city from points hundreds of miles distant, expressly and avowedly to beg the means of buying a homestead. I wish I were certain that none of these had more success with others than with me.

Begging for churches, for seminaries, for libraries, has been one of our most crying nuisances. If there be two hundred negro families living in a city, they will get up a Baptist, a Methodist, and perhaps an Episcopal or Congregational Church; and, being generally poor, they will undertake to build for each a meeting-house, and support a clergyman, — in good part, of course, by begging, — often in distant cities. A dozen boys attending a seminary will form a library association, or debating club, and then levy on mankind in general for the books they would like to possess. Thus, in addition to our resident mendicancy, New York is made the cruising-ground, the harvest-field, of the high-soaring beggary of a whole continent; while our princely merchants, at some seasons, are waited upon by more solicitors of contributions than purchasers of goods. Hence, our rich men generally court and secure a reputation for meanness, which may or may not be deserved in a particular instance, but which, in any case, is indispensable as a protection, like the shell of a tortoise. Were they reputed benevolent and free-handed, they would never be allowed time to attend to their business, and could not enjoy an hour's peace in the bosom of their respective families.

The chronic beggars are a bad lot; but the systematic borrowers are far worse. What you give is gone, and soon forgotten, — there is the end of it. It is presumable that you can spare, or you would have withheld it. But you lend (in your greener days) with some expectation of being repaid; hence, disappointment and serious loss, — sometimes, even disgrace, — because of your abused faith in human nature. I presume no year passes wherein the solvent business men of this city lose so little as Ten Millions of Dollars borrowed of them, for a few hours or days, as a momentary accommodation, by neighbors and acquaintances, who would resent a suggested doubt of its punctual repayment; yet who never *do* repay it. I am confident that good houses have been reduced to bankruptcy, by these most irregular and improvident loans.

Worse still is the habit of borrowing and lending among clerks and young mechanics. A part of these are provident, thrifty, frugal, and so save money; another, and much larger class, prefer to "live as they go," and are constantly spending in drink and other dissipation that portion of their earnings which they should save. When I was a journeyman, I knew several who earned more than I did, but who were always behind with their board. Men of this class are continually borrowing five dollars or ten dollars of their frugal acquaintances to invest in a ball, a sleigh-ride, an excursion, a frolic; and a large proportion of these loans are never repaid. Millions of dollars, in the aggregate, are thus transferred from the pockets of the frugal to those of the prodigal; depriving the former of means they are sure to need when they come to furnish a house or undertake a business, and doing the latter no good, but rather confirming them in their evil ways. Such lending should be systematically discountenanced and refused.

I hate to say anything that seems calculated to steel others against the prayers of the unfortunate and necessitous; yet an extensive, protracted experience has led me to the conclusion that nine tenths of those who solicit loans of strangers or casual acquaintances are thriftless vagabonds, who will never be better off than at present, or scoundrels, who would not pay if they were able. In hundreds of cases, I have been importuned to lend from one dollar up to ten dollars, to help a stranger who had come to the city on some errand or other, had here fallen among thieves (who are far more abundant here than they ever were on the road from Jerusalem to Jericho), been made drunk, and plundered of his last cent, and who asked only enough to take him home, when the money would be surely and promptly returned. Sometimes, I have lent the sum required; in other cases, I have refused it; but I cannot remember *a single instance* in which the promise to repay was made good. I recollect a case wherein a capable, intelligent New-England mechanic, on his way from an Eastern city to work two hundred miles up the Erie Railroad, borrowed of me the means of saving his children from famine on the way, promising to pay it out of his first month's wages; which he took care never to do. This case differs from many others only in that the swindler was clearly of a better class than that from which the great army of borrowers is so steadily and bounteously recruited.

In one instance, a young man came with the usual request, and was asked to state his case. "I am a clerk from New Hampshire," he began, "and have been for three years employed in Georgia. At length, a severe sickness prostrated me; I lost my place; my money was exhausted; and here am I, with my wife, without a cent; and I want to borrow enough to take me home to my father's house, when I will surely repay it." "Stranger," was the response, "you evidently cannot stay here, and I must help you get away; but why say anything about paying me? You know, and *I* know, you will never pay a cent." My visitor protested and remonstrated; but I convinced, if I did not convert, him. "Don't you see," I rejoined, "that you cannot have been three years a clerk in a leading mercantile house in Georgia without making the acquaintance of merchants doing business in this city? Now, if you were a person likely to pay, you would apply to, and obtain help from, those merchants whom you know; not ask help of me, — an utter stranger." He did not admit the force of my demonstration; but of course the sequel proved it correct.

I consider it all but an axiom, that he who asks a stranger to lend him money will never pay it; yet I have known an exception. Once, when I was exceedingly poor and needy, in a season of commercial revulsion or "panic," I opened a letter from Utica, and found therein five dollars, which the writer asked me to receive in satisfaction of a loan of that sum which I had made him — a needy stranger — on an occasion which he recalled to my remembrance. Perplexed by so unusual a message, and especially by receiving it at such a time, when every one was seeking to borrow, — no one condescending to pay, — I scanned the letter more closely, and at length achieved a solution of the problem. The writer was a patient in the State lunatic asylum.

A gushing youth once wrote me to this effect: —

"Dear Sir: Among your literary treasures, you have doubtless preserved several autographs of our country's late lamented poet, Edgar A. Poe. If so, and you can spare one, please enclose it to me, and receive the thanks of yours truly."

I promptly responded, as follows: —

"Dear Sir: Among my literary treasures, there happens to be exactly *one* autograph of our country's late lamented poet, Edgar A. Poe. It is his note of hand for fifty dollars, with my indorsement across the back. It cost me exactly $50.75 (including protest), and you may have it for half that amount. Yours, respectfully."

That autograph, I regret to say, remains on my hands, and is still for sale at first cost, despite the lapse of time, and the depreciation of our currency.

I once received a letter from an utter stranger, living two hundred miles away, asking me to lend him a large sum on a mortgage of his farm, and closing thus:—

"P. S. My religious views are radically antagonist to yours; but I know no member of my own church of whom I would so readily, and with such confidence, ask such a favor, as of you."

This postscript impelled me, instead of dropping the letter quietly into the waste-basket, as usual, and turning to the next business in order, to answer him as follows:—

"Sir: I have neither the money you ask for, nor the inclination to lend it on the security you proffer. And your P. S. prompts the suggestion that, whenever *I* shall be moved to seek favors of the members of some other church, rather than of that to which I have hitherto adhered, I shall make haste to join that other church."

—I trust I have here said nothing calculated to stay the hand or chill the spirit of heaven-born Charity. The world is full of needy, suffering ones, who richly deserve compassion; not to speak of the vagrants, who, though undeserving, must not be allowed to starve or freeze. I was struck with the response of a man last from St. Louis, who recently insisted on being helped on to Boston, which he said was his early home, and to whom I roughly made answer,—"You need not pretend to me that the universe is bankrupt: I know better,—know that a man of your natural abilities, if he only behaved himself, need not be reduced to beggary." "Well, sir," he quickly rejoined, "I don't pretend that I have always done the right thing,—if I did, you would know better,—all I say is, that I am hungry and penniless, and that, if I can only get back to Boston, I can there make a living.

That's my whole story." I felt that he had the better reason on his side.

There must, there will, be heavy drafts made on the sympathies and the means of all who can and will give, especially during a hard, dull Winter or a "panic." Every prosperous man should ask himself, "How much can I afford to give?" and should set apart from a tenth to a third of his income for the relief of the needy and suffering. Then he should search out the most effective channels through which to reach those whose privations are greatest, and on whom private alms can be wisely and usefully expended. There are thousands who ought to go to the Almshouse at once, — who will be more easily supported there than elsewhere, — and it is no charity to squander your means on these. A great majority of the destitute can be far better dealt with by associations than by individuals; and of good associations for philanthropic purposes there is happily no lack in any great city. There remains a scanty residuum of cases wherein money or food must be given at once, by whomsoever happens to be nearest to the sufferer; but two thirds of those who beg from door to door, or who write begging letters, are the very last persons who ought to be given even a shinplaster dime. And, as a general rule, the importunity of a beggar is in inverse ratio to his deserving, or even to his need.

— "Then you condemn borrowing and lending entirely?"

No, I do not. Many a man knows how to use, wisely and beneficently, means that he does not, while others do, possess: lending to such, under proper safeguards, is most commendable. Many a young farmer, who, by working for others, has earned one thousand dollars, and saved a good part of it, is now prepared to work a farm of his own. He who lends such a youth from one thousand to two thousand dollars, wherewith to purchase a farm, taking a mortgage thereon for the amount, and leaving to the young farmer his own well-earned means wherewith to buy stock and seed, provisions and implements, will often enable him to work his way into a modest independence, surrounded and blessed by a wife and children, — himself a useful member of society, and a true pillar of the State, — when he must, but for that loan, have remained years longer single and a hireling. So, a young mechanic may often be wisely and safely aided to establish himself in business by a timely and well-secured loan; but this should never be accorded him till, by years of patient, frugal industry, he has qualified himself for mastery, and proved himself worthy of trust. (Of traders, there will always be too many, though none should ever be able to borrow a dollar.) But improvident borrowing and lending are among our most prevalent and baneful errors; and I would gladly conduce to their reformation.

I hold that it may sometimes be a duty to lend; and yet I judge that at least nine of every ten loans to the needy result in loss to the lender, with no substantial benefit to the borrower. That the poor often suffer from poverty, I know; but oftener from lack of capacity, skill, management, efficiency, than lack of money. Here is an empty-handed youth who wants much, and must have it; but, after the satisfaction of his most urgent needs, he wants, above all things, ability to earn money and take good care of it. He thinks his first want is a loan; but that is a great mistake. He is far more certain to set resolutely to work without than with that pleasant but baneful accommodation. Make up a square issue, — "Work or starve!" — and he is quite likely to choose work; while, provided he can borrow, he is more likely to dip into some sort of speculation or traffic. That he thus almost inevitably fools away his borrowed money concerns only the unwise lender; that he is thereby confirmed in his aversion to work, and squanders precious time that should fit him for decided usefulness, is of wider and greater consequence. The widow, the orphan, the cripple, the invalid, often need alms, and should have them; but to the innumerable hosts of needy, would-be borrowers the best response is Nature's, — "Root, hog, or die!"

XXIV.

DRAMATIC MEMORIES.

I KNOW not that the instinctive yearning of human beings for dramatic representations, and the delight with which these are witnessed, alike by cit and savage, may not be a dictate of Man's innate and utter depravity, inspired by the great author of evil; yet I bear unhesitating testimony to its existence. It is very nearly half a century since my father, lying on a sick-bed, and supposed to be asleep, was intensely amused, as I afterward heard him relate, by witnessing the gambols of his three younger children, — all between eight and three years old, — who rudely recast into a dramatic form the nonsensical old song of "A frog he would a-wooing go," and enacted it — each personating one of the animals mentioned therein — for their own mutual delectation; supposing that no one else was cognizant of the performance. I have no reason to suppose that one of them had ever heard of a theatre or play prior to that unique effort.

Four or five years later, after we had migrated to Vermont, what was called an "exhibition" — that is, a play — was set on foot in our Westhaven school district, prompted by the master, and I was allotted a part therein. The drama was entitled, I think, "The Fall of Bonaparte," and was intensely saturated with detestation of the great but fallen Corsican, who, I believe, was still living, though in reduced circumstances. I recollect that my part was that of either General or Captain Lescourt (both were in the play, and I have forgotten which was mine); I only recollect that it was as full of execration of the destroyer of French liberty, the betrayer of the hopes of the untitled millions, as even *I* could wish to utter. I recollect that we had several recitations, and that the play nearly spoiled our studies for that Winter; but I cannot be certain of the consummation. I believe our play was played — badly, of course; for the performers did not average twelve years old, and not one of them had ever seen a drama really enacted. If any one asserts from knowledge that that long-expected and intently prepared-for "exhibition" failed, for some reason, to come off, I shall not contradict him, though my impression is different.

More years passed; and at length, while an apprentice at Poultney, an "exhibition" was advertised to come off one evening in the church at Wells, six miles south of us: so a party was made up to attend it, — I being one of that party. Wells had rather a hard reputation in those days (perhaps from the ill behavior of those who went thither from neighboring towns to "carry on"); which fame, I trust, it has since outgrown. It was late in Winter, with deep snow, but thawing; so that, to protect us from the balls of ice and snow constantly thrown at us from our horse's feet, a long board had been set up on edge across the front of our rude sleigh, or, rather, sled; and this, in passing a point of rock which projected into the narrow road through the forest which skirted "Lake St. Austin" (otherwise Wells Pond), was caught and held; so as to rake the sled clear of its human freight. I received a hurt on my right shin which remained unhealed for years. But no one complained, all laughed; and we were soon all on board and in motion again; reaching Wells in good time for the "exhibition." The church was crowded with eager, and not very critical, auditors; the players were considerably older than we of Westhaven were at the date of our maiden effort; and I presume the playing was better, mainly because it could not easily be worse. There were several pieces (most of them literally so) on the bills, and all were duly undergone; yet even their names have escaped me. One peculiarity remains firmly imbedded in my memory. There was a scene in one of the plays wherein a man snugly hidden amid the thick branches of an evergreen tree overhears a plot to commit robbery, and perhaps murder also. Whereupon he bides his time, and duly precipitates himself on the robber (or robbers) in the very act, putting him (or them) to death or flight, and gallantly rescuing the intended victim. Well: here is where the laugh comes in: The tree — a substantial pine or hemlock, some eight inches through, and twenty feet high — had been firmly implanted in the stage before the "exhibition" began; and there it remained to the end, — forming a noticeable, but not very congruous, portion of the furniture of every parlor, boudoir, prison-cell, court-room, &c., &c., from first to last. If city audiences were less fastidious, I suspect that managers might have learned how to retrench their expenses for furniture, fixtures, scenery, attendants, &c., by studying that Wells "exhibition."

Unluckily, some of my companions on that excursion were of the "won't go home till morning" stamp, and could not see why any one should go to Wells unless to have a "high old time." They controlled the team, and would neither set it on the road to Poultney, nor permit the rest of us to do so, until late the next day, Meantime, they would neither sleep nor tolerate slumber on the part of any one else. The performances of the latter half of the night were a little wilder and rougher than any I was ever before or since implicated in, however innocently, and Wells was nowise to blame therefor. I never saw that respected village save during that single visit; and I sincerely trust that my reputation there is not based on the average conduct of my party on that exceptionally boisterous occasion. It was never before nor since so hard for me to work as during the afternoon and evening following our return to Poultney.

More years passed; I had migrated to this city; and, in December, 1831, I was first a spectator of a genuine dramatic performance. The place was the Old Bowery; the play was William Tell; the hero's son was personated by a Miss Mestayer, then in her early teens, and still, I think, on the stage, though I have not seen her these many years. The night was intensely cold, in-doors as well as out; the house was thin; the playing from fair to middling; yet I was in raptures from first to last. I have since thought that the wise way would be to choose a fit occasion, go *once* to a good theatre, and never darken the doors of any playhouse again. I never yet entered a green-room, and have no desire to enter one; but, dim as is my eyesight, I cannot now help seeing boards, and paint (coarsely laid on), and spangles, and general tawdriness, where I once saw glory, and beauty, and splendor, and poetry, — life idealized, and Paradise realized. Yes; unless to recall lost dreams while watching the ecstasies of children on their first visit, I judge that the wise man is he who goes but once to the theatre, and keeps the impression then made on his mind fresh and clear to the close of life.

During that, my first Winter in New York, a new theatre was opened at Richmond Hill (corner of Charlton and Varick Streets), in what was said to have been Aaron Burr's country-seat thirty years before, and was still deemed far up town, though now far below the bulk of our population. There were no street-cars, and scarcely an omnibus, in those days; Richmond Hill was away from the great thoroughfares; so, though the house was small, it was seldom well filled; and we journeymen printers, who worked on newspapers that helped the theatres to auditors, were admitted on orders from the editors respectively on Saturday evenings, when audiences were habitually and emphatically thin. I think I thus attended ten or twelve times, — oftener than in any five consecutive years thereafter. The manager was a Mr. Russell, — gossip said *Mrs.* Russell, who was certainly the better player, and presumptively a cleverer person, than her husband, whose talents were nevertheless respectable. Here I saw Mrs. Duff personate Lady Macbeth better than it has since been done in this city, though she played for $30 per week, and others have received ten times that amount for a single night. I doubt that any woman has since played in our city, — and I am thinking of Fanny Kemble, — who was the superior of Mrs. Duff in a wide range of tragic characters. I am not sufficiently familiar with the present stage to render my judgment of much value; yet it seems to me that Henry Placide at the Park was a better general comedian than we now have, though John S. Clarke and Joseph Jefferson probably each surpass him in a certain round of characters, and Sothern stands alone as Lord Dundreary. Barney Williams is a clever Irishman of his kind; so is William J. Florence: but is not this decidedly a poorer kind than the genial, gentlemanly Irishman of the lamented Power? I have seen fellows (none of these) personating Irishmen on our stage, — and with a rude, Chinese fidelity to a low, vulgar type of Irish character, — who seemed to me deserving of indictment as libellers of an unlucky race, who, with all their faults, never yet made themselves despicable.

A glad vision is evoked from the long-buried past as I recall and review the playing I have seen, — that of Naomi Vincent, who appeared at the Old Bowery, became Mrs. Hamblin, and died while still very young. I never saw her off the stage; am not sure that she was beautiful, nor even that she had the elements of a great actress in her nature; but beauty of mind she must have had, or her face greatly belied her. I never saw another walk the stage with such an ingenuous, trustful, confiding manner, evincing either artlessness or the perfection of art, — in her case, I am sure, it must have been the former. Yet her dramatic capacities were barely in the bud — hardly in the blossom — when she was called away by inexorable Death.

While in Europe, I attended some half a dozen plays, — mainly operatic, — but the only one that much impressed me was that wherein several popular authors took part, in behalf of the fund for the relief of their luckless and decayed brethren. The Duke of Devonshire had fitted up a theatre in his London palace, — a very large and fine one, — Bulwer had written "Not so Bad as we Seem" for the occasion; and the leading parts in it were presented by Douglas Jerrold, Mark Lemon, Charles Dickens, &c., &c. I believe the actresses were drawn from the ranks of the profession; so that their playing was less bad than that of the men, who were for the most part — not to speak it profanely — sticks. I never witnessed more melancholy failures than the attempts at dignity and courtesy of those who stood for noblemen. The demonstration of Thackeray's theory that the British plebeian is essentially a snob was perfect. But we had for afterpiece a farce, written by Dickens and Mark Lemon conjointly; and the chief part — that of a smart, garrulous, conceited lawyer, named Gabblewig — was played by Dickens most admirably. Though it was not concluded till after midnight, I suspect most of the auditors found this play entirely too short.

I witnessed the *début* in America of Fanny Kemble and her father, — she being in her spring-time of youth and its comeliness; he either a man of little genius, or suffering from the premature decay of his physical powers. I heard the first notes that Jenny Lind condescended to exchange for our dollars, — either of them of greater worth than those of to-day. As I never heard Malibran, I cannot say that Jenny Lind's vocal power exceeded that of any other woman who ever lived, though I suspect such was the fact. I saw and heard Forrest in his later prime, and judged him effective in a round of characters by no means the highest. When in Paris, I attended several representations at the Théâtre Français, and, though I understood little that was said, I could not fail to notice the wide difference between French and Anglo-Saxon acting, — a difference nowise creditable to the latter. Off the stage, the French are more demonstrative and theatrical than the English. Why is it that their positions are reversed before the foot-lights? — that the Frenchman is there quiet, simple, natural, and the Anglo-Saxon quite otherwise. Why does the "star" of our kin walk as though on stilts, and speak like an auctioneer's bellman? Can any one explain this strange incongruity?

Of late years, I have seldom visited the theatre, unless to accompany some country friend to whom a play was a novelty and a luxury; having been repelled by its habitual leaning to the side of Slavery, Tippling, and other iniquities whereby some men derive profit from others' weaknesses. The stage was of old a powerful ally of Liberty; yet, throughout our long and arduous struggle against the vilest and grossest system of oppression ever known, it had ever so many sneers and slurs to each cheering, sympathizing word for the champions of Man's right to his own limbs and sinews. Why this was, I stop not here to inquire: I rest on the shameful fact. And the Temperance Reform has likewise been confronted at every step by scurrilous jests, insidious flings, and mean insinuations, from before the foot-lights. Hence thousands, impatient of constant misrepresentation and insult, have abandoned the theatre.

I believe that it is even yet possible to restore the failing prestige of the stage, — to revive its by-gone glories in the ages when eminent moralists, like Addison and Dr. Johnson, were its steadfast patrons, and when actors like Garrick and John Philip Kemble were the honored and intimate friends of the proudest nobles in the land. But, to achieve this, we must have a manager who can nowise be bribed or tempted to minister to prurient appetites, nor pettifog the cause of the oppressor. We must have a stage which commands the respect of the wise and good, of the philanthropic and humane, by never varnishing villany, never sneering at virtue, never pandering to lewd impulses, nor gilding with sophistry the car of triumphant wrong. I know that "confidence is a plant of slow growth," — that, once justly forfeited, it is not easily regained; yet I feel sure that there will yet be a stage which, by years of patient, self-sacrificing devotion to right and justice, to freedom and humanity, will win the favor and support of the noble and worthy, and will exert a benign influence over the earthly progress and destiny of our race.

XXV.

"OLD ZACK."

OUR Whig anticipations of malign results from the defeat of Clay by Polk, in the Presidential contest of 1844, were fully justified by the result. The XXIXth Congress, elected with Polk, was strongly Democratic; Mr. Robert J. Walker, of Mississippi, who was made Secretary of the Treasury, devoted his first annual Report to an elaborate and skilful attack on the Protective policy, and on the Tariff of 1842; and Congress proceeded thereupon to pass a new Tariff, substantially as drafted by Mr. Walker, which not only effaced or modified the Protective features of the Tariff of 1842, but substituted Ad Valorem for nearly every Specific duty embodied in the latter. In other words: where the Tariff of 1842 imposed a duty of so many dollars per ton on a particular kind of iron (for instance), that of 1846 substituted one of 30 per cent. on its value; so that, whenever iron brought a high price, the duty on its importation was correspondingly high; but, when the price ran down to zero, the duty was diminished in proportion; being thus highest when it was least needed by our iron-workers, and lowest when their need of Protection was greatest. And this act, though opposed by every representative of Pennsylvania in Congress but one, was carried through the Senate by the casting vote of Vice-President Dallas, whose nomination had been harped upon in the Presidential canvass as a guaranty to Pennsylvania, that the Tariff of 1842 would stand unaltered! Thus the very staff on which she leaned proved a spear to pierce her.

In 1844, that State had chosen 12 Democrats, 10 Whigs,

and 2 Natives, as her representatives in the XXIXth Congress; electing the Democratic Governor by 4,397 majority. We took an appeal to her people in the election of 1846, and they reversed their verdict of 1844, or, rather, attested that they had been deceived in rendering it; choosing the Whig over the Democratic candidate for Canal Commissioner (the only office filled at that election by a general vote of her people) by a majority of 8,894, on a light vote. At this election, she chose 16 Whigs and 1 Native to 8 Democrats, to represent her in the XXXth Congress. New York, New Jersey, North Carolina, and even Virginia, also showed decided Whig gains; so that, though Maine, New Hampshire, Indiana, Illinois, Missouri, and Michigan remained strongly Democratic, along with the Cotton States, the new House had a small Whig majority, whereby Robert C. Winthrop, of Boston, was chosen Speaker. This was a clear verdict against Mr. Polk's Administration, and more especially against its dealings with the Tariff question in acquiring and in wielding power.

Mr. Polk had not yet been inaugurated when the indorsement and momentum given to the Annexation policy by his election carried a bill, providing equivocally for the acquisition of Texas, through both Houses of the expiring Congress,—the Senate being with difficulty, and not without intimidation, induced to concur therein by a bare majority. President Tyler eagerly signed it, and despatched an agent post-haste to Texas to secure her assent, which was as eagerly given. Mr. Polk, soon after his inauguration (March 4, 1845), despatched a considerable part of our little army, under General Zachary Taylor, to the southern limit of the territory actually possessed by the Texans, near Corpus Christi, where the General halted, and awaited explicit orders — which were finally sent him — to cross the intervening desert, and advance to the Rio Grande del Norte, nearly opposite Matamoros. When he had thus invaded a region which had, except for a very few days, been in peacefully undisturbed possession of Mexicans for at least a century, he was attacked by a Mexican force, under

Ampudia and Arista, which he easily routed, first at Palo Alto;* then, pursuing, at Resaca de la Palma;† whence the Mexicans were driven across the river in disorder; evacuating Matamoros, when General Taylor crossed, without making a shadow of resistance. And the war thus begun was prosecuted with such manifest disproportion of resources and of military prowess, that New Mexico and Upper California were yielded to our arms without a serious contest. General Taylor defeated Santa Anna with an army thrice as numerous as his own at Buena Vista,‡ in the heart of Northern Mexico, where fell Henry Clay, Jr., at the head of his Kentucky regiment, and Hon. John J. Hardin, of Illinois, also commanding a regiment of volunteers, with many others of our bravest and best. The Mexicans' loss was, as usual, considerably heavier than ours. Further advance on this line being impracticable, — the country being in the main a rugged, waterless desert, — General Scott was despatched with an army considerably larger than General Taylor's to Vera Cruz, which he soon reduced;§ advancing thence, with 10,000 men, directly on the city of Mexico; being opposed by Santa Anna, with 15,000 men, at a difficult and strongly fortified pass in the mountains, fifty miles inland, known as Cerro Gordo, which he carried after severe fighting;‖ the Mexicans losing five generals and 3,000 men. Scott thence advanced by easy marches, wholly unopposed, through Xalapa and Perote, to Puebla, where he waited some time in expectation of peace; but none was offered, and he again advanced to the vicinity of the capital, where Santa Anna had collected 30,000 men to stop the march of Scott's 12,000, behind such intrenchments, and in positions of such natural strength, that he deemed them impregnable. But those works were partly turned by a flanking movement toward the South, when that at Contreras was assaulted at 3 A. M.,¶ and carried by the bayonet; the Mexicans losing 22 guns, 700 killed, and 1,500 prisoners. Pursuing their advantage, our soldiers next attacked the Mexicans

* May 8, 1846.
† May 9.
‡ February 22, 1847.
§ March 27.
‖ April 18.
¶ August 20.

at Churubusco (or San Pablo), where the latter were again beaten, after a protracted resistance, with a loss of 1,000 on our side to 5,000 on theirs. The battle closed at the gates of the city of Mexico, which General Scott might at once have entered; but he chose to remain outside, while a volunteer effort at peace-making, by Mr. Nicholas P. Trist, was made, without immediate result. Meantime, the Mexicans had strongly intrenched themselves at Chepultepec, on the south side of the city; and another fight took place at Molino del Rey,* near Tambago, where General Worth's division routed a force of twice its own numbers, inflicting a loss of 3,000, but suffering one of 700, including Colonels Martin Scott and Graham. Chepultepec was next bombarded and assaulted; † the Mexicans being driven from it with great loss, and pursued to the gates of the city, where they were met at midnight by commissioners, who gave notice that Santa Anna was escaping with the remnant of his forces, and that the capital was at General Scott's mercy. Our soldiers — reduced by so many bloody conflicts to about 6,000 effectives — marched in without further resistance, and the Stars and Stripes floated over the "halls of the Montezumas!" Peace — despite the difficulty of finding a responsible government wherewith to make it — was at length negotiated; ‡ Mexico ceded New Mexico and upper California to the United States; abandoned all her rights in or claim to Texas; and received from us an indemnity of $ 15,000,000, whereof $ 3,000,000 were to be reserved, and applied to the payment of our citizens who had claims against her for spoliations. So ended — when our forces had been withdrawn, and the stipulated payments made — our war upon Mexico.

The Presidential canvass of 1848 opened directly thereafter. General Zachary Taylor — a native of Virginia, but long resident in Louisiana — had evinced qualities in the war which strongly commended him to many as a candidate for

* September 8. † September 12, 13. ‡ February 2, 1848.

our highest civil office. Though his part in it was less brilliant, less important, than that of General Scott, he had commended himself far more widely to popular favor. Quiet, resolute, sententious, unostentatious, he was admired by multitudes who profoundly detested the war wherein he had so suddenly achieved renown; and many of them gloated over the prospect of hurling from power the politicians who had so wantonly plunged us into a contest of aggression and invasion by means of the very instrument which they had employed to consummate their purposes.

I non-concurred in this view, most decidedly. General Taylor, though an excellent soldier, had no experience as a statesman, and his capacity for civil administration was wholly undemonstrated. He had never voted; had, apparently, paid little attention to, and taken little interest in politics; and, though inclined toward the Whig party, was but slightly identified with its ideas and its efforts. Nobody could say what were his views regarding Protection, Internal Improvement, or the Currency. On the great question — which our vast acquisitions from Mexico had suddenly invested with the gravest importance — of excluding Slavery from the yet untainted Federal Territories, he had nowise declared himself; and the fact that he was an extensive slaveholder justified a presumption that he, like most slaveholders, deemed it right that any settler in the Territories should be at liberty to take thither, and hold there as property, whatever the laws of his own State recognized as property. We desired to "take a bond of fate" that this view should not be held by a *Whig* President, at all events.

And then I (with many others) wanted to try over again the issue on which I thought we had been defrauded in 1844. It seemed impossible that Pennsylvania (in view of her recent experience) should *again* be persuaded that any Democrat was as good a Protectionist as Henry Clay. True, we had not defeated Governor Shunk's reëlection in 1847; but the running of distinct Whig and Native candidates for Governor rendered our defeat inevitable. New York we had carried in

1847 by a very large majority,—the Free-Soil section of the Democratic party withholding its votes from the pro-Slavery or "Hunker" State ticket. The Whigs of our State were mainly for Clay; we could give him her electoral vote; and this, with Pennsylvania, made his election morally certain. Hence I worked hard to secure his nomination.

The attempt to run a parallel between this case and that of 1840 failed in the most material point. General Harrison may not have been so able as Mr. Clay, but he was not less earnestly and unequivocally a Whig. No one could indicate a shade of difference in their political views. General Harrison's military career was brief and casual; his life had been that of a civilian, honored and trusted by all Administrations between 1800 and 1828,—a Territorial Governor, United States Senator, and Ambassador to Colombia. General Taylor, now an old man, had been in the regular army from boyhood, and was in all things a veteran soldier. His slender acquaintance with and interest in politics was nowise feigned, but was usual and natural with men of his class and position.

The Whig National Convention met at Philadelphia on the 1st of June. There was a pretty full, but not extraordinary, attendance. I believe ex-Governor Morehead, of North Carolina, presided. It was very soon apparent that the shrewd, influential, managing politicians were generally for Taylor, who had a plurality, but not a majority, on the first ballot, and gained steadily on the two following, viz.:—

	1st.	2d.	3d.
Taylor,	111	118	133
Clay,	97	86	74
Scott,	43	49	54
Webster,	22	22	17
Scattering,	6	—	—

An adjournment was now had till next morning; but the issue was already decided, and General Taylor was nominated on the next ballot; when the vote stood: Taylor, 171; Clay, 35; Scott, 60; Webster, 14. All that we Clayites achieved was the substitution of Millard Fillmore as Vice-President for Abbott Lawrence, of Boston, who was on the Taylor slate; but the evidences of dissatisfaction induced the managers to take him off, and let Mr. Fillmore be nominated.

The Democrats had met at Baltimore, May 22, and, after a spirited contest, nominated General Lewis Cass, of Michigan, for President, and General William O. Butler, of Kentucky, for Vice-President. This ticket was respectable both as to character and services, yet its prospects were marred by the fact that that faction of the New York Democracy which had been known as "Barnburners," or Free-Soil men, resenting the admission of their competitors to seats in the Convention, had bolted, and refused to be governed by the result. Ultimately, they united with the Abolitionists, and with sympathizing Democrats in other States, in holding a National Convention at Buffalo, which nominated Martin Van Buren, of New York, for President, and Charles Francis Adams, of Massachusetts, for Vice-President. This ticket, though it obtained no single electoral vote, blasted the hopes of General Cass and the regular Democracy. Running General Dix for Governor of this State, with Seth M. Gates (Abolition) for Lieutenant-Governor, it polled a larger popular vote than was given to Cass; while General Taylor — though he received many thousands fewer of the people's votes than Mr. Clay did four years previous — carried the State by 98,093 plurality. He carried Pennsylvania likewise by 13,357 plurality, and 2,274 majority over all. Vermont and Connecticut gave him pluralities only; while Massachusetts, Rhode Island, New Jersey, Delaware, Maryland, North Carolina, Georgia, Kentucky, Tennessee, Louisiana, and Florida gave him absolute majorities: making fifteen States in all that went for him, giving him 163 electoral votes. General Cass had pluralities only in Maine, Ohio, Indiana, Illinois, Michigan, Wisconsin, and Iowa, just carrying the two last named; he was run very close by Taylor in Virginia, Alabama, and Mississippi, but carried them by majorities, as there was no third party in either. New Hampshire, Texas, and Arkansas were all the States that went strongly for him; making fifteen States in all, casting 127 electoral votes. General Cass received the vote of every State lying north and west of the Ohio and Missouri rivers. General Taylor had a plurality of the popular vote in the Free, and a small majority of that cast in the Slave States; carrying seven of the former and eight of the latter. In the entire Union, the popular vote stood: Taylor, 1,361,450; Cass, 1,221,920; Van Buren, 291,342. (South Carolina choosing her electors by the Legislature, no return of her popular vote can be given.)

In the event, I think the anticipations of those who had favored and those who had opposed General Taylor's nomination as the Whig candidate for President were both realized. He proved an honest, wise, fearless public servant, — true to his convictions, but yielding all proper fealty and deference to those whose votes had placed him in the White House. None more keenly regretted his sudden, untimely death — which occurred on the 9th of July, 1850, after he had been sixteen months President — than those who had most strenuously resisted his nomination.

Yet the fact remains, that the Whig party was demoralized by that nomination, and lost ground thereby in the confidence of the masses. We had fought through our great struggle of 1844 on well-defined, important principles of national policy, whereon we were at odds with our adversaries. We had challenged them to meet us, and had met them, in face-to-face discussion of our respective views, and had shown the people how and why their personal prosperity and well-being would be promoted by the triumph of our ideas, our measures. Beaten in the declared result, the Whig party never stood so strong in the popular conviction that its aims were just and its policy beneficent, as at the close of the canvass of 1844, — as was evinced in our carrying the next House of Representatives. On the other hand, our success in 1848 was the triumph of General Taylor, not of our principles. It showed that a majority preferred General Taylor to General Cass for President: that was all. We had fought the contest, not on our principles, but on our candidates; hence, many who accepted our candidates were indifferent or averse to our principles; and the very House elected with or under General Taylor chose a Democratic Speaker, and was organized to oppose his Administration. The Whigs could not say with Pyrrhus, "Another such victory, and I am ruined!" This one sufficed to disintegrate and destroy their organization. They were at once triumphant and undone.

I think I never saw General Taylor save for a moment at the Inauguration Ball, on the night after his accession to the Presidency. I was never introduced and never wrote to him; and, while I ultimately supported and voted for him, I did not hurry myself to secure his election. In fact, that of 1848 was my easiest and least anxious Presidential canvass since 1824. When a resolve opposing the Wilmot Proviso was laid on the table at the Convention that nominated him, I felt that my zeal, my enthusiasm for the Whig cause was also laid there. Yet I have little faith in third-party movements, — which are generally impelled by an occult purpose to help one of the leading parties by drawing off votes from the other. General Taylor at length avowed himself "a Whig, but not an ultra Whig"; and I believe that was about the literal truth. Zealous Whigs apprehended that he might, if elected, shrink from discharging the officeholders appointed by Tyler and Polk; but, after giving him a trial, they were constrained to admit that he "turned out better than had been expected." He was a man of little education or literary culture, but of signal good sense, coolness, and freedom from prejudice. Few trained and polished statesmen have proved fitter depositaries of civil power than this rough old soldier, whose life had been largely passed in camp and bivouac, on the rude outskirt of civilization, or in savage wastes far beyond it. General Taylor died too soon for his country's good, but not till he had proved himself a wise and good ruler, if not even a great one.

XXVI.

CONGRESS.—MILEAGE.

IN our State Election for 1846, David S. Jackson (Democrat) had been chosen to represent the upper district of our city in the XXXth Congress, by a small majority over Colonel James Monroe (Whig). That majority was obtained by bringing over from Blackwell's Island and polling in the XIXth Ward the adult male paupers domiciled in the Almshouse — not merely those who had resided in our district before they honored our city by condescending to live at her expense, but those who had been gathered in from other districts. Colonel Monroe objected to this as carrying a joke too far; and, on his contesting the return of Mr. Jackson, the House sustained the objection, and unseated Jackson without replacing him by Monroe. The people were required to vote again.

By this time, it was 1848,—the year of General Taylor's election. Colonel Monroe confidently expected to be the Whig candidate, not merely for the vacancy, but for the ensuing (XXXIst) Congress. The delegates, however, were "fixed" for Mr. James Brooks, editor of The Express, who was duly nominated for the XXXIst, while Colonel Monroe was tendered the nomination for the remaining ninety days (at $8 per day) of the XXXth Congress. He declined indignantly; whereupon, that fag-end of a term was tendered to me. I at first resolved to decline also,—not seeing how to leave my business so abruptly for a three months' sojourn at Washington; but the nomination was so kindly pressed upon me, with such apparently cogent reasons therefor, that I accepted it.

There was never any doubt of the result. A politician soon called on me, professing to be from Mr. Brooks, to inquire as to what should be done to secure our election. "Tell Mr. Brooks," I responded, "that we have only to keep so still that no particular attention will be called to us, and General Taylor will carry us both in. There are not voters enough in the district who care about either of us, one way or the other, to swamp the majority that the Taylor Electors cannot fail to receive." The returns proved the correctness of this calculation; the vote of the district standing as follows:—

Electors	Taylor	11,066
XXXth Congress	Greeley	9,932
XXXIst Congress	Brooks	9,709

My Cass competitor had 6,826 votes; my Van Buren ditto, 1,681.

General Taylor received but a plurality of the vote of our entire State, while Mr. Van Buren's popular vote exceeded that for General Cass; but in our city the case was quite otherwise; the aggregates being: Taylor, 29,057; Cass, 18,884; Van Buren, 5,106. I believe that was the very last election wherein our city ever gave a clear majority against the Democratic party, save that in 1854 her vote was pretty evenly divided between the Democratic, Whig-Republican, and Know-Nothing parties. Owing to the Democratic split, nearly or quite all the Representatives elected from our city to the XXXIst Congress were Whigs.

The district from which I was chosen included all our city above Fourteenth Street, with the XIth, XVth, and XVIIth Wards lying below that street. It then contained about one third of the city's entire population; it now contains at least two thirds. When, soon after taking my seat, I introduced a bill authorizing each landless citizen of the United States to occupy and appropriate a small allotment of the National Domain free of charge, a Western member wanted to know why *New York* should busy herself as to the disposal of the Public Lands. I responded that *my* interest in the matter was stimulated by the fact that I represented more landless men than any other member on that floor.

When the pay of Members of Congress was originally fixed, railroads and steamboats as yet were not; stage-coaches ran on a few, and but a few, great highways of travel; most of the members came part of the way on horseback, as some came all the way. It was therefore deemed just, in fixing their compensation at $6 per day, to stipulate that a like sum should be allowed as mileage, or the cost in time and money of journeying each twenty miles on the roads to and from Washington.

Congress, in time, raised its own pay to $8 per day, and $8 for every twenty miles in coming to and returning from Washington. In 1816, the pay was changed to $1,500 per annum, the mileage remaining as before; but the people revolted at this, and swept out nearly every member who had voted for it. Henry Clay had not voted at all on the question; but he was Speaker when the bill passed, and was, therefore, held responsible for its passage, — a responsibility which he gallantly met. Opposed for reëlection by one-armed John Pope, — one of the ablest men then living in Kentucky, but who labored under the serious disadvantage of having been a Federalist, — Mr. Clay had all he could do, by popular addresses and personal appeals, to stem the tide of discontent raised by the passage of the Compensation Act; even his barber — a naturalized Irishman, who had hitherto been one of his most enthusiastic, efficient supporters — maintaining an ominous silence on the subject, until Mr. Clay himself canvassed him, saying: "I trust I may count on *your* hearty support, as usual?" when he responded: "Faith, Mr. Clay, I think I shall vote *this* time for the man who can get but one hand into the Treasury."

Mr. Clay triumphed, as he ever did when a candidate for the House; but he had to promise to favor a repeal of the Compensation Act, which was carried without serious opposition. I think it was at this time that the pay was advanced from $6 to $8 per day: mileage to correspond.

But the introduction and rapid multiplication of steamboats, especially on our great trans-Alleghany network of rivers and lakes, rendered this mileage absurdly too high. A member now traversed a distance of two thousand miles about as quickly as, and at hardly more expense than, his predecessor by half a century must have incurred on a journey of two hundred miles, for which the latter was paid $80, and the former $800.

Nor was this all. The steamboat routes, though much more swiftly and cheaply traversed, were nearly twice—sometimes thrice—the length of the stage and horseback roads they superseded. And—as the law said at first, and continued to say, that they were to charge Mileage "by the usually travelled route"—they now charged and received twice as much for travelling five days in a sumptuous cabin, replete with every luxury, as their fathers paid for roughing it over the mountains in fifteen to twenty days, at a far greater cost.

Colonel Benton,—who deemed himself, and meant to be, an honest man,—somewhere about 1836, made a claim on the Treasury for about $2,000, which (he computed) was required to bring up his Mileage in past years to a par with the charges of others!—and this amount was allowed and paid him.

Said First Comptroller Elisha Whittlesey to me, near the close of his long, upright, and useful public life: "Even Mr. Calhoun has increased his charge for Mileage since the old horseback and stage-coach days: and there is just one man in Congress who charges Mileage now as all did then. That man is HENRY CLAY."

Getting into the House, I had access to the schedules of Compensation and Mileage, which (though they are said to be printed) were not (and *are* not) easily found by outsiders; and I resolved to improve my opportunity. So I hired a reporter to transcribe them, and (using as a basis of comparison the United States Topographer's official statement of the distances from Washington, by the most direct mail-route, of each post-office in the country) I aimed to show exactly how much could be saved, in the case of each member, by computing Mileage on the most direct post-route instead of "the usually travelled route." This *exposé*, when prepared, was transmitted to New York, duly appeared in The Tribune, and so came back to Washington.

I had expected that it would kick up some dust; but my expectations were far outrun. It happened that two of our Whig members from Ohio had been run out by close votes at the recent election (October, 1848), and that the crooked Mileage they charged had been used with effect by their opponents in the canvass. It might be all right for them to charge Mileage from the heart of Ohio around by Lake Erie to Washington, when the Government had constructed a first-rate national road from the vicinity of Baltimore due west through Zanesville and Columbus to Indianapolis; but the people did n't or would n't see it. These beaten sore-heads were specially prompt and eager in preaching a crusade against me on the floor.

Good and true men shared, to some extent, their feelings. Rarely, for example, has our country been served by a purer, more upright man than Hon. Jacob Collamer, of Vermont. "Mr. Greeley," said he to me, "is it not hard that I should be held up to the public as a swindler? Look at the facts: I live in Woodstock. I take the stage to Windsor, — twenty-two miles, — where I strike the nearest railroad. I ride thence by rail to Boston; from Boston to New York; from New York to Washington. It is the easiest and quickest route I can take, — the natural route of travel. I charge for the miles I actually travel, — not one more. Why is not this right?"

"Judge," I responded, "now hear *me*. Your predecessors, I happen to know, took stage from Woodstock to Rutland; from Rutland to Troy; thence steamboat to New York; thence railroad to Washington. It is now cheaper and easier for you to go by Boston, — three hundred miles farther. Will you tell me why you should be paid $240 more per annum because this cheaper and easier route has lately been opened? I concede you the advantage of the improved transit. I protest against your charging $240, and the people paying it, therefor. That is not just."

The only answer I ever received to this way of putting the case was, "Such is the law." But Congress was *master* of the law,—able, at any time, to make it just,—therefore *bound* to make it just. It was the object of my *exposé* to compel such adjustment.

General J. J. McKay, of North Carolina, once came across to my seat. He was a stern, pro-Slavery Democrat, and it was not the habit of such to waste civilities on me.

"Mr. Greeley," he said, "you have printed me as charging seven miles more than the actual distance from my home to Washington. The fact is not so. I charge precisely as you say is just,—by the shortest mail-route; but I live seven miles beyond my post-office, and I charge from my own house."

"How could I know that?" I inquired.

"You could not," he replied. "I am not blaming you; on the contrary, I thank you for what you have done. It was needed, and will do good. I only wished that you should know the facts."

As I remember, the Mileage *exposé* was first brought formally to the notice of the House by Hon. William Sawyer, of Ohio,—a very bitter Democrat, who had been annoyed, ere this, by the strictures of a correspondent of The Tribune on his habit of eating a luncheon in the House behind the Speaker's chair. He had a new grievance in the Mileage *exposé*,—in that, though the *exposé* correctly stated the difference between *his* Mileage as charged, and what it would be if computed by the most direct mail-routes, there was a blunder in the case of his nearest Whig neighbor, Hon. Robert C. Schenck, whose overcharge was not made nearly so much as it should be. Schenck promptly rose and offered to swap with his colleague, if *that* would afford him any satisfaction. It did n't.

There was one shabby dodge of those who stretched their Mileage to the utmost, that challenged, but did not command, my admiration: Each of them would find out which old stager living near him had crowded his Mileage up to the highest high-water mark; and, upon being asked by the Chairman of the Committee on Mileage to state his distance from Washington, would respond, "I live —— miles beyond [or this side of] Mr. ——." The Chairman would make out his Mileage accordingly; and now the indignantly virtuous beneficiary would say, "*I* had nothing to do with the matter. The Chairman made out my Mileage as he saw fit, and I took whatever he allowed me."

The cleverer wounded pigeons knew a great deal better than to take issue with me directly on the Mileage question; whereon (as I told them) they were a party of ten-score, confronted by twenty-odd millions. Their true expedient was a back-fire; and they contrived to set one. This Congress had, at its former session (when I was not a member), voted itself the books which it had for years been the custom to purchase for each new member, consisting of American Archives, Debates in Congress, etc., now swelled (by enormous charges) to a cost of about $1,000 per man. Those books had been ordered and bought; nothing remained but to pay for them. I had resolved to vote against this item when the bill which contained it came up in the House, though I knew it must be paid; for I apprehended that the advocates of what are called liberal appropriations would seek to make capital out of my voting for such an item. Yet, when the usual Deficiency Bill was rapidly going through the House in Committee of the Whole, the members being called on a dozen times in twenty minutes to vote (by rising) for or against some motion or item, a mischievous neighbor called out to me, "There,—you 've voted for the books!" I presume it was so; and his exultation was based on his knowledge that it was my purpose to vote against them. And yet (as I had often said) had those books been bought at fair prices, and deposited as public property by the receivers in public libraries and county clerk's offices in their respective districts, the outlay would have been judicious and proper. It was well known, however, that many to whom the books were voted never took nor saw them,—merely drawing an order for them and selling it to the book-suppliers for so much cash in hand,—less than half what the books cost the Treasury. In one case, a member well known to me was reputed to have sold his order, and gambled away the proceeds, before going to his lodging the night after the appropriation was voted.

A concerted effort was made to involve me in glaring inconsistency on this subject,—A. testified that I had justified the book-buying,—B. that I had denied having intended to vote for it,—and so on. I presume that what each so asserted was true, or nearly so; a very slight explanation might have harmonized statements which were so made as to seem in conflict. For a time, it looked as though the Mileage men had the upper hand of me; and I was told that a paper was drawn up for signatures to see how many would agree to stand by each other in voting my expulsion, but that the movement was crushed by a terse interrogatory remonstrance from Hon. John Wentworth, then a leading Democrat.

"Why, you blessed fools!" warmly inquired 'long John,' "do you want to make him President?"

They did n't, and so subsided.

Much has been said on sundry occasions about the time *I* wasted, the trouble *I* made, in the House, concerning Mileage. In fact, I did not introduce the subject there,—made no move regarding it,—and scarcely alluded to it. Hon. Elijah Embree, of Indiana, moved an amendment to the proper Appropriation Bill, providing that Mileage should thenceforth be charged by the most direct mail-route,—a clause which would have saved to the Treasury more than $100,000 per annum,—and I voted for it; but it was beaten in Committee of the Whole, and I think never came to the yeas and nays. At all events, the abuse was not corrected, and has not yet been; though the last Congress, in raising its own pay from $3,000 to $5,000 per annum, had the grace to cut down Mileage from forty to twenty cents per mile by "the usually travelled route." But I think it is no longer "usual" for a man living in central Ohio, Indiana, or Illinois to "swing around the circle," *via* Detroit, Buffalo, Albany, and New York, in travelling from home to Washington city; in fact, railroads are generally straightening and shortening the "usual" routes of travel. I presume, therefore, that the worst excesses of the Mileage swindle have ere this been abated. So mote it be!

I do not imply that legislation, whether in Congress or elsewhere, is purer and cleaner now than it was twenty or forty years ago. On the contrary, I judge that it is oftener swayed, to the prejudice of the public interest, by considerations of personal advantage, and that the evil tends strongly to increase and diffuse itself. The chartering of railroads through public lands which are required (as is clearly just) to contribute to their construction, whether by liberal grants of territory or by direct subsidies in cash, and many kindred devices for promoting at once public and private prosperity, have strongly tended to render legislation mercenary, whether in Congress, in State legislatures, or in municipal councils. When I was in the House, there were ten or twelve members — not more than twelve, I am confident — who were generally presumed to be "on the make," as the phrase is; and they were a class by themselves, as clearly as if they were so many black sheep in a large flock of white ones. I would gladly believe that this class has not since increased in numbers or in impudence; but the facts do not justify that presumption.

XXVII.

CONGRESS AS IT WAS.

WHEN I first saw the Congress of the United States, in the Summer of 1836, I judge that the Senate was the ablest body of its numbers on earth. Though there were scarcely more than fifty Senators in all, among them were Henry Clay, Daniel Webster, John C. Calhoun, Silas Wright, John Forsyth, John M. Clayton, George B. Poindexter, Thomas Ewing, William C. Preston, Nathaniel P. Tallmadge, and James Buchanan. The House, though less noticeably strong, contained many able and eminent members, headed by the "old man eloquent," John Quincy Adams, who had been — with James K. Polk and Franklin Pierce, of whom each was to be — President of the United States.

When I entered the House twelve years later, Mr. Adams had recently died in the Capitol, and been succeeded by Horace Mann, who won much honor in his educational, but little distinction in his parliamentary, career. The Senate was decidedly weaker than when I first looked down on it from the gallery; but Messrs. Webster, Calhoun, and Clayton were still members, while Messrs. Wright, Forsyth, Poindexter, and Preston had passed away, and Mr. Ewing was living (as he still is) in retirement. Mr. Polk was President, and Mr. Buchanan was his Secretary of State. Mr. Clay had resigned in 1842, and had not since been in public life, save that he was a candidate for President in 1844; but he was reëlected to the Senate that winter, and served thenceforth till his death, June 29, 1852. Mr. Pierce, after serving four years in the House, and five in the Senate, had resigned in 1843, and had since been in retirement, save that he took part in the Mexican War. He had been so completely lost to public life that his nomination for President, three or four years afterward, seemed nearly equivalent to a resurrection.

Abraham Lincoln and Andrew Johnson (each then about forty years old) were members of the House to which I was chosen, as Mr. Johnson had been of the two preceding and remained through the two following, when he was translated to the Senate. Mr. Johnson, being a Democrat, seldom visited our side of the hall, and I saw much less of him than of Mr. Lincoln, who was a Whig, and who, though a new member, was personally a favorite on our side. He seemed a quiet, good-natured man, did not aspire to leadership, and seldom claimed the floor. I think he made but one set speech during that session, and this speech was by no means a long one. Though a strong partisan, he voted against the bulk of his party once or twice, when that course was dictated by his convictions. He was one of the most moderate, though firm, opponents of Slavery Extension, and notably of a buoyant, cheerful spirit. It will surprise some to hear that, though I was often in his company thenceforward till his death, and long on terms of friendly intimacy with him, I never heard him tell an anecdote or story.

I judge that Massachusetts had, relatively, the strongest delegation in the House; as hers included Robert C. Winthrop (Speaker), Julius Rockwell, Joseph Grinnell, Charles Hudson, George Ashmun, Horace Mann, and John G. Palfrey. Ohio probably ranked next; being in part represented by Samuel F. Vinton (then Chairman of Ways and Means), Robert C. Schenck (who now fills that post), Joshua R. Giddings, and Joseph M. Root. Of the Democrats in that House, those whom I recollect as strongest were James J. McKay and Abraham W. Venable of North Carolina, Howell Cobb of Georgia, John Wentworth of Illinois, Jacob Thompson of Mississippi, and George W. Jones of Tennessee. Messrs. Alexander H. Stephens and Robert Toombs of Georgia were conspicuous members, but both then Whigs, though they have since been quite otherwise. Vermont had already been reduced to three representatives; but two of these were Jacob Collamer and George P. Marsh. Virginia had (I believe) more Whigs in that House than in any before or since; and among them were John M. Botts, William L. Goggin, and John S. Pendleton. I judge that A. H. Stephens was the most acute, and perhaps the ablest, member of that House; but one of the cleverest, if he had known how to take good care of himself, was William T. Haskell of Tennessee, of whom the world never heard. He was not reëlected, and died a few years afterward.

I do not propose to give here a history of the little that was achieved or the much that was said at that short session. As those were the last sands of an Administration already superseded, the old heads of either party were indisposed to have much done beside passing the necessary Appropriation bills; and they were able to have substantially their own way.

It used to be a standing topic of complaint, in Congress as well as out of it, that too much time was wasted there in debate on abstractions, and especially on questions relating to Slavery. I was repeatedly asked, "Don't you want the floor for a speech on the Slavery question?" — to which I answered that I did not, — that my views on that subject were already tolerably well known, and that I did not see how I could use the time of the House to public advantage by haranguing it on the threadbare topic. I think I did once speak some twenty minutes on the ruling theme; but it was on an evening set apart for general debate, and when the time was to be thus wasted anyhow. Yet, one day, when the House was in Committee on some bill having no necessary or proper connection with Slavery, a member rose and said, "Mr. Chairman, I propose to improve this opportunity to give my views on the Slavery question." Hereupon another rose and said, "Mr. Chairman, I object. The subject of Slavery is not now in order. The rule of the House is plain and imperative: the only subject that can be debated is that expressly before us. I insist that the gentleman shall proceed, if at all, in order." The Chairman decided that, since it had long been the tolerated practice to discuss anything pertaining to the state of the Union when in Committee on that subject, he should rule that the gentleman was *in* order; and, though we rallied a respectable force to overrule this decision, it was triumphantly sustained, — those who were frequently denouncing "Slavery agitation" taking the lead in its support.

Sundry attempts at reforming what were considered abuses were made that Winter, but without brilliant success. We tried to abolish flogging in the Navy, but were beaten. I think it was Mr. (now General) Schenck who raised a laugh against us by proposing so to amend that the commander of a ship of war should never order a sail spread or reefed without calling all hands and taking a vote of his crew on the question. We were temporarily successful in voting in Committee to stop dealing out strong drink to the sailors and marines in our Navy, though this, too, was ultimately defeated; but, in the first flush of our delusive triumph, a member sitting near me, who had voted to stop the grog ration, said to a friend who (I believe) had voted the same way, — "Gid, that was a glorious vote we have just taken." "Yes, glorious," was the ready response. "Gid," resumed the elated reformer, "let us go and take a drink on the strength of it." "Agreed," was the willing echo; and they went.

I had been but a few days on the floor, when a leading member on our side came along canvassing in behalf of an embryo proposition that the House should pay from its contingent fund seven dollars and a half per column each to The Union and The National Intelligencer respectively for reporting and printing our debates. "You can't pass that scheme here," I said, somewhat abruptly. "Well, sir, I believe you have been a member of this House some four or five days," he retorted; "and you seem to begin early to decide what measures can and what cannot pass." "No matter," I rejoined, "you can't pass that measure here." Nevertheless, he tried, but could n't. Up to this period, I had been favorably regarded and kindly treated by Messrs. Gales and Seaton, the excellent but unthrifty editors of The National Intelligencer; but they wasted no more civilities nor smiles on me so long as they lived respectively. They evidently could not realize that any one could oppose such a proposition from any impulse other than one of personal hostility or general malignity.

An abuse had crept in, a few years before, at the close of a long, exhausting session, when some liberal soul proposed that each of the sub-officers and attachés of Congress (whose name is Legion) be paid two hundred and fifty dollars extra because of such protracted labor. Thenceforth, this gratuity was repeated at the close of each session, — the money being taken by the generous members, not from their own pockets, but Uncle Sam's, and the vote being now that "The *usual* extra compensation," &c. As our session was a light as well as a short one, some of us determined to stop this Treasury leak; and we did it once or twice, to the chagrin of the movers. At length, came the last night of the session, and with it a magnificent "spread," free to all members, in one of the Committee-rooms, paid for by a levy of five dollars per head from the regiment of underlings who hoped thus to secure their "usual" gratuity; giving each a net profit on the investment of two hundred and forty-five dollars. After the House had been duly mellowed and warmed, a resolve to pay the "usual extra compensation" was sprung, but failed, — two thirds in the affirmative being necessary to effect the requisite suspension of the rules. Nothing daunted, the operators drew off to repair damages; and soon there was moved a resolve to pay the chaplain of the House his stipend from the Contingent Fund, and to suspend the rules to accord this resolve an immediate consideration.

"I object, Mr. Speaker," I at once interposed; "we all know that the chaplain's salary has not been left unprovided for to this time. This is a *ruse*, — I call for the Yeas and Nays on suspending the rules."

"Shame! shame!" rose and reverberated on every side; "don't keep the chaplain out of his hard-earned money! Refuse the Yeas and Nays!"

They were accordingly refused; the rules were indignantly suspended, and the resolution received.

"And now, Mr. Speaker," said the member who had been cast for this part, "I move to amend the resolve before us by adding the usual extra compensation to the sub-clerks, door-keepers, and other *employés* of the House."

No sooner said than done; debate was cut off, and the amendment prevailed. The resolve, as amended, was rushed through; and our *employés* pocketed their two hundred and fifty dollars each, less the five dollars so recently and judiciously invested as aforesaid.

I was placed by the Speaker on the Committee on Public Lands, whereof Judge Collamer of Vermont was chairman, and which was mainly composed of worthy, upright men, intent on standing up for public right against private greed. Various fair-seeming bills and claims came before us, some of which had passed the Senate, yet which we put our heel on as barefaced robberies. Virginia land-claims (for additional bounty lands to her Revolutionary soldiers), a preemption to part of Rock Island, a preëmption claim to Eelgrass Island, etc., were among the jobs remorselessly slaughtered by us: our self-complacency — not to say, self-conceit — steadily augmenting. At length, there came along a meek, innocent-looking stranger, by whom we were nicely taken in and thoroughly done for. It was a bill to cede to the several New States (so called) such portions of the unsold public lands within their limits respectively as were submerged or sodden, and thus rendered useless and pestilential, — that is, swamps, marshes, bogs, fens, etc. These lands, we were told, were not merely worthless while undrained: they bred fevers, ague, and all manner of zymotic diseases, shortening the lives of the pioneers, and rendering good lands adjacent unhealthy and worthless. But cede these swamp lands to the States including them respectively, on condition that they should sell them and devote the proceeds to draining and improving them, and everything would be lovely, — the neighboring dry lands would sell readily, and the Treasury be generously replenished, etc. There was never a cat rolled whiter in meal; and I, for one, was completely duped. As I recollect, the bill did not pass at that session; but we reported strongly in its favor; and that report, doubtless, aided to carry the measure through the next Congress. The consequence was a reckless and fraudulent transfer to certain States of millions on millions of choice public lands, whole sections of which had not muck enough on their surface to accommodate a single fair-sized frog; while the appropriation of the proceeds to draining proved a farce and a sham. The lands went, — all of them that had standing water enough on a square mile of their surface to float a duck in March, with a good deal more beside; while never a shake of ague has any pioneer been spared by reason of all the drainage done under this specious act. I can only hope that some of us learned a wholesome lesson of distrust.

The last night of a session is usually a long one; and ours was not only long, but excited. The two Houses were at variance: The House desiring (at least, voting) to prohibit the introduction of Slavery into the vast territories just then acquired from Mexico; the Senate dissenting from that policy. Of course, we who voted for the restriction could not carry it through nor over the Senate. But that body was not content to stand on the defensive: it attached to the great Civil and Diplomatic Appropriation bill (since divided) a provision for the organization of the new Territories, — of course, without the restriction against Slavery, — and, in effect, said to us, "You shall agree to this, or the new [Taylor] Administration shall not have a dollar to spend after the 1st of July ensuing." We had one or two conferences by committee; but neither House would give way. Finally, the bill came back to us on this last evening, — the Senate insisting on its Territorial amendment. Each side had rallied in full force (there were but three of all the representatives chosen from the Slave States who were not in their seats), and we were morally certain to be beaten on a motion to recede, — three or four weak brethren changing their votes rather than leave the Government penniless; when some one on our side — I believe it was Richard W. Thompson of Indiana — got in a motion to *concur, with an amendment.* This amendment accepted the Senate's project of organizing the new Territories, barely adding a stipulation that *the existing laws thereof should remain in force till changed by consent of Congress.* (The existing laws were those of Mexico, and forbade Slavery.) This motion prevailed (as I recollect, the vote on one important division stood one hundred and eleven to one hundred and ten), and completely changed the whole aspect of the matter. The pro-Slavery men were now as anxious to expunge the Territorial clause as they had previously been determined to insert it at all hazards; and the Senate struck out its cherished provision, and let the Appropriation bill pass as it originally was, leaving the question of Slavery in the new Territories as a legacy of trouble to the incoming Administration. Never was a parliamentary move more clever than that motion to concur with an amendment.

When it had been carried through our House, and while the Senate was chewing upon it, there ensued a hiatus or interregnum, — the House having really nothing to do but wait. At such times, any member who has a pet project or bill asks a suspension of the rules in favor of its consideration. Among these motions was one by Mr. Robert W. Johnson of Arkansas, who wished the House to consider a bill providing payment for horses lost by his constituents while acting as volunteers in Indian wars. His motion to suspend the rules failed; when I drew from my drawer a resolve, which had lain there for weeks, proposing that our country take the general name of COLUMBIA, in honor of the great discoverer. I was making a few remarks introductory to my motion to suspend the rules, — which I knew would be defeated, — when, as the affair was afterward explained to me, Mr. R. W. Johnson, my predecessor on the floor, turned upon Mr. O. B. Ficklin of Illinois, who sat very near him, and angrily said: "Ficklin, why do you always oppose any motion I make?" "I did not oppose your motion," was the prompt and true reply. "You lie!" rejoined Johnson, whose powers of observation were not then in their best estate, and he sprang forward as though to clutch Ficklin; when Mr. Samuel W. Inge of Alabama rushed upon the latter, and struck him two or three blows with a cane. "Order! Order! — Sergeant-at-arms, do your duty!" interposed the Speaker; and the affray was promptly arrested. "Why, Inge, what did you fall upon Ficklin for?" inquired one of his neighbors; Ficklin being an intensely pro-Slavery Democrat, as were Inge and Johnson. "Why, I thought," explained Inge, "that the fight between the North and the South had commenced, and I might as well pitch in." I did not hear him say this; but it was reported to me directly afterward, and I have no doubt that he said and thought so.

Mr. Giddings went over to the Democratic side of the House that night, and made some jocular remark to an acquaintance on the change of aspect since we had made and sustained our motion to concur with an amendment, — when he was assaulted, and was glad to get away quite rapidly. I am confident I could not have passed quietly through that side of the House between ten and two o'clock of that night without being assaulted; and, had I resisted, beaten within an inch of my life, if not killed outright. Yet I had proposed nothing, said nothing, on the exciting topic; I was obnoxious only because I was presumed earnestly hostile to Slavery.

I believe it was just 7 A. M. of the 4th of March, 1849, — the day of General Taylor's inauguration, — when the two Houses, having finished all the inevitable business of the session, were adjourned without day, and I walked down to my hotel, free thenceforth to mind my own business. I have not since been a member, nor held any post under the Federal Government; it is not likely that I shall ever again hold one; yet I look back upon those three months I spent in Congress as among the most profitably employed of any in the course of my life. I saw things from a novel point of view; and, if I came away from the Capitol no wiser than I went thither, the fault was entirely my own.

XXVIII.

GLAMOUR.

I BELIEVE I heard vaguely of what were called "The Rochester Knockings" soon after they were first proclaimed, or testified to, in the Spring of 1848; but they did not attract my attention till, during a brief absence from New York, — perhaps while in Congress, — I perused a connected, circumstantial account of the alleged phenomena, signed by several prominent citizens of Rochester, and communicated by them to The Tribune, wherein I read it. It made little impression on my mind, though I never had that repugnance to, or stubborn incredulity regarding, occurrences called supernatural which is evinced by many. My consciousness of ignorance of the extent or limitations of the natural is so vivid, that I never could realize that difficulty in crediting what are termed miracles, which many affirm. Doubtless, the first person who observed the attraction of iron by the magnet supposed he had stumbled upon a contradiction to, or violation of, the laws of nature, when he had merely enlarged his own acquaintance with natural phenomena. The fly that sees a rock lifted from its bed may fancy himself witness of a miracle, when what he sees is merely the interposition of a power, the action of a force, which transcends his narrow conceptions, his ephemeral experience. I know so very little of nature, that I cannot determine at a glance what is or is not supernatural; but I know that things do occur which are decidedly superusual, and I rest in the fact without being able, or feeling required, to explain it.

I believe that it was early in 1850 that the Fox family, in

which the so-called Knockings had first occurred or been noted,—first at the little hamlet known as Hydesville, near Newark, Wayne Co., N. Y.,—came to New York, and stopped at a hotel, where I called upon them, and heard the so-called "raps," but was neither edified nor enlightened thereby. Nothing transpired beyond the "rappings"; which, even if deemed inexplicable, did not much interest me. In fact, I should have regretted that any of *my* departed ones had been impelled to address me in the presence and hearing of the motley throng of strangers gathered around the table on which the "raps" were generally made.

I had no desire for a second "sitting," and might never have had one; but my wife—then specially and deeply interested in all that pertains to the unseen world, because of the recent loss of our darling "Pickie"—visited the Foxes twice or thrice at their hotel, and invited them thence to spend some week or so with her at our house. There, along with much that seemed trivial, unsatisfactory, and unlike what might naturally be expected from the land of souls, I received some responses to my questions of a very remarkable character, evincing knowledge of occurrences of which no one, not an inmate of our family in former years, could well have been cognizant. Most of these could have no significance or cogency to strangers; but one of them seems worth narrating.

It was the second or third day after the Foxes came to our house. I had worked very hard and late at the office the night before, reaching home after all others were in bed; so I did not rise till all had had breakfast and had gone out, my wife included. When I rose at last, I took a book, and, reading on a lounge in our front parlor, soon fell into an imperfect doze, during which there called a Mrs. Freeman, termed a clairvoyant, from Boston, with her husband and an invalid gentleman. They had together visited Niagara Falls, had seen the Foxes at Rochester on their way; and now, returning, had sought them at their hotel, and followed them thence to our house. As they did not inquire for me, being unaware of, as well as indifferent to, my presence in the house, they were shown into the back parlor, separated by sliding-doors from that in which I was, and they there awaited the return of the Foxes, which occurred in about half an hour. The sliding-doors being imperfectly closed, I drowsily heard the strangers urge the Foxes to accompany them to their hotel; saying, "We feel like intruders here." This impelled me to rise and go into the back parlor, in order to make the strangers welcome. Mrs. Freeman had been already, or was soon afterward, magnetized by her husband into the state termed clairvoyance, wherein she professed to see spirits related to those who were put into magnetic *rapport* with her. What she reported as of or from those spirits might be ever so true or false for aught *I* know. At length — merely to make the strangers feel more at their ease — I said, "Mr. Freeman, may not *I* be put into communication with spirits through Mrs. Freeman?" to which he readily assented, placed my hand in hers, made a few passes, and bade me ask such questions as I would. As she had just reported the presence of spirit brothers and sisters of others, I asked, "Mrs. Freeman, do you see any brothers or sisters of *mine* in the spirit world?" She gazed a minute intently, then responded, "Yes, there is one; his name is Horace," and then proceeded to describe a child quite circumstantially. I made no remark when she had concluded, though it seemed to me a very wild *guess*, even had she known that I had barely one departed brother, that his name was identical with my own, though such was the fact. I resumed, "Mrs. Freeman, do you see any *more* brothers or sisters of mine in the spirit world?" She looked again as before; then eagerly said, "Yes, there is another; her name is Anna — no — her name is Almira — no (perplexedly), I cannot get the name exactly, — yet it begins with A." Now the only sister I ever lost was named *Arminda*, and she, as well as my brother, died before I was born, — he being three, and she scarcely two, years old. They were buried in a secluded rural graveyard in Bedford, N. H., about sixty years ago, and no stone marks their resting-place. Even my wife did not know their names, and certainly no one else present but myself did. And, if Mrs. Freeman obtained one of these names from my mind (as one theory affirms) why not the other as well? since each was there as clearly as the other.

Not long after this, I had called on Mademoiselle Jenny Lind, then a new-comer among us, and was conversing about the current marvel with the late N. P. Willis, while Mademoiselle Lind was devoting herself more especially to some other callers. Our conversation caught Mademoiselle Lind's ear, and arrested her attention; so, after making some inquiries, she asked if she could witness the so-called "Manifestations."

I answered that she could do so by coming to my house in the heart of the city, as Katy Fox was then staying with us. She assented, and a time was fixed for her call; at which time she appeared, with a considerable retinue of total strangers. All were soon seated around a table, and the "rappings" were soon audible and abundant. "Take your hands from under the table!" Mademoiselle Jenny called across to me in the tone and manner of an indifferently bold archduchess. "What?" I asked, not distinctly comprehending her. "Take your hands from under the table!" she imperiously repeated; and I now understood that she suspected me of causing, by some legerdemain, the puzzling concussions. I instantly clasped my hands over my head, and there kept them until the sitting closed, as it did very soon. I need hardly add that this made not the smallest difference with the "rappings"; but I was thoroughly and finally cured of any desire to exhibit or commend them to strangers.

Not long afterward, I witnessed what I strongly suspected to be a juggle or trick on the part of a "medium," which gave me a disrelish for the whole business, and I have seen very little of it since. I never saw a "spirit hand," though persons in whose veracity I have full confidence assure me that they have done so. (I do not say that they were or were not deluded or mistaken.) But I have sat with three others around a small table, with every one of our eight hands lying plainly, palpably, on that table, and heard rapid writing with a pencil on paper, which, perfectly white, we had just previously placed under that table; and have, the next minute, picked up that paper with a sensible, straightforward message of twenty to fifty words fairly written thereon. I do not say by whom, or by what, said message was written; yet I am quite confident that none of the persons present, who were visible to mortal eyes, wrote it.

And here let me deal with the hypothesis of jugglery, knee-joint rattling, toe-cracking, &c. I have no doubt that pretended "mediums" have often amazed their visitors by feats of jugglery, — indeed, I am confident that I have been present when they did so. In so far as the hypothesis of spirit agency rests on the integrity of the "mediums," I cannot deem it established. Most of them are persons of no especial moral elevation; and I know that more than one of them has endeavored to simulate "raps" when the genuine could not be evoked. Let us assume, then, that the "raps" prove just nothing at all beyond the bare fact that sounds have often been produced by some agency or impulse which we do not fully understand, and that all the physical phenomena have been, or may be, simulated or paralleled by such jugglers as Houdin, Blitz, the Fakir of Ava, &c. But the amazing sleight of hand of these accomplished performers is the result of protracted, laborious training, by predecessors nearly or quite as adroit and dexterous as themselves; while the "mediums" are often children of tender years, who had no such training, have no special dexterity, and some of whom are known to be awkward and clumsy in their movements. The jugglery hypothesis utterly fails to account for occurrences which I have personally witnessed, to say nothing of others.

Nor can I unreservedly accept the hypothesis which ascribes the so-called "spiritual" phenomena to a demoniac origin. That might account satisfactorily for some of them, but not for all. For instance: In the township of Wayne, Erie Co., Pa., near the house of my father and brother, there lived, twelve or fifteen years ago, a farmer well known to me, named King, who had many good traits, and one bad habit, — that of keeping a barrel of whiskey in his house, and dealing out the villanous fluid at so much per quart or pint to his thirsty neighbors. Having recently lost a beloved daughter, he had recourse to "spiritualism," (abominable term!) and received many messages from what purported to be his lost child, — one or more of which insisted that the aforesaid whiskey-barrel must be expelled from his premises, and never reinstated. So said, so done, greatly to the benefit of the neighborhood. Now, I feel confident that the Devil never sent nor dictated *that* message; for, if he did, his character has been grossly belied, and his biography ought to be re-written.

The failures of the "mediums" were more convincing to my mind than their successes. A juggler can do nearly as well at one time as another; but I have known the most eminent "mediums" spend a long evening in trying to evoke the "spiritual phenomena," without a gleam of success. I have known this to occur when they were particularly anxious — and for obviously good reasons — to astound and convince those who were present and expectant; yet not even the faintest "rap" could they scare up. Had they been jugglers, they could not have failed so utterly, ignominiously.

But, while the sterile "sittings" contributed quite as much as the other sort to convince me that the "rappings" were not *all* imposture and fraud, they served decidedly to disincline me to devote my time to what is called "investigation." To sit for two dreary, mortal hours in a darkened room, in a mixed company, waiting for some one's disembodied grandfather or aunt to tip a table or rap on a door, is dull music at best; but so to sit *in vain* is disgusting.

I close with a few general deductions from all I have seen or known of "spirit-rapping."

I. Those who discharge promptly and faithfully all their duties to those who "still live" in the flesh can have little time for poking and peering into the life beyond the grave. Better attend to each world in its proper order.

II. Those who claim, through the "mediums," to be Shakespeare, Milton, Byron, &c., and try to prove it by writing poetry, invariably come to grief. I cannot recall a line of "spiritual" poetry that is not weak, if not execrable, save that of Rev. Thomas L. Harris, who *is* a poet still in the flesh. After he dies, I predict that the poetry sent us as his will be much worse than he ever wrote while in the body. Even Tupper, appalling as is the prospect, will be dribbling worse rhymes upon us after death than even *he* perpetrated while on earth.

III. As a general rule, the so-called "spiritual communications" are vague, unreal, shadowy, trivial. They are not what we should expect our departed friends to say to us. I never could feel that the lost relative or friend who professed to be addressing me was actually present. I do not doubt that foolish, trifling people remain so (measurably) after they have passed the dark river; I perceive that trivial questions must necessarily invite trivial answers; but, after making all due allowance, I insist that the "spiritual" literature of the day, in so far as it purports to consist of communications or revelations from the future life, is more inane and trashy than it could be if the sages and heroes, the saints and poets, of by-gone days were really speaking to us through these pretended revelations.

IV. Not only is it true (as we should in any case presume) that nearly all attempts of the so-called "mediums" to guide speculators as to events yet future have proved melancholy failures, but it is demonstrated that the so-called "spirits" are often ignorant of events which have already transpired. They did not help fish up the broken Atlantic Cable, nor find Sir John Franklin, nor dispel the mystery which still shrouds the fate of the crew and passengers of the doomed steamship President, — and so of a thousand instances wherein their presumed knowledge might have been of use to us darkly seeing mortals. All that we have learned of them has added little or nothing to our knowledge, unless it be in enabling us to answer with more confidence that old, momentous question, "If a man die, shall he live again?"

V. On the whole (though I say it with regret) it seems to

me that the great body of the "Spiritualists" have not been rendered better men and women — better husbands, wives, parents, children — by their new faith. I think some have been improved by it, — while many who were previously good are good still, — and some have morally deteriorated. I judge that laxer notions respecting Marriage, Divorce, Chastity, and stern Morality generally, have advanced in the wake of "Spiritualism." And, while I am fully aware that religious mania so-called has usually a purely material origin, so that revivals have often been charged with making persons insane whose insanity took its hue from the topic of the hour, but owed its existence to purely physical causes, I still judge that the aggregate of both Insanity and Suicide has been increased by "Spiritualism."

VI. I do not know that these "communications" made through "mediums" proceed from those who are said to be their authors, nor from the spirits of the departed at all. Certain developments strongly indicate that they do; others, that they do not. We know that they *say* they do, which is evidence so far as it goes, and is not directly contradicted or rebutted. That *some* of them are the result of juggle, collusion, or trick, I am confident; that others are *not*, I decidedly believe. The only certain conclusion in the premises to which my mind has been led is forcibly set forth by Shakespeare in the words of the Danish prince: —

> "There are more things in heaven and earth, Horatio,
> Than are dreamt of in your philosophy."

VII. I find my "spiritual" friends nowise less bigoted, less intolerant, than the devotees at other shrines. They do not allow me to see through my own eyes, but insist that I shall see through theirs. If my conclusion from certain data differs from theirs, they will not allow my stupidity to account for our difference, but insist on attributing it to hypocrisy, or some other form of rascality. I cannot reconcile this harsh judgment with their professions of liberality, their talk of philosophy. But, if I speak at all, I must report what I see and hear.

XXIX.

LAKE SUPERIOR. — MINING. — CHICAGO. — THE PRAIRIES.

ABOUT the year 1836, when the Territory of Michigan was crystallizing into a State, there arose a dispute between her and Ohio concerning a small but important corner, which included the then village — now city — of Toledo. Military — or rather militia — demonstrations were made on both sides, wherein much whiskey was consumed, but no blood shed; and at length the vastly preponderant weight of Ohio in the national councils prevailed, and insured her the peaceful possession of the contested corner; while Michigan was indifferently consoled by the preposterous addition to her natural area of a vast, wild region lying north and northwest of Lake Michigan, since known as her "Upper Peninsula." This region, when it came to be surveyed and mapped for settlement, proved rich in superficial indications of mineral wealth, mainly Copper and Iron; and a small crowd of adventurers rushed thither in quest of suddenly acquired riches, in the Summer or Fall of 1844. The early closing of navigation on Lake Superior and the St. Mary's River compelled a part of these to remain on Keewenaw Point throughout the ensuing Winter; and, being without advices from elsewhere later than the preceding August or September, the Whig portion of this crowd celebrated, on the 4th of March, 1845, Mr. Clay's presumed inauguration as President, — an inauguration which, unhappily, failed to come off, as they sanguinely believed it would do, — nay, did, — because it should have done. When Spring opened, several of them came down, bringing wondrous accounts of the riches of the Superior region in copper and silver, if not also in gold, and organized in our city several companies for the development of the wealth thus laid open to human appropriation. An old backwoodsman, named Bailey, who had heard my name, — possibly, read my paper, — had set apart for me some stock in a projected company, to be located on a copper-vein or outcrop of his discovery; requesting me to act in his behalf as a trustee or director of said company; to which I, in my yet complete ignorance of mining, acceded. For some three years thereafter, I acted accordingly; coaxing several assessments from unwilling stockholders (who, in their primeval innocence, had expected to receive dividends from their stock instead of paying assessments thereon), and applying the proceeds, as well as I could, to the opening of our mine. At length, in the Spring of 1847, I made a business visit to our property, — taking along the gold required to pay off our workmen, and buying at Detroit a yoke of oxen, a supply of hay and grain, a good stock of provisions, &c., &c., and taking them with me to their and my destination.

I had never before been farther in that direction than Detroit; and this journey considerably enlarged my acquaintance with the northwest. Lake Huron was shrouded in fog and mist, and our steamboat traversed its entire length slowly and cautiously; thence feeling our way up the St. Mary's only by daylight, — the channel being too shallow, rocky, and intricate for navigation by night. At the Sault Ste. Marie we found a small but smart young village, to whose assembled inhabitants two of us made temperance addresses, which I think some of them needed; and, when our goods had been wagoned across the portage, we took the only old propeller which had, as yet, been got across and launched on Lake Superior, and started up the lake: but it soon came on to blow a fair, fresh breeze, which was too much for our rickety craft; and her captain (very properly) ran her behind Point Keewenaw, and lay there some thirty hours, while we passengers traversed the coast for a mile or so, picking agates and other fancied, curious bits of fragmentary rock from the enormous quantity of pebbles which filled, almost to the exclusion of sand, the narrow strip of debatable ground between land and water. Next day — the wind having lulled — we rounded the Point, and ran down its longer (northwest) coast to Eagle Harbor; where, in default of piers, my oxen had to be pushed off the steamboat into the ice-cold water, and compelled to swim ashore; my goods being taken off in a small boat. That was the 15th of June; and the shallow water of the harbor was frozen over next morning for some distance from shore. There were possibly two hundred acres in all then cleared of timber on Keewenaw Point, a dozen of them adjoining this harbor, which, but for that clearing and the two taverns located thereon, remained very much as when Indians alone possessed or approached it. During the bright, warm day that followed that night's hard frost I made my way through the dense woods, unbroken save by our rough road, to our location, some six miles east of the harbor, and six hundred feet above it, where I paid off our men, and next day made, with others, an excursion of ten or twelve miles to the Bohemian and other kindred locations across the Point on Bay de Gris, and back again to our place in the afternoon, — a pedestrian journey of hardly more than twenty miles in all; yet across such a succession of brooks, bogs, and other impediments, that I — unused these sixteen years to walking more than an hour per day — was utterly fagged out, and fell my full length repeatedly in the course of the last two miles. Thence I visited, in the course of the next three or four days, the locations farther down the point, then known as Copper Falls, Pittsburg and Boston (Cliff), National, Forsyth, &c., encountering — especially around Sand Bay — denser and more ferocious clouds of mosquitoes and gnats than ever before or since presented me their bills, and insisted on immediate satisfaction. I remember an instance in which several of us fled half a mile from their haunts to a hut, which we filled with a thick and pungent smoke, with very little abatement of their numbers or their appetite.

The Point was not, in those days, calculated to attract a

Sybarite, nor even a gourmand; yet its white-fish and lake trout relieved admirably the more usual and quite substantial fare of pork, bread, beans, and potatoes; there were speckled trout in its multitudinous brooks for those who had time to catch them; while the prevailing forest of yellow pine, maple, beech, &c., covered a soil generally well adapted to potatoes, turnips, grass, &c., though not to the grains most acceptable for human food. Winter wheat or rye was generally smothered by the snows, which began to fall early in November, and kept coming till the aggregate fall often exceeded thirty feet,—the whole being settled meantime to a medium depth of six to seven feet. Sometimes, they said, a chopper, who fell from the trunk he was cutting in two, seemed in danger of disappearing, and being smothered in earth's fleecy vesture. Indian corn could rarely be matured: the nights, even in midsummer, being so sharp that seldom did a mosquito venture to pursue his human (or other) prey much after sunset. No copper of any account had yet been obtained from any but the Pittsburg or Cliff mine, nor was any of consequence shipped from the Point, save as aforesaid, while I was interested there. Shareholders, who had raised their $10,000 to $50,000 in fond expectation of early returns, found in time that every cent, and generally more, had been expended in constructing a rude pier whereon to land their supplies, cutting a road thence to their location, building a few rude shanties, drawing up their tools, powder, edibles, &c., and beginning to scratch the earth; another, and still another assessment being required,—not to secure returns, but to sink a shaft on the vein far enough to determine that they had any ore or metal to mine. By this time, their patience, or their faith, or their means, had generally failed, and they were ready to sell out for a song, or abandon the enterprise in despair and disgust. Such is, in essence, the history of most mining enterprises on Lake Superior; and I suspect it is not essentially different elsewhere. I presume there were not in 1859 so many deserted habitations throughout all the rest of our country as in California and the adjacent mining districts; and some of these were quite decent houses. All I ever realized by mining was a conviction that digging Gold, or Silver, or Copper, or Iron, or — best of all — Coal, is a fair business for those who bring to and invest in it the requisite capacity, knowledge, capital, experience, perseverance, and good luck, and that the rarely encountered "big strikes" are as one to a million. As a rule, there are many easier ways of gaining gold than digging it from the earth; yet let all dig who will. The possibility of large and sudden gains gives to the business that element of chance or gaming which so fascinates the average mind; yet, if all the gold-diggers on earth were to work faithfully throughout next year, and exchange their products respectively for wheat, I doubt that their recompense would average a peck each per day. And what is true of gold is nearly or quite so of copper, and of most other minerals as well.

I may here say that I made another journey to Lake Superior on the same errand the next year (1848), but considerably later in the season, or at the close of August, when encouraging progress had been made since my previous visit. I now tested an assertion which I had repeatedly heard, but never believed, — that, except in certain shallow bays, and even there only after a succession of hot, still days, — the water of that lake is too cold to bathe in. Going alone to the headland west of Eagle Harbor, on a bright Summer noon, when a fresh northern breeze was rolling in a very fair surf, I stripped and plunged in; but was driven out as by a legion of infuriated hornets. The water was too cold to be endured; and I never thereafter doubted the current assertion, that a hot day was never known on that Lake at a distance of a mile or more from land.

On this second visit, I waited and watched a day at the mouth of Eagle River, while our propeller made a gallant fight for dear life against a very moderate gale. She had failed to get in; if, indeed, it were safe to do so, — did not dare to go out boldly, if she could, — but, with both anchors down and full steam up, lay head to the wind, and did her best to hold her ground and resist being drifted on the rugged rocks at length barely two or three hundred yards astern. She dragged her anchors steadily, in spite of her best efforts, but slowly; so that we, expectant passengers ashore, took observations on her from hour to hour, and predicted that she would or would not ride out the gale. She did it handsomely, however; and, the next morning, her boat took us off, shipping a sea midway back to her that thoroughly drenched and nearly swamped us. Once on board, she weighed anchor and put out; and, in a few hours, I had looked my last (as yet) on the bold shores of the Father of Lakes, which stand forth green and fair in my memory evermore.

My earlier trip to the upper Lakes was concluded by a visit, per steamboat, *via* Mackinac, Sheboygan, and Milwaukee, to Chicago, then a smart and growing village, where some thousands of us gathered from the East and from the West in a grand River and Harbor Convention, which was organized on the 4th of July, 1847. Edward Bates, of St. Louis, — who had been in Congress twenty years before, and is still living, more than twenty years afterward, — was President of that Convention, and made from the chair a magnificent speech on our country's progress, genius, and destiny. Other able and good men were there, and many good speeches were made; but Mr. Bates's alone commanded general admiration. I presume that the cause of Internal Improvement, with the subsequent growth of Chicago, received a considerable impetus from that Convention.

When it had closed its deliberations, Mr. John Y. Scammon, then a rising young lawyer, since an eminent banker of Chicago, took his carriage and pair, and drove with me for three days over the prairies west of that city; crossing Fox River, at Geneva, proceeding to what is now Sycamore, and returning by Elgin to the City of the Lakes. I had, eight years earlier, traversed eastern Michigan, and there made the acquaintance of what were called "wet prairies," by which I had not been fascinated. But the prairies of Illinois are of another order; and, though by no means that dead, unbroken level which many suppose them, but cut up by brook-beds, sloughs, and roads, which were merely wagon-tracks in a deep, black soil, wore a generally delightful aspect. Forests were less frequent than seemed desirable; but "openings," or scattered trees, were never out of sight; and the small and scanty settlements were usually surrounded by promising fields of wheat and Indian corn. I presume we did not see one human habitation where a traveller over our route would now see fifty; while the average value or cost of the rude cabins we passed would hardly exceed $ 200, where that of the present houses would reach at least $ 2,000. Teamsters conveying grain to Chicago, or returning with lumber, we frequently met; yet inns were decidedly scarce; since few teamsters could afford to pay money for food or shelter, while the great mass stopped for rest or meals under almost any tree, turned out their horses to graze, or fed them from their wagons, while they ate of the substantial, wholesome food they had brought from home. I was told that a load of wheat taken sixty miles to Chicago in those days just about paid for a return load of fence-boards, leaving the farmer who made the exchange little or nothing wherewith to pay tavern-bills. Few of the early pioneers of Illinois took thither more than a fair wagon-load of worldly gear and $ 100 in money; many lacked the $ 100, and had but half a load of household stuff in the wagon, the other half being composed of wife and children; yet all found somehow enough to eat, and did not suffer intolerably from cold: and now those children enjoy comforts and may revel in luxuries which their parents scarcely aspired to. Do they realize and fitly honor the self-forgetting courage and devotion to which they are so deeply indebted?

Milwaukee was then a smart but struggling country village, consisting of some three to four hundred new houses clustered about a steamboat-landing at the mouth of a shallow, crooked creek. Wisconsin had then less than One Hundred Thousand inhabitants, which the twenty subsequent years have increased to nearly or quite One Million. Sheboygan was then relatively of far greater consequence and promise than now; but, going back thence a dozen miles inland to visit my father's brother, Leonard, I was traversing the wilderness within two miles from the steamboat-landing, and I travelled under the shade of the primitive forest through most of the succeeding ten miles. But the soil was generally good, and the timber excellent, being largely composed of Hickory, Elm, and other valuable trees; while the clearings, though new and small, were full of promise, not only in their thick-set, velvet grass, and their springing grain, but in their wealth of rugged, active, coarsely clad, but intelligent, vigorous children. Wisconsin has scarcely been surpassed by any State in her subsequent growth in population, production, and wealth; and I predict that the close of this century will see her the home of Three Millions of people as energetic, industrious, worthy, and happy, as any on earth.

At that time, no mile of railroad terminated in Chicago, and barely one line (the Michigan Central) pointed directly at that young city. Even this one proposed to stop at New Buffalo (mouth of St. Joseph's River), its passengers reaching thence its present proper terminus by steamboat in Summer, and by stage-coach in Winter. Of course, they soon saw reason to change their plans; and New Buffalo, deserted, became one of our many American victims of blighted hopes. Yet, after years of desolation, her denizens have discovered that their district is admirably adapted to peach-culture; the cold, northwest winds of later Autumn and Winter reaching them softened by passing over the adjacent lake, and so leaving her fruit-buds unblighted by their shrivelling breath. Landing here from Chicago, I took stage to Kalamazoo, or thereabout, where we met a just-completed section of the Michigan Central, on which I was brought to Detroit, and thence came homeward by steamboat to Buffalo, railroad to Albany, and steamboat to this city.

XXX.

THE GREAT SENATORS. — THE COMPROMISE OF 1850.

OUR great triumvirate — Clay, Webster, Calhoun — last appeared together in public life in the Senate of 1849 – 50: the two former figuring conspicuously in the debates which preluded and resulted in what was termed the Compromise of that year, — Mr. Calhoun dying as they had fairly opened, and Messrs. Clay and Webster not long after their close. This chapter is, therefore, in some sort, my humble tribute to their genius and their just renown.

I best knew and loved Henry Clay: he was by nature genial, cordial, courteous, gracious, magnetic, winning. When General Glascock, of Georgia, took his seat in Congress as a Representative, a mutual friend asked, "General, may I introduce you to Henry Clay?" "No, sir!" was the stern response; "I am his adversary, and choose not to subject myself to his fascination." I think it would have been hard to constitute for three or four years a legislative body whereof Mr. Clay was a member, and not more than four sevenths were his pledged, implacable opponents, whereof he would not have been the master-spirit, and the author and inspirer of most of its measures, after the first or second year.

Mr. Webster was colder, graver, sterner, in his general bearing; though he could unbend and be sunny and blithe in his intercourse with those admitted to his intimacy. There were few gayer or more valued associates on a fishing or sailing party. His mental calibre was much the larger; I judge that he had read and studied more; though neither could boast much erudition, nor even intense application. I believe each was about thirty years in Congress, where Mr. Clay identified his name with the origin or success of at least half a dozen important measures to every one thus blended with Mr. Webster's. Though Webster's was far the more massive intellect, Mr. Clay as a legislator evinced far the greater creative, constructive power. I once sat in the Senate Chamber when Mr. Douglas, who had just been transferred from the House, rose, to move forward a bill in which he was interested. "We have no such practice in the Senate, sir," said Mr. Webster, in his deep, solemn voice, fixing his eye on the mover, but without rising from his seat. Mr. Douglas at once varied his motion, seeking to achieve his end in a somewhat different way. "That is not the way we do business in the Senate, sir," rejoined Mr. Webster, still more decisively and sternly. "The Little Giant" was a bold, ready man, not easily overawed or disconcerted; but, if he did not quiver under the eye and voice of Webster, then my eyesight deceived me,—and I was very near him.

Mr. Calhoun was a tall, spare, earnest, evidently thoughtful man, with stiff, iron-gray hair, which reminded you of Jackson's about the time of his accession to the Presidency. He was eminently a logician,—terse, vigorous, relentless. He courted the society of clever, aspiring young men who inclined to fall into his views, and exerted great influence over them. As he had abandoned the political faith which I distinguish and cherish as National while I was yet a school-boy, I never met him at all intimately; yet once, while I was connected with mining on Lake Superior, I called on him, as on other leading members of Congress, to explain the effect of the absurd policy then in vogue, of keeping mineral lands out of market, and attempting to collect a percentage of the mineral as rent accruing to the Government. He received me courteously, and I took care to make my statement as compact and perspicuous as I could, showing him that, even in the Lead region, where the system had attained its full development, the Treasury did not receive enough rent to pay the salaries of the officers employed in collecting it.

"Enough," said Mr. Calhoun; "you are clearly right. I will vote to give away these lands, rather than perpetuate this vicious system." "We only ask, Mr. Calhoun," I rejoined, "that Congress fix on the lands whatever price it may deem just, and sell them at that price to those lawfully in possession; they failing to purchase, then to whomsoever will buy them." "That plan will have my hearty support," he responded; and it did. When the question came at length to be taken, I believe there was no vote in either House against selling the mineral lands.

Mr. Clay had failed to be chosen President in 1844, in part because he tried to reconcile to his support those whose views on the Texas question conflicted with his. General Taylor, on the other hand, had succeeded in 1848, while saying very little as to the pending questions affecting Slavery, or even seeming to care that adverse opinions should *be* conciliated. There was an anecdote current in the canvass to this effect: A planter wrote Old Zack, saying, "I have worked hard all my life, and the net product is a plantation with one hundred negroes, — slaves. Before I vote, I want to know how you stand on the Slavery question." The General at once responded: "Sir, I too have worked faithfully these many years, and the net product remaining to me is a plantation with *three* hundred negroes. Yours truly." The planter was satisfied.

The National Convention which nominated General Taylor had laid on the table a resolve approving, if not demanding, the exclusion of Slavery from the Territories; and this probably lost us the votes of Ohio, Illinois, Wisconsin, and Iowa. On the other hand, Alabama, Mississippi and Arkansas all voted, by small majorities, for Cass: Jefferson Davis, though a son-in-law of General Taylor, declining, on political or Slavery grounds, to support him. Had he been clearly understood to be for or against the so-called Wilmot Proviso, he would have both gained and lost votes; but I judge that, with reference to success, his silence was wisdom.

Being elected and inaugurated, he called to his cabinet Messrs. Clayton of Delaware, Crittenden of Kentucky, Ewing of Ohio, Meredith of Pennsylvania, G. W. Crawford of Georgia, Ballard Preston of Virginia, Collamer of Vermont, and Reverdy Johnson of Maryland, and proceeded to deal cautiously with the grave questions impending. It was soon evident to keen-sighted observers, that the new Administration aimed to tide over the breakers just ahead by securing the newly acquired Territories practically to free labor, through a quiet discouragement of the transfer of slaves thereto, and the speedy transformation of each Territory into a State. Dissension and division on the Wilmot Proviso were thus to be avoided by achieving expeditiously the *end* whereto that Proviso was but a means. Thus, California was rapidly metamorphosed into a free State even before she had been provided with a regular Territorial organization; while yet the Administration could fairly protest with Macbeth,—

> "Thou canst not say *I* did it! Never shake
> Those gory locks at *me!*"

The pro-Slavery interest soon felt that it was being undermined and circumvented. In the elections for Congress, next after General Taylor's inauguration, the South, which had given him both a popular and an electoral majority, chose but twenty-nine Representatives to support, with sixty-two to oppose, his Administration.

At the North, the new Administration was likewise distrusted by the more zealous champions of Free Soil, though with less reason. In the election of 1849, the Democrats of Vermont united with the Abolitionists in framing and supporting a common State ticket, on an unequivocally Free-Soil platform, with the watchword, "Free Democracy"; and, as the coalescing parties had outnumbered the Whigs in the preceding vote for President, the prospect looked squally. I was invited by the Whigs to canvass their State, and did so; beginning at Brattleborough, in the southeast, passing up to Montpelier and across to Burlington, thence down by Rutland to Bennington. One anecdote of this trip is characteristic of the times, and will bear reviving:

As, when previously asked by friends in the State what they should do for me, I had stipulated for a committee of thirteen to let me alone, and persuade others to do so, I enjoyed unusual exemption from bother, and, after speaking one rainy afternoon at some town in Orange County (Royalton, as I recollect), I took the cars, and was soon borne to Montpelier, where I was to speak the next day. The rain poured heavily, and I made my way *solus* from the railway station to a hotel, where I obtained a room, and sat down in it to my solitary reflections. I must here explain that two brothers, Vermonters, named respectively Charles G. and E. G. Eastman, then edited the Democratic State organs at Montpelier and at Nashville respectively. The Vermont Eastman, being in league with the Abolitionists, labored day by day to prove that the Taylor Administration was managing to secure the new Territories to Slavery; while the Tennessee Eastman, seeking capital for his party on the other tack, as strenuously insisted that that same Administration was doing its utmost to *exclude* Slavery from those same Territories. As The Tribune exchanged with both these candid journalists, I had recently taken a leading article from each, cut it into paragraphs, copied first from one charging the Administration as aforesaid, and then, simply premising, "Now we will hear what t' other Eastman has to say on this point," I would quote the exact opposite from the Tennessee or the Vermont brother, as the case might be. So, having seated myself in my room in the hotel at Montpelier, which I had never before been near, and where I knew no one, I looked drearily out at the furious rain for half an hour, and was about falling asleep in utter desperation, when my door opened, and a tall, sturdy mountaineer, unannounced, walked in. "Good afternoon, Mr. Greeley," was his cordial salutation. "Good afternoon," I less cordially responded; "though I do not happen to know you." "Not know me?" he incredulously asked: "why, I am t' other Eastman."

When Congress met in December following, and Howell

Cobb, [Dem.] of Georgia, had, after a long struggle, been chosen Speaker,* because the distinctively Free-Soil members would not support Winthrop, the Whig candidate, General Taylor, in his Annual Message (already published during the long struggle for Speaker), avowed that he desired and expected the early admission of both California and New Mexico as States, under such constitutions as their people should see fit to frame,— which constitutions, it was already notorious, would forbid Slavery.

Mr. Clay soon submitted† to the Senate his plan for a comprehensive settlement of all the mooted questions regarding Slavery. It contemplated: 1. The prompt admission of California as a State, under her anti-Slavery Constitution; 2. The organization of the remaining Territories, without allusion to Slavery; 3. The limitation of Texas to a defined Northern boundary, ignoring—or rather buying off—her claim to nearly all New Mexico; 4. Paying her a sum (afterward fixed at $10,000,000) for consenting to the limitation aforesaid; 5. No abolition of Slavery in the District of Columbia; 6. Exclusion by law of the traffic in slaves from said District; 7. A denial of the right of any State to obstruct or embarrass the traffic in slaves between other States, or their removal from one to another. As the second of these propositions has an abiding significance, in view of the Nebraska bill afterward avowedly based thereon, I quote it *verbatim*:—

"2. *Resolved*, That *as Slavery does not exist by law* [in,] and is not likely to be introduced into, any of the territories acquired by the United States from the republic of Mexico, it is inexpedient for Congress to provide by law either for its introduction into, or [its] exclusion from, any part of the said territory, and that appropriate territorial governments ought to be established by Congress in all the said territories not assigned as within the boundaries of the proposed State of California, without the adoption of any restriction or condition on the subject of Slavery."

* Under the plurality rule: Cobb, 102; Winthrop, 99; scattering (mainly Free-Soil), 20.

† February 13, 1850.

The gist of this proposition, as I apprehend it, is, that Slavery had not then a *legal* existence in the newly acquired Territories. In other words: Mr. Clay (in opposition to Mr. Calhoun and his followers, who maintained that the Federal Constitution necessarily became the fundamental law of any region acquired by the United States, and thus legalized Slavery in that region, and every part of it,) held, with the Free-Soil party, that Slavery must be *established* by positive law in any Territory, before it could be legal therein. I felt that we could afford to accept this as a basis of adjustment, especially when we gained therewith the instant admission of California as a Free State, and the extrusion of slaveholding Texas from nearly all New Mexico, whereof she claimed every acre lying eastward of the Rio Grande del Norte. Mr. Clay's proffer seemed to me candid and fair to the North, so far as it related to the newly acquired territories. I do personally know that Mr. Clay himself regarded it as a capitulation on the part of the South, wherein she merely stipulated for the honors of war. And it was instantly assailed by Senators Jefferson Davis and Henry S. Foote of Mississippi, James M. Mason of Virginia, William R. King of Alabama, S. U. Downs of Louisiana, and A. P. Butler of South Carolina, as proposing to the South a surrender at discretion. They all repelled the suggestion that Slavery could not legally exist in a Territory till expressly established there by law, affirming the opposite or Calhoun doctrine. Mr. Clay met them frankly and squarely; replying to Mr. Jefferson Davis as follows: —

"I am extremely sorry to hear the Senator from Mississippi say that he requires, first, the extension of the Missouri Compromise line to the Pacific; and, also, that he is not satisfied with that, but requires, if I understand him correctly, a positive provision for the admission of Slavery south of that line. And now, sir, coming from a Slave State, as I do, I owe it to myself, I owe it to the truth, I owe it to the subject, to state that no earthly power could induce me to vote for a specific measure for the introduction of Slavery where it had not before existed, either south or north of that line. Coming, as I do, from a Slave State, it is my solemn, deliberate, and well-matured determination that no power — no earthly power — shall compel me to vote for the positive introduction of Slavery, either south or north of that line. Sir, while you reproach, and justly, too, our British ancestors for the introduction of this institution upon the continent of America, I am, for one, unwilling that the posterity of the present inhabitants of California and New Mexico shall reproach *us* for doing just what we reproach Great Britain for doing *to* us. If the citizens of those Territories choose to establish Slavery, I am for admitting them with such provisions in their constitutions; but then it will be their own work, and not ours; and their posterity will have to reproach them, and not us, for forming constitutions allowing the institution of Slavery to exist among them. These are my views, sir, and I choose to express them; and I care not how extensively and universally they are known. The honorable Senator from Virginia (Mr. Mason) has expressed his opinion that Slavery exists in these Territories; and I have no doubt that opinion is sincerely and honestly entertained by him; and I would say, with equal sincerity and honesty, that *I* believe that Slavery nowhere exists within any portion of the territory acquired by us from Mexico. He holds a directly contrary opinion to mine, as he has a perfect right to do; and we will not quarrel about the difference of opinion."

The debate thus inaugurated was prosecuted at great length. Mr. Webster, in the course of it, startling the country by an elaborate speech,* wherein he took ground against what were termed Slavery agitation and agitators; against the asserted right of legislatures to instruct senators; against legislation to exclude Slavery from Federal Territories, &c., &c. In so doing he said:—

"Now, as to California and New Mexico, I hold Slavery to be excluded from those Territories by a law even superior to that which admits and sanctions it in Texas, — I mean the law of Nature, — of physical geography, — the law of the formation of the earth. That law settles forever, with a strength beyond all terms of human enactment, that Slavery cannot exist in California or New Mexico. . . . I will say further, that, if a resolution or a bill were before us, to provide a Territorial government for New Mexico,

* March 7, 1850.

I would not vote to put any prohibition into it whatever. Such a prohibition would be idle as it respects any effect it would have on the Territory; and I would not take pains uselessly to reaffirm an ordinance of Nature, nor to reënact the will of God. I would put in no Wilmot Proviso for the mere purpose of a taunt or a reproach. I would put into it no evidence of the votes of a superior power, exercised for no purpose but to wound the pride of the citizens of the Southern States."

I cannot here follow the great debate through the weary months in which the Senators and Representatives of California awaited permission to take the seats to which they had been chosen. The compromise or adjustment proposed by Mr. Clay was assailed from either side, — by zealous anti-Slavery men like Hale, Chase, and Seward; by zealous, aggressive *pro*-Slavery men like Calhoun, Jeff. Davis, Mason, and Butler, — while it was sustained by the more moderate members of either great party. A grand committee of thirteen, whereof Mr. Clay was chairman, was raised on the subject, wherefrom the chairman reported* his plan, modified so as to be less objectionable to pro-Slavery men: the vital assertion that Slavery had then no legal existence in the new territories being omitted. In the progress of the debate, further modifications of the plan were made, — all tending in the same direction; and the sudden death of General Taylor,† allowing the Presidency to devolve on Mr. Fillmore, powerfully aided the triumph of the Compromise, which had, a few days before, seemed all but hopeless. Ultimately, bills admitting California, organizing New Mexico and Utah as Territories, fixing the northern boundary of Texas, and giving her $10,000,000 for consenting thereto, providing more effectually for the recovery of fugitive slaves, and prohibiting the bringing of slaves into the Federal district for sale, were severally passed,—though with very diverse support, —and became laws of the land: thus, it was fondly, but most mistakenly, calculated, putting an end to Slavery agitation, and ushering in a long era of fraternity and domestic peace.

* May 18. † July 11.

Meantime, Mr. Calhoun had died, March 31, 1850, at Washington, where Mr. Clay likewise died, June 29, 1852. Mr. Webster survived his great compeer less than four months; dying at his home in Marshfield, Mass., October 24th of that year. These three left no statesmen among us who were their equals in general ability or in power to fix the attention of the country. We still read speeches in Congress, though generally quite satisfied with telegraphic summaries of their contents, but we no longer impatiently await, eagerly enjoy, and carefully treasure them, as we did those of the great departed.

The question is often asked, "Were the traditional great men of the past *really* greater than their living successors?" I can only answer that, while I presume the average intellect of our day is not inferior to that of the last generation, I judge that the master minds of different periods are attracted to different spheres of activity, and are impelled to different stages of development. Had Henry Clay or Daniel Webster been born and lived fifty years earlier, he could not have failed to be distinguished and honored by those who knew him; but he would probably have achieved distinction as a Revolutionary soldier, or in some other sphere than that of legislation.

"Is it not hard," I was once asked by the Governor of an important Western State, "that my salary should be far less than that of a railroad president or chief engineer?" "I infer from it," I replied, "that our age realizes more keenly its need of competent railroad men than that of capable governors of States." In this, as in many things, the intensity of the demand creates or regulates the supply. If we now lack great political debaters, it is because they are not greatly required, or because talent is more in demand and better rewarded in some other field of intellectual exertion.

XXXI.

LIBELS AND LIBEL-SUITS.

EDITORIAL life has many cares, sundry enjoyments, with certain annoyances; and prominent among these last are libel-suits. I can hardly remember a time when I was absolutely exempt from these infestations. In fact, as they seem to be a main reliance for support of certain attorneys, destitute alike of character and law, I suppose they must be borne for an indefinite period. The fact that these suits are far more common in our State than elsewhere cannot have escaped notice; and I find the reason of that fact in a perversion of the law by our judges of thirty to fifty years ago.

The first notable instance of this perversion occurred on the trial of Root *v.* King, at Delhi, about 1826. General Erastus Root was a leading Democrat through the earliest third of this century, and was, in 1824, a zealous supporter of William H. Crawford for President. As President of the Senate, he presided at the joint meeting of the two Houses, wherein electors of President were chosen; when, to his and his friends' sore disappointment, a large number of Adams, and but few Crawford men, received the requisite majority, — the friends of Adams and those of Clay having privately united on a common ticket. When the votes for this ticket began to be counted out, presaging a Crawford defeat, General Root attempted to break up the joint meeting, and thus invalidate the election. For this, and other such acts, he was severely handled by The New York American; whose editor, Charles King, was thereupon sued by Root for libel, and — the case being tried at Delhi, where Root resided and was lord-paramount — the jury, under the rulings of a Democratic judge, gave the plaintiff $1,400 damages. It was a most unjust verdict, based on a perversion of the law, which, if sustained, left the press no substantial liberty to rebuke wrong-doing or chastise offenders. And the perversion of justice thus effected naturally led to still further and worse aberrations.

Ten or a dozen years afterward, Mr. J. Fenimore Cooper returned from a long residence abroad, during which many of his novels had been written. A man of unquestioned talent, — almost genius, — he was aristocratic in feeling and arrogant in bearing, altogether combining in his manners what a Yankee once characterized as "winning ways to make people hate him." Retiring to his paternal acres near Cooperstown, N. Y., he was soon involved in a difficulty with the neighboring villagers, who had long been accustomed, in their boating excursions on the Lake (Otsego), to land and make themselves at home for an hour or two on a long, narrow promontory or "point," that ran down from his grounds into the lake, and whom he had now dissuaded from so doing by legal force. The Whig newspaper of the village took up the case for the villagers, urging that their extrusion from "The Point," though legal, was churlish, and impelled by the spirit of the dog in the manger; whereupon Cooper sued the editor for libel, recovered a verdict, and collected it by taking the money — through a sheriff's officer — from the editor's trunk. By this time, several Whig journalists had taken up the cudgels for the villagers and their brother editor; and, as Mr. Cooper had recently published two caustic, uncomplimentary, self-complacent works on his countrymen's ways and manners, entitled "Homeward Bound," and "Home as Found," some of these castigations took the form of reviews of those works. One or more of them appeared in The Courier and Enquirer, edited by James Watson Webb; at least one other in The Commercial Advertiser, edited by William L. Stone; while several racy paragraphs, unflattering to Mr. Cooper, spiced the editorial columns of The Albany Evening Journal, and were doubtless from the pen of its founder and then editor, Mr. Thurlow Weed. Cooper sued them all; bringing several actions to trial at Fonda, the new county-seat of Montgomery County. He had no luck against Colonel Webb, because, presuming that gentleman moneyless, he prosecuted him criminally, and could never find a jury to send an editor to prison on his account. Colonel Webb was defended in chief by Ambrose L. Jordan, afterward Attorney-General of the State, an able and zealous advocate, who threw his whole soul into his cases, and who did by no means stand on the defensive.

In one of his actions against Mr. Weed, he was more fortunate. Weed had not given it proper attention; and, when the case was called for trial at Fonda, he was detained at home by sickness in his family, and no one appeared for him; so a verdict of $400 was entered up against him by default. He was on hand a few hours afterward, and tried to have the case reopened, but Cooper would not consent; so Weed had to pay the $400 and costs. Deeming himself aggrieved, he wrote a letter to The Tribune, describing the whole performance; and on that letter Cooper sued *me*, as for another libel.

And here let me say, that Weed was forced to pay some $2,500 to Cooper, and as costs in his various suits, most unjustly. Weed was a profound admirer of Cooper's novels,— an extravagant one, in *my* judgment,—and was so fond of quoting them, that jokers gravely affirmed that he evidently had never read but three authors,—Shakespeare, Scott, and Cooper. (At a later day, they were obliged to add Dickens to the list.) The paragraphs that provoked Cooper's libel-suits were intended by Weed rather to admonish the American novelist that he was acting absurdly, suicidally, in quarrelling with his neighbors, to preclude their landing on "The Point"; with his countrymen by his harsh, supercilious criticisms on their manners; and with the Press by his innumerable libel-suits. Not a shred, a spice of malice, nor even of ill-will, impelled the paragraphs which Cooper resented so litigiously.

The first writ wherewith *I* was honored "By the Author of the 'Pioneers,' &c.," cited me to answer at Ballston, Saratoga County, on the first Tuesday (I believe) in December, 1842; and I obeyed it to the letter. I employed no lawyers, not realizing that I needed any. In its turn, the case was called, and opened in due form by Richard Cooper (nephew of Fenimore) for the plaintiff. No witnesses were called, for none were needed. I admitted the publication, and accepted the responsibility thereof: so the questions to be tried were these, "Was the plaintiff libelled by such publication? If so, to what amount was he damaged?" When Richard had concluded, I said all that I deemed necessary for the defence; and then Fenimore summed up his own cause in a longer and rather stronger speech than Richard's, and the case was closed. So far, I felt quite at my ease; but now the presiding judge (Willard) rose, and made a harder, more elaborate, and disingenuous speech against me than either Richard or Fenimore had done; making *three* against one, which I did not think quite fair. He absolutely bullied the jury, on the presumption that they were inclined to give a verdict for the defendant, which he told them they were nowise at liberty to do. I had never till that day seen one of them, and had never sought to effect any intimacy or understanding with them; so I must say that the judge's charge seemed to me as unfair as possible. The jury retired at its close; and, on balloting, seven of them voted to make me pay $100, two voted for $500, one for $1,000, and two for nothing at all,— or very nearly so. They soon agreed to call it $200, and make it their verdict; which they did. When all the costs were paid, I was just $300 out of pocket by that lawsuit. I have done better and worse in other cases; but, having been most ably and successfully defended in several, maugre the proverb that, "He who pleads his own cause has a fool for a client," I am satisfied that, could I have found time, in every case wherein I was sued for libel, to attend in person, and simply, briefly state the material facts to the jury, I should have had less to pay than I have done. There is always danger that the real merits of your case will be buried out of sight under heaps of legal rubbish. But it is not possible for a business man to spend his whole life in court-rooms, waiting for his case to be called; and I have often been sued in distant counties, where I could scarcely attend at all.

I left Ballston in a sleigh directly upon the rendering of the verdict, caught a steamboat, I think, at Troy, and was at my desk in good season next morning; so that, by 11 P. M., I had written out and read in proof, besides other matter, my report of the trial, which filled eleven columns of the next morning's Tribune. I think that was the best single day's work I ever did. I intended that the report should be good-natured, — perhaps even humorous, — and some thought I succeeded; but Fenimore seems not to have concurred in that opinion; for he sued me upon the report as a new libel, — or, rather, as several libels. I was defended against this new suit by Hons. William H. Seward and A. B. Conger, so cleverly, that, though there were hearings on demurrer, and various expensive interlocutory proceedings, the case never came to trial. Indeed, the Legislature had meantime overborne some of the more irrational rulings of our judges; while our Judiciary itself had undergone important changes through the political revolution in our State, and the influence of our Constitution of 1846; so that the Press of New York now enjoys a freedom which it did not in the last generation.

I say the Press, — yet only the journals of one party were judicially muzzled. Rather more than forty years ago, Mr. Weed, then living at Rochester, was positively and generally charged, through the Democratic journals, with having shaved off or pulled out the whiskers of a dead man, in order to make the body pass for that of the long-missing and never-recovered William Morgan, of anti-Masonic fame. The charge was an utterly groundless calumny, having barely a shred of badinage to palliate its utterance. Mr. Weed sued two or three of his defamers; but the courts were in the hands of his political adversaries, and he could never succeed in bringing his cases to trial. Finally, after they had been kicked and cuffed about for ten or a dozen years, they were kicked out, as too ancient and fishlike to receive attention.

This was probably the best disposition for him that could have been made of them. If he had tried them, and recovered nominal verdicts, his enemies would have shouted over those verdicts as virtually establishing the truth of their charges; while, if he had been awarded exemplary damages, these would have been cited as measuring the damages to be given against *him* in each of the hundred libel-suits thereafter brought against him. This consideration was forcibly brought home to me when, years afterward, having been outrageously libelled with regard to a sum of $1,000, which it was broadly intimated that a railroad or canal company in Iowa had given me for services rendered, or to be rendered, I ordered suits commenced against two of the most reckless libellers. But, when time had been allowed for reflection, I perceived that I could afford neither to lose nor to win these suits; that such verdicts as I ought to recover would be cited as measuring the damages that I ought to pay in all future libel-suits brought against me; so I gladly accepted such retractions as my libellers saw fit to make, and discontinued my suits. Henceforth, that man must very badly want to be sued who provokes *me* to sue him for libel.

Passing in silence several recent cases of interest wherein I was chosen defendant,—cases on which I could not dilate without annoyance to persons yet living,—I close with a statement of points in difference, as I understand them, between sundry judges and certain editors touching the Law of Libel.

I have often heard it asserted from the Bench that editors claim impunity to libel,—which is not the truth. What I claim and insist on is just this: *That the editor shall be protected by the nature and exigencies of his calling to the same extent, and in the same degree, that other men are pro-*

tected by the exigencies, the requirements, of THEIR *callings or positions respectively.*

For instance: A judge on the bench, a lawyer at the bar, may libel atrociously; and I hold may be fairly held responsible for such libel; but the law will not *presume* him a libeller from the mere fact that he speaks disparagingly of some person or persons. A householder applied to for the character of his late servant may respond: "I turned him off because I found him an eye-servant, a drunkard, and a thief"; yet the law will presume no malice not specifically proven; because it avers that, in giving his ex-servant's character, that householder was acting in the line of his duty. Had he posted up those precise words in a public place, the law *would* have presumed malice, because no duty required such posting.

Now let us apply the principle above enunciated to the actual case in hand: Jefferson Jones posts up in a bar-room, livery-stable, or on the town-pump, these words: "Clifford Nokes was last night caught stealing a hog, and was committed by Justice Smith, to await indictment and trial." The law will presume that posting malicious, and will deal harshly with Jones if he should fail to prove it literally true. And why? Clearly, because no duty required him to make any such proclamation of his neighbor's alleged frailty,—because of the fair, natural presumption, that he was moved so to post by hate or malevolence. But that same paragraph might appear in the columns of any journal that habitually printed police intelligence, without justifying or rendering plausible a kindred presumption. It might, indeed, be *proved* that the editor had inserted the item with malicious intent to injure Nokes; and then I say: "Punish the libeller to the extent of the law." But I protest against *presuming* an editor a libeller, because, in the routine of his vocation, the line of his duty, he prints information which may prove inaccurate or wholly erroneous, without fairly exposing him to the presumption that he was impelled to utter it by a malevolent spirit, a purpose to injure or degrade. Am I understood?

Twice, in the course of my thirty-odd years of editorship, I have encountered human beings base enough to require me to correct a damaging statement, and, after I had done so to the extent of their desire, to sue me upon that retracted statement as a libel! I think this proves more than the depravity of the persons implicated, — that it indicates a glaring defect in the law or the ruling under which such a manœuvre is possible. If the law were honest, or merely decent, it would refuse to be made an accomplice of such villany.

Ere many years, I hope to see all the reputable journals of this city, if not of the entire State, unite in an association for mutual defence against vexatious and unreasonable libel-suits. They ought to do this; employing a capable and painstaking lawyer, to whom every suit for libel against any member of the association should at once be referred, with instructions to investigate it candidly, and decide whether its defence ought or ought not to devolve on the press generally. If not, let it be remitted to the counsel for the journal prosecuted; but, if the prosecution be clearly unreasonable and vexatious, — a lawyer's dodge to levy black mail, — then let no money or effort be spared to baffle and defeat the nefarious attempt. Such a combination for mutual defence would arrest the prevailing habit of paying $50 or $100 to buy off the plaintiff's attorney as the cheapest way out of a bother, would soon greatly reduce the number of suits for libel, and would result in a substantial and permanent enlargement of the Freedom of the Press. It should have been formed long ago.

XXXII.

EUROPE. — THE WORLD'S EXPOSITION.

THE year 1851 was signalized by the first grand Exposition of the products of All Nations' Art and Industry. It was held in Hyde Park, London, once at the extreme west end of that metropolis, but long since enveloped by her steady, imperial growth in commerce, wealth, and population. Prince Albert, the Queen's husband, having been placed at the head of the enterprise, the Queen did her best to insure its success; and her influence, exerted to the utmost, extended far beyond her Court and those who aspire to bask in its beams. A portion of the Tory Aristocracy stood aloof, or only visited the Exposition as careless sight-seers; but the Royal Family, the Liberal Aristocracy, the Manufacturing, Commercial, and more intelligent Laboring classes, were united and enthusiastic in their efforts to secure the success of the grand undertaking. I judge that the habitual frigidity of British bearing toward foreigners was never before so thoroughly put aside or overcome. "You foreigners," said Earl Granville at a great dinner given at Richmond to the Foreign Commissioners and Jurors, "complain that we English are icy and repulsive; but you never give us a fair chance to be otherwise. We try to be courteous and hospitable whenever we are afforded an opportunity. Don't we make heroic, though luckless, attempts to speak your several languages? Don't we try in every way to make ourselves agreeable? Give us a fair trial before you condemn us as exclusive and unsocial." In this spirit, the great mass of the educated, thrifty classes treated their many foreign visitors throughout that long

Summer. I doubt that the hospitality which is evinced in entertainments and festivities was ever more widely displayed anywhere, or with more persistent generosity.

And I doubt that another exhibition, so comprehensive, so instructive, has since been or ever will be presented, though several have been, and many doubtless will be, so planned, so weeded, as to embody only articles of decided merit, as this did not. For, as all nations were invited to send samples of their exportable products to this Exposition, all had done so, without at all considering the figure these would cut when compared with the kindred products of other countries. Side by side with the subtlest and most elaborate devices of British and American locksmiths to guard the hoards of bankers and capitalists from spoliation, were the rude contrivances of Tunisian or Thibetan blacksmiths, clumsily hammered out of poor iron, on a very rude anvil, and doing no credit to the workmanship, even after all due allowances had been made. The striking contrasts thus presented in almost every department of the Exposition gave it a piquancy and zest which are henceforth unattainable; for the contributors of sorry specimens, having thus been made aware of their own relative demerits, refuse thenceforth to appear as foils for their brilliant rivals; and any attempt to replace them by samples gathered from the ends of the earth, on purpose to be derided and ridiculed, must almost necessarily prove a failure. Hereafter, we shall find in kindred expositions only the best products of the cleverest, most ingenious of the world's artificers; while the worse, and even worst, by which their worth was so admirably set off and illustrated in 1851, will remain in their coveted oblivion.

The Crystal Palace, wherein the Exhibition was held, was constructed wholly of iron and glass, and was one of the noblest, most magnificent, most graceful edifices ever seen. Its grand avenue, traversing its centre from end to end, was studded with some of the rarest and costliest articles exhibited, including Powers's statue of "The Greek Slave," the Queen's matchless "Koh-i-Noor," or Mountain of Light, said to be next to the largest diamond in existence, and hundreds more of the most admirable products of Art and Nature. Several stately and gracious elms, which were among the chief ornaments of the Park, grew on the site chosen for the Palace, and were a chief obstacle to its concession, as this was supposed to involve their destruction; but the stately edifice was made to include and cover them, so that they put forth their ample foliage and stood green and graceful throughout the Exhibition under its transparent roof, each of them "a thing of beauty" and a positive enhancement of the fairy spectacle on every side presented. Aladdin's fabled palace may have been richer in gold and gems; but ours far exceeded his in the extent and multiplicity of its devices for the sustenance, comfort, enjoyment of mankind, — its numberless steam-driven spindles, looms, &c., would have far outworked all the genii or gnomes of the Arabian romance; while the vast crowds of human beings, especially of sumptuously, picturesquely apparelled women, who thronged that grand avenue throughout day after day for weeks and months, had no rival even in the most gorgeous creations of Oriental fancy.

Having left New York in the stanch American steamship Baltic, Capt. J. J. Comstock, on the 11th of April, when a strong and cold northeaster had just set in, we took it with us across the Atlantic, rarely blest with a brief glimpse of the watery sun during our rough passage of twelve days and some hours, encountering a severe gale on our first night out, and another as we reached soundings on the Irish coast; and being surfeited with rain and head-winds during our entire passage, I was sick unto death's door for most of the time, eating by an effort when I ate at all, and as thoroughly miserable as I knew how to be; so that the dirty, grimy little tug that at last approached to take us ashore at Liverpool seemed to me, though by no means white-winged, an angel of deliverance; and my first meal on solid, well-behaving earth will long be remembered with gratitude to the friends who provided and shared it. I have since repeatedly braved the perils and miseries of the raging main, and have never found the latter so intolerable as on that first voyage; yet the ocean and I remain but distant, unloving acquaintances, with no prospect of ever becoming friends.

Reaching London just before the Exposition opened, I was accorded by the partiality of my countrymen who had preceded me (somewhat strengthened, I believe, by their jealousy of each other) the position of Chairman of one of the Juries, — each of the countries largely represented in the Exposition being allowed one Chairman. My department (Class X.) included about three thousand lots (not merely three thousand articles), and was entitled, I believe, Hardware; but it embraced not only metals, but all manner of devices for generating or economizing gas, for eliminating or diffusing heat, &c., &c. The duties thus devolved upon me were entirely beyond my capacity; but my vice-Chairman, Mr. William Bird, a leading British iron-master and London merchant, was as eminently qualified for those duties as I was deficient; and between us the work was so done that no complaint of its quality ever reached me. We had several most competent colleagues on our jury, among them M. Spitaels, of Belgium, a director of the Vielle Montaigne Zinc Mines, and one of the wisest and best men I ever knew.

Revisiting England four years thereafter, I called on my friend Bird, and he told me this anecdote: —

"You may remember," he premised, "that I paid special attention to foreign iron throughout our service as jurors in the Exposition, and that I dwelt on the admirable quality of certain of the Austrian products which came within our purview. Well: two years thereafter, when Summer brought its usual dulness of trade, I thought I would run over and see how those products were made. So, providing myself with as good letters as I could command, I, in due time, waited on Lord Westmoreland, our Ambassador at Vienna. He received me courteously, but soon said: 'I perceive, Mr. Bird, that the letters you hand me from Lord Palmerston, Lord John Russell, &c., imply something more than ordinary civilities. What do you desire?' 'I seek an order from the Austrian Minister of Industry [or whatever the designation may be], authorizing me to visit all the great iron-works in the Empire.' 'Why, Mr. Bird,' rejoined the Ambassador, 'you cannot be aware of the jealousy wherewith British predominance in iron-working is here regarded, or you would as soon request me to ask the Minister to cede you Hungary. I cannot present your request.' So (continued Mr. B.), I left the Ambassador, thoroughly rebuffed, and returned to my carriage, in which I had left an Austrian friend, who had been a commissioner at our Exposition. 'What is the matter, Mr. Bird?' he at once inquired; 'you seem to have met with a disappointment.' I certainly had, as I proceeded to explain. 'But why not *yourself* ask the Minister for the privilege you desire?' 'Because he never heard of me.' 'There you are mistaken,' said the Austrian; and, opening his official report on the London Exposition, he pointed therein to repeated and hearty acknowledgments of the highly important services rendered to the Austrian exhibitors by Mr. Bird, of the tenth jury. He offered at once to introduce and commend me to the Minister, and I gladly assented. Having been introduced accordingly in the most flattering terms, the Minister soon asked, 'Mr. Bird, can I do nothing to make your visit agreeable?' — when I indicated my wish to visit the iron-works of Austria. 'With the greatest pleasure,' he responded, and at once wrote me the desired order, couched in most emphatic and sweeping terms. Thereupon, I left him, and spent my next month in a tour through the iron-producing districts of the empire, — everywhere received most hospitably, and shown all that I asked or wished to see. Returning, at last, to Vienna, I made a parting call on Lord Westmoreland; and, in reply to his inquiry, informed him that I had spent my time, since my previous call, among the iron-works of Carinthia, Styria, &c. 'But how did you obtain the needful order?' he inquired. 'I asked the Minister for it in my own name, and he readily granted it.' 'Very well, Mr. Bird,' rejoined the puzzled Ambassador, 'should I ever have any great favor to ask of the Austrian Government, I may be glad to avail myself of your influence.'"

The council of the Exposition was composed of the chairmen of the several juries; its president was Lord Canning (son of the great Canning), who died Governor-General of India some ten years thereafter. I regarded him with deep interest for his father's sake, — that father having been England's foremost man for years within my recollection. The son seemed a man of decided cleverness and geniality, while his countenance denoted wit, though I recollect nothing said by him that confirmed my prepossession. Of the higher aristocracy, I remember only the Duke of Argyle, — a small, slight, sandy-haired person, gentle in manner, modest in bearing, and nowise exacting the servile deference generally paid by personal merit to inherited rank in Great Britain. I am sure Lord Canning, who had evidently a keen sense of the ridiculous, must have been nauseated by the genuflexions and prostrations, — "If your lordship will permit me to remark," "If I may presume to claim your lordship's attention for a moment," &c., &c. — wherewith he was habitually addressed by men whose achievements in Science and its applications were elements at once of England's glory and of her prosperity and greatness. I may have seen a favorable sample of the British nobility, but those I met were simply and eminently gentlemen, — and none more so than Arthur, Duke of Wellington, — *the* Duke, then more than eighty years old, who was one of the earliest and most frequent visitors to our American quarter, and one of the very first to proclaim — while the great London journals were jeering at the poverty and shabbiness of our department—its eminent and remarkable excellence. He not merely visited, he studied and inquired; and no more unpretending, fair-minded seeker of practical information was among our visitors. He was one of those privileged, with the jurors, to enter and examine during

18

the early morning hours, when the public was excluded, and when the queen, with her attendants, spent hours there, day after day, — in part, doubtless, to satisfy a legitimate interest, but in part, also, to commend and render popular the Exposition; so that, as my friend Charles Lane aptly remarked, "You could not exactly say whether she stood on this side of the counter or on that." I am sure, few labored more earnestly, more indefatigably than she did to make the enterprise a success, and no one with more decided efficiency.

British self-complacency and British fairness were both strikingly evinced in the conduct of the Exhibition. The chairman of the Agricultural jury was Mr. Philip Pusey, M. P. (brother of the clergyman of Tractarian fame), who inhabited and enjoyed a generous estate in Berkshire, which had been likewise inhabited and enjoyed by his ancestors for generations preceding the Norman conquest. Repeatedly, he brought up to the council a request from his jury that they might be authorized to award prizes to the best, and the second-best, American, Belgium, French, &c., ploughs, — and so of other implements, — a request evidently prompted by apprehensions that they would otherwise be constrained by the general superiority of British implements to award prizes to them only. "Mr. President," I urged in opposition, "we are asked to destroy the practical value of our awards altogether. It will be idle for this body to award a prize to one American as better for a given purpose than another American plough, — we can settle that point at home. Nor do we wish you to award a prize to an American, as best adapted, say, to working stiff clay soils, if there be a much better plough for that purpose sent here from some other country. We do not wish to be confirmed in our errors, but warned to forsake them. Let your prizes be awarded only to what is *absolutely* best, and we shall then be enabled, if other nations have better ploughs than ours, to adopt and profit by them." Others urged the same views more forcibly; and the Agricultural, like all other juries, was ultimately obliged to conform to the original programme.

When the council had met, late in July, for what was intended to be its last sitting, Mr. Pusey said, " I am constrained to ask, on behalf of the Agricultural jury, that another meeting of this body be held some fortnight hence. We have, this week, been testing reapers at Tiptree Hall (M. Mechi's), and one of the American machines (Mr. C. H. McCormick's) surprised us by the efficiency and the excellence of its operation. But the day was rainy and the grain unripe; so we do not feel sure that its triumph was not owing to those circumstances. We require another trial on a fair day, with ripe, dry grain; and, should this machine then do as well as it has already done under our eyes, we must ask for it the very highest award." The request was granted; the trial repeated under the conditions required, with a success fully equal to that previously achieved; and a Council Medal solicited and awarded accordingly.

I travelled hastily, that Summer, through France, from Calais, by Paris, to Lyons and across Savoy and Mount Cenis, into Italy, — visiting Turin, Genoa, Rome, Florence, Ferrara, Bologna, Padua, Venice, and Milan; recrossing the Alps by the St. Gothard pass, and thence coming down through Altorf and Lucerne to the Rhine at Basle; and so down the great river to Cologne; thence, across Belgium, by Aix-la-Chapelle and Brussels, into Northern France, and back to London, by Paris, Dieppe, and New Haven. I soon after journeyed northward through Newcastle-on-Tyne, York, and Berwick-on-Tweed, to Edinburgh; thence, by Glasgow, to Belfast and Dublin; thence westward, through Athlone to Galway; and, after returning to Dublin, through Wexford and Tipperary, so far southward as Limerick; returning, through Wales, to Liverpool, and there taking the Baltic for home. The very few deductions from such hasty journeyings that I may hazard will be submitted in future chapters.

XXXIII.

THE DISSOLUTION OF THE WHIG PARTY.

DIEDRICH KNICKERBOCKER, the most sagacious and most popular historian of the Dutch era of our city and State, notes one grave error of the New Netherland magnates, and their pushing, meddling, encroaching Yankee neighbors, in that, having wisely stopped fighting and betaken themselves instead to negotiation, they did not protract indefinitely that amiable and hopeful procedure, but terminated it abruptly by a treaty; over the interpreting of which their quarrel instantly broke out afresh, and raged with greater fury than before.

Their blunder has been often repeated.

The Compromise of 1850 had been carried through the XXXIst Congress, not long after President Taylor's death, mainly by virtue of the $10,000,000 given therein to Texas for the relinquishment of her preposterous claim to New Mexico. That donation raised the value of several millions of outstanding Texas bonds from ten or fifteen cents on the dollar to par. A Western Governor told me, a few years afterward, that he administered on the estate of one of the Senators from his State who helped pass the Compromise measure, and who soon after died, and that among said Senator's assets he found nearly $30,000 of those Texan bonds, with no scratch of pen to indicate how he came by them, or how much he gave for them. Had he been a Crœsus, this would have been extraordinary; as he was a politician and legislator of moderate means, it could be accounted for in but one way.

The Compromise measures had been carried by the votes of all the Northern Democrats but a few decided opponents of the Slave Power, all the Southern Whigs, with scarcely an exception, a minority of the Southern Democrats, and a decided minority of the Northern Whigs, — a minority absolutely inconsiderable until decidedly strengthened by Mr. Fillmore's accession to the Presidency. Having now the National Administration on their side, the Compromisers endeavored to make devotion to their measure a touchstone of political orthodoxy; and a manifesto was drawn up and signed by forty or fifty members of Congress, pledging themselves to support no man for any office who did not sustain the Compromise.

A Whig State Convention met at Syracuse in the Autumn of 1850, and nominated a State Ticket headed by Washington Hunt for Governor. Francis Granger was President of that Convention. Its resolves said nothing pro or con of the Compromise, but one of them approved the course of Governor Seward in the United States Senate (which he had entered on the day of President Taylor's inauguration); and this was vehemently resisted by the "Conservative" or Compromise minority of the delegates, who, headed by its President, vacated their seats on its adoption. In the contest which followed, Hunt was barely chosen over Horatio Seymour; but the Democrats carried their Lieutenant-Governor (Church), with most, if not all, of their remaining State officers. It was clear that the "Silver Grays," (or Conservative Whigs,) had either refused to vote, or gone over to the Democracy; though Governor Hunt was in fact one of themselves, and, after running once more for Governor, and being badly beaten by the "Silver Grays," he went openly over to them, and assiduously sought, but never found, promotion at their hands and those of the Democrats, with whom he had by this time become completely affiliated.

Connecticut was, in like manner, barely carried over to the Democrats by the "Silver Grays" in the Spring of 1851, and Hon. Roger S. Baldwin, who had opposed the Compromise in the Senate, was supplanted by Isaac Toucey. Thus the usually doubtful or closely contested Free States were generally carried by the Democrats, who elected United States Senators from nearly all of them between 1850 and 1854; giving their party an overwhelming preponderance in the upper House for the six years prior to 1861.

In the South, the opponents of the Compromise attempted to make head under the banner of State Rights. Mississippi having been represented in the Senate of 1850 by Jefferson Davis, who strongly opposed, and by Henry S. Foote, who as vehemently supported, the Compromise, that State divided into two new parties, termed "Union" and "State Rights" respectively, and nominated the two Senators as rival candidates for Governor. A most spirited contest resulted in the polling of an unprecedented vote, — nearly 60,000 in all, — and the choice of Foote, "Union," by more than 1,000 majority. The residue of the Union Ticket was carried by a still larger average majority.

In South Carolina, the new parties were essentially the same, but the names were different; "Coöperation" — that is, a resolve to solicit and await the concurrence of other Slave States before initiating forcible resistance to the Compromise acts — being adopted as the watchword of the more moderate party. As their election did not come off till Mississippi and other Southern States had unequivocally decided against the "Chivalry," or "Fire-Eaters," these were beaten here also by a large majority, and the hope of dragging the South into an attitude of Nullification or Disunion on this issue shown to be utterly futile.

And now the two great parties held their several Presidential Conventions, — that of the Whigs assembling at Baltimore, about the 1st of June, 1852. Mr. Fillmore was supported for reëlection by nearly all the Southern, as General Scott was by the great body of the Northern, adherents of the drooping flag. The delegates friendly to either were 130 to 134 in number, while 30 to 36 preferred Mr. Webster to either of them. Mr. Webster had been the Ajax of Compromise, had been chosen by Mr. Fillmore as his Secretary of State, and in that capacity had given character and dignity to the Administration. There was reason, therefore, for Mr. Webster's sanguine hope, that, when Mr. Fillmore's nomination was proved clearly hopeless, his name would be withdrawn, and his strength transferred to his illustrious premier. This hope was doomed, however, to disappointment. Forty or fifty ballots were had without result; when the supporters of Webster gradually went over to Scott, who was thereupon nominated, with William A. Graham, of North Carolina, for Vice-President.

But the friends of Fillmore and Webster, though differing as to candidates, were a unit as to platform; and they framed one which pledged the party unequivocally to the support and maintenance of the Compromises of 1850. General Scott made haste to plant himself squarely on this platform, which was in undoubted accordance with his own prepossessions. He thus alienated thousands of Anti-Slavery Whigs, whose detestation of the new and stringent Fugitive Slave law was uncontrollable; while the Conservative or "Silver Gray" Whigs, would not support him because the great body of Anti-Slavery Whigs did, and because they foresaw that his counsellors must necessarily be chosen in good part from among these.

The delegates to the Democratic National Convention were divided in their preferences for President, — General Cass and Mr. Buchanan being the leading favorites, but a good many votes being scattered upon others. Finally, Franklin Pierce, of New Hampshire, was brought forward, and nominated with substantial unanimity. He had been a representative in, and finally Speaker of, the more popular branch of the Legislature of his State, a Representative and Senator in Congress, and then a volunteer and Brigadier-General in the Mexican War, but had passed the last eight years mainly in retirement. A pleasing canvasser, of popular address and manners, he could not be said to have achieved eminence, whether in his civil or his military career; indeed, General Cass, who had served with him two or three years as fellow-Democrats in the Senate, had not made his acquaintance up to the hour of his nomination. Hon. William R. King, of Alabama, who had long been United States Senator from that State, was nominated with him for Vice-President.

The ensuing canvass was short, tolerably spirited, but one-sided from the start. The Democrats, who were quietly ploughing with the "Silver Gray" heifer throughout, *knew* they were backed to win, — that there could be no mistake about it. The Whigs tried hard to stem the tide; but the nomination of John P. Hale for President by the Abolitionists was a heavy side-blow, as he was sure to take thousands of votes which, but for the Compromise platform, would have been given for Scott. Maine and California in September, Pennsylvania, Ohio, and Indiana in October, gave majorities or decisive pluralities for the Democrats. The Whigs were thus prepared for defeat, but not for the overwhelming rout which overtook them, when, at the closing of the polls in November, it was found that they had carried precisely four States, — Massachusetts, Vermont, Kentucky, and Tennessee, — all the rest having chosen Pierce electors, — New York by some 25,000 plurality; Pennsylvania, Ohio, Virginia, &c., by majorities equally conclusive. True, the popular vote showed no such disparity as the electoral; but the preponderance exceeded 200,000 in an aggregate poll of about Three Millions. The Whig party had been often beaten before; this defeat proved it practically defunct, and in an advanced stage of decomposition.

XXXIV.

THE SLAVERY CONTROVERSY.

"I AM *naturally* anti-Slavery. If Slavery is not wrong, then nothing is wrong. I cannot remember when I did not so think and feel." So said Abraham Lincoln to Governor Bramlette, ex-Senator Dixon, and Editor Hodges, when they waited on him with Kentucky's remonstrance against the arming of Blacks to put down the Rebellion, and against the Emancipation policy, too tardily adopted on the part of the Union.

I believe Mr. Lincoln thus forcibly gave expression to what was the very general experience of American boys reared in the Free States forty to sixty years ago, while the traditions and the impulses of our Revolutionary age were still vivid and pervading, — at least, of those trained by intelligent Federal mothers. In the South, it may have been otherwise; though nearly all the great Southrons of our country's purer days, from George Washington and Thomas Jefferson down to Henry Clay, were at least theoretical emancipationists. As the fires of the Revolution never burned so deeply, nor shone so vividly, in the South as in the North, it is natural that they should there have sooner been stifled, if not extinguished; yet I was fifteen years old when the avowal of pro-Slavery sentiments by a Northern Representative * in Congress called forth an instant and indignant rebuke from several eminent natives † and champions of the South.

* Edward Everett of Massachusetts.

† Churchill C. Cambreleng, of North Carolina (removed to New York); J. C. Mitchell, of Tennessee; John Randolph, of Virginia.

Though but a child of seven to ten years, I was an omnivorous reader throughout the progress of the great Missouri struggle, and intensely sympathized with the North in her effort to prevent the admission of Missouri as a Slave State. The defeat of that effort showed that it had been made too late, — that the North should have insisted on the exclusion of Slavery from at least her share of Louisiana immediately after its purchase from France, or when it came to be organized as a Territory (or Territories) of the Union. "Just as the twig is bent the tree's inclined," is an axiom of the widest scope; and letting Slavery (or any other evil) creep into a vast region, and there quietly establish and fortify itself, while that region is called a Territory, intending and expecting to extrude and exclude it when said region shall present itself for recognition and admission as a State, is a manifest futility. The problem involved is neatly set forth in the hackneyed old Parliamentary epigram: —

"I hear a lion in the lobby roar;
Say, Mr. Speaker, shall we shut the door,
And keep him out? or shall we let him in,
And see if we can turn him out again?"

Mr. Jefferson, in his purer, nobler days, — before he became the leader and oracle of a great party which, in spite of his unconcealed prepossessions, gave him the votes for President of nearly all the essentially Slave States, and thenceforth leaned more and more upon the Slave Power for support, so long as that Power had a substantial existence, — had proposed, and nearly carried, in the Continental Congress of 1784, the absolute exclusion of Slavery from all the territory then belonging to, or likely to be acquired by, the old Confederation. The Revolutionary War was then barely ended; the British troops still held the city of New York; and the accidental absence of a member from New Jersey probably prevented the adoption at that time of a policy which would have realized the hopes of our Revolutionary heroes and sages, by quietly, gradually tending to and insuring the peaceful, bloodless extirpation of Human Bondage from our country. To have confined it, as Mr. Jefferson purposed and proposed, to the existing States which saw fit to maintain it, making their bounds a limit beyond which it could not pass, would not have been an expeditious nor heroic, but would have been a cheap, quiet, and certain mode of ridding the country of its most gigantic wrong and peril. But Mr. Jefferson was soon sent envoy to France, and the next Congress reduced his statesmanlike programme so as merely to exclude Slavery from all the territory then possessed by the Confederation; viz., the region lying between the Ohio and the Mississippi. And when the vast, wild country then known as Louisiana came to be acquired from France, though few years had passed, and Mr. Jefferson was then at the zenith of his power, no potent voice was raised in favor of consecrating at least its still virgin soil, or even the Northern half of it, to Free Labor forever. There is a sad pathos in the simple Scriptural narration, "Another king arose, who knew not Joseph"; but in these faster ages we do not need to await the transformation wrought by death; our kings forget, not merely their Josephs, but whatever was best and noblest of themselves.

Mr. Jefferson having thus, in 1784, proposed, and all but carried, the exclusion of Slavery absolutely and forever from all the territory contained within our National Boundaries, and not yet embraced within the jurisdiction of our thirteen States, though much of it was still the especial property of North Carolina and Georgia, both Slave States; Congress, in 1787, unanimously adopted Mr. Jefferson's prohibition, but confined its application to such territory as had already been ceded to, and was then possessed by, the Confederation. The next Congress was chosen and met under the Federal Constitution; and this, without a dissenting voice, ratified and confirmed the prohibition, as already made; but the Territories, soon thereafter cut off from North Carolina and Georgia, to be ultimately moulded into the States of Tennessee, Alabama, and Mississippi, were expressly shielded, in the acts or ordinances whereby they were ceded, from the operation of the anti-Slavery proviso of 1787, and thus fastened to the car of Bondage.

And thenceforth no new National effort was made in the right direction until the Missouri struggle, which resulted in our defeat on the main point, through the medium of a Compromise; the make-weight being a stipulation that Slavery should thenceforth be excluded from all United States territory north of the line of 36° 30′ north latitude, — that is, the southern boundary of Missouri. In other words, it was agreed and stipulated that — Missouri being admitted as a Slave State — all our remaining territory, and consequently all our States still in embryo, north of the southern boundary of that State, should be evermore free.

"After a storm comes a calm." From 1821 to 1835, or from my tenth to my twenty-fourth year, the Northern people — busy, usually prosperous, and pretty steadily increasing in numbers, wealth, and power — very generally ignored the subject of Slavery. The convictions of that portion of them who may be said to have had any were not materially changed; but what use in parading a conviction which can have no other effect than that of annoying your proud and powerful neighbor? True, Benjamin Lundy had already begun the agitation for Slavery's overthrow, which William Lloyd Garrison and others, during this period, continued and methodized; but the handful of proclaimed, aggressive Abolitionists were as one to a thousand, even at the North; while none were tolerated at the South. And, in fact, whatever of impunity they enjoyed throughout the greater portion of the North was accorded them rather through contempt for their insignificance than willingness to let them be heard. Had it been imagined that the permanence of Slavery was endangered by their efforts, they would scarcely have escaped with their lives from any city or considerable village wherein they attempted to hold forth: even as it was, hootings, howlings, blackguard revilings, rotten eggs, stoned windows, &c., &c., were among the milder demonstrations of repugnance to which they were habitually subjected.

And, while I could not withhold from these agitators a certain measure of sympathy for their great and good object, I was utterly unable to see how their efforts tended to the achievement of their end. Granted (most heartily) that Slavery ought to be abolished, how was that consummation to be effected by societies and meetings of men, women, and children, who owned no slaves, and had no sort of control over, or even intimacy with, those who did?

Suppose the people of Vermont all converted to Abolition, how was *that* to bring about the overthrow of Slavery in Georgia? I could not say nor see; and therefore I was never a member of any distinctively Abolition society, and very rarely found time to attend an Abolition meeting. Conservative by instinct, by tradition, and disinclined to reject or leave undone the practical good within reach, while straining after the ideal good that was clearly unattainable, I clung fondly to the Whig party, and deprecated the Abolition or Third Party movement in politics, as calculated fatally to weaken the only great National organization which was likely to oppose an effective resistance to the persistent exactions and aggressions of the Slave Power. Hence, I for years regarded with complacency the Colonization movement, as looking to the establishment of a respectable, if not formidable, Christian republic on the western coast of Africa, and vaguely hoped that a day might ultimately dawn, wherein the rudely transplanted children of Africa might either be restored to her soil, or established, under a government and flag of their own, in some tropical region of our own continent.

Two events, of nearly simultaneous occurrence, materially modified these preconceptions. One was the irruption of certain Western filibusterers, of whom Sam Houston may be regarded as the leader and type, into the Mexican province of Texas, under the pretence of colonization and settlement, but with deliberate intent to wrest that province, under the pretence of a revolution, from its rightful owners, and then annex it to the United States; thus expanding the area and enhancing the power of American Slavery, — a programme which was thoroughly realized in the course of ten or twelve years.

It is easy to sever the acts of this drama so as to ignore their continuity and interdependence; but I, who read the exulting anticipations of the end from the beginning, having no motive for self-delusion, never affected it. In my view, the whole business was one of gigantic spoliation, — of naked villany, — and its "being's end and aim" were the aggrandizement of the Slave Power.

The coördinate event was the martyrdom of Elijah P. Lovejoy, — a young Congregational minister, sent out from Maine to St. Louis as an evangelist in 1832, and soon impelled to start in that city an Orthodox Protestant newspaper, wherein Slavery, like Intemperance and other social evils, was treated as an impediment to the spread and sway of vital godliness. Perhaps his aggressive Protestantism had some influence in arousing the resolute, menacing opposition which at length destroyed his establishment, and drove him from the city and the State.* At all events, Mr. Lovejoy was urged, and in effect compelled, to remove his establishment to Alton, Illinois; where he fondly trusted a religious journal would be tolerated, even though it should occasionally expose and reprobate the iniquities necessarily inherent in or flowing from man-selling and man-owning.

Vain hope! there is, there can be, no Free State in a nation which allows its people to be bought and sold, held and treated, like cattle. Soon, Mr. Lovejoy was ordered to "move on"; and, failing to do so, his press was a second time destroyed by a mob. Again he resolved to renew and refit his establishment; and was proceeding to do so, when, surrounded by a few friends, he stood to arms for the defence of his property and his right of utterance, at the warehouse where his third press had just been landed from Cincinnati, and was shot dead † by one of the pro-Slavery ruffians, who thus attested their devotion to the Union and to "Southern Rights." And no legal justice was ever meted out to his murderers, —

* In May, 1836.

† November 7, 1837.

no restitution made to his bereaved family for his press and type, which constituted "the spoils of victory." He had dared, as a Christian minister, to argue the incompatibility of Slavery with the Golden Rule; and the mob had dealt him therefor what the messages of President Jackson, of Governor Marcy, &c., &c., set forth as his substantial deserts.

If I had ever been one of those who sneeringly asked, "What have we of the North to do with Slavery?" the murder of Lovejoy would have supplied me with a conclusive answer. A thousand flagrant outrages had been, and were, committed upon the persons and property of men and women guilty of no crime but that of publicly condemning Slavery; but these were usually the work of irresponsible mobs, acting under some sort of excitement; but Lovejoy was deliberately, systematically, hunted to his death, simply because he would not, in a nominally Free State, cease to bear testimony as a Christian minister and journalist to the essential iniquity of slaveholding. It was thenceforth plain to my apprehension, that Slavery and true Freedom could not coexist on the same soil. And this conviction was deepened and strengthened by the progress and issue of the struggle which resulted in the Annexation of Texas and the consequent War upon Mexico.

That Slavery, having thus extended her power in and over the Union, should not reap a further advantage, through the extension of her sway over the whole or any portion of the territory beyond Texas, most unrighteously wrested from Mexico, was my earnest resolution. To break the dangerous hold which the Slave Power had already gained in New Mexico, through the preposterously impudent, but not therefore impotent, claim of Texas to the ownership of that country, through the committal of the Democratic party, if not of the Federal Government also, to the support of that claim, through the advance of General Taylor, by President Polk's express orders, to the Rio Grande, near Matamoras, and the consequent outbreak of actual hostilities, was the cardinal point which I kept steadily in view while in Congress, and which moved me to give a qualified support to so much of Mr. Clay's original programme of Compromise as contemplated the admission of California and the organization of the remaining acquisitions from Mexico.

This general survey has seemed essential to a clear comprehension of the circumstances under which a new and more pervading excitement was aroused at the North by the shape ultimately given by Senator Douglas to his bill for the organization of the new Territories of Kansas and Nebraska, — an excitement which recast the great parties, and gave a new phase to our National career.

In politics, as in nature, great events may seem to result from inadequate causes, because a long series of preëxisting causes are unnoted or ignored. The North gave a majority of its Electoral votes to Polk, against Clay, not because of the Texas issue, but in spite of it. The more intelligent, considerate, conscientious Democrats did not approve of the proposed Annexation of Texas under existing circumstances; but they were too intent on beating Mr. Clay to give much thought or weight to the Texas issue; and, beside, they were able to convince themselves that there was little difference as to Texas between Polk and Clay. But, the struggle being over, and their ancient grudge satisfied, the celerity wherewith Annexation was effected — the election of Polk being triumphantly quoted as justifying and even requiring it — made a deep impression on their minds. They could not now effectually breast the sweeping current; but they saw, reflected, and quietly bided their time. In the Democratic triumph of 1844 was the germ of future Democratic disasters and humiliations.

XXXV.

THE NEW ERA IN POLITICS.

THE Presidential contest of 1852 had witnessed — if I should not rather say attested — the practical dissolution of the Whig party, — dissolved not by popular aversion to its principles or its leaders, but by the ever-increasing and ultimately absorbing importance acquired by questions to which those principles bore no direct relation. A majority of the voters of Pennsylvania, of Ohio, of Maryland, of North Carolina, Kentucky, and several other States, still agreed with the Whigs in favoring Protection to Home Industry, National Internal Improvements, &c., &c.; but other questions had assumed greater prominence or imminence in the minds of many of them; and these, by dividing and distracting those who had been Whigs, had not merely overthrown the former Whig ascendency, but precluded all rational hope of its reëstablishment. The veterans who had fought their best campaigns under the lead of Clay, Harrison, or Webster, might not realize this, — might persist in holding conventions, framing platforms, nominating candidates, and even achieving local successes; but the young, the ambitious, the unprejudiced, had already perceived by instinct that the party which triumphed in 1840 and in 1848 — which was barely, even if fairly, outnumbered in 1844 — was so paralyzed by divisions and defections founded on new or alien issues, that it could hardly be expected ever to carry the country again. And its virtual dissolution left the ground open and inviting for new combinations and developments.

The first of these in the order of time was the "American,"

familiarly characterized as the "Know-Nothing," movement. It had its origin in this city; where a similar, but less vigorous, less formidable, organization had been effected in 1843–44, as also at an earlier day. It now assumed the shape of a secret Order, hostile in profession to foreign domination, and in effect to the naturalization of immigrants until after a residence in this country of twenty-one years, and more especially to Roman Catholic influence and ascendency. Hitherto, this movement had been confined to a few of our great cities and their vicinage, and had, after a brief career, subsided; but now it pervaded most of our States, achieving temporary triumphs in Kentucky, Maryland, and Delaware, and stoutly battling for ascendency even in Virginia, as in nearly every Eastern State; and for a brief season it seemed destined to sweep all before it, and remodel our institutions into conformity with its ideas. But its apparent strength was largely factitious,—men of diverse parties, of radically incompatible views and purposes, using its machinery to further their several ends, and discarding it whenever such use was precluded or defeated. The fact that almost every "Know-Nothing" was at heart a Whig or a Democrat, a champion or an opponent of Slavery, and felt a stronger, deeper interest in other issues than in those which affiliated him with the "Order," rendered its disruption and abandonment a question, not of years, but of months. It claimed to have carried the Legislature of our State in 1854; but that Legislature reëlected to the Senate William H. Seward, who had no sympathy with any of its purposes; it actually chose the State officers elected in our State in 1855, though it polled less than three eighths of the entire vote,—running its candidates in between those of the two adverse parties; but its attempt to choose a President in 1856 resulted in disastrous rout; the only State carried by it being Maryland, though Millard Fillmore was its candidate for President, with Andrew J. Donelson, the nephew and heir of General Jackson, for Vice-President. Thenceforth, it dwindled rapidly, until its members had been fully absorbed into one or the other of the great rival parties some four years thereafter.

The simultaneous — in fact, concurrent at the outset, but widely divergent — movement which has since so deeply influenced our national career had its origin in the attempt to organize the territories lying directly west of the State of Missouri and Iowa, under the name of *Nebraska*. The leading facts in the premises are so widely known, and have been so thoroughly discussed, that I may pass over them hurriedly; yet they excited so powerful an influence over my own subsequent course that I cannot wholly ignore them.

Stephen Arnold Douglas, a Vermonter by birth, had made Illinois his home; and, though his education was limited, and his means moderate, aspired to fortune and power as a lawyer and politician. A Democratic candidate for Congress in 1838, in a district which included the northern two thirds of the area of the State, and now contains at least 1,500,000 inhabitants, he was beaten 68 votes by his Whig competitor in a poll of 36,742, though the Democratic Governor had therein a decided majority. But Mr. Douglas evinced in the canvass qualities that endeared him to his party, by which he was soon made a judge, in a few years chosen a Representative in Congress, and in due course transferred to the Senate, where he was placed on the Committee on Territories, and in time became its Chairman. As such, he had already (at the short session of 1852 – 53) introduced a bill to organize the Territory of Nebraska, which Senator Atchison, of western Missouri, had opposed and obstructed, — notoriously in the interest of Slavery, — the territory in question having been expressly, undeniably, consecrated to Free Labor by the Missouri Compromise of 1820.

At the next long session of 1853 – 54, Mr. Douglas reintroduced his bill to organize the territory in question; and now for the first time did he seek to deprecate the hostility evinced through Mr. Atchison by an intimation that the Compromise of 1850 had superseded and annulled the interdict of 1820. Hereupon, Mr. Dixon, of Kentucky, interposed a direct proposition that the interdict be repealed and cancelled. Mr. Douglas did not at once acquiesce, and The

Union (the Democratic organ at Washington) pointedly denounced the Dixon amendment; but Mr. Douglas, after some hesitation, accepted it in principle, and interpolated it into his bill, in terms which declared "the true intent and meaning" thereof to be "neither to legislate Slavery into the territory in question, nor to exclude it therefrom," but to leave the people thereof perfectly free to establish or exclude "the peculiar institution," as to them should seem advisable. And President Pierce, though he at first resisted and protested, was ultimately induced to sustain this proposition, and to give a written pledge (as I am well assured) that he would do so to the end.

Soon after the bill had taken this shape, and while the North was beginning to be aroused to resist it, I was traversing Ohio; and, visiting either Newark or Lancaster, I was there introduced to Hon. William Stanberry, who, years before, had been an eminent representative in Congress, but was now old and retired from public life. "What do you think of this Nebraska bill?" he eagerly inquired. "I think it bound to pass," was my response. "Ah! I see you don't understand it," he confidently rejoined: "Frank Pierce has had this project introduced, in order that he may veto it; and then nothing can prevent his reëlection." I might have assured Mr. Stanberry that a Democratic President who should lead his party into such a quagmire for his own personal advantage would not be long for this world; but he was much older than I, and I left him firm in his original faith.

I do not propose to trace here the history of the Nebraska bill, which was at length so modified by its author as to provide for two distinct Territories, — that lying directly westward of Missouri being designated *Kansas*, while the residue of that originally contemplated became *Nebraska*. In this shape, it passed the Senate by 35 Yeas to 13 Nays, and the House by 113 Yeas to 100 Nays, — *nine* of the latter from Slave States. And thereupon commenced a practical struggle between Freedom and Slavery for the possession of Kansas, which lasted down to her final admission as a Free State, after the Southern representatives had abandoned their seats in Congress, in obedience to their States' respective Ordinances of Secession.

As I gave, from first to last, whatever of strength I possessed, and of effort that I was capable of making, to the work of arousing the people of the Free States to resist and baffle, step by step, the attempt to open to Slavery the region already solemnly pledged to Free Labor, I desire briefly to set forth the grounds of that resistance whereon conservative Unionism and radical Anti-Slavery seemed to meet and coincide.

Slavery, as a local institution, was primarily the business of the States which saw fit to uphold it. We of the North, under our Federal Constitution as it then stood, had the same right to deprecate and oppose it that we had to oppose drunkenness in Canada, or polygamy in Turkey, — no less, no more. Only when it transcended the limits of those States, and challenged favor and support as a matter of National or general concern, did it (in our view) expose itself to our political antagonism. Only when it sought to involve us in a common effort, a common responsibility, with its upholders and champions, did it force us into an attitude of active, determined antagonism. This view had been succinctly and forcibly set forth, with immediate reference to Texas, so early as February, 1838, by Daniel Webster, in a speech at Niblo's Garden, New York, and was held (I presume) by a large majority of those citizens of the Free States who supposed that conscience and morality have any business in the sphere of politics.

Yet the rulers of opinion at the South seemed never to comprehend, nor even to consider it. In their view, whoever evinced repugnance to Slavery anywhere, under any circumstances, was an Abolitionist, and an enemy of their section, — a wanton aggressor upon their rights. What they in effect required of us, and what those whom they heeded and trusted at the North accorded them, was partnership in the extension and fortification of Slavery and the Slave Power. "True, we hold and work the slaves," they virtually said; "but as much for your profit as for our own. You buy our crops, and sell us whatever we need or fancy in return. You own the vessels that fetch and carry for us; you supply our fabrics, and make a part of them: help us to diffuse our institution over more territory, and we will grow more cotton and buy more goods, to your satisfaction and profit: Why not?" The answer given to this question by her Northern factors, servitors, political allies, the South heard and rejoiced in: the very different response made by the conscience of the North, she did not, because she would not, hear and comprehend.

The passage of the Nebraska Bill was a death-blow to Northern quietism and complacency, mistakingly deeming themselves conservatism. To all who had fondly dreamed or blindly hoped that the Slavery question would somehow settle itself, it cried, "Sleep no more!" in thunder-tones that would not die unheeded. Concession and complacency were plainly doomed to subserve none other than the most transient purposes. Every new surrender on the part of the North was seen to provoke a new exaction in the name of the South. Louisiana, Missouri, Texas, Kansas, — the more that was conceded, the more was still required. As, in the ascent of a mountain,

"Hills peep over hills, and Alps on Alps arise,"

so a long vista of future exactions and concessions was opened by this latest and fullest triumph of aggressive Slavery. Systematic, determined resistance was now recognized as imperative duty. That resistance could only be rendered effective through a distinct, compact political organization. That organization was therefore resolved on, spontaneously and simultaneously, by a million Northern firesides. It was earliest effected in the West, but had pervaded nearly every Free State before the close of 1854, and had assumed almost everywhere a common designation, — that of the Republican party.

XXXVI.

MY FARM.

I SHOULD have been a farmer. All my riper tastes incline to that blessed calling whereby the human family and its humbler auxiliaries are fed. Its quiet, its segregation from strife, and brawls, and heated rivalries, attract and delight me. I hate to earn my bread in any calling which complicates my prosperity in some sort with others' adversity, — my success with others' defeat. The farmer's floors may groan with the weight of his crops, yet no one else deems himself the poorer therefor. He may grow a hundred bushels of corn or forty of wheat to every arable acre, without arousing jealousy or inciting to detraction.

I am content with my lot, and grateful for the generosity wherewith my labors have been rewarded; and yet I say that, were I now to begin my life anew, I would choose to earn my bread by cultivating the soil. Blessed is he whose day's exertion ends with the evening twilight, and who can sleep unbrokenly and without anxiety till the dawn awakes him, with energies renewed and senses brightened, to fresh activity and that fulness of health and vigor which are vouchsafed to those only who spend most of their waking hours in the free, pure air and renovating sunshine of the open country.

I *would* have been a farmer, had any science of farming been known to those among whom my earlier boyhood was passed. We New-Englanders supposed ourselves, even then, an educated, intelligent people, and, relatively considered, were so: there was no person among us, over twelve years old, who had not enjoyed the privileges of common schools, and learned therein to read, write, and cipher; we all read books and newspapers, and *I* read nearly all of both that were to be found in our neighborhood; yet I cannot remember that I had ever seen a periodical devoted to farming, up to the day wherein, in my sixteenth year, I abandoned the farm for the printery. A book treating of Agriculture, or seeking to set forth the *rationale* of its processes, the natural laws on which they are based, I certainly had not seen. Nay, more: during the ten or twelve years in which I attended school, more or less, I never saw a treatise on Chemistry, Geology, or Botany, in a school-room. I hardly saw one anywhere. That true Agriculture is a grand, ennobling science, based on other sciences, and its pursuit a liberal, elevating profession, was not even hinted, much less inculcated, in any essay, speech, or sermon, any book, pamphlet, or periodical, so far as I then knew. Farming, as understood and practised by those among whom I grew up, was a work for oxen; and for me the life of an ox had no charms. Most of those I knew seemed to till the earth mainly because they could not help it; and I felt that *I could* help it. So I shook from my brogans the dust of the potato-patch, and stepped out in quest of employment better suited to an intelligent, moral being.

It was a quarter of a century after this before I felt able to buy or make the farm whereon to abide the coming of decay and death. I had been some twenty years a resident of the city, and fifteen the head of a household. Six children had been born to me, and four of them had died, — as I am confident some of them would not so prematurely have done, had they been born and reared in the country.

I had earned and bought a small but satisfactory house in the very heart of the city; but who, if he has any choice, prefers to grow old and die at No. 239, unknown to, and uncared for by, the denizens of Nos. 237 and 241? For my family's sake, if not for my own, a country home was required: so I looked about and found one.

The choice was substantially directed by my wife, who

said she insisted on but three requisites,—1. A peerless spring of pure, soft, living water; 2. A cascade or brawling brook; 3. Woods largely composed of evergreens. These may seem light matters; yet I was some time in finding them grouped on the same small plat, within reasonable distance from the city.

I *did* find them, however; and those who object to my taste in choosing for my home a rocky, wooded hillside, sloping to the north of west, with a bog at its foot, cannot judge me fairly, unless they consider the above requirements.

My land was previously the rugged, mainly wooded, outskirt of two adjacent farms, whereof my babbling brook formed the boundary.

Nine miles above White Plains, and thirty-five N. N. E. of our City Hall, the Harlem Railroad, when nearly abreast of the village of Sing-Sing, and six miles east of it, just after entering the township of Newcastle, crosses a quite small, though pretty constant, mill-stream, named by the Indians *Chappaqua,* which is said to have meant falling or babbling water, and which, here running to the southeast, soon takes a southwesterly turn, recrosses under the railroad, and finds its way into the Hudson, through the Sawmill or Nepperhan creek, at Yonkers. A highway, leading westward to Sing-Sing, crosses the railroad, just north of the upper crossing of the brook, and gives us, some twenty rods from the northwest corner of my farm, a station and a post-office, which, with our modest village of twenty or thirty houses, take their name from our mill-stream. Chappaqua is not a very liquid trisyllable, but there is comfort in the fact that it is neither Clinton, nor Washington, nor Middletown, nor any of the trite appellations which have been so often reapplied, that half the letters intended for one of them are likely to bring up at some other. (How *can* a rational creature be so thoughtless as to date his letter merely "Greenfield," or "Jackson," or "Springfield," and imagine that the stranger he addresses can possibly guess whither to mail the answer?)

My brook has its source in wooded, granite hills, on the east southeast, and comes tinkling or brawling thence to be lost in the Chappaqua, a few rods south of the road to Pleasantville, which forms my southwestern boundary. As to springs, there are not less than a dozen, which no drouth exhausts, breaking out along the foot of my hill, or at the base of a higher ridge which forms its crest.

My woods are the pride of the farm, which without them would never have been *my* farm. They cover about twenty-five of the seventy-five acres which compose it; and I say to them, with Oriental courtesy, and more than Oriental sincerity, "May your shadow never be less!" For the ground they cover is in good part an irregular, sideling granite ledge, or portions of a ledge, thinly covered by a granitic, gravelly soil, which could not be made to grow anything but wood to the profit of the grower; whereas, it grows wood better than a rich Illinois or Kansas prairie often condescends to do. Its trees are mainly Hemlock and Red Cedar (my evergreens), White and Red Oak, Whitewood, Chestnut, White and Blue Beech, Dogwood, White Ash, Sugar and Soft Maple, Elm, Hickory, Tulip, Butternut, Black, Yellow, and White Birch. There were just two trees that I could not name, after twenty years' absorption in the city; one of them is known as Pepperidge, the other as Yellow Poplar. There were a good many wild Black Cherries; but these I have nearly exterminated, as they bred caterpillars to infest my Apple-trees. Of shrubs, there are many that I cannot name. Witch Hazel, Bunch Willow, Choke Cherry, Hazel, Sassafras, and Sumac, are among those that I readily recognized. Swamp Alder infested the springy, rocky, boggy ground at the foot of one of my hills, till I extirpated it, and the Dogwood is marked for speedy destruction. It beautifies — nay, glorifies — the woods while in blossom for a week or so early in May; but it is of no account as timber, while it sows its seed everywhere, and tends to monopolize a good deal more ground than it will pay for.

My first care, on getting possession of my farm, was to shut cattle out of the greater part of the woods, where they had been free to roam and ravage throughout the two preceding centuries that this region had felt the presence of civilized man. Pasturing woods is one of the most glaring vices of our semi-barbarian agriculture. Cattle browse the tender twigs of delicate, valuable young trees, while they leave the coarse and worthless unscathed. I have, to-day, ten times as many of the Sugar Maple, White Ash, etc., coming on in my woods as there were when I bought and shut the cattle out of them.

I have no blind horror of cutting trees. Any fairly grown forest can always spare trees, and be benefited by their removal. But I protest most earnestly against the reckless waste involved in cutting off and burning over our forests. In regions which are *all* woods, ground must of course be cleared for cultivation; but many a farmer goes on slashing and burning long after he should halt and begin to be saving of his timber. Many of our dairymen are beginning to say, "Down with the rest of our woods! we can buy all the coal we need for fuel, with half the butter and cheese we can make on our lands, now covered with wood." Friends, that is a sad miscalculation. With one fourth of your land in wood, judiciously covering the crests of your ridges, the sides of your ravines, your farms will grow more grass than if wholly denuded and laid bare to the scorching sun. Protracted, desolating drouths, bleak, scathing winds, and the failure of delicate fruits like the Peach and finer Pears, are part of the penalty we pay for depriving our fields and gardens of the genial, hospitable protection of forests.

Of tree-planting, other than for fruit, I have as yet done little. A row of Rock Maples along the highways that skirt my farm, and a clump of evergreens just north of my garden, are nearly all I have to show. Any one can grow Sugar Maples who will try. To prove it, I need only say that I have lost but two in over a hundred, and these by accident, though my trees mainly came from Rochester, were opened on a warm, sunny day, and left thus with their roots exposed till thoroughly dry. I came upon the planter just then, and told him he had killed the trees; but I was mistaken. I would, however, advise no one to try the experiment of drying the roots of trees while transplanting them; but, if he *will* be so careless, he may better take the risk on the Sugar Maple than on any other tree within my knowledge.

As there is a stout hill just south of my farm, my lower land is overshadowed by hills in the two wrong directions, and so inclines to be cold. Just north of where my brook dances out of the glen which it has worn down the face of

My Evergreen Hedge.

the hill is my garden, with a slight elevation or ridge just north of it.

This low ridge I have planted with evergreens, as a shelter or wind-break for the garden. Part of them are Hemlocks and Red Cedars, transplanted from the woods just at hand; perhaps as many are Norway and other Pines, with Balsam and other Firs, obtained from nurseries. These latter have the more luxuriant growth, but all have done well; and the copse or clump — possibly forty rods in length by three or four in width — is (at least in Winter) the pleasantest object seen on the farm. The little greenhouse which nestles beneath it is flanked by strawberry beds, a few grape-vines, and room for early vegetables, which, sloping gently southward, enjoy an average temperature several degrees higher than they would if the evergreens were away; and the acre or so of level garden farther south is also, but less considerably, warmed and sheltered by this belt of evergreens, which not only verifies the apothegm of Keats, that "A thing of beauty is a joy forever," but is a positive reënforcement to the productive capacity of the farm.

I hope this narration will induce some — I wish it might induce many — to plant trees, and especially evergreens. Not merely as ornamental drapery to dwellings, but as mollifiers of the harshness of our capricious climate, they have a value as yet too narrowly appreciated. A few choice trees, just old enough to transplant, cost but a trifle; and whoever plants a dozen such judiciously, and shields them from injury, has provided a source of healthful enjoyment, not only for his own lifetime, but for that of generations yet to be.

But we need tree-planting on a broader scale than this. Wherever a ledge or giant rock impedes thorough tillage, there should be a tree, if not trees. Men of means and of thrift should buy up sterile tracts that are offered for sale at low rates, and promptly cover them with White Oak, Hickory, White Pine, Locust, Chestnut, &c. They can no otherwise so safely and profitably invest their means for the benefit of their children, while benefiting also future generations. Timber grows steadily dearer and dearer; streams become desolating torrents at intervals, and beds of dry sand and pebbles for weeks in Summer and Fall, because our hills have been too generally stripped and denuded of trees. Let us unitedly cease to do evil and learn to do well in relation to trees.

XXXVII.

MY FARMING.

THOSE who have read my account of my farm will have judged that it is not well calculated to enrich its owner by large, easily produced crops, and that it was bought in full view of this fact. I wanted a place near a railroad station, and not too far from the city; my wife wanted pure air, agreeable scenery, reasonable seclusion, but, above all, a choice, never-failing spring, a cascade, and evergreen woods, as I have already stated. Having found these on the thirty-odd acres which comprised our original purchase, we were not so unreasonable as to expect to secure also the fertility and facility of a dry, gently rolling Western prairie, or of a rich intervale of the Connecticut or Hudson. We knew that our upland was in good part hard, steep, and rocky, and that its productive capacity — never remarkable — had been largely reduced by two centuries of persistent and often excessive pasturing. Sheep may thus be fed a thousand years, yet return to the soil nearly as much as they take from it; not so with milch cows, when their milk is sent away to some city, and nothing returned therefor that enriches the fields whence that milk, in the shape of grass or hay, was drawn. And so, measurably, of Fruit: whereas Apples have long been a leading staple of our region, — Newcastle having formerly boasted more Apple-trees than any township of its size in America. But an Apple-tree cannot forever draw on the bank of Nature without having its drafts protested, if nothing is ever deposited there to its credit; and caterpillars have so long been allowed to strip most of our trees unresisted, that many have grown prematurely old and moss-covered. One year with another, Newcastle does not grow half so many Apples as her trees call for; and she never will till she feeds her trees better and fights their enemies with more persistent resolution than she has done. I have seen five thousand of those trees, in the course of a brief morning ride in June, with more caterpillars than remaining leaves per tree; and very little reflection can be needed to show that trees so neglected for a few years will have outlived their usefulness.

The woods are *my* special department. Whenever I can save a Saturday for the farm, I try to give a good part of it to my patch of forest. The axe is the healthiest implement that man ever handled, and is especially so for habitual writers and other sedentary workers, whose shoulders it throws back, expanding their chests, and opening their lungs. If every youth and man, from fifteen to fifty years old, could wield an axe two hours per day, dyspepsia would vanish from the earth, and rheumatism become decidedly scarce. I am a poor chopper; yet the axe is my doctor and delight. Its use gives the mind just enough occupation to prevent its falling into revery or absorbing trains of thought, while every muscle in the body receives sufficient, yet not exhausting, exercise. I wish all our boys would learn to love the axe.

I began by cutting out the Witch Hazels, and other trash not worth keeping, and trimming up my trees, especially the Hemlocks, which grow limbs clear to the ground, and throw them out horizontally to such a distance that several rods of ground are sometimes monopolized by a single tree. Many of these lower limbs die in the course of time, but do not fall off; on the contrary, they harden and sharpen into spikes, which threaten your face and eyes as if they were bayonets. These I have gradually cut away and transformed into fuel. Many of my Hemlocks I have trimmed to a height of at least fifty feet; and I mean to serve many others just so, if I can ever find time before old age compels me to stop climbing.

But the Hemlock so bristles throughout with limbs that it

can easily be climbed by a hale man till he is seventy; and, working with a hatchet or light axe, you commence trimming at the top, — that is, as high as you choose to trim, — and, without difficulty, cut all smooth as you work your way down. Limbs to the ground may be graceful in the edge of your wood; but your tree will not make timber nearly so fast as if trimmed, and you cannot afford it so much space as it claims in the heart of your patch of forest.

If I linger proudly among my trees, consider that here most of my farm-work has been done, and here my profit has been realized, in the shape of health and vigor. When I am asked the usual question, "How has your farming paid?" I can truthfully answer that *my* part of it has paid splendidly, being all income and no outgo, — and who can show a better balance-sheet than *that?*

Seriously — I believe there is money to be made by judicious tree-planting and forest-culture, now that railroads have so greatly cheapened the cost of transportation. If any man has or can buy a tract of woodland, or land too poor or broken to be profitably tilled, let him shut out cattle, and steadily plant choice trees while cutting out poorer; let him cut every tree that stops growing and begins to decay, or shed its limbs; let him not hesitate to thin as well as trim up; let him cut out Red Oak, for instance, and sow the acorns of White; let him, when half a dozen or more sprouts start from a single stump, cut away all but two or three, and by and by cut again; and I am confident that he may thus grow timber twice as rapidly as where it is neglected, and grow trees far more valuable than those that come by chance. Nay: if near a city, he can make a thousand dollars far more easily, though less quickly, by growing Timber than by growing Grain.

The land I ultimately bought included part of an old orchard, which I estimated worth a little more than the firewood that might be made of it; but there I was mistaken. Old Apple-trees, never grafted, or grafted with indifferent

Phot. by Rockwood.

MY HOUSE IN THE WOODS.

fruit, and which have been suffered to grow out of proper shape to a height of forty or fifty feet, so that caterpillars flourish in their tops with impunity, are simply nuisances. If you buy or inherit such, cut them down remorselessly the moment you can obtain fruit for your own use from others.

On the land I first purchased was a young orchard of two acres, mainly Russets, — small fruit, but not inviting to worms, while it keeps splendidly, — in fact, hardly becomes eatable till April or May. The Russet yields bounteously and pretty constantly; so that, if I were planting for profit in this region, I should give this sort the preference. I should carefully avoid the common error (which I, when greener, committed) of planting many sorts together; indeed, I would prefer to have but one sort in an orchard, for the convenience of gathering and marketing.

My young orchards are just fairly beginning to bear. The ground was not ploughed so deeply as it should be, — in fact, the ground on which Apple-trees are to be set should be trenched three feet deep, — but it has been well fertilized; and I hope for good crops in the years close at hand.

In the little dell or glen through which my brook emerges from the wood wherein it has brawled down the hill, to dance across a gentle slope to the swamp below, is *the* spring, — pure as crystal, never-failing, cold as you could wish it for drink in the hottest day, and so thoroughly shaded and sheltered that, I am confident, it was never warm and never frozen over. Many springs on my farm are excellent, but this is peerless. It determined the location of my house, which stands on a little plateau or bench of level ground half-way down the hill, some twenty rods north of, and forty feet higher than, itself. I never saw a sweeter spot than was the little plat of grass which my house has supplanted, with tall woods all around, and a thrifty growth of young hemlocks starting thickly just west and south of it. I do not now regard this as a judicious location: it is too much shaded and shut in; it is too damp for health in a wet time; it tempts the chimney to smoke, especially when the atmosphere is so heavy that the wind beats down over the wooded hill that rises directly on the north and east; but the hottest day is cool here; dust is unknown; and no rumble from any highway disturbs meditation or piques curiosity. My house is not much, — hastily erected, small, slight, and wooden, it has at length been almost deserted for one recently purchased and refitted on the edge of the village, just where my private road emerges from the farm, on its way to the station; but the cottage in the woods is still *my* house, where my books remain, where I mean to garner my treasures, and wherein I propose to be "at home" to my friends at stated seasons, and "not at home" to any one when I address myself to work, and especially to the consummation of a yet unaired literary project. But these are dreams, which opportunity may never be afforded to realize. As yet, I am a horse in a bark-mill, and tread his monotonous round; never finding time to do to-day what can possibly be postponed to the morrow.

The woodless portion of my upland has been patiently improved by digging, blasting, and picking out rock and stone, by running under-drains where they seemed to be needed, by ploughing deeper than it was ever ploughed before, though not yet nearly deep enough, and by persistent fertilizing with composted swamp muck, lime, salt, gypsum, bone-dust, and artificial, as well as mineral, manures, until it is to-day in very fair condition, or only needs deepening six to twelve inches more to make it so. Already, it produces almost unfailingly good crops of Indian Corn, Oats, Turnips, and especially of Grass. I have repeatedly grown fair crops of Wheat, especially of Spring, and never decidedly failed but once. Most of our lands that have long been devoted to the production of milk are in special need of phosphates, which are most readily supplied in the shape of ground bones, — the finer the better. With land in proper condition, Wheat is as sure a crop in Southern New York as in Wisconsin or Minnesota. Roots have generally done well with me on ground properly prepared; but the Potato is an exception; and I doubt that it

Phot. by Rockwood.

MY PRESENT HOME.

will hereafter produce so plenteously on our seaboard as on the breezy slopes of the Green Mountains, the Catskills, or of our high inland counties like Madison or Steuben.

My swamp (whereof successive purchases have increased the area to fully twenty acres) has been my chief difficulty. Originally, a muddy, oozy fen, thickly dotted with "hassocks" or "tussocks" of coarse bog-grass, I have cut these and (tired of awaiting their natural decay) burned them to fertilizing ashes for my upland; have seamed the entire flat with under-drains; have cut down the little runnel that permeated its centre, and the open ditch that for some distance ran parallel to it on the east, collecting the waters of a dozen springs, obliged to join it ere it was lost in my brook, that comes brawling down my hillside, and have spared no effort, grudged no cost, to render it completely arable. But the fall is so slight, not only on my own land, but for nearly a mile below it, that my success is still partial and unsatisfactory. Though I have been allowed to straighten, as well as deepen, the brook on my neighbors' land, below me, I am still flooded at intervals with back-water, which chokes my drains and threatens to inundate my fattest acres. If I live, I shall surely triumph in the end; and I am now profiting by the engineering of Mr. James Gall, whose experience in the Central (New York) and Prospect (Brooklyn) Parks is of decided value. But a good outlet, or fall, is so essential to easy success in draining, that every one who shall hereafter attempt to drain a swamp ought to begin with this, and be sure of at least two feet fall from his lowest point at flood-time in Spring before he cuts his first drain. Of all unprofitable work, burying tiles where water will run sometimes one way, sometimes the other, until they choke with mud and become utterly useless, is most discouraging. But thorough under-draining is the basis of all lasting improvement in farm or garden culture; and we should either drain our swamps thoroughly, or provide for flooding them in Winter and lay them down to cranberries. I do not doubt that this latter is in many cases the wiser disposition, except where the vicinity of a city or village forbids it, from due regard to others' health. But *my* swamp is close by a hamlet which is soon to be quite a village: so it must and shall be drained; and, that thoroughly done, it will be cheap at five hundred dollars per acre, since it needs little *but* draining to assimilate it in fertility to a patch of Western prairie. If I live, it shall yet come to.

My Barn.

My barn is a fair success. I placed it on the shelf of my hill, nearest to the upper (east) side of my place, because a barn-yard is a manufactory of heavy fertilizers from materials of lesser weight; and it is easier to draw these down hill than up. I built its walls wholly of stones gathered or blasted from the adjacent slope, to the extent of four or five thousand tons, and laid in a box with a thin mortar of (little) lime and (much) sand, filling all the interstices and binding the whole into a solid mass, till my walls are nearly one solid rock, while the roof is of Vermont slate. I drive into three stories, — a basement for manures, a stable for animals, and a story above this for hay — while grain is pitched into the loft or "scaffold" above, from whose floor the roof rises steep to a height of sixteen to eighteen feet. There should have been more windows for light and air; but my barn is convenient, while impervious to frost, and I am confident that cattle are wintered in it at a fourth less cost than when they shiver in board shanties, with cracks between the boards that will admit your hand. No part of our rural economy is more wasteful than the habitual exposure of our animals to pelting, chilling storms, and to intense cold. Building with concrete is still a novelty, and was far more so ten years ago, when I built my barn. I could now build better and cheaper; but I am glad that I need not. I calculate that this barn will be abidingly useful long after I shall have been utterly forgotten; and that, had I chosen to have my name lettered on its front, it would have remained there to honor me as a builder, long after it had ceased to have any other significance.

"You will be sick of living in the country within two years," I was confidently told when I bought; "and your place will be advertised for sale." "Then the sheriff's name will be at the foot of the advertisement," I responded. The mere fact that *I* am not yet sick of it proves nothing, since I only try to spend Saturdays upon it, and am often unable to do even that; but my wife, who spends most of each year there, and has done so ever since it was bought, is equally constant in her devotion; and the bare idea of exchanging our place for any other has never yet suggested itself to either of us. With a first-rate stone or brick house to shut out the cold, I doubt if either of us would, of choice, live elsewhere, even in Winter. For, while the young may love to wander, and may feel that they enjoy the fragrance of others' flowers, the stately grace of their woods, I think we all, as we grow old, love to feel and know that some spot of earth is peculiarly our own, — ours to possess and to enjoy, — ours to improve and to transmit to our children. As we realize the steady march of years in the thinning of our blanched locks, the deepening of our wrinkles, we more and more incline to shun travel and crowds and novelties, and concentrate our affections on the few who are infolded by "that dear hut, our home."

"But what of the *profits* of your farming? You have said nothing of *them*," I often hear. Well: it is not yet time to speak of them, — in fact, they are, as yet, unspeakably small. Thus far, I have been making a farm, rather than working one; and the process is not yet complete. The first Apple-trees of my planting, are just beginning to bear; my best land, having been recently bought, and as yet imperfectly drained, is still unproductive. Nor do I expect that farming — or anything else — will pay without better oversight than I have yet been able to accord it.

"Do you not perceive," said one near to me, "that your man there does not more than half work?" "Certainly," I replied; "I am quite aware of it. Were he disposed to be efficient, he would work his own land, not mine." You can scarcely hire any work well done, to which you cannot give personal attention. Publishing newspapers by proxy would be still more ruinous than farming.

But I close with a confident assertion that *good farming* WILL *pay* — yes, *does* pay — right here by New York, — pay generally, and pay well. Of course, he who lacks capital must work to disadvantage in this as in everything else; and a little capital will go further in the Far West than on the crowded seaboard; but I feel certain that even *I* could make money by farming in Westchester County, if I could give my time and mind to it; and that a good farmer, with adequate means, can, in following his vocation, do as well near this city as a reasonable man could expect, or wisely desire.

XXXVIII.

"SEWARD, WEED, AND GREELEY."

AS I had first engaged conspicuously in political strife at the invitation of Mr. Thurlow Weed, and had thus been brought, very soon afterward, into familiar and confidential relations with his next friend, Mr. William H. Seward, I was measurably identified with, if not thoroughly devoted to, their mutual fortunes, for the next fifteen or sixteen years. While editing The Jeffersonian in Albany, I wrote and reported (imperfectly) legislative proceedings for Mr. Weed's paper, The Albany Evening Journal; and, though I had no part in nominating Mr. Seward for Governor in 1838, I did whatever I could to help elect him; and so at his reëlection in 1840. (He had previously been State Senator, elected in 1830; but had been badly defeated by William L. Marcy, when first a candidate for Governor, in 1834.) When, after four years of obscuration, the Whig star was again in the ascendant, in 1846 – 48, I was a zealous, if not very effective, advocate of his election to the United States Senate.

Apart from politics, I liked the man, though not blind to his faults. His natural instincts were humane and progressive. He hated Slavery and all its belongings, though a seeming necessity constrained him to write, in 1838, to this intensely pro-Slavery city, a pro-Slavery letter, which was at war with his real, or at least with his subsequent, convictions. Though of Democratic parentage, he had been an Adams man, an Anti-Mason, and was now thoroughly a Whig. The policy of more extensive and vigorous Internal Improvement had no more zealous champion. By nature, genial and averse to pomp, ceremony, and formality, few public men of his early prime were better calculated to attract and fascinate young men of his own party, and holding views accordant on most points with his.

Yet he had faults, which his accession to power soon displayed in bold relief. His natural tendencies were toward a government not merely paternal, but prodigal, — one which, in its multiform endeavors to make every one prosperous, if not rich, was very likely to whelm all in general embarrassment, if not in general bankruptcy. Few Governors have favored, few Senators voted for, more unwisely lavish expenditures than he. Above the suspicion of voting money into his own pocket, he has a rooted dislike to opposing a project or bill whereby any of his attached friends are to profit. And, conceited as we all are, I think most men exceed him in the art of concealing from others their overweening faith in their own sagacity and discernment.

Mr. Thurlow Weed was of coarser mould and fibre, — tall, robust, dark-featured, shrewd, resolute, and not over-scrupulous, — keen-sighted, though not far-seeing. Writing slowly and with difficulty, he was for twenty years the most sententious and pungent writer of editorial paragraphs on the American press.

In pecuniary matters, he was generous to a fault while poor; he is said to be less so since he became rich; but I am no longer in a position to know. I cannot doubt, however, that if he had never seen Wall Street or Washington, had never heard of the Stock Board, and had lived in some yet undiscovered country, where legislation is never bought nor sold, his life would have been more blameless, useful, and happy.

I was sitting beside him in his editorial room soon after Governor Seward's election, when he opened a letter from a brother Whig, which ran substantially thus: —

"DEAR WEED: I want to be a Bank Commissioner. You know how to fix it. Do so, and draw on me for whatever sum you may see fit. Yours truly."

In an instant, his face became preternaturally black with mingled rage and mortification. "My God!" said he, "I knew that my political adversaries thought me a scoundrel, but I never till now supposed that my friends did." He at once responded to the overture to this effect:—

"Sir: I have received your letter, and shall lay it before the Governor elect, with whom it will doubtless have the influence it deserves. Yours."

Though generally in hearty accord, these fast friends were not entirely so. Seward, born in comfortable circumstances, and educated a gentleman, had none of the "Poor White" prejudice against Blacks; while it was otherwise with Weed, whose origin and training had been different. *My* New England birth and Federal antecedents saved me from sharing this infirmity, to which the poverty and obscurity of my boyhood might else have exposed me.

I was early brought into collision with both my seniors on the subject of a Registry Law. Every Whig who had been active in the political contests of this city was instinctively and intensely a champion of a registration of legal voters; knowing well, by sad experience, that, in its absence, enormous frauds to our damage are the rule, and honest and legal voting the exception. So, in the first legislature of our State that was Whig all over, a bill was introduced, with my very hearty assent and active support, which provided for a registration of voters here; and it had made such headway before it attracted the serious attention of Messrs. Seward and Weed, that all their great influence could not prevent the Whig members supporting and passing it. Yet the measure was so intensely deprecated by them, as tending to alienate the undistinguished poor, and especially those of foreign birth, from our side, by teaching them to regard the Whigs as hostile to their rights, that the purpose of vetoing it was fully formed and confidentially avowed; and, though it was at length abandoned, and the bill signed, Mr. Weed assured me that the Governor would have preferred to lose his right hand.

On one important question, Mr. Weed and I were antipodes. Believing that a currency in part of paper, kept at par with specie, and current in every part of our country, was indispensable, I was a zealous advocate of a National Bank; which he as heartily detested, believing that its supporters would always be identified in the popular mind with aristocracy, monopoly, exclusive privilege, &c. He attempted, more than once, to overbear my convictions on this point, or at least preclude their utterance, but was at length brought apparently to comprehend that this was a point on which we must agree to differ.

The political canvass of 1854 in our State was unlike any other ever known. The advocacy and passage of the Nebraska Bill had disorganized and seriously weakened the Democrats; the Whig party had wasted to a shadow, yet an august, imposing, venerable shade; the question of Liquor Prohibition, grown suddenly prominent by reason of its success in Maine, was rapidly effacing, or at least overriding, party lines; while the American, or "Know-Nothing" movement had not only a considerable, though ill-defined, genuine strength, but had attracted crowds of nominal adherents, intent on diverse special ends. Though the State had been two or three years under Democratic rule by large majorities, no one could safely guess how this year's election would result.

I was a member of the first anti-Nebraska or Republican State Convention, which met at Saratoga Springs in September; but Messrs. Weed and Seward for a while stood aloof from the movement, preferring to be still regarded as Whigs. We made no nominations at that time, but provided for a nominating convention at a later day; meantime, the Whigs held theirs, and nominated Myron H. Clark for Governor, with Henry J. Raymond for Lieutenant. The Republicans and the Prohibitionists severally held conventions thereafter, and adopted these candidates, finding them all they could ask. The Democrats had been rent afresh by their old feud respecting Slavery in the Territories: the "Softs" running the incumbent, Horatio Seymour; the "Hards," Greene C. Bronson, for Governor. The "American" candidate was Daniel Ullmann. When the vote was canvassed, it was found thus divided:—

Gov. Clark	156,804	*Lt.-Gov.* Raymond	157,166
Seymour	156,495	Ludlow (*Soft*)	128,833
Ullmann (*Am.*)	122,282	Scroggs (*Am.*)	121,037
Bronson	33,851	Ford (*Hard*)	52,074

The Whigs had both branches of the Legislature by large majorities, and they had like majorities for every candidate on their State ticket but their Governor, who was barely elected. And, though the "Americans" claimed many of the members elect, and with reason, we, who had been laboring to secure the return of Governor Seward to the Senate, *knew* that *we* had succeeded,—that many of the votes confidently counted on by his adversaries were sure for him. There were some members who actually voted against him, who would have voted for him had their votes been needed.

When all was beyond contingency, I wrote Governor Seward a private letter, intended for his eye alone; but the pointed and misleading allusions to it by certain of the Governor's devoted followers, after his failure to be nominated for President at Chicago in 1860, impelled me to demand it for publication, and to print it. It is, *verbatim*, as follows:—

HORACE GREELEY TO WILLIAM H. SEWARD.

NEW YORK, Saturday Evening, November 11, 1854.

GOVERNOR SEWARD: The Election is over, and its results sufficiently ascertained. It seems to me a fitting time to announce to you the dissolution of the political firm of Seward, Weed, and Greeley, by the withdrawal of the junior partner,—said withdrawal to take effect on the morning after the first Tuesday in February next. And, as it may seem a great presumption in me to assume that any such firm exists, especially since the public was advised, rather more than a year ago, by an editorial rescript in The Evening Journal formally reading me out of the Whig party, that I was esteemed no longer either useful or ornamental in the concern, you will, I am sure, indulge me in some reminiscences which seem to befit the occasion.

I was a poor young printer and Editor of a Literary Journal, — a very active and bitter Whig in a small way, but not seeking to be known out of my own Ward Committee, — when, after the great Political Revulsion of 1837, I was one day called to the City Hotel, where two strangers introduced themselves as Thurlow Weed and Lewis Benedict, of Albany. They told me that a cheap Campaign Paper of a peculiar stamp at Albany had been resolved on, and that I had been selected to edit it. The announcement might well be deemed flattering by one who had never even sought the notice of the great, and who was not known as a partisan writer; and I eagerly embraced their proposal. They asked me to fix my salary for the year; I named $ 1,000, which they agreed to; and I did the work required, to the best of my ability. It was work that made no figure, and created no sensation; but I loved it, and I did it well. When it was done, you were Governor, dispensing offices worth $ 3,000 to $ 20,000 per year to your friends and compatriots, and I returned to my garret and my crust, and my desperate battle with pecuniary obligations heaped upon me by bad partners in business and the disastrous events of 1837. I believe it did not then occur to me that some one of these abundant places might have been offered to me without injustice; I now think it should have occurred to *you*. If it did occur to me, I was not the man to ask you for it; I think that should not have been necessary. I only remember that no friend at Albany inquired as to my pecuniary circumstances; that your friend (but not mine), Robert C. Wetmore, was one of the chief dispensers of your patronage here; and that such devoted compatriots as A. H. Wells and John Hooks were lifted by you out of pauperism into independence, as I am glad I was not; and yet an inquiry from you as to my needs and means at that day would have been timely, and held ever in grateful remembrance.

In the Harrison campaign of 1840, I was again designated to edit a campaign paper. I published it as well, and ought to have made something by it, in spite of its extremely low price; my extreme poverty was the main reason why I did not. It compelled me to hire press-work, mailing, &c., done by the job, and high charges for extra work nearly ate me up. At the close, I was still without property and in debt; but this paper had rather improved my position.

Now came the great scramble of the swell mob of coon minstrels and cider-suckers at Washington, — I not being counted in. Several regiments of them went on from this city; but no one of the whole crowd — though I say it who should not — had done so much toward General Harrison's nomination and election as yours respectfully. I asked nothing, expected nothing; but you, Governor Seward, ought to have asked that I be postmaster of New York. Your asking would have been in vain; but it would have been an act of grace neither wasted nor undeserved.

I soon after started The Tribune, because I was urged to do so by certain of your friends, and because such a paper was needed here. I was promised certain pecuniary aid in so doing; it might have been given me without cost or risk to any one. All I ever had was a loan by piecemeal of $1,000 from James Coggeshall, God bless his honored memory! I did not ask for this; and I think it is the one sole case in which I ever received a pecuniary favor from a political associate. I am very thankful that he did not die till it was fully repaid.

And here let me honor one grateful recollection. When the Whig party under your rule had offices to give, my name was never thought of; but when, in 1842–43, we were hopelessly out of power, I was honored with the party nomination for State Printer. When we came again to have a State Printer to *elect* as well as nominate, the place went to Weed, as it ought. Yet it is worth something to know that there was once a time when it was not deemed too great a sacrifice to recognize me as belonging to your household. If a new office had not since been created on purpose to give its valuable patronage to H. J. Raymond, and enable St. John to show forth his Times as the organ of the Whig State Administration, I should have been still more grateful.

In 1848, your star again rose, and my warmest hopes were realized in your election to the Senate. I was no longer needy, and had no more claim than desire to be recognized by General Taylor. I think I had some claim to forbearance from you. What I received thereupon was a most humiliating lecture in the shape of a decision in the libel-case of Redfield and Pringle, and an obligation to publish it in my own and the other journal of our supposed firm. I thought, and still think, this lecture needlessly cruel and mortifying. The plaintiffs, after using my columns to the extent of their needs or desires, stopped writing, and called on me for the name of their assailant. I proffered it to them, — a thoroughly responsible name. They refused to accept it, unless it should prove to be one of the four or five first men in Batavia! — when they had known from the first who it was, and that it was neither of them. They would not accept that which they had demanded; they sued me instead for money; and money you were at liberty to give them to your heart's content. I do not think you *were* at liberty to humiliate me in the eyes of my own and your* public as you did. I think you exalted your own judicial sternness and fearlessness unduly at my expense. I think you had a better occasion for the display of these qualities when Webb threw himself untimely upon you for a pardon which he had done all a man could do to demerit. (His paper is paying you for it now.)

I have publicly set forth my view of your and our duty with respect to Fusion, Nebraska and party designations. I will not repeat any of that. I have referred also to Weed's reading me out of the Whig party, — my crime being in this, as in some other things, that of doing to-day what more politic persons will not be ready to do till to-morrow.

Let me speak of the late canvass. I was once sent to Congress for ninety days, merely to enable Jim Brooks to secure a seat therein for four years. I think I never hinted to any human being that I would have liked to be put forward for any place. But James W. White (you hardly know how good and true a man he is) started my name for Congress, and Brooks's packed delegation thought I could help him through, so I was put on behind him. But this last Spring, after the Nebraska question had created a new state of things at the North, one or two personal friends, of no political consideration, suggested my name as a candidate for Governor, and I did not discourage them. Soon, the persons who were afterward mainly instrumental in nominating Clark came about me, and asked if I could secure the Know-

* If I am not mistaken, this judgment is the only speech, letter, or document, addressed to the public, in which you ever recognized my existence. I hope I may not go down to posterity as embalmed therein.

Nothing vote. I told them I neither could nor would touch it, — on the contrary, I loathed and repelled it. Thereupon, they turned upon Clark.

I said nothing, did nothing. A hundred people asked me who should be run for Governor. I sometimes indicated Patterson; I never hinted at my own name. But by and by Weed came down and called me to him, to tell me why he could not support me for Governor. (I had never asked nor counted on his support.)

I am sure Weed did not mean to humiliate me, but he did it. The upshot of his discourse (very cautiously stated) was this: If I were a candidate for Governor, I should beat not myself only, but you. Perhaps that was true. But, as I had in no manner solicited his or your support, I thought this might have been said to my friends, rather than to me. I suspect it is true that I could not have been elected Governor as a Whig. But had he and you been favorable, there *would* have been a party in the State, ere this, which could and would have elected me to any post, without injuring myself or endangering your reëlection.

It was in vain that I urged that I had in no manner asked a nomination. At length, I was nettled by his language — well intended, but *very* cutting, as addressed by him to me — to say, in substance, "Well, then, make Patterson Governor, and try my name for Lieutenant. To lose this place is a matter of no importance, and we can see whether I am really so odious."

I should have hated to serve as Lieutenant-Governor, but I should have gloried in running for the post. I want to have my enemies all upon me at once, — I am tired of fighting them piecemeal. And, although I should have been beaten in the canvass, I know that my running would have helped the ticket and helped my paper.

It was thought best to let the matter take another course. No other name could have been put upon the ticket so bitterly humbling to me as that which was selected. The nomination was given to Raymond, — the fight left to me. And, Governor Seward, *I have made it*, though it be conceited in me to say so. What little fight there has been, I have stirred up. Even Weed has not been (I speak of his paper) hearty in this contest, while the journal of the Whig Lieutenant-Governor has taken care of its own interests and let the canvass take care of itself, as it early declared it would do. That journal has (because of its milk-and-water course) some twenty thousand subscribers in this city and its suburbs; and of these twenty thousand, I venture to say, more voted for Ullmann and Scroggs than for Clark and Raymond; The Tribune (also because of its character) has but eight thousand subscribers within the same radius; and, I venture to say that, of its habitual readers, nine tenths voted for Clark and Raymond, very few for Ullmann and Scroggs. I had to bear the brunt of the contest, and take a terrible responsibility, in order to prevent the Whigs uniting upon James W. Barker, in order to defeat Fernando Wood. Had Barker been elected here, neither you nor I could walk these streets without being hooted, and Know-Nothingism would have swept like a prairie-fire. I stopped Barker's election at the cost of incurring the deadliest enmity of the defeated gang, and I have been rebuked for it by the Lieutenant-Governor's paper. At the critical moment, he came out against John Wheeler in favor of Charles H. Marshall (who would have been your deadliest enemy in the House); and even your Colonel-General's paper, which was even with me in insisting that Wheeler should be returned, wheeled about at the last moment, and went in for Marshall, — The Tribune alone clinging to Wheeler to the last. I rejoice that they who turned so suddenly were not able to turn all their readers.

Governor Seward, I know that some of your most cherished friends think me a great obstacle to your advancement, — that John Schoolcraft, for one, insists that you and Weed shall not be identified with me. I trust, after a time, you will not be. I trust I shall never be found in opposition to you; I have no further wish but to glide out of the newspaper world as quietly and as speedily as possible, join my family in Europe, and, if possible, stay there quite a time, — long enough to cool my fevered brain and renovate my overtasked energies. All I ask is that we shall be counted even on the morning after the first Tuesday in February, as aforesaid, and that I may thereafter take such course as seems best, without reference to the past.

You have done me acts of valued kindness in the line of your profession, — let me close with the assurance that these will ever be gratefully remembered by

Yours,

HORACE GREELEY.

HON. WM. H. SEWARD, Present.

Seeing nothing in this letter that requires explanation, I simply add that my personal relations with Governor Seward were wholly unchanged by it. We met frequently and cordially after it was written, and we very freely conferred and coöperated during the long struggle in Congress for Kansas and Free Labor. He understood as well as I did that my position with regard to him, though more independent than it had been, was nowise hostile, and that I was as ready to support his advancement as that of any other statesman, whenever my judgment should tell me that the public good required it. I was not his adversary, but my own and my country's freeman.

In the Spring of 1859, Governor Seward crossed the Atlantic; visiting Egypt, traversing Syria and other portions of Asia Minor, as well as much of Europe. Soon after his return, he came one evening to my seat in Dr. Chapin's church, — as he had repeatedly done during former visits to our city, — and I now recall this as the last occasion on which we ever met. The Scripture lesson of the evening was the thirty-first chapter of Proverbs, which recounts the merits and proclaims the honors of the virtuous woman; enumerating, among the latter, that "Her husband is known in the gates, when he sitteth among the elders of the land." "Two months ago," thereupon observed Governor Seward, "I was travelling in Syria, with a Turkish firman and other documents, which proclaimed me, I infer, a person of some consequence; since the head functionary of a village where I halted and presented my papers received me with the greatest distinction, and, as a final proof of his regard, invited me to sit with him in the gate, as, flanked by the elders, he heard complaints and defences, and rendered judgment thereon." So unchanging are the essential habits and usages of the Asiatics, that foreign conquest — Egyptian, Assyrian, Persian, Greek, Roman, Saracen, Crusader, and Osmanli — had, along with more than thirty centuries, rolled their effacing surges over that region, yet here are the chiefs of the respective villages or tribes judging the people as of old, surrounded and counselled by the elders; and any eminent stranger is invited, as a mark of honor, to sit with them, as he was in (or before) the reign of Solomon.

Ross Browne found but one man doing anything in Syria; and he was falling off a house. It is well to be usefully busy; yet quiet and tenacious contentment with

> "The good old ways, — *all* ways, when old, are good,"

is not devoid of recommendation, and even advantage.

I have often, during these later years, been unable to agree with Governor Seward, — have sometimes quite pointedly dissented from his views of great public questions. It is not probable that we shall ever again be as near to each other as we have been. That his ends have ever been patriotic, I will not doubt; that his means have sometimes been mistaken, I think his warmest friends must admit. That he once aspired to the Presidency is a truth, but no reproach; able, wise, and good men have done so, without impeachment of their patriotism or abatement of their usefulness. Still, one who has all but clutched the glittering prize, yet failed to secure it, always thereafter seems to have suffered from the aspiration or the failure, — possibly from both. Great, intellectually, as Daniel Webster was, he would have been morally greater, and every way more useful and honored, had he sternly responded "Get thee behind me, Satan!" to every suggestion that he might yet attain the Presidency. I hope Mr. Seward will outlive, if he has not already outlived, his ambition, and will find leisure and incitement to write of what he has seen and known during his all but a half-century of devotion to public affairs. Doubtless, he could clear up points which now seem obscure and puzzling; and I will hope he would succeed in showing that, even when most denounced and execrated, he was, however mistaken, faithful in heart and purpose to Justice, to Freedom, and the inalienable Rights of Man.

XXXIX.

EUROPE REVISITED. — PARIS. — SWITZERLAND.

IN the Autumn of 1854, my wife took passage, with our two surviving children, for Europe, under a pledge that I should follow and rejoin her the ensuing Spring. As those children were less than six and four years old respectively, I did not believe she had the courage to start on such a journey without me to a continent whereon she had scarcely an acquaintance; but when I at length said to her, "If you are really going, I must engage your passage," she replied, "Engage it, then"; and I did so. She went accordingly, and spent the ensuing Winter quietly in London; where I joined her late in April ensuing. In a few days, I ran over in advance to Paris, where I hired a little cottage just outside of the then western barrier l'Etoile or *octroi* gate, which separates the Avenue Champs Elysees from the street outside, which leads to the Bois de Bolougne, to Passy, and to Neuilly. Here my wife soon rejoined me with our children, two female friends, and the husband of one of them; and here we remained till late in June, visiting the second World's Exposition, the Louvre, the Garden of Plants, the Invalides, Notre Dame, the Field of Mars, the Madeleine, Père-la-Chaise, &c., &c., and making (or renewing) a very few French with many American acquaintances. The Spring was remarkably cold, backward, cloudy, and rainy, — very unlike our preconceptions of "sunny France," and our enjoyment of Paris did not fulfil our expectations; yet the six weeks thus spent are fixed in my memory as the nearest approach to leisure I have known during the last thirty years. For, though still occupied, and even busy, throughout nearly every day, I was less so than in any former six weeks since I first landed in New York. I spent much time in the Exposition, trying to comprehend it; but I was not a juror, as I had been in London four years previously, and I did not feel required to study this Exposition so persistently, so systematically, as I had studied the former. Besides, it did not impress me so favorably nor interest me so deeply as that did. The edifice was of stone; hence, far more massive, gloomy, crypt-like, than the Hyde Park marvel; and the French seemed to me inferior in the skill required for lucid arrangement and classification. This judgment may have been the dictate of prejudice or ignorance; I only speak as I felt, and record an abiding impression. Two hours of impulsive wandering and gazing in the Paris Exposition fatigued me more than four hours' steady work as a juror in its London precursor; and I learned immeasurably more from that of '51 than I did from that of '55. In fact, the only point on which my little all of knowledge seems to have been permanently enlarged by the latter is that I think I obtained here some faint, rude conception of the peculiarities and merits of the school of art termed "pre-Raphaelite,"—I cannot say how aptly. I was deeply, though not altogether favorably, impressed by the works of J. E. Millais, Holman Hunt, and other apostles of this school, whose works here first arrested my attention; and I now recall a picture of "The Dead Ophelia" (by Millais, if I rightly remember), which evinced a pains-taking fidelity, and made a vivid, though unpleasant, impression. I trust that this school has not yet attained its fulness of development, or at least had not in 1855; if it had, the grand achievements of Raphael, of Titian, and of Murillo are in little danger of being eclipsed or superseded by those of its disciples or devotees. Still, the fact remains, that, of the many pictures exhibited in the Fine Arts division of the Paris Exposition, I remember none beside so distinctly, so vividly, as those of the British pre-Raphaelites, so called, though several of the French painters of our day evince decided merit.

Paris is the Paradise of thoughtless boys with full pockets; but I, if ever thoughtless, had ceased to be a boy some time ere I first greeted the "gay, bright, airy city of the Seine." I presume I could now enjoy a week of the careless, sunny life of her mob of genteel idlers; but a month of it would sate and bore me. To rise reluctantly to a late breakfast; trifle away the day, from noon to 5 P. M., in riding and sight-seeing; dine elaborately; and thenceforward spend the evening at theatre, opera, or party, is a routine that soon tells on one who is indurated in the habit of making the most of every working-hour. I envy no man his happiness; I envy least of all the pleasure-seeker, who chases his nimble, coquettish butterfly, year in, year out, along the Boulevards and around the "Places" of the giddy metropolis of France.

And here let me turn aside to say that the very common aspiration of our young men to spend a year or more in foreign travel seems to me inconsiderate and mistaken. No one is fit to travel in foreign lands till he has made himself pretty thoroughly acquainted with his own; and the youth who — ignorant of History, of Art, of Languages, and very slenderly versed even in Natural Science — fancies that he can pay his way while traversing Europe by writing for the Press, evinces inordinate, preposterous presumption. If I seem, in saying this, to condemn myself, so be it; but remember I was more than forty years old, and had had a full dozen years' familiarity with public affairs, before I set my face toward the Old World; yet, even thus, I doubt not that my letters abounded in blunders and *gaucheries* which a riper knowledge, a better preparation, for foreign travel, would have taught me to avoid. As it was, I wrote for a circle of readers of whom many were glad to look through my eyes because they *were* mine, — that is, because, having read my writings for years, they were interested in knowing how Europe would impress me, and what I should find there to admire or to condemn. Had not this been the case, — had I addressed readers to whom I was unknown or indifferent, — I could not have deemed my letters worth their attention, nor likely to attract it.

I say, then, most earnestly, to every youth anxious to go abroad, traverse Europe, and pay his way by writing for some journal, "Tarry at Jericho till your beard be grown." I never knew but one of your class — Bayard Taylor — who achieved a real success in thus travelling; and he left home a good type-setter, with some knowledge of modern languages; so that he stopped and worked at his trade whenever his funds ran short; yet, even thus, he did not wholly pay his way during the two years he devoted to his delightful "Views Afoot." I know it; for I employed and paid him all that his letters were fairly worth, though not nearly so much as his letters *now* righteously command. He practised a systematic and careful economy; yet he went away with money, and returned with the clothes on his back, and (I judge) very little more. My young friend, if you think yourself better qualified than he was, go ahead, and "do" Europe! but don't ask me to further your scheme; for I hold that you may far better stay at home, apply yourself to some useful branch of productive industry, help pay our National Debt, and accumulate a little independence whereon, by and by, to travel (if you choose) as a gentleman, and not with but a sheet of paper between you and starvation. It is bad to be ragged and hungry at home; it is infinitely worse to be destitute in a foreign country, where every one feels that you have no moral right to subtract from his means or add to his burdens. Even if willing to be a beggar and a vagabond, be content to burden your country, and go not abroad to disgrace her! The borrowing Yankee is a nuisance anywhere; but he is a frightful, hideous pest in those portions of Europe most frequented by Americans.

If I were to spend a year at leisure in the Old World, I think I should give a month of it to London, another to the residue of the British Isles, a third to France, a fourth to Germany, a month to Rome, another to the realm of Victor Emmanuel, or what the Pope terms "the sub-Alpine kingdom," and the remaining half of the year to Switzerland,—not political, but geographical, Switzerland, which includes Savoy and the Tyrol. I would cross the ocean in June, land at Havre or Antwerp, make my way directly to the Alps, and there remain until driven down their southward sloping vales by the coming on of Winter. Then I would descend to Milan, pass eastward to Venice, and back, by Bologna and Florence, to Rome; hieing therefrom to Naples to greet the advent of Spring; steaming thence to Marseilles, and crossing France by Lyons and Paris, to finish my tour in Great Britain and Ireland.

I crossed the Alps twice in my former visit to Europe; first by Mont Cenis, from Lyons to Turin; returning, *via* Milan, across the pass of St. Gothard to Lucerne and Basle. The long June day in which I traversed, by diligence, Savoy, from the frontier (alas! the frontier no longer) of France to the crest of Mont Cenis, is one of the brightest that lives in my memory; next to that stands that wherein I left Milan at 5 A. M., travelled fifteen miles by rail to Monza, and thence skirted by diligence Lake Como, crossed into the valley of the Ticino, which we wound steadily up to the little village or hamlet of Airolo, at the foot of the pass of St. Gothard, very near the upper limit of cultivation. Resting here for the night, and crossing the summit of the pass about noon, we rattled down to the Lake of Altorf, whereon a tiny steamboat conveyed us to Lucerne before nightfall. Though the plains of Italy glowed beneath a July sun, and the Vine, the Maize, and the Chestnut clung tenaciously to the valley of the Ticino, still they were successively constrained, by the increasing cold, to abandon it. We found little besides Oats, Potatoes, and Grass growing around Airolo; and these forsook us a little further up; so that, at the summit of the pass, a chill storm was piling new snow upon the still formidable drifts of the preceding Winter (perchance of a thousand Winters), and the tumbling, roaring brooks were frequently seen emerging from beneath ice of ample thickness and solidity.

On my later visit to Europe, I left Paris with my family in June; travelled by rail to Dijon, capital of the kingdom of Burgundy that was, — the palace of whose kings is now a museum of deeply interesting relics of that monarchy, — and, after spending a bright day there, we took diligence at 9 P. M., were toiling up the Jura next forenoon, and were soon rattling down their southeastern slope, whence we reached Geneva before night. Passing thence up the valley of the Arve to Chamonix, we spent five days there in deeply interested observation of the adjacent peaks and glaciers. I gave one day to a visit to Montanvert and the Mer de Glace (Sea of Ice), across which cattle are annually driven — a practical path being first made by cutting ice and filling crevices — to a sunny southern slope ("the Garden"), 9,000 feet above tide-level, on an adjacent mountain, where they are pastured till snow falls and lies, and then driven back to the valley whence they came. The ice of the Mer de Glace is so frequently seamed with deep cracks and crevices as to afford most unsafe footing for novices in Alpine pedestrianism; and I, for one, was glad to turn about, when I had gone but half-way across it, and regain the solid ground I had eagerly left. You climb thence nearly a thousand feet to the perch known as Montanvert, whence a good view is had, in clear-weather, of several lofty peaks, Mont Blanc included; and, when I had thence made my way down to Chamonix (you ascend on horse or mule back, but descend slowly on foot), I was as weary as any one need wish to be.

During my absence on this trip, my wife had undertaken to visit, with our children, the Glacier de Boissons, which seems scarcely a mile distant from the hotels at Chamonix, and easily accessible; but she had failed to reach it, lost her way, and been obliged to hire a peasant-woman to pilot her, and carry our fagged-out younger child, back to our hotel. I laughed at this misadventure when we met, and volunteered to lead the party next morning straight up to the glacier aforesaid, so that they might put their hands on it; but, on trying it, I failed miserably. So many deep ravines and steep *moraines* were found to bar our way, where all seemed smooth and level from our hotel, and the actual was so much greater than the apparent distance, that I gave up, after an hour's rugged clambering, and contented myself with asserting that I *could* reach the glacier by myself,—as I still presume I could, though I never tried. Either of the great glaciers is so large that it dwarfs everything around it; belittling obstacles and distances to an extent elsewhere incredible.

The Glacier des Bois is said to measure over fifty miles from the giant snow-drift wherein it originates, filling an indentation or gully leading down the east side of Mont Blanc, to the very bed of the Arve in the Chamonix valley. Indeed, the Mer de Glace itself may be considered a branch, if not the principal source, of the little river, and is approached by following up the bed of the stream for a couple of miles or so above the village, then stepping from one to another of the giant boulders, brought down by the glacier from the icy region above, and which here fill the spacious bed of the stream. I spent a forenoon here, watching the gradual dissolution of the ice by the warm breath of the valley, and noting how *moraines* are made.

A *moraine* is a ridge or bank of earth and stones, averaging four to eight feet high, and perhaps ten to twenty in width at the base, which is uniformly found bordering a glacier on either side, with one far larger—oftener two or more—at its lower extremity. It is so unfailingly separated by distances of ten to twenty feet from the glacier, that the green observer finds it difficult to comprehend that it is naturally formed of the points and fragments of rock broken off by the giant masses of ice in their imperceptible, yet constant, progress—at the average rate of six feet or so per day—from the snow-drifts cradled between the higher peaks to the deep valleys, green with grass, and crimson with Alpine flowers.

But steady observation detects a constant wearing away, in warm weather, of the lower part of the glacier facing the valley, and a consequent formation of cavities and channels therein, whereby the stones are loosened and allowed to precipitate themselves. But, while the water falls directly downward, the stones fall outward, or, striking a lower slope of ice, are so deflected from the perpendicular that they rest at last at some distance outward from the base of the glacier. Hence *moraines.*

We were in Chamonix, I believe, from the 20th to the 25th of June,—too early by a month. Snow fell repeatedly, though lightly; rain frequently and heavily; the mountain-tops were usually shrouded in cloud and fog; and we only caught a clear view of the summit of Mont Blanc on the morning of our departure. Swamp Alder (a large shrub with us) here attaining the size of a considerable tree, so that it is frequently split into fence-rails; and stretches of meadow, carpeted and blazing with the deep scarlet of innumerable flowers,—are among my recollections of that lofty, high-walled valley, so deeply embosomed in the Alps, and so rich in everything that renders the vicinage of mountains attractive to civilized man.

Returning to Geneva, we took steamboat on Lake Leman to Lausanne, whence we journeyed by diligence to Berne, and were to start thence at 4 one morning for Interlachen and the Bernese Oberland; but the sudden illness of a child forbade; and we returned to Lausanne,—a lovely little city, nested half-way up the side of a long, steep, verdant hill, which would elsewhere be deemed a mountain,—where I left my family in a rented cottage, and hastened back, by Neufchatel, Basle, and Strasburg, to Paris, where business urgently required my presence; leaving France two or three weeks later for London, Liverpool, and home. I embarked at Liverpool under a deep impression that something had gone wrong with my family (which returned in the Autumn to Paris, thence repaired to Germany, and spent the ensuing Winter at Dresden; returning, *via* England, to New York the following Summer). On reaching home, I learned that my mother had died on the day of my departure from Liverpool. Though but sixty-eight years old, she had long been worn out in mind and body by hard work and rugged cares, and had rarely spoken or evinced a clear perception of what was going on around her for many months before her death.

As this was my last passage of the Atlantic, I may barely say that, of all my experiences of protracted physical discomfort, sea-sickness is decidedly the most vivid and enduring. Though not now so easily prostrated as when I first traversed, per steamboat, a corner of Lake Erie, over forty years ago, I am never tossed on ocean billows without intense misery; and, while my first sea-passage was decidedly my worst, owing to the tempestuous weather which prevailed throughout, yet my very latest reminiscence of the "stormy main"—that of my passage from Aspinwall, *via* Key West, to this city in September, 1859—is just the reverse of "a joy forever." The Caribbean Sea is not often furrowed so deeply as the Atlantic; but its coral reefs, its weeping skies, its high temperature, with the crowds which usually throng its California steamers, make it a terror to the land-lubbers from whom Neptune exacts tribute so persistently and distressingly as from me, to whom an ocean voyage is never an enjoyment, is seldom less than a torture. What science and mammoth ships may do for us, I will not predict; but he who shall teach us to vanquish sea-sickness will deserve to be honored and crowned as one of the greatest benefactors of the human race.

XL.

TWO DAYS IN JAIL.

THERE are many ways of studying human nature; many diverse lights wherein this motley world is or may be contemplated; I judge that one of the most instructive glimpses of it is that which we obtain through grated windows. I forget, this moment, who characterizes the poet of beggary and ruffianism, Crabbe, as

> "Nature's sternest painter, but the best";

yet I am quite sure that one of the most wholesome and profitable, though least pleasant, experiences of my life, is that afforded by my confinement for forty-eight hours (with a good prospect of permanence) in the spacious debtors' prison in Paris, No. 70 Rue de Clichy, known to misfortune as "the Maison Clichy," and more familiarly to its inmates as "Clichy" merely. It happened thus:—

In the years 1852–53, an association of mainly wealthy and public-spirited New-Yorkers undertook to imitate, if not rival, the first great Exposition of the World's Industry at London in 1851. So they subscribed capital, obtained a charter from the State, and a plot of vacant ground from the city, employed architects and builders, and at length constructed on Reservoir Square (Sixth Avenue and Fortieth to Forty-second Streets), by far the most symmetrical and spacious edifice which our country has yet seen. The materials employed were almost wholly iron and glass, as in the case of its London prototype; but, though the British was a superb structure, ours was still more graceful and imposing. I doubt that many are yet born who will see New York graced by a finer building than was her Crystal Palace, until destroyed by fire in 1858.

Yet the Exhibition was doomed to failure from the start. It was located much too far up town, — as much out of the way as it would to-day be at Harlem or Hoboken, — it was but half finished, and nowise ready, when opened, — and it steadily dragged, after the first few days, until, at the close of the season, it was found that the million or more of capital stock was all sunk, and the half-million of bonds a very dubious investment.

A desperate effort was made to retrieve its fallen fortunes next Spring; and I, with others, was then induced to take a hand in it as a director and (in a small way) bondholder. Mr. P. T. Barnum was our most active, efficient leader in this desperate effort at resurrection. There were several more directors who did their very best; but the year (1854) was one of pecuniary pressure and revulsion, which combined with other influences to render success impossible. I gave much hard work and a little money to the attempt, while Mr. Barnum gave much more, but to no purpose; we barely paid our heavy current expenses; and the Exposition closed with the season, nearly as bankrupt as when we undertook to resuscitate it.

I went to Europe the next Spring (1855) without a suspicion that I should there be held accountable for our inability to wrest victory from defeat; yet, about 4 P.M. of the 2d day of June, after I had returned from a day's observation in the French "Palace of Industry," I was waited on at my little cottage by four French strangers, who soon gave me to understand that they were officers of the law, bearing a writ issued by Judge de Belleyme, of the Court of Premier Instance, at the suit of one M. Lechesne, a Parisian sculptor, who swore that he had contributed to our New York Exhibition a statue (in plaster) which had there been broken, or mutilated; for which he claimed of me, as a director, "represontant et solidaire," of the Exhibition, "douze mille francs," or $2,500 in gold. When we had, by the help of my courier, arrived at some approach to a mutual understanding, one element of which was my refusal to pay M. Lechesne $ 2,500, or any sum whatever, they said that I must enter their carriage and accompany them forthwith to the Judge, some three miles away; which, attended by my courier, I did. We had to call for Lechesne and his lawyer by the way, which consumed nearly an hour,— they being in no hurry; and, when we had told the Judge our respective stories, I proposed to go to the American Legation and persuade Don Piatt, Esq., Secretary of Legation, to guarantee my appearance for trial when wanted. The Judge pronounced this sufficient; so we set forth on another long ride to the Legation; where not only Judge Piatt, but another friend, Maunsel B. Field, Esq., offered himself as security for my appearance at court; but now Lechesne and his lawyer refused, on the ground of Mr. Piatt's exemption from arrest on civil process, to take him as security, or (in fact) to take anything but the cash they were intent on. High words passed, and a scuffle was imminent, when I insisted on being driven at once to prison,— my guardians having affected a fear that I would escape them. Crossing the Avenue Champs Élysée, densely thronged at that hour (6 P. M.), our carriage came into violent collision with another, and was disabled; when a very superfluous display of vigilance and pistols was made by my keepers, who could not be persuaded that I was intent on sticking to them like a brother. At last, a little before 7 P. M., we reached our destination, and I was admitted, through several gigantic iron doors, with gloomy crypts between them, to the office of the prison, where I was told that I must stay till 9½ P. M., because the Judge had allowed me so long to procure bail. Here my guardians left me in safe-keeping, while I ordered a frugal dinner, instead of the sumptuous public one at the Trois Frères, given by Mr. M. B. Field, which I had been invited, and had fully expected, to attend; and I sent my courier home to quiet the apprehensions of my family, who as yet knew only that some strangers had called for me, and that I had gone off with them.

Very soon, Judge Mason (John Y.), our Ambassador, called,

and was admitted to see me, though it was now too late by the regulations. I explained the matter to him, assured him that I wanted nothing but a good lawyer, and insisted on viewing the whole matter in a more cheerful light than it wore in his eyes. "But your wife will surely be distressed by it," he urged; "she being an utter stranger here, with two young children." "No," I replied; "a trifle might annoy her; but this matter looks serious, and it will only calm and strengthen her. I have sent our courier to assure her that it is all right, and request her to keep away from this, and go on with her visiting and sight-seeing, as though nothing had happened." "I have heard you called a philosopher, and I now see that you deserve the distinction," was the Judge's rejoinder, as, at my request, he left me.

Half an hour had scarcely passed, giving me barely time to eat my dinner, when my wife was ushered in, accompanied by Mrs. Piatt and our little son, whose eyes were distended with grave wonder at the iron barriers through which he had reached me. "Good woman," I observed to Mrs. Greeley, "I have been bragging to Judge Mason how quietly you would take this mischance; but here you are in jail at nightfall, when visitors are not allowed, as though you were addicted to hysterics." "But consider," she urged in mitigation, "that I first heard of your position from Francis [our courier], who comes flying home to assure me that there is nothing serious, to urge me not to be frightened, when he is trembling all over with anxiety and terror. Hardly had he left the room, when Mrs. Piatt comes in equal haste to beg me to fear nothing,— that all is but a trifle,—and *she* is quite as agitated and panic-stricken as Francis. Neither of them seems to understand the matter; so I thought I must come to you for an explanation." This I gave; when they departed; and I was at last allowed to go up to my lodging, which I find thus described in my letter thence to The Tribune:—

"By 10 o'clock, each of us lodgers had retired to our several apartments (each eight feet by five), and an obliging functionary came around and locked out all rascally intruders. I don't think

I ever before slept in a place so perfectly secure. At 6 this morning, this extra protection was withdrawn, and each of us was thenceforth required to keep watch over his own valuables. We uniformly keep good hours here in Clichy, which is a virtue that not many large hotels in Paris can boast of.

"The bedroom appointments are not of a high order, as is reasonable, since we are only charged for them four sous (cents) per night, — washing extra. The sheets are rather of a hickory sort, but mine were given to me clean; the bed is indifferent, but I have slept on worse; the window lacks a curtain or blind, but in its stead there are four strong upright iron bars, which are a perfect safeguard against getting up in the night, and falling or pitching out, so as to break your neck, as any one who fell thence would certainly do. (I am in the fifth or highest story.) Perhaps one of my predecessors was a somnambulist. I have two chairs, two little tables (probably one of them extra, through some mistake), and a cupboard which may once have been clean. The pint wash-bowl, half-pint pitcher, &c., I have ordered, and am to pay extra for. I am a little ashamed to own that my repose has been indifferent; but then I never *do* sleep well in a strange place."

As it was Saturday evening when I was taken to jail, I could not expect a release before Monday; in fact, the lawyers who were applied to in my behalf had all gone out of town, and could not be found till that day. I rose on Sunday morning in a less placid frame of mind than I had cherished overnight, and devoted a good part of the day to concocting an account of the matter meant to be satirical, and to "chaff" mankind in general by contrasting the ways of Clichy with those of the outside world, to the dispraise of the latter. Here is a specimen: —

"I say nothing of 'Liberty,' save to caution outsiders in France to be equally modest; but 'Equality' and 'Fraternity' I have found here more thoroughly than elsewhere in Europe. Still, we have not realized the social millennium, even in Clichy. Some of us were wont to gain our living by the hardest and most meagrely rewarded labor; others to live idly and sumptuously on the earnings of others. Of course, these vices of an irrational and decaying social state are not instantly eradicated by our abrupt transfer to this mansion. Some of us can cook; while others only know how to eat, and so require assistance in the preparation of our food, as none is cooked or even provided for us, and our intercourse with the outer world is subject to limitations. Those of us who lived generously aforetime, and are in for gentlemanly sums, are very apt to have money; while the luckless chaps who were sent here for owing a beggarly hundred francs or so, and have no fixed income beyond the single franc per day which each creditor must pay, or his debtor is turned loose, are very glad to earn money by doing us acts of kindness. One of these attached himself to me immediately on my induction into my apartment, and proceeded to make my bed, bring me a pitcher of water and wash-bowl, matches, lights, &c., for which I expect to pay him, — these articles being reckoned superfluities in Clichy. But no such aristocratic distinction as master — no such degrading appellation as servant — is tolerated in this community: this philanthropic fellow-boarder is known to all here as my 'auxiliary.' Where has the stupid world outside known how to drape the hard realities of life with fig-leaf so graceful as this?

"So of all titular distinctions. We pretend that we have abjured titles of honor in America; and the consequence is that every one has a title, — either 'Honorable,' or 'General,' or 'Colonel,' or 'Reverend,' or, at the very least, 'Esquire.' But here in Clichy all such empty and absurd prefixes or suffixes are absolutely unknown; even names, Christian or family, are discarded as useless, antiquated lumber. Every lodger is known by the number of his apartment only, which no one thinks of designating a cell. Mine is 139: so, whenever a friend calls, he gives two cents to a 'commissionaire,' who comes in from the outer regions to the great hall sacred to our common use, and begins calling out cent-trente-neuf (phonetically 'son-tran-nuf') at the top of his voice, and goes on, yelling as he climbs, in the hope of finding or calling me short of ascending to my fifth-story sanctuary. To nine-tenths of my comrades in adversity I am known only as 'son-tran-nuf.' My auxiliary is No. 54; so I, when I need his aid, go singing 'sankon-cat,' after the same fashion. Equality being thus rigidly preserved, maugre some diversities of fortune, the jealousies, rivalries, and heart-burnings, which keep the mass of mankind in a ferment, are here absolutely unknown. I never before talked with so many people intimate with each other without hearing something said or insinuated to one another's prejudice; here, there is nothing of the sort. Some folks outside are fitted with reputations which they would hardly consider flattering, — some laws and usages get the blessing they so richly deserve, — but among ourselves is naught but harmony and good-will. How would the Hotel de Ville, or even the Tuileries, like to compare notes with us on this head?"

A Yankee prisoner, who had seen me in New York, recognized me as I came down stairs on Sunday morning, and blazoned his inference that I was in jail by some mistake, — so I was soon surrounded by sympathizing fellow jail-birds, several of whom were no more justly liable to imprisonment than I was. In a little while, M. Vattemare, well known in his day as the projector of systematic international exchanges of books and documents, having heard of my luck at Mr. Field's dinner the evening previous, made his way in, with proffers of service, which I turned to account by obtaining, through him, from some great library, copies of the Revised Statutes and Session Laws of New York, which clearly demonstrated my legal irresponsibility to M. Lechesne for his damaged statue. Soon, other friends began to pour in, with offers of money and service; but I could not afford to be bailed out nor bought out, as fifty others would thereby be tempted to repeat M. Lechesne's experiment upon me, — so I was compelled to send them away, with my grateful acknowledgments.

Among my visitors was M. Hector Bossange, the well-known publisher, who had been accustomed to call at my rooms each Sunday, as he did on this one, and was soon asked by my wife, "Have you seen Mr. Greeley?" "Seen him!" he perplexedly responded, "I do not understand you; have I not called to see him?" "Then you have not heard that he is in prison?" "In prison?" he wildly inquired; "what can that mean?" "I do not well understand it myself," she replied; "but it has some connection with our New York Crystal Palace." "O, it is *money*,— is it?" joyfully rejoined M. Bossange; "then we will soon have him out, — I feared it was *politics!*" He knew that I was a furious anti-Imperialist, and feared that I had rashly involved myself in some plot that exposed me to arrest as an apostle of sedition,—an enemy of "Order."

Our remaining visitors having been barred out when the clock struck 4 P. M., we two Americans, with two Englishmen, a Frenchman, and an Italian, sent out our order, and had our dinner in the cell of one of us, who, being an old settler, had an apartment somewhat more roomy and less exalted than mine. Each brought to the common "spread" whatever he had of table-ware or pocket-cutlery; and the aggregate, though there were still deficiencies, answered the purpose. The dinner cost fifty cents per head, of which a part went as toll to some officer or turnkey, and there was still a good margin of profit to the restaurateur. Still, there was wine for those who would drink it; but stronger liquors are not allowed in Clichy, in spite of the assurance, so often heard, that prohibitory legislation is unknown in France. A flask of cut-throat-looking brandy had, however, been smuggled in for one of our party; and this was handed around and sipped as though it were nectar. Men love to circumvent the laws for the gratification of their appetites; and yet I judge that not one gill of spirits is drank in Clichy, where quarts were poured down while every one was free to order and drink so long as he could pay.

I presume I had had more calls that day than any other prisoner, though Sunday is specially devoted to visits; and, though grateful for the kindness and zeal for my release evinced by several of my friends, I was thoroughly weary when the lingerers were invited to take their departure, and the doors clanged heavily behind them. I could then appreciate the politeness with which M. Ouvrard, Napoleon's great army-contractor, after he had fallen into embarrassments and been lodged in Clichy by his inexorable creditors, was accustomed, when visitors called, to send to the grating his faithful valet, who, with the politest bow and shrug whereof he was master, would say, "I am sorry, sir,—very sorry; but my master, M. Ouvrard, is *out*." This was not even the "white lie" often instigated by good society; since the visitor could not fail to understand that the great bankrupt could be out in none other than that conventional, metaphorical sense which implies merely preoccupation, or unwillingness to be buttonholed and bored.

No prisoner in Clichy is obliged to see a visitor unless of his own choice; and, as one is frequently called down to the grating to have a fresh writ served on him, thereby magnifying the obstacles to his liberation, the rule that a visitor must make a minute of his errand on his card, and send it up, before an interview is accorded, is one founded in reason, and very generally and properly adhered to. Yet a fellow-prisoner, who received notice that he was called for at the grate, went recklessly down on the day after my incarceration, only to greet a tip-staff, and be served with a fresh writ. "Sir," said the beguiled and indignant boarder at this city hermitage, "if you ever serve me such a trick again, you will go out of here half killed." Some official underling was violently suspected of lending himself to this stratagem; and great was the indignation excited thereby throughout our community; but the victim had only himself to blame, for not standing on his reserved rights, and respecting the usages and immunities of our sanctuary.

I was puzzled, but not offended, at a question put me the moment I had fairly entered the prison: "Have you ever been confined here before?" I respectfully, but positively, replied in the negative, — that this was my first experience of the kind. I soon learned, however, that the question was a prescribed and necessary one, — that, if I had ever before been imprisoned on this allegation of debt, or on any other, and this had been lodged against me, I was not liable to a fresh detention thereon, but must at once be discharged. The rule is a good one; and, though I was unable *then* to profit by it, it may serve me another time.

My general conclusion, from all I observed and heard in Clichy, imports that imprisonment for debt was never a bar to improvidence, nor a curb to prodigality; that, in so far as it ever aided or hastened the collection of honest debts, it wrenched five dollars from sympathizing relatives and friends for every one exacted from the debtors themselves; and that it was, and could not fail to be, fruitful only in oppression and extortion, — much oftener enforcing the payment of unjust claims than of just ones. Let whoever will sneer at human progress and uneasy, meddling philanthropy, I am grateful that I have lived in the age which gave the death-blow to Slavery and to Imprisonment for Debt.

To get into prison is a feat easy of achievement by almost any one; it is quite otherwise with getting out. You cannot fully realize how rigid stone walls and iron doors are till they stand between you and sunshine, impeding locomotion, and forbidding any but the most limited change of place. The restless anxiety of prisoners for release, no matter how light their cares, how ample their apartments, how generous their fare, can never be appreciated by one who has not had a massive key turned upon him, and found himself on the wrong side of an impregnable wall. Doubtless, we hear much nonsense whereof "Liberty" is the burden; but, if you are sceptical as to the essential worth of Freedom, just allow yourself to be locked up for a while, with no clear prospect of liberation at any specified or definite time. Though I was but forty-eight hours in Clichy, time dragged heavily on my hands, after the friends who, in generous profusion, visited me on Sunday had been barred and locked out, and I was left for a second night to my fellow jail-birds and my gloomy reflections. "I can't get out" was the melancholy plaint of Sterne's starling; and I had occasion to believe that so many detainers or claims similar to Lechesne's would, on Monday, be lodged against me, as to render doubtful my release for weeks, if not for months.

It was late on Monday morning before my active friends outside could procure me the help I needed; but, when they did, I had, through M. Vattemare's valued aid, the books I required, and had my references and citations all ready for service. With these in hand, my lawyers went before Judge de Belleyme to procure my release; but M. Vattemare had been there already, as well as to M. de Langle, the judge of a still higher court, to testify that the Americans were generally indignant at my incarceration, and were threatening to leave Paris in a body if I were not promptly liberated. Even M. James Rothschild, I was told, had made an indignant speech about it at a dinner on Saturday evening; saying to his friends: "We are most of us directors in the Exposition now in progress here, and of course liable to be arrested and imprisoned in any foreign country we may visit, on a complaint that some one has had articles damaged or lost here, if Mr. Greeley may be so held in this action."

These representations impelled M. de Belleyme to say, in perfect truth, that he had not ordered my imprisonment,— on the contrary, he had directed the plaintiff and his lawyer to take Mr. Don Piatt's guaranty that I should be on hand, when wanted, to respond to this action. So when, at the instance of my lawyers, M. Lechesne and his attorney were called to confront them before the Judge on Monday, and were asked by him how they came to take me to Clichy, under the circumstances, they could only stammer out that they had reflected that Mr. Piatt was not subject to imprisonment in like case,—therefore, his guaranty was no security. This, of course, did not satisfy the Judge, who ordered my release on the instant; so by 4 P. M. all formalities were concluded, and my lawyers appeared with the documents required to turn me into the street. Meantime, I had had so many visitors, who sent up good-looking cards, and wore honest faces, that I had manifestly risen in the estimation of my jailers, who had begun to treat me with ample consideration.

The neighboring servants, who were intimate with ours, had witnessed my departure with the officers, and knew, of course, that this was an arrest, but pretended to our servants not to understand it. One after another of them would call on our *employées* to ask, "Why, where is Mr. Greeley?" "He has gone over to London on a little business," was the prompt reply, "and will be back in a day or two." This was accepted with many a sly wink and gentle shrug; the inquisitors having obviously united in the conclusion that I was a swindler, who had robbed some bank or vault, and fled from my own country to enjoy the fruits of my depredations. When, however, I came quietly home in a cab about the time indicated by our servants, they greatly exulted over the hoped-for, rather than expected, *dénouement*, while their good-natured friends were correspondingly disconcerted by the failure of *their* calculations. On our part, we resumed at once our round of visiting and sight-seeing, as though nothing had happened; but my little son's flying hair and radiant face, as he rushed down stairs to greet my return, will not soon be forgotten. He had been told that it was all right, when he found and left me in prison, and had tried hard to believe it; but my return, unattended and unguarded, he *knew* to be right.

I had a tedious legal squabble thereafter, — for my liberation did not, of course, abate M. Lechesne's suit against me, — and had to send to New York for documents and affidavits; meantime going to Switzerland with my family, as I have already related, — and I was signally aided in my defence by Hon. Elihu B. Washburne, of Illinois, who happened to be in Paris at the time; but, as there was really no case against me, I was at length enabled to demonstrate that fact to the satisfaction of the functionary who had been deputed to hear and report on the suit to the Tribunal of Commerce, before which I had been cited by Lechesne, — a proceeding wholly illegal, my lawyers asserted, as neither party to the action was a merchant. My counsel wished to demur to the jurisdiction, saying that the Tribunal was not a court of law, and always decided for a Frenchman against a foreigner, no matter how unjustly. At length, however, when my documents arrived from New York, they could hold off no longer, but went before the officer in question, where my opponents were most reluctant to meet them, asking for time to send to America for documents also! We understood that this was only a pretext to avoid a judgment for costs,—they did not really want to send to America, and did not send. We let them off on that excuse, however, and I came away,—leaving the suit stone dead.

I rejoice that imprisonment for debt was recently abolished in France,—I trust forever. I doubt that it ever made one debtor even outwardly honest; I am sure it often compelled the relatives and friends of prodigals to pay debts which should never have been contracted. It is wrong—it is immoral—to trust those who do not deserve credit,—it is doubly wrong to impose the payment of such debts upon some frugal uncle or brother of the debtor, in pity for that debtor's weeping wife and children. "Let every tub stand on its own bottom" is a sound rule, which imprisonment for debt tends strongly to subvert. Men are trusted who should not be, on the calculation, "I can get my pay out of his relatives by putting him into jail"; hence tavern-scores and merchants' accounts where cash down would have precluded extravagance and dissipation. The civilized world is not yet prepared for the repeal of all laws designed to enforce the collection of simple debts (not trusts); but this reform must come in due time, when mankind will wonder why it could so long have been resisted. False credit—credit to those who do not deserve, and will be rather harmed than helped by it—is the bane of our civilization. Every second man you meet is struggling with debts which he should never have contracted. We need a legal reform, which will greatly diminish our current facilities for running into debt.

XLI.

"THE BANKS CONGRESS." — THE LONG CONTEST FOR SPEAKER.

I HAD often, since the establishment of The Tribune, run down to Washington for a very few days; but never, save when for ninety days a member of the House, had I been tempted to protract my stay there; and my associates had repeatedly regretted that I could not be induced to spend more time at the political metropolis. Reflecting on this, and on the probabilities of a long and doubtful struggle for the Speakership of the XXXIVth Congress, I resolved, while staying in Paris in the Summer of 1855, that I would visit Washington before the opening of that Congress, and remain there until requested by my associates in business to return to New York, — a resolve of which I gave them due notice. When the roll of the new House was first called, at noon on Monday, December 3, I was looking on from a reporter's desk; and I remained in observation for many weeks thereafter.

That House was constituted as no other has ever yet been. No party had a majority of its members, while two separate organizations *seemed* to have. The "Americans" had chosen a majority; so had the "Republicans," or opponents of the policy embodied in the Nebraska Bill; but the lines of these two organizations ran into and crossed each other. We Republicans who were anti-"Know-Nothing" were perfectly willing to support an anti-Nebraska "American" for Speaker; but nearly all the Southern "Americans" would support no candidate who was in principle a Republican. Thus, there was in fact no majority of any party, and a long, bitter, exciting struggle for the organization was inevitable.

The Democrats held a caucus, as usual, and nominated William A. Richardson, of Illinois, for Speaker; but they could give him, at the utmost, but 80 votes, and actually did give him, on the first ballot, but 74. The Southern "Americans" mainly supported Humphrey Marshall, of Kentucky, who had 30 votes on the first ballot; but they were ready to vote for any Northern "Know-Nothing" who was not in principle a Republican, and Henry M. Fuller, of Pennsylvania, had 17 votes, mainly from the South. The Republicans and anti-Nebraska "Americans" had held no caucus and made no nominations; but they cast, on the first ballot, 53 votes for Lewis D. Campbell of Ohio, 21 for Nathaniel P. Banks of Massachusetts, 7 for Alexander C. M. Pennington of New Jersey, and there were 23 scattering votes, mainly theirs. Four ballots were taken that day, with no material variation from the foregoing result; when the House adjourned. The next day, five ballots were taken, — Mr. Richardson's vote being increased (by a fresh arrival) to 75, Mr. Banks's to 31, and Mr. Fuller's (at the expense of Humphrey Marshall's) to 21; when the House again adjourned. The next day, Mr. Campbell's vote was run up to 81, at Mr. Banks's expense; but he thenceforth began to fall off; and on Friday, having just received 75 votes, he formally declined; stating that he was satisfied that he could not be elected without either repudiating his well-known American and anti-Nebraska principles, or making pledges regarding the formation of Committees that would justly expose him to public contempt. Mr. Banks now received 41 votes; thence steadily and rapidly increasing, until, on the thirty-seventh ballot, he had 107; still lacking six more to elect him; Richardson having 76 and Fuller 28, with 13 scattering, mainly Southern "Americans." Thenceforth, the struggle went on, with no change but that caused by occasional absences of members of either party, generally paired, but relieved by fitful debates on party questions, — sometimes lasting through a day or more, until, on the 22d, Mr. Stanton, of Ohio, first moved that a *plurality* vote (the highest) should thereafter suffice to elect; which was promptly laid on the table, by 114 Yeas to 107 Nays, — the latter being the Republicans or Banks men, outvoted by the combined strength of all the other parties. This motion was repeatedly renewed by Republicans, with no better success; and the House once voted not to adjourn till a Speaker should be chosen; but, after a tedious and excited night session, this resolve was rescinded, and the debating, with occasional ballotings, continued. On the 27th, so many members, mainly Southern, had gone home to spend Christmas, that Mr. Banks needed a change of but 3 votes to elect him, — he having 100 to 105 for all others. On several of the succeeding ballots during the holidays, Mr. Banks lacked but 3 and then 4 votes of a majority; but, as the absent members returned, the prospect of an election receded. At length, on the 21st of January, Mr. Albert Rust (since a Rebel Brigadier) of Arkansas moved the following: —

"*Whereas,* One hundred and eighteen ineffectual efforts to elect a Speaker, in which the votes have been divided among Mr. Banks, Mr. Richardson, Mr. Fuller, and Mr. Pennington, must have made it manifest to those gentlemen and this Congress that neither of them is the choice of a majority of the members of this House for its presiding officer, and that a longer persistence on the part of their respective friends in urging their names for this office will only delay the organization of this House, and thereby prevent immediate legislation, when the common interests of the whole country require it: Therefore,

"*Resolved,* That it is the sense of this House that Messrs. Banks, Richardson, Fuller, and Pennington, by withdrawing their names, and forbidding their use as candidates for the Speakership, would remove certain and insurmountable obstacles to its organization, and that the public interests would be greatly promoted by their doing so."

Hereupon, Messrs. Fuller and Pennington promptly gave notice that they were no longer candidates for Speaker. Mr. Rust, finding impediments to their present consideration, withdrew his preamble and resolve, giving notice that he would reoffer them on the morrow.

I listened to his proposition with intense indignation. It was based on an assumption notoriously false, — namely, that the organization of the House was impeded by personal aspirations and rivalries, — when all knew that the conflict was one of principles, and that Rust himself was invincibly hostile to Banks only because Banks represented resistance to the further diffusion of Slavery. And Mr. Banks's supporters, with his hearty concurrence, had once and again offered to let a plurality choose, so that his and their opponents would be compelled to concentrate their strength or submit to a defeat. So far as the Republicans were concerned, they had long stood ready and eager to close the contest in the only practicable way; and it was a wrong and an insult for the antagonist parties, who could not unite on a candidate, to combine their forces for the purpose of driving from the field the chosen candidate of the Republicans. This dictating by one side who should or should not be supported by the other seemed to me a gross outrage; and I so characterized it in my despatches and letters to The Tribune.

Mr. Rust renewed his proposition on the 23d; when the House refused to order the main question upon it, and it went over under the rule to the next day; when, on motion of Mr. Pringle, of New York, it was laid on the table by 100 to 99.

I believe it was on this day that, just after the House had adjourned, and while all in attendance were returning to their respective lodgings, I was accosted by a stout, athletic man whom I did not then know, but afterward ascertained to be Rust, with the abrupt question, "Would you resent an insult?" "That depends on circumstances" was my answer. The words were scarcely spoken when a powerful blow, that I neither saw nor anticipated, temporarily stunned and staggered me; but I brought up against the wooden railing of the walk down through the public grounds, from the Capitol to the Avenue. Dozens of all parties were around, but no one interposed; and Rust, whirling on his heel, proceeded on his way. Soon recovering my consciousness, I followed; and, just before reaching my (National) hotel, overtook Rust and his party, who were probably awaiting me. He turned, with three or four friends flanking him, and again assaulted me; this time with a heavy cane, which he broke over my arm,—raised to guard my head, as I was trying to close with him. My arm was badly swelled by the blow, as my head was by its predecessor, but I neither fell nor recoiled; and Rust, soon whirling again, went on his way, while I repaired to my room in the hotel, which I was obliged to keep for some days thereafter. The only excuse or pretext for this assault was afforded by my strictures in The Tribune on his baffled attempt to coerce his political opponents into voting for some one else than the man of their choice for Speaker.

I cannot now remember that I was ever seriously assaulted since my boyhood except by Rust as aforesaid. Writing the plainest and squarest Anglo-Saxon I know, and often speaking of political opponents, their works, ways, and words, in terms that could by no tolerable stretch of courtesy be deemed flattering,—terms, doubtless, sometimes misjudging and undeserved,—I suppose I ought to deem myself fortunate in having so seldom been subjected to personal violence. Still, if Rust's assaults were intended to convince me that his proposition was fair and manly, they certainly failed to subserve their purpose.

Some weeks after these assaults, I was waited on at the Capitol by the Marshal of the District, who wished me to go before the Grand Jury as a witness against Rust. This I declined to do, unless compelled by due process of law; for, I urged, there were fully a score who witnessed either assault, all under circumstances more favorable to observation than mine; and, if these did not see fit to testify, why call on me? I did not choose to figure as an informer or complainant. I decidedly preferred not to have the wrath of the law placated by a fine of $25 or $50. So nothing was ever done in the premises. I do not even remember that Rust was ever presented by his admirers with a cane, as Mr. Brooks of South Carolina was with several by those who exulted over his far more savage and damaging attack, a few weeks later, on Senator Sumner, — a crime for which a Washington court fined the Hon. culprit $300.

If there happens to be any one who decides that Rust's proposal did not justify my strictures (which, I assume, were severe), I ask him to pass judgment on one that was submitted, directly after Rust's was disposed of, by Hon. Charles James Faulkner of Virginia, afterward President Buchanan's Minister Plenipotentiary to London. It is as follows: —

> "*Resolved*, That the persistent adherence of the Republican party to the Hon. Nathaniel P. Banks as its candidate for the office of Speaker, after the repeated manifestations by the majority of the members of this House that he does not possess their confidence for that situation, exhibits a determination to sacrifice the public interests of the country to the triumphs of a personal and sectional party; and that the further continuance of his name before this body, as the candidate of his party for the office of Speaker, justly attaches to his supporters the responsibility for a failure to organize this House."

I do not believe in the Rust style of argumentation; yet I cannot see how such propositions as the above could be appropriately met by any other.

And still the balloting for Speaker went fitfully on, alternated with debates.

President Pierce having sent in his Annual Message on the 25th, though the House was in no condition to receive it, — Mr. Banks now generally lacking six or seven votes of being chosen, — while all manner of back-stairs intrigues were fomented by the twenty or thirty nominal Republicans of whom each fancied that *he* would stand a good chance for the Speakership if Banks were withdrawn; and one or two serious but unsuccessful attempts having been made to concentrate the entire anti-Republican vote on Hon. James L. Orr (Dem.), of South Carolina; at length, on the 1st of February, a motion by Hon. John Hickman, of Pennsylvania, to adopt a plurality rule, was defeated by the close vote of 108 Yeas to 110 Nays; so that it was evident an election was not far off. Next day, Mr. Samuel A. Smith (Dem.), of Tennessee, renewed the proposition in this shape: —

"*Resolved*, That the House will proceed immediately to the election of a Speaker *viva voce*. If, after the roll shall have been called three times, no member shall have received a majority of all the votes cast, the roll shall again be called, and the member who shall then receive the largest number of votes, provided it shall be a majority of a quorum, shall be declared duly elected Speaker of the House of Representatives of the XXXIVth Congress."

A motion to lay this proposition on the table was promptly voted down, — 114 to 104, — and the resolution then adopted, under the Previous Question, — Yeas, 113; Nays, 104. The Democrats who supported it were Messrs. Barclay of Pennsylvania, Clingman of North Carolina, Herbert of California, Kelly of New York, Andrew Oliver of New York, S. A. Smith of Tennessee, and John Williams of New York. Several attempts to rescind the above rule were successively made and voted down; and then the House, rejecting all motions to adjourn, proceeded to vote under it, with the following result: —

	130th ballot.	*131st.*	*132d.*	*133d.*
Nathaniel P. Banks, of Massachusetts	102	102	102	103
William Aiken, of South Carolina	93	93	92	100
Henry M. Fuller, of Pennsylvania	14	13	13	6
Scattering,	6	6	6	5

The House thereupon, on motion of Mr. Clingman of North Carolina, resolved, by 155 to 40, that Mr. Banks had been duly elected Speaker; and the long struggle was over. It is memorable as the very first in our National history wherein Northern resistance to Slavery Extension ever won in a fair, stand-up contest, without compromise or equivocation. *Nine weeks* had been spent — I think, not unprofitably — in producing this result; and there were not over seventy-five decided Republicans in the House of 234 members in which it was achieved. Day after day, those who still insisted on holding on to Banks had been inveighed against as perilling the cause for their favorite; when, in fact, had Banks been dropped, it would have been found impossible to concentrate so many votes on any one else, as were nearly (or quite) a hundred times cast for him. The readiness of his friends, at all times, to adopt the plurality rule, and abide the result, shielded them from all just reproach as wantonly protracting the contest. If appropriations were needed, it became the supporters of the Administration to let the House be organized under that rule, so that the public need might be satisfied. The long contest had proved the "American" organization a myth, a fog-bank, an illusion; and the new-born Republican party, consolidated and united by this struggle, mustered heartily and formidably at its first National Convention, which assembled at Pittsburg, Pa., on the 22d of that month.

Mr. Banks, though then in his second term, proved an excellent Speaker, — prompt, vigorous, decided, and just. Though a majority remained politically hostile to him, and the waves of party passion ran very high, I believe but one of the many decisions made by him as Speaker was overruled; and the House, on calmer consideration, reconsidered its overruling vote. Abler men may have filled that difficult post; but no man, I judge, ever gave himself more unreservedly to the discharge of its arduous duties. I have heard that Mr. Banks was a schoolmaster in his youth, and his manner in the chair often countenanced the tradition. If he had a fault, it was that of overdoing, impelled by absorbing anxiety to keep in order a body essentially turbulent, and inclined to resent and baffle any attempt to draw the reins too tightly. The temptations to an opposite course are very strong, and presiding officers far oftener err on the side of laxity than on that of rigor.

XLII.

FREMONT. — BUCHANAN. — DOUGLAS.

THE popular elections of 1854–55 had made manifest the fact that the Opposition, if united on one ticket, was strong enough to oust the Democratic party from power at Washington; the long and arduous struggle for Speaker had shown that such combination could only be effected with great difficulty, if at all. The "American" party was first in the field, — selecting as its candidates Millard Fillmore, of New York, for President, with Andrew J. Donelson (nephew and namesake of "Old Hickory"), of Tennessee, for Vice-President, — men of decided personal strength, but impossible candidates for the Republicans, because radically hostile to their cardinal principle. The Democrats next held their Convention, and nominated James Buchanan, of Pennsylvania, for President, with John C. Breckinridge, of Kentucky, for Vice-President. President Pierce and Senator Douglas were Mr. Buchanan's competitors, and were wisely defeated, — each of them being conspicuously identified with the Nebraska bill; while Mr. Buchanan, having been, throughout President Pierce's term, Envoy to Great Britain, had escaped all complication in the popular mind with that measure. And, as Pennsylvania was the probable pivot of the contest, it was manifestly wise to present a Pennsylvanian for the first office. The Republicans, meeting last, nominated Colonel John C. Fremont, of California, for President, with William L. Dayton, of New Jersey, for Vice-President. They were strongly urged to present John McLean, of Ohio, then a Justice of the Supreme Court, for the first office, with the assurance that he could secure the bulk of the "American" vote, — at least in the Free States, — and thus probably carry Pennsylvania and Indiana. This assurance seemed to rest on no certain or tangible data, and was overruled, — a mistake (if such it were) for which I accept my full share of responsibility. I felt that Colonel Fremont's adventurous, dashing career had given him popularity, with our young men especially; and I had no faith in the practicability of our winning many votes from those "Americans" who were not heartily Republicans.

Our canvass was very animated, and our hopes, for a season, quite sanguine, especially after Maine had gone for us in September, by 25,000 plurality; but the October elections gave us a cold chill, — Pennsylvania choosing the Democratic State officers, by 3,000 majority, over the vote of the combined Opposition, with 15 of the 25 representatives in Congress, and a majority in the Legislature. Indiana likewise went against the combined Opposition, by an average majority of more than 6,000; and when it transpired that the "American" leaders, rejecting all offers to run combined tickets, persisted in running distinctive Fillmore tickets for Electors in each of these (as in most other) States, it was clear that we were doomed to defeat, — all the States that we could still rationally hope to carry casting less than half the Electoral votes. Yet we fought on with much resolution, though with little hope; giving Fremont and Dayton the six New England States, by clear majorities; New York, by 80,000 plurality; and Ohio, by nearly 17,000; while Michigan, Iowa, and Wisconsin went decidedly for us, as Illinois would have done had there been no third ticket. Pennsylvania and Indiana each gave Mr. Buchanan a bare majority over the two opposing tickets. Mr. Fillmore received the 8 electoral votes of Maryland only; Colonel Fremont had 114 votes, — those of eleven Free States; while Mr. Buchanan was elected by 112 votes from fourteen Slave States, and 62 from five Free States, — 174 in all, or a clear majority. The aggregate popular vote stood: Buchanan, 1,838,232; Fremont, 1,341,514; Fillmore, 874,707. Buchanan's inauguration (March 4, 1857) was swiftly followed by the since famous Dred Scott decision of the Supreme Court, which denied the right of Congress to prohibit slaveholding in the Territories of the Union, and proclaimed it the notion of our Revolutionary fathers that Blacks have no rights that Whites are bound to respect. Mr. Buchanan foreshadowed this decision in his Inaugural, gave it his hearty indorsement, and commended it to general approval.

Kansas had begun to be settled in 1854, directly after the passage of the Nebraska bill, and had inevitably become an arena of strife and violence. Colonies were sent thither from the Free States expressly to mould her to the uses of Free Labor; while weaker colonies were sent thither from the South, to bind her to the car of Slavery. These would have been of small account had they not been largely supplemented by the incursions of Missourians, who, thoroughly armed, swarmed across the unmarked border whenever an election was impending; camping in the vicinity of most of the polls, whereof they took unceremonious possession, and voting till they were sure that no more votes were needed; when they decamped, and returned to their Missouri homes. As the Free-State settlers refused to be thus subjugated, there were soon two Territorial legislatures, with sheriffs and courts to match; and these inevitably led to collisions of authorities and of forces, resulting in general insecurity and turmoil, with occasional sacrifices of property and of life. Congress had tried to end these disorders; but no plan could be agreed upon by the two Houses, and nothing was effected. At length, in the Summer of 1857, the pro-Slavery minority, powerfully aided by the "Border Ruffians," elected a Convention, framed a Pro-Slavery Constitution, adopted it after their fashion, and sent it to Congress for approval and ratification. It was known as the "Lecompton" Constitution, from the place where it was fabricated.

Mr. Buchanan at first hesitated to indorse or be complicated with this procedure; so that there was trouble in the camp;

and it was currently reported that his less scrupulous Secretary of the Treasury, — Howell Cobb, of Georgia, — being asked by a visitor what was the matter, carelessly replied, "O, not much; only Old Buck is opposing the Administration." Senator Douglas, on the one hand, at first seemed inclined to the side of the Missourians, whose cause he had upheld with signal ability and energy in the preceding Congress; but he soon demonstrated in favor of genuine "Popular Sovereignty," in Kansas, which was his more natural and consistent position. Reports of this change had preceded his appearance in Washington as a member of the XXXVth Congress; so that, on his calling to pay his respects to the President, an animated and spicy colloquy on the ruling topic was at once commenced by his host. "Mr. Douglas," said the President, "how are we to allay the contention and trouble created by this strife over the Lecompton Constitution?" "Why, Mr. President," replied his guest, "I do not see how *you* should have any trouble in the premises. The Constitution says, '*Congress* shall make all needful rules and regulations respecting the Territories,' &c., but I cannot recall any clause which requires *the President* to make any." Thus the conversation ran on, until the President, waxing warm, saw fit to warn his visitor that his present course would, if persisted in, soon carry him out of the Democratic party. "Mr. Senator," he inquired, "do you clearly apprehend the goal to which you are now tending?" "Yes, sir," promptly responded the Little Giant; "I have taken a through ticket, and checked all my baggage." Further discussion being obviously useless, Mr. Douglas soon left the White House, and I believe he did not visit it again during Mr. Buchanan's administration.

The XXXVth Congress, which had been mainly chosen simultaneously with Mr. Buchanan, or nearly so, was decidedly Democratic, and still more strongly pro-Slavery, — the Senate impregnably so, by about two to one, — and yet, so flagrant were the enormities of the Lecompton measure, and so conspicuous the ability and the energy of Mr. Douglas, who led the resistance to it, and threw his whole soul into the work, that the attempt to make Kansas a Slave State under the Lecompton Constitution (which her people were forbidden to change to the detriment of Slavery for several years to come) was fairly beaten; being vitally amended in the House by a vote of 120 to 112, after it had passed the Senate by 35 to 23. The Senate at first refused to concur by 34 to 22; whereupon a conference was had, and an equivocal compromise measure thereby devised and carried through both Houses by nearly a party vote. But, as this measure gave the people of Kansas a chance indirectly to vote upon and reject the Lecompton scheme, such a vote was thereupon had, and the scheme rejected by an overwhelming majority. Kansas thus remained a Territory until after the secession from Congress of most of the Southern Senators, early in 1861, when she was admitted as a Free State, with the hearty assent of three fourths of her inhabitants.

Mr. Douglas's second term as Senator expired with the Congress in which he made his gallant and successful struggle against what I deemed a great and perilous wrong, — a wrong so palpable that the eminent Senator Hammond, of South Carolina, who supported it at every step, afterward publicly declared that the Lecompton bill should at once have been kicked out of Congress as a fraud. It seemed to me that not only magnanimity, but policy, dictated to the Republicans of Illinois that they should promptly and heartily tender their support to Mr. Douglas, and thus insure his reëlection for a third term with substantial unanimity. They did not concur, however, but received the suggestion with passionate impatience. Having for a quarter of a century confronted Mr. Douglas as the ablest, most alert, most effective, of their adversaries, they could not now be induced to regard him in a different light; and, beside, their hearts were set on the election, as his successor, of their own especial favorite and champion, Abraham Lincoln, who, though the country at large scarcely knew him as for a single term a Representative in Congress, was endeared to them by his tested efficiency as a canvasser and his honest worth as a man. Four years before, the Whig portion of them had wished to make him Senator; but the far fewer anti-Nebraska Democrats held the balance of power, and they decisively said, "You will elect *our* leader, Lyman Trumbull, or you will not elect at all." Having given way then, the great body of the party had fully resolved that Lincoln should be their candidate now, and that, at all events, Douglas should *not* be. So Lincoln was nominated, and accepted in a memorable speech; and the State was canvassed by him and Douglas as it had never before been,— they repeatedly speaking alternately from the same stand to gatherings of deeply interested and intently listening thousands. In the event, Mr. Douglas secured a small majority in either branch of the Legislature, and was reëlected; but Mr. Lincoln's friends claimed a considerable majority for their favorite in the aggregate popular vote. They did not, for a while, incline to forgive me for the suggestion that it would have been wiser and better not to have opposed Mr. Douglas's return; but I still abide in that conviction.

Mr. Douglas was the readiest man I ever knew. He was not a hard student; if he had been, it would have been difficult to set limits to his power. I have seen him rise in the Senate quite at fault with regard to essential facts in controversy, and thence make damaging blunders in debate; but he readily caught at and profited by any suggestion thrown out by friend or foe; and no American ever excelled him in off-hand discussion: so that, even if worsted in the first stages, he was apt to regain his lost ground as he went on. Once, as I sat with the senior Francis P. Blair and one or two others outside the bar of the Senate in 1856, he made us the text of an amusing dissertation on the piebald, ring-streaked, and speckled materials whereof the new Republican party was composed; and, passing us soon afterward, he hailed me familiarly with the interrogation, "Did n't I give you a good turn just now?" At a later day, when the Lecompton struggle was in progress, a mutual friend, remembering that my strictures on Mr. Douglas in former years had been of a *very* caustic sort, inquired of him whether he had any objections, on account of those strictures, to meeting me on a friendly footing. "Certainly not," was his instant response; "I always pay that class of debts as I go along." Our country has often been called to mourn severe, untimely losses; yet I deem the death of Stephen A. Douglas, just at the outbreak of our great Civil War, and when he had thrown his whole soul into the cause of the country, one of the most grievous and irreparable.

Mr. Buchanan, though born nearly a quarter of a century earlier, survived Mr. Douglas by fully seven years; dying in 1868, when he had long outlived whatever influence or consideration he may once have enjoyed. Alike ambitious and timid, his conduct throughout the initial stage of the Rebellion is yet unaccountable on any hypothesis but that of secret pledges, made by him or for him, to the Southern leaders when he was an aspirant to the Presidency, that fettered and paralyzed him when they perverted the power enjoyed by them as members of his Cabinet to the disruption and overthrow of the Union. That, during those last mournful months of his nominal rule, he repeatedly said to those around him, "I am the last President of the United States," I firmly believe; that he proclaimed and argued that the Federal government had no constitutional right to defend its own existence against State secession, is matter of public record. Though he had spent what should have been the better part of a long life in working his way up to the Presidential chair, I think the verdict of history must be that it would have been far better for his own fame, as well as better for the country, that he had failed to obtain it.

XLIII.

A RIDE ACROSS THE PLAINS.

FROM the hour when, late in 1848, the discovery of rich gold *placers* in California had incited a vast and eager migration thither, insuring the rapid growth of energetic and thrifty settlements of our countrymen on that remote and previously unattractive, thinly peopled coast, the construction of a great International Railway from the Missouri to the Pacific seemed to me imperative and inevitable. I could not deem it practicable to retain permanently under one government communities of many millions of intelligent, aspiring, imperious people, separated by fifteen hundred miles of desert, traversed by two great mountain-chains, beside innumerable clusters, spurs and isolated summits, and compelling a resort, for comparatively easy, cheap, and speedy transit, to a circuit of many thousands of miles. A Pacific Railroad was thus accepted by me at a very early day as a National necessity, alike in its political and its commercial aspects; and, while others were scoffingly likening it to a tunnel under the Atlantic or a bridge to the moon, I was pondering the probabilities and means of its early construction. I resolved to make a journey of observation across the continent, with reference to the natural obstacles presented to, and facilities afforded for, its construction; but no opportunity for executing this purpose was afforded me prior to the year 1859. I then hoped, rather than confidently expected, that, on publicly announcing my intention, some friend might offer to bear me company on this journey; but my hope was not realized. One friend did propose to go; but his wife's veto overruled his not very stubborn resolve. I started alone, on the 9th of May, and travelled rapidly, *via* Cleveland, Chicago, Quincy, and the North Missouri Railroad, to St. Joseph; thence dropping down the Missouri to Atchison, and traversing Kansas, by Leavenworth and Wyandot, to Osawatomie; thence visiting Lawrence and returning to Leavenworth, whence the "Pike's Peak" stage carried me, through Topeka, Manhattan, and Fort Riley, to Junction City, then the western outpost of civilization in that quarter.

We stopped overnight at the said city, and I visited a brother editor, who was printing there a little Democratic weekly, for which he may possibly have had two hundred subscribers; but, if so, I am confident that not one half of them ever paid him the first cent. He was, primarily, as I remember, a Texan; but, having spent two years in California, he gave me the most rapturous commendations of the beauties, glories, and delights of that region. "It is the greatest, the finest, the most attractive country that man ever saw," he concluded. "Then why are you not still in California?" I inquired, glancing around his doleful little shanty. "Because I am a great fool," he bluntly replied. I did not see how profitably to protract the discussion.

We left Junction City on a bright morning late in May, following a new trail, which kept within sight of the Solomon's or middle fork of the Kansas River for the next two hundred miles. The country was, in the main, gently rolling prairie, covered with luxuriant young grass, and fairly glowing with flowers. Antelopes, though shy, were frequently seen at a distance, which they rapidly increased. Streams running into the Solomon, across our track, were at first frequent, and often skirted with trees; but grew scarcer and more scanty as we proceeded. There was some variety of timber in the wet bottoms at first; but soon the species dwindled to two, — Cottonwood and a low, wide-branching Water Elm; at length, upon passing a wide belt of thin soil, covering what seemed to be a reddish sandstone, both wood and water almost entirely vanished, save as we descried the former at intervals in the bottoms of the Solomon, some miles to the left (south) of us. The Cayota or Prairie Wolf (a mean sort of stunted or foreshortened fox) was infrequently seen; the bolder and quite formidable Gray Wolf more rarely; soon, the underground lodges of the Prairie Dog (a condensed gray squirrel) covered roods of the ground we traversed, — our newly located path lying right across several of their "towns," which it had not yet impelled them to desert. I refused, at first, to credit the plainsmen's stories that an Owl and a Rattlesnake were habitually, if not uniformly, fellow-tenants of his "hole" with the Prairie Dog, though I had already seen many Owls sitting, as we came near, each at the mouth of a hole, after the Prairie Dog had barked his quick, sharp note of alarm at our approach, and dropped into it; but I was finally compelled to succumb to testimony that could not be gainsayed. The *rationale* of the odd partnership is this: the Rattlesnake wants a lodging, and cannot easily dig one in that compact soil; the Prairie Dog *does n't* want to be dug out and eaten by the Cayota, as he quickly and surely would be but for the protection afforded by the Rattlesnake's deadly fangs. What the Owl (a small particolored one) makes by the association, I do not so clearly comprehend; but I suspect the Hawk would pounce upon and devour *him* but for the ugly customer presumed to be just at hand, and ready to "mix in," if any outsider should venture to meddle with the Owl; whose partnership duties are plainly those of a watch-dog or lookout.

Beyond the sterile sandstone belt, we struck a wide stretch of almost woodless, gently rolling prairie, thickly reticulated by tortuous buffalo paths, with frequent skeletons and still more plenteous skulls, — the soil being covered by a mere sward of the short, strong buffalo-grass; and soon we came in sight of galloping, fleeing herds of first three and four, then twenty to a hundred and fifty, buffaloes, generally running southward, in their alarm at our appearance, to seek safety in more familiar haunts, — the entire host being at this time in movement northward. Twenty or thirty miles farther on, having reached the summit of a gentle slope, we looked down its western counterpart to the pretty brook at its base, perhaps five miles distant, and thence up the opposite "rise," — the eye taking in at a glance at least a hundred square miles of close-fed velvet glade, whereof nearly or quite half was covered by buffalo, not "as thick as they could stand," but as close together as they could comfortably feed. Say that there were but twenty (instead of fifty) square miles of buffaloes in sight, and that each one had four square rods of ground to himself, the number in sight at once was 512,000. And for three days we were oftener in than out of sight of these vast herds, and must have seen several millions of buffaloes. In fact, we could with difficulty avoid them, — our driver being once obliged to stop his team, or allow it and us to be overwhelmed and crushed by a frightened, furious herd, which, having commenced its stampede southward across our path forty or fifty rods ahead of us, continued to follow each other in blind succession until we must have gone down and rolled over beneath their thundering charge (as an empty stage did a few days afterward), if we had not halted, and so avoided them. A day or two before, an agent of the line, who was riding a horse along the track, unthinking of danger, was borne down by a herd started by some emigrants the other side of an elevation, and instantly hurled to the earth. Though badly hurt, he saved himself from death by firing all the barrels of his revolver at the great brutes careering madly over his prostrate form; but his horse was instantly killed.

Emerging from the buffalo region, the soil became visibly thinner, and the vegetation poorer and poorer, until — the head sources of the Solomon having been passed — we bore rather north of west across several tributaries to the Republican or main northern branch of the Kansas, which we found here a rapid, shallow stream, perhaps a hundred yards wide by one to two feet deep, rippling over a bed of coarse sand

and gravel, with a very few cottonwoods thinly dotting its banks at long intervals, — precious little thin, coarse grass being occasionally discernible. A mule, bitten in the jaw by a rattlesnake, lying dead beside a station-tent, was one of the fresher features of this dreary region. A stunted cactus — which reared its small, prickly leaves barely above the ground — here began to be manifest. Following up the dwindling river, we soon came to a "sink," — the entire stream percolating for fifteen or twenty miles hence through its gravelly bed far below the surface of the earth, — a teamster, who dug through eight feet of sand and gravel in quest of water for his fainting beasts, being obliged to desist without finding any. Most of the tributaries we crossed on the Republican were simply broad beds of coarse, loose, dry sand, into which our mules often sank to a depth of several inches; though in Winter and Spring I presume these are considerable brooks. Wood here became so scarce that, to supply one station, it had to be carted sixteen miles. At length, we left the head springs of the Republican on our right, and struck, a few miles on, a northern tributary of the Arkansas, known as the "Big Sandy," which we ascended some twenty or thirty miles; finally leaving it on our left. Its bed was dry, of rather coarse sand, and often covered with a white, alkaline efflorescence; but, occasionally, a small stream ran gently aboveground, under one of its banks, where the channel had been worn exceptionally deep.

Soon after leaving the Big Sandy, we crossed the head waters of Bijou Creek, which runs northward into the South Platte. "Pike's Peak," snow-crowned, had for some time been visible nearly west of us; soon, we found deeper ravines and steeper hills than we had seen since we left the Missouri, with thin clumps of Yellow or Pitch Pine, — outposts of the Rocky Mountain forests, — occasionally covering patches of their sides or crests: the soil being sterile, and the grass too scanty to nourish sweeping fires at any season. After a few hours of this, we descended to the valley of Cherry Creek, near the point where it emerges from the mountains, and, following down its east bank to its entrance into the South Platte, saluted, one bright morning in June, after a rough, chilly, all-night ride, the rising city of DENVER.

Denver was then about six months old; but the rival city of Auraria (since absorbed by it), lying just across the bed of Cherry Creek (which suddenly dried up at this point during one night of my brief sojourn), had already attained an antiquity of nearly a year. As there was no saw-mill within several hundred miles, none of the edifices which composed these rival cities could yet boast a ground-floor; but I attended Divine worship the next Sunday (in Auraria) on the first second-story floor that was constructed in either of them. It may at first blush seem odd that a second-floor should precede a first; but mother Earth supplied a first-floor that did very well, while nature has not yet condescended to supply man-made dwellings with chamber-floors.

I suppose there were over a hundred dwellings in the two cities, when I reached them. I judge that they averaged fully ten feet square, though probably the larger number fell short of that standard. In material, none could boast over its neighbors, as all were built of cottonwood logs from the adjacent bank of the South Platte; but some of these were rudely squared on one side, with an axe; while others were left as God made them. I believe there was a variety in roofs also, — some being constructed of "shooks," or pieces split with an axe from a cottonwood log, while others were of cottonwood bark. I seem to remember that all the chimneys were of sticks and mud; but then some were without chimneys; and, while several had windows (I mean one apiece) composed of four to six lights of seven-by-nine glass, others were content with the more primitive device of a rude wooden shutter, closed at night, and during severe, windy, driving storms. Most of these cabins had known as yet only male housekeepers; and nearly half of them had been deserted by their creators and owners, some of whom were off prospecting for gold; while quite a number — disappointed, hopeless, homesick — had left for the States early in Spring, convinced that gold in the Rocky Mountains was a myth, a humbug, or that (in the vernacular) "Pike had n't got any peak." But the recent discoveries on Clear Creek had given matters a new and more cheerful aspect; so that, while two thirds of those who started for "the diggings" that Spring never went within sight of the Rocky Mountains, — many of them not halfway to them, — while some barely reached Denver, and then took the back track, the rival cities were gaining population quite rapidly during the ten days that I spent in or near them, and some good families were among the acquisitions. Cabins that would gladly have been sold for $25 two months earlier now ran rapidly up to $100; and the market could fairly be quoted as active and advancing. There were as yet few or no servants to be hired at any price; but a considerable band of Arapahoes were camped in Denver; and, while the braves were thoroughly worthless, their squaws were willing to do anything for food. True, they could do very little; but lugging water from the South Platte was the first requisite in housekeeping, and this they did faithfully. We lived mainly on bread, bacon, beans, coffee, and nettles, the last being boiled for greens; but those who were not particular as to dirt could often buy a quarter of antelope just brought in by an Arapahoe; or, more probably, killed by the hunter and backed in by his squaw. Whiskey was in good supply (I know nothing as to the quality) at a quarter (silver) per drink. There were several rude bedsteads just constructed in the Denver House, — the grand hotel of the city, — on which you were allowed to spread your blankets and repose for a dollar a night; but mine, being bottomed with rough slats nearly a foot apart, almost broke my back, proving far less luxurious than the bosom of mother Earth. Two blacklegs rented opposite corners of the public room, and were steadily swindling greenhorns at three-card monte, from morning till bedtime: one stage-driver, who was paid off with $207 at noon, having lost the last cent of it to one of these harpies by 2 P.M. The gamblers and other rough subjects had an unpleasant habit of quarrelling and firing revolvers at each other in this bar-room when it was crowded, and sometimes hitting the wrong man, — by which phrase I certainly do not indicate any of their own number. On the whole, therefore, I soon tired of hotel-life in Denver. It was not dull, — quite otherwise, — but I am shy by nature and meditative by habit, and some of the ways of the Denver House did not suit me. They were unmistakably Western, and I was journeying to study Western character; but, even though distance might not lend enchantment to the view of these mining-region blacklegs and ruffians, I am sure that they can be studied to better satisfaction out of pistol-shot than at close quarters.

"Suppose you jump a cabin?" suggested the friend to whom I intimated my preference for a less popular lodging. I did not understand; but he explained, and I saw the point. Several cabins were still standing vacant, as many had been; and no one knew whither their owners had gone, so whoever wanted one of these empty tenements just helped himself. I at once followed the fashion, and was happy in my choice. I was thenceforth lodged very eligibly till the owner of my cabin, returning from a prospecting tour, put in an appearance. He was evidently embarrassed at the thought that his advent must seem abrupt and unceremonious; but I cut short his apologies by insisting that the cabin afforded ample accommodation for two; and we thenceforth shared it very comfortably for the few days that I tarried in Denver.

While thus snugly and cheaply lodged, I boarded with a widow lady from Leavenworth, who had been keeping a mail-station on the plains, but, tiring of that, had just migrated to Denver, and jumped a cabin. She, with her little son, slept on a sort of shelf nearer the roof than the floor of her single room; while two male boarders, waiting outside while she made her toilet, spread their blankets on the earth-floor of her tenement. At daylight, they turned out, giving her a chance to dress, clear up, and get breakfast, which they duly returned to eat. Such was life in Denver in June, 1859.

XLIV.

THE ROCKY MOUNTAINS. — THE GREAT BASIN.

I MADE a flying visit, directly after reaching Denver, to the then new "Gregory Diggings," on Clear Creek, where is now Central City. A good road, I hear, now winds thither through the mountains, mainly keeping close to Clear Creek; but that was impossible in 1859; as even an empty wagon would have been capsized into or toward the creek at least a hundred times before making the distance. Our route lay across the South Platte, the prairie and Clear Creek (where Golden City has since sprung up), and then right up the face of the first ridge, rising 1,600 feet in a mile and a half, — an ascent so steep as to appear impossible to teams, however lightly loaded; and even saddle-horses seemed in great peril of falling off and rolling to the bottom. After two miles of level path through an open pine forest on the summit, we had to descend a declivity nearly as steep; then ascend a second mountain; and so on, till we camped at sunset, weary enough, seven miles short of the diggings, which we reached about nine next morning; spending the day and night with the pioneers, and returning to the Platte Valley the day after. I saw enough on that trip to convince me that the Rocky Mountains abound in Gold and nearly all other metals, but that these must be earned before they can be enjoyed.

I bade adieu to Denver about the 18th of June; having hired an "ambulance," or wagon and four mules, to convey me to the Overland Mail-route at Fort Laramie, on the North Platte, 200 miles northward. I judge that there were twenty considerable streams to cross in that distance, — all then in flood, from the melting snows of the inner and higher mountains. Several of these streams were forded with difficulty by our team, — one of them (the Cache le Poudre) being as large as the Charles at Cambridge. I think we saw four huts on the way, but only three of them were occupied. There was no White person then living within fifty miles of Cheyenne, where the Pacific Railroad now enters the Rocky Mountains; and only a deserted fort or military camp spoke of civilization. Yet most of the region between the two Plattes and the base of the Rocky Mountains — a district equal in area to Connecticut, if not to Vermont — has good soil, is tolerably timbered, grows fine grass luxuriantly, and will yet subsist a large farming population. It is subject to drouth, but may easily be irrigated; and then its product of Wheat, Oats, Barley, and Roots will be immense. I judge that nearly all the larger tributaries of the Missouri traverse a good farming region directly under the Rocky Mountains wherein they take rise. This region lies from 4,500 to 6,000 feet above tide, and hence is subject to frost, hail, and late snow, as well as to drouth; yet I predict its rapid settlement and growth. I wish I could see how to save its Aboriginal inhabitants from sure and speedy extinction.

After waiting five days at Fort Laramie, I took the mail stage (then weekly) which traversed the old Oregon as well as California emigrant trail up the Platte and its northern tributary, the Sweetwater, to that wide gap in the Rocky Mountains known as the South Pass, — the Sweetwater heading on the west side of the mountains, and sending (in Summer) a scanty mill-stream through the Pass. Much of this region is quite sterile; snow lay deep in a ravine of the Pass on the 5th of July; while there is one large swamp, thirty or forty miles this side, which remains frozen a foot or two below the surface perpetually. There are small lakes on this route that look most inviting, yet so surcharged with alkaline minerals that to drink freely of their water is death to man or beast. There is some Yellow Pine on the hills, with less Cottonwood and Quaking Asp, mainly skirting, at long intervals, the streams; but this region is, for the most part, unless rich in minerals, good for nothing. I learn that bounteous mines of Gold have lately been found here; and I know that the indications of Gold were quite palpable on the hills in the Pass, where we camped and spent a day beside a runnel which brings its scanty tribute to the Sweetwater. But, a few miles beyond the South Pass, where the mountains disappear, and the road to Utah and California diverges from the old trail to Oregon, and where each begins to descend toward the Pacific, the country is utterly worthless for at least two hundred miles; in the midst of which we crossed Green River, running swiftly southward, in a very deep, narrow valley, which yields a little grass and less Cottonwood. On either side of this valley stretch dreary wastes of thirsty sand, shaded only by the two low shrubs, known locally as Greasewood and Sagebrush, which, together, enclose a thousand miles of the Overland Wagon-route, and probably cover half a million square miles of the interior of our continent. Greasewood is a species of Artemisia, and derives its vulgar name from a waxy or resinous property, which causes it to burn freely, even while green; but it grows in bunches or stools six or seven feet apart, with naked, glittering sand between them; and so defies destruction by fire. Sagebrush exhibits a number of shoots, twelve to twenty inches long, from a common stalk or stump of about equal height; each shoot somewhat resembling a stalk of Sage in appearance and color. There is a Sage-Hen that eats this plant; but who, unless famishing, would thereafter choose to eat the Sage-Hen?

Fort Bridger was the first village we had seen since we left Laramie; like which, it owes its existence to a military post. It is traversed by a brawling mill-stream (Ham's Fork) which is rushing to be lost in Green River, and is said to have some arable land in its vicinity. We were still considerably north of the present route of the Pacific Railroad, which we had crossed and left near Cheyenne; but soon, crossing a high divide, we bore southward, and, descending rapidly, forded Bear River, here a swift stream one or two hundred yards wide, but scarcely more than two feet deep. It is unfortunate that the Pacific Railroad cannot follow this river hence to Salt Lake; but the course of the stream is so tortuous and so shut in by mountains and difficult precipices that this may not be. I judge that, next to the Sierra Nevada, already nearly vanquished, the stretch from Green River to Salt Lake — some three hundred miles — is the most difficult section of the entire work. But the route we traversed, leaving that of the railroad far on our right (north), rises easily out of the valley of Bear River, and thence follows down a long, narrow, grassy valley or glen known as Echo Cañon, with steep cliffs on either side, emerges from it to cross Weber River (also a tributary of Salt Lake), and thence crosses two difficult ridges of the Wahsatch and Uintah mountains, whence it winds down a ravine known as Emigration Cañon till that opens into the valley of the River Jordan and of Salt Lake; and soon we roll into the city of the many-wived prophet, the capital of his sacerdotal and political empire, and the most conspicuous trophy of his genius and his power.

That city has so changed since I saw it, — being now probably at least thrice its size nine years ago, — that I will speak of it briefly, and only as to certain permanent phases of its character. My present belief is that, like most strangers, I was more favorably impressed by it than I should have been. Not that its more intelligent people received me kindly and treated me with emphatic hospitality, — I have been thus welcomed to other cities, which nevertheless did not specially impress me. But a thousand miles of parched, mountainous desert (counting from Denver only) on which I had seen no single productive farm, and nothing that could be fairly termed a house but a few cheap structures for officers' lodgings at Forts Laramie and Bridger — no vegetables, no furniture, no beds, — had predisposed me to greet even the ruder appliances of urban life with uncritical satisfaction. Our civilization, regarded as an end, is faulty enough, and open to objections from every side; but, considered as a stage in our progress from the *status* of the Esquimaux, the Digger, the Hottentot, I submit that it may be contemplated with a complacency by no means unreasonable. Soon after leaving the last Kansas settlement, I noted the rounds of the ladder I had descended during the preceding fortnight, and photographed them as follows:—

"*May* 12*th*, *Chicago.* — Chocolate and morning journals last seen on the hotel breakfast-table.

23*d*, *Leavenworth.* — Room-bells and bath-tubs make their final appearance.

24*th*, *Topeka.* — Beef-steaks and wash-bowls (other than tin) last visible. Barber ditto.

26*th*, *Manhattan.* — Potatoes and eggs last recognized among the blessings that "brighten as they take their flight." Chairs ditto.

27*th*, *Junction City.* — Last visitation of a boot-black, with dissolving views of a board bedroom. Beds bid us good by.

28*th*, *Pipe Creek.* — Benches for seats at meals disappeared, giving place to bags and boxes. We (two passengers of a scribbling turn) write letters to our journals at nightfall in the express-wagon that has borne us by day, and must serve us as bedchamber for the night. Thunder and lightning, from both south and west, give strong promise of a shower before morning. Our trust, under Providence, is in buoyant hearts and a rubber blanket. Good night!"

I descended somewhat farther afterward, and I did not think of hardship, though the water was often scanty, as well as bad, and the pilot-bread had been so long exposed to the drying air of the Plains that human teeth could hardly penetrate it. Those who fancy army "hard-tack" dry eating would devour it thankfully, after being rationed a single week on that which I confronted on the Sweetwater and the Colorado. But hard-tack is wholesome, if not toothsome; while the bread made on the Plains, of nearly equal parts of flour and saleratus, baked in a frying-pan or spider, and eaten hot, though I ate it with facility, destroyed my digestion, and made me sick,—there being nothing to relish it but poorly smoked pork, except tea and coffee, which I declined. With good water, I could stand almost anything; but this was often unattainable, and I suffered for want of it.

Salt Lake City suddenly restored us to abundance and comfort,—rooms, beds, sheets, towels, vegetables, dried fruits, shade, &c.; while the water was beautiful and good. The Mormons have faults; but they are more uniformly industrious and (after their fashion) pious than any other people I ever visited. I doubt whether there is another city on the continent wherein family worship is so general, and profanity so rare, as in Salt Lake City, so far as its Mormon inhabitants are considered. I must believe the authors of their revelations either knavish or self-deluded; but I have such a liking for solid, steady, *bona fide* work, that the rank and file have my most hearty good wishes. Nowhere else are there so few idlers (Brigham Young assured me that there was none but himself; and he is kept busy in his vocation of prophet and ruler), and nowhere else have so few poor and ignorant people achieved so much that remains to benefit future generations, as in Utah. I cherish the hope that their spiritual vision will soon be cleared, and that they will yet, ceasing to be polygamists, become better Christians,—retaining the habits of industry, frugality, and thrift, which command my hearty admiration. "He builded better than he knew" is a truth of very wide application; and I am confident that the Pacific Railroad, of which Brigham Young is grading the thirty miles next northeast of his metropolis, is destined to work changes which it is well that he does not foresee, and which will render his dominions more populous and his people far less docile to his guidance than they now are. I judge our age inauspicious to prophets and new revelations from on high; and, though the past history of Utah seems to refute my theory, I confidently expect that of the next twenty years to confirm it.

XLV.

UTAH.—NEVADA.

A PORTION of our little army, despatched from Kansas late in 1857 to put down a threatened (or apprehended) revolt of the Mormons, had stopped for the Winter at Fort Bridger, after its trains, following carelessly in its rear, had, not far from the Colorado, been surprised and burned by a Mormon force, rendering its Winter sojourn in that desolate region one of great hardship, especially for its animals; but it finally marched into the Mormon settlements unopposed,—the chief Saints protesting that they had never purposed rebellion against the National authority. The expedition, which had threatened a bloody tragedy, was thus transformed into a most expensive farce; for, though the regulars were hardly more out of place in Utah than they had been in Kansas, they were a far more costly nuisance. Every pound of their sustenance had been hauled across twelve hundred miles of desert and mountain at a cost of $400 or $500 per ton,—or, at any rate, was charged for as if it had been. And, when I visited Camp Floyd, where it was stationed, forty-five miles south-west of Salt Lake City, officers were engaged, under orders from Washington, in selling its heavy trains at auction, at prices possibly averaging one half the actual value of the mules and one tenth that of the wagons,—the bidders being few, and evidently combined to give Uncle Sam the worst bargains possible. Governments are made to be plundered,—at all events, are regularly used to that end. I presume that, when the army was ordered from Camp Floyd to Texas the next year, part of these same wagons were bought back from their purchasers at generous prices, — which by no means implies any generosity on the part of those who bought them of the government and sold them back again.

I spent a day at Camp Floyd as the guest of my oldest army acquaintance, Lieutenant-Colonel D. C. Ruggles, 5th Infantry, whom I had first known in 1835 as a Massachusetts cadet, just appointed to a lieutenancy; and who, having married in Virginia, afterward became a General of the Southern Confederacy. We dined with the commander of the post, Colonel Albert Sidney Johnston, — a grave, deep, able man, with a head scarcely inferior to Daniel Webster's, — who, less than two years afterward, left Texas overland to take part in the Rebellion, and finally found death on the bloody field of Shiloh or Pittsburg Landing, where he led the Rebel host with a gallantry and soldiership worthy of a better cause. If some wizard had foreshadowed to us the future, as we sat around his hospitable board not three years before, who would have believed him?

Camp Floyd had been located beside a small but constant stream, with considerable stunted, bushy Cedar covering the low mountains adjacent, whence it issued; but the stage-route thence to California rose gradually from its valley into a hilly, burnt-up region southwestward; and thenceforth, till we bore up to strike the Humboldt at Gravelly Ford, some three hundred miles westward, I can remember seeing but three brooks of any account, — neither of those carrying water enough to render it a decent mill-stream; and neither, I judge, running more than five miles from the clustered mountains between which it was cradled, till the arid, thirsty plain had drank the last drop, and left its shallow bed thenceforth in Summer a stretch of dry, hot gravel and sand. We may have passed a dozen springs in this distance, though I believe we did not. In one place, there was a stretch of fifty miles from water to water, save that some had been carted in barrels to quench the thirst of our jaded mules at a point half-way from one station to another. Twice, as I recollect, we sat down to our noonday meal of pork and bread beside springs by courtesy, where water had been found by shallow digging in depressions or "sinks" below the usual surface of the plains; but the warm, sulphurous fluid thence obtained required intense thirst to render it potable. In one place, I recollect several miles of the all-pervading Grease-wood and Sage-brush which had been killed stone-dead, — dried up, apparently, though their power of resisting drouth is unparalleled; yet stunted Bunch Cedar and some Indian Pine thinly covered the brows or the crests of many hills and low mountains; seeming able to resist a drouth even of successive years. The country is so broken and mountainous that I presume Artesian wells have since been, or will easily be, dug in the rockless clay of the valleys, which will supply water, not only for drinking, but for irrigation; and the valleys need but this to render their alkaline clay bounteously productive. I judge that the surface of most of them has been raised twenty to fifty feet by earth washed down, in the course of ages, from the circumjacent mountains, and that, when irrigated, they will be cultivated with facility, and with ample success. The Mormons raise bounteous crops, especially of Wheat, wherever they can coax a stream to meander across and percolate through a portion of one of their valleys; and I presume most of those between the Wahsatch and the Sierra Nevada need but water to prove them equally fertile. Many of the mountains, I doubt not, will prove rich in minerals; but they are rarely or never arable, produce a very little grass in Spring only; and their scanty, fitful covering of wood, once cut off, would not be reproduced in a century.

Bear in mind that the route I travelled rather skirts than pierces the desert of deserts which spreads southwestward of Salt Lake, nearly or quite to the Colorado; covering many thousands of square miles. A friend, now deceased, once found himself "at sea" on this desert, and likely to perish of thirst; but he had a noble horse, to which he gave a free rein; and that horse brought him off alive, — that was all. He crossed miles on miles of pure rock salt, — how deep, he could not say; but he brought away a fragment which had been washed and worn into a nearly round log, as large as a man's thigh, and three or four feet long, which I saw. Another friend, who explored a route from Austin, Nevada, to the Colorado (on the western verge of this desert), rode, for days, down the bed of what had once been a considerable river, but which seemed to have been absolutely dry for years.

There is ample corroborating proof that the Great Basin has been far less parched than it is; and I trust that a more generous rain-fall will again be accorded it. Probably, re-clothing it with timber would renew its rains; but then the rains seem to be needed to start and sustain the timber. Two or three hundred miles north, several streams take rise that make their way northward to the Columbia; as the Humboldt, issuing from the west side of the same mountainous region, runs over three hundred miles W.S.W., to be lost in a sandy, reedy marsh, not a hundred miles from the Sierra Nevada; but, southward of this strange river of desolation, there is rarely a stream large enough to turn a grindstone, till you are very near the banks of the almost equally lonesome Colorado.

I rode more than two hundred miles down the south or left bank of the Humboldt. In that distance, I judge that all the water it receives from tributaries might be passed through a nine-inch ring; and the stream, of course, grew smaller and smaller as it flowed. Possibly, three springs were passed in all that distance, though I cannot remember so many; while I *do* right well remember my scarcely modified thirst. The alkaline water of the Humboldt I could not drink, though others did; in Spring, when its volume is greater, its quality is probably better. Once, we stopped by a small brook tumbling down from high adjacent mountains on the left, and I drank my fill of its warm, sweet water; but for this, I must have remained thirsty throughout. And, in all the two hundred miles, I believe I did not see wood enough to keep a Yankee farmer's fire going through a Winter.

Willow-bushes, skirting the little river, were nearly all. Even the mountain ranges, from one to five miles distant on either side, showed no timber, or next to none. And, when we came at length to that expansion of the stream which is called a lake, no raft, boat, or even canoe, floated on its bosom or was moored to either bank, and a cottage built of stones and clay constituted the mail-station at its foot. Thence, we crossed a waste of sand forty miles wide, which separates the "sink" of the Humboldt from the kindred marsh that drinks up the waters of the Carson, which comes down from the Sierra; and, following up the latter, by what is now Virginia City, but then was nothing, we stopped to eat at Genoa,—then the only considerable village in what has since become Nevada,—and rested our weary limbs at dark, after a night-and-day ride of four hundred miles (five days and four nights from Shell Creek in Western Utah), in a wooden hotel, at the very foot of the Sierra Nevada.

There was then no Austin, and no real mining in what is now Nevada. The auriferous and argentiferous deposit or vein now known as the Comstock lode had just been discovered,—that was about all. The natural grass of the upper end of Carson Valley had previously attracted a few settlers, who were weary of mining in California, or worn out with travel across the desert and reluctant to scale the Sierra; and, though the valley must be fully six thousand feet above the sea, and must inevitably be frosty, its beauty and verdure fully justify their partiality. I estimate that three hundred habitations, mainly log, are quite as many as existed in the entire region which is now the State of Nevada, that its civilized population did not exceed five thousand, and that its aggregate product was barely adequate to the subsistence even of this number. To-day, Nevada produces more silver, and little less gold, than any other State or Territory; and the next census will give her a population of at least two hundred thousand.

XLVI.

THE SIERRA NEVADA. — THE YOSEMITE. — THE BIG TREES.

A CLEAR, warm, golden 1st of August — such a day as the Pacific slope of our continent abounds in — took us across the Sierra Nevada by the double-summit route that follows up one branch of the Carson to its source, then descends rapidly into the valley of Lake Bigler, thence climbs diagonally the mountain west of it by a steep ascent of two miles, crosses its summit, and descends again, following a depression in which springs give birth to rills, which speedily collect into a brook, which goes brawling and leaping down the western declivity of the Sierra, and has become quite a little river (South Fork of the American) at a point twenty or thirty miles down, where we crossed its valley from the northern to the southern bank, and, rising thence to the summit of a ridge or "divide" on the south, ran rapidly down it to the thriving city of Placerville, at the base of the range, in California's great central valley of the Sacramento.

The Sierra Nevada is probably more heavily timbered than any other range of mountains on the continent. On the Nevada side, this timber is of moderate size, and almost wholly of Yellow or Pitch Pine, with a few deciduous trees in the narrow ravines of the streams; while, on the far longer slope that looks toward the Pacific, immense Yellow and Sugar Pines, often eight feet through, thickly cover thousands of square miles, interspersed with White Cedars from four to six feet in diameter, stately Balsam Firs, a considerable variety of White, Red, Live, and Rock Oaks, with a few other trees. Such a wealth of magnificent timber profoundly impresses the traveller, who has seen nothing like it since he left the eastern slope of the Rocky Mountains, and a plentiful lack of trees everywhere else since he bade adieu to the Kansas, now so many hundred miles away. The valleys and lower slopes of California are often quite bare, though wide-branching Oaks are thinly scattered over a portion of the latter; and I saw here — what I never saw elsewhere — living trees (Buckeye) six to eight inches through, with every leaf killed by drouth on the 1st of August, so that they would exhibit no sign of verdure again till after the heavy rains of the ensuing Winter. The dryness of earth and atmosphere on the Pacific slope in Summer and Autumn can only be realized by those who have experienced it. I saw the Mormon farmers cutting heavy grass by the margin of Salt Lake; but they found no process of hay-making necessary. Though its color was still a bright green, they raked it up unspread, and stacked it without ceremony, knowing that the atmosphere would meantime have sucked every atom of superfluous moisture out of the greenest of it. I presume this is the case, southward of Oregon, nearly or quite to the Isthmus of Darien.

My visit to the chief wonders of California — the Yosemite and the Big Trees — was necessarily hurried, but otherwise satisfactory. The sky was cloudless, as that of California almost uniformly is from May till October; the days were warm, but not excessively so; the journey was made on horseback, and in good part under the shade of giant evergreens. There were hundreds of acres covered almost exclusively by the Balsam Fir, sixty to eighty feet high, and one to two feet in diameter, growing at an elevation of fully 5,000 feet above tide, where the snows of Winter are so heavy and so many that the limbs of the Fir are depressed at their extremities, so as to form a series of umbrellas (as it were) rising one above another. Two high, steep mountains — one on either side of the South Merced — are surmounted by what, in 1859, were difficult bridle-paths, ere you strike at "Grizzly Flat," the source of a little runnel which meanders through an upland meadow or grassy morass to the brink of the great chasm, into which it pours itself by a fall of some 2,500 feet, which dissolves it into a white foam, whence it is afflicted with the lackadaisical appellation of "The Bridal Veil." The fall is not to blame for this, but some of its early visitors are.

The Yosemite is the grandest marvel of the continent. It is a rift or cleft in the Sierra Nevada, ten miles long, averaging half a mile wide at the bottom, and perhaps a mile at the top; its depth ranging from 3,000 to 4,000 feet, though one or two of the peaks on the north are said to rise 5,000 feet above the surface of the Merced. There are three points at which access is had to the valley,—one of them by clambering down the rocks near its head; the other two by zigzagging down either brink near its lower end. These are bridle-paths; the other, a foot-path only. That on the side of Mariposa is two miles long; and we were two good hours in winding down it through woods, with the moon's rays obscured to us by the interposition of the mountain whose north face we were descending. It was midnight when we reached its foot, and halted in the narrow, grassy valley of the stream, right in front of a perpendicular wall of gray granite 3,000 feet high, with a few Yellow Pines rooted in the crevices which at long intervals creased it, and seeming, with the mountain itself, about to be precipitated upon us.

Nothing else dwells in my memory that is at all comparable in awe-inspiring grandeur and sublimity to this wondrous chasm. I judge that the soft granite frequently found in streaks or belts by the miners of California—granite in chemical composition, but of the consistency of a rather solid boiled pudding—here existed on a much larger scale, until the little river (in Summer, a large mill-stream only) gradually dug it out, and bore it away, till the last of it had disappeared. I was told in the valley that repeated efforts of miners to dig down to the "bed-rock," in quest of mineral, had proved failures,—the sand and gravel, interspersed with bowlders, appearing unfathomable. The little streams from either brink which, at several points, leap into the valley, have, by the aid of frost and freshet, hurled millions of tons of rock and earth into the chasm, forming gigantic deposits of *débris*, over which the road up the valley carries you, generally through woods, affording difficult footing for men or animals, especially by night. Fording brooks, stumbling over rocks, winding among trees, it seemed to me that the six miles from the point where we entered the Valley to the two cottages or huts near its centre would never end; but they *did* end at last, about 2 A. M.; and I dismounted, and lay down to a welcome, though unquiet, slumber. I was covered with boils (the penalty of drinking the alkaline waters of Colorado, Utah, and Nevada), and had ridden in torture since noon, bearing my weight on my toes, barely stuck into Mexican stirrups far too small for me, whereby my feet had been so lamed that I could scarcely walk; hence, the prospect of soon rising to resume my travels was by no means alluring. I did rise, however; took breakfast; rode to the head of the Valley; examined with some care the famous fall; dined; and, at 2 P. M., started homeward; reaching Clark's ranche, on the South Merced, at 10 P. M.

Let me explain that the Yosemite fall is not that of the Merced, which enters the valley, at its head, by several successive leaps in a wild, rocky gorge or cañon, and leaves it by one even more impracticable, — giant blocks of granite being piled for hundreds of feet above the surface of the boiling current, and completely hiding it from view. The Yosemite is a side-stream or tributary, coming from the north or higher mountains, and, having itself worn down its bed to a depth of a thousand feet, leaps thence 2,600 feet into the chasm, making a single plunge of 1,600 feet. When I saw it, there was barely water in the Yosemite to turn the wheels of an average grist-mill; but in Winter and Spring there is probably twenty to forty times as much. The spectacle is rather pleasing than sublime, — the Mississippi, when in highest flood, having scarcely sufficient volume to save such a descent from seeming disproportioned and trivial.

Of Big Trees, there are two principal groups in California, — the Calaveras and the Mariposas. The former is more widely known, because quite accessible; and it boasts two or three of the largest trees; but it has barely 250 in all, while the

Mariposas has 600. They stand in a shallow valley or depression on the mountains, some 5,000 feet above the sea level, and 2,500 above the South Merced at Clark's, five miles distant.

That which was clearly largest fell several years ago, burying itself in the stony earth to a depth of four feet, and exhibiting a length of nearly or quite 400 feet. Formerly, two horses were ridden abreast for some 200 feet through the cavity, which successive fires had enlarged in it. It is still easy thus to ride through it, but the hollow has been burned out, so that it is now much shorter. Several of the trees still standing and alive are said to be over 100 feet in circumference; many are 80 to 90 feet, with a bark at least eighteen inches thick, a very little sap (white) under it, — the residue of the enormous bulk being a light, dry, reddish heart, which burns easily, even while the tree is green, but is scarcely prone to natural decay. Several of these giants rise a full hundred feet before putting forth a limb; none have many branches, but some of these are six feet through. They are a species of Cedar, — identical with the Cedars of Lebanon, our guide asserted; but I presume he only guessed so. Their foliage is scarcely, if at all, larger than that of the Yellow Pines and White Cedars growing among or near them; many of these being six to eight feet in diameter near the earth.

Within the next two years, the Central Pacific Railroad will have been completed, when passengers will leave New York on Monday morning, and dine in San Francisco the sixth evening thereafter. Then the trip, which I found tedious and rugged, will be rapid and easy, with every needed comfort and luxury proffered on arid stretches of desert, where I washed down the Mail Company's ancient pork and hot saleratus bread with more unwholesome and detestable warm alkaline water than (I trust) I shall ever be constrained to swallow hereafter. I hope to be one of the party who make the first excursion through trip to San Francisco, there to rejoice with my countrymen in the completion of the grandest and most beneficent enterprise ever inaugurated and perfected by man.

XLVII.

THE FUTURE OF CALIFORNIA.

I LINGER yet by the shores of the vast Pacific; for I feel that the general mind is still inadequately impressed with the majestic promise that impels the resistless tendency of our Gothic race toward the sands of that mighty sea. I do grievously err, if the historian of a future century does not instance the discovery of the Columbia by a Yankee, and the finding of Gold in Upper California so soon after that country had fallen into our hands, as among the most memorable and fortunate incidents in the annals of our continent, and hence of mankind.

On Gold *per se*, I place no high estimate. If all the science and labor which have been devoted by our people to the discovery and extraction of the Precious Metals had been as faithfully applied to the production of Iron, Coal, Copper, Lead, Tin, Salt, Gypsum, Marble, Slate, &c., I believe our country would have been richer and our people wiser and happier. Even if we could regard the abundant possession of Gold and Silver as a chief good, it is plain that the countries which produce are not those which most amply retain and enjoy them.

But mines or deposits of Gold and Silver are prominent among the means whereby attention and population are drawn to a region previously unpeopled, or thinly peopled by savages. Men rush madly and in thousands to a district reported auriferous; defying famine, heat, cold, pestilence, and even death itself. Mining or washing for Gold combines the fascinations of gambling — the chance of sudden riches —

with the sober incitements of regular and laudable industry: hence, it always did, and always will, allure vast numbers to brave peril and privation in its behoof. In time, the bubble bursts; the glamour is dispelled; but thousands have meantime found new homes and formed new habits; hence, a new civilized community.

I judge that gold-mining in California is nearly "played out." True, there are many good veins there which will continue to be worked at a profit for hundreds of years yet, during which many more and some better will doubtless be discovered and opened; but this is sober business, requiring capital, science, luck, patience, to insure success; while the jovial, free-handed heroes of pick and pan have passed away forever, — some to Nevada; some to Arizona; others to Montana, Idaho, &c., &c., — many to the land of shadows, — and the river-beds and "gulches" that knew them shall know them no more. California still exports Gold largely; but most of it is produced in Nevada, Montana, British Columbia, &c., &c. She for years produced Fifty Millions per annum; she has fallen off at least half; she is likely soon to fall still lower. I presume the child is born who will live to see her annual product fall below Ten Millions.

Yet her natural wealth will still be great, being varied, vast, and indestructible. I group it under these heads: —

I. *Soil.* — Of her ninety millions of acres, I should deem not over twenty millions decidedly arable; but these are, for the most part, exceedingly fertile. I judge that her great valleys were once arms of the sea, since gradually filled up by the continual abrasion and wearing away of the slopes of her omnipresent mountains. Many of them have now from 100 to at least 1,000 feet in depth of warm, mellow soil, — a marine deposit of sand, clay, and vegetable mould, in nearly equal proportions, wherein the plough very rarely disturbs a stone. I never saw land better calculated to produce large crops, year after year, with a moderate outlay of labor. The absence of rain in Summer and early Autumn keeps down weeds; while the unclouded, fervid sun hastens growth and insures perfection. I am confident that Cotton, and even Cane, might be grown to profit throughout the southern half of the State, in which the Fig, the Olive, and the Apricot grow luxuriantly and ripen unfailingly.

II. *Water.* — Though I saw large fields of heavy Indian Corn which grew and ripened without receiving a drop of rain, I nevertheless realize and admit that water is a desirable facility to vegetable growth and maturity. And, as cultivation is here mostly confined to valleys and the lower slopes of mountains, water is abundantly procurable. Artesian wells are easily dug; their flow is apt to be generous, as well as constant; and a small stream, well managed, amply irrigates a very large field. Trees and vines root deep in that rich, facile mould; the grape needs a very little water for two years, and none thereafter; while its culture requires but half the work needed here or in Europe, because our frequent rains evoke innumerable weeds. I estimate that a ton of Grapes may be produced in California with half the labor required to grow them in Italy; and that Silk, most semi-tropical Fruits, and I trust Tea, also, may be produced with equal facility. Wheat and other small grains yield largely and surely. I saw thousands of acres that had been two months cut and shocked, yet still awaited the coming of the circulating thresher; other fields were yet uncut (September 1), though long so dead-ripe that a large portion of the grain must be shelled out and lost in the field, even under the most careful handling. I saw fifty acres of choice tree-fruits — mainly Peaches and Apples — in a single patch; the Peaches rotting by hundreds of bushels, because they could not be gathered and marketed so fast as they ripened. I saw vast tracts of good Mustard, self-sown and growing wild from year to year, though apparently as good an article as ever ripened. The intense drouth of her long, cloudless, dewless Summer produces cracks and fissures in the earth, into which grains and other seeds drop when dead-ripe; rains come and close the fissures in November and later; the self-sown seed germinates, and produces a "volunteer" crop, — a full one of

Mustard, but a half crop of Wheat, &c. I saw, at the Mission of San José, giant pear-trees, planted some scores of years ago by the Jesuits, and producing largely, but of indifferent fruit, till a Yankee acquired and grafted them, when he sold in San Francisco their product, the next year but one, so as to net him $100 from each tree. I look forward to a day when this country's supply of Raw Silk, as well as of Raisins and other dried fruits, will reach us from our own Pacific coast.

The rains of California are ample, but confined to Winter and Spring. In time, her streams will be largely retained in her mountains by dams and reservoirs, and, instead of descending in floods to overwhelm and devastate, will be gradually drawn away throughout the Summer to irrigate and refresh. For a while, water will be applied too profusely, and injury thus be done; but experience will correct this error; and then California's valleys and lower slopes will produce more food to nourish and fruit to solace the heart of man than any other Twenty Millions of acres on earth.

III. *Timber.*—Most of her highlands are valuable for timber and pasturage only. There are more tons of valuable timber in the Sierra Nevada than in our whole country east of the Rocky Mountains, and southward of the latitude of Chicago. Railroads will yet render much of it commercially available, and incite its diffusion to every country and island washed by the great ocean. Its value will be found to surpass that of all the minerals covered by it, or ever exposed to the avaricious gaze of man.

The Pacific Railroads—for there must soon be three distinct lines, and in time at least three more—will be to California what the Erie Canal is to New York, the Mississippi to the great valley. It is barely possible to over-estimate their importance and value. While they render New York that focus of the world's commerce which London has so long been, they must build up, on our Pacific coast, a traffic with China, Japan, Australia, such as Tyre or Carthage never conceived. California has hitherto seemed, even to her own people, on one side of the earth; they have too generally felt as strangers and sojourners, and talked of "going home," — that is, to the Atlantic slope; but the Pacific Railroads, bringing them within a week's journey of New England, and placing them in daily mail communication with the friends of their childhood, will make thousands contented with their lot, and, after a good visit to the old, familiar firesides, they will return, contented to end their days on the Pacific slope, and will draw their younger brothers and cousins after them. I predict that California will have Three Millions of people in 1900, and Oregon at least One Million.

I close with a mere glance at San Francisco; because her age has nearly doubled since I saw her, and her population, wealth, and business, as well. At the mouth of the only considerable river that enters the Pacific from our continent, — the Columbia and the Youkon excepted, — with a fair entrance, and an ample, safe harbor, I judge that the Pacific Railroad fixes and assures her destiny as the second city of America, — the emporium wherein the farthest East will exchange its products with the remotest West. I dislike her chilly August fogs and winds, her blowing, drifting sands; I might wish her relieved of the giant sand-bank which centuries have piled up between her and the Pacific; but then her Western gales would be fiercer and sharper than now; so it is best to leave her as she is. Since twenty years have raised her from a naked beach to a city of 100,000 souls, who can doubt that eighty more will see these swelled to, at least, One Million? May Intelligence and Virtue keep even step with her material progress! may the great-grandchildren of her adventurous pioneers rejoice in the knowledge that her stormy, irregular youth has given place to a sober, respected, beneficent maturity! may her influence on the side of Freedom, Knowledge, Righteousness, be evermore greatly felt and greatly blest throughout the awaking, wondering, plastic Western world!

XLVIII.

THE PRESIDENTIAL ELECTION OF 1860.

THE events of 1858–59, with certain demonstrations against Senator Douglas and his doctrine of "Squatter Sovereignty," by nearly all his Democratic brethren in the Senate, early in the session of 1859–60, plainly portended a disruption of the dominant party; creating a strong probability that the Republicans might choose the next President. I had already, for months, contemplated that contingency, and endeavored to fix on the proper candidate for President, in view of its probable occurrence.

My choice was Edward Bates, of St. Louis. He had been sole Representative of Missouri in Congress fully thirty years before, when he had heartily supported the administration of John Quincy Adams. He had since been mainly in retirement, save that he had presided with eminent ability over the River and Harbor Convention held at Chicago in 1847, and had held a local judgeship. Born in Virginia, a life-long slaveholder, in politics a Whig, he was thoroughly conservative, and so held fast to the doctrine of our Revolutionary sages, that Slavery was an evil to be restricted, not a good to be diffused. This conviction made him essentially a Republican; while I believed that he could poll votes in every Slave State, and, if elected, rally all that was left of the Whig party therein to resist Secession and Rebellion. If not the only Republican whose election would not suffice as a pretext for civil war, he seemed to me that one most likely to repress the threatened insurrection, or, at the worst, to crush it. I did not hesitate to avow my preference, though I may have withheld some of my reasons for it.

Many Republicans dissented from it most decidedly; one of them said to me, "Let us have a candidate, *this* time, that represents our most advanced convictions."

"My friend," I inquired, "suppose each Republican voter in our State were to receive, to-morrow, a letter, advising him that he (the said voter) had just lost his brother, for some years settled in the South, who had left him a plantation and half a dozen slaves, — how many of the two hundred and fifty thousand would, in response, declare and set those slaves free?" "I don't think I could stand *that* test myself!" was his prompt rejoinder. "Then," I resumed, "it is not yet time to nominate as you propose."

The Republican National Convention was called to meet at Chicago, May 16, 1860, and I attended it, having been requested by the Republicans of Oregon to act as one of their delegates therein. Governor Seward was the most prominent candidate for the Presidential nomination, warmly backed by the delegations from New York, Michigan, and several other States, including most of those from Massachusetts. I was somewhat surprised to meet there quite a number who, in conversations with me and others, had unhesitatingly pronounced his nomination unadvisable, and likely to prove disastrous, now on hand to urge it. I strongly felt that they had been right before, and were wrong now; and I did what I could to counteract their efforts; visiting, to this end, and briefly addressing, the delegations from several States. I did much less than was popularly supposed; being kept busy for ten or twelve of the most critical hours just preceding the ballotings in the committee of one delegate from each State represented that framed and reported the platform. An effort to concentrate, prior to the balloting, all the anti-Seward votes on one candidate, proved unsuccessful; and the probability of Seward's success seemed thereafter so decided, that one of his leading supporters urged me, just before we began to ballot, to name the man whose nomination for Vice-President would be most effective in reconciling those with whom I acted to the support of Governor Seward. I advised, through him, the Seward men to make the whole ticket satisfactory to themselves. We soon proceeded to vote for a candidate for President, with the following result:—

	1st ballot.	*2d ballot.*	*3d ballot.*
William H. Seward, of New York, ...	173½	184½	180
Abraham Lincoln, of Illinois, ...	102	181	231½
Simon Cameron of Pennsylvania, ...	50½	—	—
Salmon P. Chase, of Ohio, ...	49	42½	24½
Edward Bates, of Missouri, ...	48	35	22
William L. Dayton, of New Jersey, ...	14	10	—
John McLean, of Ohio, ...	12	8	5
Jacob Collamer, of Vermont, ...	10	—	—
Scattering, ...	6	4	2

Mr. Lincoln having very nearly votes enough to nominate him on the third ballot, others were rapidly transferred to him, until he had 354 out of 466 in all, and his nomination was declared. On motion of William M. Evarts, on the part of New York, seconded by John A. Andrew on behalf of Massachusetts, the nomination was then made unanimous. On the first ballot for Vice-President, Hannibal Hamlin, of Maine, received 194 votes, which the next ballot swelled to 367 against 99,—when he, too, was unanimously nominated; and the Convention adjourned with nine hearty cheers for the ticket.

The "Constitutional Union" (late "American") party, met by delegates three days later in Baltimore, declared its platform to be "the Constitution of the country, the Union of the States, and the enforcement of the Laws," and nominated thereon John Bell, of Tennessee, for President, and Edward Everett, of Massachusetts, for Vice-President.

The Democratic National Convention* had met originally at Charleston, South Carolina; had quarrelled over a platform for a week or more; and had finally been disrupted by the withdrawal of a majority of the delegates from Slave States, because of the adoption (by a vote of 165 to 138) of a platform which was held to favor, or at least not explicitly to condemn, Senator Douglas's "Squatter-Sovereignty" dogma.

* April 23.

After taking 57 ballots for President, whereon Mr. Douglas had a decided majority of all the votes cast on every ballot, and a majority of a full Convention, that body, by a vote of 195 to 55, adjourned* to reassemble at Baltimore, June 18; at which time (the places of most of the seceders having meantime been filled) Mr. Douglas received on the first ballot 173½, and on the second 181½ votes, which was less than two-thirds of a full Convention (303). He was thereupon, on motion of Sanford E. Church, of New York, declared the nominee.

Hon. Benjamin Fitzpatrick, of Alabama, was unanimously nominated for Vice-President; but he declined, and Hon. Herschel V. Johnson, of Georgia, was put up in his stead.

The bolters at Charleston met in Baltimore on the 11th of June, but adjourned to the 25th; at which time, Hon. John C. Breckinridge, of Kentucky (then Vice-President), was unanimously nominated for President, with General Joseph Lane, of Oregon, for Vice-President.

The quadrangular contest thus inaugurated has had no parallel but a very imperfect one in 1824. It seems clear that the bolting Democratic ticket was intended to render the success of the Republicans inevitable; and the probability of that success was openly exulted over in 4th of July toasts at various celebrations in South Carolina, where no other candidate than Breckinridge had even a nominal support. Yet in New York the supporters of Douglas, of Bell, and of Breckinridge united on a common ticket, which was defeated, but only after a most determined canvass. In other States, the "fusion" was incomplete or non-existent, rendering Mr. Lincoln's success a foregone conclusion. Mr. Douglas, alone among the Presidential candidates, took the stump, and spoke with vigor and energy in several States, but to little purpose. The popular vote in the Free States was mainly divided between Lincoln and Douglas; in the Slave States, between Breckinridge and Bell: the totals in either section being, as nearly as they can be apportioned, as follows:—

* May 3.

	Lincoln.	Douglas.	Breckinridge.	Bell.
Free States, ...	1,831,180	1,128,049	279,211	130,151
Slave States, ...	26,430	163,525	570,871	515,973
Total, ...	1,857,610	1,291,574	850,082	646,124

Mr. Lincoln had 180 electoral votes to 123 for all others; he having the full vote of all the Free States but New Jersey, which gave him 4. Mr. Douglas had barely 3 in New Jersey, with the 9 of Missouri, — 12 in all, — while Breckinridge, with a much smaller popular vote, had 72 electors; barely missing those of Virginia, also Kentucky and Tennessee, making 39 in all.

Mr. Lincoln's popular and electoral vote were each a little larger than those of Mr. Buchanan in 1856; but, practically, the one result had strong points of resemblance to the other. In the former, a united South triumphed over a divided North; in the latter, a United North succeeded over a divided South. But the division affected only the Presidency; the anti-Republicans still held the Supreme Court, with the Senate, and were morally certain of a large majority also in the new House of Representatives, whereof two thirds of the members were chosen with or before the Presidential Electors.

Thus stood the country on the day after that which recorded the popular verdict for Lincoln and Hamlin.

It is true that the moral weight of that verdict was diminished by the consideration that it was pronounced by barely two fifths of the legal voters. Antagonist on other points as the defeated factions were, it was notorious that they were a unit in opposition to the cardinal Republican principle of No Extension of Slavery, which, by acting in concert, they could at any time arrest and defeat. Yet the election of Lincoln, by placing the Executive patronage of the Government in the hands of a Republican, had done much toward the development throughout the South of that latent anti-Slavery sentiment which her aristocracy abhorred and dreaded. In that election, therefore, many slaveholders saw foreshadowed the doom of their cherished "institution."

XLIX.

SECESSION,—HOW CONFRONTED.

THE popular vote * in each State for Presidential Electors having rendered inevitable the success of Lincoln and Hamlin, the result — immediately ascertained and disseminated by means of the telegraph — was nowhere received with more general expressions of satisfaction than in South Carolina, whose ruling caste had, months before, but especially on the preceding 4th of July, indicated their wish and hope that the election would have this issue. Indeed, we Republicans had been fully aware, throughout the canvass, that the division of the Democratic party effected at the Charleston Convention was designed to assure our success, — not as an end, but as a means, — and that those who supported Breckinridge, while they would have regarded his election with complacency, were quite as well satisfied with that of Lincoln. Much as they disliked — nay, detested — the "Black Republicans," they regarded Senator Douglas and his "Squatter Sovereignty" with an intenser aversion, and were bent on their absolute discomfiture at all hazards.

All revolutionary movements derive their momentum from diverse sources, and are impelled by very different agencies. Of the four and a half millions of voters for President in 1860, it is quite safe to say that all who desired Disunion were included within the 850,000 † who voted for Breckin-

* November 6, 1860.

† As South Carolina then chose her electors by her Legislature, her people do not count in this aggregate, which they would probably have swelled to about 900,000.

ridge; but even this fraction should, in justice, be divided into classes, as follows:—

I. The Disunionists, pure and simple, who, believing Slavery the only natural and stable basis of social order, and noting the steady advance of the Free States in relative wealth, population, and power, deemed the Secession and Confederation of the Slaveholding States the only course consistent with their interests or their safety. I doubt whether this class numbered half a million of the fifteen hundred thousand legal voters residing in the Slave States, while it could count no open adherents in the Free States.

II. Those who, while they perceived neither safety nor sense in Secession, did not choose to be stigmatized as Abolitionists nor hooted as cowards, but preferred the remote, contingent perils even of civil war to the imminent certainty of persecution and social outlawry, if they should be pointed out as lacking the courage or the will to risk all, dare all, in defence of "Southern rights."

III. Those who, while at heart hostile to Disunion,—deeming it no remedy for existing ills, while it opened a new vista of untold, awful calamities,—yet regarded the *menace* of Secession with complacency, as certain to frighten "the North" into any and every required concession and retraction to avert the threatened disruption.

It was this third class—I judge more numerous than, while superior in wealth and social consideration to, the first and second combined—that I deemed it our first duty to resist and baffle.

I had for forty years been listening, with steadily diminishing patience, to Southern threats of Disunion. Whatever an awakened conscience, or an enlightened apprehension of National interest, commended to a majority of the North as just and politic, was—if not equally acceptable at the South—apt to be met by the bravado, "Do what you propose, and we will dissolve the Union!" I had become weary of this, and desirous of ending it. In my cherished conception, the Union was no boon conferred on the North by the South, but a voluntary partnership, at least as advantageous to the latter as to the former. I desired that the South should be made to comprehend and respect this truth. I wished her to realize that the North could do without the South quite as well as the South could do without the North.

For the first breath of Disunion from the South fanned into vigorous life the old spirit of compromise and cringing at the North. "What will you do to save the Union?" was asked of us Republicans, as if we had committed some enormity in voting for and electing Lincoln, which we must now atone by proffering concessions and disclaimers to the justly alarmed and irritated South.

At once, the attitude of the North became alarmed, deprecatory, self-abasing. Every local election held during the two months succeeding our National triumph showed great "Conservative" gains. Conspicuous Abolitionists were denied the use of public halls, or hooted down if they attempted to speak. Influential citizens, through meetings and letters, denounced the madness of "fanaticism," and implored the South to stay her avenging arm until the North could have time to purge herself from complicity with "fanatics," and demonstrate her fraternal sympathy with her Southern sister, — that is, attest her unshaken loyalty to the Slave Power. An eminent Southern Conservative (John J. Crittenden) having proposed, as a new Union-saving compromise, the running of the line of 36 degrees 30 minutes North latitude through our new territories to the Pacific, and the positive allotment and guaranty of all South of that line to Slavery forever, the suggestion was widely grasped as an olive-branch, — even the veteran Thurlow Weed commending the proposal to popular favor and acceptance as fair and reasonable. The Republican party — which had been called into existence by the opening of free soil to Slavery — seemed in positive danger of signalizing its advent to power by giving a direct assent to the practical extension of Slavery over a region far larger and more important than that theoretically surrendered by the Kansas-Nebraska bill. In fact, the attitude of the North, during the two last months of 1860, was foreshadowed in four lines of Collins's Ode to the Passions: —

> "First, Fear his hand, its skill to try,
> Amid the chords bewildered laid;
> And back recoiled, he knew not why,
> E'en at the sound himself had made."

And the danger was imminent that, if a popular vote could have been had (as was proposed) on the Crittenden Compromise, it would have prevailed by an overwhelming majority. Very few Republicans would have voted for it; but very many would have refrained from voting at all; while their adversaries would have brought their every man to the polls in its support, and carried it by hundreds of thousands.

My own controlling conviction from first to last was, — There must, at all events, be no concession to Slavery. Disunion, should it befall, may be calamity; but complicity in Slavery extension is guilt, which the Republicans must in no case incur. It had for an age been the study of the slaveholding politicians to make us of the North partners with them in the maintenance, diffusion, and profit or loss of their industrial system. "Slavery is quite as much your affair as ours," they were accustomed to say in substance: "we own and work the negroes; you buy the cotton and sugar produced by their labor, and sell us in return nearly all we and they eat, drink, and wear. If they run away, you help catch and return them: now set us off a few hundred thousand miles more of territory whereon to work them, and help us to acquire Cuba, Mexico, &c., as we shall say we need them, and we will largely extend our operations, to our mutual benefit." It was this extension that I was resolved at all hazards to defeat.

But how?

Good and true men met the Disunionists (whether earnest or affected) in this square, manly way: "You must obey the laws. The Union will not be tamely surrendered, and cannot be dissolved by force. Whoever shall attempt thus to dissolve it will have reason to repent of his temerity. Behave yourselves, or you will rue your turbulence!"

To me, as to some others, a different course seemed advisable. We said in substance: "You Disunionists claim to be the Southern people, and rest your case on the vital principle proclaimed in our fathers' immortal Declaration of Independence, — 'Governments derive their just power from the consent of the governed.' We admit the principle, — nay, we affirm, we glory in it; but your case is not within it. You are *not* the Southern people; you are not even a majority of the Southern Whites; you are a violent, unscrupulous, desperate minority, who have conspired to clutch power and wield it for ends which the overawed, gagged, paralyzed majority at heart condemn. Secure us a fair opportunity to state our side of the case, and to argue the points at issue before your people, and we will abide their decision. We disclaim a union of force, — a union held together by bayonets; let us be fairly heard; and, if your people decide that they choose to break away from us, we will interpose no obstacle to their peaceful withdrawal from the Union."

Whether this was, or was not, in the abstract, sound doctrine, it is clear that those who uttered it exposed themselves to ready misapprehension and grave obloquy, which were counterbalanced by no advantage or profit to themselves. Their consolation was that they had done something toward arresting the spring-tide of Northern servility that set strongly in favor of "conciliation" through the adoption of the Crittenden Compromise.

They were right at least in their fundamental assumption of fact. The South was *not* for Secession. Though its partisans had previously made skilful use of the machinery of the Democratic party to secure Governors, Legislatures, &c. in their interest, and the Federal officers — appointed by Pierce and Buchanan while Jefferson Davis, Jacob Thompson, John B. Floyd, Howell Cobb, John Slidell, &c., were their trusted advisers — were nearly all implicated in their conspiracy, the Disunionists, wholly unresisted by President Buchanan, were enabled, by their utmost efforts, to alienate but a minority of the Southern States or People from the

Federal Union. South Carolina, Georgia, Alabama, Mississippi, Louisiana, Florida, and Texas — seven States in all, entitled to but twenty-eight representatives in Congress — were claimed as having seceded, up to the hour wherein War was formally inaugurated by an order from the Confederate War Department to open fire upon the Federal fortress named Sumter, in Charleston harbor. In no one of these States but Texas had the ordinance of Secession been submitted to, and ratified by, a direct popular vote. The eight other Slave States, which had double their free population and double their representation in Congress, had not merely declined to secede, — Virginia, Kentucky, Tennessee, and Missouri, had given such majorities against it as they never gave before; North Carolina and Arkansas had expressly voted it down; while Maryland and Delaware refused even to take the matter into consideration. In fact, the people of the South, like those of the North, were as yet unripe for Disunion, and shuddered at the prospect of civil war. The bombardment of Sumter, which summoned the Nation to arms, was impelled by a consciousness that the mushroom Confederacy would otherwise collapse and disappear. Said Jeremiah Clemens, formerly United States Senator from Alabama, at a Union meeting at Huntsville, March 13, 1864: —

"I wish to state a fact in relation to the commencement of this war. Some time after the ordinance of Secession was passed I was in Montgomery, and called on President Davis, who was in that city. Davis, Memminger, the Secretary of War [Leroy Pope Walker], Gilchrist, the member from Lowndes County, and several others, were present. As I entered, the conversation ceased. They were evidently discussing the propriety of firing on Fort Sumter. Two or three of them withdrew to a corner of the room; and I heard Gilchrist say to the Secretary of War: '*It* MUST *be done. Delay two months, and Alabama stays in the Union. You must sprinkle blood in the faces of the people.*'"

So said, so done, — except that the "sprinkle" swelled into a cascade, the cascade into a river, which inundated and reddened the whole breadth of our country.

L.

OUR CIVIL WAR, — ACTUAL AND POSSIBLE.

HOSTILITIES on the part of the Confederacy had been inaugurated weeks before Mr. Lincoln's accession to the Presidency. The Federal forts, arsenals, armories, sub-treasuries, &c., &c., located in the seceding States, had, in good part, thus changed hands, — often with the hearty assent and coöperation of their custodians, — always without serious resistance offered by them or commanded from Washington. Fort Sumter, Key West, and Fort Pickens (at Pensacola) were all that held out for the Union. General Twiggs's surrender* of the greater part of our little Army, then posted along the exposed frontiers of Texas, with all the forts, arms, munitions, stores, &c., occurred two weeks before the close of Mr. Buchanan's term. Still, the fact that war existed, or even that it was inevitable, was not generally realized in the Free States, till the telegraph flashed far and wide the startling news that fire had been opened† on Fort Sumter from the Rebel forts and batteries whereby it was half encircled, — following this, next day, with the tidings that the feebly manned and nearly foodless fort had surrendered. Hereupon, Virginia was promptly plunged by her Convention into the widening vortex of Secession; and was soon followed by Arkansas,‡ North Carolina,§ and ultimately by Tennessee.‖

Meantime, President Lincoln, directly on hearing of the fall of Sumter, had summoned the new Congress to meet in

* February 18, 1861.
† April 12, 1861.
‡ May 6, 1861.
§ May 20, 1861.
‖ June 8, 1861.

extraordinary session on the 4th of July ensuing, and had called on the Governors of the presumptively loyal States for their respective quotas of a volunteer force of 75,000 men to defend the capital and public property of the Union. The Governors, not only of Virginia (which was then on the point, if not in the act, of seceding), but of North Carolina, Tennessee, Missouri, Kentucky, and even Delaware, responded only with "railing accusations," implying amazement that any President should ask or expect their help in the nefarious work of "coercion." From the Governors of the Free States (nearly or quite all Republicans) very different responses were received, swiftly followed by the required volunteers. One of the first regiments on foot was from Massachusetts, and was fiercely assailed* on its passage through Baltimore by a vast pro-Slavery mob, whereby three of its men were slain and eight seriously wounded. The residue made their way through the city, and proceeded to Washington; but a Pennsylvania regiment, just behind it, was roughly handled by the mob, and constrained to take the back track to Philadelphia. Baltimore thereupon ranged herself on the side of Secession, stopping the trains and cutting the wires that connected Washington with the still loyal States; the Federal Arsenal at Harper's Ferry, being menaced, was fired and abandoned; the Navy Yard at Norfolk was culpably deserted, leaving two thousand cannon and large supplies of munitions to the exulting Confederates; a Confederate camp was established near St. Louis, under the auspices of Governor Jackson, and men openly enlisted and drilled there for the work in prospect; the South was closed to Northern travel and commerce, and everything portended a formidable, bloody, devastating war.

Yet President Lincoln persisted in what seems to me his second grave mistake,—that of underestimating the spirit and power of the Rebellion. He had called for but 75,000 men when apprised that Fort Sumter had fallen; he called for no more when assured that Virginia and North Carolina had been swept into the vortex of Secession by that open

* April 19, 1861.

defiance of the National authority and assault on the National integrity; that Arkansas and Tennessee were on the point of following their bad example; and that even Maryland and Missouri were, at least for the moment, in the hands of those who fully shared the *animus* and sympathized with the aims of the Disunionists. It was now plain that the Slave Power was the Nation's assailant, and that its motto was, "War to the knife!" I think the President should have changed his tactics in view of the added gravity of the public danger. I think he should have invited the people to assemble on a designated early day in their several wards and townships, then and there to solemnly swear to uphold the Government and Union, and to enroll themselves as volunteers for the war, subject to be called out at his discretion. Each man's age, as well as name, should have been recorded; and then he should have called them out in classes as they should be wanted,—say, first, those of 20 to 25 years old; secondly, those between 25 and 30; and so on. I judge that not less than One Million able-bodied men would have thus enrolled themselves; that the first two calls would have provided a force of not less than two hundred thousand men; and that subsequent calls, though less productive, would have supplied all the men from time to time required, without cost and without material delay.

The Confederate Congress had met at Montgomery, Alabama, held a brief session, and adjourned to reconvene at Richmond on the 4th of July. I hold that it should not have been allowed so to meet, but that a Union army, One Hundred Thousand strong, should have occupied that city early in June,—certainly before the close of that month. Richmond was not yet fortified; it was accessible by land and by water; we firmly held Fortress Monroe; the designated capital of the Confederacy should never have received its Congress, but should have witnessed such a celebration of the anniversary of American Independence as had never yet thrilled its heart. The war-cry, "Forward to Richmond!" did not originate with me; but it is just what should have been uttered, and the words should have been translated into deeds.

Instead of energy, vigor, promptness, daring, decision, we had in our councils weakness, irresolution, hesitation, delay; and, when at last our hastily collected forces, after being demoralized by weeks of idleness and dissipation, were sent forward, they advanced on separate lines, under different commanders; thus enabling the enemy to concentrate all his forces in Virginia against a single corps of ours, defeating and stampeding it at Bull Run, while other Union volunteers, aggregating nearly twice its strength, lay idle and useless near Harper's Ferry, in and about Washington, and at Fortress Monroe. Thus what should have been a short, sharp struggle was expanded into a long, desultory one; while those whose blundering incapacity or lack of purpose was responsible for those ills united in throwing the blame on the faithful few who had counselled justly, but whose urgent remonstrances they had never heeded. "Forward to Richmond!" was execrated as the impulse to disaster, even by some who had lustily echoed it; and weary months of halting, timid, nerveless, yet costly warfare, naturally followed. Men talk reproachfully of the heavy losses incurred by Grant in taking Richmond, forgetting that his predecessors had lost yet more in *not* taking it. In war, energy — prompt and vigorous action — is the true economizer of suffering, of devastation, and of life. Had Napoleon or Jackson been in Scott's place in 1861, the Rebellion would have been stamped out ere the close of that year; but Slavery would have remained to scourge us still. Thus disaster is overruled to subserve the ends of beneficence; thus the evil of the moment contains the germ of good that is enduring; and thus is freshly exemplified the great truth proclaimed by Pope: —

> "In spite of pride, in erring Reason's spite,
> One truth is clear, — WHATEVER IS, IS RIGHT."

LI.

ABRAHAM LINCOLN.

THERE are those who say that Mr. Lincoln was fortunate in his death as in his life: I judge otherwise. I hold him most inapt for the leadership of a people involved in desperate, agonizing war; while I deem few men better fitted to guide a nation's destinies in time of peace. Especially do I deem him eminently fitted to soothe, to heal, and to reunite in bonds of true, fraternal affection a people just lapsing into peace after years of distracting, desolating internal strife. His true career was just opening when an assassin's bullet quenched his light of life.

Mr. Lincoln entered Washington the victim of a grave delusion. A genial, quiet, essentially peaceful man, trained in the ways of the bar and the stump, he fully believed that there would be no civil war, — no serious effort to consummate Disunion. His faith in Reason as a moral force was so implicit that he did not cherish a doubt that his Inaugural Address, whereon he had bestowed much thought and labor, would, when read throughout the South, dissolve the Confederacy as frost is dissipated by a vernal sun. I sat just behind him as he read it, on a bright, warm, still March day, expecting to hear its delivery arrested by the crack of a rifle aimed at his heart; but it pleased God to postpone the deed, though there was forty times the reason for shooting him in 1860 that there was in '65, and at least forty times as many intent on killing or having him killed. No shot was then fired, however; for his hour had not yet come.

Almost every one has personal anecdotes of "Old Abe."

I knew him more than sixteen years, met him often, talked with him familiarly; yet, while multitudes fancy that he was always overflowing with jocular narrations or reminiscences, I cannot remember that I ever heard him tell an anecdote or story. One, however, that he *did* tell while in this city, on his way to assume the Presidency, is so characteristic of the man and his way of regarding portents of trouble, that I here record it.

Almost every one was asking him, with evident apprehension if not perturbation: "What is to be the issue of this Southern effervescence? Are we really to have civil war?" and he once responded in substance as follows:—

"Many years ago, when I was a young lawyer, and Illinois was little settled, except on her southern border, I, with other lawyers, used to ride the circuit; journeying with the judge from county-seat to county-seat in quest of business. Once, after a long spell of pouring rain, which had flooded the whole country, transforming small creeks into rivers, we were often stopped by these swollen streams, which we with difficulty crossed. Still ahead of us was Fox River, larger than all the rest; and we could not help saying to each other, 'If these streams give us so much trouble, how shall we get over Fox River?' Darkness fell before we had reached that stream; and we all stopped at a log tavern, had our horses put out, and resolved to pass the night. Here we were right glad to fall in with the Methodist Presiding Elder of the circuit, who rode it in all weather, knew all its ways, and could tell us all about Fox River. So we all gathered around him, and asked him if he knew about the crossing of Fox River. 'O yes,' he replied, 'I know all about Fox River. I have crossed it often, and understand it well; but I have one fixed rule with regard to Fox River: I never cross it till I reach it.'"

I infer that Mr. Lincoln did not fully realize that we were to have a great civil war till the Bull Run disaster. I cannot otherwise explain what seemed to many of us his amazing tameness when required by the Mayor and by the Young

Christians of Baltimore to promise not to have any more volunteers marched across the State of Maryland on their way to the defence of Washington. Had he then realized that bloody strife had become a dire necessity, I think he would have responded with more spirit.

When we were at length unmistakably launched on the stormy ocean of civil war, Mr. Lincoln's tenacity of purpose paralleled his former immobility. I believe he would have been nearly the last, if not the very last, man in America to recognize the Southern Confederacy, had its arms been triumphant. He would have much preferred death.

This firmness impelled him to what seemed to me a grave error. Because he would never consent to give up the Union, he dreaded to recognize in any manner the existence of the Confederacy. Yet such recognition, after the capture of several thousands of our soldiers, became inevitable. Had Fortune uniformly smiled on our arms, we might have treated the Rebellion as a seditious riot; but our serious loss in prisoners at Bull Run rendered this thenceforth impossible. We were virtually compelled to recognize the Confederates as belligerents, by negotiating an exchange of prisoners. Thenceforth (it seems to me) we were precluded from treating them as felons. And I could see no objection, not merely to receiving with courtesy any overtures for peace they might see fit to make, but even to making overtures to them, as Great Britain so publicly did to our Revolutionary fathers in the Summer of '76.

War has become so fearfully expensive, through the progress of invention and machinery, that to protract it is to involve all parties in bankruptcy and ruin. Belligerents are, therefore, prone to protest their anxiety for Peace, — in most cases, sincerely. Napoleon, though often at war, was always proclaiming his anxiety for peace. It seemed to me, throughout our great struggle, that a more vigorous prosecution; alike of War and of Peace, was desirable. Larger armies, in the average more energetically led, more ably handled, seemed to be the National need, down to a late stage of the contest. And I deemed it a mistake to put aside any overture that looked to the achievement of peace. Instead of repelling such overtures, however unpromising, I would have openly welcomed any and all, and so treated each as to prove that the continuance of war was not the fault of our side. And so, when Henry May, Colonel Jacquess, and others, solicited permission to go to Richmond in quest of Peace, I would have openly granted them every facility, asking them only to state distinctly that I had not sent nor accredited them. And I judge that Mr. Lincoln slowly came to a conclusion not dissimilar to mine, since Mr. F. P. Blair's two visits to Richmond were made with his full knowledge; while his own visit to Fortress Monroe, there to meet Confederate Commissioners and discuss with them terms of pacification, was a formal notice to all concerned of his anxiety to stay the effusion of blood. I believe that this conference did much to precipitate the downfall of the tottering Confederacy. I doubt whether any one of Sherman's nearly simultaneous successes did more. And, while Mr. Lincoln would have been a tenacious champion of the authority and dignity of the Union and the rights and security of all its loyal people, I am sure the vanquished Rebels would have found him a generous conqueror.

Mr. Lincoln died for his country as truly as any soldier who fell fighting in the ranks of her armies. He was not merely killed for her sake, — because of the high responsibilities she had a second time devolved on him, and the fidelity wherewith he fulfilled them, — he was worn out in her service, and would not, I judge, have lived out his official term, had no one sought his immolation. When I last saw him, a few weeks before his death, I was struck by his haggard, care-fraught face, so different from the sunny, gladsome countenance he first brought from Illinois. I felt that his life hung by so slender a thread that any new access of trouble or excess of effort might suddenly close his career. I had ceased to apprehend his assassination,—had ceased even to think of it; yet "the sunset of life" was plainly looking out of his kindly eyes and gleaming from his weather-beaten visage.

I believe I neither enjoy nor deserve the reputation of favoring exorbitant allowances or lavish expenditures; yet I feel that my country has been meanly parsimonious in its dealings with Mr. Lincoln's family. The head of that family was fairly elected and inaugurated President for a second term; and he had scarcely entered upon that term when he was murdered because he was President. I hold that this fact entitled his family to the four years' salary which the people had voted to pay him; that the manner of his death took his case entirely out of the category of mere decease while in office; and that they should have been paid the $100,000 which, but for Booth's bullet, would have been theirs, instead of the one year's salary that was allowed them. I am quite aware that Mrs. Lincoln was and is unpopular,—I need not inquire with what reason, since I am not pleading for generosity, but for naked justice. Buchanan, trembling at the rustle of a leaf, served out his term, and was paid his full salary; dying, seven years later, of natural decay. To withhold Mr. Lincoln's pay because he invoked the hatred of assassins by his fearless fidelity, and was therefore bereft of life when in the zenith of his career, is to discourage fidelity and foster pusillanimity. May not the wrong be redressed even yet?

Mr. Lincoln was emphatically a man of the people. Mr. Clay was called "The Great Commoner" by those who admired and loved him; but Clay was imperious, even haughty, in his moods, with aristocratic tastes and faults, utterly foreign to Lincoln's essentially plebeian nature. There never yet was man so lowly as to feel humbled in the presence of Abraham Lincoln; there was no honest man who feared or dreaded to meet him; there was no virtuous society so rude that, had he casually dropped into it, he would have checked innocent hilarity or been felt as a damper on enjoyment. Had he entered as a stranger a logger's camp in the great woods, a pioneer's bark-covered cabin in some new settlement, he would have soon been recognized and valued as one whose acquaintance was to be prized and cultivated.

Mr. Lincoln was essentially a growing man. Enjoying no advantages in youth, he had observed and reflected much since he attained to manhood, and he was steadily increasing his stock of knowledge to the day of his death. He was a wiser, abler man when he entered upon his second than when he commenced his first Presidential term. His mental processes were slow, but sure; if he did not acquire swiftly, he retained all that he had once learned. Greater men our country has produced; but not another whom, humanly speaking, she could so ill spare, when she lost him, as the victim of Wilkes Booth's murderous aim.

Though I very heartily supported it when made, I did not favor his re-nomination as President; for I wanted the War driven onward with vehemence, and this was not in his nature. Always dreading that the National credit would fail, or the National resolution falter, I feared that his easy ways would allow the Rebellion to obtain European recognition and achieve ultimate success. But that "Divinity that shapes our ends" was quietly working out for us a larger and fuller deliverance than I had dared to hope for, leaving to such short-sighted mortals as I no part but to wonder and adore. We have had chieftains who would have crushed out the Rebellion in six months, and restored "the Union as it was"; but God gave us the one leader whose control secured not only the downfall of the Rebellion, but the eternal overthrow of Human Slavery under the flag of the Great Republic.

LII.

JEFFERSON DAVIS.

THE President of the Southern Confederacy was chosen by a capable, resolute aristocracy, with express reference to the arduous task directly before him. The choice was deliberate, and apparently wise. Mr. Davis was in the mature prime of life; his natural abilities were good; his training varied and thorough. He had been educated at West Point, which, with all its faults, I judge the best school yet established in our country; he had served in our little army in peace, and as a Colonel of volunteers in the Mexican War; returning to civil life, he had been conspicuous in the politics of his State and the Nation; had been elected to the Senate, and there met in courteous but earnest encounter Henry Clay and his compeers; had been four years Secretary of War under President Pierce; and had, immediately on his retiring from that post, been returned to the Senate, whereof his admirers styled him "the Cicero," and whereof he continued a member until — not without manifest reluctance — he resigned and returned to Mississippi to cast his future fortunes into the seething caldron of Secession and Disunion. As compared with the homely country lawyer, Abraham Lincoln, — reared in poverty and obscurity, with none other than a common-school education, and precious little of that; whose familiarity with public affairs was confined to three sessions of the Illinois Legislature and a single term in the House of Representatives, — it would seem that the advantage of chieftains was largely on the side of the Confederacy.

The contrast between them was striking, but imperfect;

for each was thoroughly in earnest, thoroughly persuaded of the justice of the cause whereof he stood forth the foremost champion, and signally gifted with that quality which, in the successful, is termed tenacity, in the luckless, obstinacy. Mr. Lincoln was remarkably devoid of that magnetic quality which thrills the masses with enthusiasm, rendering them heedless of sacrifice and insensible to danger; Mr. Davis was nowise distinguished by its possession. As the preacher of a crusade, either of them had many superiors. But Mr. Davis carefully improved — as Mr. Lincoln did not — every opportunity to proclaim his own undoubting faith in the justice of his cause, and labored to diffuse that conviction as widely as possible. His successive messages and other manifestoes were well calculated to dispel the doubts and inflame the zeal of those who regarded him as their chief; while, apart from his first Inaugural, and his brief speech at the Gettysburg celebration,* Mr. Lincoln made little use of his many opportunities to demonstrate the justice and necessity of the War for the Union.

Mr. Davis, after the fortunes of his Confederacy waned, was loudly accused of favoritism in the allotment of Military trusts. He is said to have distrusted and undervalued Joseph Johnston, which, if so, was a grave error; for Johnston proved himself an able and trustworthy commander, if not a great military genius, — never a blunderer, and never intoxicated by success nor paralyzed by disaster. His displacement in 1864 by Hood, as Commander-in-Chief of the Army of Georgia, was proved a mistake; but it was more defensible than the appointment of Halleck as General-in-Chief of our armies, directly after his failure on the Tennessee. Bragg is named as first of Davis's pets; but Bragg seems to me to have proved himself a good soldier, and to have shown decided capacity at the Battle of Stone River, though he was ultimately obliged to leave the field (and little else) to Rosecrans. Pemberton was accounted another of Davis's overrated favorites; but Pemberton, being of Northern birth, was never fully trusted,

* November 19, 1863.

nor fairly judged, by his compatriots. On a full survey of the ground, I judge that Davis evinced respectable, not brilliant, capacities, in his stormy and trying Presidential career; and that his qualifications for the post were equal to, while his faults were no greater than, Mr. Lincoln's.

This, however, was not the judgment of his compatriots, who extravagantly exaggerated his merits while their cause seemed to prosper, and as unjustly magnified his faults and short-comings from the moment wherein their star first visibly waned. They were ready to make him Emperor in 1862; they regarded him as their evil genius in 1865. Having rushed into war in undoubting confidence that their success was inevitable, they were astounded at their defeat, and impelled to believe that their resources had been dissipated and their armies overwhelmed through mismanagement. They were like the idolater, who adores his god after a victory, but flogs him when smarting under defeat.

A baleful mischance saved Mr. Davis from the fate of a scapegoat. After even he had given up the Confederacy as lost, and realized that he was no longer a President, but a fugitive and outlaw, he was surprised and assailed, while making his way through Georgia to the Florida coast with intent to escape from the country, by two regiments of Union cavalry, and captured. I am confident that this would not have occurred had Mr. Lincoln survived, — certainly not, if our shrewd and kind-hearted President could have prevented it. But his murder had temporarily maddened the millions who loved and trusted him; and his successor, sharing and inflaming the popular frenzy, had put forth a Proclamation charging Davis, among others, with conspiracy to procure that murder, and offering large rewards for their arrest as traitors and assassins. Captured in full view of that Proclamation, he might have been forthwith tried by a drum-head Court-Martial, "organized to convict," found guilty, sentenced, and put to death.

This, however, was not done; but he was escorted to Savannah, thence shipped to Fortress Monroe, and there closely imprisoned, with aggravations of harsh and (it seems) needless indignity. An indictment for treason was found against him; but he remained a military prisoner in close jail for nearly two years, before even a pretence was made of arraigning him for trial.

Meantime, public sentiment had become more rational and discriminating. Davis was still intensely and widely detested as the visible embodiment, the responsible head, of the Rebellion; but no one now seriously urged that he be tried by Court-Martial and shot off-hand; nor was it certain that a respectable body of officers could be found to subserve such an end. To send him before a civil tribunal, and allow him a fair trial, was morally certain to result in a defeat of the prosecution, through disagreement of the jury, or otherwise; for no opponent of the Republican party, whether North or South, would agree to find him guilty. And there was grave doubt whether he *could* be legally convicted, now that the charge of inciting Wilkes Booth's crime had been tacitly abandoned. Mr. Webster * had only given clearer expression to the general American doctrine, that, after a revolt has levied a regular army, and fought therewith a pitched battle, its champions, even though utterly defeated, cannot be tried and convicted as traitors. This may be an extreme statement; but surely a rebellion which has for years maintained great armies, levied taxes and conscriptions, negotiated loans, fought scores of sanguinary battles with alternate successes and reverses, and exchanged tens of thousands of prisoners of war, can hardly fail to have achieved thereby the position and the rights of a lawful belligerent. Just suppose the case (nowise improbable) of two Commissioners for the exchange of prisoners, — like Mulford and Ould, for example, — who had for years been meeting to settle formalities, and exchange boat-loads of prisoners of war, until at length — the power represented by one of them having been utterly vanquished and broken down — that one is arrested by the victors as a traitor, and the other directed to prosecute him to conviction and

* In his first Bunker Hill Oration.

consign him to execution, — how would the case be regarded by impartial observers in this later half of the Nineteenth Century? And suppose this trial to take place two years after the discomfiture and break-down aforesaid, — what then?

Mr. Andrew Johnson had seen fit to change his views and his friends since his unexpected accession to the Presidency, and had, from an intemperate denouncer of the beaten Rebels as deserving severe punishment, become their protector and patron. Jefferson Davis, in Fortress Monroe, under his proclamation aforesaid, was an ugly elephant on Johnson's hands; and thousands were anxious that he should remain there. Their view of the matter did not impress me as statesmanlike, nor even sagacious.

The Federal Constitution expressly provides* that,

> "In all criminal prosecutions, the accused shall enjoy the right to a speedy and public trial, by an impartial jury of the State and district wherein the crime shall have been committed," &c.

In times of war and grave public peril, Constitutions cannot always be strictly heeded; but what national interest required that this provision should be persistently, ostentatiously defied?

An Irishman, swearing the peace against his three sons for pertinaciously assaulting and abusing him, made this proper reservation: "And your deponent would ask your honor to deal tenderly with his youngest son, Larry, who never struck him when he was down." I confess to some fellow-feeling with Larry.

Mr. George Shea, the attorney of record for the defence in the case of The United States *versus* Jefferson Davis, indicted for treason, is the son of an old friend, and I have known and liked him from infancy. After it had become evident that his client had no immediate prospect of trial, if any prospect at all, Mr. Shea became anxious that said client be liberated on bail. Consulting me as to the feasibility of procuring some names to be proffered as bondsmen of persons who had

* Amendments, Art. VI.

conspicuously opposed the Rebellion and all the grave errors which incited it, I suggested two eminent Unionists, who, I presumed, would cheerfully consent to stand as security that the accused would not run away to avoid the trial he had long but unsuccessfully invoked. I added, after reflection, "If *my* name should be found necessary, you may use that." He thanked me, and said he should proffer it only in case the others abundantly at his command would not answer without it. Months passed before I was apprised, by a telegram from Washington, that my name *was* needed; when I went down and proffered it. And when, at length, the prisoner was brought before the United States District Court at Richmond,* I was there, by invitation, and signed the bond in due form.

I suppose this would have excited some hubbub at any rate; but the actual tumult was gravely aggravated by gross misstatements. It was widely asserted that the object of giving bail was to screen the accused from trial, — in other words, to enable him to run away, — when nothing like this was ever imagined by those concerned. The prisoner, through his counsel, had assiduously sought a trial, while the prosecution was not ready, because (as Judge Underwood was obliged to testify before a Committee of Congress) no conviction was possible, except by packing a jury. The words "straw bail" were used in this connection; when one of the sureties is worth several millions of dollars, and the poorest of them is abundantly good for the sum of $5,000, in which he is "held and firmly bound" to produce the body of Jefferson Davis whenever the plaintiff shall be ready to try him. If he only *would* run away, I know that very many people would be much obliged to him; but he won't.

It was telegraphed all over the North that I had a very affectionate meeting and greeting with the prisoner when he had been bailed; when in fact I had never before spoken nor written to him any message whatever, and did not know him, even by sight, when he entered the court-room. After the bond was signed, one of his counsel asked me if I had any

* May 13, 1867.

objection to being introduced to Mr. Davis, and I replied that I had none; whereupon we were introduced, and simply greeted each other. I made, at the request of a friend, a brief call on his wife that evening, as they were leaving for Canada; and there our intercourse ended, probably forever.

When the impeachment of President Johnson was fully resolved on, and there was for some weeks a fair prospect that Mr. Wade would soon be President, with a Cabinet of like Radical faith, I suggested to some of the prospective President's next friends that I had Jefferson Davis still on my hands, and that, if he were considered a handy thing to have in the house, I might turn him over to the new Administration for trial at an hour's notice. The suggestion evoked no enthusiasm, and I was not encouraged to press it.

I trust no one will imagine that I have made this statement with any purpose of self-vindication. To all who have civilly accosted me on the subject, I trust I have given civil, if not satisfactory, answers; while most of those who have seen fit to assail me respecting it, I have chosen to treat with silent scorn. I believe no one has yet succeeded in inventing an unworthy motive for my act that could impose on the credulity of a child, or even of my bitterest enemy. I was quite aware that what I did would be so represented as to alienate for a season some valued friends, and set against me the great mass of those who know little and think less; thousands even of those who rejoiced over Davis's release, nevertheless joining, full-voiced, in the howl against me. I knew that I should outlive the hunt, and could afford to smile at the pack, even when its cry was loudest. So I went quietly on my way; and in due time the storm gave place to a calm. And now, if there is a man on earth who wishes Jefferson Davis were back in his cell, awaiting, in the fourth year of his detention, the trial denied him in the three preceding, he is at liberty to denounce me for my course, in the assurance that he can by no means awake a regret or provoke a reply.

LIII.

AUTHORSHIP.—WRITING HISTORY.

ALMOST every one who can write at all is apt, in the course of his life, to write something which he fancies others may read with pleasure or with profit. For my own part, beyond a few boyish letters to relatives and intimate friends, I began my efforts at composition as an apprentice in a newspaper office, by condensing the news, more especially the foreign, which I was directed to put into type from the city journals received at our office; endeavoring to give in fewer words the gist of the information, in so far, at least, as it would be likely to interest our rural readers. Our Editor, during the latter part of my stay in Poultney, was a Baptist clergyman, whose pastoral charge was at some distance, and who was therefore absent from us much of his time, and allowed me a wide discretion in preparing matter for the paper. This I improved, not only in the selection, but in the condensation, of news. The rudimentary knowledge of the art of composition thus acquired was gradually improved during my brief experience as a journeyman in various newspaper establishments, and afterward as a printer of sundry experimental journals in this city; so that I began my distinctive, avowed editorial career in The New-Yorker with a considerable experience as a writer of articles and paragraphs. I had even written verses,—never fluently nor happily,—but tolerably well measured, and faintly evincing an admiration of Byron, Mrs. Hemans, and other popular writers,—an admiration which I never mistook for inspiration or genius. While true poets are few, those who imagine themselves capable of becoming such are many; but I never advanced even to this grade. I knew that my power of expression in verse was defective, as though I had an impediment in my speech, or spoke with my mouth full of pebbles; and I very soon renounced the fetters of verse, content to utter my thoughts thenceforth in unmistakable prose. It is a comfort to know that not many survive who remember having read any of the few rhymed effusions of my incautious youth.

I had been nearly twenty years a constant writer for the newspaper press ere I ventured (in 1850) to put forth a volume. This was entitled "Hints toward Reforms," and consisted mainly of Lectures and Addresses prepared for delivery before village lyceums and other literary associations from time to time throughout the preceding six or eight years. Most of them regarded Social questions; but their range was very wide, including Political Economy, the Right to Labor, Land for the Landless, Protection to Home Industry, Popular Education, Capital Punishment, Abstinence from Alcoholic potations, &c., &c. My volume was an ordinary duodecimo of 425 pages, compactly filled with the best thoughts I had to offer; all designed to strengthen and diffuse sympathy with misfortune and suffering, and to promote the substantial, permanent well-being of mankind. When I had fully prepared it, I sent the copy to the Harpers; and they agreed to publish it fairly, on condition that I paid the cost of stereotyping (about $400), when they would give me (as I recollect) ten cents per copy on all they sold. I cheerfully accepted the terms, and the work was published accordingly. I believe the sales nearly reimbursed my outlay for stereotyping; so that I attained the dignity of authorship at a very moderate cost. Green authors are apt to suffer from disappointment and chagrin at the failure of their works to achieve them fame and fortune. I was fairly treated by the press and the public, and had no more desire than reason to complain.

I have given these unflattering reminiscences so fully, because I would be useful to young aspirants to authorship, even at the cost of losing their good-will. I have been solicited by many — O, so many! — of them to find publishers for the poems or the novel of each, in the sanguine expectation that a publisher was the only requisite to his achievement of fortune and renown; when, in fact, each had great need of a public, none (as yet) of a publisher. You are sure, O gushing youth! that your poems are such as no other youth ever wrote, — such as Pindar, or Dante, or Milton would read with delight, — and I acquiesce in your judgment. But the great mass of readers have not "the vision and the faculty divine"; they are prosaic, plodding, heavy-witted persons, who read and admire what they are told others have read and admired before them, — if the discovery of new Homers and Shakespeares were to rest with them, none would henceforth be distinguished from the common herd. You, we will agree, are such a genius as Heaven vouchsafes us once in two or three centuries; but can you dream that such are discerned and appreciated by the great mass of their cotemporaries? How much, think you, did Homer, or Dante, or Milton receive from the sale of his works to the general public? Nay: how much did Shakespeare's poetry, *as* poetry, contribute to his sustenance? Nay, more: do *you*, having acquired the greenback-cost of adding a volume to your library, buy the span-new verses of Stiggins Dobbs or C. Pugsley Jagger? You know that you do not, — that you buy Shelley, or Béranger, or Tennyson, instead. Then how can you expect the great mass of us, who have not the faintest claim to genius or special discernment, to recognize *your* untrumpeted merit and buy your volume? You ought to know that we shall follow your example, and buy — if we ever buy poems at all — those of some one whose fame has already reached even our dull ears and fixed our heedless attention. Hence it is that no judicious publisher will buy your manuscript, nor print it, even if you were to make him a present of it. He can't afford it. And your talk of the stupidity, the incompetency, the rapacity, or the cruelty of publishers is wholly aside from the case. Not one first work in a hundred ever pays the cost of its publication. True, yours *may* be the rare exception; but the publisher is hardly to blame that he does not see it.

A year or two later, on my return from my first visit to Europe, I was surprised by an offer to publish in a volume the letters I had written thence to The Tribune, and pay me copyright thereon. I knew, right well, that they did not deserve such distinction, — that they were flimsy and superficial, — things of a day; to be read in the morning and forgotten at night. But it seems that some who had read them in The Tribune wished to have them in a more compact, portable shape; while it was highly improbable that any others would be tempted to buy them: so I consented, and revised them; and they duly appeared as "Glances at Europe" in 1851 – 52. I recollect my share of the proceeds was about $500; for which I had taken no pecuniary risk, and done very little labor. Had the work been profounder, and more deserving, I presume it would not have sold so well, — at all events, not so speedily.

Years passed; I made my long-meditated overland journey to California; and the letters I wrote during that trip, printed from week to week in The Tribune, were collected on my return, and printed in a volume nearly equal in size to either of my former. As a photograph of scenes that were then passing away, of a region on the point of rapid and striking transformation, I judge that this "Overland Journey to California in 1859" may be deemed worth looking into by a dozen persons per annum for the next twenty years. Its publishers failed, however, very soon after its appearance; so that my returns from it for copyright were inconsiderable.

And now came the Presidential contest of 1860, closely followed by Secession and Civil War, whereof I had no thougnt of ever becoming the historian. In fact, not till that War was placed on its true basis of a struggle for liberation, and not conquest, by President Lincoln's successive Proclamations of Freedom, would I have consented to write its history. Not till I had confronted the Rebellion as a positive, desolating force, right here in New York, at the doors of earnest Republicans, in the hunting down and killing of defenceless, fleeing Blacks, in the burning of the Colored Orphan Asylum, and in the mobbing and firing of The Tribune office, could I have been moved to delineate its impulses, aims, progress, and impending catastrophe.

A very few days after the national triumph at Gettysburg, with the kindred and almost simultaneous successes of General Grant in the capture of Vicksburg, and General Banks in that of Port Hudson, with the consequent suppression of the (so called) "Riots" in this city, I was visited by two strangers, who introduced themselves as Messrs. Newton and O. D. Case, publishers, from Hartford, and solicited me to write the History of the Rebellion. I hesitated; for my labors and responsibilities were already most arduous and exacting, yet could not, to any considerable extent, be transferred to others. The compensation offered would be liberal, in case the work should attain a very large sale, but otherwise quite moderate. I finally decided to undertake the task, knowing well that it involved severe, protracted effort on my part; and I commenced upon it a few weeks later, after collecting such materials as were then accessible. I hired for my workshop a room on the third floor of the new Bible House, on Eighth Street and Third and Fourth Avenues, procured the requisite furniture, hired a secretary, brought thither my materials, and set to work. Hither I repaired, directly after breakfast each week-day morning, and read and compared the various documents, official reports, newspaper letters, &c., &c., that served as materials for a chapter, while my secretary visited libraries at my direction, and searched out material among my documents and elsewhere. The great public libraries of New York, — Society, Historical, Astor, and Mercantile — all cluster around the Bible House; the two last-named being within a bowshot. I occasionally visited either of them, in personal quest of material otherwise inaccessible. When I had the substance of my next chapter pretty fairly in mind, I began to compose that chapter; having often several authorities conveniently disposed around me, with that on which I principally relied lying open before me. I oftener wrote out my first draft, merely indicating extracts where such were to be quoted at some length; leaving these to be inserted by my secretary when he came to transcribe my text; but I sometimes dictated to my secretary, who took short-hand notes of what I said, and wrote them out at his leisure. My first chapter was thus composed at one sitting, after some days had been given to the arrangement of materials; but, usually, two days, or even three, were given to the composition of each of the longer chapters, after I had prepared and digested its material. Our rule was to lock the door on resuming composition, and decline all solicitations to open it till the day's allotted task had been finished; and this was easy while my "den" was known to very few; but that knowledge was gradually diffused; and more and more persons found excuses for dropping in; until I was at length subject to daily, and even more frequent, though seldom to protracted, interruptions. I think, however, that if I should ever again undertake such a labor, I would allow the location of my "den" to be known to but one person at The Tribune office, who should be privileged to knock at its door in cases of extreme urgency, and I would have that door open to no one beside but my secretary and myself. Even my proof-sheets should await me at The Tribune office, whither I always repaired, to commence a day's work as Editor, after finishing one as Author at the "den."

A chapter having been fairly written out or transcribed by my secretary, while I was "reading up" for another, I carefully revised and sent it to the stereotyper, who sent me his second and third proofs, which were successively corrected before the pages were ready to be cast. Sometimes, the discovery of new material compelled the revision and recast of a chapter which had been passed as complete. And, though the material was very copious, — more so, I presume, than that from which the history of any former war was written, — it was still exceedingly imperfect and contradictory. For instance: when I came to the pioneer Secession of South Carolina, I wished to study it in the proceedings and debates of her Legislature and Convention as reported in at least one of her own journals; and of these I found but a single file preserved in our city (at the Society Library), though four years had not yet expired since that Secession occurred. A year later, I probably could not have found one at all. Of the score or so of speeches made by Jefferson Davis, often from cars, while on his way from Mississippi to assume at Montgomery the Presidency of the Confederacy, I found but two condensed reports; and one of these, I apprehend, was apocryphal. In many cases, I found officers reported killed in battles whom I afterward found fighting in subsequent battles; whence I conclude that they had not been killed so dead as they might have been. Some of the errors into which I was thus led by my authorities were not corrected till after my work was printed; when the gentlemen thus conclusively disposed of began to write me, insisting that, though desperately wounded at the battle in question, they had decided not to give up the ghost, and so still remained in the land of embodied rather than that of disembodied souls. Their testimony was so direct and pointed that I was constrained to believe it, and to correct page after page accordingly. I presume a few, even yet, remain consigned to the shades in my book, who nevertheless, to this day, consume rations of beef and pork with most unspiritual regularity and self-satisfaction. There doubtless remain some other errors, though I have corrected many; and, as I have stated many more particulars than my rivals in the same field have usually done, it is probable that my work originally embodied more errors of fact or incident than almost any other.

Yet "The American Conflict" will be consulted, at least by historians, and I shall be judged by it, after most of us now living shall have mingled with the dust. An eminent antagonist of my political views has pronounced it "the fairest one-sided book ever written"; but it is more than that. It is one of the clearest statements yet made of the long train of causes which led irresistibly to the war for the Union, showing why that war was the natural and righteous consequence of the American people's general and guilty complicity in the crime of upholding and diffusing Human Slavery. I proffer it as my contribution toward a fuller and more vivid realization of the truth that God governs this world by moral laws as active, immutable, and all-pervading as can be operative in any other, and that every collusion or compromise with evil must surely invoke a prompt and signal retribution.

The sale of my history was very large and steady down to the date of the clamor raised touching the bailing of Jefferson Davis, when it almost ceased for a season; thousands who had subscribed for it refusing to take their copies, to the sore disappointment and loss of the agents, who had supplied themselves with fifty to a hundred copies each, in accordance with their orders; and who thus found themselves suddenly, and most unexpectedly involved in serious embarrassments. I grieved that they were thus afflicted for what, at the worst, was no fault of theirs; while their loss by every copy thus refused was twenty times my own. I trust, however, that their undeserved embarrassments were, for the most part, temporary, — that a juster sense of what was due to them ultimately prevailed, — that all of them who did not mistake the character of a fitful gust of popular passion, and thereupon sacrifice their hard earnings, have since been relieved from their embarrassments; and that the injury and injustice they suffered without deserving have long since been fully repaired. At all events, the public has learned that I act upon my convictions without fear of personal consequences; hence, any future paroxysm of popular rage against me is likely to be less violent, in view of the fact that this one proved so plainly ineffectual.

LIV.

MY DEAD.

"I DO not wear my heart upon my sleeve," and shrink from the obtrusion of matters purely personal upon an indifferent public. I have aimed, in the series herewith closed, to narrate mainly such facts and incidents as seemed likely to be of use, either in strengthening the young and portionless for the battle of life, or in commending to their acceptance convictions which I deem sound and important. My life has been one of arduous, rarely intermitted, labor,—of efforts to achieve other than personal ends,—of efforts which have absorbed most of the time which others freely devote to social intercourse and to fireside enjoyments. Of those I knew and loved in youth, a majority have already crossed the dark river, and I will not impose even their names on an unsympathizing world. Among them is my fellow-apprentice and life-long friend, who, after long illness, died in this city in 1861; my first partner, already named, who was drowned while bathing in 1832; and a young poet of promise who was slowly yielding to consumption when the tidings of our Bull Run disaster snapped short his thread of life,—as it would have snapped mine had it been half so frail as his. The faces of many among the departed whom I have known and loved come back to me as I gaze adown the vista of my half-century of active life; but I have no right to lift the veil which shrouds and shields their long repose. I will name but those who are a part of myself, and whose loss to earth has profoundly affected my subsequent career.

Since I began to write these reminiscences, my mother's

last surviving brother, John Woodburn, has deceased, aged seventy-two, leaving the old Woodburn homestead, I understand, to some among his children; so has my father's brother, Isaac, aged eighty, leaving, so far as I know, but one of the nine brothers (John) still living. My father himself died on the 18th of December last, aged eighty-six. He had, for twelve years or more, been a mere wreck, first in body only; but his infirmities ultimately affected his mind; so that, when I last visited him, a year before his death, he did not recognize me till after he had sat by my side for a full half-hour; and he had before asked my oldest sister, "Did you ever know Henry Greeley?" — alluding to one of her sons, then several years dead. He had fitful flashes of mental recovery; but he had been so long a helpless victim of hopeless bodily and mental decay that I did not grieve when I learned that his spirit had at length shaken off the encumbrance of its mortal coil, which had ceased to be an instrument, and remained purely an obstruction. Of his protracted life, forty-two years had been spent in or on the verge of New England, and forty-four in his deliberately chosen, steadily retained, Pennsylvanian home.

My son, Arthur Young ("Pickie"), born in March, 1844, was the third of seven children, whereof a son and daughter, severally born in 1838 and in 1842, scarcely opened their eyes to a world which they entered but to leave. Physically, they were remarkable for their striking resemblance in hair and features to their father and mother respectively.

Arthur had points of similarity to each of us, but with decided superiority, as a whole, to either. I looked in vain through Italian galleries, two years after he was taken from us, for any full parallel to his dazzling beauty, — a beauty not physical merely, but visibly radiating from the soul. His hair was of the finest and richest gold; "the sunshine of picture" never glorified its equal; and the delicacy of his complexion at once fixed the attention of observers like the late N. P. Willis, who had traversed both hemispheres without having his gaze arrested by any child who could bear a comparison with this one. Yet he was not one of those paragons sometimes met with, whose idlest chatter would edify a Sunday school,—who never do or say aught that propriety would not sanction and piety delight in,—but thoroughly human, and endued with a love of play and mischief which kept him busy and happy the livelong day, while rendering him the delight and admiration of all around him. The arch delicacy wherewith he inquiringly suggested, when once told a story that overtaxed his credulity, "I 'pose that aint a lie?" was characteristic of his nature. Once, when about three years old, having chanced to espy my watch lying on a sofa as I was dressing one Sunday morning, with no third person present, he made a sudden spring of several feet, caught the watch by the chain, whirled it around his head, and sent it whizzing against the chimney, shattering its face into fragments. "Pickie," I inquired, rather sadly than angrily, "how *could* you do me such injury?" "'Cause I was nervous," he regretfully replied. There were ladies then making part of our household whose nerves were a source of general as well as personal discomfort; and this was his attestation of the fact.

There were wiser and deeper sayings treasured as they fell from his lips; but I will not repeat them. Several yet live who remember the graceful gayety wherewith he charmed admiring circles assembled at our house, and at two or three larger gatherings of friends of Social Reform in this city, and at the N. A. Phalanx in New Jersey; and I think some grave seigniors, who were accustomed to help us enjoy our Saturday afternoons in our rural suburban residence at Turtle Bay, were drawn thither as much by their admiration of the son as by their regard for his parents.

Meantime, another daughter was given to us, and, after six months, withdrawn; and still another born, who yet survives; and he had run far into his sixth year without one serious illness. His mother had devoted herself to him from his birth, even beyond her intense consecration to the care of her other children; had never allowed him to partake of animal food, or to know that an animal was ever killed to be eaten; had watched and tended him with absorbing love, till the perils of infancy seemed fairly vanquished; and we had reason to hope that the light of our eyes would be spared to gladden our remaining years.

It was otherwise decreed. In the Summer of 1849, the Asiatic cholera suddenly reappeared in our city, and the frightened authorities ordered all swine, &c., driven out of town, — that is, above Fortieth Street, — whereas our home was about Forty-eighth Street, though no streets had yet been cut through that quarter. At once, and before we realized our danger, the atmosphere was polluted by the exhalations of the swinish multitude thrust upon us from the densely peopled hives south of us, and the cholera claimed its victims by scores before we were generally aware of its presence.

Our darling was among the first; attacked at 1 A. M. of the 12th of July, when no medical attendance was at hand; and our own prompt, unremitted efforts, reënforced at length by the best medical skill within reach, availed nothing to stay the fury of the epidemic, to which he succumbed about 5 P. M. of that day, — one of the hottest, as well as quite the longest, I have ever known. He was entirely sane and conscious till near the last; insisting that he felt little or no pain and was well, save that we kept him sweltering under clothing that he wanted to throw off, as he did whenever he was permitted. When at length the struggle ended with his last breath, and even his mother was convinced that his eyes would never again open on the scenes of this world, I knew that the Summer of my life was over, that the chill breath of its Autumn was at hand, and that my future course must be along the downhill of life.

Yet another son (Raphael Uhland) was born to us two years afterward; who, though more like his father and less like a poet than Arthur, was quite as deserving of parental love, though not so eminently fitted to evoke and command general admiration. He was with me in France and Switzerland in the Summer of 1855; spending, with his mother and sister, the previous Winter in London and that subsequent in Dresden; returning with them in May, '56, to fall a victim to the croup the ensuing February. I was absent on a lecturing tour when apprised of his dangerous illness, and hastened home to find that he had died an hour before my arrival, though he had hoped and striven to await my return. He had fulfilled his sixth year and twelve days over when our home was again made desolate by his death.

Another daughter was born to us four weeks later, who survives; so that we have reason to be grateful for two children left to soothe our decline, as well as for five who, having preceded us on the long journey, await us in the Land of Souls.

My life has been busy and anxious, but not joyless. Whether it shall be prolonged few or more years, I am grateful that it has endured so long, and that it has abounded in opportunities for good not wholly unimproved, and in experiences of the nobler as well as the baser impulses of human nature. I have been spared to see the end of giant wrongs, which I once deemed invincible in this century, and to note the silent upspringing and growth of principles and influences which I hail as destined to root out some of the most flagrant and pervading evils that yet remain. I realize that each generation is destined to confront new and peculiar perils, — to wrestle with temptations and seductions unknown to its predecessors; yet I trust that progress is a general law of our being, and that the ills and woes of the future shall be less crushing than those of the bloody and hateful past. So, looking calmly, yet humbly, for that close of my mortal career which cannot be far distant, I reverently thank God for the blessings vouchsafed me in the past; and, with an awe that is not fear, and a consciousness of demerit which does not exclude hope, await the opening before my steps of the gates of the Eternal World.

MISCELLANIES.

LITERATURE AS A VOCATION.

THE world is a seminary; Man is our class-book; and the chief business of life is Education. We are here to learn and to teach,—some of us for both of these purposes,—all at least for the former. Happy he, and greatly blest, who comes divinely qualified for a Teacher,—fitted by nature and training to wrestle with giant Ignorance and primal Chaos, to dispel unfounded Prejudice, and banish enshrouding Night. To govern men, in the rude, palpable sense, is a small achievement; a grovelling, purblind soul, well provided with horsemen and artillery, and thickly hedged with bayonets and spears, may do this. Nero ruled the Roman world at the height of its power and glory, and ruled it so sternly that no man dared speak of him, while he lived, save in the language of abject flattery. Caligula did it likewise; and so, in an uncouth, second-hand, deputizing way, did (or might have done) Caligula's horse; but which of these, think you, could have *instructed* the millions he so sternly swayed? Alaric had no difficulty in cutting off ten-score thousand heads; but he leaves to our own Everett the writing of the poem wherein the nature of his exploits is duly celebrated. Had he been obliged to slice off as many more heads, or write such a poem, he would have chosen the former task without hesitation or self-distrust.

The true king, then,—the man who *can*,—from which root I would derive also *ken* and *cunning*,—is he who sways the mighty realm of Thought; whose achievements mimic those of the Infinite Father by building out into void space, and peopling Chaos with living and beneficent, though bodiless, creations. Who knows or cares what was the name of Homer's temporal sovereign? The world could not spare Cicero's Orations, but what recks it of his consulate? George III. ruled respectably a mighty realm through the most memorable half-century in the history of man; yet his age will be known to remote posterity, not as his by any means, nor even as that of Napoleon or Wellington, but as that of Goethe, Wordsworth, and Byron. Bonaparte himself was a reality and no sham; yet he missed his best chance of earthly immortality when he allowed Fulton to leave France with the steamboat still in his brain. The burning of Moscow was unlucky for the conqueror of Austerlitz; but this non-comprehension of our great countryman was a betrayal of incapacity, — a downright discomfiture, of which no Grouchy can be made the scapegoat.

Inevitable, then, is it, and by no means to be lamented, that, in an age so eventful and stirring as ours, an innumerable multitude should aspire to Write, — that is, to Teach. Nay, it is greatly to be desired, and every way to be encouraged, that the largest possible number should aspire to sing and shine as enlighteners and monitors of their fellow-beings. Brother in the tow frock and ragged unthinkables! have you an idea humming in your brain, that seems to you fitted to cure even the lightest of human maladies? Out with it, I pray you, in mercy to a benighted, heart-sick, and blindly suffering race! Sister in linsey-woolsey, and wearing a red-cotton handkerchief by way of diadem, have you aught to say, that, if uttered, would cheer and bless the weary steps whereby we are all measuring off the little span which divides us from the grave? For sweet Charity's sake, do not withhold it, but let your light shine, even though the darkness be sure *not* to comprehend it, — a by no means novel nor uncommon case. Heed not the croaker's warning that the world overflows with books and authors, — so it did in Solomon's time; yet how many very good ones, that mankind could hardly spare, have been written since! Truly, the universe is full of light, and has been these thousands of years; yet, for all that, we could not dispense with the sunshine of to-morrow, whether as a realization or as an assuring prediction. Never believe those who tell you that our Race are surfeited with teachers, — that their present needs are material only, not spiritual, — and that your humble lay will be drowned by the crashing volume of the world's great choral harmonies, — for if you have something to say, and do really *say* it, never doubt that it will find or make its way to the eyes and hearts of those fitted to appreciate and enjoy it.

But the real perplexity, the one great source of disappointment and mortification in the premises, is this, — Of the legions who aspire to teach and sing, only a very small proportion do so from any hearty, intrinsic, essential love of the work, while the great multitude seek primarily and mainly their own glory or aggrandizement, rather than the good of their kind. They aspire to be teachers, not because the world needs to be taught, but because they must somehow be fed. Minim's "lays" are inspired by his laziness, and not by any of the Muses, who would be tortured by his invocations if they paid any sort of heed to his twanging. Crotchet's treatise on Hydraulics and Dynamics was impelled by the vacuum in his own stomach, rather than by any painful sense of deficiency or error in popular conceptions of natural science. Van Roamer's "Travels" were constrained by the stern alternative of quitting his native soil or cultivating it; he is enabled to tell us how the Camanches grow corn, or the Mohaves harvest beans, through his own invincible repugnance to assisting in either process at home. And thus the domain of letters is continually infested, is wellnigh overrun, by a swarm of adventurers who are only intellectual in their pursuits and tendencies because they dread being, and so have not fitted themselves to be, material, — as Talleyrand accounted all men Military who were not Civil. Hence, the patient earth groans beneath the weight of books written from as grovelling a motive as ever sent a truant whimpering to school, and the moon and stars are persecuted with flatulent apostrophes and impertinent staring by bards whose main incitement to thus tormenting the night is a constitutional abhorrence of getting up and swinging an axe in the morning.

It is high time the current cant affirming the misfortunes of authorship, "calamities of genius," the miserable recompense of intellectual effort, &c., were scouted from the earth. Its groundwork is a total misconception of the relations of things intellectual to things physical, — of Mind to Matter, Time to Eternity. Milton, they say, sold Paradise Lost for ten pounds to its original publisher, Mr. Simmons. Begging your pardon, gentlemen, he did no such thing; if he had done, the mighty epic would have henceforth been *Simmons's* Paradise Lost, no longer Milton's. No such poem was ever written for pounds, few or many, nor ever can be. The author sold only the privilege of multiplying copies for the few years wherein his right of property in his work was protected by law; but the poem was still Milton's, and so must remain while Time shall endure. Trade and Law are mighty in their several spheres; but both together are powerless to vest the proper ownership of Paradise Lost in anybody else than John Milton.

I am not palliating the injustice done to authors by our laws of Copyright; they are indeed gross and indefensible. Their original sin inheres in their attempt to draw a distinction where the laws of the Universe make none, — between Property in the creations of the Brain and in those of the Hands. The distinction is at best imperfect. A poem, as given by the author to the press, is the joint production of intellect and muscles, — so is a plough or a boot-jack. The difference is one of proportion only, — in the poem, the labor of Production is mainly brain-work; the reverse is the case with the plough. The poet's work, *as* poet, is one of creation purely, so far as finite beings can create; while the mechanic's achievement is one of accommodation or shaping merely. No man ever made, no man *can* make, a flour-barrel so thoroughly his as Childe Harold was and is Byron's. On what principle, then, do human laws say that the flour-barrel belongs to the maker, his heirs or assigns, so long as it shall exist, and wherever it may be found, but that Childe Harold was Byron's property only within a narrow territorial radius and for a brief term of years? Clearly, on no principle at all. The law plunders the author while pretending to protect him. It ought to know nothing of Copyright save to require the author to give fair notice that he regards his production as a property, and forbids the multiplication of copies by any other than a publisher expressly authorized by him. Then, if it were deemed expedient to confiscate the author's right of property, at the expiration of fifty or a hundred years from the date of his work's first appearance, he ought to be fairly compensated for his book, if the demand for it were still active, so as to justify a claim to indemnity on the part of his heirs.

The Law of Copyright is pernicious in all its restrictions on the natural right of property, — wrong in denying that right in one country to the citizen of another, and thereby bribing the author to pander to local and provincial prejudices, instead of speaking to all Humanity. A book which finds readers in all or many lands is presumptively worth far more than one which finds admirers only in the country which produced it. This law is doubly wrong in virtually saying to the author, "Cater to the prejudices, the follies, the passions of the hour; for the approval of future generations may indeed pile marble above your unconscious dust, but will give no bread to your famishing offspring!" It is very true that the pecuniary recompense is not the main impulse to the production of works which the world does not willingly let die; but the State has no moral right to rob a man merely because he leaves his doors unlocked. It is bound to render to each his due; and it sets an evil example in divesting any of what is rightfully his own.

But, to ninety-nine of every hundred literary aspirants, it makes no difference practically whether the copyright accorded to their works is or is not limited both in time and space. Out of every hundred books published, not ten are ever read out of the country which produced them; hardly one will be heard of by the author's own grandchildren. "Come like shadows, so depart," is the motto that would fitliest illustrate the title-page of our booksellers' annual catalogues of their new issues. Like an April snow-shower, they are poured upon us till they threaten to cover, if not transform, the earth; but soon the sun shines out, and, the next hour, they have vanished forever.

Now, while it is quite true that Milton did not write Paradise Lost for Mr. Simmons's ten pounds, nor for any number of anybody's pounds, it is none the less certain that the State has no moral right to bribe its authors to strive for momentary popularity rather than enduring regard. It has no moral right to say to them, "Write skilfully on a level with the passions and prejudices of the day, and you shall have wealth and present fame; but, if you write what the vicinage may condemn, yet what the Ages and the Race must approve and embalm, you shall be punished with poverty for yourself and beggary for your children." That "ye cannot serve God and Mammon" was true enough in the nature of things, before the State undertook to aggravate, as against Mammon's despisers, the severity of the sentence and the intensity of the punishment.

The World of Thought! how vast its extent! how majestic its triumphs! I am not surprised that literary fame is the object of such general aspiration; I should be surprised indeed if it were otherwise. Just consider how potent, how vast, is the sway to-day exercised by Plato, and Virgil, and Tacitus, now so many centuries in their graves, and compare it with the narrow, transient, imperfect dominion of Alexander or Augustus, so omnipotent in his own age and sphere, so impotent elsewhere, and ever after. Xenophon the leader has long been undistinguishable dust, while Xenophon the narrator is still in the zenith of his power and renown. Julius Cæsar holds his place in the world's regard far more by means of his Commentaries than of his victories, and Bonaparte's first campaign electrified Europe not more by his battles than his bulletins. We cannot wonder, then, that men have sacrificed ease and pleasure, youth and strength, grace of motion and power of vision, to win a name among those who worthily wielded that "weapon mightier than the sword"; for, indeed, there is no other field of effort, no other arena for ambition, so inviting, so dazzling, as this. Wolfe on the Heights of Abraham admiringly recited Gray's Elegy, and declared that he would rather be its author than the conqueror of Montcalm and Canada. "All for love and the world well lost," is the surrender of the grandest possibilities to a fleeting delirium of the senses; but well might the conqueror of an empire, the heir of a dynasty, exchange his circumscribed and vanishing dominion for a seat among the Kings of Mind,—the rulers of that World of Ideas, whose sway each year expands and strengthens, though their bones have enriched, centuries ago, the soil with which they wrestled for a meagre subsistence as Homer the mendicant or Æsop the slave.

But have the true Kings of Thought in fact realized their own might, and actually aspired to and struggled for the preeminence which Mankind has so cordially assigned them? Did Shakespeare, for instance, know himself the intellectual prodigy he truly was, and apprehend that the lines he dashed off with such facile rapidity would be read in delighted awe and wonder on isles of the Southern main, far beyond the African cape, which in his day bounded in that direction the known world? I find in his writings the presence of amazing power, but not the consciousness of it. Nay: I cannot help suspecting that, had he really known how great a man he was and is, he would have refrained from acting and talking so often like a little one. The world has known men who profoundly esteemed themselves great, and justified that consciousness by every act of their lives. I could not have dared to ask Michael Angelo to build me a tavern-stable out of the crumbling walls of a deserted monastery or fortress; I should have cowered before the glance of his eye as he turned upon me with the question, "Do you think I was sent into the world to build stables?" Yet I would not have hesitated — would you? — to ask Shakespeare to write me, for a consideration, an epithalamium, a monody, a pasquinade, an epigram; and should not have feared rebuke or refusal, if the price named were sufficient. For I see the man working and delving from day to day like any journeyman among us, — with immense courage, certainly, and capacity, and consciousness of power, — but still working up the ordinary play-house rubbish into his grand, airy new structure, as any skilful mason might fill up the centre of his wall with the commonest brickbats, until the difference between him and other playwrights seems one of degree purely, and not of kind. But, reading him thoughtfully, I am arrested by passage after passage evincing an almost Divine faculty, — a faculty in which I discern nothing of the playwright, but rather the inspiration of the soul-rapt prophet, who looks straight through all things; for to him the universe is without opacity, and past, present, and future are mere lines of demarcation across the great plain lying lucid and level before him. This man's nature is a riddle which I, very palpably, cannot read; so I turn away, perplexed and overmastered, to resume the thread of my discussion. If he were *always* unapproachable, I could comprehend, though I might not accurately measure him; if he were only a clever play-house poet, I could more easily and surely estimate him; but his starry flights and his paltry jokes — his celestial penetration and his contemptible puns — form together a riddle entirely too hard for me. I read him; I admire him; but I do not know him; and all the commentators and critics serve only to render darkness more visible, — *my* darkness, I freely admit; but is it not also in some part their own?

The great soul like Milton's, finding utterance through Authorship because utterance is a necessity of its being, and because it feels impelled benignly to assure its weaker, more opaque brethren, that evil is phenomenal and transitory, — the murky exhalation of a chill night, which heaven's sunshine will in due time dissipate, — for this I take to be the burden of all true Literature, as of true Prophecy, — this is, to my eye, the grandest, noblest spectacle beheld on earth. But the literary hack also, — whereof I hold Shakespeare to be the highest type yet revealed to us, — perhaps the highest ever *to* be seen, — he who, finding authorship to be the work directly in his way, takes hold of it and *does* it, heartily, manfully, capitally, with all his might, as he would do anything else that thus planted itself across his path; always evincing talent, energy, resolution; sometimes irradiating these with the celestial fire of genius — he, too, is at least a respectable personage; and contemplating him shall give us added strength and vivacity for the discharge of our own duties, whatsoever they be. But the literary mendicant, — the aspirant to live by literature, while literature begs to be excused from his obsequious and superserviceable attentions, — of him and his works be the heavens mercifully oblivious, be the earth compassionately delivered! He is just the sorriest sight the sun looks down upon, and fills us with the dismalest conceptions of the lower possibilities of human infirmity.

Do but contemplate him, at twenty, thirty, forty, fifty years of age, — a hale, stout, broad-shouldered man, with thews that might chop cord-wood or do some other creditable service to his kind, — at all events, with fingers terminating either fore-arm that would answer for gathering apples or picking up potatoes, — to see him, thus generously furnished, insisting on Authorship as his vocation, when nobody wants to hear or read him, — wandering from publisher to publisher to petition for the printing of his poem or novel, or besieging editor after editor for employment on his journal, — this is a spectacle of human degradation which angels may well weep over. And then to hear *him* talk of the Calamities of Genius! — he whose chief calamity is, manifestly, a total lack of genius, and not of genius merely, but of self-respect, energy, or manhood. Had he but one spark of true genius, it would develop in him a healthful, proper pride, whereof the first dictate would be a revolt against such hawking and auctioneering of his Diviner faculties. "No," he would say, "I need bread, and am not ashamed to solicit the privilege of earning it by such means as naturally bring bread, — by hireling labor in the corn-field, the meadow, the ditch, or the mine; for that is the natural resort of all those who have no estate of their own. I can proudly ask my neighbor to let me saw his wood for a dinner, since such is the obvious way of earning dinners, and sawed wood ministers to a physical necessity akin to my urgent need of victual; but to ask any man to give me a dinner or a dollar for a poem or essay which he never asked me to write, — to beg of him an exchange of his bread for my thoughts, my ideas, — this I cannot stoop to do. If my book be printed, either with my own means or those of a publisher who believes it will do, let any man buy it and pay for it who will; but, if I urgently want bread, let me produce something which is bread's natural equivalent, or let me beg it, if reduced to that dire extremity, in the direct, honest way; but to degrade my faculty of uttering thoughts, such as they are, into a means of indirect beggary, that lowest deep of humiliation, I cannot, dare not, descend to."

Perhaps there is not in all Literature any monument of human perversity and self-exposure more emphatic than the grand chorus of complaint and remonstrance which every year forces its way through some muddy channel or other to the public ear, of which the burden is the stolidity, incapacity and niggardliness of publishers, in not discerning unrecognized merit in the works of young or unknown authors, buying their manuscripts at a generous price, and introducing them, with appropriate ceremonies, to the reading public. There are never less than thousands of these unprinted authors, whose fame is yet in the egg, but who fancy that they need only a spirited and appreciating publisher to cause it to chip the shell and soar away on eagles' wings to immortality. Every year, some hundreds of fresh aspirants to literary distinction contrive to overleap the hated barrier and rush into print; when perhaps the books of ten of them repay the cost of the adventure; two or three are encouraged to try again; and possibly one proves a man of mark, wins popular approbation, and is ever after solicited by publishers, instead of needing to solicit their partiality and favor. But it was not by this one, nor yet by the two or three, that the howl was prolonged as to the obtuseness and rapacity of publishers,— their drinking rare wines out of the skulls of their plundered, starving authors, &c., &c. No: it is from the ranks of the great unpublished, or, if published, unread, that this hideous dissonance goes up,—men who, far from being victims of publishers, have victimized *them,* and will do it again whenever they shall induce one to bring out another of their dreary inanities. All the wine that will ever be made by publishers out of these plaintive gentlemen's productions might be drank out of *their own* skulls, while they are yet living, and leave abundant room therein for all the brains they have to fulfil their ordinary functions undisturbed and unstimulated.

Authors of this stamp rarely consider that not creditable writing only, but true publishing also, is an intellectual vocation,—that as much ability is often evinced in bringing out and selling a book as in writing it. Publishing is a pursuit requiring various talents, ripe scholarship, large capital, and rare sagacity. Of original publications, but a small portion prove profitable, while the great majority involve positive loss. The instances of undeserved or inordinate success in publishing are quite as rare as in authorship.

And you, my unfledged bard! who croak over the stupidity of publishers, and the indifference of the reading class to unlaurelled merit, out of your own mouth shall you be condemned! You complain that others are deaf and blind to such merit; yet *you* are not one whit less so yourself! *You,* Mr. Epaphroditus Sheepshanks, who grumble that Thackeray or Tennyson is read, yet your novel or poem untouched,—is tacitly condemned by thousands who cannot *know* that it is not excellent,—do *you* buy or read the novels of Snooks or the poems of Pettibone, in preference to those of the great celebrities of our day? You know well that you do no such thing,—that you have never looked through them, have scarcely given them a thought. You say, very naturally, "They *may* be good; but my time for reading is limited; and I choose to devote it first to those whose works I have already some reason to *know* are good. Snooks and Pettibone may be clever fellows, I dare say they are, but they must await a more convenient season." And in this you talk and act sensibly; quite otherwise when you grumble that more would-be authors do not succeed in getting printed, and that those who do fail to extract more money as copyright from publishers in addition to that which they have already squandered in paper, typography, and binding.

True, there appear at long intervals men decidedly in advance of their time, — who come to their own, and are not recognized and made welcome, — who write, like Wordsworth or Emerson, for a public which their genius must create or their patience await, — authors whose works would sell better if they were less profoundly good. But this class accept their fortune unmurmuringly, and never repine over their inability to serve at once God and Mammon, and so grasp the rewards of both Time and Eternity. They do their own work calmly, uncomplainingly, almost unconsciously, like the stars and the mountains, and are content to gladden and bless as they may, without striking for an advance of wages. They know, without seeking it, that their message of good-will finds its way to the hearts fitted to receive and assimilate it; they would be amazed by an intimation that their efforts were unappreciated and unrewarded. Not laboring mainly for popularity or pelf, they cannot regard the absence of both as an evidence that their effort is defeated and their labor in vain.

"But," says an ingenuous youth, "I aspire to eminence, fame, popularity, — nay, sir, to usefulness, — as an author; which, I trust, is no ignoble aspiration. Then why may I not seek to sell the fruits of my intellectual efforts in order to cultivate and improve my faculties, and qualify me for the career I meditate? Why may I not seek to sell the poem or story I wrote yesterday, in order to win me bread and opportunity to write a better one to-morrow?" The question is a fair one, and shall be fairly answered.

The ever-present and fearful peril of the Literary vocation is compliance, — the sacrifice of the eternal verity to the temporary necessity. To write to-day for to-day's bread involves the necessity of writing what to-day will appreciate, accept, and buy. This is to set your faculty of thought and utterance up at auction to the best cash bidder, agreeing to do whatever Divine or diabolic work he may have in hand; and it is most unlikely that he who bids highest in current coin for to-day's work, payable to-night, will have Divine work for you to do. Of course, it is understood that you do not *directly* sell yourself to whomsoever will pay highest; but that is the palpable *tendency* of going needily into the market to barter brains for bread. You cannot afford to be nice respecting the use to which your mental faculties are to be turned, if you must sell them to-day, or go hungry to-morrow. The natural drift, therefore, of sending your head into the market for sale is toward moral indifference and debasement, — toward the sale of your talents for the most they will fetch, without regard to what use they will be required to subserve. This tendency may be resisted, baffled, overborne; but it can never cease to be a reality and a peril. Sensual appetite is always ready to pay generously for a present gratification; while Virtue is constitutionally austere and provident. And, beside, there is a very great mistake widely prevalent which confounds the continual *use* with the *improvement* of the faculties essential to Authorship; whereas, use is as often exhausting as strengthening. Washington, Bonaparte, Byron, Wellington, — in fact, nearly all the great men of the last age, — evinced qualities as admirable and eminent in the outset as in the maturity of their several careers. Their opportunities, their responsibilities, may have afterward been broader; but Washington on Braddock's fatal field, Bonaparte in Italy, Byron in Childe Harold, Wellington in India, while still young men, evinced the great qualities which have rendered their names immortal. They there gave promise of all that they afterward performed. If such qualities inhere in you, they will find or make their way out; if they do not, you cannot create them by years of imitative, mechanical drudgery as a journeyman in the vocation you are anxious to master.

I would say, then, to aspiring young men: "While you seek the ladder that leads up to renown, preserve, as above all price, your proper independence, mental and physical. Never surrender yourself to what is termed an intellectual vocation until you have first laid the foundations of independence in the knowledge of a good trade or handicraft, to fall back on whenever you shall find yourself unable to maintain at once your position as a brain-worker and your perfect self-respect. Take your place in the field or the shop, and make yourself master of its duties, — fasten yourself to some patch of ground on some slope of the Alleghanies, the Catskills, the Ozarks, — do anything which will make you a self-subsisting, skilful, effective worker with the hands, while you have the full control of your mental powers, and may apply your hours won from toil to their improvement, until you shall be called thence to intellectual pursuits by some other need than your own. Then you may accept the new opportunity in perfect security, and in the proud consciousness that your instructed sinews can earn you a livelihood by manual labor, should it ever happen that you can no longer maintain your integrity and your self-respect in that other vocation to which a hope of wider usefulness, and the request of those you serve, will have drawn you. Now, you need no longer consider how much truth the public will bear, but what is the particular truth it needs to have expounded and enforced to-day. You will serve mankind as a benefactor, not now as a slave.

It is one of the most venerable of jokes, — patronized, I dare say, by Mr. Joseph Miller and other ancient collectors of good things, and yet so pat to my argument that I cannot refrain from quoting it, — that a London ship was once captured off the Spanish coast by an Algerine rover, and her crew and passengers mustered before the Dey, to be put to the best use respectively as slaves. Each, as he entered the immediate presence of the head pirate, was required to name his trade or calling; which, being duly interpreted, he was assigned to the workshops, the ship-yard, the gardens, or the galleys, according as his past experience had fitted him for efficiency in one vocation or another. At length, there came one who answered the usual question by avowing himself an author, and this was finally translated so as to render it comprehensible to the Dey; who, after puzzling his brains for some time to devise a better use for so helpless an object, finally ordered him to be provided with a pair of feather inexpressibles, and set to hatching out chickens. Here the story stops, leaving us in tantalizing darkness as to the success of the literary gentleman in this new field of production; but, as the employment so compelled must have been sedentary and irksome to the last degree, it serves to enforce my moral, that a youth should thoroughly qualify himself to earn his own bread with his hands before he risks himself on the precarious enterprise of ministering to the intellectual needs of others.

Having thus protested, as I could not in conscience fail to do, against the baseness which aspires to authorship as an escape from ruder labor, and then whimpers because its flimsy intellectual wares cannot be exchanged for wholesome bread-corn, or substantial beef, let me not fail to remonstrate also against the crying injustice done, more especially by the laws of *our* country, not to her worthless but to her worthier, nobler Authors, through the denial of International Copyright. We nationally and systematically steal the works of Bulwer, Dickens, Thackeray, Macaulay, Browning, Tennyson; boldly claiming the right and exerting the power of taking, using, enjoying, their products, without rendering the authors any equivalent; and we thereby deprive our own authors of the fair and just reward of *their* labor as well. Our Irving, Bryant, Hawthorne, Longfellow, &c., are less widely read and less fully recompensed than they should be, because the works on which they are paid a copyright must be sold in direct competition with those of their European rivals, whom we refuse to pay at all. "Are they not paid by their own countrymen?" I hear triumphantly asked. "No, sir!" I reply; not paid by Europe for the service they render *us*, not paid by anybody else for the instruction or entertainment *we* derive from their works. This instruction we have no moral right to appropriate without paying for it, any more than we might honestly clothe ourselves in unbought European fabrics which a wrecking storm had strewn along our shores. That we *can* take them without redress, and for the present with impunity, is undoubted; but *that* no more proves our *right* to do it than the impunity long enjoyed by the corsairs of the Barbary coast in plundering Christian vessels in the Mediterranean, proved the justice of *that* shameful atrocity. The day will yet dawn wherein Man everywhere shall profoundly realize that no essential advantage can ever be obtained through injustice, — that the constitution of the Universe is such that no product of human effort can be obtained cheaper than by honestly buying and fairly paying for it. In that day, it will be felt and admitted that we have seriously injured and imperilled our country, by intrusting the formation of its mind, morals, and manners mainly to Foreign Authors, through the relative cheapening and consequent diffusion of their works inevitably resulting from the denial of International Copyright.

Perhaps there is no chapter in the history of Literature more amusing, and yet none which is essentially more melancholy, than that which acquaints us with the frailties of Authors, and especially of those of decided genius. That Shakespeare was arraigned for deer-stealing, — a most poetical and delicate sort of theft, all admit; — that the great Bacon, father of modern Philosophy, was disgraced and cashiered for corruption as Lord Chancellor, the most responsible and one of the most lucrative as well as honorable posts in the kingdom; that Burns was irregular in love and immoderate in drink; that Byron was a libertine, and Chatterton a cheat; that some bards have run away with other men's wives, while a good many have run away from their own, — these, and like deplorable facts, are reiterated and gloated over by millions, who are much better acquainted with the vices and errors of the greatly gifted than with their writings. Too many of us find an ignoble, if not malicious, pleasure in reducing those whose intellectual stature threatens to dwarf us at least to our own *moral* level; we catch at the evidences of their frailty, in order to assure ourselves that we too are spiritually deathless as they, or they at least mortal as we are. And their lives are necessarily so public, so transparent, so scrutinized, that the least flaw attracts observation; they seem worse than others at least as bad as they, only because they are better known. How many follies, meannesses, vices, sins, in the lives of the common-place, are charitably hidden from public view by the friendly oblivion which screens the majority from observation in shielding them from public interest or curiosity! How many have stolen deer, and been convicted and whipped or imprisoned for it, and had the matter all over and forgotten within a year or two; while here stands great Shakespeare, still in the stocks for deer-stealing, though he has stood there so patiently — a little disdainfully, perhaps, yet quite exemplarily — for almost three centuries! O, it is a fearful thing for one greatly gifted to cherish vices or yield to temptations! his errors cover and deform him like writhing, hissing snakes, whose scaly sides and gleaming crests shine in the refulgence by which his genius has surrounded him, from the towering height to which his achievements have lifted him, so that the whole world sees them; the good with pitying sorrow, the thoughtless with mirthful levity, the bad with ill-concealed exultation. Vice is lamentable in any, — is the source, not merely of moral degradation, but of physical suffering; but saddest of all are the offences, most signal and enduring the punishments, of those fitted by Nature to be great, — the Kings of the mighty realm of undying Thought!

The necessities, the perplexities, the pecuniary distresses, of authors, — these, too, have afforded the multitude an inexhaustible fund of anecdote and entertainment. In fact, the obvious contrast between the novelist or poet in his garret, lying abed for the day, perhaps, to have his linen washed, while he considers whether to let his hero marry the great heiress and inherit his principality just yet, or tantalize the reader's impatience with new machinations or impediments through two or three chapters more, — this is antithesis too pungent, too comic, not to be enjoyed. The great majority have ceased to read such "slow," tame essays as those of The Spectator and The Tatler; yet the story of Dick Steele's embarrassments, follies, arrests for debt, and irreclaimable prodigalities, have recently been retold to our city audiences by Thackeray with inimitable felicity, and enjoyed with unexampled zest. An author's thoughts, it would seem, may perish or be supplanted, but the mementos of his thoughtlessness will endure forever.

Yet there is exaggeration in the current notion of the constitutional poverty and squalor, the desperate shifts and average seediness, of authors, which ought to be exposed, since there is just truth enough at the bottom of it to render it mischievous. The great, the radical difference between our age and the centuries which preceded the invention of printing, ought to be explained and realized. In those ages, the cost of multiplying books was so great that very few copies, even of the best, were made or could be afforded; and the author's right of property in his work — that is, his rightful control over the privilege of reproducing it — was of slender or doubtful pecuniary value. Homer, of course, received nothing for his masterly and immediately, universally popular works, beyond the few pence flung to him here and there in requital for the pleasure he afforded by singing them. Cicero was paid for his orations by his clients, never by his readers. And thus it chanced that the *dedication* of books, now so absurd and unmeaning, had once a real force and significance. Authors, as a class, were never rich, and those who were poor had yet inherited a prejudice against living on air. And, since their works had no pecuniary value when completed, they were very poor security, while yet unwritten, for the bread that *must* be eaten, and the wine which *would* be drank, by the authors while writing them. So each poor aspirant for literary distinction was obliged, at the outset of his undertaking, to seek and find a *patron,* wealthy, and fond of doing public-spirited acts, or at least of the fame thence arising, who would be willing to subsist him while at his work and reward him at its close. The Dedication, then, was the author's public and formal acknowledgment of his obligation to his patron,—his avowal that the credit of the work ought to be divided between them,—just as to-day the inventor of a mechanical improvement, and the capitalist who supplies the money wherewith to perfect and secure it, often take out a patent jointly. But the Art of Printing, and the general diffusion of knowledge and literary appetite, have abolished patrons, by abolishing the necessity which evoked them; so that there is now but one real patron, The Public, and nearly all dedications to particular individuals are affected, antiquated, and unmeaning.

It is a very common but a very mischievous notion, that the writing of a book is creditable *per se.* On the contrary, I hold it *dis*creditable, and only to be justified by proof of lofty qualities and generous aims embodied therein. To write a book when you have nothing new to communicate,—nothing to say that has not been better said already,—that is to inflict a real injury on mankind. A new book is only to be justified by a new truth. If Jonas Potts, however illiterate and commonplace, has been shipwrecked on Hudson's Bay, and has travelled thence overland to Detroit or Montreal by a route previously unknown, then he may give us a book—if he will attempt no more than to tell us as clearly as possible what he experienced and saw by the way,—which will have a genuine value, and which the world may well thank him for; and so of a man who, having manufactured charcoal all his days, should favor us with a treatise on burning charcoal, showing what was the relative value for that use of the various woods; how long they should be on fire respectively; how much wood should be burned in one pit, and how the burning should be managed. Every contribution, however rude and humble, to our knowledge of nature, and of the means by which her products may most advantageously be made subservient to our needs, is beneficent, and worthy of our regard. But the fabrication of new poems, or novels, or essays, or histories, which really add nothing to our stock of facts, to our fund of ideas, but, so far as they have any significance, merely resay what has been more forcibly, intelligibly, happily, said already, — this is a work which does less than no good, — which ought to be decried and put down, under the general police duty of abating nuisances. I would have every writer of a book cited before a competent tribunal and made to answer the questions: "Sir, what proposition is this book intended to set forth and commend? What fact does it reveal? What is its drift, its purport?" If it embodies a new truth, or even a new suggestion, though it seem a very mistaken and absurd one, make way for it! and let it fight its own battle; but if it has really *no* other aim than to be readable, therefore salable, and thus to win gold for its author and his accomplices, the printer and publisher, then let a bonfire be made of its manuscript sheets, so that the world may speedily obtain from it all the light it is capable of imparting.

I once received a letter from a somewhat noted novelist, pressing me to read thoroughly one of his works just issued, which the cover proclaimed his "greatest novel," and which he wished me to commend to general favor, saying he was anxious to do his part toward the emancipation of the poor from their unmerited degradations and miseries. I was not able to read the book, — editors receive too many requests like this; but I replied to the letter; saying, in substance: "You wish to improve the condition of the poor. Well: allow me to suggest a way. Take hold of the first piece of vacant earth you can gain permission to use, plant an acre with potatoes, cultivate and gather them, give one half to such poor creatures as really need them, and save the balance for your own subsistence while you grow more next year. In this way, you will do more toward meliorating the condition of the poor than you could by writing novels from July to eternity." My philanthropic friend did not take my advice, — he did not even thank me for it; but he soon after started a newspaper, whereof he sent me the first five numbers, in every one of which I received a most unmerciful flagellation. The paper is since dead; but I have no doubt its editor continued his castigations to the last, and died laying it on with whatever vigor he had left. *I* could not help that. I never made any reply; but my convictions, as expressed in my letter to him, remain unchanged to this day.

Yet let us not seem to disparage the Author's vocation; nay: we dare not, we cannot. There is no other earthly exercise of power so Olympian, pervasive, enduring. Reflect how many generations, dynasties, empires, have flourished and vanished since the Book of Job was written; and how many more will rise and fade, leaving that sublime old poem still fresh and living. See Cicero, Virgil, Horace, Livy, still studied and admired by the patrician youth of nations unknown to Rome in her greatness, while all other power pertaining to the Pagan era of the Eternal City has long since passed away forever. Nay: consider how Plutarch, Æschylus, Plato, living in a world so very different from ours, — in many respects, so infantile compared with ours, — can still instruct the wisest and delight the most critical among us, and you may well conclude that to write nobly, excellently, is a far loftier achievement than to rule, to conquer, or to kill, and that the truly great author looks down on the little strifes and agitations of mankind from an eminence which monarchs can but feebly emulate, and the ages can scarcely wear away.

But eminence in any good or great undertaking implies intense devotion thereto, — implies patient, laborious exertion, either in the doing or in the preparing for it. He who fancies greatness an accident, a lucky hit, a stroke of good fortune, does sadly degrade the achievement contemplated, and undervalue the unerring wisdom and inflexible justice wherewith the universe is ruled. Ask who among modern poets have written most admirably, so far as manner and finish are regarded, and the lover of Poetry least acquainted with Literary History will unhesitatingly answer, — Pope, Goldsmith, Gray, Moore, Campbell, Bryant, Longfellow, Tennyson. He may place others above any or all of these in power, in genius, in force; but he cannot doubt that these have most smoothly, happily, faultlessly, sung what they had to sing, — that their thoughts have lost less than almost any others' by inharmony or infelicity of expression. Then let him turn to Biography, and he will find that these men have excelled nearly or quite all others in patient study, in fastidious determination to improve, so long as improvement was practicable; in persistent labor, so long as labor could possibly avail. It was quite easy for Pope to say, "The things I have written fastest have always pleased most"; for he always studied and thought himself full of a subject before he began to write about it, and his composition was merely a setting down and arranging of ideas already present in his mind. And yet I apprehend that Posterity has not ratified his judgment; I mean, that his works which "pleased most" when first published have not stood the test of time as well as some others. The world of letters knew him as a pains-taking, laborious, correct writer, even before he had established his claim to be honored as a great one. And the works he wrote so rapidly he afterward revised, corrected, altered, recast, before allowing the public to see them, to the sad encouragement of blasphemy among his printers, so that on one occasion his publisher decided that it would be easier to compose in type afresh than attempt to correct one of his proofs. No man ever wrote better, so far as style is regarded; because no man was ever more determined to publish nothing that he could improve. So Goldsmith considered four lines of his "Deserted Village" a good day's work, and the world has ratified his judgment. With the kindred "Elegy" of Gray, this belongs to a school of poetry which I do not transcendently admire; but its excellence after its kind, I presume, no one has ever doubted. And it is related of Moore, the most fastidious and the most melodious writer of our time, that a friend once travelled with him all day, and was surprised by his taciturn moodiness and abstraction, until, just before night, his face lighted up, and he exclaimed, like the old Greek: "I have it! That will do!" — then explained to his startled companion that he had been all day trying to adjust a rhyme or counterpart to a line in one of his then unfinished poems, and had but just now succeeded. It is thus that works which the world prizes and embalms are composed. A style termed "easy" is generally obtained at great expense of time and effort, whether in the immediate composition or in the lifelong preparation for it; and he who calculates on storming the ramparts of literary fame by the audacity, the impetuosity, of his genius, will very certainly be repulsed and discomfited. The "kingdom of heaven" may "suffer violence," but the republic of letters resents and repels it.

O, my erring friend! delighted that your son of fourteen years or your daughter of twelve has written a page of not intolerable verses, I pray you to lay this lesson to heart! I can sympathize with your paternal partiality; I do not wonder that you are proud of your child's achievement, — for the writing even of bad verses at so tender an age *is* an achievement in one sense, and may plausibly be deemed by you a sign of promise, — but you are thinking of the figure *those verses* would cut in the Poet's Corner of some journal, of the praises they would elicit and the distinction they would confer on their writer; and against these fond, foolish, perilous fancies I most earnestly protest and warn you. If your child has any talent — which is possible, though not probable; for precocity in any but secret authorship argues a low idea of the difficulties of creditable composition, and a taste easily satisfied, because of the poverty of its conceptions of excellence, — still, it is possible your child *has* talent, (which I am confident he did not inherit); and, *if* he has, you are taking the very course to ruin him. Puff him up with the conceit that he is an author at fourteen, and he will pretty surely have proved himself a fool before he is twenty-five. But read over his composition with him, and kindly point out its faults or weaknesses; encourage him to try again, and avoid these errors if possible, but studiously withhold his productions from publicity, and impress him with the truth that to write feebly or badly, — as he cannot now help doing if he writes at all, — is only creditable or noteworthy as it renders possible his writing well after he shall have attained intellectual and physical maturity. Thus cultivate, chasten, and ripen his faculty, but never stimulate it; and there is a possibility that it may ultimately ally him to the great and good of past ages; but let him set out with the conceit that he is a prodigy, and his wreck and ruin are inevitable.

It only remains to me to speak more especially of my own vocation, — the Editor's, — which bears much the same relation to the Author's that the Bellows-blower's bears to the Organist's, the Player's to the Dramatist's, Jullien or Listz to Weber or Beethoven. The Editor, from the absolute necessity of the case, cannot speak deliberately; he must write to-day of to-day's incidents and aspects, though these may be completely overlaid and transformed by the incidents and aspects of to-morrow. He must write and strive in the full consciousness that whatever honor or distinction he may acquire must perish with the generation that bestowed them, — with the thunders of applause that greeted Kemble or Jenny Lind, with the ruffianism that expelled Macready, or the cheerful laugh that erewhile rewarded the sallies of Burton or Placide. No other public teacher lives so wholly in the present as the Editor; and the noblest affirmations of unpopular truth, — the most self-sacrificing defiance of a base and selfish Public Sentiment that regards only the most sordid ends, and values every utterance solely as it tends to preserve quiet and contentment, while the dollars fall jingling into the merchant's drawer, the land-jobber's vault, and the miser's bag, — can but be noted in their day, and with their day forgotten. It is his cue to utter silken and smooth sayings, — to condemn Vice so as not to interfere with the pleasures or alarm the consciences of the vicious, — to praise and champion Liberty so as not to give annoyance or offence to Slavery, and to commend and glorify Labor without attempting to expose or repress any of the gainful contrivances by which Labor is plundered and degraded. Thus sidling dexterously between somewhere and nowhere, the Able Editor of the Nineteenth Century may glide through life respectable and in good case, and lie down to his long rest with the non-achievements of his life emblazoned on the very whitest marble, surmounting and glorifying his dust.

There is a different and sterner path, — I know not whether there be any now qualified to tread it, — I am not sure that even one has ever followed it implicitly, in view of the certain meagerness of its temporal rewards and the haste wherewith any fame acquired in a sphere so thoroughly ephemeral as the Editor's must be shrouded by the dark waters of oblivion. This path demands an ear ever open to the plaints of the wronged and the suffering, though they can never repay advocacy, and those who mainly support newspapers will be annoyed and often exposed by it; a heart as sensitive to oppression and degradation in the next street as if they were practised in Brazil or Japan; a pen as ready to expose and reprove the crimes whereby wealth is amassed and luxury enjoyed in our own country at this hour, as if they had only been committed by Turks or Pagans in Asia some centuries ago. Such an Editor, could one be found or trained, need not expect to lead an easy, indolent, or wholly joyous life, — to be blessed by Archbishops or followed by the approving shouts of ascendant majorities; but he might find some recompense for their loss in the calm verdict of an approving conscience; and the tears of the despised and the friendless, preserved from utter despair by his efforts and remonstrances, might freshen for a season the daisies that bloomed above his grave.

Let me conclude by restating the main propositions which pervade and vivify this essay. Literature is a noble calling, but only when the call obeyed by the aspirant issues from a world to be enlightened and blessed, not from a void stomach clamoring to be gratified and filled. Authorship is a royal priesthood; but woe to him who rashly lays unhallowed hands on the ark or the altar, professing a zeal for the welfare of the Race only that he may secure the confidence and sympathies of others, and use them for his own selfish ends! If a man have no heroism in his soul, — no animating purpose beyond living easily and faring sumptuously, — I can imagine no greater mistake on his part than that of resorting to authorship as a vocation. That such a one may achieve what he regards as success, I do not deny; but, if so, he does it at greater risk and by greater exertion than would have been required to win it in any other pursuit. No: it cannot be wise in a selfish, or sordid, or sensual man to devote himself to Literature; the fearful self-exposure incident to this way of life, — the dire necessity which constrains the author to stamp his own essential portrait on every volume of his works, no matter how carefully he may fancy he has erased, or how artfully he may suppose he has concealed it, — this should repel from the vestibule of the temple of Fame the foot of every profane or mocking worshipper. But if you are sure that your impulse is not personal nor sinister, but a desire to serve and ennoble your Race, rather than to dazzle and be served by it; that you are ready joyfully to "shun delights, and live laborious days," so that thereby the well-being of mankind may be promoted, — then I pray you not to believe that the world is too wise to need further enlightenment, nor that it would be impossible for one so humble as yourself to say aught whereby error may be dispelled or good be diffused. Sell not your integrity; barter not your independence; beg of no man the privilege of earning a livelihood by Authorship; since that is to degrade your faculty, and very probably to corrupt it; but, seeing through your own clear eyes, and uttering the impulses of your own honest heart, speak or write as truth and love shall dictate, asking no material recompense, but living by the labor of your hands, until recompense shall be voluntarily tendered to secure your service, and you may frankly accept it without a compromise of your integrity or a peril to your freedom. Soldier in the long warfare for Man's rescue from Darkness and Evil, choose not your place on the battle-field, but joyfully accept that assigned you; asking not whether there be higher or lower, but only whether it is here that you can most surely do your proper work, and meet your full share of the responsibility and the danger. Believe not that the Heroic Age is no more; since to that age is only requisite the heroic purpose and the heroic soul. So long as ignorance and evil shall exist, so long there will be work for the devoted, and so long will there be room in the ranks of those who, defying obloquy, misapprehension, bigotry, and interested craft, struggle and dare for the redemption of the world. "Of making many books there is no end," though there is happily a speedy end of most books *after* they are made; but he who by voice or pen strikes his best blow at the impostures and vices whereby our race is debased and paralyzed may close his eyes in death, consoled and cheered by the reflection that he has done what he could for the emancipation and elevation of his kind.

POETS AND POETRY.

WE are all born poets. Not that every tenanted cradle holds an undeveloped Shakespeare, — far from it. *Demonstrated* intellectual greatness is the prerogative of the few; it is "the vision," not "the faculty divine," which is the birthright of the many. The grime of smoke and care and sin heavily inwraps, incases, japans, many souls, even in early childhood, — as we see children of seven years prematurely haggard with suffering, squalor, and vice, — but there was a time when these imps were poets, lacking only the power of expression. The child who conjectured that the stars were but chinks or crannies of heaven, — gimlet-holes bored in the adamantine firmament to let God's glory through; the prattler who watched the darkening evening sky, until, espying the first bright speck through its dusky medium, she rapturously exclaimed, "There! God has made a star!" — were happy only in expressing the common impulses of childhood. As all young children are actually theists, — believers in a veritable, personal, conscious, omniscient, omnipotent Author and Ruler of all things, and utterly averse to substituting for this natural, tangible conception any thin attenuation of Pantheistic fog or "fire-mist," any blank Atheistic assumption, which gives to blind Chance or inexorable Fate the name of Law, — so the uncorrupted child instinctively perceives the poetic element in Nature, realizes that we are not the mere combinations of gases and alkalies to which the chemist's crucible would reduce us, but beings of mysterious origin and untold spiritual force, inhabiting a world only less weird and wondrous than ourselves. The Frenchman, who was astounded by the discovery that he had been talking prose all his life, might have been equally amazed by the assurance that he formerly thought, if he did not utter, poetry, — and this was as true as the other. Every close observer must have noted how naturally the talk of unschooled, unspoiled children takes on poetic vestments, — becomes dramatic not merely, but hyperbolic and imaginative in a high degree. Emerson truly says that the first person who called another *puppy* or *ass* was a poet, — perceiving in the individual contemplated a spiritual aptitude to bark or bray, as the case might be. I only add that the first child who ever saw a man making an ass of himself, — which, with all deference to our common progenitor, I apprehend was the first child that ever clearly saw anything whatever, — at once perceived the spiritual similitude, and probably blurted out the ungracious truth. All savage tribes — that is, all nations still in their mental childhood — have a poetic literature, if any; their legends, their traditions, their romances, their chronicles, are all poetic, alike in substance and in diction. Of this truth our Aborigines afford a ready demonstration. A stagnant or decrepit race, like the Chinese, may have their prosaic ordinances, statutes, records, statistics, philosophies; not so a vigorous, elastic, Teutonic tribe or Saracenic empire.

Thus we naturally find some of the most admired and remarkable poems — the Book of Job, the Hebrew Psalms, the Iliad, and the Bagavhat Geta of the Hindoos — dating back to the infancy of Society, as the Inferno, and Shakespeare's and Milton's masterpieces, ally themselves with the infancy of modern civilization, or of the Protestant development thereof. We laugh at Nimrod Wildfire and kindred etchings of the hyperbolic or exaggerated modes of speech indicative of a new country, — new, that is, to the race now inhabiting it; the story of a Western soil so fertile that a crowbar, carelessly thrust into it overnight, is found bristling with spikes and tenpenny nails next morning; of the pumpkin-vine, that outran the steed of the rather astonished traveller; of the

Vermonter, whose chance companion in the cutter behind a rather lively nag at length perplexedly inquired, "What grave-yard is this we are passing through?" and was answered, "Only the milestones along the road," — but a new people are irresistibly prone to these exaggerations. The young American, who goes abroad, finds himself obliged to moderate and tone down his ordinary conversation to adapt it to the general level; to speak of Niagara, or Lake Superior, or the glaciers of Switzerland, in the language that rises spontaneously to his lips, would jar the nerves of his polished listeners, and he would very possibly be reminded, by some highly respectable citizen, that the view from the foot of the great cataract at Niagara could not possibly be that of a falling ocean, since the narrowest ocean is three thousand miles across, while Niagara is hardly a mile. The well-bred Englishman of to-day is so fenced in, incrusted, barricaded, with respectabilities, proprieties, decencies, that the poetic element — nay, even the faculty of appreciating it — seems choked out of him; hence, the British poets of to-day find a warmer and more general appreciation with us than at home; and I cannot doubt that there are many more Americans than Britons familiar with the works of Scott, Byron, and I think even Shakespeare. Yet the English are our kinsmen; equal, but dissimilar, in mental capacities and aptitudes, — only we are still in the poetic phase of our national life, out of which they have passed. We are too cultivated and critical to produce a great epic, — our Washington is no Achilles, no Alexander, no demigod, but a sensible, conscientious, conservative Virginia planter, heartily loyal to Church and King; yet one whom insane tyranny and regal folly converts at last into a rebel, — of course, a more formidable rebel than any natural agitator, leveller, demagogue, or even philosophizing democrat, could be; for, when *he* draws the sword against the throne he has revered and prayed for from childhood, be sure there are not many left to draw *for* it whose support carries either moral weight or physical power — the weight of numbers — along with it. For Washington, though a model man in his way, is not a representative American. His calm, sedate, orderly frame of mind is not that which is habitual with or prized by the mass of our people. He is such a man as the multitude accept as a leader in a perilous and trying emergency, when they feel a pressing need of the sympathy and aid of the solid "men of property and standing" in their imminent struggle; but, had not Washington led the army of the Revolution, he would never have been chosen President; as a plain Virginia gentleman, he would have been beaten in a canvass for the Legislature by some Davy Crockett, Sam Houston, or Larry Keitt of his day, and would thereupon have forsworn politics in disgust, and devoted his after life to his family, his farm, and his stock, and been known only to a hundred or two of the next generation as an upright incorruptible justice of the peace, and a very capable and soldierly captain of the militia company of his neighborhood. No: Washington, in an age of peace and thrift, would never have been "the gray-eyed Man of Destiny," — never been cheered at the theatre, nor glorified in the star-spangled journals. We heap such honors on men of a stamp very different from his.

But to return to Poetry.

The most vulgar error of the vulgar mind with respect to Poetry is that which somehow confounds it with *verse,* and even with *rhyme;* supposing that a measured distich or quatrain, ending with words of similar but not identical sound, is necessarily poetic. Proud mothers will often draw forth from the deepest recess of closet or bureau some metrical effusion of budding son or daughter, which is supposed to be instinct with poetry, because measured into feet and tagged with rhyme; when in fact there is no more poetry in it than in the request, "Pass me the baked potatoes." Rhymed couplets of regularly measured and accented lines are a fashion of our poetry, but no more essential to it than a silk or fur hat is to the character of a gentleman. It is barely possible that the child who has an addiction to and knack of making verses may nevertheless possess some share of the poetic faculty, —

the Divine afflatus, — but the presumption against it is almost overwhelming. The poetic genius naturally disdains the fetters of rhyme, or only consents to wear them at the beck of stern necessity. To the fresh, unhackneyed soul, kindling with rapture inspired by its first perceptions of the beauty inhering in the wonder-works of God, rhyme is as unnatural and repulsive as the fool's cap and bells. For, not merely is it true that there have been great poets who never dreamed of such a thing as rhyme, and clever rhymsters who had not the faintest conception of poetry, but there have been genuine poets who failed miserably as rhyming poetasters. John Bunyan, for example, whose Pilgrim's Progress is the epic of Methodism, — (I know, good reader, that he was not technically a Methodist, and that I ought to have said Evangelicalism, had there been such a word,) — and one of the truest, if not the greatest, of British poems, wrote hideous doggerel whenever he attempted verse, as the introduction to that same epic bears testimony. There can hardly be a more certain evidence that a child has ceased to be poetic than the fact that he has begun to rhyme.

The oldest and most natural — I should rather say, the least unnatural — form of poetic expression, when poetry ceased to be a purely spontaneous utterance of exalted and overmastering emotions, and became, in some sense, an art, is that of *parallelism*, or the expression of the same idea or sentiment through two succeeding images or affirmations; the second being merely cumulative or confirmatory of the former. The Hebrew Scriptures embody some of the earliest and most familiar examples of this parallelism, of which I cite Ruth's appeal to Naomi as a beautiful exemplification: —

"And Ruth said:
'Entreat me not to leave thee,
Nor to return from following after thee:
For whither thou goest I will go,
And where thou lodgest I will lodge:
Thy people shall be my people,
And thy God my God:
Where thou diest will I die,
And there shall I be buried.'"

I am inclined to deem this parallelism, which informs all the poetry of the Bible, not exclusively Hebrew, but a mode of poetic expression natural to the primitive stages of Society, the intellectual puberty of the Race; though I at this moment recall few examples of it outside of Hebrew lore. Mungo Park, the explorer of Central Africa, relates that, as he lay sick and suffering in the Great Desert, the negro women, who mercifully ministered to his sore necessities, gave utterance to their sympathy in a rude song, of which the burden ran thus:—

> "Let us pity the poor white man:
> He has no mother to bring him milk,
> No wife to grind his corn."

A parallelism as palpable, though not so perfect, as any in Job or Ecclesiastes.

"The Poet," says Emerson, "is the man without impediment." If so, I apprehend that the Poets of our world's infancy enjoyed certain marked advantages over their modern successors. Not only was the whole range of poetic imagery then fresh and unused, so that the bard was never constrained to discard a happy simile occurring to his mind because some other bard had used it before him, but, moreover, his utterance was nowise impeded or shackled by the necessity of obeying the rules or formulæ established by preceding bards and their critics, for the government of the realm of Poetry. If the soul of the universe found expression through his burning words,—if their perusal inspired the reader with a deeper and truer perception of the infinite reason which inheres in seeming dissonance, as well as obvious harmony and good,—if he were impelled by it to love and practise virtue, to loathe vice, yet pity its victims, and to count nothing a defeat or disaster which did not involve a surrender of his own high purpose, his generous aspiration for human well-being,—then was he a true poet, whom the ages were waiting to crown, though Fadladeen should demonstrate unanswerably his ignorance of the first rudiments of the minstrel's art. But the poet of our day must be an obedient vassal to an inexorable rule, — must shun ruggedness or wilfulness of expression as a mortal sin, — must respect the unities, and be loyal to rhythm and rhyme, — or he cannot induce the critics even to blast him with their thunders. True, a wild colt of a bardling will now and then revolt against this despotism, and go prancing and kicking, and displaying his ill-conditioned, shaggy coat across Nature's wide, bare common; but the critical shrug ultimately kills if it does not tame him, and he is left but the sorry choice between subsiding into a patient dray-horse, and being cut up for dog's meat. MacDonald Clarke, twenty years ago, and "Walt. Whitman," just now, undertook to be poets in defiance of the canons of the art; but, though the latter received the unmeasured indorsement of Emerson, and obtained an immediate currency on the strength of it, I doubt whether even he, despite his unquestionable originality, and dazzling defiance of what men have been accustomed to regard as decency, will ever achieve the distinction of being knocked on the head with a volume of the Edinburgh Review.

The earliest poets were, I apprehend, the shepherds of Arabia, Chaldea, and that westernmost jut of the great Asian continent, wherein so large a share of the events memorable in Man's history have transpired. All shepherds are naturally poets; or rather, the loneliness, the silence, and the seriousness, of the shepherd's life naturally predispose him to poetry. He is not necessarily and constantly absorbed in his daily duties, which yet require of him a wakeful, alert understanding, and senses sharpened to acuteness by the necessity of keen perception and watchful observation. When at length his flock have sunk, at early evening, to rest, and the shepherd crouches, wrapped in his blanket-cloak, beside them, his mind awakens to a loftier activity ere his senses are sealed in slumber: from his mountain-side elevation, he looks abroad across rolling river and twinkling city — across valleys where the fog begins to gather and wooded ridges fluttering in the chill night-breeze — to other mountains, vast and towering as his own, and to heaven, vaster and higher than them all, and the feelings of immensity, of awe, and of reverence are stirred within his soul: if of a cold, calculating, mathematical nature, he becomes an astronomer, and begins to weigh the stars in his balance; if of a fervid, impulsive genius, his meditations melt and glow into poetry. From shepherd races and shepherd climes have come forth the instructors, conquerors, bards, and civilizers of the barbarian world.

But the mountainous ruggedness, the "cloudless climes and starry skies," of Chaldea, Syria, and Arabia, so unlike the vast plains of Sarmatia and Scythia, are especially favorable to the development of the poetic fire; hence, the Book of Job, so manifestly pastoral in its origin as well as its imagery, is one of the sublimest, as it probably is the very oldest, of surviving poems. True, the author is palpably a scholar, an observer, a traveller, who has gathered all the world knew in his day of astronomic as of terrestrial lore; but his hero is a Chaldean or Hebrew herdsman, living by the side of the great Arabian desert, and subject to the mischances and sudden reverses which constantly threaten and frequently befall the shepherds of that region, even in our own day. In its magnificent imagery, as well as in its characters and incidents, Job is the simplest and grandest, as well as oldest, of pastoral poems.

A shepherd boy, keeping his flock on the sterile mountains of Judea, in constant peril from the savage beasts and not less savage men of the desert, — "a cunning player on an harp," sought out by King Saul's servants to expel the evil spirit which had taken possession of their master (alas that the evil spirits which gain control of rulers cannot always be thus exorcised!), — a battler for his race and faith and native land, volunteering to encounter, while still a mere lad, the giant champion of their mortal foe, and vanquishing him in deadly combat, — a fugitive from the jealous madness of his royal master, into whom the Evil One seems to have again entered, and there intrenched himself beyond dislodgement by the powers of music, — a needy and desperate wanderer and outlaw for years, carrying his life in his hand, — then the anointed monarch and idolized hero of his nation, — then dethroned and put to flight by the ingratitude and perfidy of his favorite son and the fickle levity of his people, — again restored to a throne of increasing splendor, and dying peacefully and regally in extreme old age, at the summit of his power and glory, — if I were required to name that one who of all men had lived the most arduous, stirring, eventful life, most full of violent contrasts and trying situations, of love and war, of glory and humiliation, I must say, David, king of Israel. A life so full of absorbing action would seem to give little chance for literary culture or achievement; and yet this warrior king, who could not be permitted to build the Great Temple to his God, because he had been a man of violence and blood, has bequeathed us so many Psalms in which the waiting, contrite souls of ages so remote and races so diverse as ours from his find a fuller and fitter expression of their aspirations and their needs than all the piety and genius of intervening ages have been able to indite. Yes, this untaught shepherd son of Jesse, this leader in many a sanguinary fight, this man of a thousand faults and many crimes, knew how to sweep the chords of the human heart as few or none have ever touched them before or since, — to take that heart, with all its frailty, its error, its sin, and lay it penitently, pleadingly, at the footstool of its Maker and Judge, and teach it by what utterances, in what spirit, to implore forgiveness and help. Other thrones have their successions, dynasties, their races of occupants; but David reigns unchallenged King of Psalmody till Time shall be no more.

Of Greek Poetry I have a right to say but little. The general impression it makes on me is that of youthfulness on the part of its authors. The most learned among us do not know those old Greeks very well; and I am often impelled to wonder whether the versatile, elastic, cheating, unreliable Greeks of our day are not lineal descendants, not of the

Spartans, perhaps, but of the Athenians and Argives of old; whether the latter did not hate work and love profit as much as the Fanariote or the Greek trader of our time; nay, whether the Spartans themselves, *plus* a few satisfactory floggings, are not reproduced in the warrior mountaineers of Albania and the fierce robber bands which infest the passes and plains of Thessaly. True, the Athenian of to-day is behind the citizens of Western Europe in culture, in courage, and in most manly virtues; but may he not be as far in advance of the Western Asiatic of Xerxes' or Darius's reign as were the countrymen of Miltiades or Alexander? Europe north of the Alps has unquestionably advanced; may not Greece have simply stood still, instead of retrograding? The solution of this doubt is to be found, not in the prowess nor the physical achievements of the old Greeks, but in their literature, and especially their tragedy.

The Greek epic held substantially the place of the modern novel; I cannot so confidently say that the novel *fills* the place of the epic. The epic embodied and presented human life under its more heroic and majestic aspects, — the life of the patriot, ready to seal his devotion with his blood. Greek life, as depicted by Homer, is rude and sterile; its pleasures, gross and sensual; its gods, men and women endowed with supernatural powers, but not at all distinguished by supernatural virtues. It would be very rash in me to pronounce Homer monotonous, and at times tedious, when the scholars, who know him so much better, say exactly the reverse; so I will not hazard the criticism, though I shall privately cherish my own opinion. I wonder if any one else ever detected or fancied a resemblance between the roll of Homer's heroes and Catlin's gallery of Indian portraits?

The Epic is the utterance of a ruder age than ours. The scholar still praises it, — he thinks he delights in it, — but it is the delight of association, of comparison, of remembrance, — not of direct and simple enjoyment. Who ever heard of an edition of the Iliad in translation being required by the *un*-classical youth of Great Britain, of this or of any other modern country? I apprehend that, for each copy of any great epic to be found in the hands or under the pillow of the youth in all our common schools, you may find ten copies of the Arabian Nights or of certain of Dickens's Novels. Only by those who have been impelled to study them as a task are the great epics still read; and by these rather as a habit or duty than as a genuine pleasure.

Yet we must be grateful to the creators of the Epic, since to them are we indebted, by direct transmission, by lineal descent, for Tragedy, the broadest, the deepest, the most vivid, expression of human emotions and aspirations. Æschylus is the true child of Homer, and that grand Athenian stage whereon the passions, the impulses, the hopes, the fears, the love, piety, guilt, revenge, remorse, which make up our strangely compounded Human Nature, were depicted so intensely as never before nor since, was the outgrowth of those lofty and stirring narrations wherewith "that blind old man from Scio's rocky isle" was wont to beguile the hours and inspire the hearts of the ancestors of Pericles and Plato. From the goat-song of the Mime, the cart of Thespis, the rude chant of the ballad-singer, the monologue of the legendary, the dialogue of the satirist, was rapidly elaborated that shapely and towering fabric of Grecian Tragedy which must awe, delight, and instruct mankind through ages yet to be.

The argument of Tragedy is the struggle of Man with Misfortune, — the spectacle of Virtue enduring the buffets of Adversity, and of Crime overtaken by the shafts of Retribution. But Greek Tragedy essayed a loftier flight than ours, and presented the suffering but undaunted human soul enduring and defying the bolts of Fate, the anger of the immortal gods. We see there Guilt hurried irresistibly to its awful doom, — inexorable Nemesis visiting the punishment of evil deeds even upon the grandchildren and great-grandchildren of the evil-doer, — the fair, the gentle, and the good, bowing to the destiny invoked by the sin of some progenitor, — and this is not unlike what experience and literature have elsewhere made familiar; but Prometheus, chained to his rock and suffering the tortures of the damned for having dared to enlighten and bless mankind, yet calm-souled and defiant, awaiting the unknown but inevitable hour which shall dethrone his jealous and fearful Olympian tyrant, and bring him deliverance and recompense, this is a conception peculiar to Greek Tragedy, and the lesson of stoical endurance and intellectual force taught by it is without a modern parallel. Nor must we rashly conclude that the great tragic poets were irreverent or hostile to the religion of their age and race. Behind the fable of Prometheus rests the grand, eternal truth, that all the forces of the universe are subject to the moral law; that Good is the measure and true end of Power; that tyranny and cruelty would still be what they are if their responsible author were armed with celestial thunders; that, if there could be a more benignant and just being than the Deity, that being would then be God.

Let me venture to cite one passage from the Agamemnon of Æschylus as rendered by Bulwer in his Athens, — not one characteristic of Greek Tragedy, but one which the reader of poetry will readily contrast with familiar passages of Scott and Byron. It is that in which Clytemnestra announces to the chorus the glad tidings of the capture of Troy, — said tidings having been transmitted by the good old fire-telegraph of primitive times: —

"A gleam, — a gleam from Ida's height,
By the fire-god sent, it came;
From watch to watch it leaped, that light,
As a rider rode the flame!
It shot through the startled sky,
And the torch of that blazing glory
Old Lemnos caught on high,
On its holy promontory,
And sent it on, the jocund sign,
To Athos, mount of Jove divine.
Wildly the while it rose from the isle,
So that the might of the journeying light
Skimmed over the back of the gleaming brine!
Farther and faster speeds it on,
Till the watch that keep Macistus' steep, —
See it burst like a blazing sun!

Doth Macistus sleep
  On his tower-clad steep?
No! rapid and red doth the wild-fire sweep.
It flashes afar on the wayward stream
Of the wild Euripus, the rushing beam!
It rouses the light on Messapion's height,
And they feed its breath with the withered heath.
    But it may not stay!
    And away, — away, —
  It bounds in its freshening might.
    Silent and soon,
    Like a broadened moon,
  It passes in sheen, Asopus green,
  And bursts on Cithæron gray.
The warder wakes to the signal rays,
And it swoops from the hill with a broader blaze,
  On — on the fiery glory rode; —
  Thy lonely lake, Gorgōpis, glowed, —
  To Mĕgara's mount it came;
    They feed it again,
    And it streams amain, —
  A giant beard of flame!
The headlong cliffs that darkly down
O'er the Saronic waters frown,
Are passed with the swift one's lurid stride,
And the huge rock glares on the glaring tide,
With mightier march and fiercer power
It gained Arachne's neighboring tower, —
Thence on our Argive roof its rest it won,
Of Ida's fire the long-descended son!
Bright harbinger of glory and of joy!
So first and last, with equal honor crowned,
In solemn feasts, the race-torch circles round.
And these my heralds! this my Sign of Peace!
Lo! while we breathe, the victor lords of Greece
Stalk, in stern tumult, through the halls of Troy!"

The Romans were never a poetic people. Epicureans, who philosophized in verse, like Horace; biting satirists, like Juvenal; happy weavers into verse of legendary lore, like Virgil, the Longfellow of that sole age, the Augustan, in which Roman literature seems to have been at all worthy of the mistress of the civilized world; concise, critical, caustic, pains-taking annalists the Romans were, but not poets. Their best metrical productions have a second-hand flavor; they smell of the lamp; they would have been different, or never have been at all, had there been no Greece.

Brownson says certain ages are termed Dark, because *we* are in the dark with regard to them. Those who will may assign a kindred reason for my assumption, that there was no poetry worth treasuring and praising written between the Augustan age and the time of Dante, and that one needs to be at least as good a Catholic as Dante to appreciate and enjoy the Inferno.

When I assume that English Poetry for us begins with Shakespeare, I must not be misunderstood. That there is merit of a certain kind in Chaucer, in Spenser, and other British rhymers before the age of Queen Bess, is of course manifest. But who in our day ever sat down to read Chaucer or Spenser otherwise than as a task, — something requisite to a competent knowledge of English literature? For my part, I say frankly that I hold The Faery Queene a bore, and never had patience to complete its perusal. Its allegorical representations of our good and evil impulses are tedious, fantastic, unreal, insufferable. They probably instructed and delighted the generation for which they were written; but their fragrance has departed. Lay them respectfully, tenderly down to their long rest, and let the gathering dust slowly bury them out of sight!

But of that vast, "myriad-minded" Shakespeare, what shall I say? True, I do not love him; but do I the less appreciate and admire his intellectual force and grandeur? Because I profoundly hate his Toryism, shall I disparage his unquestioned and, in its way unequalled, genius? Because I am compelled to perceive that his jokes are often sorry and his puns mainly detestable, must I be presumed to deny that his humor is delicious and his imaginative faculty beyond that of any other mortal? By no means.

I am provoked by his ingrain Toryism, because it seems at once unnatural and irrational. I will not deny that the mass of men are base, — possibly *as* base as he represents them, — I will only insist that there are capacities, possibilities, in this abused nature of ours, beyond our actual achievement, or beyond his apprehension of that achievement. Even if it were otherwise, he, a child of the people, the son of a woollen-draper, should not have been first to discover and proclaim the deplorable fact. Yet, no autocrat born in the purple nourished a more profound contempt for the rabble, the canaille, the *oi polloi*, than this vagabond by statute and venison-thief by conviction. In his game, only the court-cards count; all the rest go for nothing. We, the untitled, undistinguished masses, are not merely clowns and poltroons, fit only for butts for knightly jests, and hardly good enough to be meat for knightly swords, but there is a constant, though quiet, assumption that this, as it ever has been, must continue to be forever. You would naturally suppose that grandest event in modern history, the discovery of the Western continent, which was still recent in his day, and which must have been the theme of many a conversation in his presence among the Raleighs, Drakes, and other daring spirits of that stirring time, who had personally visited the New World, would have inspired even in his breast some hope of a fairer future for Humanity on earth, — some aspiration, at least, for a Social Order wherein Rank and Wealth should not be everything, and Man nothing, — but no: I cannot recall even a passing allusion to America, save that most inaccurate one, "the still vext Bermoothés," and never once an intimation, a suspicion, that the common lot might be meliorated through the influence of the settlement and civilization of this side of the globe. Of course, the actor-manager-author meant no disrespect to us Anglo-Americans in prospect, nor yet to our Franco-American neighbors just north, nor to the Spanish and Portuguese Americans south of us; it was only a way he had of viewing everything with an eye which, though it oft, "in fine frenzy rolling," might "glance from heaven to earth, from earth to heaven," never penetrated laterally much beyond the fogs of London and the palace of Whitehall, and not only saw in the million merely the counters wherewith kings and nobles played their gallant game, but refused to see in them the possibility of becoming anything better.

Whether Shakespeare the monarchist or Milton the republican were intellectually the greatest Englishman who ever lived, I will not judge; but none can doubt that, morally, Milton was by far the superior. His purity of life and nobleness of aim; his constancy to the republican cause after it had been irretrievably ruined; in short, his every act and word, prove his immeasurably the nobler nature. Shakespeare, the Tory and Courtier, had he lived an age later, could never have dared and suffered for his convictions as Milton did for his. Nor, though he has written many finer passages, which have found ten times as many delighted readers as aught of Milton's has found, or perhaps will ever find, can I recall one passage from Shakespeare, which does his manhood such honor as is reflected on Milton's by his two sonnets on his blindness, which, however familiar, I shall make no apology for citing:—

ON HIS BLINDNESS.

When I consider how my light is spent
Ere half my days, in this dark world and wide,
And that one talent which is death to hide,
Lodged with me useless, though my soul more bent
To serve therewith my Maker, and present
My true account, lest he returning chide;
"Doth God exact day-labor, light denied?"
I fondly ask: But Patience, to prevent
That murmur, soon replies, "God doth not need
Either man's work or His own gifts; who best
Bear His mild yoke, they serve Him best: His state
Is kingly; thousands at His bidding speed,
And post o'er land and ocean without rest;
They also serve who only stand and wait."

TO CYRIAC SKINNER.

Cyriac, this three years, day these eyes, though clear,
To outward view, of blemish or of spot,
Bereft of light, their seeing have forgot,
Nor to their idle orbs doth sight appear
Of sun, or moon, or star, throughout the year,
Or man, or woman. Yet I argue not

Against Heaven's hand or will, nor bate a jot
Of heart or hope; but still bear up and steer
Right onward. What supports me, dost thou ask?
The conscience, Friend, t' have lost them overplied
In Liberty's defence, my noble task,
Of which all Europe rings from side to side.
This thought might lead me through the world's vain mask
Content, though blind, had I no better guide.

Such sentiments, not only uttered but *lived*, the efflux of a serene, majestic soul, which calamity could not daunt, nor humiliation depress, not merely honor our common nature, — they exalt and ennoble it. Shakespeare could no more have written thus of himself than Milton could have created and gloated over the character of Falstaff.

Of later English poets, prior to those of the reign of George III., I regard Pope alone as deserving of remark; and he mainly because of the unmeasured eulogies of Byron and others, who certainly should be judges of poetry. For myself, while esteeming him a profound philosopher and moralist, and the king of verse-makers, I should hardly account him a poet at all. "The Rape of the Lock" is undoubtedly a clever poem of the slighter or secondary order; but very much of Pope's verse, had it been cast in the mould of prose, would never have struck us as essentially poetic. For all the poetry they contain, some of his satirical verses might better have taken the form of prose, not to speak of those which, for the sake of decency, had better not been written at all. And so I say of Goldsmith, Thomson, Cowper, Young, and their British cotemporaries: they understood the knack of verse-writing; they did well what they undertook; their effusions — "The Deserted Village," especially — may still be read with a mild and temperate enjoyment; but a thousand such bards would never have created a National Poetry, — never have produced anything which other nations would eagerly translate and delightedly treasure. Essentially, they are not poets, but essayists, sometimes moralists or sermonizers; at others, romancers or story-tellers; but they produced nothing which mankind could not easily spare. Let them glimmer awhile in their decent, inoffensive mediocrity, then sink into a kind oblivion.

The credit of ushering in the brightest era of British Poetry belongs to the Scotch ploughman and rustic, Robert Burns. This man of many faults and sins, who little deemed himself summoned to do the work of a literary reformer, was yet fated to brush aside the sickly sentimentalisms and fantastic conceits of an artificial age, and teach Poetry to speak once more to the soul in accents of Truth and Nature. At the sound of his honest, manly, burly voice, the nymphs and goddesses, the Chloes and Strephons, of a dawdling and unreal generation vanished, and Poetry once more spoke from heart to heart in her own unmuffled, undisguised voice, and was joyfully recognized and welcomed. I know that citations may be made from Burns which would seem to contradict this statement; but they prove only that he was at times fitfully ensnared by the Delilahs whose sorceries he was nevertheless destined to vanquish and conclude. "A man's a man for a' that," "The Twa Dogs," "The Cottar's Saturday Night," and many more such, will for generations be read and admired in the gas-lighted drawing-room, and by the log-cabin fireside, as vindications of the essential and proper nobility of Human Nature, and of the truth that virtue and vice, worth and worthlessness, fame and shame, are divided by no pecuniary, no social, line of demarcation, but may each be found in the palace and in the hovel, — under the casque of a noble or the cap of a boor. In the character and works of Robert Burns is the first answer of the dumb millions to the taunts and slurs of Shakespeare.

The great French Revolution — if I should not rather say, the great mental world-revolution which preceded and impelled the French — ushered in a new era in Literature, and especially in Poetry. Burns was the herald or forerunner of this era, but he did not live to mark its advent.

I do not rank Walter Scott with the poets of our century. Though chronologically his place is among them, he belongs essentially to another epoch, or at least to the period of transition. The morning-star of this era was Keats; its lurid and oft-clouded sun was Byron. Keats was a dreamy and sensitive youth, whose soul found in poetry its natural expression; but who had not attained the maturity of his genius, the perfection of his utterance, when a harsh and withering criticism killed him. Byron was a wild and dissolute young lord, who had made one tolerably good, and many weak, if not inexcusably bad, attempts at poetry, when a severe but just critique stung him to madness, and his wrath and bitterness flashed and glowed into enduring verse. His indignation was volcanic; but the lava it ejected was molten gold,—sulphurous, as volcanic discharges are apt to be. As the death-freighted thunderbolt, which often stuns and slays, has been known to unseal the ears of the deaf and the reason of the idiot, so the harsh discipline which crushed the poet Keats made a poet of the second-rate poetaster Byron.

When I assign to Byron a very high, if not the highest, place among modern English poets, I will only ask those who differ from me to instance another whose writings have been so widely read, or have exerted so marked an influence on the age in which they appeared and the generation then in their teens. I do not commend that influence,—I realize that it does not, on the whole, conduce to a more confiding faith in either God or man. Byron's poems, equally with his life, letters, and conversation, excuse, if they do not justify, De Staël's savage characterization, "He is a demon." Read Cain and Manfred considerately, then take up Goethe's "Faust," and study the *rôle* of Mephistopheles, and you will be tempted to guess, since Goethe could not well have modelled his demon after Byron's life, that Byron must have modelled his character on that of Goethe's devil.

It would be a difficult task to write an honest life of Byron that would be adapted to the use of Sunday schools, unless you were to do as he promised in the opening of Don Juan, but failed to perform, when he gave out that his story would be a moral one, because, before he ended it, he meant—

"to show
The very place where wicked people go."

Yes, this sceptical, cynical, irreverent, law-deriding libertine Byron has made his mark deeply on our century, and not wholly for evil. His honest, profound, implacable hatred of tyranny in every shape, where has it been surpassed, either in intensity or in efficacy? Do you believe Holy Inquisitions and other machinery for torturing and killing men and women for the honest avowal of their religious convictions could endure another year, if every one had read "The Prisoner of Chillon?" You or I may loathe his way of looking at the great problem of Evil; but tell me who ever presented the argument against what is currently termed the Evangelical view of this problem more tersely, strongly, startlingly, than he has done in "Cain, a Mystery"? And his remark that, "if Satan is to be allowed to talk at all, you must not expect him to talk like a clergyman," is obviously just. You must let him fairly present his view of "the great argument," as Milton does not, as Byron does, but with too manifest a leaning to the infernal side. Bind up "Paradise Lost" and "Cain" in one volume, and you will have therein the best condensed statement of the pro and con of the theology currently accounted Orthodox or Evangelical that can be found in the English language.

I think Moore has somewhere said before me, that the Third Canto of Childe Harold contains some of the noblest poetry we have. Waterloo, the Alpine thunder-storm, and scores of passages equally vivid, will at once present themselves to the reader's mind. "Description is my forte," said Byron; and Bayard Taylor, sailing through the Adriatic and the Ægean, along the rugged coast of Dalmatia, and among the ruin-strown, yet flower-mantled, "Isles of Greece," remarks that he finds himself continually recalling or repeating the descriptive stanzas of Childe Harold, suggested by a similar voyage; for nothing else could so truly, forcibly, aptly, embody his own impressions and emotions. Remember that Homer and Æschylus had gazed on much of this same panorama, and written from minds full of the thoughts it excited, and you are prepared to estimate the tribute paid by our American traveller to the genius of Byron. Let me quote one familiar passage — how could I quote any that is *not* familiar? — from Manfred. I cite that respecting the Coliseum, because, having myself seen the moon rise through its ruined arches while Italian devotees were praying and chanting within, and French cavalry prancing and manœuvring without, its enormous walls, I feel its force more vividly than though I had seen this mightiest monument of ancient Rome in imagination only. Yet what could I say of that grandest of ruins to equal this?

"MANFRED.

"The stars are forth, the moon above the tops
Of the snow-shining mountains. — Beautiful!
I linger yet with Nature, for the night
Hath been to me a more familiar face
Than that of man; and in her starry shade
Of dim and solitary loveliness,
I learned the language of another world.
I do remember me, that in my youth,
When I was wandering, — upon such a night
I stood within the Coliseum's walls,
'Midst the chief relics of almighty Rome;
The trees which grew along the broken arches
Waved dark in the blue midnight, and the stars
Shone through the rents of ruin: from afar,
The watch-dog bayed beyond the Tiber; and,
More near, from out the Cæsars' palace came
The owl's long cry, and, interruptedly,
Of distant sentinels the fitful song
Began and died upon the gentle wind.
Some cypresses beyond the time-worn breach
Appeared to skirt the horizon; yet they stood
Within a bowshot. — Where the Cæsars dwelt,
And dwell the tuneless birds of night, amidst
A grove which springs through level battlements,
And twines its roots with the imperial hearths,
Ivy usurps the laurel's place of growth; —
But the gladiator's bloody circus stands,
A noble wreck, in ruinous perfection!
While Cæsar's chambers, and the Augustan halls,
Grovel on earth in indistinct decay.—
And thou didst shine, thou rolling moon, upon

All this, and cast a wide and tender light,
Which softened down the hoar austerity
Of rugged desolation, and filled up,
As 't were anew, the gaps of centuries;
Leaving that beautiful which still was so,
And making that which was not, till the place
Became religion, and the heart ran o'er
With silent worship of the great of old! —
The dead but sceptred sovereigns, who still rule
Our spirits from their urns."

Of Coleridge, Southey, Campbell, Rogers. and other cotemporaries of Byron, Wordsworth excepted, I shall say very little. Each did some things well; but, beyond a few stirring lyrics by Campbell, and perhaps the Christabel and Genevieve of Coleridge, I think our literature could spare them all without irreparable damage.

Wordsworth's ultimate triumph is a striking proof of the virtue of tenacity. Here is a studious, meditative man, of no remarkable original powers, who quietly says to himself, "Intensity of expression, vehemence of epithet, volcanic passion, profusion of superlatives, are out of place in Poetry, which should embody the soul's higher and purer emotions in the simplest and directest terms which the language affords." So he begins to write and the critics to jeer, but he calmly perseveres; and, when it is settled that he *won't* stop writing, the critics conclude to stop jeering, and at length admit that he was a poet all the while, but that their false canons or perverted tastes precluded their discovery of the fact for a quarter of a century. I do not accept Wordsworth's theory, — I believe there are ten persons born each year who are fitted to derive both pleasure and instruction from the opposite school to one who can really delight in and profit by the bare, tame affirmations which are characteristic of Wordsworth (for he, like the founders of other schools, is not always loyal to his own creed), — but that Wordsworth's protest against the intensity of the Byronic school was needed and wholesome, I cannot doubt.

Yet it was not Wordsworth, not "the Lake school," as it

was oddly designated, that led and inspired the reaction against "the Satanic school," so called, of Poetry, by which the later morning of the XIXth century was so mildly irradiated. The credit of that reaction is primarily due to a woman, — to Felicia Hemans. When Byron, still young, was dying in Greece of disappointment, and the remorse which a wasted life engenders, she was just rising into fame among the purest and happiest homes of England, like a full moon rising calmly, sweetly, at the dewy close of a torrid and tempestuous day. It was *her* influence that hushed the troubled waves of doubt and defiance and unrest, and soothed the heaving breast into renewed and trusting faith in virtue, eternity, and God.

I apprehend that Mrs. Hemans finds fewer readers, with far fewer profound admirers, to-day than she had thirty years ago; and in this fact there is a strong presumption that we, who so admired her then, assigned her a higher station than her writings will maintain. A pure and lovely woman, unhappy in her domestic relations, and nobly struggling by literature to subsist and educate her children, is very apt to arouse a chivalry, among readers not only, but critics, that is unfavorable to sternness of judgment. I would gladly believe that the girls of 1868 read Mrs. Hemans as generally, and esteem her as highly, as their mothers did in *their* girlhood; but I fear their brothers, for the most part, neither read nor admire her. Let me venture, therefore, for the sake of my older readers, to cite one of her minor poems, which must recall to many minds hours of pure and tranquil pleasure passed in the perusal of the author's fresh effusions. Forty years ago, had you opened a thousand American weekly newspapers, — presuming that so many then existed, — you would have found the "Poet's Corner" of at least one third of them devoted to one of the latest productions of Mrs. Hemans, and not one fourth so many given up to the verses of any other person whatever. Now, you might open three thousand journals without discovering therein even her name. Bryant, Tennyson, Longfellow, Whittier, Lowell, Holmes, now fill her accustomed place; as, forty years hence, alas! some fresher favorites will fill *their* places. So flows and ebbs this transitory world! But let not us, her old admirers, suffer her name to drift by us into Oblivion's murky sea without a parting cup of remembrance. We will recall

THE ADOPTED CHILD.

"Why wouldst thou leave me, O gentle child?
Thy home on the mountain is bleak and wild, —
A straw-roofed cabin, with lowly wall;
Mine is a fair and pillared hall,
Where many an image of marble gleams,
And the sunshine of picture forever streams."

"O, green is the turf where my brothers play,
Through the long, bright hours of the Summer's day!
They find the red cup-moss where they climb,
And they chase the bee o'er the scented thyme,
And the rocks where the heath-flower blooms they know;
Lady, kind lady, O let me go."

"Content thee, boy! in my bower to dwell;
Here are sweet sounds which thou lovest well:
Flutes on the air in the stilly noon,
Harps which the wandering breezes tune,
And the silvery wood-note of many a bird,
Whose voice was ne'er in thy mountain heard."

"O! my mother sings at the twilight's fall,
A song of the hills far more sweet than all;
She sings it under our own green tree,
To the babe half slumbering on her knee;
I dreamt last night of that music low, —
Lady, kind lady! O, let me go."

"Thy mother is gone from her cares to rest;
She hath taken the babe on her quiet breast;
Thou wouldst meet her footstep, my boy, no more,
Nor hear her song at the cabin door.
Come thou with me to the vineyards nigh,
And we 'll pluck the grapes of the richest dye."

"Is my mother gone from her home away?
But I know that my brothers are there at play:
I know they are gathering the foxglove's bell,
Or the long fern-leaves by the sparkling well;

Or they launch their boats where the bright streams flow,
Lady, kind lady! O, let me go."

"Fair child, thy brothers are wanderers now;
They sport no more on the mountain's brow;
They have left the fern by the spring's green side,
And the streams where the fairy barks were tied.
Be thou at peace in thy brighter lot;
For thy cabin home is a lonely spot."

"Are they gone, *all* gone, from the sunny hill?
But the bird and the blue-fly rove over it still;
And the red-deer bound in their gladness free;
And the heath is bent by the singing bee,
And the waters leap, and the fresh winds blow:
Lady, kind lady! O, let me go!"

I do not know how many ever suspected, during his life, that THOMAS HOOD was a poet of rare and lofty powers. I apprehend, however, that they were, at least till near the close of his career, a "judicious few," — fewer, even, than the judicious are apt to be. For this true bard was nevertheless a man, — though delicate in frame, and for the most part frail in health, he had physical needs, — more than all, he had a wife and children, who looked to him for daily bread, and must not look in vain. Poet as he was, he knew that mankind not only stone their prophets before building their tombs, but starve their poets before glorifying them; and he declined to sacrifice his children's bread to his own glory. The world would not pay cash down for poems, but freely would for fun; so he chose to mint his golden fancies into current coin that would pass readily at the grocer's and baker's, rather than fashion it daintily into cameos and filigree-work, which he must have pledged at ruinous rates with the pawnbroker. And we, generation of blockheads! thought him a rare buffoon, because he sported the cap and bells in our presence, knowing this, though by no means the best thing he could do, decidedly that for which we would pay him best. If his "Whims and Oddities" imply the degradation of a great faculty, is not the fault, the shame, rather ours than his? If a modern Orpheus could only find auditors by fiddling for bacchanal dancers in bar-rooms, could *we* justly reproach him for his vulgar tastes and low associations?

We who so long read and laughed at Hood's puns and quips, — read and only laughed, when we should have thought and sighed, — we might have seen, if we had sought instruction, and not mere recreation, that a great moralist, teacher, philanthropist; an earnest hater of tyranny and wrong; a warrior, with Damascus blade, on cant, and meanness, and servility, — was addressing us in parables which were only wasted, as others' parables have been, because our ears were too gross, our understandings too dull and sordid, to perceive, or even seek, their deeper meaning. We might have discerned the lesson, but did not, because the laugh sufficed us.

Have I seemed to regret or condemn the law whereby the true poet is divorced from the hope of gain by his faculty? I surely did not mean it. Wisely, kindly devised is that Divine ordinance, "Ye cannot serve God and Mammon." The law is steadfast and eternal, — the seeming exceptions few and factitious. The greatest benefactors of mankind have waited till after death for the recognition of their work and their worth. If to speak the highest truths and do the noblest deeds were the sure way to present fame and pelf, what merit would there be in virtue, what place for heroism on earth? If Poetry were the Pennsylvania Avenue to fortune and present fame, how could our earth upbear the burden of her poets? No: it were better for Poetry that there had never been a Copyright Law, so that the Poet's utterances were divorced from all hope of pecuniary recompense. We should then have had far fewer poems, perhaps, but not half the trouble in unburying them from the avalanche of pretentious rhythmical rubbish whereby they are overlaid and concealed. Let aspiring youth evermore understand that writing Poetry is not among the Divinely appointed means for overcoming a dearth of potatoes. I do not say that potatoes were never gained in this way, though I doubt that any were ever thus *earned.* Be this as it may, I am quite sure that no one ever undertook to write Poetry *for* potatoes, — to satisfy his personal need of potatoes by writing Poetry, — who thereby truly succeeded. He may have achieved the potatoes, but not the Poetry. So Hood did manfully and well in writing "Whims and Oddities" for a livelihood, and Poetry for fame alone. Do you suppose the hope of money could ever have impelled any man to write "The Song of the Shirt"?

Let us refresh our remembrance of him with the simplest and best-known of his minor effusions, — one ten thousand times quoted, familiar to almost every school-child, yet not worn out, because it cannot be: —

I REMEMBER, I REMEMBER.

I remember, I remember
The house where I was born,
The little window where the sun
Came peeping in at morn;
He never came a wink too soon,
Nor brought too long a day;
But now I often wish the night
Had borne my breath away!

I remember, I remember
The roses, red and white,
The violets, and the lily-cups, —
Those flowers made of light!
The lilacs where the robin built,
And where my brother set
The laburnum on his birthday, —
The tree is living yet!

I remember, I remember
Where I was used to swing,
And thought the air must rush as fresh
To swallows on the wing;
My spirit flew in feathers then,
That is so heavy now,
And summer-pools could hardly cool
The fever on my brow!

I remember, I remember
The fir-trees dark and high;
I used to think their slender tops
Were close against the sky.
It was a childish ignorance,
But now 't is little joy
To know I 'm farther off from heaven
Than when I was a boy.

How many years is it since he who is England's Laureate first dawned upon us? It seems to me scarcely twenty; yet he must have been writing and printing for nearly twice that period. It is a slow as well as arduous labor for even excellence to make itself felt across an ocean; yet I believe there are to-day as many Americans as Englishmen who honor and delight in the poems of Alfred Tennyson. One of their best characteristics is the carefulness, the evident labor and extreme polish, with which they are produced. After thirty years devoted to Poetry, — almost exclusively, I believe, — his writings may all be compressed within a moderate volume. In an age when many a by no means old man has turned out his twenty volumes, and many a Miss in her teens has nearly finished her third novel, this is a virtue indeed to be commended. To one who has achieved the public ear — for whose future issues eager publishers have checks of generous amount ready to be exchanged for the unread manuscript — the temptation to overwrite is hard to be resisted. Poets are popularly supposed to be, as a class, neither rich nor frugal; the more honor, then, to one who refuses to dilute his nectar like a milkman to whom the pump is convenient. I was deeply interested in Bayard Taylor's anecdote of the German poet Uhland, when in a green old age, who, to the traveller's natural inquiry as to what work he was now composing or meditating, replied that he had not recently felt constrained to write anything, — in other words, that nothing now pressed upon his mind for utterance with irresistible force. Would that authors, as a class, could truly say that they write only under the spur of thoughts burning for expression, — not of appetites clamoring for satisfaction.

Though Tennyson has written sparingly, he has yet covered much ground. "In Memoriam," "The Princess," "Maud," — I hardly know who in our day has produced three poems so unlike, yet each so excellent. "In Memoriam" is probably the best expression of a profound and lasting, yet temperate and submissive, sorrow to be found in our language. Yet his minor poems had made him a world-wide reputation

— made him the Queen's Laureate — before one of these was written, at least before it was published. And they are worthy of their fame. So rich and pure in imagery, so dainty and felicitous in expression, so musical and mellifluous in their rhythm and cadence, — they are rightly ranked among the gems of English literature. Let me cite a part of one of them which is not the most popular, but which seems to me among the happiest. The fable, if fable it be, that eating the lotus brings forgetfulness of care, answering almost to the old Greek's draught from Lethe, is not novel; but who before has ever treated it so well as this?

THE LOTUS-EATERS.

I.

"Courage!" he said, and pointed tow'rd the strand;
"This mounting wave will roll us shoreward soon."
In the afternoon, they came unto a land
In which it seeméd always afternoon.
All 'round the coast, the languid air did swoon,
Breathing like one that hath a weary dream.
Full-faced above the valley stood the moon;
And, like a downward smoke, the slender stream
Along the cliff to fall and pause and fall did seem.

II.

A land of streams! some, like a downward smoke,
Slow-dropping vails of thinnest lawn, did go;
And some through wav'ring lights and shadows broke,
Rolling a slumb'rous sheet of foam below.
They saw the gleaming river seaward flow
From th' inner land: far off, three mountain-tops,
Three silent pinnacles of aged snow,
Stood sunset-flushed: and, dewed with showery drops,
Up-clomb the shadowy pine above the woven copse.

III.

The charméd sunset lingered low adown
In the red West: through mountain-clefts, the dale
Was seen far inland, and the yellow down
Bordered with palm, and many a winding vale
And meadow, set with slender galingale;
A land where all things always seem'd the same!
And 'round about the keel, with faces pale,
Dark faces pale against that rosy flame,
The mild-eyed, melancholy Lotus-eaters came.

IV.

Branches they bore of that enchanted stem,
Laden with flower and fruit, whereof they gave
To each; but whoso did receive of them,
And taste, to him the gushing of the wave
Far, far away did seem to moan and rave
On alien shores; and if his fellow spake,
His voice was thin, as voices from the grave;
And deep-asleep he seemed, yet all awake,
And music in his ears his beating heart did make.

V.

They sat them down upon the yellow sand,
Between the sun and moon, upon the shore;
And sweet it was to dream of Father-land,
Of child and wife and slave; but evermore
Most weary seemed the sea, weary the oar,
Weary the wandering fields of barren foam.
Then some one said, "We will return no more";
And all at once they sang, "Our island home
Is far beyond the wave; we will no longer roam."

* * * * *

Of Robert Browning the reading public knows too little; it shall yet know more. Even in England, I found few whose delight in him equalled my own; and I fairly startled judicious friends by insisting that he is not inferior, on the whole, to Tennyson. But there are obvious reasons why *this* prophet should be denied honor in his own country of all others. For Browning's verse too often lacks clearness; his fancies are piled one upon another in wild confusion; he is fitfully fantastic and mystical; and John Bull has, of all men, the most intense aversion to what is called Transcendentalism. There is an anecdote afloat of Douglas Jerrold meeting a friend in the street soon after Browning's "Sordello" was issued, and thrusting the book into his hands with the fierce command, rather than entreaty, "Read that!" The puzzled friend read a few lines of the opening, and desisted, with the remark, "Why, this is rank nonsense!" "O, thank God!" exclaimed Jerrold; "then I am not mad! I was sure, if that was sense, that I ought to be sent to Bedlam at once." Another anecdote makes Browning gravely relate to an intimate friend that he had tested in Sordello a favorite theory, by omitting in the published copy each alternate line of the poem as written; but he candidly added, the experiment was a failure.

Browning's best issue was that which opens with "The Blot on the Scutcheon," and contains "Pippa Passes," "Luria," and "Paracelsus." The first-named is one of the purest, sweetest, most affecting dramatic poems in our literature; the action hastens to its catastrophe as resistlessly as, and more naturally than, that of Hamlet or Macbeth; and the heroine's dying wail over her lost innocence, her early doom, —

> "I had no mother, — God
> Forsook me, — and I fell,"

has a condensed force and pathos rarely exceeded.

I am apt to have little sympathy with the complaint that an author is obscure. It very often implies only indolence and lack of earnestness in the complainant. We are prone to read too drowsily, and expect writers to spell out their meaning to us, as if we were four-year-olds, still busy with our "a-b-abs" and "baker." There is an anecdote current to this effect, that when Emerson first began to lecture transcendental-wise in Boston, one of his most constant auditors was the able and veteran conservative lawyer, Jeremiah Mason, accompanied by his daughters. His brethren at the bar were puzzled by this addiction on the part of so distinguished a conservative, and wonderingly inquired of him whether he understood what Emerson uttered. He candidly responded that he did not; but added that his daughters (girls of thirteen and fifteen) understood it perfectly. There was probably more truth in this reply than was intended. The kingdom of heaven stands not alone in being easier of access to little children than to adults. Comprehension is not the result of knowledge solely, but of receptivity, of sympathy. It was not nearly so easy for the old lawyer as for the young damsels to attain the same plane of thought with the lecturer, and to travel in the same direction. He might possibly have learned more had he been less wise.

Yet it is deplorably true that our newest literature too often lacks simplicity, lucidity, straightforwardness. It speaks in riddles, when it should be natural, direct, and open as the day. Carlyle is not half so obscure as his contemners declare him; yet his "Sartor Resartus" cannot be thoroughly mastered and enjoyed by the average reader short of three or four perusals; and how many will have patience to give it that number? Whatever requires so many involves the pursuit of knowledge under difficulties. Emerson, though he is no longer opaque, did formerly try the patience, as well as the discernment, of his admirers; and I can quite credit the story told of one who stopped him in the street and recited a passage from one of his essays, asking what he meant by it; to which the author of "Brahma" and "The Sphinx," after pondering the passage a moment, calmly replied that he certainly *had* a meaning in his mind when he wrote that sentence, though it had now unfortunately escaped him. But Browning's fault seems to inhere rather in utterance than in conception; his mind is full of materials ill stowed, which come rushing against and trampling over each other when summoned to daylight, and so choke the aperture and prevent egress, or rush forth an incongruous, confused mass, muddily sweeping all before them. His later writings are half spoiled by this chaotic whirl, and are thence inferior on the whole to their immediate predecessors. Yet what a wealth of allusion, a mine of meaning, a daguerreotype of the intellectual tendencies of the age, are found in "Bishop Blougram's Apology"! And what have we clearer and purer in our language than this? —

EVELYN HOPE.

Beautiful Evelyn Hope is dead!
  Sit and watch by her side an hour.
That is her book-shelf, this her bed;
  She plucked that piece of geranium flower,
Beginning to die, too, in the glass.
  Little has yet been changed, I think;
The shutters are shut; no light may pass,
  Save two long rays through the hinges' chink.

Sixteen years old when she died!
  Perhaps she had scarcely heard my name, —

It was not her time to love; beside,
  Her life had many a hope and aim;
Duties enough, and little cares,
  And now was quiet, now astir,
Till God's hand beckoned unawares,
  And the sweet white brow is all of her.

Is it too late, then, Evelyn Hope?
  What! your soul was pure and true;
The good stars met in your horoscope,
  Made you of spirit, fire, and dew, —
And, just because I was thrice as old,
  And our paths in the world diverged so wide,
Each was nought to each, must I be told?
  We were fellow-mortals, nought beside?

No, indeed! for God above
  Is great to grant, as mighty to make,
And creates the love to reward the love, —
  I claim you still, for my own love's sake!
Delayed, it may be, for more lives yet,
  Through worlds I shall traverse, not a few;
Much is to learn and much to forget,
  Ere the time be come for taking you.

But the time *will* come, — at last it will,
  When, Evelyn Hope, what meant, I shall say,
In the lower earth, in the years long still,
  That body and soul so pure and gay;
Why your hair was amber, I shall divine,
  And your mouth of your own geranium's red, —
And what you would do with me, in fine,
  In the new life come in the old one's stead.

I have lived, I shall say, so much since then,
  Given up myself so many times;
Gained by the gains of various men,
  Ransacked the ages, spoiled the climes:
Yet one thing — one — in my soul's full scope,
  Either I missed or itself missed me, —
And I want and find *you*, Evelyn Hope!
  What is the issue? let us see!

I loved you, Evelyn, all the while,
  My heart seemed full as it could hold, —
There was place and to spare for the frank young smile,
  And the red young mouth, and the hair's young gold.
So, hush! — I will give you this leaf to keep —
  See, I shut it inside the sweet, cold hand;
There — that is our secret! go to sleep;
  You will wake, and remember, and understand.

I envy the biographer of Robert and Elizabeth Barrett Browning. Twenty years ago they were poets, unknown to each other, undistinguished; he poor, and each by no means young. I have heard that their first acquaintance came through their published works, which revealed a sympathy destined to make them one forever. Reversing the usual order, they loved, they became personally acquainted, and were married. Thenceforward, each wrote better, more acceptably, — in the main, more lucidly, — than before; wrote, doubtless, by the help of the other's happy suggestions as well as loving criticisms. And so each won larger and still widening audience, and more generous appreciation, and ampler recompense; and a fair son was born to them; and a wealthy friend, nowise related to either, left them a modest fortune; and they spent their wedded years partly in their native England and partly in their beloved Florence, which inspired both of them, but especially the wife, with some of her noblest and most enduring poems, — "Casa Guidi Windows" for instance, and "Aurora Leigh," — and there, I believe, she died, leaving her husband and son not to lament, but to rejoice over and thank God for, the abiding memory of her worth and her love.

I close this hurried survey without having attempted to consider the claims of any among our countrymen to the character and designation of Poets. I should prefer to consider American Poetry by itself, and in its relations to that which preceded and that which is cotemporary with it. In so doing, we should find, I judge, that, while it has grave faults, — faults of imitation, of poverty, of crudity, of exaggeration, — it has decided merits and excellences also, — merits not only eminent in themselves, but such as give promise of still loftier achievement in the future. If we have contributed our full share to the bounteous Anglo-Saxon stock of shallow and sham poetry, we have also contributed our full quota — considering our youth as a nation, and our prosaic preoccupations, our lack of leisure, and of the highest intellectual culture — to that which the world will not willingly let die. I waive this discussion for the present, however, and close with a more direct consideration of the problem, "What is the essential nature and true office of Poetry?"

Of course, I need waste no more time on the pitiable ignorance which confounds Poetry with Verse, — the eternal essence with the occasional form or garb, — though this delusion has still many votaries, — I might say, victims. The young lady who corrected a friend's allusion to Shakespeare as a Poet with the smilingly confident assurance that his plays were not poetry, not being rhymed, has still sharers in her sad misapprehension. Poetry is at least four thousand years old, — as old as extant literature, if not older; while Rhyme, I suspect, can hardly be traced beyond the time of the Troubadours of western and southern Europe, in the days of the Crusades. Verse, Metre, or Rhythm is of course much older. I presume some rude trace of this may be found in the very oldest writings extant, — the chant or speech in Genesis of Lamech to his wives, for instance, and the oldest Hindoo or Chinese Poems. But, though it may seem natural, and almost necessary, that poetic utterances should flow into harmonious or rhythmical numbers, this is not inevitable. Chateaubriand, one of the greatest poets of the last generation, wrote rarely in verse. Willis has written good verses, but his finest poem is "Unwritten Music," — in structure, a prose essay. That Rhyme is not essential to Poetry, all probably know who clearly know anything; but that measured and duly accented lines, each beginning with a capital letter, do not constitute Poetry, though it may be generally, is by no means universally understood. But we cannot define by negations alone; and the question still recurs, What *is* Poetry?

I understand by Poetry that mode of expression or averment which lifts the soul above the region of mere sense, — which reaches beyond the merely physical or mechanical aspects of the truth affirmed, and apprehends that truth in its universal character and all-pervading relations, so that our own natures are exalted and purified by its contemplation. For instance, I affirm that the Creation was a wondrous, beneficent work, which all intelligent, moral beings cognizant thereof must have regarded with admiration, but that the plans and purposes of God are entirely above the comprehension of Man, — that is plain prose. Now let us see a poetic statement of that same truth, and mark its immensely superior vividness and force: —

"Then the Lord answered Job out of a whirlwind, and said, —
Where wast thou when I laid the foundations of the earth?
Declare, if thou hast understanding!
Who hath laid the measures thereof? if thou knowest?
Or who hath stretched the line upon it?
Whereupon are the foundations thereof fastened?
Or who laid the corner-stone thereof, —
When the morning stars sang together,
And all the sons of God shouted for joy?"

Or I am impelled to observe that the creations of the mind, unlike all corporeal existences, are essentially indestructible, and so fitted to abide and exert influence forever, — that is a prosaic statement of an obvious fact; let us note how Byron presents it in poetry: —

"The beings of the mind are not of clay;
Essentially immortal, they create
And multiply in us a brighter ray,
And more beloved existence — that which Fate
Prohibits to dull life in this our state —
Of mortal bondage, by these spirits supplied
First exiles, then replaces, what we hate,
Watering the hearts whose early flowers have died,
And with a greener growth replenishing the void."

Or I observe that the midnight thunder, during a violent Summer tempest, is echoed from mountain-top to mountain-top, forming a chorus of awful sublimity; but the poet seizes the thought, and fuses it in the glowing alembic of his numbers thus: —

"Far along,
From crag to crag the rattling peaks among,
Leaps the live thunder, — not from one lone cloud,
But *every* mountain now hath found a tongue;
And Jura answers, through his misty shroud,
Back to the joyous Alps, that call to her aloud."

Such instances speak more clearly than the plainest or the subtlest definitions. They show that, to the poetic conception, Nature is no huge aggregation of senseless matter, warmed into fitful vitality by sunbeams only to die and be resolved into its elements, but a living, conscious, vital universe, quivering with deathless aspiration because animated by the breath of God.

Nor must we regard Poetry merely as an *intellectual* achievement, — a trophy of human genius, an utterance from the heart of Nature, fitted to solace its votaries and strengthen them for the battle of Life. Poetry is essentially, inevitably, the friend of Virtue and Merit, the foe of Oppression and Wrong, the champion of Justice and Freedom. Wherever the good suffer from the machinations and malevolence of the evil, — wherever Vice riots, or Corruption festers, or Tyranny afflicts and degrades, there Poetry is heard as an accusing angel, and her breath sounds the trump of impending doom. She cannot be suborned nor perverted to the service of the powers of darkness: a Dante or a Körner, lured or bribed to sing the praises of a despot, or glorify the achievements of an Alva or a Cortes, could only stammer out feeble, halting stanzas, which mankind would first despise, then compassionately forget. But to the patriot in his exile, the slave in his unjust bondage, the martyr at the stake, the voice of Poetry comes freighted with hope and cheer, giving assurance that, while Evil is but for a moment, Good is for ever and ever; that all the forces of the Universe are at last on the side of Justice; that the seeming triumphs of Iniquity are but a mirage, Divinely permitted to test our virtue and our faith; and that all things work together to fulfil the counsels and establish the kingdom of the all-seeing and omnipotent God.

REFORMS AND REFORMERS.

THIS hard, cold, rocky planet, on whose surface we exist, toward whose centre we gravitate, seems to evince but a rugged and wayward kindness for her step-child, Man. Even to the savage, whom she takes to her rough breast with some show of maternal fondness, she says, "Take your chance with my varying moods, — to-day, sunshine, flowers, and bounty; to-morrow, wintry blasts, bare hills, and destitution." What wonder if the poor Esquimaux, shivering in his foodless lodge, which bleak wastes of drifting snow environ, should misread even the serenely benignant skies, and fancy that diabolic was at least equally potent with Divine agency in creating such a world?

To civilized man, unless fenced about and shielded by that purely artificial creation we term Property, Nature presents a still sterner aspect. He may know, even better than the savage, how to extract sustenance and comfort from the elements everywhere surrounding him; but he finds those elements appropriated, — monopolized, — *tabooed,* — the private, exclusive possessions of a minority. To cut in the forest a dead, decaying tree, wherewith to warm his shivering, scarce-clad limbs, — to dig edible roots from the swamp, or gather berries from the beetling crag to stay his gnawing hunger, — is a trespass on the rights of some proprietor, property-owner, landlord, which legally subjects him to the assiduous but disagreeable attentions of the justice and the constable. Doomed to fight his way through this thorny jungle, he finds the weapons all chained out of his reach, or pointed against him. Born into a state of war, he must first forge or buy the requisite implements for the fray, though his adversaries are under no sort of obligation to wait till he is ready. The fertile prairie often produces sour, ungenial grasses; and the giant forest, so luxuriant in its panoply of tender foliage, affords but a grudging subsistence to the few birds and animals which inhabit or traverse it. Everywhere is presented the spectacle of diverse species of animated beings struggling desperately for subsistence, and often devouring each other for food.

Into this unchained menagerie Man is thrust, to fight his way as best he can. The forest, the prairie, the mountain, the valley, the lakes, and the ocean, must be tamed to hear and heed his voice ere they can be relied on to satisfy his urgent needs. The river long obstructs his progress ere he learns the secret of making it bear him swiftly and cheaply on his course; the soil that shall ultimately yield him the amplest harvests is a quaking bog, useless, and hardly passable, until he succeeds in draining and tilling it. The lion or tiger, whom he ultimately regards as a raree-show, and carts about for his diversion, is primarily quite other than amusing, and, though exhibiting himself at less than the "half price" at which children are elsewhere admitted to the spectacle, attracts no curious children of Adam to any exhibition but that of their own heels. The waterfall that propels the civilizee's mill arrests the savage's canoe. In short, Nature, though complaisant at seasons, is yet, in the larger view, grudging and stern toward our race, until transformed and vivified by Labor and Science.

Man, therefore, is by primal necessity a Transformer, — in other words, a Reformer. He must first, by resolute effort, fix his bit in the mouth of Nature, his saddle on her back, and his spurs in her sides, ere he is prepared to run his nobler race and achieve his higher destiny. Though mental development and moral culture be the admitted *ends* of his mundane existence, yet to *begin* with the pursuit of these is to court and insure defeat, by invoking frost and starvation. If the philosopher or divine were to visit the pioneer just slashing together his log hut in the wilderness, and accost him with, "Why wear out your life in such sordid, grovelling, material drudgery, when the gorgeous canopy of heaven overarches you, the glad sun irradiates and warms you, and all Nature, ministering gratuitously to your gross, bodily wants, invites to meditation and elevating self-communion?" the squatter's proper answer, should he deign to give any answer at all, would be: "Sir, I provide first for my bodily needs, and against the fitful inclemencies of the now genial skies, in order that I may by and by have leisure and opportunity for those loftier pursuits you eulogize so justly, though inappositely. I could not fitly meditate on God, the Universe, and Human Destiny, with a shivering wife looking me sadly in the face, nor with the cries of hungry children ringing in my ears. Nay: I could not so meditate this balmy June morning, in full view of the truth that, if I were content with meditation to-day, such *would be* the appeals of those dependent on me ere June should greet us again. What you suggest, then, is excellent in its time and place; but I must hew and delve to-day, in order that my season for contemplation and culture may ultimately come."

Now, this obvious response of the pioneer to the philosopher is in essence the material or circumstantial Reformer's answer to the Stoic and the Saint. "Wealth is dross; Power is anxiety, — is care; Luxury enervates the body and debases the soul," these remonstrate in chorus: "Know thyself, and be *truly* wise; chasten your appetites, and be rich in the *moderation* of your physical wants," adds the Stoic; "Know God, and find happiness in adoring and serving Him," echoes the Saint. "True, O Plato! true, divinest Cecilia! but everything in its order. To render fasting meritorious, one should have meat at command; and great spiritual exaltation springs not naturally from a body gaunt with enforced hunger. Let me surround myself with what is needful for me and mine in the way of food, and clothing, and shelter; not forgetting meantime the nobler ends of my existence, but looking also to these; thus will I achieve for myself Opportunity for that loftier plane of being whereto you so justly invite me. I am not forgetting nor disobeying the injunction to 'Seek first the kingdom of God and His righteousness"; I am only affirming that, until the legitimate physical needs of those dependent on my exertions are provided for, it would not be righteous in me to surrender myself to contemplation, nor even to devotion." And this is substantially the answer of the Reformer of Man's external circumstances to those who insist that the end he meditates is to be attained from *within*, rather than from *without*, — in the apt phrase of Charles Lane, by improvement, not of this or that *circum*stance, but of the vital *centre*-stance. We readily admit this; but what then? The question still recurs, "How is the desired end to be attained?" and we hold that there is no practical cure for the vital woes of the pitiable which does not involve a preliminary change in their outward conditions. You may shower precepts and admonitions, tracts and Bibles, on the squalid, filthy, destitute thousands who tenant, thick as knotted adders, the cellars and rookeries of our great cities, and all will run off them like water from a duck's back, leaving them exactly as it found them. But first take them out of these lairs and lazar-houses, wash them, clothe them decently, and place them where they may, by honest, useful labor, earn a fair subsistence; *now* you may ply them with catechisms and exhortations with a rational hope of advantage. To attempt it sooner, even with seeming success, is only to cover their filthiness with a tenacious varnish of hypocrisy, rendering it less hateful to the eye, but more profound and ineradicable.

But not the Worker only — the robust, earnest Thinker also — is of necessity a Radical. He sees his less fortunate brethren oppressed and degraded, debased and enslaved, through the malign influences of selfish Cunning and despotic Force; and his very soul is stirred within him as was that of Moses by the spectacle of his people's sufferings under the rule of their Egyptian taskmasters. No matter what is the extent or nature of Man's abstract, inherent depravity, he cannot fail to see that men are actually better or worse as they have better or worse instructors, rulers, and institutions. Before condemning Human Nature as incorrigible, and thereupon justifying those who nevertheless contrive to make its guidance and government a gainful trade, he inquires whether this same abused Nature has not done better under other auspices, and becomes satisfied that it has. Then he says to the banded decriers of Human Nature and to the conservatives of old abuses who take shelter under their wing: "You say that Man cannot walk erect; remove your bandages from his feet, your shackles from his limbs, and let us see! You say that he cannot take care of himself; then why compel him, in addition, to take such generous care of *you?* You say he is naturally dishonest and thievish; but how could he be otherwise, when he cannot fail to perceive that you, who set yourselves up for his guides and exemplars, are perpetually and enormously robbing him? Begin by giving back to him the earth which you have taken from under his feet, the knowledge you have monopolized, the privileges you have engrossed; and we can better determine whether he needs anything, and what, from your charity, after he shall have recovered what is rightfully his own."

It is a fearful gift, this of moral prescience,—the ability and the will to look straight into and through all traditions, usages, beliefs, conventionalities, garnitures, and ask: What is this *for?* What does it signify? If it were swept away, what would be really lost to mankind? This baptism, or whatever may be the appliance,—does it really cleanse? Does it even tend to the desiderated result? or does it not rather fortify with a varnish of hypocrisy and a crust of conceit the preëxisting impurity and vice? Is there the old unrighteousness left, with only self-righteousness superadded? Well does a deep thinker speak of the spirit of reform as walking up and down, "paving the world with eyes,"—eyes which not merely inquire and pierce, but challenge, accuse, arraign also. Happily was the prophet of old named a *seer;* for he who rightly and deeply sees thence foresees. Your brawling demagogue is a very empty and harmless personage, — "a voice, and nothing more"; but a silent, unimpassioned thinker, though uttering only the most obvious and universal truths, sets the social caldron furiously seething and bubbling. "Think not that I am come to send peace on earth," says the Prince of Peace; "I am not come to send peace, but a sword." All the rebels, conspirators, Messianic impostors, of that turbulent age, were not half so formidable to Judean conservatism, Roman despotism, as the Sermon on the Mount. And so in our day, a genuine, earnest reformer, no matter in what manger cradled, in what Shaker garb invested, sets all things spinning and tilting around him.

The true Reformer turns his eyes first inward, scrutinizing himself, his habits, purposes, efforts, enjoyments, asking, What signifies this? and this? and wherein is its justification? This daily provision of meat and drink, — is its end nourishment and its incident enjoyment? or are the poles reversed, and do I eat and drink for the gratification of appetite, hoping, or trusting, or blindly guessing, that, since it satiates my desires, it must satisfy also my needs? Is it requisite that all the zones and continents should be ransacked to build up the fleeting earthly tabernacle of this immortal spirit? Is not the soul rather submerged, stifled, drowned, in this incessant idolizing, feasting, pampering of the body? These sumptuous entertainments, wherein the palate has everything, the soul nothing, — what faculty, whether of body or mind, do they brighten or strengthen? Why should a score of animals render up their lives to furnish forth my day's dinner, if my own life is thereby rendered neither surer nor nobler? Why gorge myself with dainties which cloud the brain and clog the step, if the common grains and fruits and roots and water afford precisely the same sustenance in simpler and less cloying guise, and are far more conducive to health, strength, elasticity, longevity? Can a man worthily surrender his life to the mere acquiring and absorbing of food, thus alternating only from the state of a beast of burden to that of a beast of prey? Above all, why should I fire my blood and sear my brain with liquors which give a temporary exhilaration to the spirits at the cost of permanent depravation and disorder to the whole physical frame? In short, why should I live for and in my appetites, if these were Divinely created to serve and sustain, not master and dethrone, the spirit to which this earthly frame is but a husk, a tent, a halting-place, in an exalted, deathless career? If the life be indeed more than meat, why shall not the meat recognize and attest that fact? And thus the sincere Reformer, in the very outset of his course, becomes a "tee-total" fanatic, represented by the knavish and regarded by the vulgar as a foe to all enjoyment and cheer, insisting that mankind shall conform to his crotchets, and live on bran-bread and blue cold water.

Turning his eyes away from himself, he scans the relations of man with man, under which labor is performed and service secured, and finds, not absolute Justice, much less Love, but Necessity on the one hand, Advantage on the other, presiding over the general interchange of good offices among mankind. In the market, on the exchange, we meet no recognition of the brotherhood of the human race. A famine in one country is a godsend to the grain-growers and flour-speculators of another. An excess of immigration enhances the cost of food while depressing the wages of labor, adding in both ways to the wealth of the forehanded, who find their only drawback in the increased burdens of pauperism. Thus the mansion and the hovel rise side by side, and where sheriffs are abundant is hanging most frequent. One man's necessity being another's opportunity, we have no right to be surprised or indignant that the general system culminates, by an inexorably logical process, in the existence and stubborn maintenance of Human Slavery.

Yes, I insist that Slavery is a logical deduction from principles generally accepted, and almost universally accounted sound and laudable. For, once admit the premises that I have a right to seek profit from my neighbor's privations and calamities; that I have a right to consume in idleness the products or earnings of half a dozen workers, if my income will justify the outlay; and that it is better to live indolently on others' earnings than industriously from the proceeds of my own, — and the rightfulness of Slavery is a logical deduction, as plain as that two and two make four. Hence the gambler, the swindler, the pander for gain to others' vices, is always pro-Slavery, or is only withheld from that side by fear of being himself enslaved. You would not on three continents find a pirate or gaming-house bully who would not gladly tramp five miles on a dark, stormy night, to help lynch an Abolitionist. And thus not only have all Reforms a sympathetic, even if ill-understood, relationship, but the *enemies* of reforms are united by a free-masonry equally potent and comprehensive. The negro-trader of Charleston or New Orleans would always help to mob a Temperance lecturer, even though he did not himself drink; for he hated and dreaded the application of ethical laws to practical life. This particular reform did not interfere with his pursuits or his gains; but he felt instinctively that all other reforms were just behind it, — that they were peering over its shoulder, and ready to rush in if this one succeeded in opening the door. So he put his shoulder against it, and held fast, — not that he objected specially to this, but that he would make seasonable resistance to the crowd that came trooping in its train.

It was very common, of old, for the members of diverse parties and sects to protest that they were not Abolitionists, — a most superfluous assurance. Essentially, radically, there are just so many Abolitionists as comprehend that it is better for themselves, better also for their children, to earn their subsistence by fair, honest service to their kind, than to have it supplied them for nothing. He only is truly, inflexibly an Abolitionist who realizes that the faculty of producing or earning bread is as much an element of man's happiness as the ability to consume and relish it. He who idly wishes that Providence had made him heir of a fortune, so that he might have fared sumptuously and lived idly, might just as well sigh outright for John Mitchell's coveted Alabama plantation and fat negroes.

Whether it shall ever be found practicable to substitute a more trustful and beneficent social order for that which now prevails, the sceptics are fully justified in doubting. So many experiments — fairly tried, so far as *they* can see — have resulted in so many failures, that they quite rationally conclude that the Family is the only, or at least the highest, social organization whereof poor, depraved human nature is capable. It is all very well, they fairly say, to talk of the great economies of some theoretic social system, — how much could be saved in fences and fuel, stowage and lights, production and distribution, by uniting five hundred families in one household, on a common domain, rather than scattering them over twice as many acres or twenty-score farms; but, since it is proved that families *cannot* or will not live and labor in this way, what use in commending it? You might as well talk of the superior pavement of the New Jerusalem seen in St. John's vision to that of Broadway or Chestnut Street, and insist that our cities shall henceforth use the former exclusively.

There is much force in this view; but there is more force in one higher and nobler. It is true that men and women educated in the selfish isolation and antagonism of our current households are not qualified — at least, the great mass of them are not — for any better form of society. It is true that this knowledge has been attained through years of patient exertion and sacrifice, — attained by earnest, ardent, self-denying men and women, who would have given their lives to perfect conclusively a contrary demonstration. And, though it is truly urged that these demonstrations were made under very imperfect and unfavorable circumstances, it is equally true that they were the most favorable that could be, and better than can now be, obtained.

We stand, then, in the presence of this state of facts:

On the one hand, it is proved difficult to create and maintain a more trustful and harmonious social structure out of such materials as the old social machinery has formed, — or rather, we may say practically, out of such materials as the old machinery has expelled and rejected; yet we know, on the other hand, that a more — yes, I will say it — Christian Social Order is not impossible. For it is more than half a century since the first associations of the gentle ascetics contemptuously termed Shakers were formed; and no one will pretend that *they* have failed. No: they have steadily and eminently expanded and increased in wealth, and every element of material prosperity, until they are at this day just objects of envy to their neighbors. They produce no paupers; they excrete no beggars; they have no idlers, rich or poor; no purse-proud nabobs, no cringing slaves. So far are they from pecuniary failure, that they alone have known no such word as fail since, amid poverty and odium, they laid the foundations of their social edifice, and inscribed "Holiness to the Lord" above their gates. They may not have attempted the highest nor the wisest achievement; but what they attempted they have accomplished. And, if there were no other success akin to theirs, — but there *is*, — it would still be a demonstrated truth that men and women can live and labor for general, not selfish, good, — can banish pauperism, servitude, and idleness, and secure general thrift and plenty, by moderate coöperative labor and a complete identity of interests. Of this truth, each year offers added demonstrations; but, if all were to cease to-morrow, the fact that it *had* been proved would remain. Perhaps no Plato, no Scipio, no Columbus, no Milton, now exists; but the capacity of the Race is still measured and assured by the great men and great deeds that have been. Man *can* work for his brother's good as well as his own: an unbroken, triumphant experience of half a century has established the fact, so that fifty centuries of contrary experience would not disprove it.

But we are not required to prove the capacity, the adaptability, of Man to a social accord so extreme as Communism.

The practicability of this involves that of every social reconstruction less radical, just as a bushel of grain contains every lesser measure thereof; but the truth of the reverse does not follow. A bank on which every human being, or even every stockholder, might fill up and draw checks at discretion, would soon be broken; but it does not follow that a well-managed joint-stock bank must inevitably fail. Man may yet, in far distant ages, become wise enough, good enough, to realize that Labor is needful to him as food, and that frugality and temperance are essential to long life and sustained enjoyment. But, far this side of that, he may become convinced that he wars on himself in seeking a selfish good, and that only in conjunction with others' happiness can his own be secured. It needs not that he be willing to share his earnings with others, in order that he may realize that every involuntary idler saps the general well-being, and that it is the interest of each to see that there is work and fair recompense for all.

I write in sad and chill November. The skies are sullen and weeping; the ground is reeking mire; and the fierce northwester lingers just behind the Highlands, ready to rush upon the tattered and thin-clad like a pack of famished wolves. Adown the street pace crowds of weary seekers,—seekers once of fame, perhaps, or power, or wealth; but now of food and raiment,—of work and wages. The shop-windows and doors are choked with ship-loads of wares adapted to their urgent physical needs,—everything requisite to eat, and burn, and wear. All these were produced by labor; and the needy are most willing to give labor in exchange for them. The owners, on the other hand, want to sell them,—bought them for that purpose, and must break if the end is not attained. Yet here the two classes stand facing, eyeing each other,—a thin plate of glass dividing them,—the man within anxious to sell, and he without eager to buy,—yet some malignant spell seems to keep them still blankly, helplessly staring at each other. Perhaps a mere combination of the hungry, thin-clad thousands who wishfully, fruitlessly gaze into those windows, would secure the desired result; for here are persons of all kinds as well as grades of ability anxiously seeking work, — that is, seeking opportunity to coin their own exertions into the bread and clothes and shelter they so pressingly need. Say there is no work for them, and their own hunger and rags give you the lie: they themselves collectively afford that very market for their labor for want of which they severally shiver and famish. But the carpenter cannot live on timber, even if he had it; he cannot even build himself the dwelling for want of which his children shiver in some damp basement; and thus the seedy tailor grows daily more ragged, and the unemployed shoemaker despairingly sees his own feet come more and more fully in contact with the frosty, flinty pavement; while the seamstress out of work creeps to her bare garret and prays God that starvation, rather than infamy, may end her long battle, now so nearly lost, for the coarsest and scantiest bread. Legislators! philanthropists! statesmen! there *must* be some way out of this social labyrinth; for God is good, and has not created men and women to starve for want of work. The precept "Six days *shalt* thou labor" implies and predicts work for all; where is it? and what shall supply it? If you cannot or will not solve this problem, at least do not defame or impede those who earnestly seek its solution!

The great, the all-embracing Reform of our age is therefore the SOCIAL Reform, — that which seeks to lift the Laboring Class, as such, — not out of labor, by any means, — but out of ignorance, inefficiency, dependence, and want, and place them in a position of partnership and recognized mutual helpfulness with the suppliers of the Capital which they render fruitful and efficient. It is easily said that this is the case now; but, practically, the fact is otherwise. The man who has only labor to barter for wages or bread looks up to the buyer of his sole commodity as a benefactor; the master and journeyman, farmer and hired man, lender and borrower, mistress and servant, do *not* stand on a recognized footing of reciprocal benefaction. True, self-interest is the acknowledged impulse of either party; the lender, the employer, parts with his money only to increase it, and so, it would seem, is entitled to prompt payment or faithful service,— not, specially, to gratitude. He who pays a bushel of fair wheat for a day's work at sowing for next year's harvest has simply exchanged a modicum of his property for other property, to him of greater value; and so has no sort of claim to an unreciprocated obeisance from the other party to the bargain. But so long as there shall be ten who would gladly borrow to one disposed and able to lend, and many more anxious to be hired than others able and willing to employ them, there always will be a natural eagerness of competition for loans, advances, employment, and a resulting deference of borrower to lender, employed to employer. He who may hire or not, as to him shall seem profitable, is independent; while he who must be hired or starve exists at others' mercy. Not till Society shall be so adjusted, so organized, that whoever is willing to work shall assuredly *have* work, and fair recompense for doing it, as readily as he who has gold may exchange it for more portable notes, will the laborer be placed on a footing of justice and rightful independence. He who is able and willing to give work for bread is not essentially a pauper; he does not desire to abstract without recompense from the aggregate of the world's goods and chattels; he is not rightfully a beggar. Wishing only to convert his own muscular energy into bread, it is not merely his but every man's interest that the opportunity should be afforded him, — nay, it is the clear *duty* of Society to render such exchange at all times practicable and convenient.

A community or little world wherein all freely serve and all are amply served, — wherein each works according to his tastes or needs, and is paid for all he does or brings to pass, — wherein education is free and common as air and sunshine, — wherein drones and sensualists cannot abide the social atmosphere, but are expelled by a quiet, wholesome fermentation, — wherein humbugs and charlatans necessarily find their level, and nought but actual service, tested by the severest ordeals, can secure approbation, and none but sterling qualities win esteem, — such is the ideal world of the Socialist. Grant that it is but a dream, — and such, as yet, it for the most part has been, — it by no means follows that it has no practical value. On the contrary, an ideal, an illusion, if a noble one, has often been the inspirer of grand and beneficent efforts. Moses was fated never to enter the Land of Promise he so longingly viewed from afar; and Columbus never found — who can now wish that he had? — that unimpeded sea-route westward to India that he sought so wisely and so daringly. Yet still the world moves on, and by mysterious and unexpected ways the great, brave soul is permitted to subserve the benignant purposes of God contemplating the elevation and blessing of Man. And so, I cannot doubt, the unselfish efforts in our day for the melioration of social hardships, though their methods may be rejected as mistaken or defective, will yet signally conduce to their contemplated ends. Fail not, then, humble hoper for "the Good Time Coming," to lend *your* feeble sigh to swell the sails of whatever bark is freighted with earnest efforts for the mitigation of human woes, nor doubt that the Divine breath shall waft it at last to its prayed-for haven!

Time will not suffice to speak fully of the efforts, but yesterday so earnest and active, now so languid and unapparent, for the abolition of the legal penalty of Death. Perhaps this effort has already succeeded so far as it was best it should succeed at present, — that is, so far that some States in the West, as others in the East, have absolutely, and others virtually, abolished the Death Penalty. If we could now forget the whole subject for ten years, we might, at the close of that period, compare carefully and searchingly the prevalence of capital crime in the States respectively which have abolished and. those which have retained the Gallows, and strike an instructive balance between them. For the present, let it suffice that no one appears now to be seriously contending that life is less safe or crime more prevalent in the States which destroy no human lives than in others. And, when Society shall for a generation have set a consistent example of reverencing the inviolability of this life, regarding it as a sacred gift from God, which He only may warrantably take away, — we may rationally hope that the example will not be lost, even on those constitutionally prone to outrage, violence, and crime.

Nay, let me venture one more suggestion. The nations, races, ages, most advanced in civilization and knowledge have ever been most reluctant to quench the light of life. Despots and oligarchies have mowed down men by wholesale, where republics and popular governments have generally been forbearing and humane. Every trial of popular sovereignty in Europe has been attended or followed by a mitigation or diminution of sanguinary penalties; and the glorious uprising of '48 would ere this have nearly dismissed the hangman or headsman from the public service, if Royal treachery, courtly conspiracy, and popular levity had not crushed it. And now, in the heyday of Reaction, we hear from time to time of one despot after another, having recovered his throne and his presence of mind, reëstablishing or reinvigorating the Gallows. I rejoice in the hope that the progress of Christianity, civilization, and liberty, will yet drive it altogether from the earth.

I will barely glance at the great problem of Educational Reform, — of the blending of Labor with Study, so as to preserve health of body and vigorous activity of mind, enable the student nearly or quite to work his way through academy and college, and send him out better qualified to wrestle with adversity, instruct the uneducated, and maintain a healthful independence, than he otherwise could be. Not to argue or commend, but simply to state the position of the Reformers, shall be the point of my aim.

The old division of mankind into a numerous, unlearned, or working, and a thinly sown but powerful thinking, directing, educated, governing class, is no longer possible, save in approximation. The principle underlying the Brahminical system of caste is alien to our laws and our intellectual condition. The masses have at least a smattering of knowledge, and more than a shadow of power. They may be educated badly, imperfectly, superficially; they will never again consent to be not educated at all. Ever-increasing millions will be spent on their instruction: shall they thereby be taught what they need to know, or what is adapted to other needs than theirs? An argument will hardly be necessary to show that the training required to make an able and efficient doctor, lawyer, or clergyman, is not that which is essential to the development of a capable and well-informed farmer, mechanic, or civil engineer. Nobody contends that the routine of our colleges is that which is best calculated to fit a youth for eminence as a military or naval commander: why, then, should it be deemed appropriate for our embryo captains of industry? None are more apt to inveigh against the shallowness or quackery of our current applications of science to agriculture, than they who bar the way to our advance to the acquisition of a science of agriculture which shall be neither shallow nor empirical.

The time when to know how to read was proof presumptive of an education for the priesthood can never be recalled. The supposition that methodized knowledge is not as important to the cultivator as to the clergyman is no longer entertained. No wise champion of classical education to-day sadly or sneeringly inquires, with the Apocryphal writer of Ecclesiasticus, "How can *he* get wisdom that holdeth the plough, that glorieth in the goad, that driveth oxen, and is occupied with the care of bullocks?" The spirit that dictated those questions may still linger in some cloistral recesses, some sepulchral caverns, but it no longer stalks abroad outspoken and defiant. It is in our age a thing of night, and must vanish with the dawning of the day.

Well, then: we need and must have a system of higher education which recognizes the truth that Man is by nature a worker, — a fashioner and ruler of matter, — that to be industrious is dictated to him by a beneficent law of his being, and that daily muscular as well as mental effort is among the conditions of his healthful and joyful existence. We need an education which recognizes that God has placed men on earth that they may work, and that every attempt to escape this destiny parallels the original offence of Jonah, and subjects the offender to calamities like to his. We need an education which shall not only regard as an end the forming of more instructed and efficient farmers and artisans than we now have, but the ultimate training of the great mass of our youth to degrees of skill in the choice and use of implements hitherto unknown. To this end, we must have seminaries which not merely provide work for their pupils, but *require* it inflexibly from all, — which educate the head and the hand together, each to be the ally and the complement of the other; which shall teach our aspiring youth, not only *how* to do better than their fathers did in every field of blended intellectual and industrial effort, but *why* this way is better than any other, and in what direction further improvement is to be made. Thus, and thus only, may we expect to elevate our industrial pursuits to that position which they are justly entitled to hold, and render them attractive to our aspiring and noble youth. Every useful vocation is respected in proportion to the measure of intellect it requires and rewards, and never can rise above this level. You may eulogize the Dignity of Labor till doomsday, without making a boot-black's calling as honorable as that of an engineer or a draughtsman; and, so long as an ignorant and stupid boor shall be esteemed wise enough, learned enough, for a competent farmer or mechanic, all spread-eagle glorification of Manual Labor will be demagogue cant and office-seeking hypocrisy. Only through a truer and nobler education can the working masses ever attain the position and the respect which the genius of our institutions predicts and requires for them. And that Education has yet its seminaries to found and its professors to train or discover.

But I must not dwell longer on special Reform movements, though many others challenge our attention. If the few bricks taken almost at random give any fair idea of the character and proportions of the edifice, you will thence perceive, — what many of you, doubtless, have not waited till now to learn, — that what the Reform Spirit of our age labors primarily and generally to establish is the equality of Human Rights, regardless of all disparities of strength, or knowledge, or caste, or creed, or color, — an equality based on the all-embracing moral obligation to consecrate every faculty, every impulse, to the highest good of Humanity. Through all its selfishness, rapacity, folly, and sin, the Genius of our Age speaks to us in tones which the discerning hear and the thoughtful heed; and the burden of its message runs thus: "It is nobler and better to teach the child than to hang the man; — it is wiser to remove temptation from the path of the weak than to punish them because they have stumbled and fallen, — easier to find the vagrant orphan a home, and teach him a trade, than to watch him as a rogue and punish him as a thief, — cheaper and better for Society to find work for all who need and seek it than to support the needy in idleness as paupers, vagrants, or criminals, — nobler to warn than to doom, — more godlike to lift up than to crush down, — and far safer to be surrounded and shielded by gratitude and love than to be walled in with batteries and hedged about by spears." Thus testifies the age of Steam-Presses, Railroads, and Lightning Telegraphs to Statesmen, Legislators, and Rulers; when shall it be fully understood and heeded?

But I have proposed to speak, not only of Reforms, but of Reformers, — a theme somewhat less grand and inspiring. For, indeed, the contrast between the work proposed and the man who proposes and undertakes it is often so broad as to partake of the ludicrous. I have met several in my day who were quite confident of their ability to correct Euclid's Geometry or upset Newton's theory of Gravitation; but I doubt whether one of them could have earned or borrowed two hundred dollars in the course of a year, and nothing stumps an average Reformer of things in general so completely as to be asked to settle his board-bill. I can guess with what awed apprehension the green disciple comes up from some rural hamlet or out-of-the-way village to the metropolis, there to meet for the first time the oracle of some great movement for the regeneration of the world, whose writings he has devoured with wondering admiration; and with what blank surprise he finds himself introduced, at some club-house or restaurant, to said oracle, — a spindling, chattering, personally insignificant entity, who discourses volubly and disjointedly of the times, the crops, and the weather; and never even blunders on a pithy saying, unless when, in the fervor of good fellowship, he orders "Pork Chops for two." But it were hardly fair to ride down Reformers in a body, as a brigade of heavy cavalry might sweep over a pulk of Cossacks; let us analyze the mass with searching and patient discrimination.

The first or lowest class among them I take to be the *envious.* The wide disparity between most men's estimate of themselves respectively, and their neighbors' valuation of the very same article, has been abundantly observed. The number who suppose themselves enormously underrated in the world's opinion is very great; and each believes that he would have long since acquired a fortune or achieved eminence if he had only passed current for all he was worth. The ambitious and conceited, thus stamped in the mint of Society at what they consider a ruinous depreciation, are naturally rebels against the authority which thus disranks and degrades them, — they know that the Social edifice is wrong end up, from the fact that they are so near the bottom of it. And thus thousands fancy themselves Reformers, while their real objection to the world as it is relates not at all to the fashion of the structure, but solely to their own place in it.

Akin to this class is that of the devotees of Sensual Appetite, whose prospective millennium is a period of general license, wherein everybody may do with impunity whatsoever his desires may prompt, — or, at least, *they* may. This class sees the Social world so covered, fettered, interpenetrated, by laws, customs, beliefs, which plant themselves firmly across the path whereon its members are severally pressing forward to the gratification of every impulse, that it is plain that either Society is or they are sadly in the wrong; and imperious Appetite forbids the conclusion that *they* are. If the world as it is would only concede them wealth without industry, enjoyment without obedience, respect without virtue, it would be as good a world now as they could ask for; but since it will not (indeed, cannot) do thus, they make desperate fight against it, just as a vicious and indiscreet bull, it is said, will sometimes butt heads with a locomotive. Byron speaks to us out of the heart of this class, and so forcibly that his statement will hardly be improved. The diction of this school is often nervous; its logic invincible, if only its premises be granted; and its rhetoric really fascinating to those who are in the heyday of youth and its passions; but the understanding is only clouded, it is not convinced, by the inculcations thus incited, and the cooling of the blood gives conscience an opportunity to reassert her long-ignored sovereignty. The free songs, so deliciously warbled and heartily delighted in by bachelor Little, become a scandal and a nuisance to respectable Mr. Thomas Moore, husband of a worthy wife, and father of piano-playing daughters; and thus Social Order, without directly replying to the sophistries or resisting the vagaries of her revolting sons, awaits patiently the inevitable hour when they shall voluntarily kneel at her feet to abjure their treason, beg her forgiveness, and seek absolution.

I think there is a small class whom mere force of will, or, rather, a spirit of antagonism, impels into the service of Reform. These mark how unequal is the battle ever waged between the contending hosts, and are prompted by a chivalrous sentiment to couch a lance on the weaker side. They see how royalties, hierarchies, aristocracies, bourgeoises, all support each other and overbear the opposing array, — how the victory so grandly won by Radicalism to-day only results at last in widening the base and increasing the power of Conservatism; and they mentally say, "Here goes for the side which must triumph, if at all, against immense odds, yet can never enjoy the fruits of a victory!" — and so rush in, to be cut down, thrust back, or metamorphosed, as chance or Providence may determine.

For indeed the argument for Conservatism is intrinsically so strong, that only the maddest unwisdom, the most preposterous displays of selfishness, on the part of its champions, could possibly overthrow it. No monarchy was ever undermined or overturned except through some monarch's own blunders or crimes, and none ever will be. If ever man of wealth were so timorous as to fear that the houseless, shivering wretches in the streets would eject the possessors of stately, comfortable mansions, and sit down securely in their places, he evinced a want of sagacity at least equal to his want of nerve. If a city could be sacked by its desperate denizens, the first set who effected a lodgement in its palaces would make haste to shoot the residue of the rabble horde for their own security, and so would weaken themselves beyond the possibility of maintaining their dizzy altitude. Radicalism is the tornado, the earthquake, which comes, acts, and is gone for a century; Conservatism is the granite, which may be chipped away here or there to build a new house, or let a railroad pass, but which will substantially abide forever.

The argument for Conservatism appeals resistlessly to all who have good digestive organs which they cherish, with anything satisfactory whereon to employ them. The natural presumption that whatever has stood the shocks and mutations of centuries is deeply grounded in Nature and the Divine purpose, is wellnigh invincible. "I grant you," says the Conservative, "that many things seem rather out of tune; but what then? Is it *my* duty to upset what so many great and good men have left untouched, and some of them have expressly commended? That the world is full of ignorance and wrong, crime and woe, is very true; but *I* cannot help that; and it will do no good to shed gallons of tears over it, and try to put others into mourning. No: let us take things as we find them; relieve distress when we can afford it, and float along as nearly with the current as will answer. Bad as the world is, a man with good fortune, (which includes health,) a reasonable self-control, a tolerably clear conscience, a well-filled store-house, and a fair balance with his banker, may extract a good deal of enjoyment from it, if he will wisely improve his opportunities, and not insist on making himself miserable by dabbling too deeply in the miseries of others." Millions *live* all of this, who do not *say* more than half of it.

Perhaps one of the most instructive spectacles is that of the impulsive young Radical undergoing a gradual transformation, or cooling off, into a staid, respectable Conservative, with property to care for, a position to maintain, and a reputation to cherish. He was honest of yore, and is honest (as the world goes) now; but circumstances alter cases. When he declaimed against the monopoly or aggregation of lands, he had none of his own; but he has since become "seized," as the lawyers say, of a snug estate, and he would not like to have any one seize it away from him. It may be larger than one man absolutely needs; but he wants to improve it, and it will cut up nicely among his rather numerous children or nephews. So he builds him an elegant mansion, surrounds and fills it with evidences of taste and ministers to luxury, and sits down to contemplate matters in general more calmly and philosophically than he did in his impulsive, headlong youth. And the great world without takes on a very different aspect when viewed through his elegant shrubbery, adown his velvet lawn, and colored rosily by the bumper of generous juice which often gets between his eyes and the distant prospect, from that it wore when viewed with naked optics, or with only a cup of crystal water between him and the sun. "Yes," he says, slowly and languidly, "there *is* need of Reform; but let it be effected prudently and decorously. These *modern* Radicals are different from those of *my* young days: they are rash, reckless, destructive, infidel; I can have no sympathy, no fellowship, with such." True, O Plutus! you can have none. But "prudently," did you say, sir? Ah no! Reforms of any depth will *never* be urged prudently and cautiously; for, if their advocates were prudent, they would not be Reformers at all. Very likely, Prudence may step in at the opportune moment, and mediate successfully between heedless Innovation and stubborn Reaction; but to wait for Prudence to *impel* a Reform is to wait for Death to originate Life.

And, indeed, the embarrassment of headlong allies is one of the chief sorrows of the Reformer's lot. He can never say "A" without some one else following with a "B" which he is sure does not belong to the same alphabet; but this the other as confidently denies; and the whole Conservative party backs the latter with all its force. Luther's career was perpetually made thorny by this sort of unwelcome allies, and Bossuet knew exactly from what armory to draw the most deadly shafts to hurl against the advancing hosts of the Reformation. "If you assert this, how will you defend your position against him who will manifestly assert that? If you put the Bible above the Church, how answer him who puts Reason above the Bible? If you insist that every *man* shall be allowed to vote, how resist the demand that every *woman* be equally enfranchised? If you repudiate *vindictive* punishments, how justify punishment at all?" I think it was Brougham who observed, that there never yet was a Reform proposed that might not have been defeated by giving adequate weight to the question, "If you go so far, why not farther? If this be right, is not more equally right? And where can you consistently stop?" And thus many a fiery Radical has been cooled down into placid (or acrid) Conservatism, by discovering that the character of his associates, the tendency of their doctrines, the ends which they contemplated, were such as he could never approve.

I presume there are not many Reformers worthy of the designation who ever anticipated fame or wealth as a result of their labors in the cause of Humanity. Yet I recollect an application once made to me by a particularly green youth, who wished employment as a writer or journalist, urging as an inducement that he thought he could indite some forcible essay in favor of the Reforms wherein I was deeply interested. "My friend," I felt constrained to reply, "I can very easily write myself quite as much in favor of those Reforms as the public will bear; another such hand at the bellows would ruin me." Conservatism has many faults, but it is a good paymaster; while Radicalism is constitutionally out at the elbows, and may toss you its purse with ever so lordly an air, but all you take by the motion is a poor sixpenny worth of dried eelskin. True, now and then a Reformer lives to fight out *his* special battle, and secure the hard-won triumph of his well-directed, persistent effort. But by this time Conservatism has taken the bantling into *her* snug house, there to fondle and cherish it as her own; while Radicalism has swept on to new efforts, new struggles, perhaps ultimately new triumphs: so the forlorn Reformer stands shivering at the remorseless door which has engulfed *his* darling; he cannot hope to overtake the rushing host, which is now far on its eager way, and indeed he has no heart for the attempt; so he commonly ends by begging admittance into the mansion, and the privilege of now and then fondling the baby, which coolly eyes the queer, old, seedy codger, and wonders how *he* ever wormed his way into the hallowed precincts of Respectability and Elegance. *He* says nothing, for his heart is too full; but gathers up his tattered garments and dies, looking fondly, sadly, on that cold, averted face to the last.

To the earnest, true Reformer, life is indeed no holiday

feast, and earth no Eden garnished with singing-birds and flowers. The most sanguine, buoyant soul, once fairly entered on this career, is not long in learning how much stronger is old Adam than young Melancthon. Not merely that his bread is apt to be coarse and his couch somewhat rugged, — he was prepared for this, — but the intractability of ignorance, the stubbornness of prejudice, the thanklessness of those arrested in a downhill career, the inefficiency of effort, and "the heart-sickness of hope deferred," are indeed appalling. Doubting, irresolute Hamlet may well be distracted, not so much by the fact that "the times are out of joint," as that *he* seems to have been "born to set things right." For the moral dangers of the Reformer's calling are even more disheartening than its pecuniary discouragements. "Do you know," said a broken-down ex-lecturer for Temperance, Anti-Slavery, &c., &c., once to me, in a tone and with a look of deep meaning, "that there is no life so *unhealthy* as that of a popular agitator?" The "patriot to a brewery" may even enjoy it; but for the proud, shy, home-bred man, who would rather see the smile on the face of the loved one than be the subject of a civic ovation, and rather hear the idle prattle of his babes than the shouts of clustered thousands responsive to his burning words, it is a cold, stern life that he leads; and he labors under constant apprehensions that, while he is striving to diffuse sentiments of benignity, generosity, and mercy, the milk of human kindness, by reason of those very efforts, is slowly drying up in his own breast, and he, while still struggling earnestly, though somewhat mechanically, to redeem the human race, is coming gradually to dislike and despise them.

The most striking, perhaps the only general, tribute ever paid to the position and merits of the true Reformer is that embodied in the universal jeer and shout which announces the exposure of the fallen aspirant or false pretender. As there was never a villain who did not hail with hearty exultation the exposure of a priest's lechery or a moralist's knavery, so the lazy, sensual, luxury-loving, money-grasping million enjoy nothing more keenly than the tidings that one who has reproved their selfishness and made them uncomfortable by his projects of social melioration or homilies on human brotherhood has at length been tempted into sin, or turned inside out by some casual revelation, and proved as selfish and venal as themselves. As the news is rapidly disseminated, the face of sensualism and self-seeking broadens into one universal grin, — peal after peal of "unextinguished laughter" disturbs the serenity of the atmosphere, — you might suspect from hearing it that everybody's uncle had died, and left him heir to a bounteous fortune. The grandest Hebrew prophet, looking on such a spectacle, might forcibly say, as of old: "Hell from beneath is stirred up to meet thee; it stirreth up its denizens to inquire exultingly, 'Art thou also become as one of us?'" And thus the Reformer who, while he stood erect, seemed beneath the meanest, — more hated, reviled, and despised, — shall prove by his fall that he was dreaded, and really honored, as well; that the devils contemplated his efforts in the spirit which believes and trembles; that those who most defamed and misrepresented, yet secretly respected and wished themselves virtuous enough to be almost, if not altogether, such as he. And thus a career which in its progress seemed despised and reprobated shall yet in its defeat and ruin prove to have been really admired and honored, even by those who lacked virtue to imitate or even commend it.

Yet this shout from the nethermost *hades* is by no means justified by the fact on which it is based. Men are often weak and fallible in action, even though their intellectual perception of the right is of the deepest and clearest. Bacon's philosophy is sound and valuable, though Bacon was a corrupt chancellor, a bribed judge. The earth *does* move, in accordance with Galileo's hypothesis, though Galileo himself was induced by ghostly fulminations and personal perils to recant it. Peter might have denied and blasphemed till doomsday without belittling or confounding that salvation of which he had been chosen a witness and an apostle. Few men are equal in their daily lives to the moral altitude of their highest perceptions; and all the confessors and martyrs might apostatize, and heap shame on their own heads, without detracting one iota from the worth of philanthropy or Christianity. Man is a reed which the slightest breeze deflects, the feeblest step prostrates; but Truth is adamant and eternal.

Yes, it is a great thing to be truly a Reformer, even one misinterpreted and scorned through life, as what genuine Reformer ever failed to be. The tombs of the dead prophets are built only of the stones hurled at them while living; and thus may we accurately measure the greatness of their daring, the force and truth of their unprecedented utterances. To speak firmly the word destined ultimately to heal Man's deadliest maladies, yet certain instantly to evoke his direst curses — this is a heroism whereof no other forlorn hope than that of Humanity is capable. Idly, weakly, shall the timidly perspicacious hope to speak the great truth, yet not offend the beneficiaries of current falsehoods; to declare the true God, yet excite no uproar among Diana's silversmiths. The world was never created, and is not governed, so that Policy and Principle, Time and Eternity, God and Mammon, can all be served together. If they could be, Virtue would be merely shrewdness, and blindness the physical synonyme of evil.

But what then? Do we say that the path of Rectitude is thorny and craggy, and that the only verdure and balmy sunshine that approach it are those of the adjacent, alluring byways of Luxury and Ease, leading down to the garden of Sensual Pleasure? By no means. What is affirmed is not that Truth's service is necessarily one of privation and suffering, but that the true soldiers never choose it as the way of ease, of ambition, or from any selfish consideration whatever, but because it is the way of Right. "Necessity is upon me," says the true Apostle; his course is one dictated to him by considerations higher than any hopes of heaven, deeper than any fears of hell. Doubtless, to the eye of sense, his career seems dwarfish, his aspirations baffled, his life a defeat and a failure. But he has never appealed to the ordeal of sense, and feels under no obligation to accept its judgments. Who shall say that Nebuchadnezzar on his throne is happier than Daniel in his prison? or that Herod in his palace, gorged with Epicurean dainties, and gloating over voluptuous music and dancing, is more blest than the uncouth, stern-souled Baptist, striding in solitary hunger over sun-scorched deserts of rock and sand, — very far from luxury, but very near to God, — or contemplating his swiftly approaching death in a malefactor's dungeon? Jerusalem and the Temple, the Palace and its gardens, are the possessions of the former; but what are they to the celestial splendors, the eternal verities, which are present to the rapt, adoring gaze of the latter, and gild the visions of his rocky couch with a glory inconceivable to the apprehension of the Sadducee?

These two can never understand each other while they remain essentially as now. The unbelief that questions, and cavils, and scruples, and doubts, and denies, seems to him incomparably less virulent and fearful than that which makes mitres and triple-crowns counters of a sordid ambition, and shakes the keys of eternal bliss or woe in the face of long-suffering millions, to make them bow their necks passively to the yoke of a soul-crushing despotism.

For, indeed, to the Reformer's apprehension, nothing can be more absurd than the dread of irreligion professed by men whose daily lives are a proclamation of indifference to the wants and wrongs of the benighted and destitute, — who are so intent on having the Poor evangelized, that they do not ask how they are to be fed, — and who act as though a plentiful distribution of tracts and Bibles would alone suffice to banish evil from the earth.

To the Conservative, Religion would seem often a part of the subordinate machinery of Police, having for its main object the instilling of proper humility into the abject, of contentment into the breasts of the down-trodden, and of enduing with a sacred reverence for Property those who have no personal reason to think well of the sharp distinction of Mine and Thine. The Reformer, on the other hand, insists on Humanity as the inevitable manifestation of all true Religion, presses the best-beloved Apostle's searching question, "If a man love not his brother, whom he *has* seen, how can he love God, whom he has *not* seen"? or, as a poet of our own day has phrased it, affirms that there

"are infidels to Adam worse than infidels to God,"

and that the effective answer to an imperfect, halting faith, is a devoted, loving life.

This earnest, angry strife shall yet be composed, — this stormy clamor be hushed, — not through the absolute defeat of either party, but through the recognition by each of the truth affirmed by the other, so that Conservatism and Reform shall take their places side by side on the same platform, and Faith and Life, Humanity and Christianity, be recognized by our enlarged vision as halves of the same unit, planets revolving around and lighted in turn by the same sun of Everlasting Truth. Meantime, let us cherish the Reformer! for his, and not the Conservative's, is the active, aggressive force through which this ultimate harmonization of the Real with the Ideal is to be achieved. Harsh and sweeping, rash and destructive, he may seem, and often is; but his fire, however blind and indiscriminate its rage, will be found at last to have left unconsumed all that was really worth preserving. With him, while we respect the proper force and legitimate function of Conservatism, we must say —

"Standing still is childish folly;
Going backward is a crime;
None should patiently endure
Any ill that he can cure:
ONWARD! keep the march of Time!
ONWARD! while a wrong remains
To be conquered by the right,

While Oppression lifts a finger
To affront us by his might,
While an error clouds the reason
Of the universal heart,
Or a slave awaits his freedom,
ACTION is the wise man's part."

And *to* him our final word of gratitude and cheer shall fitly be—

"We thank thee, watcher on the lonely tower,
For all thou tellest of the coming hour
When Error shall decay and Truth grow strong,
And Right shall rule supreme and vanquish Wrong."

And, indeed, though the life of the Reformer may seem rugged and arduous, it were hard to say considerately that any other were worth living at all. Who can thoughtfully affirm that the career of the conquering, desolating, subjugating warrior, — of the devotee of Gold, or Pomp, or Sensual Joys; the Monarch in his purple, the Miser by his chest, the wassailer over his bowl, — is not a libel on Humanity and an offence against God? But the earnest, unselfish Reformer, — born into a state of darkness, evil, and suffering, and honestly striving to replace these by light, and purity, and happiness, — he may fall and die, as so many have done before him, but he cannot fail. His vindication shall gleam from the walls of his hovel, his dungeon, his tomb; it shall shine in the radiant eyes of uncorrupted Childhood, and fall in blessings from the lips of high-hearted, generous Youth. As the untimely death of the good is our strongest moral assurance of the Resurrection, so the life wearily worn out in doubtful and perilous conflict with Wrong and Woe is our most conclusive evidence that Wrong and Woe shall yet vanish forever. Luther, dying amid the agonizing tears and wild consternation of all Protestant Germany, — Columbus, borne in regal pomp to his grave by the satellites of the royal miscreant whose ingratitude and perfidy had broken his mighty heart, — Lovejoy, pouring out his life-blood beside the Press whose freedom he had so gallantly defended, — yes, and not less majestic, certainly not less tragic, than either, the lowly and lonely couch of the dying 'Uncle Tom,' whose whole life had been a brave and Christian battle against monstrous injustice and crime, — these teach us, at least, that all true greatness is ripened, and tempered, and proved, in life-long struggle against vicious beliefs, traditions, practices, institutions; and that not to have been a Reformer is not to have truly lived. Life is a bubble which any breath may dissolve; Wealth or Power a snow-flake, melting momently into the treacherous deep across whose waves we are floated on to our unseen destiny; but to have lived so that one less orphan is called to choose between starvation and infamy, — one less slave feels the lash applied in mere wantonness or cruelty, — to have lived so that some eyes of those whom Fame shall never know are brightened and others suffused at the name of the beloved one, — so that the few who knew him truly shall recognize him as a bright, warm, cheering presence, which was here for a season and left the world no worse for his stay in it, — this surely is to have really *lived*, — and not wholly in vain.

THE GROUNDS OF PROTECTION.*

MR. PRESIDENT AND RESPECTED AUDITORS: —

IT has devolved on me, as junior advocate for the cause of Protection, to open the discussion of this question. I do this with less diffidence than I should feel in meeting able opponents and practised disputants on almost any other topic, because I am strongly confident that you, my hearers, will regard this as a subject demanding logic rather than rhetoric, the exhibition and proper treatment of homely truths, rather than the indulgence of flights of fancy. As sensible as you can be of my deficiencies as a debater, I have chosen to put my views on paper, in order that I may present them in as concise a manner as possible, and not consume my hour before commencing my argument. You have nothing of oratory to lose by this course; I will hope that something may be gained to my cause in clearness and force. And here let me say that, while the hours I have been enabled to give to preparation for this debate have been few indeed, I feel the less regret in that my *life* has been in some measure a preparation. If there be any subject to which I have devoted time, and thought, and patient study, in a spirit of anxious desire to learn and follow the truth, it is this very question of Protection; if I have totally misapprehended its character and bearings, then am

* Speech at the Tabernacle, New York, February 10, 1843, in public debate on this resolution: —

Resolved, That a Protective Tariff is conducive to our National Prosperity.

Affirmative:	JOSEPH BLUNT,	Negative:	SAMUEL J. TILDEN,
	HORACE GREELEY.		PARKE GODWIN.

I ignorant, hopelessly ignorant indeed. And, while I may not hope to set before you, in the brief space allotted me, all that is essential to a full understanding of a question which spans the whole arch of Political Economy, — on which abler men have written volumes without at all exhausting it, — I *do* entertain a sanguine hope that I shall be able to set before you considerations conclusive to the candid and unbiassed mind of the policy and necessity of Protection.

Let us not waste our time on non-essentials. That unwise and unjust measures have been adopted under the *pretence* of Protection, I stand not here to deny; that laws *intended* to be Protective have sometimes been injurious in their tendency, I need not dispute. The logic which would thence infer the futility or the danger of Protective Legislation would just as easily prove *all* laws and all policy mischievous and destructive. Political Economy is one of the latest-born of the Sciences; the very fact that we meet here this evening to discuss a question so fundamental as this proves it to be yet in its comparative infancy. The sole favor I shall ask of my opponents, therefore, is that they will not waste their efforts and your time in attacking positions that we do not maintain, and hewing down straw giants of their own manufacture, but meet directly the arguments which I shall advance, and which, for the sake of simplicity and clearness, I will proceed to put before you in the form of Propositions and their Illustrations, as follows: —

Proposition I. A NATION WHICH WOULD BE PROSPEROUS, MUST PROSECUTE VARIOUS BRANCHES OF INDUSTRY, AND SUPPLY ITS VITAL WANTS MAINLY BY THE LABOR OF ITS OWN HANDS.

Cast your eyes where you will over the face of the earth, trace back the History of Man and of Nations to the earliest recorded periods, and I think you will find this rule uniformly prevailing, that the nation which is eminently Agricultural and Grain-exporting, — which depends mainly or principally on other nations for its regular supplies of Manufactured fabrics, — has been comparatively a *poor* nation, and

34

ultimately a *dependent* nation. I do not say that this is the *instant* result of exchanging the rude staples of Agriculture for the more delicate fabrics of Art; but I maintain that it is the inevitable *tendency.* The Agricultural nation falls in debt, becomes impoverished, and ultimately subject. The palaces of "merchant princes" may emblazon its harbors and overshadow its navigable waters; there may be a mighty Alexandria, but a miserable Egypt behind it; a flourishing Odessa or Dantzic, but a rude, thinly peopled southern Russia or Poland; the exchangers may flourish and roll in luxury, but the producers famish and die. Indeed, few old and civilized countries become largely exporters of grain until they have lost, or by corruption are prepared to surrender, their independence; and these often present the spectacle of the laborer starving on the fields he has tilled, in the midst of their fertility and promise. These appearances rest upon and indicate a law, which I shall endeavor hereafter to explain. I pass now to my

Proposition II. THERE IS A NATURAL TENDENCY IN A COMPARATIVELY NEW COUNTRY TO BECOME AND CONTINUE AN EXPORTER OF GRAIN AND OTHER RUDE STAPLES AND AN IMPORTER OF MANUFACTURES.

I think I hardly need waste time in demonstrating this proposition, since it is illustrated and confirmed by universal experience, and rests on obvious laws. The new country has abundant and fertile soil, and produces Grain with remarkable facility; also, Meats, Timber, Ashes, and most rude and bulky articles. Labor is there in demand, being required to clear, to build, to open roads, &c., and the laborers are comparatively few; while, in older countries, Labor is abundant and cheap, as also are Capital, Machinery, and all the means of the cheap production of Manufactured fabrics. I surely need not waste words to show that, in the absence of any counteracting policy, the new country will import, and continue to import, largely of the fabrics of older countries, and to pay for them, so far as she may, with her Agricultural staples. I will endeavor to show hereafter that she will continue to do this long after she has attained a condition to manufacture them as cheaply for herself, even regarding the *money* cost alone. But that does not come under the present head. The whole history of our country, and especially from 1782 to '90, when we had no Tariff and scarcely any Paper Money, — proves that, whatever may be the Currency or the internal condition of the new country, it will continue to draw its chief supplies from the old, — large or small according to its measure of ability to pay or obtain credit for them; but still, putting Duties on Imports out of the question, it will continue to buy its Manufactures abroad, whether in prosperity or adversity, inflation or depression.

I now advance to my

Proposition III. IT IS INJURIOUS TO THE NEW COUNTRY THUS TO CONTINUE DEPENDENT FOR ITS SUPPLIES OF CLOTHING AND MANUFACTURED FABRICS ON THE OLD.

As this is probably the point on which the doctrines of Protection first come directly in collision with those of Free Trade, I will treat it more deliberately, and endeavor to illustrate and demonstrate it.

I presume I need not waste time in proving that the ruling price of Grain (as of any Manufacture) in a region whence it is considerably exported, will be *its price at the point to which it is exported, less the cost of such transportation.* For instance: the cost of transporting Wheat hither from large grain-growing sections of Illinois was last fall sixty cents; and, New York being their most available market, and the price here ninety cents, the market there at once settled at thirty cents. As this adjustment of prices rests on a law obvious, immutable as gravitation, I presume I need not waste words in establishing it.

I proceed, then, to my next point. The average price of Wheat throughout the world is something less than one dollar per bushel; higher where the consumption largely exceeds the adjacent production, — lower where the production largely exceeds the immediate consumption (I put out of view in this statement the inequalities created by Tariffs, as I choose at this point to argue the question on the basis of universal Free Trade, which is of course the basis most favorable to my opponents). I say, then, if all Tariffs were abolished to-morrow, the price of Wheat in England — that being the most considerable ultimate market of surpluses, and the chief supplier of our manufactures — would govern the price in this country, while it would be itself governed by the price at which that staple could be procured in sufficiency from other grain-growing regions. Now, Southern Russia and Central Poland produce Wheat for exportation at thirty to fifty cents per bushel; but the price is so increased by the cost of transportation that at Dantzic it averages some ninety and at Odessa some eighty cents per bushel. The cost of importation to England from these ports being ten and fifteen cents respectively, the actual cost of the article in England, all charges paid, and allowing for a small increase of price consequent on the increased demand, would not, in the absence of all Tariffs whatever, exceed one dollar and ten cents per bushel; and this would be the average price at which we must sell it in England in order to buy thence the great bulk of our Manufactures. I think no man will dispute or seriously vary this calculation. Neither can any reflecting man seriously contend that we could purchase forty or fifty millions' worth or more of Foreign Manufactures per annum, and pay for them in additional products of our Slave Labor — in Cotton and Tobacco. The consumption of these articles is now pressed to its utmost limit, — that of Cotton especially is borne down by the immense weight of the crops annually thrown upon it, and almost constantly on the verge of a glut. If we are to buy our Manufactures principally from Europe, we must pay for the additional amount mainly in the products of Northern Agricultural industry, — that is universally agreed on. The point to be determined is, whether we could obtain them abroad cheaper — *really* and positively cheaper, all Tariffs being abrogated — than under an efficient system of Protection.

Let us closely scan this question. Illinois and Indiana, natural grain-growing States, need Cloths; and, in the absence of all Tariffs, these can be transported to them from England for two to three per cent. of their value. It follows, then, that, in order to undersell any American competition, the British Manufacturer need only put his cloths at his factory *five* per cent. below the wholesale price of such cloths in Illinois, in order to command the American market. That is, allowing a fair broadcloth to be manufactured in or near Illinois for three dollars and a quarter per yard, cash price, in the face of British rivalry, and paying American prices for materials and labor, the British manufacturer has only to make that same cloth at three dollars per yard in Leeds or Huddersfield, and he can decidedly undersell his American rival, and drive him out of the market. Mind, I do not say that he *would* supply the Illinois market at that price *after* the American rivalry had been crushed; I know he *would not;* but, so long as any serious effort to build up or sustain Manufactures in this country existed, the large and strong European establishments would struggle for the additional market which our growing and plenteous country so invitingly proffers. It is well known that in 1815 – 16, after the close of the Last War, British Manufactures were offered for sale in our chief markets at the rate of "*pound for pound,*" — that is, fabrics of which the first cost to the manufacturer was $ 4.44 were offered in Boston market at $ 3.33, duty paid. This was not sacrifice, — it was dictated by a profound forecast. Well did the foreign fabricants know that their self-interest dictated the utter overthrow, at whatever cost, of the young rivals which the war had built up in this Country, and which our Government and a majority of the People had blindly or indolently abandoned to their fate. William Cobbett, the celebrated Radical, but with a sturdy English heart, boasted upon his first return to England that he had been actively engaged here in promoting the interests of his country by compassing the destruction of

American Manufactories in various ways which he specified, — "*sometimes* (says he) *by Fire*." We all know that great sacrifices are often submitted to by a rich and long-established stage-owner, steamboat proprietor, or whatever, to break down a young and comparatively penniless rival. So in a thousand instances, especially in a rivalry for so large a prize as the supplying with Manufactures of a great and growing Nation. But I here put aside all calculations of a temporary sacrifice; I suppose merely that the foreign manufacturers will supply our Grain-growing States with Cloths at a trifling profit so long as they encounter American rivalry; and I say it is perfectly obvious that, if it cost three dollars and a quarter a yard to make a fair broadcloth in or near Illinois, in the infancy of our arts, and a like article could be made in Europe for three dollars, then the utter destruction of the American manufacture is inevitable. The Foreign drives it out of the market and its maker into bankruptcy; and now our farmers, in purchasing their cloths, "buy where they can buy cheapest," which is the first commandment of Free Trade, and get their cloth of England at three dollars a yard. I maintain that this would not last a year after the American factories had been silenced, — that then the British operator would begin to think of *profits* as well as bare cost for his cloth, and to adjust his prices so as to recover what it had cost him to put down the dangerous competition. But let this pass for the present, and say the Foreign Cloth is sold to Illinois for three dollars per yard. We have yet to ascertain how much she has gained or lost by the operation.

This, says Free Trade, is very plain and easy. The four simple rules of Arithmetic suffice to measure it. She has bought, say a million yards of Foreign Cloth for three dollars, where she formerly paid three and a quarter for American; making a clear saving of a quarter of a million dollars.

But not so fast, — we have omitted one important element of the calculation. We have yet to see what effect the purchase of her Cloth in Europe, as contrasted with its manufacture at home, will have on the price of her Agricultural staples. We have seen already that, in case she is forced to sell a portion of her surplus product in Europe, the price of that surplus must be the price which can be procured for it in England, *less* the cost of carrying it there. In other words: the average price in England being one dollar and ten cents, and the average cost of bringing it to New York being at least fifty cents and then of transporting it to England at least twenty-five more, the net proceeds to Illinois cannot exceed thirty-five cents per bushel. I need not more than state so obvious a truth as that the price at which the surplus can be sold governs the price of the whole crop; nor, indeed, if it were possible to deny this would it at all affect the argument. The real question to be determined is, not whether the American or the British manufacturers will furnish the most cloth for the least *cash,* but which will supply the requisite quantity of Cloth for the least *Grain in Illinois.* Now we have seen already that the price of Grain at any point where it is readily and largely produced is governed by its nearness to or remoteness from the market to which its surplus tends, and the least favorable market in which any portion of it must be sold. For instance: if Illinois produces a surplus of five million bushels of Grain, and can sell one million of bushels in New York, and two millions in New England, and another million in the West Indies, and for the fifth million is compelled to seek a market in England, and that, being the remotest point at which she sells, and the point most exposed to disadvantageous competition, is naturally the poorest market, that farthest and lowest market to which she sends her surplus will govern, to a great extent if not absolutely, the price she receives for the whole surplus. But, on the other hand, let her Cloths, her Wares, be manufactured in her midst, or on the junctions and waterfalls in her vicinity, thus affording an immediate market for her Grain, and now the average price of it rises, by an irresistible law, nearly or quite to the average of the world. Assuming that average to be one dollar, the price in Illinois, making allowance for the fertility and cheapness of her soil, could not fall below an average of seventy-five cents. Indeed, the experience of the periods when her consumption of Grain has been equal to her production, as well as that of other sections where the same has been the case, proves conclusively that the average price of her Wheat would exceed that sum.

We are now ready to calculate the profit and loss. Illinois, under Free Trade, with her "workshops in Europe," will buy her cloth twenty-five cents per yard cheaper, and thus make a nominal saving of two hundred and fifty thousand dollars in her year's supply; but, she thereby compels herself to pay for it in Wheat at thirty-five instead of seventy-five cents per bushel, or to give over *nine* and one third bushels of Wheat for every yard under Free Trade, instead of *four* and a third under a system of Home Production. In other words, while she is making a quarter of a million dollars by buying her Cloth "where she can buy cheapest," she is losing nearly Two Millions of Dollars on the net product of her Grain. The striking of a balance between her profit and her loss is certainly not a difficult, but rather an unpromising, operation.

Or, let us state the result in another form: She can buy her cloth a little cheaper in England, — Labor being there lower, Machinery more perfect, and Capital more abundant; but, in order to pay for it, she must not merely sell her own products at a correspondingly low price, but enough lower to overcome the cost of transporting them from Illinois to England. She will give the cloth-maker in England less Grain for her Cloth than she would give to the man who made it on her own soil; but for every bushel she sends him in payment for his fabric, she must give two to the wagoner, boatman, shipper, and factor, who transport it thither. On the whole product of her industry, two thirds is tolled out by carriers and bored out by Inspectors, until but a beggarly remnant is left to satisfy the fabricator of her goods.

And here I trust I have made obvious to you the law which dooms an Agricultural Country to inevitable and ruinous disadvantage in exchanging its staples for Manufactures, and involves it in perpetual and increasing debt and dependence. The *fact*, I early alluded to; is not the *reason* now apparent? It is not that Agricultural communities are more extravagant or less industrious than those in which Manufactures or Commerce preponderate,—it is because there is an inevitable disadvantage to Agriculture in the very nature of all distant exchanges. Its products are far more perishable than any other; they cannot so well await a future demand; but in their excessive bulk and density is the great evil. We have seen that, while the English Manufacturer can send his fabrics to Illinois for less than five per cent. on their first cost, the Illinois farmer must pay two hundred per cent. on his Grain for its transportation to English consumers. In other words: the English manufacturer need only produce his goods five per cent. below the American to drive the latter out of the Illinois market, the Illinoian must produce wheat for *one third* of its English price in order to compete with the English and Polish grain-grower in Birmingham and Sheffield.

And here is the answer to that scintillation of Free Trade wisdom which flashes out in wonder that *Manufactures* are eternally and especially in want of Protection, while Agriculture and Commerce need none. The assumption is false in any sense,—our Commerce and Navigation cannot live without Protection,—never did live so,—but let that pass. It is the interest of the whole country which demands that that portion of its Industry which is *most exposed* to ruinous foreign rivalry should be cherished and sustained. The wheat-grower, the grazier, is protected by ocean and land; by the fact that no foreign article can be introduced to rival his except at a cost for transportation of some thirty to one hundred per cent. on its value; while our Manufactures can be inundated by foreign competition at a cost of some two to ten per cent. It is the grain-grower, the cattle-raiser, who is protected by a duty on Foreign Manufactures, quite as much as the spinner or shoemaker. He who talks of Manufactures being protected and nothing else, might just as sensibly complain that we fortify Boston and New York, and not Pittsburg and Cincinnati.

Again : You see here our answer to those philosophers who modestly tell us that their views are liberal and enlightened, while ours are benighted, selfish, and un-Christian. They tell us that the foreign factory-laborer is anxious to exchange with us the fruits of his labor, — that he asks us to give him of our surplus of grain for the cloth that he is ready to make cheaper than we can now get it, while we have a superabundance of bread. Now, putting for the present out of the question the fact that, though *our* Tariff were abolished, *his* could remain, — that neither England, nor France, nor any great manufacturing country, would receive our Grain untaxed though we offered so to take their goods, — especially the fact that they never *did* so take of us while we were freely taking of them, — we say to them, " Sirs, we are willing to take Cloth of you for Grain : but why prefer to trade at a ruinous disadvantage to both ? Why should there be half the diameter of the earth between him who makes coats and him who makes bread, the one for the other ? We are willing to give you bread for clothes ; but we are not willing to pay two thirds of our bread as the cost of transporting the other third to you, because we sincerely believe it needless and greatly to our disadvantage. We are willing to work for and buy of you, but not to support the useless and crippling activity of a falsely directed Commerce : not to contribute by our sweat to the luxury of your nobles, the power of your kings. But come to us, you who are honest, peaceable, and industrious ; bring hither your machinery, or, if that is not yours, bring out your sinews ; and we will aid you to reproduce the implements of your skill. We will give you more bread for your cloth here than you can possibly earn for it where you are, if you will but come among us and aid us to sustain the policy that secures steady employment and a fair reward to Home Industry. We will no longer aid to prolong your existence in a state of semi-starvation where you are ; but we are ready to share with you our Plenty and our Freedom here." Such is the answer which the friends of Protection make to the demand and the imputation: judge ye whether our policy be indeed selfish, un-Christian, and insane.

I proceed now to set forth my

Proposition IV. THAT EQUILIBRIUM BETWEEN AGRICULTURE, MANUFACTURES AND COMMERCE, WHICH WE NEED, CAN ONLY BE MAINTAINED BY MEANS OF PROTECTIVE DUTIES.

You will have seen that the object we seek is not to make our country a Manufacturer for other nations, but for herself, — not to make her the baker and brewer and tailor of other people, but of her own household. If I understand at all the first rudiments of National Economy, it is best for each and all nations that each should mainly fabricate for itself, freely purchasing of others all such staples as its own soil or climate proves ungenial to. We appreciate quite as well as our opponents the impolicy of attempting to grow coffee in Greenland or glaciers in Malabar, — to extract blood from a turnip or sunbeams from cucumbers. A vast deal of wit has been expended on our stupidity by our acuter adversaries, but it has been quite thrown away, except as it has excited the hollow laughter of the ignorant as well as thoughtless. All this, however sharply pushed, falls wide of our true position. To all the fine words we hear about "the impossibility of counteracting the laws of Nature," "Trade regulating itself," &c., &c., we bow with due deference, and wait for the sage to resume his argument. What we *do* affirm is this, *that it is best for every nation to make at home all those articles of its own consumption that can just as well — that is, with nearly or quite as little labor — be made there as anywhere else.* We say it is not wise, it is not well, to send to France for boots, to Germany for hose, to England for knives and forks, and so on; because the real cost of them would be less, — even though the nominal price should be slightly more, — if we made them in our own country; while the facility of paying for them would be much greater. We do not object to the occasional importation of choice articles to operate as specimens and incentives to our own artisans to improve the quality and finish of their workmanship, — where the home competition does not avail to bring the process to its perfection, as it often will. In such cases, the rich and luxurious will usually be the buyers of these choice articles, and can afford to pay a good duty. There are gentlemen of extra polish in our cities and villages who think no coat good enough for them which is not woven in an English loom, — no boot adequately transparent which has not been fashioned by a Parisian master. I quarrel not with their taste: I only say that, since the Government *must* have Revenue and the American artisan *should* have Protection, I am glad it is so fixed that these gentlemen shall contribute handsomely to the former, and gratify their aspirations with the least possible detriment to the latter. It does not invalidate the fact nor the efficiency of Protection that foreign competition with American workmanship is not entirely shut out. It is the *general* result which is important, and not the exception. Now, he who can seriously contend, as some have seemed to do, that Protective Duties do not aid and extend the domestic production of the articles so protected might as well undertake to argue the sun out of the heavens at mid-day. All experience, all common sense, condemn him. Do we not know that our Manufactures first shot up under the stringent Protection of the Embargo and War? that they withered and crumbled under the comparative Free Trade of the few succeeding years? that they were revived and extended by the Tariffs of 1824 and '28? Do we not know that Germany, crippled by British policy, which inundated her with goods yet excluded her grain and timber, was driven, years since, to the establishment of her "Zoll-Verein" or Tariff Union, — a measure of careful and stringent Protection, under which Manufactures have grown up and flourished through all her many States? She has adhered steadily, firmly, to her Protective Policy, while we have faltered and oscillated; and what is the result? She has created and established her Manufactures; and in doing so has vastly increased her wealth and augmented the reward of her industry. Her public sentiment, as expressed through its thousand channels, is almost unanimous in favor of the Protective Policy; and now, when England, finding at length that her cupidity has overreached itself, — that she cannot supply the Germans with clothes yet refuse to buy their bread, — talks of relaxing her Corn-Laws in order to coax back her ancient and profitable customer, the answer is, "No; it is now too late. We have built up Home Manufactures in repelling your rapacity, — we cannot destroy them at your caprice. What guaranty have we that, should we accede to your terms, you would not return again to your policy of taking all and giving none so soon as our factories had crumbled into ruin? Besides, we have found that we can make cheaper — really cheaper — than we were able to buy, — can pay better wages to our laborers, and secure a better and steadier market for our products. We are content to abide in the position to which you have driven us. Pass on!"

But this is not the sentiment of Germany alone. All Europe acts on the principle of self-Protection; because all Europe sees its benefits. The British journals complain that, though they have made a show of relaxation in their own Tariff, and their Premier has made a Free Trade speech in Parliament, the chaff has caught no birds; *but six hostile Tariffs* — all Protective in their character, and all aimed at the supremacy of British Manufactures — were enacted within the year 1842. And thus, while schoolmen plausibly talk of the adoption and spread of Free Trade principles, and their rapid advances to speedy ascendency, the practical man knows that the truth is otherwise, and that many years must elapse before the great Colossus of Manufacturing monopoly will find another Portugal to drain of her life-blood under the delusive pretence of a commercial reciprocity. And, while Britain continues to pour forth her specious treatises on Political Economy, proving Protection a mistake and an impossibility through her Parliamentary Reports and Speeches in praise of Free Trade, the shrewd statesmen of other nations humor the joke with all possible gravity, and pass it on to the next neighbor; yet all the time take care of their own interests, just as though Adam Smith had never speculated nor Peel soberly expatiated on the blessings of Free Trade, looking round occasionally with a curious interest to see whether anybody was really taken in by it.

I have partly anticipated, yet I will state distinctly, my

Proposition V. PROTECTION IS NECESSARY AND PROPER TO SUSTAIN AS WELL AS TO CREATE A BENEFICENT ADJUSTMENT OF OUR NATIONAL INDUSTRY.

"Why can't our Manufacturers go alone?" petulantly asks a Free-Trader; "they have had Protection long enough. They ought not to need it any more." To this I answer that, if Manufactures were protected as a matter of special bounty or favor to the Manufacturers, a single day were too long. I would not consent that they should be sustained one day longer than the interests of the *whole* Country required. I think you have already seen that, not for the sake of Manufacturers, but for the sake of all Productive Labor, should Protection be afforded. If I have been intelligible, you will have seen that the purpose and essence of Protection is LABOR-SAVING, — the making two blades of grass grow instead of one. This it does by "planting the Manufacturer as nearly as may be by the side of the Farmer," as Mr. Jefferson expressed it, and thereby securing to the latter a market for which he had looked to Europe in vain. Now, the market of the latter is certain as the recurrence of appetite; but that is not all. The Farmer and the Manufacturer, being virtually neighbors, will interchange their productions directly, or with but one intermediate, instead of sending them reciprocally across half a continent and a broad ocean, through the hands of many holders, until the toll taken out by one after another has exceeded what remains of the grist. "Dear-bought and far-fetched" is an old maxim, containing more *essential* truth than many a chapter by a modern Professor of Political Economy. Under the Protective policy, instead of having one thousand men making Cloth in one hemisphere, and an equal number raising Grain in the other, with three thousand factitiously employed in transporting and interchanging these products, we have over two thousand producers of Grain, and as many of Cloth, leaving far too little employment for one thousand in making the exchanges between them. This consequence is inevitable : although the production on either side is not confined to the very choicest locations, the total product of their labor is twice as much as formerly. In other words, there is a double quantity of food, clothing, and all the necessaries and comforts of life, to be shared among the producers of wealth, simply from the diminution of the number of non-producers. If all the men now enrolled in Armies and Navies were advantageously employed in Productive Labor, there would doubtless be a larger dividend of comforts and necessaries of life for all, because more to be divided than now and no greater number to receive it: just so in the case before us. Every thousand persons employed in needless Transportation and in factitious Commerce are so many subtracted from the great body of Producers, from the proceeds of whose labor all must be subsisted. The dividend for each must, of course, be governed by the magnitude of the quotient.

But, if this be so advantageous, it is queried, why is any legislation necessary? Why would not all voluntarily see and embrace it? I answer, because the apparent individual advantage is often to be pursued by a course directly adverse to the general welfare. We know that Free Trade asserts the contrary of this; maintaining that, if every man pursues that course most conducive to his individual interest, the general good will thereby be most certainly and signally promoted. But, to say nothing of the glaring exceptions to this law which crowd our statute-books with injunctions and penalties, we are everywhere met with pointed contradictions of its assumption, which hallows and blesses the pursuits of the gambler, the distiller, and the libertine, making the usurer a saint and the swindler a hero. Adam Smith himself admits that there are avocations which enrich the individual but impoverish the community. So in the case before us. A B is a farmer in Illinois, and has much grain to sell or exchange for goods. But, while it is demonstrable that, if *all* the manufactures consumed in Illinois were produced there, the price of grain must rise nearly to the average of the world, it is equally certain that A B's *single act*, in buying and consuming American cloth, will not raise the price of grain generally, nor of *his* grain. It will not perceptibly affect the price of grain at all. A solemn compact of the whole community to use only American fabrics would have some effect; but this could never be established, or never enforced. A few Free-Traders standing out, selling their grain at any advance which might accrue, and buying "where they could buy cheapest," would induce one after another to look out for No. 1, and let the public interests take care of themselves: so the whole compact would fall to pieces like a rope of sand. Many a one would say, "Why should I aid to keep up the price of Produce? I am only a *consumer* of it," — not realizing or caring for the interest of the community, even though it less palpably involved his own; and that would be an end. Granted that it is desirable to encourage and prefer Home Production and Manufacture, a Tariff is the obvious way, and the only way, in which it can be effectively and certainly accomplished.

But why is a Tariff necessary after Manufactures are once established? "You say," says a Free-Trader, "that you can Manufacture cheaper if Protected than we can buy abroad: then why not do it *without* Protection, and save all trouble?" Let me answer this cavil: —

I will suppose that the Manufactures of this Country amount in value to One Hundred Millions of Dollars per annum, and those of Great Britain to Three Hundred Millions. Let us suppose also that, under an efficient Protective Tariff, ours are produced five per cent. cheaper than those of England, and that our own markets are supplied entirely from the Home Product. But at the end of this year, 1843, we,—concluding that our Manufactures have been protected long enough and ought now to go alone,—repeal absolutely our Tariff, and commit our great interests thoroughly to the guidance of "Free Trade." Well: at this very time the British Manufacturers, on making up the account and review of their year's business, find that they have manufactured goods costing them Three Hundred Millions, as aforesaid, and have sold to just about that amount, leaving a residue or surplus on hand of Fifteen or Twenty Millions' worth. These are to be sold; and their net proceeds will constitute the interest on their capital and the profit on their year's business. But *where* shall they be sold? If crowded on the Home or their established Foreign Markets, they will glut and depress those markets, causing a general decline of prices and a heavy loss, not merely on this quantity of goods, but on the whole of their next year's business. They know better than to do any such thing. Instead of it, they say, "Here is the American Market just thrown open to us by a repeal of their Tariff: let us send thither our surplus, and sell it for what it will fetch." They ship it over accordingly, and in two or three weeks it is rattling off through our auction stores, at prices first five, then ten, fifteen, twenty, and down to thirty per cent. below our previous rates. Every jobber and dealer is tickled with the idea of buying goods of novel patterns so wonderfully cheap; and the sale proceeds briskly, though at constantly declining prices, till the whole stock is disposed of and our market is gorged to repletion.

Now, the British Manufacturers may not have received for the whole Twenty Millions' worth of Goods over Fourteen or Fifteen Millions; but what of it? Whatever it may be is clear profit on their year's business in cash or its full equivalent. All their established markets are kept clear and eager; and they can now go on vigorously and profitably with the business of the new year. But more: they have crippled an active and growing rival; they have opened a new market, which shall erelong be theirs also.

Let us now look at our side of the question:—

The American Manufacturers have also a stock of goods on hand, and they come into our market to dispose of them. But they suddenly find that market forestalled and depressed by rival fabrics of attractive novelty, and selling in profusion at prices which rapidly run down to twenty-five per cent. below cost. What are they to do? They cannot force sales at any price not utterly ruinous; there is no demand at any rate. They cannot retaliate upon England the mischief they must suffer,—her Tariff forbids; and the other markets of the world are fully supplied, and will bear but a limited pressure. The foreign influx has created a scarcity of money as well as a plethora of goods. Specie has largely been exported in payment, which has compelled the Banks to contract and deny loans. Still, their obligations must be met; if *they* cannot make sales, *the Sheriff* will, and must. It is not merely their surplus, but their whole product, which has been depreciated and made unavailable at a blow. The end is easily foreseen: our Manufacturers become bankrupt and are broken up; their works are brought to a dead stand; the Laborers therein, after spending months in constrained idleness, are driven by famine into the Western wilderness, or into less productive and less congenial vocations; their acquired skill and dexterity, as well as a portion of their time, are a dead loss to themselves and the community; and we commence the slow and toilsome process of rebuilding and rearranging our industry on the one-sided or Agricultural basis. Such is the process which we have undergone twice already. How many repetitions shall satisfy us?

Now, will any man gravely argue that we have *made* Five or Six Millions by this cheap purchase of British goods,—by "buying where we could buy cheapest?" Will he not see that, though the *price* was low, the *cost* is very great? But the apparent saving is doubly deceptive; for the British manufacturers, having utterly crushed their American rivals by one or two operations of this kind, soon find here a market, not for a beggarly surplus of Fifteen or Twenty Millions, but they have now a demand for the amount of our whole consumption, which, making allowance for our diminished ability to pay, would probably still reach Fifty Millions per annum. This increased demand would soon produce activity and buoyancy in the general market; and now the foreign Manufacturers would say in their consultations, "We have sold some millions' worth of goods to America for less than cost, in order to obtain control of that market; now we have it, and must retrieve our losses,"—and they *would* retrieve them, with interest. They would have a perfect right to do so. I hope no man has understood me as implying any infringement of the dictates of honesty on their part, still less of the laws of trade. They have a perfect right to sell goods in our markets on such terms as we prescribe and they can afford; it is *we*, who set up our own vital interests to be bowled down by their rivalry, who are alone to be blamed.

Who does not see that this sending out our great Industrial Interests unarmed and unshielded to battle against the mail-clad legions opposed to them in the arena of Trade is to insure their destruction? It were just as wise to say that, because our people are brave, therefore they shall repel any invader without fire-arms, as to say that the restrictions of other nations ought not to be opposed by us because our artisans are skilful and our manufactures have made great advances. The very fact that our manufactures are greatly extended and improved is the strong reason why they should not be exposed to destruction. If they were of no amount or value, their loss would be less disastrous; but now the Five or Six Millions we should make on the cheaper importation of goods would cost us One Hundred Millions in the destruction of Manufacturing Property alone.

Yet this is but an item of our damage. The Manufacturing classes feel the first effect of the blow, but it would paralyze every muscle of society. One hundred thousand artisans and laborers, discharged from our ruined factories, after being some time out of employment, at a waste of millions of the National wealth, are at last driven by famine to engage in other avocations, — of course, with inferior skill and at an inferior price. The farmer, gardener, grocer, lose them as customers to meet them as rivals. They crowd the labor-markets of those branches of industry which we are still permitted to pursue, just at the time when the demand for their products has fallen off, and the price is rapidly declining. The result is just what we have seen in a former instance: all that any man may make by buying Foreign goods cheap, he loses ten times over by the decline of his own property, product, or labor; while to nine tenths of the whole people the result is unmixed calamity. The disastrous consequences to a nation of the mere derangement and paralysis of its Industry which must follow the breaking down of any of its great Producing Interests have never yet been sufficiently estimated. Free Trade, indeed, assures us that every person thrown out of employment in one place or capacity has only to choose another; but almost every working-man knows from experience that such is not the fact, — that the loss of a situation through the failure of his business is oftener a sore calamity. I know a worthy citizen who spent six years in learning the trade of a hatter, which he had just perfected in 1798, when an immense importation of foreign hats utterly paralyzed the manufacture in this country. He travelled and sought for months, but could find no employment at any price, and at last gave up the pursuit, found work in some other capacity, and has never made a hat since. He lives yet, and now comfortably, for he is industrious and frugal; but the six years he gave to learn his trade were utterly lost to him, — lost for the want of adequate and steady Protection to Home Industry. I insist that the Government has failed of discharging its proper and rightful duty to that citizen, and to thousands and tens of thousands who have suffered from like causes. I insist that, if the Government had permitted without complaint a foreign force to land on our shores and plunder that man's house of the savings of six years of faithful industry, the neglect of duty would not have been more flagrant. And I firmly believe that the people of this country are One Thousand Millions of Dollars poorer at this moment than they would have been had their entire Productive Industry been constantly protected, on the principles I have laid down, from the formation of the Government till now. The steadiness of employment and of recompense thus secured, the comparative absence of constrained idleness, and the more efficient application of the labor actually performed, would have vastly increased the product,—would have improved and beautified the whole face of the country; and the Moral and Intellectual advantages thence accruing would alone have been inestimable. A season of suspension of labor in a community is usually one of aggravated dissipation, drunkenness, and crime.

But let me more clearly illustrate the effect of foreign competition in raising prices to the consumer. To do this, I will take my own calling for an example, because I understand that best; though any of you can apply the principle to that with which he may be better acquainted. I am a publisher of newspapers, and suppose I afford them at a cheap rate. But the ability to maintain that cheapness is based on the fact that I can certainly sell a large edition daily, so that no part of that edition shall remain a dead loss on my hands. Now, if there were an active and formidable Foreign competition in newspapers,—if the edition which I printed during the night were frequently rendered unsalable by the arrival of a foreign ship freighted with newspapers early in the morning,—the present rates could not be continued: the price must be increased or the quality would decline. I presume this holds equally good of the production of calicoes, glass, and penknives as of newspapers, though it may be somewhat modified by the nature of the article to which it is applied. That it does hold true of sheetings, nails, and thousands of articles, is abundantly notorious.

I have not burdened you with statistics,—you know they are the reliance, the stronghold, of the cause of Protection, and that we can produce them by acres. My aim has been to exhibit not mere collections of facts, however pertinent and forcible, but the *laws* on which those facts are based, — not the immediate manifestation, but the ever-living necessity from which it springs. The contemplation of these laws assures me that those articles which are supplied to us by Home Production alone are relatively cheaper than those which are rivalled and competed with from abroad. And I am equally confident that the shutting out of Foreign competition from our markets for other articles of general necessity and liberal consumption which can be made here with as little labor as anywhere would be followed by a corresponding result, — a reduction of the price to the consumer at the same time with increased employment and reward to our Producing Classes.

But, Mr. President, were this only on one side true, — were it certain that the price of the Home product would be permanently higher than that of the Foreign, I should still insist on efficient Protection, and for reasons I have sufficiently shown. Grant that a British cloth costs but $3 per yard, and a corresponding American fabric $4, I still hold that the latter would be decidedly the cheaper for us. The Fuel, Timber, Fruits, Vegetables, &c., which make up so large a share of the cost of the Home product, would be rendered comparatively valueless by having our workshops in Europe. I look not so much to the nominal price as to the comparative facility of payment. And, where cheapness is only to be attained by a depression of the wages of Labor to the neighborhood of the European standard, I prefer that it should be dispensed with. One thing must answer to another; and I hold that the farmers of this country can better afford, as a matter of pecuniary advantage, to pay a good price for manufactured articles than to obtain them lower through the depression and inadequacy of the wages of the artisan and laborer.

You will understand me, then, to be utterly hostile to that idol of Free Trade worship, known as Free or unlimited Competition. The sands of my hour are running low, and I cannot ask time to examine this topic more closely; yet I am confident I could show that this Free Competition is a most delusive and dangerous element of Political Economy. Bear with a brief illustration: At this moment, common shirts are made in London at the incredibly low price of *three cents per pair.* Should we admit these articles free of duty and buy them because they are so cheap? Free trade says Yes; but I say No! Sound Policy as well as Humanity forbids it. By admitting them, we simply reduce a large and worthy and suffering class of our population from the ability they now possess of procuring a bare subsistence by their labor to unavoidable destitution and pauperism. They must now subsist upon the charity of relatives or of the community,—unless we are ready to adopt the demoniac doctrine of the Free Trade philosopher Malthus, that the dependent Poor ought to be rigorously starved to death. Then what have we gained by getting these articles so exorbitantly cheap? or, rather, what have we not lost? The labor which formerly produced them is mainly struck out of existence; the poor widows and seamstresses among us must still have a subsistence; and the imported garments must be paid for: where is the profits of our speculation?

But even this is not the worst feature of the case. The labor which we have here thrown out of employment by the cheap importation of this article is now ready to be employed again at any price,—if not one that will afford bread and straw, then it must accept one that will produce potatoes and rubbish; and with the product some Free-Trader proceeds to break down the price and destroy the reward of similar labor in some other portion of the earth. And thus each depression of wages produces another, and that a third, and so on, making the circuit of the globe,—the aggravated necessities of the Poor acting and reacting upon each other, increasing the omnipotence of Capital and deepening the dependence of Labor, swelling and pampering a bloated and factitious Commerce, grinding down and grinding down the destitute, until Malthus's remedy for Poverty shall become a grateful specific, and, amid the splendors and luxuries of an all-devouring Commercial Feudalism, the squalid and famished Millions, its dependants and victims, shall welcome death as a deliverer from their sufferings and despair.

I wish time permitted me to give a hasty glance over the doctrines and teachings of the Free Trade sophists, who esteem themselves *the* Political Economists, christen their own views liberal and enlightened, and complacently put ours aside as benighted and barbarous. I should delight to show you how they mingle subtle fallacy with obvious truth, — how they reason acutely from assumed premises, which, being mistaken or incomplete, lead to false and often absurd conclusions, — how they contradict and confound each other, and often, from Adam Smith, their patriarch, down to McCulloch and Ricardo, either make admissions which undermine their whole fabric, or confess themselves ignorant or in the dark on points the most vital to a correct understanding of the great subject they profess to have reduced to a Science. Yet even Adam Smith himself expressly approves and justifies the British Navigation Act, the most aggressively Protective measure ever enacted, — a measure which, not being understood and seasonably counteracted by other nations, changed for centuries the destinies of the World, — which silently sapped and overthrew the Commercial and Political greatness of Holland, — which silenced the thunder of Van Tromp, and swept the broom from his mast-head. But I must not detain you longer. I do not ask you to judge of this matter by authority, but from facts which come home to your reason and your daily experience. There is not an observing and strong-minded mechanic in our city who could not set any one of these Doctors of the Law right on essential points. I beg you to consider how few great practical Statesmen they have ever been able to win to their standard, — I might almost say none; for Huskisson was but a nominal disciple, and expressly contravened their whole system upon an attempt to apply it to the Corn Laws; and Calhoun is but a Free-Trader by location, and has never yet answered his own powerful arguments in behalf of Protection. On the other hand, we point you to the long array of mighty names which have illustrated the annals of Statesmanship in modern times, — to Chatham, William Pitt, and the Great Frederick of Prussia; to the whole array of memorable French Statesmen, including Napoleon the first of them all; to our own WASHINGTON, HAMILTON, JEFFERSON, and MADISON; to our two CLINTONS, TOMPKINS, to say nothing of the eagle-eyed and genial-hearted LIVING master-spirit* of our time. The opinions and the arguments of all these are on record; it is by hearkening to and heeding their counsels that we shall be prepared to walk in the light of experience and look forward to a glorious National destiny. My friends! I dare not detain you longer. I commit to you the cause of the Nation's Independence, of her Stability and her Prosperity. Guard it wisely and shield it well; for it involves your own happiness and the enduring welfare of your countrymen!

* Henry Clay.

SUNDRY LECTURING REMINISCENCES.

A DAY'S RIDE IN MAINE.

AUGUSTA, MAINE, March 24, 1849.

THREE days had glided away rapidly, and pleasantly, and not very idly, among the heartiest of friends in Bangor, — days bright as Italy, and pure as the breath of mountains. The still abundant snow gradually melted into the rivulets from the streets, the adjacent roads, and the southern exposures, in the beams of the ascendant sun; but the nights were crisp and bracing, and the frequent appearance of lighter sleighs in the streets bespoke the obstinacy with which Winter's fleecy mantle still held its ground in the surrounding country. The ice still bound the Penobscot nearly to Frankfort, fourteen miles below; holding the business of Bangor and vicinity in its rugged embrace, and even tempting the foolhardy to travel with teams on its now treacherous surface. But on Tuesday the clear azure of several preceding days was gradually obscured by the portents of a coming storm, which, in the course of the following night, became quite unequivocal, and the pattering of rain on the roof of the Hatch House through the small hours gave premonition of a moist ride to Waterville on the morrow. It was not, however, till the stage-coach (a naked, open wagon) drew up at the door, between six and seven in the morning (Wednesday, 21st), that the fun of it became entirely palpable. The wind came strong from the southwest; the skies were black; the rain was coming faster and faster; in short, a Down-East Equinoctial was upon us.

There were six of us passengers, not forgetting the driver, the best roadsman of all, whom no obstacle could daunt and no botheration disconcert, and who, protected in part by his rubber over-all, looked the day's driving wind and driven rain in the face with buoyant philosophy. The six amused themselves, when they could stay in the wagon, by turning a part of the water from one to the other by means of four umbrellas, which would have been of some account had not the course of the descending fluid been so greatly deflected from the perpendicular by the sweeping gale, and had there not been entirely too much of it. Even as it was, the man in a red-flannel shirt and glazed outer garments, who occupied the most sheltered position (leeward of the umbrellas), and seemed to have been taught by some bird the secret of oiling himself, contrived to maintain a comparatively dry look to the end.

Ten miles — mainly of mud — had slid rapidly and merrily behind us, before we encountered the first formidable snow-drift still occupying the road, over which hundreds of teams had travelled securely for weeks, but into which, softened by the rain, ours plunged, and in it wallowed. The next moment, the leaders were down in a tangled pile; the off one rolled clear over the nigh one, and was extricated, and got up on the near side. The passengers (the heaviest having been thrown out rather suddenly as we came to a halt, the wagon barely not upsetting) walked ahead in quest of help and shelter; (perhaps it did n't pour!) the wheel-horses were also taken off, and four oxen obtained to draw the wagon out of the drift, and on to the changing-place, not far distant.

Soon, all were on board again, — all as good as before, except that the buffaloes were wet on both sides, and the seats had rather a clammy feeling; and we went on merrily as ever — meeting few decided obstacles for the next twelve miles — to the second changing-place (North Dixmont).

So far, we had made good time, in spite of wind and weather. "And now," said the driver, "you may expect to see some bad going." The testimony was confirmed by others, but we did not need their assurance. Two miles more were got over pretty well, one bad place being avoided by letting down the fence, and making a detour through the field; but soon we were brought to a dead halt again. The horses were floundering in a rather profound drift; the wagon was "stuck"; and no resource remained but to beat up the neighborhood for oxen to draw it on, while the passengers went ahead in quest of dinner. The portliest of the number (weighing good two hundred), who had already twice taken his own portrait by a flying-leap into a snow-drift, and had received some severe contusions and a hard wrench in the later operation, when he narrowly missed breaking a leg in clearing the wagon, alone lingered behind to pick up some bits of rides between the worst snow-drifts, of which, I think, there were a hundred within that next two miles. Yet, the wagon was, by six oxen, got through or around them somehow in a little more than two hours, — the horses following behind, and coming through with a beaten and sorry look. I had no idea it could be done so soon by an hour.

Dinner (at Troy) in a hurry, and all aboard again; and henceforward to Waterville we were enabled to take the rain sitting instead of walking for nearly all the time. Some drifts had to be walked over, of course; some snow had to be shovelled away from before the wheels; once or twice, we had to take hold and help propel the wagon through a drift, that need not have been so deep, so far as any practical utility was regarded in its construction; and twice more our solid friend was half thrown, half jumped, into the snow-drifts, as the wagon keeled up on one side, and seemed intent on going over. The last time, one arm went through the drift into about two feet of coolish water, and he, already racked and sore, was on the point of losing temper. The others were more nimble, or, rather, more lucky; generally making a clean jump, and alighting perpendicularly and right end up. Finally, at 6 P. M., we drove rapidly into Waterville, — fifty good miles from Bangor, — and found warm rooms and various comforts awaiting us. Lecturing that evening was a little up hill; but, since the hearers did not audibly complain, I sha' n't. I thought the village dancing-school at our hotel ought to have broken up at midnight, considering that some of us were to be called for the Augusta stage at 5 A. M.; but the young folks seemed to enjoy it to a much later hour; and, if their parents don't object, I probably should be quiet. Still, I *do* say that dancing — which ought to be a healthful, innocent, and approved recreation for all — is made unpopular with the grave and devout by the outrageously late hours to which mere infants in years are kept up by it, in hot and crowded rooms, whence they are suddenly transferred, when utterly exhausted, to the outdoor cold and their fireless homes. It was not the creaking of that fiddle, the heavy pounding of unskilled feet on the ball-room floor, and the annoying rattle of my door-latch in consequence, till some time this morning, that put this into my head; but these served to confirm me in my earlier conviction.

A RIDE ACROSS THE ALLEGHANIES.

WASHINGTON, Monday, December 3, 1851.

It was 10 o'clock on Saturday morning when our steamboat reached Wheeling, in two days from Cincinnati. That was a bad sample of Western steamboat management. I had promised at home to be here the evening before the Session opened; and it was essential that I should be punctual. I ought to have stopped but one day instead of two at Cincinnati. I ought to have travelled by land from that city, and so been at Wheeling six hours sooner. The boat ought to, and might have been there some hours earlier. But here it was 10 o'clock, and the stages to connect at Cumberland with the Baltimore and Ohio train next morning had all been gone some four hours. No other train would leave Cumberland till Monday morning, — twenty-four hours later. I jumped ashore with my baggage, and sped to the stage-office. One of the Members of Congress, for self and company, got there at the same moment, and spoke: "Can you send us through to Cumberland in time for to-morrow's train?" "No, sir, it is too late." The Congressman returned to report progress. Not comprehending the impossibility of driving 193 miles in 22 hours, even over a hilly road, with relays of good horses every ten or twelve miles, I hung on, and had the resident proprietor summoned. I put the question to him, varied as follows: "Will money put us through to Cumberland in time for to-morrow's cars?" "Yes, money will, — money enough." "How much?" "If five of you will pay for a full stage (nine seats) and twenty dollars extra, you shall be taken through." I hurried down to the boat in search of the Congressmen, but looked it over without finding them. At last, I discovered one of the Senators: "Mr. R., call your friends; we can be taken to Cumberland in season, for about twenty dollars each."

He would not listen, — said it could not be done, — he had tried it once, and failed. (I suspect he did not try the extra price, "No cure, no pay.") He turned away, and the boat put off. I went back to the stage-office alone. "Mr. S., what is your price for taking me through to Cumberland in season?" "Regular fare to Baltimore, eleven dollars; forty dollars extra for gaining time, — in all, $ 51." I put down the change, and he got up his horses. In ten minutes we were on the road. The gentleman who drove stands at the head of his profession. He understood, by experience or instinct, that the perfection of driving is not to seem or need to drive at all. By a slight and easy motion of his wrist, he thridded his way through a drove of cattle, around a carriage, and among the piles of broken or to be broken stone everywhere encumbering the road, now on one side, then on the other, and again in the middle or on both. He knew just when to hold in, and when to let out, but seemed to do more of the former than of the latter; hardly using a persuasion to speed in the course of the ride. He drove at no time over eleven, nor under ten, miles per hour. The day was bright, though cool; the air crisp and bracing. We had a light carriage, with fresh horses every ten to twelve miles. Whatever craft we espied ahead was sure to be hull down astern in the course of five minutes. We drove sixty-two miles in a trifle short of six hours, but lost nearly an hour more in making changes, as we were not expected at the stations. It was 10.40 (Baltimore time) when we started. At half past 5 we overhauled the Mail Stages half-way between Brownsville and Uniontown, Pa., 62 miles from Wheeling. I threw my baggage upon one, and followed it; bidding a hearty farewell to my driver, who turned back to Brownsville for the night, on his way to Wheeling. We were in Uniontown to tea 15 minutes past 6; left at 7; and drove straight ahead over the Alleghanies, only stopping to change or water, and making the five changes in less than twenty minutes, all told. The night was cold, and snow contrived to fall from about midnight, though less profusely than on the plains this side. I think the cold prevented. But each stage was just full of passengers, and little discomfort was felt from the cold. I don't consider riding through a cold night without a halt the summit of human felicity; but it does very well, if you don't waste your time and strength in trying to go to sleep. That is absurd. We drove into Cumberland at 7 A. M.; had breakfast, and abundant time for outward renovation, before the cars started at half past 8. The storm continued through the day, changing from snow to sleety hail and almost rain as we neared the coast. We met with a bad accident at 4 P. M., — when 45 miles from Baltimore, our snow-scraper catching against some part of the track, so that it was broken and turned under the forward engine, which was thrown off the track, and the one behind it partly followed the example. Both were disabled and considerably injured. Happily, we had still a third engine, pushing behind, which was detached and run back to Frederick for help to clear away the wreck and mend the track, which had been torn up by our disaster. After four hours' delay, we got under headway again, but came on very slowly, and only made the Relay House at

11 P. M., — too late for any chance to reach this city till morning. But we were in here before 9 A. M., three hours before Congress convened, and in ample season to look into whatever was going on. Governor Brown of Mississippi, whom I left on the boat at Wheeling, incredulous as to the practicability of getting through to Cumberland in season, was of course not here to vote for his friend, Howell Cobb, when even one vote was no slight consideration. I presume he is in, *via* Pittsburg, to-night.

A NIGHT-RIDE ACROSS THE PRAIRIES.

SOUTH BEND, INDIANA, October 18, 1853.

I LEFT New York on Monday morning of last week, reached Lafayette, *via* Erie Railroad, Buffalo City, the steamboat Queen of the West to Cleveland, and the railroad thence by Galion, Bellefontaine, and Indianapolis, at noon on Wednesday. Having given the residue of that day and all the next to the State Agricultural Fair, and fulfilled the engagement that drew me to Indiana, I returned to Indianapolis on Friday morning, spoke there in the evening, and started back *via* Lafayette, on Saturday morning, to fulfil a promise to speak on the evening of that day at Laporte, where I should reach the Northern Indiana and Southern Michigan Road, and set my face homeward. How we were delayed on our way back to Lafayette, and how, on reaching that smart young village, I was misled, by the kind guidance of a zealous friend, into waiting for the Northern cars at a place half a mile distant from that where they then actually were; how I at last broke over all assurances that they always started from this point, and must come here before leaving, and made for their out-of-the-way station just in time to be too late, — it were a fruitless vexation to recall. Suffice it that at noon I stood on the platform where I might and should have been twenty minutes before, just in time to see the line of smoke hovering over the rapidly receding train, to realize that any seasonable fulfilment of my promise to Laporte was now impossible, and to learn that the next regular train would leave on Monday, and take me to Laporte just two days after I should have been there. I wandered back to the village, in no enviable mood, to telegraph my mishap to Laporte, and had the privilege of cooling my heels for an hour and a quarter on the steps of the office, while the operators were leisurely discussing and digesting their dinner. They came at last, just too late to enable me to stop the sending of a carriage eleven miles from Laporte to meet me at Westville; and I retraced my steps to the out-of-town depot, to see what chance remained or might turn up.

As quite a number had been deceived and left as I was, owing to the recent change in railroad arrangements, the agent said he would send out an extra train that afternoon, if he could procure an engine; but none came in that could be spared, and at four o'clock our extra train was adjourned to next morning at ten; and I returned to the telegraph office to apprise Laporte that I would speak there for Temperance the next (Sunday) evening, and then walked over to the Bramble House, and laid in a stock of sleep for future contingencies.

I was at the depot in ample season next morning; but the train that was to start at ten did not actually leave till noon, and then with a body entirely disproportioned to its head. Five cars closely packed with live hogs, five ditto with wheat, two ditto with lumber, three or four with live stock and notions returning from the Fair, and two or three cattle-cars containing passengers, formed entirely too heavy a load for our asthmatic engine, which had obviously seen its best days in the service of other roads, before that from New Albany to Michigan City was constructed. Still, we went ahead; crossed the Wabash; passed the Tippecanoe Battle-ground; ran our engine partly off the track, and got it back again; and by three o'clock had reached Brookston, a station fourteen miles from Lafayette, with a fair prospect of traversing our whole ninety-odd miles by the dawn of Monday morning.

But here we came to a long halt. The engine was in want of both wood and water; and, though woods and sloughs were in sight in various directions, neither were accessible. So our engine was detached, and ran ahead some five miles for water, and still farther for wood, and a weary two hours were tediously whiled away before its return.

It came at last, hitched on, and started us; but, before it had moved us another half-mile, the discharge-cock of the boiler flew out, letting off all our water and steam, and rendering us hopelessly immovable for hours to come.

We got out to take an observation. The village of Brookston consists of three houses and no barn, with a well (almost dry) for the use of the railroad; but neither of the houses is a tavern, nor more than one-story high; and their aggregate of accommodation fell far short of the needs of the hungry crowd so unexpectedly thrown upon their hospitality. Two or three more houses of like or inferior calibre were gleaming in the rays of the setting sun at various distances on the prairies; but these were already surfeited with railroad hands as boarders, not to speak of sick women or children in nearly every one; for disease has been very rife this season on these prairies. Still, a friend found an old acquaintance in one of the nearest residents, whose sick wife spread a generous table forthwith for as many of us as could sit around it; and, having supped, we turned out on the prairie to make room for a family party, including two women, one of them quite sick,—as she had been all the way up, and at Lafayette for some days before. Our conductor had started a hand-car back to Lafayette in quest of the only engine there,—a weak, old one, needing some repairs before it could be used. It was calculated that this engine would be up about eleven o'clock, and would then drag us back to Lafayette to spend the remainder of the night, and take a fair start in the morning. This I, for one, had resolved not to submit to, though the only alternative were a camp-fire on the prairie.

But now a bright thought struck the engineer, for which I think he was indebted to *my* good angel. He recollected that a good engine was stationed at a point named Culvertown, forty-three miles ahead; and he decided to take a hand-car and make for this, so that our bow should have two strings to it. The hand-car was dragged over the rough prairie around our long train, and launched,— I following with my carpet-bags, on the lookout for chances. In a trice, it was duly manned; I had coaxed my way to a seat upon it; and we were off.

The full moon rose bright over the eastern woods as, with the north star straight ahead, we bade adieu to the embryo City of Brookston.

We were seven of us on the hand-car; four propelling by twos, as if turning a heavy, two-handed grindstone; but we let off one passenger after traversing a few miles. The engineer and I made up the party; and the car — about equal in size to a wheelbarrow and a half — just managed to hold us and give the propellers working-room. To economize space, I sat a good part of the time facing backward, with my feet hanging over the rear of the car, knocking here and there on a tie or bridge-timber, and often tickled through my boots by the coarse, rank weeds growing up at intervals between the ties, and recently stiffened by the hard October frosts. As a constant effort to hold on was required, the position was not favorable to slumber, however it might be to cogitation. Our Irish steam was evolved from Yankee muscles, and proved of capital quality. We made our first five miles, heavily laden as we were, in twenty-five minutes; our first ten miles in an hour; but our propellers grew gradually weary; we stopped twice or thrice for oil, water, and perhaps one other liquid; so that we were five hours in making the forty-three miles, or from 7 P. M. till midnight. I only tried my hand at propelling for a short mile, and that experience sufficed to convince me that, however it may be as a business, this species of exercise cannot be conscientiously commended as an amusement. The night was chilly, though clear; the dead-ahead breeze, though light, was keen, and I, by no means dressed for such an airy ride, felt it most sensibly.

Our course lay across the east end of Grand Prairie, which stretches westward from the bank of the Wabash across Indiana and Illinois, to the Mississippi, and thence through Iowa and Nebraska, perhaps to Council Bluffs and the Rocky Mountains. The ground we traversed was nearly level, often marshy, and for the most part clear of wood; but we frequently crossed belts or spurs, on higher, dryer soil, of the great forest on our right, with occasional clumps of sturdy oaks, — islets of timber in the prairie sea, — to which the belts aforesaid served as promontories. Four prairie-fires, — two on either hand, — at intervals of miles, burned brightly but lazily; for the wind was not strong enough, nor the vegetation dry and crisp enough, to impel a rapid, roaring, sweeping fire.

Now a flock of geese flew by, murmuring subduedly; then a great heron rose before us, and flew heavily over the marshes; an opossum was frightened by our noisy approach, and fled eagerly into the prairie, under an evident mistake as to the nature of our business; and again an odorous skunk, keeping his carcass unseen, gave pungent evidence of his close proximity. Finally, a little after midnight, chilled and weary, we reached the one-horse village of Culvertown, and found the engine missing, — run down to Michigan City for repairs, — so that my companions had had their rugged ride for nothing. The landlady of the only house in sight got up and made a fire; the engineer decided to await the return of the fugitive engine; and I began to drum up the means of farther conveyance; for I was still twenty-odd miles from any public conveyance that would speed me on my way. Horses, I learned, were not easily to be had; and, even if I had a team, the roads across the great marsh and small river just north of us were rather shy. But the engineer lent me the hand-car which had already done such good service, and I evoked from slumber two Dutchmen, who were persuaded to act as my crew; and by 1 A. M. I was again under headway northward; the air keener, and I more vulnerable to its assaults in my loneliness, than when six of us were so closely huddled together. But my Dutchmen propelled with a will, and my good craft sped briskly onward.

From Culvertown, a prairie-marsh stretches thirteen miles northward, and I think no building, and hardly a cultivated acre, were visible through all that distance. The dense fog, beaten down by the cool air, lay low on this marsh, and was heavily charged with prairie-smoke for a part of the way. Three miles from C., we crossed, on a pokerish bridge of naked timbers, the slough-like bed wherein the Kankakee oozes and creeps sluggishly westward to join the Fox and form the Illinois. They say the Kankakee has a rapid current, and dry, inviting banks, from the point where it crosses the Illinois line, which might tempt one to regret that it did not cross that line forty miles higher up. Happily, the keen air had done for the mosquitoes, so that we had no more music than I had fairly bargained for; but Bunyan might have improved his description of the Slough of Despond had he been favored with a vision of the Kankakee marshes. At 4 A.M., my good craft brought up at Westville, and I was gratified by the sight of half a dozen houses at once for the first time since leaving Lafayette, seventy-eight miles below. I doubt that all the houses visible on that seventy-eight miles would amount to a hundred; and I am sure they would be dear at two hundred dollars each, on the average. Yet there are much fine timber and excellent land on that route, and he who passes over the railroad ten years hence will see a very different state of things. If efficient plans of drainage can but be devised and executed, that region will yet be one of the most productive in the world. Still, the financiering which conjured up the means of building that New Albany and Michigan City Railroad is worthy of a brazen monument. At Westville, I was but eleven miles from Laporte, and four from the crossing of the great Northern Indiana Road from Chicago: so, having accomplished sixty-four miles by hand-car since dark, and arrived within striking distance of a civilized railroad, I went to bed till breakfast-time; took passage by wagon at 7; was in Laporte by 9; spoke for Temperance at 1; took the railroad at 3; and came here to fulfil my engagement to lecture last evening; and thus, having reopened my communications, I close this hurried account of A Night Ride Across the Prairies.

A WINTER FLOOD IN ILLINOIS.

GALESBURG, ILLINOIS, February 7, 1857.

I LEFT the train from Chicago on this (the Burlington) Road at 7 A.M. yesterday at "Oquawka Junction," the last station this side of the Mississippi, and took the stage in due season for Oquawka ($5\frac{1}{2}$ miles north), on the bank of the great river, and the shire town of Henderson County. It had been raining and thawing for a day or so hereabout; and, though there was little snow to melt, the hard-frozen earth threw off the water like a glass roof. The creeks were all over their banks, wandering at their own sweet will,—"South Henderson," "Main Henderson," and "North Henderson" vying with each other in encroachments on the people's highway, and all the "sloughs" and depressions transformed into temporary lakes; but our stage crossed them all safely,—there being a solid frost bottom to each,—and reached Oquawka in due season.

But the rain poured harder as the day wore on, and the evening was as inclement and forbidding as could well be imagined. I said my say to a rather thin house,—yet a large gathering for such a night,—and then looked about for the means of making good my promise to be in Galesburg (only 33 miles distant, 27 of it railroad) this evening.

The prospect was not cheering. The rain was pouring, the wind howling, and the creeks rising. Already, the stage had been stopped by the creeks on its evening trip to the cars; and it was plain that to wait till morning was to prolong my stay indefinitely. Now, Oquawka is a nice place, as its mellifluous name would indicate, and has many excellent people whose acquaintance I should have been glad to improve; but the telegraph is not among its advantages, and I could not let the people of Galesburg, and other towns to which I was due, know what had become of me, nor why I disappointed them; so I resolved to dig out, if possible; and, as the creeks were still rising rapidly, the only course was to start at once. A council of wise friends decided that I could not reach Oquawka Junction, if I were ever so bent upon it, and should find no train there if I did; and that the only hopeful course was to take the highest or eastern road, and steer for Monmouth (half-way to Galesburg) at once. By taking this course, I should turn several vicious creeks, leaving only "Main Henderson" really formidable. So a buggy and capital span were procured from a livery-stable, with their shrewd and capable owner as pilot, and, at a little past 10 o'clock, we put out into the storm, resolved to see Monmouth (18 miles, by our route) before daylight, if possible. Though the clouds were thick, the wind blew, and the rain poured, there was a good moon above all, which, though obscured, gave about all the light that was really necessary.

Though Oquawka is built on the sand, we crossed wide stretches of water before we had cleared it; and, of the miles of high sand-ridge that intervened between it and "Main Henderson," I judge that fully a fourth lay under water. Still, hoofs and wheels brought up on frost; and it was not till we descended into the bottom of "Main Henderson" that matters began to wear a serious aspect.

Forty rods west of the ordinary channel of the creek, we plunged into the water, which grew gradually deeper, until our boots and baggage had drunk of it to satiety. Just at this point, the driver's quick and wary eye caught sight of some plank or timber which had formed part of a bridge over one of the ordinary side-cuts of the stream when over its bank,—said plank or timber-head being even with the surface of the flood, with such an angle of inclination as indicated that the bridge was a wreck, and had probably in good part floated off. He reined up his horses before reaching it, and turned them face about, and in a minute we were half-way back,—not to dry, but to unflooded land. Here we took sweet counsel together, and I offered to return to Oquawka if he considered it foolhardy to persist in going forward. He studied a moment, and concluded to make another attempt; which he did, and went through above the treacherous bridge, though I don't believe any man could have done it two hours later. We were soon in shallower water, found the main bridge all right, and no deep water east of it, though "Smith's Creek" (a tributary which enters "Main Henderson" just below the bridge) set back upon and covered our road with a swift current for perhaps a quarter of a mile. The driver was familiar with the road, and thought it had never been so covered before. Soon, however, we ascended a long, badly gullied hill of the very worst clay, and breathed more freely on the high, level prairie, covered in good part with water, and not pretty wheeling, but never threatening to float us bodily off, like that raving "Main Henderson."

Having reached "Stringtown," five or six miles on our way, the driver called up a wayside friend, and borrowed dry socks, while I made researches in my baggage for a like creature-comfort, but with very unsatisfactory results. "Main Henderson" had been there before me, and had made everything fit for his wear, and unfit for mine. I closed valise and leathern bag with a shiver, and we resumed our weary way.

I do like the prairies, though their admirers won't admit it; and I cheerfully certify that the best going we found was on the virgin turf. True, the "sloughs" were many and wide; yet, there was frost and ice at the bottom of them, which seldom cut through; but, whenever it did, it gave horses, buggy, and riders, a racking. My pilot picked our way with great judgment, and we were nevermore stopped, and hardly checked, until we came out on the main road westward from Monmouth, three miles distant.

That three miles of dense prairie was the heaviest travelling I ever underwent; and, if our jaded horses traversed it in an hour and a quarter, they did passing well. On the naked prairie, we felt little anxiety; for, if the slough seemed too deep straight ahead, we could sheer right or left *ad libitum*, only taking care to keep some landmark in view, if possible. But roads imply bridges over the water-courses; and these bridges were far more perilous than the water-courses themselves.

Still the wind blew, still the rain fell, in spite of our repeated predictions that it would soon hold up; and still our horses plodded slowly onward, until those three miles seemed to me interminable. Our main business was to watch the bridges just ahead, and see that they had not been washed out; and they generally seemed to stand remarkably well. At last, Monmouth was in sight; the last bridge was passed; no, not the last, for our horses were in a deep gully this instant. A second more, and they sprang out, and jerked the buggy in with a crash that is still audible. The nigh fore-wheel snapped its tire, and went down, an armful of oven-wood; the tongue split, but held on, and the driver was pitched across my knees head downward into the deep mortar-bed termed the road. I went forward on my face, but clung to the wreck, with my feet entangled in apron and blankets; and, as the horses started to run, the look ahead for an instant was not flattering.

Only for an instant, however. The idea of running with that wreck through such mud, after a heavy night-drag of eighteen miles, was so essentially ridiculous that no well-bred horse could have entertained it. Ours perceived this instinctively, and soon slacked up, while the driver recovered his feet and his reins, if he had ever fully lost the latter. I cannot say how I came out of the dilapidated vehicle, nor could the driver give me any light on the subject; but I soon found myself resuming the perpendicular, and facing rearward in quest of my hat, which I found in a wayside pond several rods back, two thirds full of water, but still floating. My blanket I fished out of the semi-liquid mud about midway between my goal and my starting-point, and, for the first time on my journey, found its company disagreeable.

Men never know when they are well off. Five minutes before, I had been industriously cherishing my cold, wet feet, fencing off the driving rain, and fancying myself an object of just compassion; now, I saw clearly that, so long as the carriage remained sound, I had been in an enviable state of ease and enjoyment. Throwing my soiled blanket over one arm, and taking my valise in the opposite hand, I pulled one foot after another out of the deep, tarry mud, losing both my well-fastened overshoes therein without knowing it, and pushed through to a tavern at the rate of a mile and a half per hour, in a state of general bedragglement and desperate jollity which Mark Tapley could not have bettered.

It was 4 A. M. when a hospitable roof overshadowed us. The house was full, and my petition for a pair of slippers, and a room with a fire in it, could not be granted. But a bar-room fire was got up, and a bed in due time provided, though a ball that night in the village — no, city — had absorbed most of the accommodations. But our noble horses found what they needed, and we had an hour's sleep or more, though I did not incline to sleep at all. I got up to breakfast, and to find all as I expected about the railroad. The Chicago night-train went down nearly on time, but did not reach Oquawka Junction, finding the track all washed out at the crossing of "South Henderson," ten miles below. But its engine came back about 9 A.M., took on board half a dozen of us, and backed up to Galesburg (seventeen miles) in less than an hour; saving me another dreaded carriage-ride of at least six hours. We crossed one washed-out place, which threatened to throw us off, but did not. I guess I am the last person who will have left Oquawka for several days, and suspect Burlington (Iowa) has parted company with the world eastward of the Mississippi for at least as many.

MORAL. — We are none of us half grateful enough for the blessings of railroads, — when the trains run, and the cars don't fly the track.

MARRIAGE AND DIVORCE.

A DISCUSSION BETWEEN HORACE GREELEY AND ROBERT DALE OWEN.

DIVORCE.—WOMAN'S RIGHTS.*

OUR Legislature is again importuned to try its hand at increasing the facilities of divorce. We trust it will ponder long and carefully before it consents. That many persons are badly mated is true; but that is not the law's fault. The law of our State says plainly to all the unmarried, "Be very careful how you marry; for a mistake in this regard is irrevocable. The law does not constrain you to marry, does not hurry you to marry, but bids you be first *sure* that you know intimately and love devotedly the person with whom you form this irrevocable union. We rectify no mistakes; it rests with you not to make any. If you do, bear the penalty as you ought, and do not seek to transfer it to the shoulders of the community." And this, we think, is, in the broad view, right, though in special cases it involves hardship.

The paradise of free-lovers is the State of Indiana, where the lax principles of Robert Dale Owen, and the utter want of principle of John Pettit (leading revisers of the laws), combined to establish, some years since, a state of law which enables men or women to get unmarried nearly at pleasure. A legal friend in that State recently remarked to us, that, at one County Court, he obtained eleven divorces one day before dinner; "and it was n't a good morning for divorces either." In one case within his knowledge, a prominent citizen of an Eastern manufacturing city came to Indiana, went through

* Editorial in The Tribune of March 1, 1860.

the usual routine, obtained his divorce about dinner-time, and, in the course of the evening was married to his new inamorata, who had come on for the purpose, and was staying at the same hotel with him. They soon started for home, having no more use for the State of Indiana; and, on arriving, he introduced his new wife to her astonished predecessor, whom he notified that she must pack up and go, as there was no room for her in that house any longer. So she went.

How many want such facility of divorcing in New York? We trust not one in a hundred. If we are right in this judgment, let the ninety-nine make themselves heard at Albany as well as the one. The discontented are always active; the contented ought not to sleep evermore.

We favor whatever may be done to mitigate the hardships endured by mismated persons in perfect consistency with the maintenance of the sanctity and perpetuity of Marriage. Cases are constantly occurring in which a virtuous and worthy girl persists in marrying a dissolute scapegrace, in spite of the most conclusive demonstrations of his worthlessness. Five years hence, when he has become a miserable loafer and sot, she will wish herself divorced from him; but the law says No, and we stand by it. But the law ought to allow her to earn for herself and her little ones, and not enable him to appropriate and squander her few hard-won shillings. This is asked for, and ought to be granted. So the law should allow the woman who is living wholly separate from her husband, by reason of his brutality, cruelty, or profligacy, to have the same control over her property and earnings as if she had never married. This is not now the case. Nay; we know an instance in which a woman, long since separated from her worthless husband, and trying hard to earn a meagre living for their children, was disabled and crippled by a railroad accident; yet the law gives her no right of action against the culpable company; her broken ankles are legally her runaway husband's, not her own; and he would probably sell them outright for a gallon of good brandy, and let the company finish the job of breaking them at its convenience.

We heartily approve of such changes in our laws as would make this deserted wife the legal owner of her own ankles; but we would not dissolve the marriage obligation to constancy for any other cause than that recognized as sufficient by Jesus Christ.

MR. OWEN'S RESPONSE.*

To the Editor of the New York Tribune:—

Sir: Retired from political life, and now disposed to address the public, if at all, through a calmer medium than the columns of a daily paper, still, I cannot read the allusion in this morning's Tribune, made in connection with an important subject, to my adopted State and to myself by name, without feeling that justice to both, and, what is of more consequence, the fair statement of a question involving much of human morality and happiness, require of me a few words. You say:—

"The Paradise of free-lovers is the State of Indiana, where the lax principles of Robert Dale Owen, and the utter want of principle of John Pettit (leading revisers of the laws), combined to establish, some years since, a state of law which enables men and women to get unmarried nearly at pleasure."

You are usually, I think, correct in your statements of fact, and doubtless always intend to be so. That in this endeavor you sometimes fail, we have a proof to-day.

So far as I recollect, the Indiana law of divorce does not owe a single section to Mr. Pettit. Be that, however, as it may, it owes one of its provisions, *and one only*, to me. I found that law thirty-four years ago, when I first became a resident of the State, in substance nearly what it now is; indeed, with all its essential features the same. It was once referred to myself, in conjunction with another member of the Legislature, for revision; and we amended it in a single point; namely, by adding to the causes of divorce "habit-

* From The Tribune of March 5, 1860.

ual drunkenness for two years." In no other particular, either by vote or proposition, have I been instrumental in framing or amending the law in question, directly or indirectly.

Do not imagine, however, that I seek to avoid any responsibility in regard to that law as it stands. I cordially approve it. It has stood the test for forty or fifty years among a people whom, if you knew them as intimately as I do, candor would compel you to admit to be, according to the strictest standard of morality you may set up, not one whit behind those of sister States, perhaps of more pretensions. I approve the law, not on principle only, but because, for more than half a lifetime, I have witnessed its practical workings. I speak of its influence on *our own citizens.* It is much to be regretted that any one should ever be compelled to seek a divorce out of his own State. But, even in alluding to abuses which *have* occurred in this connection, you failed to tell your readers, what perhaps you did not know, that our law has of late years been so changed that the cases you state cannot possibly recur. No one can now sue for a divorce in Indiana, until he has been during one year, at least, a resident of the State; and the provision regarding timely notice to the absent party is of the strictest kind.

You speak of Indiana as "the Paradise of free-lovers." It is in New York and New England, refusing reasonable divorce, that free-love prevails; not in Indiana. I never even heard the name there. You locate the Paradise, then, too far west.

And does it not occur to you, when a million of men,— chiefly plain, hardy, industrious farmers, with wives whom, after the homely old fashion, they love, and daughters whose chastity and happiness are as dear to them as if their homes were the wealthiest in the land,— does it not occur to Horace Greeley that, when these men go on deliberately for half a century maintaining unchanged (or, if changed at all, made more liberal) a law of divorce which he denounces as breeding disorder and immorality,— that the million, with their long experience, may be right, and that Horace Greeley, without that experience, may be wrong?

You talk of my "lax principles." I think that, by my past life, I have earned the right to be believed when I say what *are* my principles and what are not.

On this subject, they go just so far as the Indiana law, and no further. I have given proof of this. I have had a hundred opportunities, and never used them, to move its amendment. I was chairman of the Revision Committee of our Constitutional Convention; but in our Constitution we incorporated nothing in regard to divorce, except a prohibition against all divorces by the Legislature. To that, I think you will not object. At the next session, I was chairman of the committee to revise the laws; but we merely reënacted the old divorce law, of which experience had taught us the benefits. It grants divorce for other causes than the one your law selects, — as for abandonment; for cruel treatment; for habitual drunkenness; and for any other cause for which the court may deem it proper that a divorce should be granted.

Are these "lax principles"? I claim to have them judged according to a Christian rule. "By their fruits ye shall know them." You have elopements, adultery, which your law, by rendering it indispensable to release, virtually encourages; you have free-love, and that most terrible of all social evils, prostitution. We, instead, have regulated, legal separations. You may feel disposed to thank God that you are not as other men, or even as these Indianians. I think that we are justified in His sight, rather than you.

Or is it, perhaps, the amendment I *did* propose and carry which seems to you lax in principle? — the provision, namely, that a wife should not be compelled to live with one who has been, for years, an habitual drunkard. You have told us that she ought to be so compelled. It constantly occurs, you say, that a "virtuous and worthy girl" marries a man who "becomes a miserable loafer and sot"; and you add: "She will wish herself divorced from him; but the law says No, and we stand to it."

Think, for a moment, what this actually involves! Let us take the "single captive," lest the multiplicity of images distract us. See the young creature, "virtuous and worthy," awaiting, late in the solitary night, the fate to which, for life, you consign her; and that for no sin more heinous than that her girl's heart, believing in human goodness, had trusted the vows and promises of a scoundrel. Is it her home where she is sitting? Let us not so desecrate the hallowed word. It is the den of her sufferings and of her shame. A bloated wretch, whom daily and nightly debauch has degraded below humanity, has the right to enter it. In what temper he will arrive, God alone knows, — all the animal within him, probably, aroused by drink. Will he beat her, — the mother of his children, the one he has sworn to love and protect? Likely enough. Ah! well if that be all! The scourge, though its strokes may cause the flesh to shudder, cannot reach the soul. But the possible outrages of this "miserable loafer and sot" may. He has the command of torments, legally permitted, far beyond those of the lash. That bedchamber is his, and the bed is the beast's own lair. It depends, too, on the brute's drunken will whether it shall be shared or not. Caliban is lord and master, by legal right. There is not a womanly instinct that he cannot outrage; not a holy emotion that he may not profane. He is authorized to commit what more resembles an infamous crime — usually rated second to murder, and often punished with death — than anything else.

And in this foul pit of degradation you would leave to a fate too horrible for infamy itself, a pure, gentle, blameless, Christian wife! Her cry thence may ascend to heaven; but, on earth, you think it should be stifled or contemned. She entreats for relief, — for escape from the pollution she abhors; you look down upon her misery, and answer her, "The law says No, and we stand to it."

God forgive you, Horace Greeley, the inhuman sentiment! I believe you to be a good man, desiring human improvement, the friend of what you deem essential to social morality. God send that you may never, in the person of a daughter of your own, and in the recital of her tortures, practically learn the terrible lesson how far you have strayed from the right!

Further to argue the general question would be an unwarrantable intrusion on your columns. Suffice it to say, that, if I differ from you as to the expediency of occasionally dissolving misery-bringing unions, it is precisely because I regard the marriage relation as the holiest of earthly institutions. It is for that very reason that I seek to preserve its purity, when other expedients fail, by the besom of divorce. No human relation ought to be suffered so to degenerate that it defeats the purpose of its institution. God imposes no laws on man merely to have the pleasure of seeing them obeyed; but, on the contrary, with special reference to His creatures' welfare and improvement. Marriage itself, like the Sabbath, was made for man; not man for marriage. It fulfils God's intentions so long as the domestic home is the abode of purity, of noble sentiment, of loving-kindness, or, at least, of mutual forbearance. But it defeats His purpose, and violates the Divine economy, when it becomes the daily cause of grievous words and heartless deeds, — of anger, strifes, selfishness, cruelty, ruffianism. That it should ever be thus degraded and perverted, all good men must lament; and all ought earnestly to seek the most effectual remedy.

In no country have I found the marriage obligation so little binding as in the nation * near whose court, as minister, I recently spent five years, — a country where Marriage is a sacrament and Divorce an impossibility; and where, indeed, on account of their "lax principles," the inhabitants neither need nor care for it. In no country have I seen marriage and its vows more strictly respected than in my adopted State, where the relation, when it engenders immorality, may be terminated by law. For the rest, divorces in Indiana are far less frequent than strangers, reading our divorce law, might be led to imagine. We find Jefferson's words to be as true of married persons as of the rest of man-

* Naples.

kind. They "are more disposed to suffer while evils are sufferable, than to right themselves by abolishing the forms to which they have been accustomed."

The question remains, whether it be more pleasing in the sight of God, and more conducive to virtue in man, to part decently in peace, or to live on in shameful discord.

I am, sir, your obedient servant,

ROBERT DALE OWEN.

NEW YORK, March 1, 1860.

REPLY BY MR. GREELEY.*

TO THE HON. ROBERT DALE OWEN, OF INDIANA: —

MY DEAR SIR: I had not expected to provoke your letter this day published; but the subject is one of the highest and widest importance, and I am very willing to aid in its further elucidation.

I do not think the issues of fact raised by you need long detain us. The country knows that you have for the last thirty years and more been a leading member of the generally dominant party in Indiana, — almost the only member who could with propriety be termed a political philosopher. As such, you have naturally exerted a very great influence over the legislation and internal policy of that State. Often a member of her Legislature as well as of Congress, and one of the revisers of her laws, you admit that the Law of Marriage and Divorce came at one time directly and distinctly under review before you, and that you ingrafted thereon a provision adding another — habitual drunkenness — to the pre-existing grounds on which divorce might legally be granted. As to "lax principles," I need not say more than that I cite your letter now before me as a sample and illustration.

But let me brush away one cobweb of your brain. You picture the case of a pure and gentle woman exposed to the

* From The Tribune of March 6, 1860.

brutalities and cruelties of a beastly sot of a husband. For such cases, *our* laws grant a separation from bed and board, — not a disruption of the marriage tie, with liberty to marry again. I think this is just right. I would not let loose such a wretch as you have depicted to delude and torture another "pure and virtuous girl." Let one victim suffice him.

Your reference to the "blameless *Christian* wife," and to what is "more pleasing in the sight of God," impels me to say that I must consider Jesus of Nazareth a better authority as to what is Christian and what pleases God than you are. His testimony on this point is express and unequivocal (Matt. xix. 9), that a marriage can be rightfully dissolved because of adultery alone. You well know that was not the law either of Jews or Romans in his day; so that he cannot have been misled by custom or tradition, even were it possible for him to have been mistaken. I believe he was wholly right.

For what *is* Marriage? I mind the Apostolic injunction, "Hold fast the form of sound words." Dr. Webster's great dictionary says: —

> "MARRIAGE: The act of uniting a man and woman *for life;* wedlock; the legal union of a man and woman *for life. Marriage* is a contract both civil and religious, by which the parties engage to live together in mutual affection and fidelity *till death shall separate them.*"

So Worcester: —

> "MARRIAGE: the act of marrying, or uniting a man and woman *for life* as husband and wife," &c., &c.

I surely need not quote to you the language of the marriage ceremony, — the mutual and solemn promise to "take each other for better, for worse," and "to live together *till death do part,*" &c., &c. You must be aware that the entire Christian, and I think most of the partially civilized pagan world, regard this solemn contract to cleave to each other *till death* as the very essence, the vital element, of Marriage.

Now it is not here necessary that I should prove this better than any possible substitute: suffice it that I insist that whoever would recommend a substitute should clearly, specifically, set forth its nature and conditions, and should call it by its distinctive name. There may be something better than Marriage; but nothing *is Marriage* but a solemn engagement to live together in faith and love *till death.* Why should not they, who have devised something better than old-fashioned Marriage, give their bantling a distinctive *name,* and not appropriate ours? They have been often enough warned off our premises; shall we never be able to shame them out of their unwarrantable poaching?

I am perfectly willing to see all social experiments tried that any earnest, rational being deems calculated to promote the well-being of the human family; but I insist that this matter of Marriage and Divorce has passed beyond the reasonable scope of experiment. The ground has all been travelled over and over: — from Indissoluble Monogamic Marriage down through Polygamy, Concubinage, easy Divorce, to absolute Free Love, mankind have tried every possible modification and shade of relation between Man and Woman. If these multiform, protracted, diversified, infinitely repeated, experiments have not established the superiority of the union of one man to one woman for life — in short, Marriage — to all other forms of sexual relation, then History is a deluding mist, and Man has hitherto lived in vain.

But you assert that the people of Indiana are emphatically moral and chaste in their domestic relations. That may be; at all events, *I* have not yet called it in question. Indiana is yet a young State, — not so old as either you or I, — and most of her adult population were born, and I think most of them were reared and married, in States which teach and maintain the Indissolubility of Marriage. That population is yet sparse; the greater part of it in moderate circumstances, engaged in rural industry, and but slightly exposed to the temptations born of crowds, luxury, and idleness. In such circumstances, continence would probably be general, even were Marriage unknown. But let Time and Change do their work, and then see! Given the population of Italy in the days of the Cæsars, with easy divorce, and I believe the result would be like that experienced by the Roman Republic, which, under the sway of easy divorce, rotted away and perished, — blasted by the mildew of unchaste mothers and dissolute homes.

If experiments are to be tried in the direction you favor, I insist that they shall be tried fairly, — not under cover of false promises and baseless pretences. Let those who will take each other on trial; but let such unions have a distinct name as in Paris or Hayti, and let us know just who are married (old style), and who have formed unions to be maintained or terminated as circumstances shall dictate. Those who choose the latter will of course consummate it without benefit of clergy; but I do not see how they need even so much ceremony as that of jumping the broomstick. "I'll love you so long as I'm able, and swear for no longer than this," — what need is there of any solemnity to hallow such a union? What libertine would hesitate to promise that much, even if fully resolved to decamp next morning? If man and woman are to be true to each other only so long as they shall each find constancy the dictate of their several inclinations, there can be no such crime as adultery, and mankind have too long been defrauded of innocent enjoyment by priestly anathemas and ghostly maledictions. Let us each do what for the moment shall give us pleasurable sensations, and let all such fantasies as God, Duty, Conscience, Retribution, Eternity, be banished to the moles and the bats, with other forgotten rubbish of bygone ages of darkness and unreal terrors.

But if — as I firmly believe — Marriage is a matter which concerns not only the men and women who contract it, but the State, the community, mankind, — if its object be not merely the mutual gratification and advantage of the husband and wife, but the due sustenance, nurture, and education of their children, — if, in other words, those who voluntarily incur the obligations of parentage can only discharge those obligations personally and conjointly, and to that end are bound to live together in love, at least until their youngest child shall have attained perfect physical and intellectual maturity, — then I deny that a marriage can be dissolved save by death or that crime which alone renders its continuance impossible. I look beyond the special case to the general law, and to the reason which underlies that law; and I say, — No couple can innocently take upon themselves the obligations of Marriage until they KNOW that they are one in spirit, and so must remain forever. If they rashly lay profane hands on the ark, theirs alone is the blame; be theirs alone the penalty! They have no right to cast it on that public which admonished and entreated them to forbear, but admonished and entreated in vain. Yours,

HORACE GREELEY.

NEW YORK, March 5, 1860.

MR. OWEN'S REJOINDER.*

TO THE HON. HORACE GREELEY: —

MY DEAR SIR: In one matter we shall not differ, and that is in the opinion that Jesus of Nazareth should be considered better authority as to what is Christian — and I will add as to what is conducive to public morals — than either you or I. The longer I live, the more I settle down to the conviction that *the* one great miracle of history is, that a system of ethics so far in advance as was the Christian System, not only of the semi-barbarism of Jewish life eighteen hundred years ago, but of what we term the civilization of our own day, should have taken root, and lived, and spread, where every opinion seemed adverse and every influence hostile. But, before we take Christ's opinion on the subject in hand, let us go a little further back.

You tell us that "the very essence of marriage" is, that

* From The Tribune of March 12, 1860.

the married should "cleave to each other till death." And, as a corollary, you insist that, if this condition is ever violated (as by the action of a divorce law), then it is *not* Marriage which prevails, but only a substitute. You add :—

"I insist that whoever would recommend such substitute should clearly, specifically set forth its nature and conditions, and should call it by its distinctive name. There may be something better than Marriage, but nothing *is Marriage* but a solemn engagement to live together *till death.* Why should not they who have devised something better than old-fashioned Marriage give their bantling a distinctive *name,* and not appropriate ours? They have been often warned off our premises; shall we never be able to shame them out of their unwarrantable poaching?" [The Italics are yours.]

This is plain. If the law regards Marriage as a contract which, under any circumstances, may be terminated, then (you allege) men and women live together under what is but a substitute for marriage, — under what should go by the name of concubinage, or some similar term. Such is the state of things, you infer, under the present Indiana law.

I do not think you reflected what a sweeping assertion you were here making. For there is not a State in the Union — not even New York — which is without a divorce law. In every State of the Union, therefore, Marriage is a contract of such a nature that contingencies *may* arise under which the married may *not* "live together until death them do part." If, then, the possible contingency of separation, legally admitted, annuls "the very essence of marriage," and converts it into concubinage, in what condition, I pray you, are married people living throughout the United States?

The same state of things prevails in all Protestant countries. Only in those which acknowledge the Pope as their religious head is Marriage an indissoluble sacrament. Is it your opinion that Catholics only are really married?

But this is a mere instalment of the difficulties which inhere in your proposition. Moses, of whom we are told (Deuteronomy v. 31) that God said to him: "Stand thou here by me, and I will speak unto thee all the commandments, and the statutes, and the judgments which thou shalt teach my people," promulgated to the Jews a law of divorce. Our divorce-law in Indiana must be, even in your eyes, a moral statute, compared to that of the Jewish lawgiver; for the latter provided: "When a man hath taken a wife and married her, and it come to pass that she find no favor in his eyes, then let him write her a bill of divorcement, and give it in her hand, and send her out of his house. And when she is departed out of his house, she may go and be another man's wife." (Deuteronomy xxiv. 1.) This, unless you deny the record, you must admit to be God's own law. It was first declared, according to the usual chronology, about 1450 years before the Christian era. It remained unchanged till Christ's day. Joseph and Mary were married under it; and the former, when he doubted Mary's fidelity, was "minded to put her away privily." For fourteen centuries and a half, then, God's chosen people, living under His law, had, according to you, a mere substitute for marriage. What distinctive name the "bantling" deserves, I leave to your judgment. We have been accustomed to regard it as "old-fashioned marriage." It is certain, however, that the contract, under such a law, was, "I will be your husband just as long as you find favor in my eyes; and, as soon as you cease to do so, you shall have a bill of divorcement, and be sent out of my house. Then you may marry whom you please."

Jesus tells us that this law was given "because of the hardness of their hearts"; or, as we should now express it, because of the low grade of morality then existing in Judea. Nevertheless, if it really be God's own law, how can you allege that it is wrong in itself? But, if it be not wrong, then divorce, even of the easiest attainment, must, in a certain state of society, be right. And hence results another important principle; namely, that there is no absolute right or wrong about this matter of divorce; but that it may properly vary in its details at different stages of civilization. It is certain that, under the Divine Economy, our modern sense of propriety and morality has been so developed, that we should not tolerate the Jewish statute giving uncontrolled license to the husband, but no right of relief whatever to the wife.

Jesus, discarding the old law, is stated to have proposed (as you remind us) to the people of his day a substitute where there was but a single cause for divorce, — the same recognized by the New York statute. But his idea of conjugal infidelity was not that entertained in our courts of law. He looked, beyond surface-morality, to the heart. In his pure eyes, the thought and the act were of equal criminality. His words were: "Whosoever looketh on a woman to lust after her hath committed adultery with her already in his heart." (Matthew v. 28.) The fair inference seems to be, that the proper cause for divorce is, not the mere physical act of infidelity, but that adultery of the heart which quenches conjugal love; thus destroying that which, far more justly than your cohabitation till death, may be regarded as "the very essence of Marriage."

I do not allege that Jesus so connected his two teachings, — that regarding divorce and that defining adultery, — that the Jews of his day, gross-minded as they were, might detect the connection and perceive its inference. If the Hebrews, in Moses' time, were so steeped in barbarism that nothing better than the bill-of-divorcement privilege was suitable for them, we may readily imagine that, even after fourteen centuries had elapsed, enough of the hardness of heart would remain to justify a law, in advance of the other, indeed, but still only adapted to a hard, material race, — a race who had not learned that the letter killeth, but the spirit giveth life, — a race who cannot be supposed to have been capable of appreciating, hardly of comprehending, a morality of standard so exalted that the thought is brought to judgment though the deed disclose it not.

I will go further and admit that, if the words of Jesus, in the text quoted by you, have come down to us reported with strict accuracy, he may have intended the men of his day to put upon them, as best adapted to their social *status*, the literally material interpretation which seems to have suggested itself to the framers of the New York divorce law. Jesus was not one who urged reform, as some modern innovators do, rashly or prematurely. Prudence was one of his distinguishing characteristics. He said not all that was in itself true and proper to be said at some time, but only all the truths which the people to whom he addressed himself were prepared to receive. That he kept back a part, we have his own words to prove: "I have yet many things to say unto you, but ye cannot bear them now; howbeit, when He, the Spirit of Truth, is come, he will guide you into all truth." (John xvi. 12, 13.)

Yet, even if your law-makers but received the same impression that was produced on the Jews by Jesus' words, it by no means follows that it is the one adapted to our wants and progress. It by no means follows that *we* should not look beyond the dead letter to the living spirit. If the divorce law promulgated from Mount Sinai was no longer adapted to a world grown fifteen hundred years older, are we to suppose that eighteen hundred years more, passed away, have brought with them no need for another advance and a more enlightened interpretation?

Thus, I think, I have shown you:—

First. That it will not do to warn us who think Divorce a moralizing engine, as poachers, off your self-enfeoffed premises; or to bid us seek some name other than Marriage wherewith to designate our legal unions. The Bible tells us that the ancestors of Christ were really married; and I never heard this denied, till your doctrine denied it.

Second. That, according to the Old Testament, easy divorce was expressly permitted, three thousand years ago, by the Deity himself.

Third. That divorce laws may properly vary, in different stages of civilization. And

Fourth. That the language of Jesus, fairly construed, designates the proper cause of divorce to be, that infidelity of the heart which defeats the true purpose of marriage.

In conclusion, permit me to say, as to the quasi-divorce to which, under the name of "separation from bed and board," you refer, and which you think "just right," that of all the various kinds of divorce it has been found, in practice, to be the most immoral in its tendency. The subjects of it, in that nondescript state which is neither married nor single, are exposed — as every person of strong affection must be who takes a vow of celibacy yet mixes with the world — to powerful temptations. Unable to marry, the chances are, that these law-condemned celibates may do worse. I think that those members of your bar with whom the procurement of legal separations is a specialty could make to you some startling disclosures on this subject.

But, be this as it may, what becomes of the "mutual and solemn vow to live together till death them do part"? What becomes of the dictionary definitions which you adduce about being "united for life," and about "affection and fidelity till death shall separate them"? Does not your policy of "separation from bed and board" as effectually extinguish these, and thus, according to your view, as completely convert Marriage into a concubinal substitute, as my remedy of Divorce?

I am, my dear sir, faithfully yours,

ROBERT DALE OWEN.

NEW YORK, March 6, 1860.

MR. GREELEY AGAIN.*

TO THE HON. ROBERT DALE OWEN OF INDIANA:—

DEAR SIR: In my former letter, I asserted, and I think proved, that

I. The established, express, unequivocal dictionary meaning of Marriage is *union for life.* Whether any other sort of union of man and woman be or be not more rational, more beneficent, more moral, more Christian, than this, it is cer-

* From The Tribune of March 17, 1860.

tain that *this is Marriage*, and that that other is something else.

II. That this is what we who are legally married — at all events, if married by the ministers of any Christian denomination — uniformly covenant to do. I distinctly remember that *my* marriage covenant was "for better, for worse," and "until death do part." I presume yours was the same.

III. That Jesus of Nazareth, in opposition to the ideas and usages current in his time, alike among Jews and Gentiles, expressly declared Adultery to be the only valid reason for dissolving a marriage.

IV. That the nature and inherent *reason* of Marriage inexorably demand that it be indissoluble except for that one crime which destroys its essential condition. In other words, no marriage can be innocently dissolved; but the husband or wife may be released from the engagement upon proof of the utter and flagrant violation of its essential condition by the other party.

And now, allow me to say that I do not see that your second letter successfully assails any of these positions. You do not, and cannot, deny that our standard dictionaries define Marriage as I do, and deny the name to any temporary arrangement; you do not deny that I have truly stated Christ's doctrine on the subject (whereof the Christian ceremonial of Marriage, whether in the Catholic or Protestant Churches, is a standing evidence); and I am willing to let your criticism on Christ's statement pass without comment. So with regard to Moses: I am content to leave Moses's law of divorce to the brief but pungent commentary of Jesus, and his unquestionably correct averment that "from the beginning, it was not so."

But you say that, if my position is sound, I make "a sweeping assertion" against the validity of the marriages now existing in Indiana and other divorcing States. O no, sir! Nine tenths of the people in those States — I trust, ninety-nine hundredths — were married by Christian ministers, under the law of Christ. They solemnly covenanted to remain faithful until death, and they are fulfilling that promise.

Your easy-divorce laws are nothing to them; their conscience and their lives have no part in those laws. Your State might decree that any couple may divorce themselves at pleasure, and still those who regard Jesus as their Divine Master and Teacher, would hold fast to his Word, and live according to a "higher law" than that revised and relaxed by you.

I dissent entirely from your dictum that the words of Jesus relative to Marriage and Divorce may have been intended to have a local and temporary application. On the contrary, I believe he, unlike Moses, promulgated the eternal and universal law, founded, not in accommodation to special circumstances, but in the essential nature of God and man. I admit that he may sometimes have withheld the truth that he deemed his auditors unable to comprehend and accept, but I insist that what he *did* set forth was the absolute, unchanging fact. But I did not cite him to overbear reason by authority, but because you referred first to Christianity and the will of God, and because I believe what he said respecting Marriage to be the very truth. Can you seriously imagine that your personal exegesis on his words should outweigh the uniform tradition and practice of all Christendom?

You understand, I presume, that I hold to separations "from bed and board"—as the laws of this State allow them—only in cases where the party thus separated is in danger of bodily harm from the ferocity of an insane, intemperate, or otherwise brutalized, infuriated husband or wife. I do not admit that even such peril can release one from the vow of continence, which is the vital condition of Marriage. It may possibly be that there is "temptation" involved in the position of one thus legally separated; but I judge this evil far less than that which must result from the easy dissolution of Marriage.

For here is the vital truth that your theory overlooks: The Divine end of Marriage is parentage, or the perpetuation and increase of the Human Race. To this end, it is indispensable—at least, eminently desirable—that each child should enjoy protection, nurture, sustenance, at the hands of a mother not only, but of a father also. In other words, the parents should be so attached, so devoted to each other, that they shall be practically separable but by death. Creatures of appetite, fools of temptation, lovers of change, as men are, there is but one talisman potent to distinguish between genuine affection and its meretricious counterfeit; and that is the solemn, searching question, "Do you know this woman so thoroughly, and love her so profoundly, that you can assuredly promise that you will forsake all others and cleave to her only until death?" If you can, your union is one that God has hallowed, and man may honor and approve; but, if not, wait till you can thus pledge yourself to some one irrevocably, invoking heaven and earth to witness your truth. If you rush into a union with one whom you do not thus know and love, and who does not thus know and love you, yours is the crime, the shame; yours be the life-long penalty. I do not think, as men and women actually are, this law can be improved; when we reach the spirit-world, I presume we shall find a Divine law adapted to its requirements, and to our moral condition. Here, I am satisfied with that set forth by Jesus Christ. And, while I admit that individual cases of hardship arise under this law, I hold that there is seldom an unhappy marriage that was not originally an unworthy one, — hasty and heedless, if not positively vicious. And, if people *will* transgress, God can scarcely save them from consequent suffering; and I do not think you or I can.

Yours,
HORACE GREELEY.

NEW YORK, March 11, 1860.

A CORRECTION.*

TO THE EDITOR OF THE N. Y. TRIBUNE: —

SIR: Your paper of yesterday, 12th inst., contains a letter bearing the signature of Robert Dale Owen. After eulogizing

* From The Tribune of March 12, 1860.

the doctrine of the New Testament, which is carried out in the law of the State of New York, and which only permits divorce in case of adultery, the writer falls foul of that "semi-barbarous" people, the Jews, and their legislator, Moses, whose law of divorce Mr. R. D. Owen professes to quote *verbatim* from Deuteronomy xxiv. 1: "When a man hath taken a wife and married her, and it come to pass that she find no favor in his eyes, then let him write her a bill of divorcement and give it in her hand, and send her out of his house." Now, I would respectfully ask of Mr. R. D. Owen, how is it, that, in transcribing these words out of the Bible, he has left out and altogether omitted the words "because he hath found some uncleanness in her," which form an integral part of the first verse in the twenty-fourth chapter of Deuteronomy, after the sentence, "find no favor in his eyes," and before the sentence, "then let him write," &c.

These words omitted by Mr. R. D. Owen form the gist of the whole law on Divorce. For the Hebrew word *ervah*, which the English version here renders "uncleanness," is throughout sacred Scripture invariably used to express illicit sexual intercourse. *Vide* Leviticus xviii., where the word occurs several times, and is rendered "nakedness."

Into the argument on Divorce it is not my intention to enter; and, as it is not parliamentary to impute motives, I must not say that Mr. R. Owen intentionally mutilated the text he quotes, leaving out words which fully prove that this Word of God, through Moses His servant, so cavalierly, not to say unfairly, treated by Mr. R. D. Owen, is identical with the law of our State, which he praises as derived from the New Testament. But I should like to know, and I ask you, Mr. Editor, what degree of confidence and consideration can be due to the assertions and opinions of a disputant who, professing to quote *verbatim* from a book so well known as the Bible, "somehow" contrives to omit the pith and marrow of a law against which he directs his assault?

Yours,

A Semi-Barbarous Rabbi.

REPLY BY MR. OWEN.*

To "A Semi–Barbarous Rabbi":—

Sir: I omitted the words in the text from Deuteronomy, to which in to-day's Tribune you refer, intentionally. If they were at all essential to the true understanding of the text, you are right in taking me severely to task for their omission. A man who would garble a quotation from any book to suit his purpose ought to forfeit all claim to public confidence.

I omitted them from what you may term a weakness, or may pronounce to be mere fastidiousness. My studies never having gone beyond Greek, the Old Testament, in its original tongue, is a sealed book to me. The expression, "because he hath found some uncleanness in her," conveyed to my mind no idea except as a phrase, couched in terms less veiled than modern usage is wont to employ, to mean disgust produced by some personal habit or idiosyncrasy. If in this I was not mistaken, the words are clearly non-essential; and I might innocently consult my feelings by omitting them in the columns of a daily paper.

But if, as you assert, the Hebrew word rendered "uncleanness" means "adultery," the omission was a grave one, even if not wilfully committed.

Does it mean adultery? If, without presumption, one who has never cultivated those roots of which that impudent fellow who indited Hudibras declared that they "flourish most on barren ground" may venture to argue the point with a Rabbi, I ask leave to take issue as to this interpretation. The subject, indeed, is a disagreeable one; but, in self-defence, I cannot now choose but follow whither you lead; namely, to the chapter cited by you, Leviticus xviii., where, as you inform us, the same word rendered "uncleanness" in Deuteronomy occurs several times, and is translated "nakedness." The first verse in which this happens reads thus: "The nakedness

* From The Tribune of March 19, 1860.

of thy father and the nakedness of thy mother thou shalt not uncover." If, as you allege, the word *ervah,* here translated "nakedness," is "throughout Sacred Scripture invariably used to express illicit sexual intercourse," or, as in a wife's case it would be, adultery; and if in the above text we substitute the one word for the other (as, if you are right, we may properly do), we shall have a text which you may comprehend, but which, to my obtuser perceptions, becomes wholly unintelligible.

I, in what your learning may set down as my simplicity, have always interpreted the text in question as referring to that offence which Shem and Japheth avoided, and for which Canaan (Genesis ix. 25) was cursed.

The word "uncleanness" does, indeed, in another text (Numbers v. 19), mean adultery; but, to give it that meaning, other defining words are expressly added. The priest, in that text, thus addresses the woman suspected of infidelity, "If no man have lain with thee, and if thou hast not gone aside to uncleanness *with another instead of thy husband,* be thou free," &c. Even in this text, however, if we were to attempt to substitute "adultery" for "uncleanness," we should not only have flagrant tautology, but a phrase that would seem to favor the idea that a wife might commit adultery with her husband as well as with other men; a thing, I must confess, I never before heard of.

But, independently of all this, the very words of the text seem to preclude your reading. Those words are: "If it come to pass that she (the wife) find no favor in his eyes because of some uncleanness," &c. Now, a wife may be said to "find no favor" in a husband's eyes, if her person or her character become disagreeable to him; but who would ever select such a phrase for a graver occasion? What would you think of saying, "Mrs. Smith found no favor in Mr. Smith's eyes, because of some acts of adultery"?

Finally, a difficulty remains which, in my eyes, as in the eyes of all Christians it must be, is insuperable; though "A

Semi-Barbarous Rabbi," perhaps, may get over it. *Jesus did not interpret the text as you do.*

Your assertion is, that Moses' law "is identical with the law of your State" (New York); that is to say, that it allowed Divorce for no other cause except adultery. If that was so, why, I pray you, did Jesus say: "Moses, because of the hardness of your hearts, suffered you to put away your wives"? And why did he add: "But in the beginning it was not so; and I say unto you: Whosoever shall put away his wife, except it be for fornication, and shall marry another, committeth adultery"? You make Moses' law and Jesus' law identical. Yet here we find Jesus discarding the one as a permission granted only because of the old Hebrews' hard hearts, and substituting the other. But was there nothing to discard? Were the law discarded and the substitute inculcated one and the same? That, as every reasonable man must see, is a sheer impossibility. For we cannot imagine Jesus' words to be meaningless, nor conclude that he was trifling with his audience, and recommending, for their adoption, the self-same thing he condemned.

We know, as well as we can know any historical fact, that, at the time when we are told that Jesus declared adultery to be the only valid cause for divorce, that declaration was, as Mr. Greeley, in his last letter, reminds us, "in opposition to the laws and usages alike among Jews and Gentiles."

I am not well informed as to how far Rabbis usually regard the words or the opinions of Jesus as authoritative. For myself, if I am in error, — if the ancient Jews, as you allege, were not permitted to divorce their wives "except it be for fornication," and if, in consequence, there was, in Christ's day, nothing to reform in the Jewish divorce law, — it is enough for me to know that, in adhering (as, after a careful survey of the whole ground, I do) to the opposite opinion, I am but adopting the views and sharing the interpretation put forth by the Author of the Christian religion.

ROBERT DALE OWEN.

NEW YORK, Saturday, March 17, 1860.

Comment by Mr. Greeley.

All this strikes us as very absurd, and based on an unaccountable lack of perception. The fundamental idea of the Mosaic law is personal and perfect *purity*. Moses, therefore, permitted the husband who had been deceived as to the chastity, *prior to marriage*, of his wife, to put her away. This Jesus disallowed, as a temporary or local permission, based on grounds peculiar to the Hebrew economy, reëstablishing in its stead the law as it was "from the beginning," that only incontinence, *after marriage*, can afford a valid reason for divorce.

MR. OWEN IN RESPONSE.*

THE WORD "ERVAH."

To the Editor of The N. Y. Tribune :—

Sir : Unwilling to rest under the imputation cast on me by you in to-day's "Tribune," namely, that my views in reply to a "Semi-Barbarous Rabbi" are "very absurd," and are "based on an unaccountable lack of perception," I have looked a little more closely into the philology of the question, and beg leave here to present to you the result.

Gesenius, than whom, you are aware, there is no better authority, in his Hebrew Lexicon, translates ERVAH, *turpitudo, fœditas;* and referring specially to the bill-of-divorcement text (Deuteronomy xxiv. 1), he renders it "*Macula aliqua in muliere reperta*"*;* that is, "a blemish (or spot) found in the woman." You can consult this Lexicon in the Astor Library.

In Luther's Translation of the Bible (to be found in the same Library), at the text above referred to, that reformer, in explaining the word "uncleanness," parenthesises thus : (*um etwas das ihm misfällt, es sey an ihrem Leibe oder Gebärden oder Sitten, die sich aber sonst züchtig verhällt ;*) which, if you are familiar with German, you know to mean : ("in re-

* From The Tribune of March 24, 1860.

gard to something which displeases him, either in her person or in her demeanor, or in her conduct, without imputation, however, on her chastity.") The word *züchtig* means strictly, *chaste, modest.* One could hardly find anything more in accordance with my interpretation than this.

Again, the learned Ewald (in his "Geschichte des Volks Israel," Vol. II. of Anhang, page 185), commenting on the Jewish bill of divorcement, says: *Und sicher enthielte ein solcher Brief keinen weitern Tadel der Frau als wäre er ein Klagebrief gewesen; sondern diente der Frau eher als ein Zeugniss dass ihrer Wiederheirath nichts im Wege stehe:* that is, "And such a document certainly imputed no further blame to the wife than if it had been a mere letter of complaint; on the contrary, it rather served as a certificate in her hands, in proof that there was no obstacle to a second marriage."

I think you will no longer deny that, if my views are "very absurd," they are at least sustained by the best Hebrew Lexicon of the day, by a writer of the highest authority on Hebrew history, and, finally, that they are indorsed, beyond all possible doubt, by the Great Reformer himself. These learned men must all have shared my "unaccountable lack of perception."

Whence you disinterred your idea that incontinence in the wife *prior to marriage* was the Mosaic ground of permission to put her away I have no idea whatever. Certainly not from the Old Testament, so far as I am acquainted with its pages. As I read there, incontinence before marriage, unless disproved (Deuteronomy xxii. 20, 21), was, according to the Mosaic law, punishable, not by a bill of divorcement, but by a cruel death.

Yours,

ROBERT DALE OWEN.

NEW YORK, Monday, March 19, 1860.

MR. OWEN RESUMES.*

DIVORCE.

To the Hon. Horace Greeley:—

My dear Sir: You derive your arguments against Divorce from two sources:

1. From Scripture.
2. From the morality of the case.

I. If you regard the Old Testament as a portion of the Word of God, you must admit that the Jewish bill-of-divorcement law was framed, not by a fallible lawgiver, but by the Deity himself, Moses being only the medium of its promulgation.

If you accept the authority of Gesenius, of Ewald, and of Luther, you must further concede to me that that bill-of-divorcement law permitted a husband to put away a faithful wife in any case in which she became personally disagreeable, or in her deportment obnoxious to him, and that he was sole judge whether she found favor in his eyes or not.

These premises conceded, it follows, that, upwards of three thousand years ago, God sanctioned a law which permitted a husband to put away his wife when she displeased him, by means of a simple bill of divorcement, drawn up by the husband himself.

The New Testament informs us, and you remind us, that Jesus, fourteen centuries later, disallowed that law. But he did not condemn it as a law which ought never to have existed; he intimates that it was rendered necessary by the "hard hearts" of those for whose guidance it was framed.

Then the law of God, enacted thirty-two centuries ago, was declared by Jesus, eighteen centuries ago, to be no longer adapted to the state of human society.

What follows? That there is no positive good or evil,—no absolute virtue or vice? Far from it. There are principles permanent as the everlasting hills, immutable as the

* From The Tribune of March 28, 1860.

laws that hold the planets to their course; principles that depend not on times and seasons, that are the same yesterday, to-day, and forever. Such, to select an eminent example, is the declaration, "Love is the fulfilling of the law." It was true from the creation; it will be true until time shall be no more.

But the details of a law are one thing, and a great, eternal principle is another. Laws properly change as the world changes. But the master principles underlying laws — the "laws of the laws," to adopt Bacon's phrase — endure while the world lasts.

Beyond the general rule, however, we have, in this particular case, the direct authority of Jesus for it, that a divorce law adapted to one age may cease to be suitable in another.

But, if the details of a Divine law three thousand years old were properly rejected in a later stage of society, is it not certain that the same *may* be true in our age of other details put forth by Jesus as suitable for the Jews of his day? for men so low in the social scale that they found in his teachings nothing but blasphemy, and rewarded them by mockings and scourgings, and a death of torture on the cross?

It follows, past all denial, that while, as Christians, we should be guided by the great principles taught by the Author of our religion, we are *not* bound by the details of a law adapted for Judea in the days of Herod the King; provided our moral sense, moulded and quickened by Christian study, leads us to the conclusion that we — less hard of heart than those who cried out, "Crucify him!" — can bear other laws and greater liberty than they.

And thus, at last, we are thrown back, for guidance, to the second source whence your arguments are derived.

II. In other words: What is the true morality of the case?

"The Divine end of Marriage," you say, "is the perpetuation and increase of the human race."

Has civilization, in our day, reached no further than this? Do we find in the holiest of human relations no higher, nobler object — no end more divine — than the operation of that instinct (common to man with the lower races) which peoples the earth? God has, indeed, ordained that, incidental to Marriage, and inseparable from it, shall be Reproduction. If, in any sense, it be true that this is *the* divine end of human marriage, it must be in the same sense which applies when the stag seeks his partner, or the dove submits to her mate. But, just in proportion as man is nobler than the bird of the air or the beast of the field, is his marriage removed to infinite distance above theirs. Woe to that bride, standing in her white robes before the altar, who is thought of, by the one at her side, only as the future bearer of his children! Woe to her, if she has not chosen a spouse whose heart is swelled with aspirations that overmaster the sensual; in whose soul there burns not a light pure enough and bright enough to quench, in such a moment as that, the lurid flames of desire?

It is one of the most beautiful and beneficent arrangements which mark the Divine economy, that an institution — a physical incident of which is the propagation of the race — should, in its higher and nobler results, be the means of calling forth all that is best and purest in the inner nature of man; love, in the broadest acceptation of that much profaned word, — love, that crushes man's innate selfishness, and teaches him the great lesson that the best happiness is to be found in cares for another, not in thoughts for himself; love that is heightened, indeed, by the warmth of earthly emotions, but has an existence above and apart from these; to remain when age has quenched passion, — to endure beyond the term of our present stage of existence.

In that higher phase of wedded life which has its origin in sentiments and aspirations such as these, not in the results of our nature's lower instincts, will a cultivated mind, in its best moments, recognize "the Divine end of Marriage." If, some day, released from the daily round and deafening whirl of politics, you give to your better instincts, in quiet, fair scope and free voice, I think they will teach you this.

Meanwhile, we are here at issue. You have one conception of the Divine end of Marriage, I another. If yours be the correct idea, then it may be that nothing except that which casts doubt on the parentage of offspring should be valid cause for the dissolution of Marriage. If, on the contrary, I have more justly interpreted the higher purposes of that institution, then whatever violates these defeats the Divine end of Marriage, and supplies rightful cause why the relation, failing in its true intent, should be discontinued. It is a sound principle in jurisprudence, that, with the termination of the cause for a law, the law also should cease.

I do not merely say, in cases where the holiest purposes for which God ordained Marriage are frustrated, its divinest ends defeated, and its inmost sanctuary defiled, by evil passions, that the relation, thus outraged, *may* not improperly cease: I say that, for the sake of virtue and for the good of mankind, in all such demoralizing cases, it *ought* to cease. Household strife is immorality; domestic hatred is immorality; heartless selfishness is immorality; inhuman treatment of the weak by the strong is terrible immorality. And that condition of things, degenerate from a noble purpose, which fosters evils such as these, has become itself immoral and demands abatement.

Why, in its vice-fostering perversion, should a life of bickering be dragged on, till death, at last, brings separation and peace? In the interests of the children, perhaps? But is that the atmosphere in which their young lives should expand? Or, is it in order that that intangible generality called SOCIETY may be propitiated and appeased? But how, I beg of you, can the true interests of Society be subserved by perpetuating immorality among its members? What sort of Moloch is this Society that demands the immolation of its own offspring?

What further objection do you interpose? In substance, this, — that men and women about to marry, exercising deliberation and discrimination, ought never to select ill; and that, if they do, "theirs is the crime and the shame, and theirs should be the life-long penalty."

If a lawgiver, directly or virtually, demands impossibilities, his laws will fail of their effect. In making his demands, then, he should have special reference to the powers likely to be at the disposal of those of whom these demands are made. It avails nothing to say that a thing ought to be, if, as a general rule, it cannot be.

But of all requirements, the most arduous — arduous even when mature thought has brought wisdom, and when age has conferred experience — is the decision whether a being, loved now, is the one of all others, intellectually, morally, physically, to whom, in a true home, we can impart permanent happiness, and from whom we are capable of receiving it. Mortal eyes, even the wisest, never fully penetrate the veil. There may be that beyond which no foresight could anticipate.

And, if such be the case, with wisdom and experience to guide, what shall we expect from unsuspicious faith, just entering a false world, serenely ignorant of its treacheries, an utter stranger to its guile? Will its goodness be its protection? The reverse. In such a trial, it is the noblest who are the most exposed. The better the nature, the more imminent the danger it encounters. The cold, the heartless, the calculating, have fair chance of escape; it is the warm, the trusting, the generous, who are the usual sufferers. What belief so blind as that of first, pure, young affection? What so easily cheated as a fresh and faithful and innocent heart?

And by what right, according to what principle, I pray you, do we decide that there is one mistake that is never to be corrected; one error, the most fatal of all, which, once committed, we shall never be permitted to repair?

A "life-long penalty" you would inflict. And for what heinous offence? Say that an honest mistake were a crime; say that a venial error were a career of shame. Even then, the sentiment would be Jewish, not Christian. "An eye for an eye, a tooth for a tooth," was the rule addressed to the hard hearts. Nowhere, in all Christ's teachings, will you find the like. The sin of your brother, sinning seven times, you would not forgive; yet, as a Christian, you ought to forgive it, even to seventy times seventy. The entrance to the father's house you would bar against the returning prodigal. His, you would declare to him, was "the sin, the shame"; his should be "the life-long penalty." No rejoicing that he was dead and is alive again; no weeping joy that he was lost and is found!

Let us dismiss abstractions, and stand face to face with the realities of life. The time may come when men and women (the eyesight of the affections opened) shall unfailingly distinguish and choose their own appropriate mates. I have heard enthusiasts argue that it will; and that there is a future before mankind, even on earth, in which conjugal separation and divorce will be unknown terms. God send it! But, meanwhile, it is with the present, and its errors, and its evils, and its sufferings, and its temptations to sin, that we have to deal. Where we fail to cure, it is our duty to alleviate. If we cannot make all the married virtuous and happy, let us do what we can, by humane laws of prevention, to relieve from immoral situations; and thus to diminish domestic misery and arrest household vice.

I thank you, my dear sir, for the opportunity afforded to discuss this subject, and am

Faithfully yours,

ROBERT DALE OWEN.

NEW YORK, Tuesday, March 20, 1860.

MR. GREELEY'S REJOINDER.*

TO ROBERT DALE OWEN:—

DEAR SIR: As you have intimated your willingness that our discussion should here close, I will endeavor to introduce no new views into this letter. I will simply sum up the controversy as it stands.

I. I have hitherto shown, and you have not attempted to

*** From The Tribune of April 7, 1860.**

disprove, that Marriage is, according to every standard dictionary, *a union for life,* indissoluble at the pleasure of those married, or either of them. I have insisted that you have no right to use this important word in a vitally different sense from that given to it by the great lexicographers. What you favor may be ever so much better than Marriage (though I believe it far otherwise), but it is manifestly not the same thing, and you ought to give it a distinctive name. When I am told that two persons are married, I understand that they have covenanted to live together as husband and wife, not during pleasure, but during life. The dictionaries, the Christian religion, the general consent of my countrymen and of the civilized world, fully justify me in that conception. When, therefore, you apply the term Marriage to a very different compact, you not merely use words unjustifiably, but you virtually confess the badness of your cause. The tradesman who counterfeits another's trade-marks virtually confesses the inferiority of his own wares. I protest, then, against your using the word Marriage to designate any other union than one for life. If A and B have agreed, with ever so much ceremony, to live as man and wife until one or both of them shall see fit to separate and form new relations, they may be ever so wisely and rationally paired, but they are not married. I made this point as strongly before; our readers will judge whether you have or have not met it. At all events, I mind the Apostle's injunction to "Hold fast the form of sound words." We who stand by Marriage as Jesus Christ established and Noah Webster defines it, have a right to the word by which that relation has ever been characterized. What you advocate is quite another thing,—be pleased to give it a distinguishing name. Then, if we call our compact by your name, the public will understand that we admit your union to be more rational, honorable, ennobling, than ours. At all events, we warn you off our premises, and insist that you shall not lay your eggs in our nest. If you demand liberty to form temporary unions, we will consider that demand; but you must not call them marriages;

for, though they may be the same to you, they are far otherwise to us.

II. As to the religious or Christian view of the subject, I rest on the simple, explicit averment of Jesus of Nazareth, as universally understood and regarded by the Christian Church for eighteen centuries. We know what Hebrew, Greek, Roman laws and customs respecting the marital union were in Christ's day; we know that Jesus propounded and his disciples accepted a very different law, — that of Marriage indissoluble but by death, or by that crime which is death to all the sanctities of Marriage. We know that Orthodox and Heretic, Catholic and Protestant, literal and liberal, with barely exceptions enough to prove the rule, have understood the Saviour's doctrine of Marriage throughout the Christian centuries as I do to-day. That this Christian doctrine of Marriage is a chief reason for the moral, intellectual, and even material, supremacy of Europe over Asia in our day, I do most firmly believe; *you* will regard it as you think fit. And, as to Moses and his law, with all you have to say of them, all the answer that seems to me needed is contained in the few words of Jesus on that very point: "Moses, for the hardness of your hearts," permitted easy divorce; "but from the beginning it was not so."

III. I have said that "the Divine end of Marriage is the perpetuation and increase of the human race." By that affirmation I abide. Of course, I did not say that Marriage has no other end than this; so all your criticism seems to me ludicrously inapposite. I do not urge that, in a true sexual union, everything else but the production, nurture, and well-being of children, must be ignored. I *do* insist that there must be nothing incompatible or inconsistent with this. If required to say whether the union of this man with this woman is true, noble, and honorable, or sensual, selfish, and debasing, I must ask, "Would they gladly have children born of it? Would they proudly acknowledge those children before the world, and undertake to fulfil toward them all the duties of parents?"

If not, their union, though impelled by mutual admiration, and signalized by a lava-flood of passion, is shameful and unblest. The sexual union which the immediate parties prefer should be childless has no right to be at all.

I was shocked when I heard an apostle of your faith say, some years since, "We hold that the parents are not to be *sacrificed* to the children." I hold, on the contrary, that the lives of true parents are filled with acts of self-sacrifice for their children, — that their lives have been well spent who have given to the world offspring nobler than themselves. And, while I admit that the conduct of a husband may be so outrageous, so brutal, as to justify the innocent wife in requiring a separation, I insist that one who truly comprehends the nature and purposes of Marriage will not seek to marry another while the father of her children is still living. I do not think she could look those children in the eye with all a mother's conscious purity and dignity while realizing that their father and her husband, both living, were different men. Nor do I feel that she could be to them all that a mother should be under such conditions.

IV. The vice of our age, the main source of its aberrations, is a morbid Egotism, which overrides the gravest social necessities in its mad pursuit of individual, personal ends. Your fling at that "intangible generality called SOCIETY" is directly in point. You are concerned chiefly for those who, having married unfortunately, if not viciously, seek relief from their bonds; I am anxious rather to prevent, or at least to render infrequent, immoral, and unfit sexual unions hereafter. The miseries of the unfitly mated may be deplorable; but to make divorce easy is in effect to invite the sensual and selfish to profane the sanctions of Marriage whenever appetite and temptation may prompt. Here are a man and a woman who know absolutely nothing of each other but that they are reciprocally pleased with each other's appearance, and think Marriage would conduce to their mutual enjoyment, — so they form a connubial partnership. Next year — perhaps next month — they have tired of each other, — discovered incompatibilities of temper, — quarrelled, — in short, they hate each other, as they very well may; so they are divorced, and ready to marry again. Gibbon intimates that, under the Roman liberty of Divorce, by which Rome was debauched and ultimately ruined, a woman had eight husbands within five years. Mr. Owen, whenever you shall have succeeded in appropriating our word Marriage as a fig-leaf for this sort of thing, you will cause us to invent or appropriate some other term to characterize what *we* mean by Marriage; and then you will very soon drop your own dishonored designation and come coveting ours again. So please leave us what belongs to us, and choose a new term for *your* arrangement now.

"It is very hard," said a culprit to the judge who sentenced him, "that I should be so severely punished for merely stealing a horse." "Man," replied the judge, "you are *not* so punished for merely stealing a horse, but *that horses may not be stolen.*" The distinction seems to me clear and vital. The wedded in soul may know each other if they will; it is impossible that others should certainly know them. To those who are thus wedded, the covenant to "take each other for better, for worse," and "to live together till death do part," has no terrors; they enter upon it without hesitation, and fulfil its conditions without regret. But to the libertine, the egotist, the selfish, sensual seeker of personal and present enjoyment at whatever cost to others, the Indissolubility of Marriage is an obstacle, a restraint, a terror; and God forbid that it should ever cease to be! Thousands would take a wife as readily, as thoughtlessly, as heartlessly, as they don a new coat or sport a new cravat, if it were understood that they might unmarry themselves whenever satiety, or disgust, or mutual dislike, should prompt to that step. But it is not so, Mr. Owen, even in Indiana. Men and women are married, even in Indiana, "for better, for worse," and under solemn covenant to "live together till death do part"; and they cannot resort to Divorce, even there, without conscious shame or general reprobation. That human laws may be everywhere conformed to the Divine, and no sexual union hallowed by

Church or State but that union for life which alone is true Marriage, is the ardent hope of

Yours,

HORACE GREELEY.

NEW YORK, March 31, 1860.

MR. OWEN'S CLOSING ARGUMENT.*

TO THE HON. HORACE GREELEY :—

MY DEAR SIR: Imitating your precaution, I shall, in summing up, avoid the introduction of new views; I shall also study strictest brevity. Had your summing up fairly presented the question at issue, the public need not have been troubled with mine.

It is a besetting weakness of our nature to imagine itself unfailingly right, its opinions infallibly true, its rules of action the only morality. If, in a discussion of principles, we yield to this, the best thing is to close it; because, conducted in such a spirit, it becomes useless, or worse.

The sole point of our discussion, and that which might be usefully, if dispassionately, debated, has been this: You advocate a divorce law with one only cause of divorce: I think it conducive to public morality that such a law should admit several causes. I took that position, and I took no other. I indorsed the divorce law of Indiana; nothing more. But how, in summing up, do you state the case? In substance, thus: Marriage under a single-cause divorce law, as in New York, *is* Marriage. There is no other Marriage. What goes by that name, under a divorce law admitting several causes, as in Connecticut or Indiana, is *not* Marriage, but concubinage. If those who are united under such laws call themselves married, they "use words unjustifiably"; they "virtually confess the badness of their cause"; they are as "tradesmen who counterfeit another's trade-marks";

* From The Tribune of April 21, 1860.

they are countenancing the Roman woman who had "eight husbands within five years," and appropriating Mr. Greeley's word Marriage "as a fig-leaf for this sort of thing." They must "choose a new term for *their* arrangement." Horace Greeley, armed with Noah Webster, declares to them, that "they may be ever so wisely and rationally paired, but they are not married," and he "protests against their using the word."

The law of Connecticut, the law of Indiana, declares, that Marriage, contracted under a divorce law admitting several causes, and by virtue of which the union *may*, in certain contingencies, terminate before death, *is* Marriage." Horace Greeley tells them it is "quite another thing." The law of Connecticut, the law of Indiana, provides, if a couple, legally divorced, contract a second marriage, such second marriage is legal. Horace Greeley insists that they "must not call that Marriage; for, though it may be the same to them, it is far otherwise to him."

Here is a conflict. The Revised Codes of Connecticut and Indiana (and of a dozen other States beside) declare one thing; Horace Greeley declares the opposite. The one or the other, it is evident, must be grievously in error.

Popes, from the Vatican, have, not unfrequently, assumed the power, as to certain laws enacted by duly constituted legal authority in various Catholic countries, by Papal Bull to override and annul them. But in our country we consider the law supreme; in force, and to be acknowledged and respected, until it be legally repealed.

This is not all. In your summing up, motives are imputed. Those who enact or approve a divorce law which admits more causes than one are told that "they are concerned chiefly for those who, having married unfortunately, if not viciously, seek relief"; and that this arises from a "morbid egotism, the vice of our age, which overrides the gravest social necessities in its mad pursuit of individual, personal ends."

Does it not occur to you, when men vote for or sanction reasonable divorce laws, they *may* do so from a conscientious motive? Does it not occur to you, that when an opponent expresses the opinion, "in cases where the holiest purposes for which God ordained Marriage are frustrated, and its inmost sanctuary defiled by evil passions, it ought for the sake of virtue to cease," — that he *may* be sincere in that opinion? Have you forgotten that there is One only who looks into the heart and reads its motives; and that no human being has a right, setting himself up as judge and ruler, to usurp His place?

The story of the horse-thief (told that he was punished not merely for his offence, but "*that horses may not be stolen*"), if it has any bearing on the subject at all, has an unfair one. Horse-stealing is a crime. To take it for granted that Divorce also is one is to prejudge the whole question under discussion. Again; if the meaning be, that the unhappily married should suffer, not merely for their mistake, but *that divorces may not be granted*, then you fall into the same error as the Jews, when they, zealous without knowledge for their Sabbath, were reminded by Jesus, in the spirit of the truest philosophy, that human institutions are made for man, not man for human institutions.

Others may have argued that children ought to be sacrificed to parents. I hold, and ever have held, that there is no duty more sacred than that which we owe to those to whom we impart existence. It is a misfortune, and a great one, that a mother should look her children in the eye, and think that their father, then living, and her husband, are different men. But far greater is the misfortune when she looks upon them with the bitter consciousness that they are daily, hourly, learning to know in their father a sot, a brute, a ruffian, the desecrator of the domestic sanctuary; far greater is the anguish to feel that that father never teaches them one lesson of virtue, never gives them one useful example, except it be such as the Helots furnished to the Spartan youth; a terrible beacon, warning from the shame and the folly of intemperance.

If you conclude that divorce laws necessarily cause young people to marry as readily and heartlessly as they don a fresh hat or sport a new bonnet, you do your fellow-creatures great injustice; and a few years' residence in Indiana would convince you of your mistake. You might be reminded of what, even at our age, we ought not to have forgotten, — what manner of thing, namely, youthful affection is; how undoubtingly it believes, how wholly it trusts; how little it calculates laws or troubles itself about Divorce, or dreams of anything except that it shall always love as it loves now; constancy a pleasure even more than a duty, and change an impossible desire. We often err in ascribing to the restraining influence of faulty laws that which is due to the faithful impulses of our better nature.

You remind us, on Gibbon's authority, that the liberty of Divorce was grossly abused in debauched Rome. I remind you that the liberty of Republicanism was terribly abused in revolutionary France. But it would be a poor argument thence to conclude, that, in this country, we ought to forbid divorce and introduce a monarchy.

The moral and intellectual supremacy of Europe over Asia you ascribe mainly to Christian Marriage. To Christian Marriage, as opposed to Polygamy, it may justly be thus ascribed. This opinion I myself, in a recent work, expressed: "Under the system of Monogamy alone have man's physical powers and moral attributes ever maintained their ascendency; while weakness and national decadence follow in the train of Polygamy, whether openly carried out, as in Deseret and Constantinople, or secretly practised, as in London and New York."*

But this has no bearing on the Divorce question. You will not assert that the morals were better before the Reformation, in Catholic countries refusing divorce, than they were after Luther's time in Protestant countries permitting it.

Briefly summing up, I remind you: —

1. That I proved, and you have not attempted to disprove, that, according to the Old Testament, God promulgated, more than three thousand years ago, a divorce law permitting a

* Footfalls on the Boundary of Another World, page 42.

husband to put away a wife who found no favor in his eyes; that that law prevailed among His chosen people from the time of Moses till long after Joseph and Mary were united subject to its provisions; and, consequently, that if Marriage, determinable by Divorce, be no Marriage, there was not a married man or woman among the Jews for fifteen hundred years.

2. I have shown, and you have admitted, that Jesus disallowed that law; not denying that it was suitable at the period it was given, yet declaring that, in his day, it ought not to prevail. I thence deduced the inference, not assailed by you, that, according to Scripture, divorce laws may properly vary in different stages of civilization.

3. I have stated, what the best legal authority * indorses, that, of the various kinds of Divorce, none has been found, in practice, so immoral as that variety, unknown to our Indiana law, but known in New York as "separation from bed and board." You think it "just right." Let the public judge between us.

4. Referring to our modern state of civilization, I have argued, that the present age is prepared to see, in the holiest of human relations, purposes far higher, infinitely more worthy the epithet divine, than the mere operation of the instinct that peoples the earth; that Marriage was designed to be, and should be, the means of calling out all that is best and purest in the inner nature of man; and that, when it becomes the daily source of anger, strife, cruelty, brutality, it defeats God's purpose, violates the Divine economy, becomes itself immoral, and ought to cease. You dissent. Again be the public the judge in the premises.

But if in these I dissent, there are other points as to which, in concluding this controversy, I am glad to agree with you. I agree that every State has a direct interest in the private morals of its members. I agree that whatever policy is found, in the end, best calculated to promote these morals, ought to prevail. I agree that it is one of the greatest of earthly blessings, when a married couple dwell together in

* Bishop, on Marriage and Divorce, § 277.

unity till death. I agree that no light or transient cause should dissolve the conjugal union. I agree that men and women ought mutually to bear and forbear "while evils are sufferable," rather than to right themselves by resort to separation or divorce. I agree, further, that a state of things which leads to Divorce is to be deprecated and lamented, and that Divorce itself is a grave misfortune. And I but add that, when a long train of abuses and immoralities, pursuing invariably the same course, clearly shows that a union has become destructive of its holy ends, then it ought to be a right, and may become a duty, to select of two evils the lesser; to acquiesce in the necessity which indicates a separation, and legally to dissolve the bands which connect the ill-mated members together.

In taking leave of you, suffer me to correct an error which crept into my second letter. I there said that there was not a State of the Union without a Divorce law. I ought to have added, "except the State of South Carolina." She boasts that "within her limits, a divorce has not been granted since the Revolution." But suspend your approbation till you learn, as Bishop will inform you, what is the concomitant: "Not only is adultery not indictable there [in South Carolina], but the Legislature has found it necessary to regulate, by statute, how large a proportion a married man may give of his property to his concubine."*

You will admit that your system of Indissoluble Marriage is dearly paid for, under such a state of things; nor have you been in the habit of asserting that the morals of divorce-denying South Carolina are superior to those of Connecticut or Indiana.

I am, my dear sir,

Faithfully yours,

ROBERT DALE OWEN.

PHILADELPHIA, April 9, 1860.

* Marriage and Divorce, § 285.

MR. GREELEY CLOSES THE DISCUSSION.*

To the Hon. Robert Dale Owen :—

Sir : I understood from you that your concluding letter would be that to which I last replied ; but, since you have deemed it necessary to write again, I necessarily, yet willingly, rejoin. As before, I shall confine myself strictly to the points made in your last.

I. You seem to complain that I consider my side of the question at issue the side of Morality and Right. But, if I did not, why should I so earnestly uphold it ? Do I complain of *your* holding your own side in similar regard ? Assuredly, I cannot change my convictions, and should not be required to conceal them. Indeed, since you admit that my conviction is grounded in a "besetting weakness of our nature," you surely cannot regard it with surprise, any more than I can deem it a reason for closing our discussion ; though I have at all times since you began it been willing to close it.

II. You think the difference between us to be simply this : I allow Divorce for a single cause (Adultery), you for several causes ; and you would thus reduce it, from a question of principle, to one of details. But you cannot deny that my one ground of Divorce is that expressly affirmed to be such by Jesus Christ, to the exclusion and negation of all others. Nor can you fail to see that if, as I hold, the paramount (not sole) Divine end of Marriage is Parentage, or the perpetuation and increase, under fit auspices, of the Human Race, then that crime which vitiates and confuses parentage may logically be deemed the sole sufficient reason for annulling a marriage. To my mind, therefore, our difference is clearly and emphatically one of principle. I do not hold that even Adultery justifies the dissolution of a marriage so far as the culpable party is concerned. It simply authorizes, but by no means requires, the faithful, exemplary husband or wife to procure a legal adjudication and declaration of the fact that

* From The Tribune of April 31, 1860.

this marriage has — solely through the infidelity of the adulterer — been dissolved, so far only as it imposes duties or obligations on the wronged and innocent party.

III. As to what constitutes Marriage, — what Marriage *is*, — I have quoted the standard lexicographers of our language, who unanimously pronounce it a union and consecration of one man to one woman *for life*, and deny the name to all other unions. Your quarrel on this point is not with me, but with the dictionaries, as well as with the Christian Church. I have made no new definitions; I have simply insisted that those which have stood unchallenged hitherto shall be recognized and respected. Not by me primarily, but by Jesus of Nazareth, and, following him, by Noah Webster and Dr. Worcester, have the definitions I rest on been set forth. If they truly define the term, then the mutual promise of a man and woman to live together until one of them shall have proved a sot, a termagant, a ruffian, or a beast, is *not* a marriage. If you insist that the authorities I quote mistake or misstate the true meaning and force of the term, why do you not quote lexicographers who favor *your* rendering? Is it not clear that you would have done so, had there been any? And, if there be none, how can you complain of me for insisting that the word Marriage shall be held to mean that, and that only, which our standard dictionaries say it *does* mean?

IV. And this disposes of your talk of "Horace Greeley" saying this or that, in opposition to your views. If any part of what I have urged rests on the naked dictum of Horace Greeley, it is, of course, of little moment; but, if it is correctly based on the explicit teachings of Jesus Christ, on the unbroken tradition and nearly universal affirmation of the Christian Church, on the lessons of Profane History (see Gibbon), the definitions of standard lexicographers, and the concurring judgment of a vast majority of the wise and good, why, then, you see, the case is bravely altered, and the fact that I reaffirm what all of these have constantly asserted, does not necessarily render it insignificant, nor subject it to ridicule.

V. You dwell on the fact that the codes of Indiana and of some other States permit Divorce for other cause than Adultery, as though this proved the people of those States not married, according to my understanding of the term. But I have already urged the fact that, in those States, as elsewhere, Christian Marriage is unqualifiedly a union for life, and that most of those who marry there are married by clergymen in a strict and open accordance with the Christian law. You know, as well as I do, that divorce, followed by another marriage, rarely fails to cover with odium the parties involved in it, or at least some of them. You may not know, however, as I do, that, in repeated instances, persons divorced under the State laws you glory in, and otherwise married, have been excommunicated therefor by Protestant churches, clergymen being silenced for the same cause. That no Catholic would even dream of contracting such second marriage, no matter in what State or under whatever permission of the secular authority, you, of course, fully understand. I must protest, then, against your inference, from the fact that the laws of certain States allow Divorce on various grounds, that their people are in verity generally educated and married, and afterward live, under the law as you would have it. The "higher law" is their safeguard.

VI. I am surprised that you could so mistake my application of the judge's remark, that he punished the horse-thief, "not for stealing a horse, but that horses may not be stolen."

My idea was, and is, that Marriage is rightfully made indissoluble, in order that unfit and unreal marriages may not be contracted. Say that a legal marriage may be nullified merely because the parties find or fancy themselves unsuited to each other, or unhappy in their union, and I defy you to guard against so-called marriages whereof the impulse is mere appetite or worldly convenience. Such unions, in fact, are made, and will be made, under whatever laws. But tens of thousands of libertines, lechers, egotists, who would take a new wife at least every Christmas, if they could legally and reputably rid themselves in season of the old one, are appalled and deterred by the stern exaction of a solemn promise to fulfil all the obligations of husband and wife "till death do part." We cannot, even thus, be sure that *all* marital unions will be genuine marriages; but I know no other touchstone which that "intangible something called Society" can apply half so searching as this.

VII. As to whatever discrepancy may exist between the teachings of Moses and of Jesus respectively, regarding Divorce, they present no difficulty to my mind. I hold the law of Moses (not the Decalogue, which says nothing of Divorce) to have been local and temporary in its application; while that of Jesus is permanent and universal. Hence my adhesion to the latter.

VIII. The vital difference between us seems to me to hinge just here: You regard primarily those who have made false marriages, — who have wedded hastily, giddily, carnally, viciously, — and seek to relieve them from the inevitable consequence of their errors. I, on the other hand, am more intent on dissuading and deterring others from following their bad example, and so plunging, like Dives, "into this torment." If you could unmarry every discordant pair to-morrow, and should thereby teach the yet single that they might marry in haste and get divorced at leisure, you would not diminish, but greatly increase, the aggregate of human woe; while, if I could convince the giddy millions of heedless youth that Marriage is the most important, serious, solemn incident of their lives, and that whoever contracts it on the strength of pleasing features and a six-weeks' acquaintance commits a crime which will assuredly and fearfully punish its perpetrators, I should do mankind the greatest service, even though I should thereby render it certain that no divorce be evermore granted. Believing that unhappy unions were mainly, in their outset, unworthy ones, and that none who marry truly and nobly ever need seek or wish for Divorce, I must continue to uphold the law given through the words of Jesus of Nazareth, which, I am happy to know, is substantially identical with the law of New York. The Puritan pioneers of New England, it is jocularly said, resolved to take the law of God for their guidance until they should find time to make a better. Lacking not merely the leisure to frame such better law, but the faith to anticipate or seek it, I propose to hold by what I clearly, undoubtingly, accord with Christendom in understanding to be the Law of Marriage as enunciated by Him who "spake as never man spake." In the hope that further reflection and observation may bring you to a realizing sense of its wisdom and benignity,

I remain, yours,

HORACE GREELEY.

NEW YORK, April 25, 1860.

NOTE:

INDIANA DIVORCE LAW, AS IN FORCE MARCH 1, 1860.

(*Revised Statutes of Indiana*, Vol. II. pp. 234 to 237.)

§ 6. Divorces may be decreed by the Circuit Courts of this State on petition filed by any person who, at the time of the filing of such petition, shall have been a *bona fide* resident of the State one year previous to the filing of the same, and a resident of the county at the time of the filing of such petition, which *bona fide* residence shall be duly proven by such petitioner to the satisfaction of the Court trying the same.

§ 7. Divorces shall be decreed, upon the application of the injured party, for the following causes: —

1. Adultery, except as hereinafter provided.
2. Impotency.
3. Abandonment for one year.
4. Cruel treatment of either party by the other.
5. Habitual drunkenness of either party, or the failure of the husband to make reasonable provision for his family.
6. The conviction, subsequent to the marriage, in any country, of either party of an infamous crime.
7. *Any other cause* for which the Court shall deem it proper that a divorce should be granted.

§ 8. Divorces shall not be granted for adultery in any of the following cases: —

1. When the offence has been committed with the connivance of the party seeking the divorce.

2. When the party seeking the divorce has voluntarily cohabited with the other, with knowledge of the fact; or has failed to file his or her petition for two years after he or she had discovered the same.

3. When the party seeking the divorce has also been guilty of adultery, under such circumstances as would have entitled the opposite party, if innocent, to a divorce.

. . . .

§ 21. The Court, in decreeing a divorce, shall make provision for the guardianship, custody, support, and education, of the minor children of such marriage.

. . . . . .

§ 23. The divorce of one party shall fully dissolve the marriage contract as to both.

§ 24. A divorce decreed in any other State by a court having jurisdiction thereof shall have full effect in this State.

. . . . . .

§ 27. Wherever a petition for divorce remains undefended, it shall be the duty of the prosecuting attorney to appear and resist such petition.

(The other sections refer to modes of procedure, legitimacy, property rights, etc. The Indiana law does not permit limited divorce.)

ANALYTICAL INDEX.

A BOOK OF SURPASSING INTEREST.

HORACE GREELEY'S AUTOBIOGRAPHY.

RECOLLECTIONS OF A BUSY LIFE.

An elegant octavo volume; a superb specimen of typography. Illustrated with the best STEEL PORTRAIT OF MR. GREELEY ever published, and with various beautiful Engravings, Pictures of his various Homes, his Farm, etc., etc., together with a beautiful Portrait of MARGARET FULLER, engraved by LINTON.

Mr. Greeley has said of it: "I shall never write anything else into which I shall put so much of *myself*, my experiences, notions, convictions, and modes of thought, as these RECOLLECTIONS. I give, with small reserve, my mental history."

The book embraces views of early New England settlement, the author's own youthful life, education, apprenticeship, adventures, professional and political reminiscences, experience in Congress, newspaper-life in New York, and much useful talk about farms and farming. It is a peculiarly entertaining and valuable work,—a look behind the scenes during an important period of the country's history,—a book to be read with interest by Business Men, Farmers, Literary Men, Young Men, Students of the Times, the Women of America, Politicians, Men of the South, Northern Loyalists, *Intelligent Thinkers of all Classes.*

PRICES: Extra Cloth, $3.50; Library Style (Sheep), $4.50; Half Morocco, $5.00; Half Calf, elegant, $6.00. Sold only by Subscription. Exclusive territory given.

J. B. FORD & CO.,

164 NASSAU ST., PRINTING-HOUSE SQUARE, NEW YORK.

☞ *Opinions of the Press, Religious and Secular, of all shades of politics, and in every section of the country, may be found on this and the following pages.*

Independent.

We venture to predict for this book a large sale. It is valuable as a truthful record of the career of one of the most remarkable men in America, and as a sketch of some of the most important events in the later history of the country.

New York Tribune.

The personal career of Mr. Greeley was brought before the public several years ago, in the lively volume devoted to his biography, by Mr. James Parton. No materials, however, were furnished for that work by Mr. Greeley himself, who had never been in the habit of preserving any memoranda relating to his own history, and the present volume, accordingly, is the first production on the subject which can claim an autobiographical character. At the same time, it of course involves copious reminiscences of the political developments of the last twenty-five years. Of the manner in which the work has been accomplished, and the points of interest which it presents to the public, we are not at liberty to speak in this journal. The mechanical execution of the work is highly creditable to the publishers. It is printed on type and paper of unusual excellence, and the binding is at once substantial and elegant. The portrait of Mr. Greeley, from Brady's photograph, is a striking likeness, and the other embellishments of the volume add both to its interest and value.

New York Times.

One of the most amusing things we have heard lately is that Mr. Greeley's just published *Recollections*, a book which began by selling furiously in the Middle and New England States, finds, out West, a serious obstacle in the bailing of Jefferson Davis. In the first place, we had supposed that everybody had come to rejoice at Mr. Greeley's conduct in helping to relieve the government of an embarrassing prisoner, whom they were not ready to try, whom they wanted within reach, and whom yet they did not wish to keep in confinement, not being able to give him — what the worst criminal may claim — a fair and speedy trial. But, aside from that, the bailing affair was but one incident in Greeley's *Busy Life*, and if his oddities are worth reading about at all, certainly that one, which so stirred up the minds of his disciples, is just the one which they ought to understand. It is funny to see how people will let their political feelings and prejudices warp their common sense.

Brick Pomeroy's Democrat.
(N. Y.)

There are many reasons why men should read books, and those which run counter to our own opinions are often quite as enjoyable and quite as instructive as those with which we agree. There is probably no intelligent man in this whole country who has not heard of Horace Greeley and of the *New York Tribune*, — for the two are inseparable, — and who does not know of the colossal influence which the man and the journal have wielded in American history. Be it for bad or good, it is a power, and one that we cannot afford to let go uncomprehended. In these *Recollections*, Mr. Greeley gives more of an insight into his life and motives than he ever has done before; and as the history of a self-made man, who, by using natural ability with industry, earnestness, and sobriety, has placed himself high among the actors of the national drama, they deserve to be read, and, we doubt not, will be.

Evangelist. (N. Y.)

For thirty years — the lifetime of a generation — he has been not only an interested spectator, but an active participant in all the controversies of the day. He has fought in every campaign from the days of Jackson. Within that time almost all the great men who were upon the stage when he began his career have passed away. Though a private citizen, no man has done more than he to set up or pull down political idols. His long observation of public men and measures is invaluable in the record which he gives. No man, since the death of John Quincy Adams, has been more familiar with the political history of the country, or has furnished to it a more valuable contribution.

New York Ledger.

There are few men — entirely apart from his political views — the study of whose lives would be so instructive to the boys and young men of the country as that of the Hon. Horace Greeley. He has risen by his own exertions, until he is now one of the most widely and most favorably known of living men. We congratulate the new house of J. B. Ford & Co. on having such a popular work to introduce them to the publishing world.

Boston Transcript.

Mr. Greeley is emphatically a self-made man, who has risen from poverty to wealth, from obscurity to eminence, without any sacrifice of self-respect or independence. He has crawled to no position he has ever gained, but has won it by fair labor or fair fight. The number of eminent public men with whom he has been associated or come into collision makes his volume a contribution to politics as well as to the cause of self-culture.

Christian Advocate and Journal.
(N. Y.)

A goodly octavo here presents to the public a pretty full, and doubtless a very accurate, autobiography of the famous "philosopher" of the *Tribune*. Mr. Greeley's has unquestionably been a busy life, and it was, perhaps, wise in him to write it out while yet his "recollections" were unimpaired by old age. For forty years he has been watching the course of public affairs, and for more than three quarters of that period he has been an active participator in them. Hence his "recollections" constitute a pretty full history of the country for those years, especially as respects politics and the newspaper press.

Scientific American. (N. Y.)

Horace Greeley is a strong man every way; strong in his likes and dislikes, in his opinions and prejudices. Mentally and physically, his powers of endurance are such as to excite the admiration of all who know the amount of work he daily gets through. . . . As a moral tonic, we have seldom seen a book that we would more readily place in the hands of a family, or one that we should expect to see sooner well thumbed.

American Journal of Mining.
(N. Y.)

The book is a delightful one, interesting on every page to the young Americans for whom it was especially intended. Who does not know how dry and dusty is the labor of extracting from files of newspapers or contemporary records that political history of the country which has not yet assumed its final form on the rolls of Clio? And, on the other hand, who does not know how charming it is to hear some hale old politician tell again the stories of his past campaigns? How eagerly we ask him about the actors who have long since left the stage! How we thrill again at the songs and watchwords of "Log-Cabin Days!" How we seem to hear again tall

Harry of the West, or Webster, built of granite fused with fire, or keen Calhoun, or dauntless Douglas! This chatty volume gives all these things, and more.

Providence (R. I.) Journal.

A handsome volume, — handsome in every particular of mechanical execution. . . . The autobiography is full of interest for every reader, and full of instruction for every young man. Whatever differences of opinion there may be in regard to the political and social theories of Horace Greeley, he stands to-day as a strong power in this country, and the influence which he exerts cannot be shaken, for it rests on the firm foundations of intellectual ability, constant work, and moral honesty.

Examiner and Chronicle. (N. Y.)

Mr. Horace Greeley's "Recollections of a Busy Life," as published in the *Ledger*, with considerable additional matter, is published by Messrs. J. B. Ford & Co. in a handsome volume. Besides this frank setting forth of the author's opinions, and the unconscious self-portraiture that one must make in such a writing, the volume is a valuable summary of some leading facts in our recent political history, as seen from his point of view, and a picture of some phases of American life, which it is well to have photographed before their final disappearance.

Washington (D. C.) Evening Star.

Since Franklin's autobiography, we know of nothing in the autobiographical way of such fascinating interest as Greeley's frank, straightforward, racily told story of his own career. We dare say that the autobiographies of the two printer-statesmen — not unlike in some respects — will be read by our grandchildren with equal favor.

Boston Advertiser.

His history of the "American Conflict" was begun soon after the decisive battle of Gettysburg, and we have here a very interesting account of the way in which that laborious work was executed. Its sale was wide and rapid until the "bailing" affair occurred, and that all but stopped it. For the "Recollections" we predict a broader and an enduring demand. Its intrinsic excellences and interest will always secure for it an honorable place on the biographical shelf.

Frederick (Md.) Republican.

This history of the struggles and triumphs of one who has achieved such marked distinction in the politics and literature of his time should be read and studied by every boy who has nothing to rely upon but his own strong hands and stout heart. The beautiful tribute to Margaret Fuller forms one of the most interesting chapters of the work, and will prove of deep and lasting interest to all admirers of this noblest type of American women.

Anti-Slavery Standard.

His account of Margaret Fuller, who was for a time an inmate of their family, is especially interesting. He speaks of her as "the most remarkable, and, in some respects, the greatest woman America has yet known."

The publishers have added materially to the value and interest of the book in securing a finely executed portrait of Margaret Fuller, by Mr. W. J. Linton, the distinguished English engraver, by whom she was personally known.

Littell's Living Age.

We shall find opportunities to make this record of a remarkable man well known to our readers. Mr. Greeley has been an important part of the late years of the Republic.

The Nation. (N. Y.)

Perhaps there is not in the United States a better known name than that of Horace Greeley. There can be no doubt, therefore, that these "Recollections" of his busy life will have readers in good store; and with better reason than many books multitudinously read. Such a career as this volume describes, conducting its hero up from the depths of an extreme though not sordid poverty to the eminent position in the world of politics and journalism which he achieved, might well make a wiser man than Mr. Greeley think more highly than he ought to think of his own share in effecting the great changes he had witnessed, and to over-estimate the importance of the part he had had in them.

Hartford (Ct.) Courant.

We are exceedingly obliged to Mr. Bonner of the *Ledger*, for asking Mr. Greeley to write these "Recollections," to Mr. Greeley for complying with the request, and to the publishers of this book for giving it to the world in so attractive a form. We who have known Mr. Greeley from the early days of the *Tribune*, nay, even back of that, through the *Log-Cabin* and *New-Yorker* days, find many things in the book which we knew very well before, but also many things which are fresh and new. . . . . We can assure those who buy this book that they will greatly enjoy it.

Springfield (Mass.) Republican.

This, doubtless, gives us a truer idea of Mr. Greeley than a more full and elaborate biography by any other hand could do. But the great majority of men are moved more by feeling than argument, and there is probably not another living writer in this country who has exerted so wide an influence as the veteran editor of the *Tribune*.

Louisville (Ky.) Journal.

These letters were very popular when appearing in the *Ledger*, and now when revised and in part rewritten by the author, and with original matter added, they cannot fail to be far more valuable in their present elegant and substantial form. To the student, the ambitious or the poor boy, these letters are full of instruction and hope. They abound in anecdotes, in humor, and wise counsel.

Philadelphia Inquirer.

All classes of American readers will find material for grave thought in this volume, originally a series of sketches written for the New York *Ledger*. Collectively, in this volume, they relate the mental history of one of the boldest thinkers and most forcible writers in this country. The "Recollections" have been changed from their original shape, by Mr. Greeley himself, for this volume; all of them have been revised; to one half of them additions have been made, and a number of entirely new topics have been added.

Packard's Monthly.

A Vigorous Publishing House.—Messrs. J. B. Ford & Co., who have recently inaugurated a subscription publishing house in this city, give evidence of fitness for their work in their first production, which happens to be Greeley's "Recollections of a Busy Life." The book is a credit to the country, and should be an everlasting reproach to certain publishers who make much money at Hartford. Compare Mr. Greeley's portrait here with the miserable caricature under which his name is printed in Mrs. Stowe's "Eminent Men," recently brought out by a Hartford house. It is like comparing day with night. And so of other points in the two publications. We trust that this new house may not expend its vigor at the start, but may persevere in well-doing and prosper in the end, as it most assuredly will.

Working Farmer.

J. B. Ford & Co., New York, have recently published several new and valuable works, which deserve special mention in our columns.

First, we have "Recollections of a Busy Life," with miscellaneous papers, by that worthy and famous farmer's son, Horace Greeley. This book ought to be in every public and private library, where it shall be accessible to every young man in the land. Mr. Greeley's farm experiences, both as boy and man, as related by his vigorous pen, are so diverting that we feel tempted to quote liberally for the delectation of our rural readers; but as lack of space compels us to forbear this month, we advise them to write to the publishers for a copy of the work.

Army and Navy Journal.

The recollections of the life of this prominent journalist, which has indeed been a busy one, must undoubtedly prove both cheering and instructive to those American boys who are struggling under difficulties incident to poverty and obscurity, and to whom his autobiographical sketches are dedicated. . . . . The present volume is the first we have received bearing the imprint of Ford & Co., who are deserving of much praise for the excellence of its typographical appearance, and also for the good taste displayed in all the mechanical details of the book.

The Methodist. (N. Y.)

Many lives are busy ones, and not a few persons are in the habit of thinking themselves overworked a great part of the time; but we venture to say that but few workers have, through so long a series of years, crowded so many hours of earnest thought and intense action into each day as has Horace Greeley during the last forty years, or, indeed, from almost the day of his birth, February 3, 1811. . . . . It would be profitable to follow Mr. Greeley through the account of his struggles with poverty and opposition, but space will not permit to thoroughly review a book so teeming with matters of present interest.

only study it thoroughly, and follow what is set down, he may with good sense and plenty of practice come in time to train and drive as well as I do. Yours truly,

D. MACE.

From Hiram Woodruff's legitimate successor, Dan Pfifer.

CYPRESS HILLS, L. I., Oct. 31, 1868.

CHARLES J. FOSTER, ESQ.: *Sir:* — Hiram Woodruff's book is sure to be of very great service to the young men of the country who have got young horses. I have read it through more than once. People who have horses should read it carefully, and follow the directions set down for the treatment, feeding, training, and driving of trotters. It makes me remember old times, when I read the story of Ripton, for I was with Hiram then.

Yours truly, D. PFIFER.

Wilkes's Spirit of the Times.

This book has been put before the public in a very handsome and complete style, by Messrs. J. D. Ford & Co., of this city, and we observe from our exchanges that it is receiving handsome notices from the press. The estimation in which we hold it is well known to our readers. We believe it to be *the most practical and instructive book that ever was published concerning the trotting horse;* and those who own or take care of horses of other descriptions may buy and read it with a great deal of profit. Besides all this, it is a work of great interest.

Mr. Bonner's New York Ledger.

Hiram Woodruff was the great trainer of his day; but, by his unsullied integrity and unequalled capacity, he rose above his profession. No man could ever say of him that he had his price. Indeed, it is the universal testimony of all who knew him, — friends and foes, — that his integrity was absolutely unassailable. In this work, which has been ably, carefully, and judiciously edited by his faithful friend Mr. Charles J. Foster, are recorded for the benefit of the public at large, his life-long experiences; his sayings and doings; his authoritative views on almost everything pertaining to the horse. *It is a book for which every man who owns a horse ought to subscribe. The information which it contains is worth ten times its cost;* and we hope for the sake of the widow who owns the copyright, that the sales may, at least, reach one hundred thousand copies.

New York Herald.

The author of this work stood at the head of his profession as a trainer and driver of the trotting horse. . . . .

The book under consideration is the matured result of forty years' labor on the part of the author in developing the speed and endurance of the trotter, and his method of training and driving is accepted by turfmen as the perfection of that art. This method is fully set forth in this volume, accompanied with abundant illustrations of its correctness by the track performances of many of our most celebrated trotting horses. To horsemen in particular the book will be found especially attractive and of great value. *It will become a standard authority on the subject of which it treats.*

New York Times.

This book will become the manual of the roadsters. Woodruff was king of the horse-trainers, and the *rationale* of his system shows that he was a man of excellent judgment, while his many successes on the course furnish the best commentary on his modes of equine management. The book is calculated to be a very popular one, for every one who drives a nag in harness will have the ambition to read it, and it has an excellent narrative style. Indeed, if this was the style of Mr. Woodruff himself, he must have been as clever in his talk with men as in his management of horses. The book is handsomely got up, with a well-executed portrait of the late New York Mareschal and Master of Horse.

New York Tribune.

This is a masterly treatise by the master of his profession, — the ripened product of forty years' experience in handling, training, riding, and driving the trotting horse. There is no book like it in any language on the subject of which it treats. It is accepted as authority by the owners of racing trotters, and of fast roadsters. Its publication has been hailed by gentlemen as critically appreciative as Robert Bonner, and by trainers and drivers as distinguished as Sam Hoagland, Dan Mace, and Dan Pfifer. The book is unquestionably one of great value. For in America and England the development of the horse has long been considered second only in importance to the development of man. This work contains the results of forty years' uninterrupted labor in bringing the trotter up to the highest speed and the greatest endurance of which he is capable. Before we read it we had seen with curious surprise very hearty commendation of it and eulogy of its author in the leading Presbyterian, Baptist, and Methodist journals. No wonder, for Hiram Woodruff's system is based on the law of love.

Brick Pomeroy's Democrat.

Hiram Woodruff, a life-like portrait of whom adorns the book, of course needs no introduction to any American who cares anything about horses. His life was one continued benefit to that noble animal, one prolonged and successful effort to improve its condition, speed, and usefulness to man. His memory is that of a man proverbially honorable and of unapproached excellence in his calling. What Hiram Woodruff did *not* know about horses, and particularly the training of good colts and the driving of trotting horses, is hardly worth the knowing. What he *did* know, he has put into this book.

The (N. Y.) Liberal Christian (Unitarian).

We have a decided distaste for everything connected with horse-racing, and when the "Trotting Horse of America" was put into our hands the book dropped of its own weight on to the table. Ashamed of this prejudice, we took it up, and soon found ourselves reading at full pace about the way colts should be raised, and horses trained, and racers cared for, and the breed improved. . . . . In reading the book we were struck with the analogy between the scientific treatment of the horse and the best treatment of the human being. . . . . What a pity parents and teachers would not learn wisdom from the horse-trainer!

Springfield (Mass.) Republican.

The volume before us contains the best results of Woodruff's large observation and matured judgment, in regard to the breaking, feeding, and training of horses. It is full of shrewd remarks and sound rules. Those who know nothing about a horse, or not much, will be surprised at the amount of information and the variety of directions contained; and to see how truly the care and handling of the horse rise to the dignity of a science.

Boston Watchman and Reflector, (Baptist).

One may read and study this book with profit, for it was written by a man who loved the horse, knew his peculiarities, and from the experience of years utters words of wisdom as to the best way of training and driving the noblest animal ever given to man for service. *The advice, the suggestions, the rules given in the book are invaluable.* If we owned a "stable," we would make our grooms study it; if we were a Vermont farmer, each son should have a copy, for, while it is specially devoted to trotting horses, the work contains valuable information for every man who owns or drives a horse.

San Francisco Times.

There are very few lovers of the trotting-turf to whom the name of Hiram Woodruff is not as familiar as a household word. For nearly forty years this veteran horseman trained, rode, drove, and talked horse, and held almost undisputed sway upon the American turf. He came from a race of horsemen, and the horse was his especial pet and favorite. With him it was no ephemeral passion, but a life-long love; and on his death-bed, true to the instincts of his nature, the last clearly articulate word that he spoke was "horse." Such was the author of the book before us, and to this his only literary effort he brought not only a great love and pride of vocation, but a keen insight into all matters connected therewith, and an experience rarely, if ever, equalled.

San Francisco Bulletin.

Not only the patrons of the turf, but all who take an interest in equine affairs, will welcome the ample volume with the above title, which has just appeared from the press of J. B. Ford & Co., New York. The author, the late Hiram Woodruff, was an eminent authority in the specialty to which he devoted his life. Probably no man of his time knew more about horses, loved them with a more ardent love, and was better qualified to do them justice.

Round Table.

There is, we repeat, a great deal of instruction in the work, and we may add, there is a great deal of spirit and piquancy as well. We should call *The Trotting Horse of America* indispensable to horsemen, and it is by no means uninteresting reading for any, not included in that category, who are capable of sympathizing at times with the enthusiasm of others in a pursuit which does not so immediately appeal to the outside observers themselves.

Boston Traveller.

The volume embraces a wonderful amount of information on its subject, admirably prepared and presented, and *really leaving little more to be desired on that subject*, till the passage of years shall have furnished new illustrations of it. Mr. Foster has edited the work well and discreetly, and the biographical sketch he gives of Mr. Woodruff is a model piece of writing; and Mr. Wilkes gives an introductory sketch of the great trainer that is worthy of his strong and lively pen. A striking portrait of Mr. Woodruff adorns the volume, which is got up in very elegant style.

Worcester Spy.

Mr. Woodruff, whose experience and observation for forty years have prepared him to discuss this subject in the best manner, has given us a book that all interested in trotting horses will be likely to study. It has the indorsement of George Wilkes and Robert Bonner, and is undoubtedly *the best book on the subject that has ever been written.*

Boston Post.

A volume which, from the glance we have given it, we should say was worthy the experience of a man who did more than any one else to raise the standard of our fast horses.

Philadelphia Press.

It may be characterized, briefly but emphatically, as the best, because the most practical and "knowledgable" book upon trotting horses ever printed.

Boston Advertiser.

A book thoroughly unique in its way.

Boston Journal.

A valuable volume for reference.

American Agriculturist.

This is the title of a very neat 12mo volume. . . . . It was published in chapters in *Wilkes's Spirit of the Times*, and now, as soon after the death of the famous trainer as possible, it is given to the public, and will be found of great interest to all who love a good horse. The first eleven chapters, together with others scattered through the book, are chiefly instructive on handling, feeding, training, etc. Others are reminiscences of the trotting-turf, told in a very pleasant way. It contains 412 pages, with a portrait of the author, and will no doubt meet, and worthily, with a very extensive sale.

Boston Cultivator.

While this book was written by one pre-eminently skilled in his art, and especially designed for all interested in the breeding, training, as well as all else that relates to the horse, it cannot fail of being attractive to the general reader. . . . . We therefore commend it as *deserving a place in all public libraries, and especially so to the notice of Farmers' Clubs*, wherever they have been organized.

St. Louis Democrat.

Everything desirable to be known of the famous trotters is found in these pages, with suggestions and instructions for rearing stock, breaking, or rather "educating" colts, and full details of practical experience. It is accompanied by a sketch and portrait of Woodruff, and *will be sought for by every owner, breeder, or lover of the horse in the land.*

Catholic World (Monthly).

It is one of those rare books which, while got up for a special purpose, and seemingly suited to the few, overleaps the narrow limits apparently prescribed, and *attracts to itself the favorable notice of the entire community.*

The American Farmer.

It is the most complete work of the kind, and possesses all the fascination of a novel, even to others than horsemen.

Working Farmer.

We commend the work under consideration to farmers in all sections of the country. It is calculated to do great good, and to teach them many things about the horse which they probably do not but ought to know.

The Nation.

The record of his experience and suggestions constitutes, therefore, a valuable accession to our knowledge, and will prove to be of *standard authority among the most skilful.* The graphic style of his descriptions, the vivid pictures he draws of the breeding and education of his favorites, and the reminiscences he recalls of incidents on the turf, form a work of great merit. . . . Those who are desirous to form an accurate idea of the characteristics of the trotting horse, for their benefit as riders or drivers, *cannot find any other work in our language so replete with useful information*, interesting hints, and readable anecdotes. Hiram Woodruff is now dead, and it will be many a year before we shall look upon his equal in his line of business.

N. Y. Evening Post.

While, as the work of an enthusiastic horseman, and with a true purpose, a large part of the book is made up of "reminiscences of the trotting-turf," there is a vast deal else exhibiting the grasp of a master in the art of training and caring for the animals he so profoundly appreciated. It is, then, not only by lovers of the horse that this book will be valued. It contains a store of observation and suggestion *valuable to every man who owns horses either for trotting or draught.*

LIFE OF JESUS, THE CHRIST.

BY

HENRY WARD BEECHER.

THE Publishers of this forthcoming work find it necessary — on account of the intense and abiding interest aroused all over the land by their announcement that the greatest living religious teacher was engaged upon so important a theme — to make some answer to the constant inquiries concerning the book. Germany, France, England, all have their schools both of orthodoxy and of scepticism, no two of which occupy the same ground or help each other in dealing with the popular mind in the different countries; and none of which is properly adapted to the wants of religious thinkers in America. This must be the work of an American, — and of a completely representative American.

It is with full confidence in the attainment of this result that the publishers of the "Life of Jesus, the Christ," to which great work MR. BEECHER is now constantly and earnestly devoting his abundant energies, are preparing for its issuance in a manner worthy the public expectancy, the universal interest in the subject, and the repute of the author.

The work is to be issued in two styles. It will be first published in a full octavo volume of about 800 pages. This, although called the "Plain Edition," will be illustrated with several valuable engravings. First, with four superb Maps, constructed expressly for this work from the very latest data, including the great English, Dutch, and French governmental surveys of Palestine, the present explorations of Jerusalem itself by LIEUT. WARREN, Royal Engineers, and every attainable source of exact geographical and topographical information. These are engraved on copper and on stone (printed in two tints) by COLTON, the famous map-maker and publisher. The other illustrations are a

Frontispiece, "Head of Christ," restored, painted, and engraved on steel by the renowned American engraver, WM. E. MARSHALL, from a photograph of LEONARDO DA VINCI'S rapidly decaying masterpiece in Milan, "The Last Supper,"—a really grand work of the engraver's art; and a beautiful Steel-plate Title-page, containing a Vignette of Bethlehem, engraved by R. HINSHELWOOD, of the Continental Bank-Note Company.

The other style will be in royal octavo size, richly illustrated. It will contain the Frontispiece, Title-page, and Maps mentioned above, a series of twenty large full-page wood-engravings, and from fifty to seventy-five smaller cuts printed in the text, the entire series being about completed.

These engravings are from *new and original drawings never before published*, having been designed expressly for this work after sketches taken directly from the places represented. They are a new and full illustration of localities, people, and customs among the scenes of our Lord's earthly labors, and, as artistic productions, are believed to be superior to anything before published on that subject. They are engraved by W. J. LINTON, the celebrated wood-engraver, now resident in New York, universally acknowledged to be the first master of his art, and his brother, H. D. LINTON, long well known and highly esteemed in Paris.

The maps were constructed and the illustrations designed by A. L. RAWSON, an artist for years resident in the Holy Land, and thoroughly conversant with its features. The drawings on wood are from the artistic pencil of HARRY FENN. The work will be printed at the University Press, Cambridge, Mass., by WELCH, BIGELOW, & Co.

Concerning the date of publication, more particular information will be given through the newspaper press in due time. It may be said, however, that the book will not be ready for canvassing by subscription agents (in which manner alone it is to be sold) before the month of May next.

J. B. FORD & CO., Publishers,

164 NASSAU STREET, PRINTING-HOUSE SQUARE, NEW YORK.

www.ingramcontent.com/pod-product-compliance
Lightning Source LLC
LaVergne TN
LVHW021058110826
845150LV00001B/103

* 9 7 8 1 4 2 5 5 6 6 4 5 6 *